THE ORIGINS OF CATHOLIC EVOLUTIONISM
1831–1950

THE ORIGINS OF CATHOLIC EVOLUTIONISM

1831–1950

KENNETH W. KEMP

The Catholic University of America Press

Washington, D.C.

TABLE OF CONTENTS

PART I

THE FOUNDATIONS LAID
(1771–1885)

PART II

THE ORIGIN OF THE HUMAN BODY I: EVOLUTION DEFENDED & RESISTED
(1885–1900)

PART III

THE ORIGIN OF THE HUMAN BODY II: DIVINE FORMATION FROM AN EVOLVED ANIMAL BODY
(1898–1909)

PART IV

OLD CONTROVERSIES & NEW:
EXTENSIVE CHRISTIAN NATURALISM TOLERATED;
BERGSONISM & POLYGENISM REJECTED

(1909–1931)

PART V

EVOLUTION ACCOMMODATED:
MIVARTIAN ANTHROPOGENESIS,
BUT NOT TEILHARDIAN
THEOLOGY OF NATURE

(1931–1955)

PART VI

CONCLUSION & AFTERWORD

APPENDICES

ACKNOWLEDGMENTS

I would like to acknowledge the assistance and encouragement that I have received over the years from many colleagues, particularly John Boyle, Ali Chamseddine, Peter Distelzweig, Robert Kennedy, Raymond MacKenzie, Zsolt Nagy, and Philip Rolnick.

NOTE ON
TRANSLATIONS
& CITATIONS

Translations from primary sources are almost always my own. When a translation has been published, I have usually included in the bibliography publication details about the translation, and sometimes an exact page number in the footnotes, for the convenience of readers who want to see the larger context of the material under discussion. In the case of secondary sources, I have, unless otherwise noted, quoted published translations.

＊ ＊ ＊ ＊ ＊

Articles published anonymously are listed in the footnotes and in the bibliography under the publication in which they appeared.

INTRODUCTION

In my earlier book, *The War That Never Was*, I argued that to present the history of the relations between science and religion (in the case of evolution) as a history of warfare is to deal in myths. It mischaracterizes two different wars. One of the wars that really did happen was a philosophical war waged by atheists against Christianity, a war in which atheists attempted to draw on science for support. The other was a war between new scientific ideas and old ones, one in which old scientific ideas were sometimes unnecessarily, and too tightly, attached to theological ideas and in which new scientific ideas were sometimes (in exposition, though not in essence) interwoven with anti-religious philosophical ideas.

The latter war was fought within churches no less than elsewhere: The Church of England included not only Samuel Wilberforce, its evolution-skeptical bishop of Oxford, but also the more evolution-friendly Frederick Temple (archbishop of Canterbury) and William Henry Flower (zoologist at the Hunterian Museum). The Presbyterian churches in the United States included not only the anti-evolution campaigner William Jennings Bryan, but the more evolution-friendly James Woodrow (theologian at Columbia [South Carolina] Theological Seminary and holder there of the first American Professorship of Natural Science in Connection with Revelation) and Asa Gray (Harvard University botanist and America's first prominent Darwinist).[1] That was true of the Catholic Church as well.

---

1 See, for example, David N. Livingstone, *Darwin's Forgotten Defenders*, and James R. Moore, *The Post-Darwinian Controversies*.

The focus of my earlier book was the evolution-related incidents and movements most commonly cited as evidence of war between science and religion—the Huxley-Wilberforce exchange at Oxford (1860), the Scopes Trial (1925), and the more recent American curricular wars over the place of evolutionary biology, Creation-Science, and Intelligent-Design Theory in the science classrooms of America's religiously neutral public schools (ongoing since about 1980). A story centered on those incidents left little room for discussion of evolutionary biology and Catholicism, where the story ran along different lines.

Andrew Dickson White, whose *A History of the Warfare of Science with Theology* (1896) is one of the foundational articulations of the idea that science and theology (though not, on his telling, non-theological religion) are in an important sense at war, speaks highly of Nicholas Cardinal Wiseman's *Twelve Lectures on the Connexion Between Science and Revealed Religion* (1836)[2] and mentions only two Catholic incidents (both minor) in his discussion of the alleged theological war on Darwinism. American Catholics generally kept their distance from both sides of the 1925 Scopes Trial.[3] William Jennings Bryan, one of the leaders in the anti-evolution campaign of the 1920s and assistant prosecutor in the Scopes Trial, had an enthusiastic Catholic supporter in Benedict Elder, editor of Louisville's diocesan newspaper, *The Record*, and later president of the Catholic Press Association.[4] Elder's strong sympathy with the Bryan campaign was not, however, shared by all of his fellow Catholics. Nor did the Catholic Church have a close association with the anti-evolutionism of the last decades of the twentieth century. Indeed, the court challenges to creation-science statutes in Arkansas and Louisiana in the 1980s found Catholics (a priest in one case, a bishop in the other) as *plaintiffs* in challenges to the anti-evolution laws. Although Catholic biochemist Michael Behe has been one of the principals in the development of Intelligent-Design Theory, other Catholics—biologist Kenneth Miller, philosopher and priest Ernan McMullin, and archbishop (and philosopher-scientist) Józef Życiński—have been prominent among the critics of that theory and among the defenders of the compatibility of mainline evolutionary biology with Christian theology.[5]

Nevertheless, some historians present opposition to biological evolution in a way that, if not explicitly asserting there was a war between the Catholic Church and science over evolution, overemphasize the presence, exaggerate the extent, or mispresent the substance of Catholic hostility to evolution. John Haught wrote that "until Pope John Paul II admitted that the evidence for biological evolution is compelling, . . . papal statements . . . seem to have condemned, ignored, or given only grudging acceptance to the ideas

---

2 White, *History*, I: 223–24. One might wonder whether John W. Draper's rather stridently anti-Catholic *History of the Conflict between Religion and Science* (1875) would not be a better source of evidence for conflict between evolutionism and the Church, but Draper's discussion of evolution (247–49) does not mention Catholicism and his polemic against the Catholic Church (e.g., ch. 10) is exclusively concerned with other issues.

3 For a contemporary confirmation of this, see the Jesuit editors' "The Middle Road to Dayton" in *America*. For a historian's account, see John L. Morrison, "American Catholics and the Crusade Against Evolution."

4 See his articles in *Commonweal* and in the *Fortnightly Review*.

5 See Miller, *Finding Darwin's God*; McMullin, *Evolution and Creation*; and Życiński, *God and Evolution*.

made famous by Charles Darwin"[6] and that "scientifically unsophisticated popes and theologians in the late nineteenth and early twentieth century, unable to distinguish clearly between science and materialist beliefs, were often appalled by Darwin's evolutionary theory."[7] Don O'Leary wrote that "many Catholics experienced great difficulties when they struggled to reconcile the narratives of Genesis with progressive developments in the historical, geological, and biological sciences."[8]

Haught's summary is a rather un-nuanced account of magisterial policy on evolution. He failed to distinguish between Darwin's ideas about animals and those about human beings and between unofficial and magisterial statements. He wrote "ignored" when it would have been better to say just "remained silent about." Does the maxim *qui tacet consentire videtur*, "silence implies consent," not apply here? Should we be surprised by a lack of enthusiasm for an idea that had been abused by enthusiastic opponents of religion ever since it had first been proposed?[9] O'Leary's "experienced great difficulties when they struggled to reconcile" is tendentious. Better would be just to say that some Catholics were unconvinced by the new ideas. For some the reason was hermeneutical, for others philosophical, and for still others scientific. Better also would be to add that other Catholics, whatever their views about the scientific merits of the new ideas, argued that there were no *theological* reasons for rejecting them.

The story of the Catholic evolutionist perhaps best known to the general public, Jesuit paleontologist Pierre Teilhard de Chardin, has become grist for the mills of the warfare theorists. An (anonymous) reviewer at *Publishers Weekly* wrote that

> Teilhard . . . succeeded in melding his life as a Jesuit priest and as a scientist at a time when the Catholic Church denied that such a thing was either possible or desirable. Teilhard's superiors prohibited him from publishing almost everything he wrote during his lifetime and forced him into exile from his native France. Published after his death, his works became classic examples of integrating religion and science.[10]

That account, as I will show, fits the Warfare Myth better than it fits the facts.

Even some historians who do not emphasize conflict between science and religion sometimes overstate the Index's resistance to evolutionary biology. Marie Claire Groessens-VanDyck and Dominique Lambert wrote that "from the end of the nineteenth century . . . the Congregation of the Index of Prohibited Books and the Holy Office had tried to prevent the publication of works which, within the Church, tried to demonstrate the compatibility of doctrine or Scripture even with a theory of transformism limited to

---

6 Haught, "Evolution," 181.

7 Haught, "Darwin and Catholicism," 485.

8 O'Leary, *Roman Catholicism and Modern Science*, 251.

9 See my "With Friends Like Those."

10 *Publishers Weekly*, "The Jesuit and the Skull," 153. These are the views of the reviewer, not of Aczel.

animal species."[11] Harry Paul said that Dalmace Leroy's work was placed on the *Index*;[12] as we shall see, it was not.

Although one cannot deny that there were Catholics (even educated Catholics in positions of responsibility) who had serious concerns about the new evolutionary theories, the range and extent of those concerns was on the whole narrower than the statements just quoted suggest. It is misleading to make claims like O'Leary's without acknowledging the truth of a sub-contrary "opposite": some (perhaps many) Catholics did not experience great difficulties in reconciling the narratives of Genesis with progressive developments in the historical, geological, and biological sciences. Objections at the Congregation of the Index were focused on the canons of hermeneutics articulated by proponents of evolutionary ideas and on the origin of the human body. Catholic works arguing for the evolutionary origins of animals were published, if not with universal assent to their ideas, then at least without incident.

＊ ＊ ＊ ＊ ＊

The story of Catholic reaction to, and reception of, evolutionary biology is different in significant ways from the debate within Protestantism that featured so prominently in my earlier book. There are several reasons why this is so.

First, Catholicism is distinctly conservative in its theology, but not literalistic in its hermeneutics. While Catholic theologians have long emphasized the importance of the "literal sense" (meaning "the precise meaning of texts as produced by their authors"[13]), Catholic hermeneutics is not literalistic.[14] First, it has always been more open to metaphorical interpretation than are some of today's Protestant literalists. In the Catholic tradition, the figurative use of language, and even metaphorical interpretations of the text, are considered to be *part of* the literal sense as the Church has traditionally used that term. Second, it has always acknowledged the place of allegorical interpretation in reading the Bible, though the allegorical sense of a passage was supplementary to, not alternative to, the literal sense (as Catholics understood that term). And finally, in the last years of the nineteenth century and the first half of the twentieth, the Church came gradually to accept the use of historico-critical and related methods of Scriptural exegesis. Unlike some branches of conservative Protestantism, it has never been committed to the kind of plain-meaning hermeneutics that made literacy (and piety, of course) a sufficient preparation for Scriptural interpretation. I elaborate on this in Appendix II-C.

Second, the Catholic debate differed from the debate within Protestantism as a result of Catholicism's nineteenth-century revival of Thomistic philosophy. The commitment of

---

11 Groessens-VanDyck and Lambert, " Darwinisme d'un chanoine," 51. Technically, the Index was not concerned with preventing the publication of works, that being the work of diocesan censors, although it did occasionally recommend that certain authors be prohibited from writing any further books. Its writ was rather prohibitions with respect to books already published.

12 Paul, *Edge of Contingency*, 74.

13 Pontifical Biblical Commission, *Interpretation*, II.B.1.

14 See the Pontifical Biblical Commission, *Interpretation*, I.F.

Pope Leo XIII to make that philosophy a prominent feature of Catholic intellectual and educational life (articulated in his 1879 encyclical *Aeterni patris*) affected the reception of evolutionary accounts of the origin of species in several ways.[15] Most importantly, it offered a philosophical defense of the exceptionalist anthropology that was central to Catholic theology and that was explicitly rejected by Darwin in *The Descent of Man* (1871), a rejection which should be seen as *the grounds for* his extension of the theory to the origin of man and not as *a mere logical consequence of* the theory articulated in his *Origin of Species*. More generally, Thomism included a larger philosophy of nature, a hylomorphism that was both essentialist and teleological.[16] Thus, in addition to the question (important to all Christians) of whether Darwinism (or other theories of biological evolution) denied the existence of souls or just ignored them, Catholic intellectuals faced such further questions as how the Darwinian concept of species related to the concept of biological species used in Thomistic (essentialist) philosophy and whether natural selection (in the judgment of some a non-teleological process) is compatible with a generally teleological philosophy of nature. That is not to say that the task is insurmountable. Indeed historian Harry W. Paul wrote, though not focusing here exclusively on the question of evolution, that "fair critics could admit that the return to Thomism was wise because Aristotelian metaphysics was capable of assimilating the results of modern science and of being adapted to Catholicism. Thomism was the only system capable of preserving the essentials of Catholicism and of assimilating relevant modern scientific developments."[17] Thomists did disagree on whether an evolutionary account of the origin of species could be assimilated at all; those who thought it could differed among themselves about how the assimilation could be effected.

Third, the Catholic response to evolutionary biology, it is helpful to keep in mind, had to be worked out at the same time as the Church fended off the attacks of an aggressively anti-clerical, when not explicitly anti-religious, liberalism (the *Kulturkampf* in Germany, the *Risorgimento* in Italy, and counterparts in France, Spain, and elsewhere).

The extent of that hostility is revealed in a comment that Jesuit entomologist Erich Wasmann culled from the many press comments about some public lectures he had delivered in Berlin in 1907. A Protestant critic, one Dr. M. Senff, wrote: "It would be better to have rather less ecclesiastical indignation [from Fr. Wasmann's critics] and rather more scientific truthfulness, even if it is a bit uncomfortable. Then, a third person would not end up in the awkward situation, of having, as a matter of honor, in a Protestant

---

15 For examples of early implementations of the project of *Aeterni patris*, see Thomas Harper, *Metaphysics*; the multivolume *Philosophia lacensis*, begun in 1880 (and in particular Tilmann Pesch's *Institutiones philosophiae naturalis*); and P. L. De San's *Institutiones metaphysicae specialis*.

16 Briefly, hylomorphism is a philosophy of nature according to which each individual thing is a composite of matter (which makes something the individual that it is) and a substantial form (which makes something the kind of thing that it is); essentialism is the idea that every individual thing has a specific essence, or is an individual of a particular kind; teleology is the idea that a full understanding of natural processes requires reference to the τέλος (i.e., end, goal, or purpose) of the process.

17 Paul, *Edge of Contingency*, 189. Paul devoted all of his chapter 6 (176–94) to a historical account of turn-of-the-century French thought on "Thomism and Science."

country, to come to the aid of a Jesuit."[18] Wasmann was writing, one might add, from his Luxembourg exile, the *Jesuitengesetz* which had expelled the Jesuits from Germany in 1872 still being in force.

In England, Thomas H. Huxley, "Darwin's Bulldog," once referred to "Our great antagonist—I speak as a man of science—the Roman Catholic Church, the one great spiritual organisation which is able to resist, and must, as a matter of life and death, resist, the progress of science and modern civilisation."[19] The "religion" that contended with science in John W. Draper's seminal *History of the Conflict between Religion and Science* (1875), the reader quickly realizes, is not religion in general, but Catholicism.

In France, Harry Paul wrote:

> there was a clear attempt to base anti-clerical republican politics on a scientistic ideology. Darwinism was most susceptible to exploitation by anti-clericals. The intellectual problem of reconciling religious beliefs with new scientific developments was thus connected with republican anti-clericalism. This meant that republicans were encouraged to accept Darwinism and that Catholics had a good political reason to be suspicious of it as an ideological weapon against Catholicism. Only the finest minds were capable of separating the purely scientific aspects of Darwinism from the wider social and political implications.[20]

Most of the challenges posed by nineteenth-century liberalism were questions of political and social philosophy (when they were not simply questions of policy and institutional structures), questions which had nothing to do with evolutionary biology. One challenge, however, was relevant to the question of the relationship between Catholic theology and evolutionary biology—the intellectual liberalism characterized by historian Joseph Altholz as "an emphasis upon the legitimacy and value of intellectual sources independent of the authority of the Church"[21] and exemplified by the Comte de Montalembert in France, by Ignaz Döllinger in Germany, and by Lord Acton in England. Most Catholic evolutionists did not directly address the general question of intellectual freedom from ecclesiastical authority in scientific inquiry. Two exceptions were John Gmeiner and St.-George Mivart, both of whom addressed the question in the Catholic periodical press.[22]

* * * * *

And so, having finished a general response to the idea of the Christian reaction to evolutionary biology as evidence for the Warfare Myth, I have written a book precisely

---

18 Senff, "Jesuitenpater Wasmann. *Pro* oder *contra*?," quoted here from Wasmann, *Kampf*, 153–54 (trans., 255–56).

19 Huxley, "Scientific Education," 120. He added: "The Catholic priest is trained to know his business, and do it effectually. The professors of ["one of the most important of the institutions in which the clergy of the Roman Catholic Church in these islands are trained"], learned, zealous, and determined men, permitted me to speak frankly with them. We talked like outposts of opposed armies during a truce—as friendly enemies."

20 Paul, *Edge of Contingency*, 21.

21 Altholz, *Liberal Catholic Movement*, 1.

22 Gmeiner, "Liberty of Catholics"; Mivart, "Modern Catholics."

about Catholic reception of the theory. I have called this book *The Origins of Catholic Evolutionism: 1831–1950*; a few words about the title are perhaps in order—about evolution, about *Catholic* evolutionism, and about the choice of dates.

First, about the term "evolution." The term can, to be sure, be applied broadly. For some people, it calls to mind "a cosmical process, one and continuous from nebula to man, from star to soul, from atom to society,"[23] But whatever broader meaning and application the term may sometimes have, my subject here is evolution as an answer to the question of the origin (or, more precisely, the differentiation) of biological species. For our purposes, the most important components of that answer are four theses—transformism itself (i.e., that species originate by the transformation of previously existing species), the common ancestry of different species, natural selection as the cause of those transformations, and the applicability of these ideas to the origin of the human race.

Second, what do I mean by "Catholic evolutionism"? The story I want to tell cannot make fundamental a distinction between Catholics who accepted "evolution" and those who rejected it—between "Catholic evolutionists" and their Catholic opponents. Despite the superficial logical appeal of such a distinction, it will founder on the historical fact that there was so much variation both among those who were in some sense evolutionists and among those who were not that it will, in the end, be best to admit that *tertium vere datur*.

Among the non-evolutionists, some rejected evolutionary ideas for reasons that quickly turned into theological hostility, asserting that Catholics *could not* embrace any of the four component theses. Some of that hostility was based on readings of Genesis far more literal than other Catholics thought necessary. Some was a reaction (an over-reaction) to the philosophical materialism that anti-Christian evolutionists have tried (and still try) to attach to the *scientific* theory of evolution.[24] Some was based on doubts about whether anything like Darwinian evolution (non-essentialist and grounded in random variation) was compatible with the Thomistic (essentialist and teleological) philosophy of nature which had been of so much service in systematizing theology.

But not all Catholics who rejected the theory did so for reasons that could be made to touch on theology. Some skepticism was based on the counter-intuitive character of the idea. Could butterflies and buffalo really have a common ancestry? Could random variation and natural selection produce eyes or wings? Some had more scientific reservations. While the first three grounds tended to lead from skepticism to theological hostility, the fourth, taken alone, generally did not.

There was also variation within what can legitimately be called Catholic evolutionism.

First, the four theses mentioned above are logically distinct. Not all transformists were selectionists. Not all transformists were willing to extend the theory to man. I think that it will be most useful to recognize as "evolutionists" any Catholic who accepted any of the four component theses mentioned above.

---

23 The phrase comes from Grant Allen, *Charles Darwin*, 191.

24 Again, see my "With Friends Like Those."

Second, most of the component theories come in weaker and stronger forms. Was there one, a few, or many first kinds? Was natural selection the main means of modification, an important one, or just one among several? Are these ideas applicable to the origin of the human race or just to the origin of the body? If the latter, are they the exclusive, or only a contributory, cause?

The very contrast between evolutionist and non- (much less anti-) evolutionist, the epistemological contrast between acceptance and rejection, is oversimplified. On which side do the intermediate verdicts—"doubtful, but not impossible," "plausible, but not proven"—fall?

A history of Catholic evolutionism, focused as it may properly be on Catholics ready to accept the truth of some of the four theses, must also give some attention to the rôle in the eventual accommodation of evolutionism within Catholic thought played by those Catholics who expressed strong scientific or philosophical reservations about the *truth* of the four evolutionary theses without thinking that there was anything *theologically* problematic about them. These might be called "mere compatibilists" or "accommodationists." Indeed, the reality of the epistemological spectrum, and the logical independence of the various theses that make up evolutionism, forces us to recognize that even a distinction between mere compatibilists and Catholic evolutionists is less sharp than a logically obsessive taxonomist might be tempted to insist.

Finally, why 1831–1950? Those dates (and the dates of this book's part and chapter titles) are only symbolic and approximate, not precise. I chose 1831 in homage to the scientist who might be called the first Catholic evolutionist, Jean-Baptiste Julien d'Omalius d'Halloy, the first edition of whose *Éléments de géologie* was published that year. I chose 1950 as the year in which Pius XII published his encyclical letter *Humani generis*, which included the universal magisterium's first public statement about evolution. I will discuss (albeit briefly) some earlier and later incidents—early condemnation of some defenses of materialistic versions of evolutionism by the Congregation of the Index, the reaction to the encyclical (particularly on the question of monogenesis) and some more recent magisterial statements on the issue. My focus, however, will be on the years specified in my title.

✳ ✳ ✳ ✳

My focus in this book will be precisely on the scientific theory of the evolutionary origin of biological species. Of three ideas loosely connectable to that theory, ones that some readers might expect, or at least hope, to find here, I have chosen not to address one at all and the other two I will address only lightly.

Perhaps closest of the three to my topic is paleoanthropology. When, in 1929, the Arkansas attorney general's office was asked whether the use of Katharine Elizabeth Dopp's *Tree Dwellers* (1904) in Arkansas's public schools did not violate the state's new anti-evolution law, that office issued an opinion that it did not. The Arkansas law prohibited only teaching the evolution of man from animals, not the evolution of modern from prehistoric man.[25] That distinction, legally correct though it was, lost its sharpness as I began to write my history of Catholic evolutionism. The question of the evolutionary *origin* of the human race cannot, of course, be separated from the evidence of the fossil record, but *which* fossils are relevant precisely to the question of animal ancestry? Peking Man? Neanderthalers? Cro-Magnon Man? That leads to the question of what to make of Paleolithic culture—tools, art, and burials. It is also loosely connected to the question of human antiquity. Partly because of the extent to which Catholic scientists were involved in the research into those questions, and partly because incidents from the history of paleoanthropology and Paleolithic archeology shed light on the more general question of the historical relations between evolution and religion, I had hoped to include a discussion of that topic in this book, but, for reasons of space, in the end chose not to do so. Perhaps I can make them the subject of another book.

I will discuss here only the two most central questions of anthropogenesis. One, perhaps the more obvious, is the origin of the human body. The other is monogenesis, the idea that the entire human race is descended from a single first human couple. *Genesis* 1–2 presents the origin of man in terms of such a couple, an idea repeated throughout the Bible. The Septuagint's version of the prayer of the young Tobias and Sarah says, "[God] made Adam and gave him Eve ... and from them brought forth the seed of mankind."[26] St. Paul drew out the theological importance of monogenesis for the doctrine of original sin, in his epistle to the Romans (5:12). There is something right about what Teilhard wrote when he said: "As a result of the factual impossibility of Science ever being able to magnify the paleontological past enough to distinguish individuals, ... mono- and polygenism are in reality *purely theological concepts*, introduced for dogmatic reasons, but extra-scientific by their nature (insofar as they are empirically unverifiable),"[27] but he was thinking precisely as a paleontologist when he said that. Polygenism is the presumptive, even if not logically necessary, consequence of Darwinian evolution. More recently, it has been defended as a consequence of the genetic diversity of the race and of points of genetic similarity between man and chimpanzee. The general scientific background is discussed in Appendix I-C and Catholic treatment of the question in chapters 2, 17, and 19.

A second topic, the one I will omit, is the question of the origin, not of species, but of life itself. Some evolutionists (e.g., Jean-Baptiste Lamarck and Ernst Haeckel) combined questions of the origin of life with questions of the origin of species; others (saliently, Charles Darwin) did not. The idea that life emerged on the planet as the product of natural processes alone is, even today, at best inchoate, a deduction from a more general philosophy of nature, but an idea still lacking enough empirical and experimental support to be considered a *product* (as opposed to a *subject*) of scientific research. Catholic authors generally noted both the claims of some authors about a fully natural origin of life and the emphasis of Darwin and others on separating the question from that of the origin

---

25 *Arkansas Gazette*, "Evolution Law Held Not Violated," 11.

26 Tobit 8:6 (the Vulgate [Tobit 8:8] does not include the second part of the sentence).

27 Teilhard, "Monogénisme et monophylétisme," 247 (trans., 209).

of (distinct) species. Some, but not all, Catholic authors did think that the origin of life was a transition that required direct divine action, but because ideas about the origin of life were not a part of the biological theory of evolution (and for that matter were more philosophical or speculative than *scientific*), I have not said much about them in this work, the theme of which I have limited to questions of theology and *science.*

Finally, I will address only briefly something else that might come to a reader's mind as a part of Catholic evolutionism, namely the comprehensively evolutionist theology of nature made most famous by Jesuit paleontologist Pierre Teilhard de Chardin. I will discuss Teilhard's work in paleoanthropology and some of his work on the connection of science and religion, but the most famous of his ideas can, I think, be characterized not so much as an attempt to establish the compatibility of scientific and theological ideas (my interest in this book) as an attempt to *build* a theological system on science-inspired foundations; it was not an attempt to *accommodate* evolutionary biology but to *extend,* and to adapt, the idea of evolution, saliently, to eschatology. A detailed history of *that* project is beyond the scope of this work. I leave it to other scholars.

✳ ✳ ✳ ✳ ✳

My research into the history of Catholic evolutionism shows that it began early and was both widespread and sustained, as can be seen by the range of authors whose work is reviewed here. Some of those authors published books on the topic; others included a defense of a Catholic evolutionism in works primarily devoted to another, or to a broader, topic. It can hardly be denied that there were many Catholics who accepted evolutionist ideas without ever expressing their thoughts in public—surely scientists who were working on other lines of research and people who simply felt that that they had nothing to add to what was already being said; possibly also clerics forbidden by their superiors from addressing the issue.

It is hard to know how exactly to measure the extent to which Catholics were open to evolutionism (not least because of the many dimensions of the controversy, identified above). Perhaps the best that one can do is to look at its treatment in the Catholic periodical press, in Catholic encyclopedias, and in textbooks, to which I devote several chapters.

This book is not, however, a history of the Catholic *debate* over evolution *per se.* I have not attempted a *systematic* presentation of Catholic *anti*-evolutionism. That view also, of course, had its proponents. It will make its appearance both in my discussion of public reactions to the work of Catholic evolutionists and in its presence in the offices of the Church as official ecclesiastical reaction to Catholic evolutionism was under consideration.

✳ ✳ ✳ ✳ ✳

I want to conclude my introduction by drawing the reader's attention to appendices that will provide useful background, but would unduly delay the commencement of the story if presented as an introduction to the book. Appendix I provides a history of the scientific aspects of the questions that Catholic authors were confronting, the general shape of the *scientific* controversy over the origin of species and of man. Appendix II presents an introduction to the relevant epistemological features of Catholic theology, including hermeneutics and the theological "notes" of certainty by which theological ideas were graded. Appendix III provides some of the institutional background (e.g., the operating procedures of the Congregation of the Index of Prohibited Books) as well as an account of the variety of places (ranging from official documents to books and articles) in which ideas connected to our topic made their appearance.

PART I
THE FOUNDATIONS LAID
(1771–1885)

CHAPTER 1

CATHOLIC THOUGHT ON EVOLUTION BEFORE DARWIN

The Jesuit who taught me Russian history used to warn against "reading history backwards." He meant starting Russian history courses with the Bolshevik Revolution, as though nothing of importance to Russian history had happened before 1917. And so, in the present book, even though it may be tempting to start a history of Catholic evolutionism with reactions to the publication of Darwin's *Origin of Species*, we have to begin by noting that there were, if not "forerunners to Darwin," at least pre-Darwinian evolutionists, including a pre-Darwinian Catholic evolutionist.

Catholics have been involved in the history of the paleoetiological sciences, the science of "ancient causes,"[1] from the start. René Descartes, it would be fair to say, invented them;[2] Bl. Niels Stensen laid the foundations for paleoetiological geology. (For details, see the introduction to Appendix I.)

What about the Bible? In 1769, John Needham, an English Catholic priest and a biologist with a strong interest in the relationship between science and religion, wrote in a letter to the Comte de Buffon that "one must take those six days of creation as six

---

1 The word "paleoetiology," albeit in a haplological version ("palætiology") which seems to me to be both less euphonious and less clear, was coined by nineteenth-century historian and philosopher of science William Whewell; see his *Philosophy of the Inductive Sciences*, 1: xxxv–xxxvi.

2 See Descartes, *Discours* V, 42–44 (trans., 107–8).

periods of unknown length."[3] Pope Pius VII was reported by some nineteenth-century French authors to have accepted as orthodox the idea that the days of the Hexaemeron are epochs of long duration.[4]

Several authors show us the open state of the question.[5] Denis de Frayssinous, titular bishop of Hermopolis and one of the leading Catholic apologists of early nineteenth-century France, uncommitted on the question, wrote:

> I shall not decide before or against this opinion; if it is not the most common, it, nevertheless, has its upholders; I might cite modern theologians who have embraced it, or who have regarded it as at least uncertain. All that is important for us to know, is that it may be opposed or maintained without endangering our faith in the general revelation made to us by means of Moses. . . . We have a right to say to geologists: Pry as deeply as you please into the bowels of the earth; if your observations do not positively require that the days of the creation should be longer than our common days, we will continue to follow the common sentiment of their duration; if, on the contrary, you discover clearly and evidently, that the terrestrial globe, with its plants and animals, must be much older than the human race, Genesis contains nothing which is opposed to that discovery; for you are allowed to regard each of the six days as a period of indefinite time, and your discoveries will then become the explanatory commentary of a passage whose sense has hitherto been undetermined.[6]

French Catholic geologist Marcel de Serres wrote in the first edition of his *De la Cosmogonie de Moïse comparée aux faits géologiques* (1838) that the question of how the six days mentioned in Genesis are to be understood and of what length must be attributed to them "seems to have been resolved in a way that leaves no doubt even among those hardest to convince. Indeed, the results obtained by a knowledge not even suspected in antiquity seem to prove that . . . the six days in question were periods of indeterminate length."[7] In the second edition, published a few years later, however, he acknowledged more explicitly the open state of the question: "In this matter, everyone has a right to

---

3 Needham, *Nouvelles recherches*, 25.

4 The remark was reportedly made in a conversation with the members of the Institut national des sciences et arts (later renamed l'Institut de France), during his visit to Paris in 1804–05. I think that that must mean during one of the pope's visits to the Muséum d'histoire naturelle, which he had made on January 8 and March 14, 1805. I have, however, found no contemporaneous reports of the remark and authors who should have known about it (and who would surely have mentioned it if they had), e.g., Wiseman in his *Twelve Lectures* (1836), do not mention it. The earliest report of the remark that I can find comes from Alexandre-Aimé Giraudet, *Nouveau Traité de géologie* (1843), 369. Giraudet was a graduate of the Institute, but an author who, having been born only in 1798, could hardly have heard the conversation himself.

    Those remarks (even if genuine) did not, however, settle the matter, even in Catholic circles. Jules Fabre d'Envieu, priest and professor of sacred history at the Sorbonne, acknowledged in his *Les Origines de la terre et de l'homme* (1873), 225–26, that the pope had given the idea a certain approval (though only "simply as a theologian"); Fabre d'Envieu did not think that the interpretation was exegetically sound.

5 For a history, see Goulven Laurent, "Catholiques face à la géologie," 77–100.

6 Frayssinous, *Défense du christianisme* (1825), 2:49–51 (trans., 2:52–54).

7 De Serres, *Cosmogonie de Moïse*, 19–20.

choose; for the Church has not made a decision. Its theologians [*docteurs*] are as divided on the question as are the scientists [*savants*]."[8]

At about the same time, Nicholas Wiseman, then a priest, later cardinal archbishop of Westminster, highlighted the accompanying theology of nature in some lectures delivered in Rome in 1835. There he said of Élie de Beaumont's theory of the origin of mountains[9] that "this theory, by its beautiful unity in cause and action, is in perfect accord with all we know of the methods used by divine Providence, which establishes a law and then leaves it to act: so the budding forth of mountain chains should be the well-timed effect of causes, constant in rule, though irregular in action."[10]

The eighteenth and early nineteenth centuries saw the appearance of paleoetiological approaches to biology as well. Benoît de Maillet's *Telliamed* (1748) and Erasmus Darwin's *Zoonomia* (1794) were not only highly speculative but thoroughly materialist works. Jean-Baptiste Lamarck's *Philosophie zoologique* (1809) and his *Histoire naturelle des animaux sans vertèbres* (1815) was at least somewhat less speculative. If it was not philosophically materialist, it was at least perceived by its critics to be so. The review of the works of these authors by the Congregation of the Index of Prohibited Books will be discussed at the end of the chapter.

The first half of the nineteenth century, however, also saw the appearance of the earliest version of Catholic biological evolutionism, in the thought and work of the important Belgian geologist, Jean-Baptiste Julien d'Omalius d'Halloy.

1. CATHOLIC EVOLUTIONISM BEFORE DARWIN: JEAN-BAPTISTE JULIEN D'OMALIUS D'HALLOY (1783–1875)

Jean-Baptiste Julien d'Omalius d'Halloy was born into a wealthy aristocratic family in Liège in 1783.[11] In 1801, his family sent him to Paris for a literary and humanistic education, but, having read Buffon in his father's library, he was quickly drawn to the Muséum d'Histoire naturelle. There he was able to listen to the lectures of both the transformist Jean-Baptiste Lamarck and the anti-transformist Georges Cuvier. He was able to establish a scientific reputation in stratigraphy with an "Essai sur la géologie du nord de la France" and a "Mémoire sur l'étendue géographique du terrain des environs de Paris." The notes from his field work promised much more to come but, reluctantly, he set aside scientific research in favor of positions of increasing responsibility in government. The Revolution of 1830 brought his political responsibilities to an end but allowed him to return to scientific work, on which he remained active for the rest of his life. He did

---

8 De Serres, *Cosmogonie de Moïse*, 2nd ed., 7.

9 Cf., e.g., Élie de Beaumont, "Recherches," the work cited by Wiseman.

10 Wiseman, *Twelve Lectures*, 1:313–14.

11 For biographical details, see J. Guequier, "Omalius d'Halloy;" or E. Dupont, "Notice sur la vie." For a more specialized account of his thoughts on evolution, see Raf De Bont, *Darwins kleinkinderen*, 29–52, and "Serpent without Teeth"; as well as Goulven Laurent, *Paléontologie et évolution en France*, 395–403.

not resume the field work that underlay his earliest contributions to geology, however, but instead finished an introductory textbook of geology that he had begun while still governor of Namur. That book, which first appeared as *Éléments de géologie* (1831), he kept up to date throughout his life; its eighth, and final, edition (retitled *Précis élémentaire de géologie*) appeared in 1868.

Although he was first and foremost a geologist, the paleontological aspects of that larger science led him to consider the question of the origin of species. One can distinguish two steps in his contribution to that question.

His first, negative, contribution came as early as 1812–13, when he rejected explanation of faunal succession by reference to catastrophes and successive creations. Such an explanation, he argued, was inconsistent with the details of the paleontological record and, more generally, with "the way nature ordinarily works."[12] His second, positive, contribution was his defense of transformism (or "reproduction," to use his term) as a better account of what he called "the succession of living things." This view he first articulated in the final sections of the first edition of the *Éléments*.[13] His views received some elaboration in lectures that he gave before the Société géologique de la France (of which, despite being Belgian, he was for many years the president) and before the Académie royale des sciences, des lettres et des beaux-arts de Belgique.[14]

The alternatives to transformism, he argued, were implausible: "The idea of a series of new creations is a purely gratuitous hypothesis not based on any analogy with phenomena which take place in historical times; it seems that one should not resort to such hypotheses except when it is absolutely impossible to explain the facts in any other way, which is not at all true in this case."[15] Partial extinction followed by migration does sometimes actually occur, but would leave as "singular coincidences" such facts as the similarity between living and extinct animals in the same region, similarities among organisms geographically adjacent to one another, and the generally progressive succession found in the geological column.

And so, one is left with transformism. Is this inconsistent with the apparent stability of species over the course of generations?

> However great the stability of species is, it is not absolute, and if we look at the history of now-existing living things in this regard, we will see that various causes can lead to changes in their forms. The principal among these causes is the attention of man, who, by augmenting, diminishing, or varying the nutrition of living beings, as well as by changing the temperature of their environment, has been able to double the flowers, to make fruits larger and more succulent, and to give domestic animals

---

12 D'Omalius, "Notice," 58–59 (or summary in *Nouveau Bulletin*, at 128).

13 D'Omalius, *Éléments*, 522–33. In the "Historical Sketch" that Darwin included in the third and later editions of the *Origin of Species*, he acknowledged d'Omalius's "excellent, though short paper" of 1846 as well as his support of the idea in 1831 (*Origin of Species*, 3rd ed., xvi).

14 These lectures include "Note sur la succession," the untitled public lecture of 1850, "Discours sur l'espèce," and "Sur le Transformisme."

15 D'Omalius, *Éléments*, 526–27.

qualities and forms so different that zoologists are obliged to admit into the species *dog* a collection of animals which differ among themselves much more that does the fox from the wolf.[16]

Those causes of variation operate in nature as well. If they do not lead to new species today, that is because the causes and effects were more intense in the past.[17] D'Omalius was thus less committed than were Lyell and Darwin to strong versions of actualism (to explaining the past exclusively on the basis of causes now in operation) and indeed attributed precisely to Darwin's actualism what d'Omalius saw as an overreliance on natural selection and the struggle for existence in the explanation of faunal succession.[18]

These were scientific arguments, but they were arguments in defense of what was widely thought to be a materialist thesis. D'Omalius, however, was a Catholic. He was on principle committed to some degree of separation between science and theology, though one that cut both ways: "Just as our religious beliefs must not prevent us from seeing the facts of nature as they are, even less may we rely on observations made with our gross senses in attacking dogmas which are of a completely different order."[19] There was not, however, a problem in this case: "None of the facts established as a result of geognostic observations undermines the account contained in Genesis."[20] Indeed, "one should see in the cosmogony of Genesis only the establishment of a few great principles, notably the existence of an omnipotent God existing anterior to matter and the creation of the latter by the former."[21]

The Bible is accommodationist in its use of language; transformism is theologically neutral. D'Omalius went one step further. It is successive creations, not transformations, that seem to be inconsistent with Scripture.[22] And, as an argument from an underlying theology of nature, he added:

> I find it hard to believe that the omnipotent being whom I consider to be the author of nature has, at different epochs, caused all living beings to perish, in order to give Himself the pleasure of creating new beings, which, on the basis of the same general plans, present successive differences tending to arrive at the present forms and sometimes reproducing the rudiments of organs that were useful to earlier beings but which have no use to the later ones.... It seems to me much more probable and more in conformity with the eminent wisdom of the Creator to admit that, just as He has given living beings the power of reproduction, so He has also endowed them with the property of modifying themselves according to circumstances—a phenomenon of which nature still gives examples.[23]

16 D'Omalius, *Éléments*, 528–29.

17 D'Omalius, *Éléments*, 529–30.

18 D'Omalius, *Précis*, 496.

19 D'Omalius, *Éléments*, 530n.

20 D'Omalius, *Éléments*, 530n.

21 D'Omalius, "De l'Accord." 556.

22 D'Omalius, *Précis*, 496.

23 D'Omalius, "Sur le Transformisme," 771–72.

In addition to the general anti-materialist concerns about transformism, there were also more particular Catholic concerns about the origin of man. Lamarck had, after all, included man also within his transformist history of life, but d'Omalius, like all Catholic evolutionists, limited the rôle of evolution in the origin of the human race. First, to draw from paleontology any conclusions about the immortality of the soul would be to confuse the physical order and the metaphysical. Second, d'Omalius did not feel, as Darwin did, the appeal of a comprehensive (monophyletic) version of the Common Ancestry Thesis and thus felt it less necessary to address in any detail the question of animal origins of man: "Although I consider the living beings of today as coming, by way of reproduction, from those of ancient times, he wrote, I do not mean to say that man must consider the polyp as the root of his noble race."[24] Man might have undergone evolutionary transformations over the course of earth history, but d'Omalius was not committed to a history of life that included the transformation of an animal into a man.

2. EVOLUTIONISM AND THE INDEX BEFORE 1859

There is no evidence of unfavorable reaction to D'Omalius's books on the part of the official Church. The years before Darwin did see three other books on evolution delated to the Congregation of the Index in the years before 1859; action was taken against two.

The first book against which action was taken was Benoît de Maillet's *Telliamed* (1748). Maillet's cosmology featured an eternal world, directed by chance. Although focused on a geology in which most of the features of the earth were attributed to a receding ocean, it devoted several chapters to the origin of animals and of man. The geological work was based on careful observation; the sections on the origin of species display a mixture of sound observation, credulity, and vivid imagination.[25] Preparation of the manuscript for publication remained incomplete at Maillet's death in 1738. In the last years of his life, he had turned the task of editing the work over to a French priest, J. B. le Mascrier, who had made a business of editing and arranging publication of books that would not otherwise have been approved by French censorship. Le Mascrier made some effort to tone down *Telliamed*'s unorthodox features and the result was published ten years after Maillet's death. The book remained extremely popular until the end of the eighteenth century.

---

24 D'Omalius, *Éléments*, 530n.

25 "Concerning the origins of terrestrial animals, I notice that there are none of them, whether walking, flying, or creeping, of which similar or closely related species do not exist in the sea, and for which the change from one of these elements to the other would not only be possible and probable, but even supported by a great number of examples.... The resemblance ... is highly worthy of our attention and it is surprising that nobody, to my knowledge, has tried to find out the reasons for this similarity."—*Telliamed*, 133–35 (Carozzi trans., 184–85). The resemblance got the attention Maillet thought it deserved in, for example, Neil Shubin's *Your Inner Fish*. But then one comes to the reports of mermen sightings, at *Telliamed*, 151–71 (Carozzi trans., 192–200).

Telliamed was reviewed by the Index, at the general congregation held on May 24, 1771,[26] on the basis of a *votum* prepared by Ambrogio Maria Erba da Milano, an Observant Franciscan.[27] Ambrogio counted the author as being among those who (in Lactantius's phrase) "not only do not want to maintain religion, but even want to destroy it."[28] He cited as objectionable Maillet's doctrine of the eternity of the world, his account of the origin of man (directly opposed to Moses's narrative of creation from dust), and his anti-providentialism. The decision was made to place the book on the *Index* but, due to what seems to be a clerical error, it was never listed correctly and eventually ceased to be listed altogether.[29]

The second book delated to the Index was Lamarck's *Histoire naturelle des animaux sans vertèbres* (1815), delated by Fr. Lorenzo Tardi Agris, for its evolutionism but also for its broader anti-providentialist materialism.[30] There is no evidence in its archives that the Congregation reviewed the book. It was never placed on the *Index*.

The third book was Erasmus Darwin's *Zoonomia* (1794–96), primarily a work of medical analysis (such as a classification of diseases) and of physiology, but also including some philosophical speculation on the nature of life. It is a materialist account, according to which "all animals have a similar origin, viz. from a single living filament; and that the difference of their forms and qualities has arisen only from the different irritabilities and sensibilities, or voluntarities, or associabilities, of this original living filament."[31] The book was translated into Italian in 1803–05 and it was that translation that was delated to the Index.[32] Albertino Bellinghi, a Camaldolese monk, wrote the *votum*. Most relevant

---

26 Diary entry, May 24, 1771 (fol. 40v–41v, Diarii 18 (1764–1807)).

27 Erba, *Votum* (fol. 19r–21r, Protocolli 1771–73/90, CL, ADDF).

28 Lactantius, *Divine Institutes*, 3.28.

29 The history of the listing and subsequent disappearance of *Telliamed* from the *Index* is as follows:

Every year or two, the Index published a decree listing the works condemned over the course of the several meetings of the Index since the issuance of the previous decree. And so, its *Decretum* of May 24, 1771 listed ten new works condemned over the previous seven months, including "*Telliamed, or Conversations of an Indian Philosopher with a French Missionary,* . . . put in order on the basis of the notes [*memoires*] of the late M. de Maillet, by J. A. G." That was copied from the title page of the 1749 edition, the one that it had reviewed. J. A. G., unknown to the Index, was Jean Antoine Guer, an obscure lawyer (Carozzi, *Telliamed*, 15).

In 1779, the decrees of the previous decade were published as a booklet entitled *Ad indicem novissimum*. Ordinarily, books in the *Index* were listed by author, but the editors of the booklet apparently thought that Maillet was not exactly the author and "J. A. G." was not really a name, so they listed the work under the title (*Telliamed*) and under the subtitle (*Entretiens d'un philosophe indien*). Worse, the compiler, perhaps partly misled by the unclear formatting of the decree but also due to clerical carelessness, thought that *Telliamed* was part of the multi-part *Évangile du jour*. The four parts of that work had been listed separately on the decree, so the booklet also listed them separately, with cross-references to the main entry for the *Évangile*. Both entries for *Telliamed* were cross-referenced in the same way. That error of was copied into next full edition of the *Index* in 1786.

Next came the gradual (unauthorized) removal of the book from the *Index*; probably an editor was attentive enough to notice that *Telliamed* was not part of the *Évangile*, but not clear about the proper correction. The 1835 edition of the *Index* dropped the "*Telliamed*" entry, though the "*Entretiens*" entry remained. In the 1841 and subsequent editions, it too was removed.

30 Agris to Index (fol. 73, Atti e documenti 1821–28/2, CL, ADDF).

31 E. Darwin, *Zoonomia*, 39.4.6.

32 Bellinghi, *Votum* (fol. 359–60 and 401–5, Protocolli 1808–19/103, CL, ADDF).

to our subject was the notice taken of Darwin's views that "the world itself might have been generated, rather than created; that is, it might have been gradually produced from very small beginnings, increasing by the activity of its inherent principles, rather than by a sudden evolution of the whole by the Almighty fiat." This passage, Bellinghi argued, contained two errors. First, "the word 'generated' connotes a division in the substance of the generating principle." Second, "if one says that the World was 'gradually produced from very small beginnings, increasing by the activity of its inherent principles,' then one excludes Moses's story of the creation in six days."[33] Bellinghi recommended that the work be prohibited.[34] On December 22, 1817, it was placed on the *Index*.[35]

The two prohibited books had embedded their evolutionism in a broader materialist philosophy of nature which, quite apart from their evolutionism, was incompatible with Catholic doctrine. The consultor who reviewed Darwin's *Zoonomia* noted his concerns about evolutionism as well, but since the Index only made an overall judgment about the book (without voting on each individual element in a consultor's expressed concerns), it is impossible to say with certainty whether the alleged inconsistency with the Mosaic Hexaemeron alone would have led to the prohibition of his book.

33 E. Darwin, *Zoonomia*, 39.4.8; quoted in Bellinghi's *Votum* (fol. 403r–v).

34 Bellinghi, *Votum* (fol. 401r).

35 Decretum (fol. 359, Protocolli 1808–19/103, CL, ADDF).

CHAPTER 2

SCIENTISTS & THEOLOGIANS
(1859–1885)

In the decades immediately following Charles Darwin's announcement of his new theory in 1858, a number of Catholic authors took up the question of the extent to which biological evolution was compatible with Catholic doctrine. Three, a paleontologist and two zoologists, were of particular importance.

Of these, the first was Albert Gaudry. His first discussion of the issue came less than a year after the paired papers of Darwin and Alfred Russel Wallace, proposing the evolutionary origin of species by natural selection, had been read to the Linnean Society of London[1] and several months before Darwin's *Origin* appeared in print. Although he subsequently engaged in occasional correspondence with Darwin, his first interest in the topic arose rather from the evolutionism of Jean-Baptiste Lamarck and of the more paleontology-minded Étienne Geoffroy Saint-Hilaire and his son Isidore. Of the three, Gaudry made the greatest scientific contributions to the new theory, indeed so much

---

1 Darwin and Wallace, "On the Tendency of Species to Form Varieties," two separate papers presented together. For more on Darwin and Wallace, see Costa, *Wallace, Darwin, and the Origin of Species*. One should note, however, that these papers do not make special reference to the faunal succession that was at the center of Gaudry's interest.

so that historian Goulven Laurent rightly called Gaudry the founder of evolutionary paleontology.[2] Indeed his work was cited by both Darwin and Lyell.[3]

The second, Filippo De Filippi, addressed the topic only in one lecture, a lecture of considerable importance in Italy—indeed he is usually credited with initiating Italian interest in Darwinism—but seemingly little noticed elsewhere. He died young, only three years after the lecture was delivered.

The third, St. George Mivart, by contrast, lived for another thirty years after his first contribution to the topic, and addressed the topic in several books (and consequently in much greater detail than had de Filippi). Perhaps for those reasons, Mivart seems to have had a broader influence on the development of a precisely Catholic evolutionism than did the other two, but all three must be added to the list of major pioneers of Catholic evolutionism.

However much all three merit our particular attention, they were not alone. I devote the middle pages of the chapter to six other early accommodationist responses to evolutionism, partly for the content of their ideas and partly just to show the geographic range of accommodationism. I conclude with an account of the *status questionis* with respect to monogenism.

1. ALBERT GAUDRY (1827–1908)

Albert Gaudry[4] was born in Germain-en-Laye in 1827. He inherited his father's (amateur) interest in geology and earned a doctorate in the subject from the Muséum d'Histoire naturelle in 1852. His interests soon focused on paleontology and he began his institutional life as an assistant to his brother-in-law Alcide d'Orbigny, first holder of the newly-created chair in paleontology at the Muséum. He was himself named to that chair in 1872 and held it for thirty years. In 1882, he was elected to the Académie des Sciences, the first paleontologist to be elected as such to that body. In 1904, he was elected president of the Académie. His major professional accomplishments include field work at Pikermi in Greece (1855 and 1860) and at Mount Léberon in the French Midi (1872). At both sites he turned up fossils of Tertiary mammal species intermediate between known species. This fieldwork was followed by a three-volume general account of evolutionist paleontology (*Les Enchaînements du monde animal* [1878–90]) and his *Essai de paléontologie philosophique* (1896). His thoughts on evolution can be subsumed under four heads.

✳ ✳ ✳ ✳ ✳

---

2 Laurent, "Gaudry, Alfred," 1802.

3 Darwin, *Origin of Species*, 5th ed., 402, and Lyell, *Principles of Geology*, 10th ed., 2:481–84.

4 For biographical details, see Laurent, "Gaudry," or Frank Bourdier, "Albert Jean Gaudry." See also Pascal Tassy, "L'émergence de la paléontologie darwinienne au XIXe siècle," and Laurent, "Albert Gaudry et la paléontologie évolutive."

First is his acceptance of transformism as the proper explanation of faunal succession. He first expressed his evolutionist sympathies in early 1859, in a retrospective article on the work of his brother-in-law written shortly after the latter's death. D'Orbigny had attributed the various fossil faunas to twenty-seven successive acts of creation. Gaudry acknowledged two alternative explanations—migration from adjacent locations, which he rejected, and "modification of species over the course of ages, with the lower beings perfected and transformed little by little into organizationally more advanced animals."[5]

Gaudry's acceptance of the idea is explicit in his reports on his excavations in Pikermi, excavations which had already begun several years before the article just mentioned, and at Mount Léberon:

> As I tried to understand the history of fossil beings, it seemed to me more and more likely that the *Author of the world* did not create the successive species of geological ages separately, but that He drew the later from the earlier ones. My studies at Pikermi confirmed this way of seeing the matter as it showed me the numerous links between forms that had at first seemed distinct.[6]
>
> These analogues reveal a certain resemblance between the fauna of the Upper Miocene and the faunas which preceded and followed it. Although this resemblance often shows itself more in general traits than in details, it must be given great weight by anyone trying to understand the plan of creation. In fact, one is either forced to admit what is called the law of imitation, that is to suppose that, in creating the beings of one geological epoch, God partly took as models the beings of preceding epochs, or one has to believe that the analogies represent blood relationships, whether near or extended. I prefer the second of those hypotheses, because most of the analogous species have such a large number of resemblances, compared to the number of differences, that it would seem to be simpler to derive the ones from the others than the destroy the earlier ones in order to remake something almost identical. . . . One can hardly be surprised by the inclination to think that one has before one's eyes not species of distinct origin but a single type that had undergone slight modifications.[7]

He summarized the relationships among fossil species by drawing properly phylogenetic trees; indeed he was among the first to do so.[8]

His finds, he thought, were "probably sufficient to prove that the transitions observed at Pikermi are related to a law common to all beings,"[9] a point that he elaborated in his three-volume *Les Enchaînements du monde animal* a few years later. There he wrote: "We can see many clues of sequences that make us think that in the same class there have been transitions from species to species, from genus to genus, from family to family, and

---

5 Gaudry, "D'Orbigny," 838.

6 Gaudry, *Mont Léberon*, 75.

7 Gaudry, *Mont Léberon*, 91–92. See also *Pikermi*, 62–63 (*Attique*, 366).

8 Gaudry, *Pikermi*, 36–46 (*Attique*, 348–55). For the historical context, see Pascal Tassy, "Trees before and after Darwin."

9 Gaudry, *Pikermi*, 60 (*Attique*, 364).

from order to order." Then he asked, "Can we go further? Do we find evidence that, within a phylum, animals of different classes have passed from one to the other?" His answer was that it was too early to do so: "It is obvious that the theriodonts, ichthyosaurs, and pterodactyls have narrowed the gap which exists between reptiles and mammals, but they have not closed it in such a way as to prove a transition between these two classes today so distinct." With regard to the most striking case, dinosaurs as a link between reptiles and birds, he wrote:

> The most reasonable conclusion, it seems to me, is to believe that dinosaurs and birds had a common ancestor which was neither a true dinosaur nor a true bird. I suppose that in general there was only a very distant relationship between animals of different classes belonging to the same phylum. Their union must go back to a remote epoch, in which they had not yet taken on the distinctive characteristics of the classes in which we now classify them. What are these presumed ancestors from which animals that have since led to different classes emerged? We do not know. Certainly we would like to see the gaps disappear and to understand the unity of the whole organic world, but our science is still too young. Workers of the first hour, we can see only vaguely, in the distance, the magnificent tableau of nature, where, under the direction of the Divine Artist, everything is coordinated, interconnected, linked together across space and through the ages.[10]

Gaudry acknowledged that there were still gaps in the fossil record, but wondered whether these were not rather gaps in our knowledge than gaps in the history of life.[11] Nevertheless, "although those who study the living world have been able to believe in the fixity of species, those who examine geological times are rather led to think that change is the essence of creatures. Divine Activity seems to be shown by the incessant modifications which, in giving variety to nature, have contributed to its beauty,"[12] an idea which he contrasted to the then more common idea of discrete, successive creative acts by calling it "continuous creation."[13]

✳ ✳ ✳ ✳ ✳

The second element in Gaudry's evolutionism is his rejection of the ideas of a struggle for existence and natural selection. Gaudry's acceptance of Darwin's ideas about the origin of species by descent with modification did not extend to acceptance of Darwin's *explanation* of those modifications.[14]

In his report on the Pikermi excavations, he wrote: "My researches have shown that, in geological times, Greece was not a scene of struggles and disorders; everything was

---

10 Gaudry, *Enchaînements: Fossile secondaires*, 300. See also his earlier *Enchaînements: Fossile primaires*, 292–93, where he sounds a little more skeptical about a unification of all lineages.

11 Gaudry, *Pikermi*, 65–66 (*Attique*, 368).

12 Gaudry, *Mont Léberon*, 96.

13 Gaudry, *Enchaînements: Fossile primaires*, 314.

14 Gaudry to Darwin, May 22, 1867, *Correspondence*, 15:274.

arranged in harmony."[15] "The carnivores that one sees there played a rôle in the economy of nature more beautiful that one would at first suppose. They served, then as now, to keep the otherwise excessive fecundity of the herbivores in check. They were not numerous enough to turn Greece into a scene of struggle, of universal violence."[16] Darwin replied to Gaudry that "you do not fully understand what I mean by 'the struggle for existence, or *concurrence vitale*.'"[17] In this, Darwin seems correct. "Nature, red in tooth and claw" was, after all, Tennyson's phrase, not Darwin's. Darwin was explicit that he was using the word "struggle" "in a large and metaphorical sense," which included "the missletoe … struggl[ing] with other fruit-bearing plants, in order to tempt birds to devour and thus disseminate its seeds rather than those of other plants."[18]

Gaudry said that he was not concerned with the mechanisms of modification, partly because it would require a wider range of scientific knowledge than he thought he possessed, partly because he thought that the cause might be entirely beyond the reach of human understanding.[19] He was, however, willing to go so far as to say that "however animals were renovated [*renouvelé*], what is certain is that no modification was due to chance." Then he added:

> If we recognize that the living [*organisé*] beings were subject to gradual transformation, we will look at them as plastic substances that an artist was pleased to mold during the immense course of ages, lengthening here, widening or decreasing there, as a sculptor with a piece of clay produces a thousand forms, according to the impulse of his genius. But we will not doubt that the artist who was doing the molding was the Creator himself, since each transformation carried a reflection of His infinite beauty.[20]

Gaudry's rejection of chance is at least an assertion of providentialism. His image of an artist suggests direct divine intervention in the history of life, but other passages seem to suggest the opposite. Elsewhere, he had written that "Change seems to be the supreme *law of nature*."[21] And: "Providence, which gave inorganic things the property of undergoing physical and chemical modifications, which gave to living [*organisé*] beings the power of reproducing by undergoing complete metamorphoses (as that of a caterpillar into a butterfly, of infusoria into polyps and then into medusae), can certainly just as well give those living things the power to generate new species."[22]

✳ ✳ ✳ ✳ ✳

15 Gaudry, *Pikermi*, 68 (*Attique*, 370).

16 Gaudry, *Pikermi*, 18 (*Attique*, 336); see also *Paléontologie philosophique*, 30.

17 Darwin to Gaudry, September 17, 1866, *Correspondence*, 14:318.

18 Darwin, *Origin*, 62–63.

19 Gaudry to Darwin, May 22, 1867, *Correspondence*, 15:274.

20 Gaudry, *Pikermi*, 68 (*Attique*, 370).

21 Gaudry, *Paléontologie philosophique*, 211–12 (italics mine).

22 Gaudry, "D'Orbigny," 838.

The third element of Gaudry's evolutionism is his assertion that it is compatible with his Catholic faith. This theme was already articulated in Gaudry's retrospective on d'Orbigny: "Some people have considered the theory of transformations to be a materialist doctrine, but that reproach seems to us to be unfounded. . . . As long as the naturalist only allows a transformation of things into other things that is determined by an original impulse emanating from the will of the Creator, he remains safe from any suspicion of materialism."[23] In general

> it is wrong to oppose the idea of successive creations to that of transformations, as if this were a debate between religious ideas and pantheism. . . . It is a question of knowing, not whether God created or did not create, but whether the successive appearances contained in potency in his creation were formations or transformations.[24]

✳ ✳ ✳ ✳ ✳

The fourth element of Gaudry's evolutionism is his views on human origins.

He clearly accepted the antiquity of man. Indeed, his most significant contribution to paleoanthropology came in 1859 when, in the midst of the controversy over Jacques Boucher de Perthes's claim to have found stone tools in the diluvial deposits of the Somme valley, evidence of the hitherto unrecognized antiquity, he went to Amiens and conducted excavations that confirmed that early man was indeed contemporaneous with several species of extinct European megafauna.[25]

Gaudry seems, however, never directly to have addressed the question of the *animal origins* of the human race, as opposed to its antiquity. Nevertheless, I think that we can make two inferences about his views.

In 1830, France's leading paleontologist, the anti-evolutionist Cuvier, had expressed his astonishment that not a single fossilized quadrumanal tooth or bone had yet been discovered,[26] but that changed in 1837. Most relevant to the question of human origins was a Middle Miocene jawbone discovered by Albert Fontan in 1856. Édouard Lartet, to whom Fontan entrusted the scientific analysis of the find, named it *Dryopithecus* and saw in it "a step of dentition intermediate between that of man and living apes."[27] Gaudry said that it was "the only anthropomorphic ape found in the fossil state that could be compared with man."[28] Was *Dryopithecus* the, or at least a, missing link?

---

23 Gaudry, "D'Orbigny," 838. The charge of materialism had been made, for example, by François-Louis-Michel Maupied in his *Dieu, l'homme, et le monde*, 3:206–7.

24 Gaudry, *Pikermi*, 61 (*Attique*, 365).

25 Gaudry, *Contemporanéité*.

26 Cuvier, *Discours*, 6th ed., 360.

27 Lartet, "Note sur un grand Singe fossile," 220.

28 Gaudry, *Le Dryopithèque*, 5.

Gaudry discussed the species twice, first in 1878, in the volume of *Enchaînements* devoted to Tertiary mammals.[29] There he followed Lartet's lead, calling it "an ape ... similar to man in many particulars."[30]

To that, Gaudry added the remark that "the question of the links and differences between man and *Dryopithecus* has taken on greater importance in recent years as a result of discoveries, thought to be traces of man, in Miocene terrains."[31] He was, cautiously, willing to defer to the experts on the question of whether the eoliths were artifacts (rather than the product of some natural process), but, every other Miocene mammal having been transformed into some descendant species over the intervening millennia, he doubted that man existed in that remote epoch. In the end, he suggested, "if it were to be demonstrated that the flints of the Beauce limestone collected by M. l'abbé Bourgeois were artifacts [*taillé*], the most natural idea that would present itself to my mind would be that they were made by dryopithecines."[32] That is not, of course, though Gaudry did not address the question explicitly, the same as saying that *Dryopithecus* was a species ancestral to man. The idea of species that were chronologically, but not genealogically, pre-Adamite, had been suggested by, for example, Jules Fabre d'Envieu, priest and theologian at the Université de Paris, as a possible way of explaining certain scientific data without creating theological problems.[33]

Gaudry's second contribution to the appraisal of *Dryopithecus* came when, in 1890, Félix Regnault asked him to study a new dryopithecine fossil. His analysis of the new find led him to revise his opinion. Focusing on what could be inferred from the shape of the jaw about the dryopithecine tongue, he wrote that the Miocene ape "does not establish an intermediary between the man who speaks and the beasts that bellow."[34] In light of the new evidence, "there was in Tertiary Europe neither man nor any creature that came close to him. Since *Dryopithecus* is the highest of the fossil great apes discovered to date, we must acknowledge that paleontology has not yet provided any evidence of linkage between man and animals."[35]

Gaudry does not, however, seem to place man completely outside the history of life that he had outlined. Imagining a time traveler surveying the history of life, he wrote on the final pages of the *Enchaînement*:

> If our traveler were not tired of his long trek through the ages, he would find in the Tertiary *Dryopithecus*, *Dinotherium* and a thousand other mammals; in the Quaternary and in the present age, he would meet man, the artist and poet; man,

29 Gaudry, *Enchaînements: Mammifères tertiaires*, 236–41.

30 Gaudry, *Enchaînements: Mammifères tertiaires*, 236.

31 Gaudry, *Enchaînements: Mammifères tertiaires*, 238. The discoveries in question, usually called eoliths, were made by priest-paleoanthropologist Louis Bourgeois in 1863–67 ("Étude sur des silex travaillés").

32 Gaudry, *Enchaînements: Mammifères tertiaires*, 241.

33 Fabre d'Envieu, *Les Origines de la terre et de l'homme*, 329–30.

34 Gaudry, *Dryopithèque*, 8.

35 Gaudry, *Dryopithèque*, 11.

who thinks and prays. The history of the world as a whole is truly the history of a progressive evolution [*développement*]. Where will this evolution end?[36]

Whatever rôle he seems to give to evolutionary processes in the formation of the human body, however, he also emphasized that there is more to man than a material body. In a letter to Darwin, he said, "as for me, transformism does not infringe on my ideas as a spiritualist or on my respect for human dignity."[37] And in his article on d'Orbigny, he had written:

> One can believe in these transformations without accepting the transformation of material principles into immaterial ones. One cannot even draw from transformations occurring in the material world the conclusion that there are analogous transformations in the immaterial world, since those worlds are quite distinct—the latter so obviously outweighs the former that the Creator can act *mediately* in the one and *immediately* in the other. Finally, the doctrine of transformations does not affect the dignity of man. God can have arrested the ordinary course of nature for his privileged creature.[38]

2. FILIPPO DE FILIPPI (1814–1867)

Filippo De Filippi[39] was born in Milan on April 29, 1814. At university, his interest turned from medicine (the profession of his father) to natural science and he eventually became one of the leading Italian naturalists of his day. The topics of his work ranged from parasitic worms and the embryology of fish to paleontology and mineralogy.[40] In 1848, he was called to the Università degli Studi di Torino to become professor of zoology and director of the zoological museum. Despite those responsibilities, he found time for both popular science writing and, being a sincere and practicing Catholic,[41] for reflection on the relationship between science and religion. His more technical work, of course, was the foundation for his reputation as a zoologist, but it was his other work that earns him a place in our story.

The controversy between Lamarck and Cuvier, between the comprehensive transformism of the former and the uncompromising fixism (and catastrophism) of the latter, centered though it may have been in France, played a formative rôle in Italian biological thought as well. De Filippi, and others, were looking for some kind of intermediate

---

36 Gaudry, *Enchaînements: Fossiles secondaires*, 305.

37 Gaudry to Darwin, January 11, 1868, *Correspondence*, 16:1, 19.

38 Gaudry, "D'Orbigny," 838.

39 For biographical details, see Michele Lessona, "Filippo De Filippi." See also Giovanni Landucci, "De Filippi," and Guido Cimino, "De Filippi."

40 For a bibliography, see Jacopo Moleschott, "Cenno biografico," 444–53.

41 Michele Lessona, De Filippi's student, and then his colleague, as well as an ardent evolutionist (Italian translator, for example, of Darwin's *Descent of Man*), testified to this, against those who have tried to deny it, in his "De Filippi," 652–54. I will say more about this below.

position. It was in that intellectual context that De Filippi proposed just such a theory, in *Il diluvio Noëtico* (1855).[42]

That book, as its name might suggest, was fundamentally a catastrophist work. Catastrophes did not, however, despite what some catastrophists seemed to think, have to be universal, and the doctrine was in any case *logically* distinct from an absolute fixism with respect to phylogenetic lineage. And so, on the basis of paleontological observation, De Filippi wrote:

> From this complex of facts and inductions it is clear that the geological revolutions by which each epoch of creation was closed . . . could not have entirely destroyed the organic beings which had flourished in that epoch; many of those beings continued to exist under the new telluric conditions of the subsequent epoch.
>
> Direct observation comes in here to show that a relatively small number preserved their primitive traits unchanged and one has to recognize that those traits are more or less profoundly modified under the changed conditions of existence. Those variations constitute, for the naturalist, indications of various true and distinct species.[43]

There were, to be sure, limits to how far those transformations could go: "We can without any hesitation make the common bear come from the cave bear; we feel some doubt as to whether mastodons are the ancestors of elephants; and we are definitely and insuperably opposed to the derivation of man from apes, as proposed by Lamarck and Geoffroy de St. Hilaire."[44]

De Filippi's views themselves evolved between 1855 and 1864, however. An early, brief review of Darwin's *Origin* in the *Rivista contemporanea*, which, according to historian Giovanni Landucci, was probably written by De Filippi, is sympathetic: "Although not accepted by all scientists, the theory is corroborated by great erudition, diligent research, and solid reasoning."[45] Otherwise, De Filippi was silent, but in 1864, perhaps prompted by the appearance of Huxley's *Evidence as to Man's Place in Nature*, in which Huxley had made explicit just what light might be shed by the theory of evolution on the origins of man, he made public his acceptance of a transformism much more extensive than he had adopted in the work cited above. On February 11 of that year, he delivered a public lecture entitled "L'uomo e le scimie," so focused precisely on the question of man and the apes. He began the lecture with a general endorsement of the ideas that constitute Darwin's *Origin*, not only transformism, but natural selection and universal common ancestry as well.[46] Then he proceeded to his discussion of man and apes, with respect to which he made two points.

---

42 De Filippi "Diluvio," 95–104 and 341. See also his *La creazione terrestre*.

43 De Filippi, "Diluvio," 98.

44 De Filippi, "Diluvio," 102.

45 Landucci, "De Filippi," 1135.

46 On natural selection, see in particular "Uomo e scimie," 12 and 59–60. On common ancestry, to pick just two passages, "Uomo e scimie," 43 and 51. Citations are to the published 1864 edition, except citations to the appendix, which are to

The argument for the first begins by urging a return to Carl Linnaeus's placement of man with apes and monkeys within a taxonomic order of Primates (the alternative system being their separation into distinct orders, Bimana [man] and Quadrumana [apes and monkeys], as was done by Johann Friedrich Blumenbach and then by Cuvier).[47] With respect to the brain (for example), he wrote that "man does not differ from the apes more than the principal systematic families of those apes differ from one another."[48] From that systematic connection, he drew a genealogical consequence:

> If man by constitution, by his configuration, is an animal belonging to the order of primates, hardly differing from apes by the distance which distinguishes one genus from another within a zoological order; if it is reasonable to derive all the primates from a single stock; if, in the chronological succession of living beings, apes had preceded man, the ultimate consequence presents itself, without our having to look for it.[49]

The ancestral primate that theoretically, if not paleontologically, presents itself would not, however, be any presently existing ape: "We can clearly derive from that the conclusion that we should not search for our primitive stock in any of today's anthropoid apes, but rather in a species lost in the pre-human epoch; in other words, present-day apes are the cadet branch. We are the principal branch of the common genealogical trunk."[50]

What is the significance of this conclusion? It is perhaps too easy to read his statement that "to say that man is descended from an ape is to do no more than to express an anatomical fact"[51] as though the emphasis were on the word "fact." It would express his larger view equally well (perhaps better) if the emphasis were put on the word "anatomical." De Filippi's second point, and in his view one even more important than the first, was that there is more to man than anatomy. The correspondences between man and ape with respect to structure are of less significance than the differences at the level of instinct and intellect.

> The more we reduce the physical inequalities between man and ape, the more the inequalities that remain, the differences in powers [*differenze virtuali*], grow in importance. . . . The place of man in nature must be determined not by the more or less of morphological characteristics subject to variation within the narrow confines of a species but by comparison of the powers proper to man with those of animals.[52]

De Filippi emphasized those differences:

---

the 1865 edition.

47 Linnaeus, *Systema naturae*, 10th ed. (1758), 1:16 and 18; Blumenbach, *Handbuch der Naturgeschichte*, 8th ed. (1807), 61; Cuvier, *Le Règne animal*, 2nd ed. (1829), 1:xxix–xxx and 69–109.

48 De Filippi, "Uomo e scimie," 37.

49 De Filippi, "Uomo e scimie," 41.

50 De Filippi, "Uomo e scimie," 45.

51 De Filippi, "Uomo e scimie," 42.

52 De Filippi, "Uomo e scimie," 46.

> When the naturalist thinks he can resolve the question of the difference between
> instinct and reason, or between animal and human reasoning, by asserting that man
> and animal have the same power [*principio virtuale*], or that there is nothing in one
> that is not in the other, then he will see common sense advancing against him like
> a heavy phalanx, and will have to cede the field of battle.[53]

The differences that everyone recognizes, he said, are sufficient to justify the establishment of a separate human kingdom, alongside those of minerals, plants, and animals: "The legitimacy of that kingdom cannot be disputed. Those who accept it and those who reject it both confirm it: … for of all of man's distinctive attributes, two are the most certain: one is that of putting himself in question and the other is the struggle with his own feelings."[54] The coat of arms of the human kingdom, he said in the last words of his lecture, contains the double crown of the moral and the teleological orders.[55]

And about religion? He made several points about religion and theology. First, on the methodological level, he said:

> Natural philosophy has nothing to do with revelation and cannot be used either for
> or against it. The rationalists make poor use of reason when they try to set scientific
> results in opposition to beliefs or to religious sentiments as though such opposition
> were in itself a probative criterion of physical truths. And theologians do a disservice
> to religion when they try to give it support that it does not request, which it does
> not need, and which, having been absolutely conceded to free discussion, can be
> overturned.[56]

Second, with respect to the theology of nature:

> The author of organic forms is also the author of the laws which govern them
> both individually and collectively. In the latter more than in the former, is mani-
> fested infinite Wisdom. It is possible to be profoundly atheistic while accepting the
> *immediate* [*di getto*] formation of organic species and a true religious sentiment is
> consistent with the doctrine of a genealogical descent of species from a primitive
> type, just as the pious [*ascetico*] exclamation "Not a leaf can fall without God's will"
> is consistent with a complete acceptance of the laws of gravity.[57]

And finally, on where his genealogy leaves the relation between Creator and man: "No one objects to saying that man is the ultimate terminus of the chain of created beings; but, when one counts and names the links of that chain, protests arise from every quarter. To

---

53 De Filippi, "Uomo e scimie," 47.

54 De Filippi, "Uomo e scimie," 50.

55 De Filippi, "Uomo e scimie," 53. The teleological order to which he referred is an extrinsic teleology, the suitability of the planet for human life.

56 De Filippi, "Uomo e scimie" (1865), Appendice, 68–69.

57 De Filippi, "Uomo e scimie" (1865), Appendice, 70 (emphasis De Filippi's).

think that the origin of man is perhaps less divine when the Biblical clod of earth turns out to be the entire organic world is a strange way of understanding human dignity."[58]

That all seems clear enough to me, but apparently the audience at his lecture wanted a simpler answer. Perhaps the confusion was caused in part by the juxtaposition of an inclusion of the human species within the order of primates and an exclusion of that same species from the animal kingdom altogether. He had confronted this apparent inconsistency in his lecture:

> One cannot avoid the dilemma. Either one takes into consideration only the material part of man, and then good zoology will not allow one to separate man and ape into two orders, the similarities between the two being too great, or one considers the powers [*virtualità*] as well, and then in better zoology, there is too much distance. So, colleagues, it would not be overly bold of us if we were to force the hand of the dispenser of taxonomic honors. Let us frankly seek investiture as a kingdom; a voice inside us says that we deserve it.[59]

One thing is certain—the audience's reaction was neither uniform nor simple. De Filippi wrote in a letter to Michele Lessona:

> I do not want to forego the pleasure of describing some of the groups in my audience. . . . Sèlla and Guerrieri were sitting together on one bench and, as I, step by step, showed how, in a purely anatomical sense, all the traits that differentiate man from apes disappeared one after another, they said "Good job, De Filippi! Great! Just right!"
>
> Behind them sat Prati and at each exclamation from them, he added, "No, wait! You'll see! I know De Filippi too well. He hasn't yet gotten to his conclusion."
>
> At last came my "but," in which I had put the principal point of the lecture; and then Sèlla and Guerrieri exclaimed "Ouch! Ouch!" and Prati, "Listen to that. Didn't I tell you? Good job, De Filippi."
>
> A little further away was a group that included Fr. Raineri and Fr. Scavia; they grimaced at every argument I made, tossed their heads, and twitched like Matteucci's frogs. My "but" came for them, too, but came uncomprehended, just as though I had been speaking Turkish.[60]

In the end, two very different groups of partisans went home unhappy. Many conservative Catholics refused to accept the relation between man and apes. Perhaps they were unhappy with De Filippi's willingness to minimize the kind of anatomical differences between man and ape that Richard Owen was still looking for in England. Perhaps they were unhappy

---

58 De Filippi, "Uomo e scimie" (1865), Appendice, 67–68.

59 De Filippi, "Uomo e scimie," 49.

60 Lorenzo Camerano, "Michele Lessona," 356n. The persons named in the letter are Quintino Sèlla (1827–84), anticlerical minister of finance, and the poet Giovanni Prati (1814–84), who, like De Filippi, was a member of the Consiglio superiore della pubblica istruzione. The other men named may have been Anselmo Guerrieri Gonzaga (a risorgimentalist politician who had an amateur interest in science) and Giovanni Scavia (a prolific author of school textbooks). Carlo Matteucci was an Italian neurophysiologist whose work on the electric induction of motion in frog legs continued the line of research begun by Luigi Galvani.

with his emphasis on behavior and powers without any explicit mention of the human soul. Many rationalists (to use a term of the day) did not want a reconciliation of science and religion. How could the new scientific ideas be used in the rationalists' war against religion if they were compatible with theological doctrine?

Darwin's *Origin* had received little notice in Italy in the years before De Filippi's lecture, but that changed in 1864. Although Giovanni Canestrini and Leonardo Salimbeni's Italian translation of the *Origin*, published the next year, avoided the ideological polemics that had marred the first French translation (Clémence Royer's), the transition from a *scientific* anthropogenesis to an *ideological* one was perhaps, if not logical, at least no less natural than was the transition from zoogenesis to anthropogenesis. It happened everywhere. In Italy, the associated tensions were only aggravated by the underlying tensions between the Catholic Church and the newly established Kingdom of Italy which, having conquered a large part of the Papal States in 1860, posed a continual threat to do the same to Rome itself. So, the debate over a scientific theory that had connections to religion and philosophy was carried on among partisans many of whom already opposed one another also on an emotionally charged *political* issue.

✳ ✳ ✳ ✳ ✳

In 1865, De Filippi accepted a government offer to join the steam-powered corvette *Magenta* in its circumnavigation of the globe. He took ill, however, while in the Far East and was put ashore at Hong Kong, where he died on February 9, 1867, but our story does not end there. The events associated with his last days on earth only set off another controversy.[61]

When the news of his death reached Italy, the government published an official notice, including the observation that "Senator De Filippi saw the advent of death with great serenity of mind and religious resignation. . . . He asked for and fervently received the comforts of religion and the administration of last rites."[62] Two Turinese preachers announced from their pulpits the good news that God had touched the heart of a great sinner at the moment of his death.[63] Some anti-clericals, by contrast, were outraged. One insisted that this "Jesuitical tale" was absolutely impossible.[64]

---

61 See Elena Canadelli, "La morte di De Filippi."

62 *Gazzetta Ufficiale*, "Ultime Notizie," 3.

63 Lessona, "De Filippi," 653–54.

64 Mauro Macchi, "Non è Possibile," 221.

23

3. ST. GEORGE JACKSON MIVART (1827–1900)[65]

Shortly after the publication of the fifth edition of *The Origin of Species* and the same year as the publication of the first edition of *The Descent of Man*, St. George Mivart published the first (and perhaps in some respects the most important) book-length articulation of Catholic evolutionism—*On the Genesis of Species*.[66]

Mivart's interest in biology had begun in his youth. His early plans for study at Oxford came to an abrupt end in 1844 when, at age seventeen, he converted to Catholicism. (Oxford still required entering students to subscribe to the Church of England's explicitly anti-Catholic Thirty-Nine Articles of Religion.) In January 1858, Mivart attended a series of lectures on "The Principles of Biology" given by Huxley at the Royal Institution. "It is almost needless to say," Mivart later wrote, "that his teaching, both its manner and matter, made a profound impression on me."[67] The next year, Mivart was introduced to Huxley and, the year following, became his student. In 1862, Mivart began a teaching career, being appointed Lecturer (and later Professor) of Comparative Anatomy at St. Mary's Hospital Medical School in London, where he remained until 1884.

His early scientific work focused particularly on comparative anatomy and systematic zoology, with a special emphasis on primates. He began publishing the results of his research in 1864 and by 1870 had written or co-authored twenty-eight books and articles.[68] During the remaining thirty years of his life, he published about thirty more technical articles as well as monographs on frogs, cats, dogs, and parrots, and some six other books on various other aspects of biology. James McMullen Rigg said of his scientific work that "in mastery of anatomical detail he had few rivals, and perhaps no superior, among his contemporaries."[69]

Although Mivart began his biological work as a protégé of Huxley, and indeed received his teaching appointment at St. Mary's on Huxley's recommendation, by 1871 Mivart's thinking had diverged from Darwin's on two key points—the importance of natural selection in the transformation of species and the origin of man. He first expressed his disagreement in a book review of the fifth (i.e., 1869) edition of Darwin's *Origin*, a review published (in accordance with the practice of the day, anonymously) in the Jesuits' *The Month*.[70] Next, under his own name, he published his book-length critique, *On the*

---

65 There are two biographies: Jacob W. Gruber, *A Conscience in Conflict*, and Christopher Blum's doctoral dissertation, *St. George Mivart*.

   It is perhaps appropriate to mention, for the benefit of readers new to the subject, that Mivart is called "*St.* George" by a decision of his (non-Catholic) parents at his birth, and not by the decision of any ecclesiastical body.

66 Several months later, also in 1871, Mivart published a second edition, in which he took note of the appearance of Darwin's *Descent of Man*. The changes are mostly in additional footnotes, without any significant change from the views he had expressed in the first edition.

67 Mivart, "Reminiscences," 988.

68 Bibliographies are available in Gruber, *Conscience in Conflict*, 249–58, and in Blum, *Mivart*, 388–96.

69 Rigg, "Mivart," 181.

70 Mivart, "Difficulties of the Theory of Natural Selection."

Genesis of Species. Finally, also in 1871, he published (again anonymously) a review of *The Descent of Man* in the *Quarterly Review.*[71]

Mivart's scientific critique of natural selection need not concern us in any detail. His thesis was "that 'Natural Selection' acts, and indeed must act, but that still, in order that we may be able to account for the production of known kinds of animals and plants, it requires to be supplemented by the action of some other natural law or laws as yet undiscovered."[72] His concerns were those articulated also by many of his contemporaries—the difficulty of accounting for the incipient stages of useful structures, the likelihood of saltations, limits to specific variability, etc.[73] He suspected that "variation can in [some] cases be proved to be subject to certain determinations in special directions by other means than Natural Selection"[74] and regarded "the whole organic world as arising and going forward in one harmonious development similar to that which displays itself in the growth and action of each separate individual organism."[75]

He also noted the attempts of others to bring theology into the evaluation of the theory, commenting, however, that "if the *odium theologicum* has inspired some of its opponents, it is undeniable that the *odium antitheologicum* has possessed not a few of its supporters."[76] His own view, however, was that both a general doctrine of evolution and the particular mechanism of natural selection were "perfectly consistent with strictest and most orthodox Christian theology"[77] and he devoted an entire chapter of his book to the defense of that compatibilist thesis. At the heart of his exposition was a distinction between absolute and derivative creation:

> In the strictest and highest sense "Creation" is the absolute origination of any thing by God without preëxisting means or material, and is a supernatural act.
>
> In the secondary and lower sense, "Creation" is the formation of any thing by God derivatively; that is, that the preceding matter has been created with the potentiality to evolve from it, under suitable conditions, all the various forms it subsequently assumes.[78]

That distinction, he argued, is sufficient to erase the alleged contradiction between the theory of evolution and the doctrine of creation:

> The conflict has arisen through a misunderstanding. Some have supposed that by "creation" was necessarily meant either primary, that is, absolute creation, or, at least,

---

71 He returned to this theme in several later books—*Man and Apes, Contemporary Evolution,* and *Lessons from Nature.*

72 Mivart, *Genesis of Species,* 17.

73 For a summary, see Mivart, *Genesis of Species,* 34.

74 Mivart, *Genesis of Species,* 32.

75 Mivart, *Genesis of Species,* 33.

76 Mivart, *Genesis of Species,* 24.

77 Mivart, *Genesis of Species,* 16.

78 Mivart, *Genesis of Species,* 269.

> some supernatural action; they have therefore opposed the dogma of "creation" in the imagined interest of physical science.
>
> Others have supposed that by "evolution" was necessarily meant a denial of Divine action, a negation of the providence of God. They have therefore combated the theory of "evolution" in the imagined interest of religion.[79]

He went on to cite St. Augustine, St. Thomas Aquinas, and Francisco Suárez in defense of his claim that *derivative* creation is consistent with the theological tradition.[80]

Although Mivart thought that Darwin's general views on evolution were theologically neutral, he held that Darwin's views on the descent of man could *not* be reconciled with orthodoxy. Darwin's *Origin of Species* had referred to the origins of *man* only obliquely, but the idea that the transformation of species was sufficient to account for that origin no less than for that of plants and animals was explicitly made in three other books within just a few years.[81] Mivart of course accepted as "a generally-received [Catholic] doctrine" the theses that "the soul of every individual man is absolutely created in the strict and primary sense of the word, that it is produced by a direct or supernatural act, and, of course, that by such an act the soul of the first man was similarly created."[82] He denied, however, that this, or any other doctrine of Catholic theology, was inconsistent with an evolutionary account of the origin of the human body:

> Scripture . . . says that "God made man from the dust of the earth, and breathed into his nostrils the breath of life." This is a plain and direct statement that man's body was not created in the primary and absolute sense of the word, but was evolved from preëxisting material (symbolized by the term "dust of the earth"), and was therefore only derivatively created, i.e., by the operation of secondary laws.[83]

Mivart's book received generally favorable notice from the British scientific community, being reviewed, for example, both in the *British Medical Journal* and in *Nature*.[84] Darwin, however, was ambivalent. He recognized the seriousness of Mivart's critique of natural selection and wrote to Wallace that "[Mivart's] work, I do not doubt, will have a most potent influence versus Natural Selection. The pendulum will now swing against us."[85] Indeed many of the revisions of the *Origin* made for the sixth (1872) edition were devoted to answering Mivart's objections. Nevertheless, Darwin also complained to several correspondents about what he saw as the unfairness of Mivart's review, an unfairness which he attributed to Mivart's bigotry (i.e., to his religious beliefs) and which he took

---

79 Mivart, *Genesis of Species*, 279.

80 Mivart, *Genesis of Species*, 281–83. This led to an exchange with Huxley in *The Contemporary Review* precisely on the point of Suárez's views.

81 For details, see Appendix I.B.

82 Mivart, *Genesis of Species*, 295n53. Mivart acknowledged that he was not using the term "supernatural" in its strict theological sense.

83 Mivart, *Genesis of Species*, 300.

84 Anonymously in the *British Medical Journal* and by Alfred W. Bennett in *Nature*.

85 Darwin to Wallace, January 30, 1871, in Wallace, *Letters*, 1: 258.

particularly personally.[86] Mivart's review of *The Descent of Man* offended Darwin and his friends and elicited a savage reply from Huxley in *The Contemporary Review*,[87] one focused rather less on the scientific issues that one would have a right to expect. By 1874, Mivart's relations with the Darwin circle suffered a complete rupture, precipitated by Mivart's reference, in another book review, to an article on eugenics written by Darwin's son George. The details of that controversy are not relevant to the subject of this book and need not detain us.[88]

Although Mivart's work came in for some criticism from Catholic anti-evolutionists,[89] it was well-received by other Catholics, including those in positions of authority. His *Genesis of Species* was favorably reviewed in the major Catholic reviews.[90] He received encouragement from St. John Henry Newman.[91] He was requested by Henry Cardinal Manning to join the faculty of the new (but short-lived) Catholic University of Kensington in 1874. In 1875–76, Cardinal Manning secured for him a doctorate in philosophy from the pope, then Bl. Pius IX, as someone "distinguished for his public refutation of unbelievers who misused the physical sciences."[92] In 1890–92, a few years after his retirement from St. Mary's, he accepted an appointment to the newly established Institut des hautes études philosophiques at the Université catholique de Louvain, where he gave lectures on "A General Introduction to the Science of Nature."[93]

It is important to acknowledge that, at two points in the last decade of his life, Mivart had problems with Church authorities—important to our story only because of the widespread but completely erroneous idea that this trouble indicated an official opposition to Mivart's ideas about evolution.

The first of Mivart's problems came as a consequence of his discussion of an unrelated theological question in three articles he wrote on the possibility of eventual happiness in Hell. These articles were placed by the Holy Office on the *Index of Prohibited*

---

86 See Darwin to J. D. Hooker, September 16, 1871, in Darwin, *More Letters*, 1:332–33, and to A. R. Wallace, January 30 and July 9, 1871, in Wallace, *Letters*, 1:257–59 and 264–65. Wallace did not agree with Darwin's assessment on this point (see Wallace to Darwin, July 12, 1871, in Wallace, *Letters*, 1:265–67).

87 Huxley, "Mr. Darwin's Critics." Mivart replied in "Evolution and its Consequences."

88 Those details, with extensive quotations from the relevant correspondence, are recounted in Gruber, *Conscience in Conflict*, 98–114. The matter is reviewed, briefly, by Janet Browne in her *Charles Darwin*, 2:355.

89 For example, in the exchange between Jeremiah Murphy and John S. Vaughan in the *Irish Ecclesiastical Record* (1884–5), discussed in chapter 4.

90 Anonymous reviews appeared in *The Month* and the *Dublin Review*. *The Tablet* also commended the book, but emphasized its anti-Darwinian character and read its treatment of anthropogenesis as a defense of mere compatibilism rather than as the presentation of the actual historical origins of the human race.

91 See Newman to Mivart, January 15 and December 9, 1871 (Newman, *Letters*, 25:268–69 and 446). In the latter, Newman wrote: "[I]t is pleasant to find that the first real exposition of the logical insufficiency of Mr. Darwin's theory comes from a Catholic. In saying this, you must not suppose I have personally any great dislike or dread of his theory, but many good people are much troubled at it."

92 Audiences (1875), 181: 2: 1059 and 1072, ASPF. Manning had requested for Mivart the degree of Doctor of Philosophy and *The Tablet* ("Catholic University College") reported him as having received that degree. The records of the Congregation for the Propagation of the Faith acknowledge the request as asking for a degree in philosophy but report the degree awarded as one in sacred theology. I think this must be a clerical error on the part of the Congregation.

93 Published as *Introduction générale à l'étude de la nature*.

Books in 1893, a judgment to which Mivart, at the time of the condemnation, submitted.[94] This had a further unfortunate consequence for him. In 1894, Mivart's name was removed from the list of Louvain faculty in the *Annuaire de l'Université Catholique de Louvain*. Mivart wrote to John-Baptiste Abbeloos, Rector Magnificus of the University, on July 23, 1894 to inquire why this had been done. A letter from Désiré Mercier to Cardinal Pierre-Lambert Goossens (July 26, 1894) suggests that his name had been removed by the Belgian bishops as a result of Mivart's articles on Hell having been placed on the *Index* and that was indeed what Mivart thought was the cause.[95] Mercier's request to Goossens that Mivart be reinstated apparently failed. On August 4 of the same year, Mivart submitted his resignation to Abbeloos.[96]

The second problem arose in 1899, when Mivart was already gravely ill with the condition that would take his life the following year. On August 29, Mivart wrote to Andreas Cardinal Steinhuber, prefect of the Congregation of the Index, expressing his concern that his articles on Hell continued to appear in the *Index*.[97] Next, in January 1900, he published two highly polemical articles criticizing the Church on issues ranging from his dissatisfaction with *Providentissimus Deus* to his views on the reformability of even such well-established doctrines as the bodily resurrection of Christ and the perpetual virginity of the Blessed Virgin Mary.[98] These articles, even when not heretical, are in places almost a paradigm of what it is to be "offensive to pious ears."

Those articles evoked a sharp (in places too sharp) rebuke in the pages of *The Tablet*[99] and a demand from Herbert Cardinal Vaughan, Mivart's bishop, that he sign a profession of faith composed by Vaughan. This Mivart refused to do.[100] Vaughan then formally excluded Mivart from the sacraments. Shortly thereafter, Mivart died. In accordance with canon law, he was refused burial in a Catholic cemetery.

A few years later, Mivart's son, with the support of his father's physician, argued that Mivart's statements during this controversy did not reflect Mivart's considered judgment,

---

94 The works in question were "Happiness in Hell," followed by "Happiness in Hell: A Rejoinder," and "Last Words on the Happiness in Hell." He returned the issue one more time, in "The Index and My Articles on Hell."

As I explain in Appendix III.B, the evaluation of articles and books was properly the work not of the Holy Office but of the Congregation of the Index. That in this case the Holy Office took the initiative was unusual, but not *ultra vires*. For details, see Mariano Artigas, *Negotiating Darwin*, 248–55.

Gruber claimed to see a consistent line of development in Mivart's work. He described Mivart as moving from an attempt to reconcile Catholic doctrine with natural science through an attempt to reconcile it with Biblical criticism, to a final attempt to reconcile it with ethics. There may be here some kind of psychological consistency, but it is not, in my judgment, a development that *logical* consistency would require.

95 Mercier to Goossens, July 26, 1894, 3 (portfolio 4, Institut des hautes études philosophiques, AUCL).

96 Mivart to Abbeloos, August 5, 1894 (Rectoral Archives XXXIII/13, AKUL).

97 Mivart to Steinhuber, August 29, 1899 (fol. 297, Protocolli 1897–99, CL, ADDF; the letter is reprinted in Artigas, *Negotiating Darwin*, 256–57).

98 Mivart, "Continuity of Catholicism," and "Recent Catholic Apologists." These, together with his correspondence with Cardinal Vaughan (mentioned below), Mivart later published in a pamphlet entitled *Under the Ban*.

99 Vaughan, "Mivart's Heresy."

100 For a history of the affair, see (in addition to Gruber's *Conscience in Conflict*, 188–213) John D. Root, "Final Apostasy"; and Artigas, *Negotiating Darwin*, 248–67.

but were caused by his illness,[101] a claim recognized by Francis Bourne, Vaughan's successor as archbishop of Westminster. Mivart was reburied in consecrated ground. The relevant question here, however, is not the *cause* of Mivart's actions, but the rôle played in all of this by Mivart's evolutionism. The question of evolution and the origin of the human race were mentioned by Mivart either in "The Continuity of Catholicism" or in "Some Recent Catholic Apologists."[102] He expressed his anger at the actions taken by the Congregation of the Index against Dalmace Leroy and John Zahm[103] and denied the teaching authority of the Church in matters that might be resolved by scientific inquiry. These comments did not, however, appear to have played a rôle in the Church's reaction. In response to Mivart's remark that "the account of the Fall" is not "in any sense, historical and true," Cardinal Vaughan required only that Mivart profess "that the first man, Adam, when he transgressed the command of God in Paradise, immediately lost the holiness and justice in which he had been constituted,"[104] but of the origin of Adam's body (the particular point which, in the 1890s, had become the center of theological controversy), much less of the theory of evolution in general, there is no mention in the profession of faith that Mivart had been expected to sign.

4. OTHER CATHOLIC EVOLUTIONISTS

D'Omalius, Gaudry, De Filippi, and especially Mivart (scientists all) were surely the most important Catholic evolutionists in the years up to about 1885, but they were not the only ones. Sympathy with the view can be found in the work of other Catholics as well—priests and laity, future bishops and seminary professors, scattered from Italy, Spain, Germany, and France to the United States and El Salvador. All of these authors rejected a fully Darwinian account of the origin of man, but all were, to varying extents, open to an evolutionary account of the origins of plants and animals, and (in some cases) of the human body. At a minimum, they were compatibilists about the relation between transformism and Catholic theology.

a. Raffaello Caverni (1837–1900)

Six years after the publication of Mivart's book, there appeared in Italy a second, but rather different, book-length attempt to articulate a Catholic evolutionism. Its author, Raffaello Caverni, a priest of the diocese of Florence, had spent ten years teaching physics and mathematics at the diocesan seminary in Firenzuola. In 1871, he was assigned to a parish in the village of Quarata Antellese, where his parochial duties left him much

---

101 That view was defended by Gregory P. Elder, *Chronic Vigour*, 109. The case for genuine apostasy was presented by Gruber, *Conscience in Conflict*, 143–47, and Root, "Final Apostasy."

102 Mivart, "Apologists," *Under the Ban*, 52–54, and "Continuity," *Under the Ban*, 84.

103 For details on these cases, see chapter 6.

104 Mivart, "Continuity," 81, and Vaughan's Formula, 6–7, both in Mivart, *Under the Ban*.

time for scholarly work and where he remained until his death in 1900. Not surprisingly, evolution being the topic of the day, Caverni worked out his own ideas on the subject and published them, first in a series of articles in the Catholic cultural review *Rivista Universale*, and then, in book form, as *De' nuovi studi della filosofia, discorsi di R. C. ad un giovane studente* (1877).[105]

The *Nuovi studi* argued for three theses. First, Darwin's account of the origin of plant and animal species is highly plausible. Second, his account of the origin of human species is not plausible. Third, a distinction must be made between divine (and infallible) passages of Scripture and passages that were of human origin and thus subject to error.

Caverni's general case for transformism was fairly standard. What was distinctive was his attempt to subsume the idea under a broader, providentialist theology of nature:

> What is impossible for blind selection by nature, what is strange in the absolute thought of pantheism, and of the idea which becomes every species, every form, every thing, seems to me to take on all the appearance of truth in the context of the dogma of a personal Being which creates prime matter from nothing and infuses into it the necessary power, which leaves it then to develop itself, though always directing the work with its assistant Wisdom. It is not, therefore, natural selection or the autonomy of a generative nature [*natura genitrice*] which bring about the progressive developments of created forms; rather God who first creates the substance, then, conserving its being and physically premoving its interior power, comes gradually to create each form Himself, without seeming to do so and without the assistance of any inferior agency.[106]

And what about the origin of man? "Man cannot be the terminus of a zoological series."[107] "The similarity of form between brute animal and man is just analogical and not genealogical."[108] Caverni argued that there were problems even with the evolution of the human body,[109] but the heart of his argument was an exceptionalism focused on human intelligence. Animals are, in the end, machines, even if they are moved by physiological forces, rather than just the physical forces of Cartesian zoology.[110] And so, "consciousness [*sentire*] is only a property of intellect [*intelligenza*] and any attribution of sensation to brute animals has to be understood in a way different from what is found in us."[111] Indeed consciousness could not precede intellect nor, more generally, could awareness of an individual object precede a knowledge of the abstract. He appealed, in his defense

---

105 For biographies, see Vincenzo Cappelletti and Federico Di Trocchio, "Caverni," and Sara Pagnini, *Profilo di Raffaello Caverni (1837–1900)*.

106 Caverni, *Nuovi studi*, 17–18.

107 Caverni, *Nuovi studi*, 17.

108 Caverni, *Nuovi studi*, 51.

109 Caverni, *Nuovi studi*, 51–53 (on the hand and brain) and 54–57 (on relative hairlessness), both arguments that had been made (with respect to natural selection, at least) a few years before by Alfred Russel Wallace in his *Contributions to the Theory of Natural Selection*, 348–50.

110 Caverni, *Nuovi studi*, 91–92.

111 Caverni, *Nuovi studi*, 113.

of this order, to the ontologism of Vincenzo Gioberti and Antonio Rosmini-Serbati.[112] So any attempt to extend the Darwinian account of the origin of species to the origin of human beings would be unsound.

Caverni's third thesis was purely theological: Divine inspiration is limited to dogmatic and moral questions; it does not extend to matters that could be investigated using the methods of the natural sciences.[113] The opening chapter of Genesis did have theological content—the creation of the world by God and God's conservation of created things in existence—but not any that could conflict with the results of scientific inquiry.

And so, to quote from his table of contents, "the new Darwinian doctrines and the natural sciences should not frighten believers" and "they should be allowed to be cultivated in peace and, if it is necessary to disprove them, to improve them [*cultivarle*] ourselves with love."[114]

The book was criticized by Francesco Salis Seewis, SJ, in a two-part review in *Civiltà cattolica*. Some of the objections were theological—the reviewer thought that the distinction between revealed doctrines and mere scientific opinion in Sacred Scripture according to the criterion proposed by Caverni could easily be used to call into question all the facts of sacred history. But the review also raised scientific and philosophical concerns. "Darwinism is an offshoot of unbelief: it comes from thinking of nature without God and from the tendency to exclude Him from nature." The review would discuss "how much there is of the scientific in that tissue of ridiculous suppositions, intolerable paralogisms, and manifest equivocations."[115]

The book was later placed on the *Index of Prohibited Books*. The story of that action will be told in chapter 3.

b. Franz von Hummelauer (1842–1914)

Franz von Hummelauer, Austrian by birth, entered the Society of Jesus in 1860 and rose to become one of the most important Catholic exegetes of the nineteenth century. He was chosen to write the *Commentarius in Genesim* (1895) for the German Jesuits' great *Cursus Sacrae Scripturae*. In 1903, he was made consultor to the Pontifical Biblical Commission.

In his *Der biblische Schöpfungsbericht: Ein exegetischer Versuch* (1877), he argued that the "days" of the Hexaemeron are not chronological time periods at all, but distinct parts of a vision in which God revealed the origin of the world to Adam. This was, needless to say, a controversial view, but it had Catholic supporters as well as Catholic opponents. His view of Darwinism is, however, separable from his interpretive approach to the Hexaemeron. He presented it directly at the end of his book:

---

112 Caverni, *Nuovi studi*, 76. Caverni cited Rosmini, *Nuovo saggio sull'origini delle idee*, and Gioberti, *Introduzione allo studio della filosofia*.

113 Caverni, *Nuovi studi*, 21–24 and 29–34.

114 Caverni, *Nuovi studi*, vi, summarizing pages 39–41.

115 Salis Seewis, "De' nuovi studi," 66 and 67.

> We here understand [by the term "Darwinism"] not that gross error which sees even in reason-endowed man nothing more than an exponentiated ape. We understand rather by the term merely the view according to which all plant and animal forms are derived from a few initial forms, or maybe even from only one completely simple original form. Naturally it is not our job either to contest this view or to support it; we only want to go so far as to state that it in no way contradicts Gen. 1. Darwinism allows only the first living beings, or the one original form of life, to come immediately from the hand of God; Genesis says that Adam saw all plants and animals emerge "according to their kinds" at God's command. From that we can only go so far as to conclude that Genesis traces the origination of all living things to God. Whether this origination extends to the Creator mediately or immediately is a point on which Genesis, which must skip over intermediate forms, if indeed there were any, will provide no elucidation.[116]

c. Manuel Francisco Vélez (1839–1901)

Manuel Francisco Vélez was born in Zacapa, Guatemala. Ordained in 1864, he taught philosophy at the Pontifical University of San Carlos Borromeo in Guatemala until the anti-clericalism of the liberal revolution of 1871 led him to leave that country for El Salvador. There he taught at the Liceo Salvadoreño and, in the 1880s, published a catechism and several textbooks on philosophy.[117] More important for our story, he also published an article entitled "El Darwinismo i la Creacion" in the Nicaraguan review *El Ateneo*, followed in 1884–85 by a book, *Antropogenia, o sea Origen del hombre según la revelación y la ciencia.*

In 1887, he was appointed bishop of Comayagua (Honduras). The last years of the nineteenth century were years of political turmoil in Honduras, characterized by a struggle for power between conservatives and generally anti-clerical liberals. Vélez's sympathies were with the conservative presidents and when Domingo Vásquez was overthrown by the liberal Policarpo Bonilla in February 1894, Vélez decided to go into exile, governing his diocese from the safety of El Salvador until Bonilla left office.[118] His troubles, however, were not yet at an end. On August 24, 1894, a Genoese traveler named Pratolongo wrote to the secretary of the Inquisition, making grave charges against the Central American Church and clergy in general, and singling out Vélez (as a lover of wealth, of drunkenness, and of women, and as an author of objectionable works) for particular criticism.[119] The

---

116 Hummelauer, *Biblische Schöpfungsbericht*, 149.

117 Four—*Lecciones de logica* (1883); *Lecciones de ideología* (1884); *Lecciones teórico-practicas de gramatica española* (1884); and *Lecciones sumarias de doctrina cristiana*, 2nd ed. (1885)—have little relevance to our topic. (The first two are fol. 3 and 4, 1896–99/13, CL, ADDF).

118 For more details on the larger issues, see Ena Yolanda Ronero Gómez, *Reforma liberal,* or Lucas Paredes, *Drama político de honduras.*

119 Copies were sent to Pratolongo's own archbishop (Tommaso Reggio), and to the Substitute at the Secretariat of State (Mario Mocenni, who had been Apostolic Delegate to Honduras at the time of Vélez's appointment). Pratolongo's letter is not in the archives of the Inquisition, as the documents that are there note (fol. 42v, 1896–99/13, CL, ADDF) nor is it in that of the Congregation for Extra-ordinary Ecclesiastical Affairs (now at the Archivio storico della Sezione dei Rapporti

Inquisition took the matter up on November 14, 1894, investigating both the charges about Vélez's character and conduct and the concerns about his the orthodoxy of his books and articles. These two matters can be, and in Rome largely were, treated separately.[120]

The extent to which the complaints about the bishop's character were justified I will leave to other historians. Suffice it to say that the bishop had enemies not only in the new government, but within the Church. Vélez's own reports to Rome indicate a serious attempt at local reforms, both in discipline of the clergy and canonical re-organization of the diocese.[121] Some local Catholics were unhappy with his inability to send priests to all parts of the diocese; others were unhappy with what they perceived as his liberalism.[122] Probably some Catholics (even among the clergy) did not share his political sympathies. Rome seems to have judged Pratolongo's complaints as being without foundation, for in July 1899 the Holy Office reported to the Congregation for Extra-ordinary Ecclesiastical Affairs that it had no objection when, the Bonilla presidency having ended, Vélez returned to his diocese.[123]

* * * * *

So, what exactly did Vélez have to say about evolution and the question of human origins? Vélez's article presented an exposition of Darwin's evolutionism and of Mivart on the various senses of the word "creation." He also tried to place the Darwinian concept of a struggle for existence into a Christian theology of nature:

> What the Darwinist school has chosen to call a *struggle for existence*, presenting it as a general and pre-existent fact in virtue of which all beings, instinctively and because of their own natural development, tend to conserve themselves in being and to destroy their competitors . . . in Christian language could be called the providential equilibrium established among all the beings of the entire creation; and rather than being called a struggle could more properly be called *the harmony of contrasts and the concert of existing things*.[124]

He remained unconvinced with respect to the evolutionary origin of species for scientific reasons, but was resolutely compatibilist, even with respect to the human body. He

---

con gli Stati della Segreteria di Stato). The gist of the letter was summarized by Ricardo Casanova y Estrada, archbishop of Guatemala, in his "Relazione di Mons. Vescovo di Guatemala intorno al popolo, clero e Vescovo di Comayagua Emanuele Francesco Vélez" (fol. 30–38).

120 On the separation, see the opening paragraphs of the *votum* of Pie de Langogne (fol. 12, 1896–99/13, CL, ADDF).

121 See his letters to Mariano Cardinal Rampolla, then secretary of state, for 1893–94 (doc. 32–34, fasc. 7, Honduras 1893–97, ASSR).

122 On the absence of pastors: Bishop Salvatore di Pietro (vicar apostolic of British Honduras) to the Congregation for the Propagation of the Faith (Propaganda Fidei), November 23, 1894; on the bishop's alleged liberalism: José Birol (a Lazarist priest in Costa Rica) to Archbishop Antonio Sabatucci (papal nuncio to Colombia), January 25, 1895. Both writers are passing on complaints that they heard from Honduran Catholics (doc. 35 and 36 respectively, fasc. 7, Honduras 1893–97, ASSR).

123 Felice Cavagnis (pro-secretary of the Congregation for Extra-ordinary Ecclesiastical Affairs) to Casimiro Gennari (assessor at the Inquisition), June 19, 1899 (fol. 69r–69v), and Minutes of the preparatory congregation, July 1, 1899 (fol. 72, 1896–99/13, CL, ADDF).

124 Vélez, "Darwinismo," 74.

33

concluded his article by saying that "the theory of the simian origin of man, then, may be scientifically false and absurd, but as long as it preserves the direct and supernatural creation of the human soul and is not applied to the intellectual and moral order, it is not opposed to the dogmas of religion or of faith."[125]

His book can be divided into two parts. The first (chapters 1–12) takes up a variety of general questions on the nature of science and revelation. There exists, Vélez said, "a real battle between religion and science, or better put, between the expositors of Christian doctrine and the partisans of modern naturalism."[126] The goal of the book, of course, was to reconcile the two parties. How? "The starting point for any true reconciliation between religion and modern science … would be the separation of those parts of the Bible which correspond to faith from those which correspond to science."[127] The first chapters of the book were devoted to laying the foundations for such a reconciliation.

The second half (chapters 13–19) addressed a variety of topics on the border between theology and the paleoetiological sciences, followed by a chapter summarizing his conclusions.

He began with the antiquity of man, a point (he said) on which the Church had said nothing and on which science was not yet in a position to offer an answer.[128] He addressed next the question of pre-Adamites, rational beings that existed before Adam. The question of whether human beings existed in the Tertiary period, or more generally the question of the provenance of early human artifacts, was theologically neutral since Catholic doctrine did not require that every human being that ever lived be descended from Adam, but only that currently existing human beings [*actual hombre*] be descended from him.[129] The question of whether there were or were not rational beings prior to or contemporaneous with Adam was not one to which theology offered any answer. What theology does teach (as necessary to the doctrine of original sin) was a unity of lineage for all human beings living now and for many generations before us—a common descent from Adam (i.e., monogenesis). Any Pre-Adamites that might have existed, and their descendants, are long extinct.

Having addressed those somewhat tangential questions, he turned directly to the central questions of whether species in general, and the human race in particular, owe their origins to natural processes or to the voluntary actions of some being external to nature. As a scientific matter, he said, the question of transformism had not yet been settled in favor of the new theories; but, insofar as it was compatible with an underlying providence, it (and, for that matter the origin of life itself) was an open question for Christians.[130] On the topic of anthropogenesis itself, he wrote:

125 Vélez, "Darwinismo," 81.

126 Vélez, *Antropogenia*, 4.

127 Vélez, *Antropogenia*, 14.

128 Vélez, *Antropogenia*, 110 and 117.

129 Vélez, *Antropogenia*, 118.

130 Vélez, *Antropogenia*, 161–63.

> In the sense in which evolution includes only the human body, separate and inde-pendent from the soul, . . . there is no reason to believe that the hypothesis of *animal origin* is opposed to divine revelation or to Catholic dogma.
>
> The same reasons which . . . prove that a spiritualist transformism is not contrary to revealed Christian principles . . . can be applied to the *animal origin* of man.[131]

Would this Mivartian resolution run afoul of the Catholic doctrine that the soul was the form of the human body? According to Vélez, Thomistic embryology showed that it would not. That embryology held that human reproduction included the transformation of the sensitive but non-rational embryo that constituted the second stage of human embryological development into a being capable of receiving a rational soul directly created by God. If a created rational soul could be implanted into the product of natural embryological development, of which it would then be the substantial form, then there could be no philosophical (or theological) objection to the idea that a created soul could be implanted in (and serve as the substantial form of) the product of evolutionary processes at some point in the course of the phylogenetic history of life on earth.[132]

In the end, Vélez was content with going no further than an insistence on com-patibilism: "I have no interest in defending Darwin or evolutionist doctrines, but only in reconciling them in general . . . with the dogmas and teachings of religion and faith."[133] The reaction of the Holy Office, which reviewed the book some fifteen years after it was published, will be discussed in chapter 6.

d. John Gmeiner (1847–1913)

John Gmeiner, a diocesan priest first of Milwaukee and then of St. Paul, had been interested in the relation between science and religion since about the time of his ordina-tion. He addressed the question of evolutionary biology in three of his published works.

He did so first in his *Modern Scientific Views and Christian Doctrine Compared* (1884), written while he was teaching at St. Francis Seminary in Milwaukee. In that book, he defended four theses. First, Darwin's Natural Selection and Common Ancestry Theses are compatible with Scripture, a point on which he cited (at least with respect to common ancestry) Hummelauer.[134] Second, these theses were anticipated by St. Augustine, who had written that all things were created "potentially and causally" in the first creation of

---

131 Vélez, *Antropogenia*, 188–89. He mentioned here Mivart's *Genesis of Species* and *Lessons from Nature* as well as John Zahm's Denver lecture, *The Catholic Church and Modern Science*, discussed in chapter 5.

132 The basis of Vélez's argument here—a theory of delayed animation, or the infusion of a *rational* soul only some time after conception into an embryonic organism that had at first been animated by a vegetative, and then by a rational, soul—is now contrary to the *sententia communis* on the question, though the idea has never been formally condemned by the Church.

133 Vélez, *Antropogenia*, 207. See also 161 and 209.

134 Gmeiner, *Modern Scientific Views*, 156–57.

matter.[135] Third, Darwin's ideas on these points are "no more than a bold hypothesis."[136] Fourth, about the origin of the first human body, he said: "I would not venture to declare Prof. Mivart's opinion inconsistent with any Christian doctrine, although great theological authorities[137] decidedly reject the same."[138]

Next, in a paper on British philosopher Herbert Spencer's comprehensive evolutionism, which he read at the first Congrès scientifique international des catholiques in Paris shortly after his transfer to St. Thomas Aquinas Seminary in St. Paul, Gmeiner argued that Spencer's work contained grave errors, but not on every point. With respect to Darwinism, he thought (as did many others, including scientists) that natural selection was not capable of causing the effects that Darwin had attributed to it. On Darwin's Common Ancestry Thesis, by contrast, he wrote:

> If, however, we assume that Creator bestowed the first simple organisms the power, over time, to produce more perfect living forms, then sound philosophy can make no valid objection against such an evolutionary hypothesis. For such a doctrine … in no way obscures our ideas of divine omnipotence, but rather increases a thousand-fold our reverence towards the Creator who can impart so many nearly infinite powers to an amorphic cell.[139]

About evolutionary anthropogenesis, he wrote:

> First, if it is a matter only of the body of the first man, from the philosophical point of view, nothing against the *possibility* of such evolution can be said. For such an evolution is not inconsistent with God's omnipotence, or with His wisdom, or with the nature of the human body. Whether such an hypothesis is in agreement with the Mosaic narration or not is a matter for theologians.
>
> Second, if, however, such an hypothesis is applied to the explanation of the origin of the human soul, then it must be rejected as philosophically false. Since the human soul is a simple substance, its origin can be neither by generation nor by evolution, but only by creation. Thus, Catholic philosophers teach that individual human souls are immediately created by God.[140]

Finally, in *Medieval and Modern Cosmology* (1893), his last discussion of the topic, he seems to be more positively disposed to the theory of evolution (both in general and with respect to the human body) without going so far as to make an explicit endorsement of the idea.[141]

---

135 Gmeiner, *Modern Scientific Views*, 157–58. He acknowledged that Carl Guettler, professor at the University of Munich, had made this point in his *Naturforschung und Bibel*, 145.

136 Gmeiner, *Modern Scientific Views*, 169.

137 He cited Hugo Hurter, *Theologiae dogmaticae compendium*, 2:180.

138 Gmeiner, *Modern Scientific Views*, 183.

139 Gmeiner, "Doctrina Spencer," 182–83.

140 Gmeiner, "Doctrina Spencer," 183.

141 Gmeiner, *Cosmology*, 50–55.

e. Charles-Maximilien Bégouën (1827–1885)

Charles-Maximilien, Count Bégouën, was by occupation paymaster general (*trésorier-payeur général*) of Toulouse. He was "a convinced and fervent Catholic"[142] as well as being the ancestor of four important French prehistorians—Henri (his son) and Henri's sons Max, Jacques, and Louis. What brings him into our story is the fact that he hosted in his home gatherings of the intellectual elite of his city. "Despite the ardor of the polemics," his son later wrote, "it was neutral ground where believers and free-thinkers, evolutionists and fixists, could meet."[143] Émile Cartailhac, one of the leading prehistorians of the day, attended; so did François Duilhé de Saint-Projet of the Institut Catholique de Toulouse.

On February 26, 1878, Count de Sambucy-Luzençon, in a presentation on prehistorism and transformism, objected that Darwinism was too conjectural to count as a scientific account of the origin of man.[144] Bégouën objected at the time and, over the course of the next two years, with the assistance of both Cartailhac and Duilhé de Saint-Projet, Bégouën wrote and published a booklet entitled *La Création évolutive*, not so much a direct reply to Sambucy-Luzençon's particular arguments as a general articulation of a view that was both creationist and evolutionist.

Bégouën began by observing that the battle between evolutionists and their opponents had, to a large extent, become a battle between materialists and spiritualists. His own view was that the gradual development of living things that is the central principle of evolutionism is compatible with the existence of a first cause and of human souls and with human exceptionalism, i.e., with the central principles of spiritualism.[145] He summarized his own philosophy and theology of nature in six points:

1. The world as we see it was not created instantaneously, but by the continuous action of an omnipotent will.
2. The changes which it has undergone are an indication of the contingent nature of matter.
3. Vital phenomena and the evolution which accompanies them are not the result of an unconscious force inherent to matter.
4. The laws of the Darwinist School, true within certain limits, are only clear and logical for those who see them as an instrument of divine will.
5. The law of progress, which departs from inorganic matter to arrive at man, is summarized in Genesis and could have been realized through an evolution directed by God.
6. The rôle of man can only be explained by the presence of an immaterial soul, making him a different kind of being in creation, which he dominates from the height of his reason and of his moral freedom.[146]

---

142 Henri Bégouën, *Quelques souvenirs*, 17.

143 Henri Bégouën, *Quelques souvenirs*, 17.

144 Sambucy-Luzençon, "Séance du 26 Février 1878," 19. See also Henri Bégouën, "Préhistoire," 102.

145 Charles Bégouën, *Création évolutive*, 3–5.

146 Bégouën, *Création évolutive*, 5–6.

Bégouën admitted more direct divine action than most twenty-first century compatibilists think is necessary, though not so much as to undermine the fundamentally evolutionary character of his account. In addition to the direct creation of each human soul, a point common to all versions of Catholic compatibilism, he thought that direct divine action was necessary in two other cases—the origin of life[147] and mutual adaptation as, for example, of orchids and bumblebees.[148] With respect to the origin of life, he surely had in mind Louis Pasteur's challenges to the possibility of spontaneous generation. On the co-occurrence of the changes in, say, orchid and bee, he thought that the action of a "superior will" was a better explanation than was chance.

Of perhaps more interest today is Bégouën's use of precisely the variability within each species as an argument against special creation. Why would independently created species be variable at all? What could be the point of variability if not the formation of new species?[149]

The most important issue, the origin of man, he left for his final chapter, where he cited the usual human capacities—civilization, language, conscience, abstract ideas—in defense of the idea that man really is distinct from all merely animal beings.[150]

In his concluding paragraphs, he made an appeal to both sides. To the Darwinists:

> Push the theory of transformism as far as your research seems to allow; but when, in following the chain of beings you get back to the starting point, recognize that beyond matter and living beings there is a superior and omnipotent intelligence, the origin of every thing and the cause of all changes. It is not a perturbing cause, but the logical explanation of all the laws which you so much admire and which are nothing more than the expression of that intelligent being's thought. Similarly, in studying man, take into account not only his analogies with other beings, but also the differences, and you will be forced to agree that the animal cannot explain the man, the meaning of whom you will only find when you see in him a superior principle, unequaled in [the rest of] creation.[151]

And to the spiritualists:

> Be unshaken in your belief in the existence of the soul and of God; but do not seek to contain the latter within the narrow limits of a creation that has been abruptly and capriciously made. And when you admire the interdependence and the logic which preside over the laws of nature, do not refuse to see in them the effects of an evolution which has God as its author; one whose principal lines are retraced in the narrative of Genesis.[152]

---

147 Bégouën, *Création évolutive*, 20.

148 Bégouën, *Création évolutive*, 36.

149 Bégouën, *Création évolutive*, 24.

150 Bégouën, *Création évolutive*, 55.

151 Bégouën, *Création évolutive*, 58.

152 Bégouën, *Création évolutive*, 58–59.

Bégouën's essay seems to have received less notice than did other French works of Catholic evolutionism, such as that of Leroy. It is rarely mentioned by later authors. Nevertheless, it was not, from the Catholic side, idiosyncratic. It appears to have been written with the encouragement of Duilhé de Saint-Projet.[153] And it surely laid out a line followed by Bégouën's much more prominent son, Henri. It is one more example of Catholic evolutionism in the first decades after the publication of Darwin's work.

f. José Mendive (1836–1906)

José Mendive, SJ, one of the leading Spanish neo-Thomists of his day, used the occasion of the publication of a Spanish translation of John William Draper's *History of the Conflict between Religion and Science* (in 1876), to prepare a long work of his own on science and religion. His *La Religión católica vindicada de las imposturas racionalistas* (1883) is, however, more than just a reply to Draper; it also takes up a discussion of the paleoetiological sciences in their own terms. It went through four editions, the last published in 1897.

Mendive's discussion of the antiquity of the world emphasized that the teaching of Genesis 1 is limited to the doctrine of creation itself (a free act of God that constitutes a temporal beginning of the world) and to the doctrine that the world was created precisely as a suitable dwelling-place for man and in a way that laid the foundation for sabbatical rest.[154] About the *mode* of creation and ornamentation, by contrast, Scripture does not provide any clarity.[155] Catholics have offered, and the Church has permitted, a number of different interpretations of the Hexaemeron—from St. Augustine (simultaneous creation) through the majority of Scholastics (successive creation over the course of 24-hour days) to the nineteenth-century interpretations of Giovanni Battista Pianciani, published originally in a long series of articles and then as a book by *Civiltà cattolica*, and of Wiseman (successive epochs). Mendive himself thought that the idea of a very old earth not only best fits the empirical evidence, but has exegetical advantages over the idea of twenty-four-hour days as well.[156] He noted the correspondence between the order of the Hexaemeron and what geologists say about the history of the earth, but refused to make too much of that correspondence: "the chronological order of geological ages established by scientists could well have to be modified in light of new discoveries."[157] Mendive recommended that the Hexaemeron be interpreted not chronologically, but philosophically, "as the different parts of a visible whole, divided methodically into seven distinct periods, whatever might be the temporal order in which they occurred."[158]

---

153 Henri Bégouën, *Quelques souvenirs*, 18.

154 Mendive, *Religión católica*, 201, 198–99, and (for the foundation of the Sabbath not depending on a chronological interpretation of the Hexaemeron) 231.

155 Mendive, *Religión católica*, 202.

156 Mendive, *Religión católica*, 224.

157 Mendive, *Religión católica*, 239. See also 232.

158 Mendive, *Religión católica*, 232.

In chapters 21 and 22, Mendive took up the topic of the origin of man—the former chapter on Catholic doctrine and the latter on transformism. Mendive accepted as a paleontological fact an appearance of man on earth that was relatively recent compared to that of other living things.[159] So where did the first human beings come from? Scripture tells us, he says, that they were made "immediately" by God.[160] He did not mean, however, that God created the body of the first man immediately, for he went on to ask:

> How did God form the first man? Did He take a soul brought into being out of nothing and infuse it all at once into unformed and inorganic dust? Or did He first produce a body organized and suited to the functions proper to our spiritual and intellectual life? Sacred Scripture does not express itself with sufficient clarity on this point. Thus we cannot say with certainty that the Creator has followed one or the other path.[161]

He reviewed the work of two earlier writers, and a contemporary—Jesuit theologian and philosopher Francisco Suárez (1548–1617), Rodrigo de Arriaga (1592–1667), and Mivart.[162] Suárez and Arriaga, of course, were too early to consider the idea that the origin of man could be attributed to the transformation of an animal species, but both had addressed the question of whether the formation of the first human body required divine action. Arriaga had said that, even if it was philosophically impossible for the angels to have formed the first human body (since, according to Scholastic consensus, they did not have power over matter), it could not be said to be either theologically erroneous or contrary to Scripture;[163] Mendive agreed.[164]

Mivart's view that natural processes might have sufficed to produce an individual with a *proximate* disposition to be infused with a human soul he rejected because it was contrary to Sacred Scripture as generally understood by the Fathers,[165] though he also raised non-theological questions about this option—whether it was consistent with scientific gradualism, whether it did not imply, among other things, that there would also be related non-human individuals (of which there seemed to be no evidence).

Could natural processes have produced at least an individual with a *remote* disposition for such an infusion? Could God not have transformed the body of an animal by supernatural action in such a way as to make it suitable for the infusion of a human soul? "There would be no absolutely invincible problems [in systematic theological anthropology], even though it is clear that we may never set aside the common interpretation [of

159 Mendive, *Religión católica*, 415.

160 Mendive, *Religión católica*, 415.

161 Mendive, *Religión católica*, 416–17.

162 Suárez, *De opere sex dierum*, III.1; Arriaga, *De opere sex dierum*, 34.1.

163 Arriaga, *De opere sex dierum*, 34.1.4–5.

164 Mendive, *Religión católica*, 419–20.

165 Mendive, *Religión católica*, 423.

Scripture] *until the necessity of the new interpretation has been proven.*"[166] Even Suárez, whose view is immediate formation from dust, recognized that the contrary view was also probable (i.e., defensible). Arriaga had taken precisely the latter view.[167] Once one has acknowledged the necessity of supernatural action, what reason could there be to prefer formation from an animal's body to formation from simple dust? Mendive conceded the force of the question, but said in reply: "Given that some naturalists have made such a great effort to derive the human body from other, more imperfect, ones which preceded it in earlier geological ages, it is good for Catholics to know how far concessions can go without in the least affecting our sacred dogmas."[168] He was not yet convinced that the transformist history of life was correct,[169] but he did not believe that the impeding theological objections were settled doctrine.

Central to Mendive's analysis of transformism was a distinction between versions that denied any essential differences among organisms and those that acknowledged such a distinction (at least between man and animals). The extent to which the former, which he called materialistic transformism, was driven by philosophical more than empirical considerations was clear, he said, from the readiness of so many to add spontaneous generation to Darwinism. Spiritualistic versions ranged from Mivart's to versions in which God (or angels) made direct modifications of species over the course of the history of life, at least in the case of the origin of the human body if not also in the case of the origin of other living things.[170] Mendive rejected Mivart's account (for reasons mentioned above) in favor of accounts that gave a greater rôle to supernatural forces, which he thought were true immediate causes of the major developments in the history of life.[171]

5. MONOGENISM AND POLYGENISM

The general question of whether evolutionary processes played any rôle at all in the origin of biological species, and the more particular question of whether they played any rôle in the origin of the bodies of the first human beings, were not the only questions that Catholic evolutionists had to confront with respect to the idea of an evolutionary anthropogenesis. At the periphery lay two further questions—the age of the human race and whether it had its origins in a single first couple (monogenesis). That second question was itself entangled with the further question of whether all human beings alive today are members of a single species, a thesis denial of which was sometimes called "pluralism." Of those two questions, the second (the question of the original, and

---

166 Mendive, *Religión católica*, 429 (emphasis mine).

167 Mendive, *Religión católica*, 431–33.

168 Mendive, *Religión católica*, 434.

169 He called it a false opinion (Mendive, *Religión católica*, 221n1).

170 Mendive, *Religión católica*, 462–64.

171 Mendive, *Religión católica*, 464–65.

specific, unity of the race) was more closely connected to the question of evolutionary origins than was the first (the question of age), and so I have incorporated a review of that, but not the other, into my history. The general history of the polygenist challenge to monogenism (mostly, but not exclusively, a scientific challenge) I review in Appendix I.C. The response of Catholics as they developed their own version of evolutionism, I will trace in the body of the book.

The raciological polygenism of the early nineteenth century, as I show in the Appendix, emerged slightly earlier than, and independent of, biological evolutionism. The first Catholic discussions of the question are, therefore, essentially pre-evolutionary.

We can begin with two of the *Twelve Lectures* (1836), which Wiseman devoted to "The Natural History of the Human Race."[172] There he framed his challenge to the views of the leading French pluralists as follows: "*Could* such varieties as we now see in the human race, have sprung up from one stock? For if this is demonstrated, we have removed the grounds whereon the adversaries of revelation deny the unity of origin which it teaches. And, moreover, every sound philosopher will, if unobjectionable, prefer the simpler to the more complex hypothesis."[173] He offered, by way of evidence that "it is certain and obvious that animals, acknowledged to form one species, under peculiar circumstances, divide into varieties as distinct as those observable in the human species."[174]

Another response can be found in Clarence A. Walworth's *Gentle Skeptic: or, Essays and Conversations of a Country Justice on the Authenticity and Truthfulness of the Old Testament Records* (1863). Walworth was a Paulist (and later a diocesan) priest whose interest in apologetics and in geology led him to address an array of issues on the relation of science and religion, ranging from the antiquity of the earth to the Flood of Noah. Although he did not address evolution itself, he did devote a chapter to "The Consanguinity of the Human Race."[175] Universal descent from a single ancestor, he said, was required by the doctrine of original sin and the necessity of a Redeemer for all.[176] Although the questions of original and specific unity (i.e., singularity of origin and commonality of species) were distinct, the former implied the latter.[177] With respect to the scientific side of the question, he argued (in defense of original unity) that the difference among human races was not beyond the reach of processes of biological variation. He also argued against the scheme of zoological provinces on which Agassiz had based his polygenism. The work of Josiah Nott and George Gliddon he dismissed as "pert and gossipy."[178]

A critique of pluralism can also be found in the work of Franz Heinrich Reusch, professor of Catholic theology at the University of Bonn. In his *Bibel und Natur: Vorlesungen*

---

172 Wiseman, *Twelve Lectures*, 1:143–258.

173 Wiseman, *Twelve Lectures*, 1:187.

174 Wiseman, *Twelve Lectures*, 1:189.

175 Walworth, *Gentle Skeptic*, 332–56.

176 Walworth, *Gentle Skeptic*, 332.

177 Walworth, *Gentle Skeptic*, 345–46.

178 Walworth, *Gentle Skeptic*, 334.

über die mosaische Urgeschichte und ihr Verhältnis zu den Ergebnissen der Naturforschung (1862), he argued that "One finds in man features that, in the animal world, are considered to be the surest sign of a single species."[179] The variation in skin color and skull shape so emphasized by those who denied the specific unity of the human race counted for little in the face of

> some other points in which all, even the most different races of men, resemble one another. These include—the same anatomical form of the body, the same limit to life expectancy, the same susceptibilities to disease, the same normal body temperature, the same average pulse, the same length of pregnancy, the same menstrual period.[180]

To this list of features Reusch added in a later passage the identity of mental powers—"reason, memory, self-consciousness, conscience, language."[181]

Specific unity does not prove original unity, however.[182] Reusch recognized that there were two possibilities. One was the traditional view of common ancestry for all human races (whether in a single couple or in multiple similar couples). The second began human prehistory with many original couples, racially different from one another from whom the various races descended. The latter possibility did not seem to him to require geographical diversity, though it would require some kind of separation of the racially distinct couples. What does he have to prove? He wrote:

> For our purposes, it is not necessary that we prove that [distinct origins for the various races] is untenable, and that [a common origin, whether in one couple or in more than one] is correct, from the standpoint of comparative anthropology. A scientific proof that a common origin is tenable will be quite enough for us. That is, that the various currently existing races can be descended from the same or identical parents and that present racial differences are explainable without the assumption of differences in their ancestors. Let such a proof be produced—and I will do it in the next lecture—and it cannot be said that the doctrine of the unity of the human race contradicts scientific anthropology.[183]

The proof is based on what we observe in other kinds of living things. On this, he quoted comparative anatomist Johannes Müller, one of the most important biologists of his day: "The successive generations of animals and plants change as they spread over the surface of the earth. These changes take place within the limits prescribed to the species and genera, but they are reproduced as variational types of the species over the course of generations. The present races of animals have sprung from the conjunction of many different conditions."[184] In the fourth edition of the book (1876), Reusch added: "I

---

179 Reusch, *Bibel und Natur*, 391 (cf. trans., 2:190).

180 Reusch, *Bibel und Natur*, 391 (cf. trans., 2:190–91).

181 Reusch, *Bibel und Natur*, 415 (cf. trans., 2:222).

182 Reusch, *Bibel und Natur*, 397–98 and 415 (cf. trans., 2:201–2, and 223).

183 Reusch, *Bibel und Natur*, 398 (cf. trans., 2:202).

184 Müller, *Handbuch der Physiologie*, 2:768; quoted in Reusch, *Bibel und Natur*, 417.

have already pointed out that in this respect the investigations initiated and carried out by Darwin have produced a result favorable to the doctrine of the unity of the human race."[185] He had not, to be sure, become a Darwinist. He had reservations about natural selection and even about a comprehensive version of common ancestry. Nevertheless, "Darwin must not be denied his due. He has again raised the question of the concept of species and of the mutability of organic species. The resultant investigations will probably show that we have drawn the limits on that mutability much too narrowly."[186]

So there is no scientific reason to believe that the racial variation found in nineteenth-century man was present in the first human beings. Further, what we know about other animals, that they originated in a single center of creation, presumably applies to man as well.[187] Finally, there is no reason to believe that the species did not originate in a single first couple.[188] Reusch, as he recognized, had not *proven* that the species originated in a single couple; he had, he said, shown that there were not *scientific* objections to the theological doctrine that this is so.

185 Reusch, *Bibel und Natur*, 4th ed., 490; see also p. 373 (trans., 2:225 and 2:60).

186 Reusch, *Bibel und Natur*, 4th ed., 372 (trans., 2:58).

187 Reusch, *Bibel und Natur*, 4th ed., 498 (trans. 2:236).

188 Reusch, *Bibel und Natur*, 4th ed., 504 (trans., 2:243–44).

CHAPTER 3

THE OFFICIAL CHURCH
(1859–1885)

Nineteenth-century Catholic intellectuals—scientists and theologians, clergy and laity, researchers and popularizers—responded to evolutionary biology with varying degrees of acceptance and skepticism. It was a lively controversy. I will begin with the official church—with bishops, councils and the curia. No less important than the statements that they made are instances in which the Church could have addressed the topic but did not (and, presumably, chose not to) do so. Arguments from silence are, to be sure, sometimes fallacious, but the writ *Qui tacet consentire videtur* still runs, at least with the qualification *ubi loqui debuit ac potuit.* If the attempt to develop a Catholic evolutionism were deeply problematic, the Church not only could have, but would have spoken in places where it in fact did not.

1. POPE BL. PIUS IX (R. 1846 TO 1878)

We can begin with Bl. Pius IX, who is sometimes said to have been hostile to the theory of evolution. It is not, however, clear what his personal views on the subject were.

The sole basis for the judgment that he was hostile to the theory seems to be a letter mentioned by Andrew Dickson White in his *History of the Warfare of Science with*

Theology in Christendom, and occasionally by other historians and polemicists since then,[1] but which played no rôle in the Catholic debate over evolution. The letter was written to French physician Constantin James in 1877. James had written an anti-evolutionist volume entitled *Du Darwinisme ou l'Homme-singe*,[2] in which he dismissed Darwinism as a fairy tale. At the suggestion of Joseph Cardinal Guibert, archbishop of Paris, James sent a copy of his book to Pope Pius IX, whose letter of thanks included a characterization of Darwinism as "a system which is repugnant at once to history, to the tradition of all peoples, to exact science, to observed facts, and even to Reason herself." The term "Darwinism" was used variously over the course of the first half-century or so of its existence, sometimes for selectionism, sometimes for evolutionary theories in general, sometimes for the descent of man from animals, and sometimes for a comprehensive materialistic cosmogony, according to the taste (or distaste) of the writer.[3] The "repugnant system" of Pope Pius's letter is presumably Darwinism as James defined it, a theory "according to which man is nothing but the progeny of an ape," one "which is false not only about the origin of man, but equally about his duties in this world and his destiny in the other."[4] There are two reasons for believing that Pope Pius was less committed on this matter than the appeal to this letter might suggest.

First, surely no less important than the contents of a personal letter was the more public conferral of a doctoral degree on Mivart. Although Cardinal Manning had not focused on Mivart's evolutionism in his request that Mivart be given the decree, this aspect of Mivart's thought was well-known, surely to Manning and presumably also to Pope Pius.

Second is an argument from silence. These were years in which the Catholic Church (and Pope Pius in particular) reacted sharply against a variety of new ideas that it (and he) judged to be incompatible with Catholic doctrine. In 1864, Pius issued his encyclical *Quanta Cura* along with "a syllabus containing the most important errors of our time."

---

1 White's treatment of the incident is found in his *History*, 1:75 and 77. This letter was discussed much more recently in Fiedler and Rabben, *Rome Has Spoken*, 178.

2 The book was reviewed by Francesco Salis Seewis in *Civiltà cattolica*.

James had been a student of the prominent French physiologist François Magendie. For a brief biographical note, see Tort, "James."

3 For an example of the broader use of the term, see Gaetano Moroni's characterization of Darwinism (in his *Indice generale*, 2:437) as "the fantasy of the transformation . . . of one animal species into another, . . . praised by the schools of Materialism and Rationalism, enemies of Catholicism, such that the profession of Darwinism and of Materialism are one and the same thing."

One should keep in mind also, when asking what Pius might have meant by the term, historian John L. Morrison's comment that by 1890 (a year cited as relevant to *his* immediate larger point), "Darwinism . . . had acquired too many connotations to be viewed [as a purely scientific subject]. Darwinism, as opposed to evolution, conjured up atheistic philosophies, threats to dogma, and heretical notions about the creation of man. It did not matter really whether these abhorrent ideas were intrinsic to Darwinism. They were inseparably associated with it in fact" (Morrison, "William Seton," 577).

For further testimony as to the use of the word (and in an Italian context), we can turn to historian Giovanni Landucci who, in a comment on the effect of De Filippi's lecture "L'uomo e le scimie," wrote that "for several decades, as a result, non-specialists, in particular, generally understood 'Darwinism' to mean the animal origin of man" ("De Filippi," 1137).

4 James, *Darwinisme*, 2–3.

Although addressed primarily to the political challenges posed by Italian anti-clerical liberalism, it began with seven theses under the heading "Pantheism, Naturalism and Absolute Rationalism." It made no mention of the new paleoetiological sciences—not of historical geology and not of biological evolution—though, to be sure, it also does not address fully evolutionary anthropogenesis, which Pius surely opposed. That absence does not, of course, show that Pius accepted the new ideas, but it does further weaken the case for the idea that Pius was a determined anti-evolutionist.

2. THE PROVINCIAL COUNCIL OF COLOGNE (1860)

The first official Catholic reaction to evolutionism came from the Prussian Rhineland. In 1860, Johannes Cardinal von Geissel, archbishop of Cologne, convened a provincial council of the bishops of his archdiocese as well as of representatives of local universities, seminaries, and religious orders.[5] Geissel had been interested in the idea of convening a provincial council since at least 1848. Particularly impressed by the approach taken at Vienna in 1858, he took a personal interest in possible doctrinal pronouncements. For that work, he secured the assistance of Wilhelm Wilmers, a theologian who was then teaching philosophy at the Jesuit college in Bonn. Wilmers had already achieved a theological reputation with his *Lehrbuch der Religion* (1851).[6] And so the acts of the Council included a wide-ranging, though not comprehensive, set of statements on points of doctrine, including "titles" on the Trinity, on creation, and on man.

The title on creation does not address the question of evolution. On the origin of plant and animal species, the Council was absolutely silent. But the following title, "On Man," began with a chapter "On the Origin of the Human Race and on Human Nature" which said: "Our first parents were made [*conditi*] immediately by God. Therefore, we declare to be clearly opposed to Sacred Scripture and to faith the opinion . . . that man, even considering only his body, was brought forth by the spontaneous change [*immutatio*] of a less perfect nature into a more perfect one in a way that is continuous and culminates in a human nature."[7] Why did the Council address precisely this question? What does the statement mean? What authority does it have?

It is not clear exactly what led the Council to decide to say what it did. One might at first think that it was a reaction to the publication, just a few months before the Council convened, of Darwin's *Origin of Species*, but that seems unlikely. The first edition of that book went on sale only in November 1859. Although it was reviewed by Heinrich Bronn in

---

5 The most thorough accounts of the history of the Council are Otto Pfülf, SJ, *Cardinal von Geissel*, 2:438–59, and, though without too much attention to *our* subject, Sebastian M. M. Cüppers, *Das Kölner Provinzialkonzil*. For a briefer introduction, see Johannes Stöhr, "Exempel Köln," and Reimund Haas, "Und an die geistlichen Personen." For brief accounts of the Council, but focused on our topic, see Artigas, *Negotiating Darwin*, 21–23, or Ernest C. Messenger, *Evolution and Theology*, 226–27.

6 See Johannes Beumer, "Pater Wilhelm Wilmers."

7 Cologne, I.IV.14, in *Acta et decreta*, 5: 292.

the *Neues Jahrbuch für Mineralogie, Geognosie, Geologie und Petrefaktenkunde* in January 1860, that review does not place any particular emphasis on Darwin's *Origin* as a solution to the question of the origin of man and in places refers rather pointedly just to plants and animals. Bronn's translation of the *Origin* itself began to appear only a few weeks before the Council's first session, and with a slight, but significant, modification of the original Darwinian title—*Über die Enstehung der Arten im Thier- und Pflanzen-Reich*, "on the origin of species *in the animal and plant kingdoms.*"[8]

The idea of the evolutionary origin of the human race was, in any case, already in the air and had been defended by other authors in ways more explicit than anything that can be found in Darwin's *Origin*. Lamarck had suggested it in his *Philosophie zoologique* (1809) and Chambers had defended it in the *Vestiges of the Natural History of Creation* (1844).[9] More immediately, Karl Vogt, though not yet himself an evolutionist, had produced a (second) German translation of Chambers's *Vestiges* in 1851, with a second edition released in 1858, just two years before the Council met. Chambers seems to have suggested precisely the kind of mixed (evolutionary-creationist) account of anthropogenesis rejected by the Council: "There is, in reality, nothing to prevent our regarding man as specially endowed with an immortal spirit, at the same time that his ordinary mental manifestations are looked upon as simple phenomena resulting from organization, those of the lower animals being phenomena absolutely the same in character, though developed within much narrower limits."[10]

Whatever might have precipitated the Council's statement, what exactly did it mean? Did the Council teach that all versions of human evolution are false, or only that some are (and if the latter, which)? We must be careful to read such statements restrictively, not expansively. As the codified code of canon law later admonished, "Nothing is to be understood as declared or dogmatically defined unless it clearly is so."[11]

First, what did the council mean by "*immediately* made"? Theological discussion of the origin of Adam's body had had a long history, even by 1860. It had been a topic of discussion in the Middle Ages[12] and it had been thoroughly discussed among the Renaissance Scholastics and their successors.[13] Many of those theologians described the formation of Adam's body as (in some sense) immediate. What did *they* mean by

---

8 The Council met from April 29 to May 17, 1860. Bronn's translation came out in three parts, reported in the *Börsenblatt für den deutschen Buchhandel* on April 4, May 2, and June 11, 1860 (pp. 683, 874, and 1166).

9 Lamarck, *Philosophie zoologique*, 349–57 (trans., 169–73); Chambers, *Vestiges*, 233–35.

10 Vogt, trans., *Natürliche Geschichte der Schöpfung*, 276. (Or see Chambers, *Vestiges*, 1st ed., 326; Vogt translated the sixth edition, but that does not affect this passage.)

For further background on evolution and Catholicism in Germany, see Hermann Josef Dörpinghaus, *Darwins Theorie und der deutsche Vulgärmaterialismus.*

11 Pius X, *Code of Canon Law*, Canon 1323, §3.

12 See William R. Doran, *De corporis Adami origine.*

13 See Carlo Brivio, *Origine del corpo umano.* The questions discussed included the matter from which Adam's body was formed, the possible rôle of created beings (here, angels) as secondary causes in that act of formation, and the mode of formation (whether instantaneous or with a certain succession, whether before or contemporaneous with the creation of the soul).

that term? Carlo Brivio wrote: "Some of the authors who used the term accepted angelic co-operation in the formation of the human body; others accepted (at least as probable) the successive [i.e., non-instantaneous] formation and organization of the body; and Silvestrus Maurus accepted even the co-operation of the celestial bodies."[14] Perhaps the Fathers at Cologne meant (in using the term "immediate") to deny that evolutionary processes played any rôle in the formation of Adam's body, but if they did so, they went farther than their predecessors had gone.

Second, what does the Council's rejection of "*spontanea* immutatio" as an account of the origin of the human body exclude? It is safe to say that the Council meant to exclude at least non-providentialist accounts of the evolution of the body. Did they, to go to the other extreme, teach that the first human body was directly formed (from inanimate matter) by God? To say so would be to impute to the Council more than it actually said. Surely the idea (advanced some three decades later by Cardinal González[15]) that God acted directly to make the first human body out of some already existing animal body, rather than out of inanimate matter, could not be considered a *spontaneous* change.

But what about the idea that the changes that transformed an animal body into a human body were the result of the operation of natural causes, but with those natural causes understood as *secondary* causes, established by and executors of Divine Providence? Would such changes be spontaneous because immediately natural or non-spontaneous because ultimately providential? The acts of the Council themselves do not answer this question; we can, however, look for clues in some late-nineteenth-century textbooks, where the terms "spontaneous evolution" or "spontaneous generation" (in a sense wider than abiogenesis) were used by several Catholic theologians, two of whom attended the Council.

Wilmers, the theological expert most responsible for the doctrinal decrees prepared by the Council, objected to the idea that man arose from animals by a spontaneous evolution [*Entwicklung*] in his *Handbuch der Religion* (1875). Since he thought that there was no spontaneous evolution even in the plant and animal world, he would surely not have accepted the idea of a spontaneous evolution of a human from an animal body. What would make an evolutionary change spontaneous? Apparently just that nature itself possessed the power to effect the change.[16]

Mathias Scheeben, present at the Council as a young observer on his way to take up a teaching position at the archdiocesan seminary (and later to become a highly respected theologian), also used the term, but without an explicit definition. He seems to have had a slightly different understanding of the term, for he emphasized that the spontaneous evolution that is (on his view) a feature of Darwinism is not fully consistent with the

---

14 Brivio, *Origine*, 28.

15 See chapter 5.

16 Wilmers, *Handbuch der Religion*, 234.

idea that the order of the material world is a work of Divine art. That latter idea would require, he said, that the origin of species bear some relation to fixed Divine ideas.[17]

There is a definition of spontaneous *generation*, but in a broad sense that includes the transformation of one species into another, in Tommaso Zigliara's *Summa philosophica* (1876). Zigliara, a Dominican priest, was one of the best of the new generation of Neo-Thomist philosophers; two years later, he would play a rôle in writing *Aeterni Patris*, Leo XIII's seminal encyclical promoting Thomistic philosophy. He would receive a cardinal's hat in 1879. He defined spontaneous *generation* as a "blind and accidental and progressive unfolding [*explicatio*] from a brute and unformed state to vitality, and successively up to rational life in man."[18] French Dominican Dalmace Leroy, whom we will meet again in chapter 5, then, seems to be on firm ground when, in his discussion of the teaching of the Council, he suggested that the point of the word "spontaneous" is to reject precisely atheistic (or at least non-providentialist) accounts. He argued that the transformations found in a providential world would not be spontaneous in the proscribed sense.[19]

Third, how must one understand the phrases "even considering only his body" and "culminates in a human nature"? Suppose that "spontaneous" natural processes created a body into which a (directly created) human soul was subsequently infused by God. Would not a Thomist have to say that the spontaneously created body would not really be a *human* body until a divinely created human soul was infused in it and that thus, in the philosophically precise (if not in the colloquial) sense, natural changes ("spontaneous" or not) cannot create a human body? Leroy made precisely this point: "In the living composite which we call the human body, it is the soul which is the form."[20] So the product of natural evolutionary processes is not, until the infusion of a rational soul, a *human* body.

Fourth, one must not overlook the significance of the words "in a way that is continuous and culminates in human nature." Perhaps Chambers's account is rejected here. It is harder to say whether Mivart's evolutionism (then still ten years in the future) is similarly rejected. Could a body without an intellectual soul be said to have a human nature? If not, then a body *with a human nature* did not originate by evolution or by a continuous process, even on Mivart's account.

What authority do the teachings of the Council of Cologne have? The acts and decrees of the Council were submitted to Rome, where, in due course, they were approved (in the sense of receiving the *recognitio* ordinarily accorded to provincial councils) and were (taken as a whole) praised by Pope Pius. Such *recognitio* does not, however, make

---

17 In his *Handbuch der katholischen Dogmatik*, 2:95 (¶260), Scheeben referred to "the gradual spontaneous evolution of species" and said (a few lines above this) that "Darwinism ascribes the origin of living things to spontaneous evolution of inorganic [matter] and does not ascribe the existence of species to a fixed divine idea."

18 Zigliara, *Summa philosophica*, 2:148 (Psychologia, 1.4.1).

19 Leroy, Évolution restreinte, 259.

20 Leroy, Évolution restreinte, 260.

them into anything more than the decrees of a provincial council.[21] Such *legal* authority as the statement about the non-evolutionary origin of the human body had, therefore, it had only in the Archdiocese of Cologne.

3. VATICAN I (1869–1870)[22]

On December 6, 1864, Pope Pius IX announced to a group of cardinals assembled for a meeting of the Congregation of Rites his intention to convene an ecumenical council, the twentieth in the history of the Church and the first in three centuries, in order "to provide for the extraordinary needs of the Christian flock."[23] Invitations to propose topics to be discussed were sent out to some (but not all) cardinals and bishops.

The Council began with an ambitious agenda. Work began with the establishment of five preparatory commissions, each with a distinct area of concern. The commission responsible for theology and dogma, for its part, decided to prepare three schemata—one on faith, one on the Church, and one on the sacrament of matrimony. The first schema, the only one relevant to our topic, bore the preliminary title "Catholic teaching against the multiple errors derived from rationalism" and anthropology was just one of the many subjects with respect to which, in the judgment of those formulating the agenda, there were errors in need of correction. Of the anthropological errors, only some concerned "man naturally considered"; the supernatural order—original justice and original sin—was also addressed.

The Council, which opened on December 8, 1869, was able to complete only a small part of that agenda before September 20, 1870, when the city fell to the armies of King Victor Emmanuel. On October 20, Pius suspended the Council. Most of its work, including a statement on the origin of the human race, was left unfinished. The Council had managed to approve a statement on creation in general,[24] but had not addressed the topic of evolution. What might it have said about that latter topic if it had had time to accomplish all that it had set out to do? The Council's work was far enough along that we can, by reviewing its preliminary work (its *Nachlaß*, one might say), at least suggest an answer to that question.

It might seem to have been an opportune time for the Council to have addressed the new evolutionary ideas. The bishops who had gathered at Cologne seem to have thought so in 1860 and, although Darwin's *Descent of Man* and Mivart's *Genesis of Species* would be

---

21 See Franz Xavier Wernz, SJ, *Ius decretalium*, 2: 2: 746.

22 For a history of the Council, see Theodor Granderath, SJ, *Geschichte des vatikanischen Konzils*, or Cuthbert Butler, *The Vatican Council*. Relevant documents can be found in Joannes Dominicus Mansi, *Sacrorum conciliorum collectio*, vols. 49–53.

23 Mansi, *Collectio*, 49:9–10.

24 "The one true God, of His own goodness and almighty power, not to increase His own happiness, . . . but to manifest His perfection by the goods which He bestows on creatures, freely, at the beginning of time and out of nothing made [*condidit*] both the spiritual and the corporeal creation, namely, the angelical and the mundane, and then the human creature, as constituted of both spirit and body" (Vatican I, *Dei Filius*, c. 1 (Alberigo, *Decreta*, 781)).

published only after the adjournment of the Vatican Council, the decade between the two councils had seen the publication of several new secular (and sometimes anti-religious) defenses of the evolutionary origin of man—by Huxley in England, Canestrini in Italy, and Haeckel in Germany—as well as Clémence Royer's decidedly anti-Christian translation of, and gloss on, *The Origin of Species* in France. Catholics had also addressed the issue, and were divided over it. De Filippi, as I mentioned in the previous chapter, had already offered a compatibilist account of the matter, though without a great deal of elaboration.

Few of the bishops who prepared responses to Pope Pius's inquiry about which topics the Council should take up made any mention of evolution. Ignaz de Senestréy, bishop of Regensburg, did, but he did not focus on the origin of the human body, identifying, the "errors of our day, . . . regarding the origin and nature of the human race" more broadly: "many modern authors deny that all men are descendants of Adam, and materialists are not ashamed to say that the human race is not essentially different from brute animals but trace their origin through some kind of natural evolution and transformation back to those animals."[25] Some of the theologians selected as *periti* for the Vatican Council had already written against the evolutionary origin of the body. These included two members of the preparatory commission on theology and dogma, Johann Schwetz[26] and Giovanni Perrone, whose textbooks will be discussed in chapter 4. Konrad Martin, bishop of Paderborn, who, as head of a suffragan see, had been in attendance at the Council of Cologne, was not only on the deputation charged with revisions of the work of the preparatory commission, but was personally charged with that revision. Joseph Kleutgen, to whom Martin delegated the actual work of revision, had also written against the evolutionary origin of the human body.[27] One might also notice the presence at the Council of Wilhelm Wilmers, though only as theologian-consultant to Jean-Gabriel Meurin, SJ, vicar apostolic of Bombay-Poona, and so in a position much less important than that of Martin.[28] There is no indication that Martin himself was committed to repeating Cologne's teaching on this point. That the Vatican Council did not address the question in as much detail as Cologne had done could not have been because the earlier statement was unknown to the participants in the later Council's work.

In fact, the documents devoted to "man naturally considered," from the first draft to the last,[29] focused on two central points. The first was the common origin of the

---

25 De Senestréy, "Responsum," in Mansi, *Collectio*, 49:138–44, at 138–39.

26 "Divine revelation says that Adam and Eve, not only their souls, but also their bodies, were immediately created by God" (Schwetz, *Theologia dogmatica*, 2:2).

27 "Because it must have a nature that would make interaction with spirit possible, its production must lie beyond the sphere of the principle of nature, and so that principle would not be able to produce the first human body without the action of the Creator" (Kleutgen, *Philosophie der Vorzeit*, 467 (¶792).

28 Beumer, "Wilmers," 145–51.

29 The Council's preparations for consideration of the origin and nature of man can be found in the following eight documents:

Three *vota* addressing the topic, prepared by consultors to the theologico-dogmatic commission:

(1–2) Two by Johann Schwetz (no. 29–30)—"Doctrina de homine" (June 1868) and "Decretum de homine" (April 1869) (Indici 1172, I–II, AAV). Mentioned, but not published, in Mansi, *Collectio*, 49:738, these are discussed in detail in Ladislao Orbán, *Theologia güntheriana et Concilium vaticanum*.

whole human race from Adam; the second was man as composed of body and rational soul (the latter being the form of the former).[30] Some of the drafts repeat the Biblical language—Franzelin's July 1869 draft, for example, includes the phrase "man, whom the LORD God formed of dust from the ground, and into whose nostrils He breathed the breath of life."[31] The two central concerns, named in that same document as a header to the relevant paragraph, did not address the evolutionary *origins* of the race, or, to state the same point differently, the question of whether man had an animal ancestry.

There were only a few expressions of interest in addressing the question of evolution and the origin of man during the deliberations of the preparatory commission. Giuseppe Pecci, a Jesuit theologian then professor at the university La Sapienza, raised the question

---

(3) One by Giuseppe Pecci (no. 54)—"De erroribus qui in primo syllabi capite recensentur" (March 1869) (mentioned in Mansi, *Collectio*, 49:739–40, published in the Dokumentenanhang to Hermann Pottmeyer, *Der Glaube vor dem Anspruch der Wissenschaft*, 3*–25*; citations below are to the document's own page numbers).

Five successive drafts of schemata proposed as constitutions for the final approval of the Council:

(4) A 47-page draft, written by Johann Baptist Franzelin, SJ (no. 32)—"Definitio doctrinae catholicae contra multiplices errores ex impio rationalismo derivatos vel contra multiplices absoluti ac temperati rationalismi errores" (July 1869) (mentioned at Mansi, *Collectio*, 49:738; published in J. M. G. Gomez-Heras, *Temas dogmáticos del Concilio vaticano I*, 1:280–302).

(5) The preparatory commission's eighteen-chapter revision of Franzelin's draft, ready by October 1869—originally "Decretum de doctrina catholica contra multiplices errores ex rationalismo derivatos (seconda forma)" (no. 33; Mansi, *Collectio*, 49:738), but submitted to the Council on December 20 as "Schema constitutionis dogmaticae de doctrina catholica, &c." (Mansi, *Collectio*, 50:59–119, with the chapter on anthropology at 70–71 and the corresponding notes at 108–12); summarized as "Brevis expositio doctrinae capitum quae continentur in schemate constitutionum sacro oecumenico concilio vaticano proponendarum." (Mansi, *Collectio*, 49: 739–50).

This second draft was not, however, well-received. The problem was not doctrinal; Charles Gay, one of the members of the dogmatic commission, said of the *schema*: "it is too concerned with German errors, many of which are hardly known outside the schools, and not enough with those that so trouble men's minds and create so much danger to society." This remark was made to Henri-Joseph Icard, another theologian at the council, who recorded it in his *Journal de mon voyage et de mon séjour à Rome*, 49 (quoted here from Fernand Mourret, *Le Concile du Vatican*, 191, the original in the archives of the Séminaire de Saint-Sulpice in Paris). And so, on January 10, after seven days of debate, it was sent for redrafting to a deputation that had been especially elected the month before precisely to revise schemata when necessary. The task was delegated to Martin and sub-delegated to Kleutgen.

(6) Kleutgen's draft, submitted to the deputation for its consideration on March 11—"Schema reformatum constitutionis dogmaticae de fide catholica patrum deputatorum examini propositum" (Mansi, *Collectio*, 53:164–77, esp. 170). The difficulties of the subject led to further revisions.

(7) A proposed revision precisely of the chapter on man, ready on March 20—"Capitis VI alterius schematis textus reformatus patribus deputatis denuo propositus" (Mansi, *Collectio*, 53:210–12).

(8) The final revision—"Schema secundae constitutionis dogmaticae *De doctrina catholica* a Deputatione pro rebus fidei reformatum" (Mansi, *Collectio*, 53:230–38). The first four chapters (on creation, revelation, faith, and reason) were submitted to the Council on March 14 and, after discussion, were promulgated as *Dei Filius*. The last five, including chapter 6 "On the Origin and Nature of Man," was ready only on April 26, 1870, but by then the Council had already turned to the question of papal infallibility (contained in another product of the theologico-dogmatic commission and ultimately issued as the constitution *Pastor aeternus*). The Council gave the question of anthropology no further consideration.

30 "Brevis expositio doctrinae capitum quae continentur in schemate constitutionum sacro oecumenico concilio vaticano proponendarum," Mansi, *Collectio*, 49:739–50, at 743. See also the content of the anathematic canons attached to some of the drafts (e.g. "Schema secundae constitutionis," Mansi, *Collectio*, 53:236).

The term "form" here is a technical term of Scholastic philosophy meaning that which makes a piece of matter the *kind* of thing that it is. The human soul, that is to say, is what makes a body precisely a *human* body with the powers (saliently, rationality) that constitute *human* being. This account of the human soul only repeats what the Church had taught at two previous ecumenical councils—"the soul is truly in itself and essentially the form of the human body" (Vienne [1312], Decree 1; Lateran V [1513], *Apostolici regiminis*).

31 Franzelin, "Definitio doctrinae catholicae," 298–99.

in a *votum* that he wrote for the preparatory commission. His explication of the error of "more recent naturalism" did not mention evolution. It did condemn De Filippi (along with such more commonly mentioned *bêtes noires* of the anti-materialists as Vogt, Jacob Moleschott, and Ludwig Büchner) for holding that "contained in the essence of matter are internal and active powers which effect all the operations of the human soul."[32] In his conclusion to this section of the *votum*, Pecci addressed evolutionism directly, recommending a canon condemning "those who say that matter, by its own powers, has so evolved that, by successive transmutations of species, it has arrived at man himself as though at its ultimate end."[33] In the course of the commission's deliberations, one member of the commission (the minutes do not say who) raised the question of evolutionary anthropogenesis again: "the observation was made that these days another error is flourishing as well, namely that man is a product and effect of the evolution of matter, or at least that he originated by a spontaneous generation of matter. Some mention of this error could be made here, one of the consultors said, with the details of how left to the deputation's editors."[34] A *relatio* submitted by János Simor, archbishop of Esztergom (Hungary) and a member of the deputation charged with revision of the constitution on faith, asked "whether there is any time other than ours which faces attack from the foul doctrine which looks for the origins of the human race in a hairy ape?"[35] Despite Pecci's recommendation, and despite the comments just mentioned, the general issue did not find explicit mention in any of the various drafts of the relevant *schema*. The second of the two points which the commission did emphasize (body-soul composition), however, created a natural opening for a further question—where did the body and soul come from?

In addressing the origin of the body, the various versions of the *schema* kept to the words of Scripture—the human body was formed "from the dust of the ground." The question of whether that formation was done immediately or by way of secondary causes was never raised. Nor was there any explicit mention of the idea condemned at Cologne—that the human body was brought forth by the spontaneous change of a less perfect nature into a more perfect one in a way that is continuous and culminates in a human nature. Nothing in the text suggests any particular view about evolutionary origins of the human body.

---

32 Pecci, "De erroribus," 40. Pecci is not the only one who thought De Filippi was a materialist. The suspicion generated by the first half of his lecture on man and apes was probably reinforced by his friendly relations with his Turin colleague Moleschott (see De Filippi, "La fisiologia di professore Moleschott") and his kind words about Vogt (*L'uomo*, 58–60n4, where he described Vogt's new *Vorlesungen über den Menschen* as "an excellent book which could serve as a very good basis for further discussions on a subject of great importance"). That some materialists also saw De Filippi as one of their own I showed above. There I also showed that these assessments of him were mistaken. In any case, Pecci seems not to have been particularly careful in his identification of materialists. He also lists, for example, one "Wagner," but whom could he have meant? Göttingen's Rudolph Wagner's critique of materialism was what precipitated nineteenth-century Germany's *Materialismusstreit*; Munich's Andreas Wagner also entered the lists on the anti-materialist side.

33 Pecci, "De erroribus," 43. See also Query IV.1 in the unattributed "De Pantheismo, rationalismo, et naturalismo: Quaeritur," in Pottmeyer, *Glaube*, 26*–27*.

34 Minutes for May 13, 1869, in Mansi, *Collectio*, 49:697.

35 Simor, "De emendationibus prooemii constitutionis dogmaticae *De fide catholica*," in *Acta et decreta: Collectio lacensis*, 7:91–95, at 92.

This lack of concern about the details stands in some contrast with the attention given to the origin of the human soul. The *schema* that the commission had presented to the Council when it opened said only that God had "breathed into Adam's nostrils the breath of life." It added a long note explaining why the commission had not included the idea that the soul was directly created by God.[36]

The idea that human souls were not directly created by God but were somehow generated by the parents had had a long, if contested, history in Christian theology. Although it had been fairly decisively rejected in medieval Scholasticism, it had made something of a comeback among Protestants and then, in the nineteenth century, among Catholics as well.[37] The commission's unwillingness to define the *creation* of each human soul met, however, with some resistance when the *schema* was discussed at the Council itself. Andon Bedros Hassoun, Armenian Patriarch of Cilicia, said: "I think it would be best if the decree were to include here . . . that the soul was immediately created by God and infused into the body. In that way, any revival of traducianism would be solemnly condemned before it spreads."[38] Jean-François-Anne Landriot, bishop of Rheims, on the other hand, urged that the matter *not* be defined since the alternative view had been judged to be possible by respected theologians in the past.[39] Hassoun, as it turned out, had been elected to the deputation charged with revising the *schema*; the final version of the revision included the phrase "sc., a soul produced *ex nihilo*."[40]

So, what can we conclude? The Council included, among the *periti*, theologians who rejected the idea of the evolutionary origin of the human body. There is, however, no evidence that they, or the bishops, attempted to include this idea in the documents of the Council; discussion on anthropological matters was focused rather on the question of the origin of the human *soul*. They gave the question of the origin of the body (and *a fortiori* biological evolution) less attention than had the bishops at Cologne, and this despite the lively debate begun (in Italy) by De Filippi with his lecture of 1862.

36 "Schema constitutionis dogmaticae" of December 20, 71 and 108–12.

37 Among the more important were Jakob Frohschammer, who taught that parents create the soul in his *Über den Ursprung der menschlichen Seelen*, and Bl. Antonio Rosmini-Serbati, in his *Psicologia*, 1:145–49 (¶¶647–59).

 Frohschammer's book was placed on the *Index* in 1857. Rosmini's work had been reviewed by the Holy Office in 1854, but no formal censure of his view was then made. (For more on Rosmini and ecclesiastical authorities, see Richard Malone, "Historical Review of the Rosmini Case.")

38 Hassoun, "Oratio," 182, in Mansi, *Collectio*, 50:180–85. It is, perhaps, no accident that it was precisely an Armenian who made this point. In 1341, in the course of working out a reunion of the Armenians with Rome, Pope Benedict XII had required (in the libellus *Cum Dudum*) that the Armenians make explicit their rejection of the traducianism of the Armenian philosopher Մխիթար (Mkhit'ar, but Mechitriz in the Latin of the libellus). For a historical overview, see Leen Spruit, *Origin of the Soul*; Robert Lacroix, *Origine de l'âme humaine*; or William Reany, *Creation of the Human Soul*.

39 Landriot, "Oratio," 241, in Mansi, *Collectio*, 50:241–46.

40 "Schema secundae constitutionis." 53:230.

4. OFFICIAL EPISCOPAL REACTIONS

The Church chose not to (or at least did not choose to) address the question of evolution at the ecumenical council called to confront (among other matters) the intellectual challenges of the day. Individual bishops did, however, occasionally speak or act in an official capacity against the new evolutionary ideas. Two cases can be cited, both from Spain; I know of no other cases in which bishops acted on their own authority, although it is of course possible that others did so less formally. Cases of bishops requesting action by Rome are discussed below.

The first case comes from Granada, where Rafael García Álvarez, director of the Instituto de Segunda Enseñanza de la provincia de Granada, had defended evolutionary ideas in the lecture with which he opened the 1872–73 academic year. Bienvenido Monzón y Martín, the archbishop of Granada, denounced the lecture in a pastoral letter and had the published version placed on a Spanish index of prohibited books.[41]

The second case, one that found a place in White's *History of the Warfare of Science with Theology in Christendom*,[42] occurred in the Canary Islands. In 1876, local naturalist Gregorio Chil y Naranjo published the first volume of his *Estudios históricos, climatológicos y patológicos de las Islas Canarias*. The local bishop, José María Urquinaona y Bidot, condemned the book and excommunicated its author.

What significance can be attributed to these two incidents? It is important to keep in mind that Spanish evolutionism, including Chil's *Estudios*, was not so much the paleoetiological *science* of Darwin as it was the monistic *philosophy* of Haeckel.[43] Manuel de la Revilla, a leading positivist, wrote in 1877 that "there are, among the positivists and the Darwinists, many thinkers who . . . construct a complete materialist metaphysics, which they present . . . as an unavoidable consequence of the theory of evolution."[44]

The introduction to Chil's book presented a materialist account of the origin of the world (along the lines of Darwin and Haeckel, Chil said[45]) in which the word "creation" had been used to mean merely "appearance in the world," and in which man was a modified ape (*simio*), though one differing from other apes insofar as it had the power of abstraction.[46] On the other hand, Bishop Urquinaona, in the *Carta Pastoral* (1876) in which he condemned Chil's book, rejected more than just Chil's materialism. Whether Urquinaona's insistence on the account of creation offered by Moses was limited to an exnihilationistic understanding of creation and the immediate divine action in the

---

41 García Álvarez, *Discurso*; Monzón, "Censura sinodal." The index was León Carbonero y Sol, ed., *Índice de los libros prohibidos*, 210. See Thomas F. Glick, "Spain," 324–25, and Francisco Pelayo López, *Ciencia y creencia en España*, 165–68. See also Rafael García Álvarez and Leandro Sequeiros San Román, *Granada y el darwinismo*.

42 White, *History*, 1:85. White, incorrectly, put "Chil y Marango."

43 For summaries of the history of the reception of Darwinism in Spain, see Glick, "Spain," or Diego Núñez, *El darwinismo en España*.

44 Revilla, "Revista crítica," 119–20.

45 Chil, *Estudios*, 14–15.

46 Chil, *Estudios*, 14.

creation of man or whether it included also direct creation of animals Urquinaona does not make clear, but it did also explicitly reject Chil's account of primitive man as a cave man lacking, for example, the use of fire.

The best account of the situation in Spain would seem to be that scientific ideas were caught in a crossfire between an overly skeptical Catholic clergy and atheistic philosophers pretending to be scientists. Indeed one contemporary observer, Joaquín Serrano Cañete, a physician at the Instituto Médico Valenciano, who accepted the theory of evolution, characterized the debate on evolution organized by the Ateneo Científico in Valencia in 1878 as a debate between "two groups of extremists, 'the party of the impatient' and that of the retrogrades, each having aggrandized Darwinian theory for its own ends."[47]

5. THE CONGREGATION OF THE INDEX[48]

The Congregation of the Index received the first complaint about a work of Catholic evolutionism only in 1877, when Caverni's *Nuovi studi* was delated by Eugenio Cecconi, archbishop of Florence, the author's ordinary. Cecconi had first requested two local reviews of the book, one (apparently) by a priest of the archdiocese and the other (apparently) not.[49] Both reviews were negative. The book's proposed canons of Biblical interpretation would reach too far—if the Biblical authors were fallible in speaking about natural phenomena, then why not also about history (including Sacred History)? It was not clear why the evolutionary processes accepted by Caverni would not extend to the origin of man, whereas Catholic doctrine held, according to the reviewers, that even the human body was formed directly by God. The tone of the book was too acrimonious.[50] Cecconi delated the book to the Congregation of the Index in Rome.

At the Index, Girolamo Saccheri, its secretary, turned the book over for review to Zigliara, then one of the consultors at the Index. Already in 1876, he had argued against evolutionary theories in his *Summa philosophica*, published just the year before.[51] For the Index, he prepared a 19-page *votum* expressing three concerns.

First, he thought that Darwinism was, in its essentials, a new version of Lamarckism—a history of life in which chemical combinations produced one or a few species of primitive cells,[52] which in turn were transformed into the many biological species existent today. It still faced the scientific objections that had been raised by Cuvier, Zigliara said, but it faced deeper, philosophical, objections as well. It was fundamentally a pantheistic and materialistic system with a logical affinity to Hegelianism. Caverni's

---

47 Quoted in *El mercantil valenciano*, February 14, 1878 (quoted here from Glick, "Spain," 325).

48 For details on the responsibilities and procedures of the Index, see Appendix III.B.

49 Florentine *vota* (fol. 4, Atti e documenti 1878–85, CL, ADDF). For a more complete summary of the *vota*, see Artigas, *Negotiating Darwin*, 39. The point about the identity of the authors was first made by Artigas.

50 Second Florentine *votum*, 6.

51 Zigliara, *Summa philosophica*, 148–53 (Psychologia, I.4).

52 Darwin was resolutely agnostic on this point, though Lamarck and Darwinists such as Haeckel were not.

attempt to introduce providentialist components made it pantheism *sui generis*, perhaps, but pantheism nonetheless.

Since Caverni's philosophical zoology played an important rôle in blocking the extension of Darwinian arguments to anthropogenesis, it would be important that he got this right; Zigliara thought that he did not. Zigliara had already written a critique of the ontologism on which Caverni had relied in his argument for the difference between man and animal.[53] In addition, it was clear, Zigliara said, both from Scripture and from experience, that animals had imaginative and estimative powers; if such powers can be attributed to Caverni's imponderable fluids in animals, then it is not clear why it could not also be so attributed for man in a way that would undermine Caverni's argument for the difference between man and animals.

There were also, Zigliara went on to say, theological problems with Caverni's book. In order to reconcile his thesis with the text of Genesis, Caverni had resorted to unacceptable canons of Scriptural interpretation. These canons, if followed to their logical conclusion, would render revelation a dead letter and would make the Vatican Council's distinction between revealed truths that are supernatural with respect to their object and those that are so with respect to their mode of being known simply a distinction without a difference.[54]

Zigliara recommended that the *Nuovi studi* be placed on the *Index* and that the archbishop of Florence tell Caverni not to publish his promised book on the origin of man.

Zigliara's recommendation was accepted by both the preparatory and the general congregations; the recommendation to condemn the book was unanimous. The final step would be approval of the decree by the pope, now Leo XIII, who had been elected a bare four months previously. In the report he prepared for the pope as secretary of the Congregation, Saccheri pointed out that "until now, the Holy See has rendered no decision on the system mentioned," and added that "if Caverni's work is condemned, as it should be, Darwinism would be indirectly condemned." Whether Saccheri meant by "Darwinism" any evolutionary account of the origin of species, or just evolutionary accounts of the origin of man, is not clear.[55] In any event, the pope approved the decision of the Congregation; Caverni, when it was presented to him, submitted. The condemnation was published on July 31, 1878, and the book itself was largely forgotten.

In what sense was this an "indirect" condemnation of Darwinism? First, of course, it was indirect because the Congregation of the Index had no authority to condemn *ideas*; it had jurisdiction only over printed material.

Second, to the extent that the condemnation was a consequence of Caverni's inability to articulate sound principles of hermeneutics that would reconcile the evolutionary origin of species with the text of Genesis, the condemnation of the book on the basis

---

53 Zigliara, *Luce intellettuale*.

54 Zigliara, *Votum*, May 25, 1878, 9 (fol. 71, Protocolli 1878–81, CL, ADDF).

55 See my discussion of this term in footnote 3 on page 46.

of Caverni's hermeneutics (if that is what it was) might be thought to be an *indirect* condemnation of the evolutionary ideas developed on their basis as well.

But the condemnation could also be seen as indirect in a third sense—it was completely opaque. The *Index* is only a *list* of prohibited books. Only in the rarest cases did it publish the reasons why individual books were prohibited. That Caverni's book defended evolutionism would be known to anyone who read the reviews of the book in *Civiltà cattolica*, but would not be at all evident to anyone who only saw the title listed in the *Index*. Neither the book nor its condemnation was ever mentioned in subsequent public debates over evolutionism. The editors of *Civiltà cattolica*, which was stridently and diligently anti-evolutionist through the end of the century, never mentioned the fate of the *Nuovi studi* as relevant to the Church's attitude towards evolution, though it would have strengthened their editorial position to have done so. Francesco Salis Seewis, who had written the critical review of Caverni's book in 1877, did not mention that book, or its fate, when he published his notice of the appearance of Zahm's *Evolution and Dogma* in 1897. Neither was it mentioned in histories of Catholic responses to evolutionism until Mariano Artigas, Thomas F. Glick, and Rafael A. Martínez recognized its relevance to this story when the archives of the Index were opened in 1998, when they saw a reference to the book in marginal notes on a copy of a *votum* for a later case.[56]

Presumably the reason for this ignorance about the book is that no one not sworn to secrecy knew exactly why the book was condemned. When rumors that the book was under investigation first began to fly in late 1877, Caverni had written to the pastor of his hometown that he thought the whole problem had originated in "a few phrases in which perhaps I openly attempted to remove from the secular [i.e., diocesan] clergy and especially the parish priests the yoke which, it seemed to me, the friars and, in particular, the Jesuits wanted to put on them."[57] Indeed, Salis Seewis complained in the final paragraph of his review of the book in *Civiltà cattolica* about the calumnious criticisms that Caverni had directed at the clergy and about his thoughtless repetition of unbelievers' complaints about its ignorance.[58] Though Caverni might have realized that that was not so when (later) he was told by his bishop not to write his book on the origins of man, later historians, until the opening of the archives in 1998, also seem to have attributed the condemnation to his criticism of contemporary ecclesiastical rivalries.[59]

Caverni did later publish his ideas on the antiquity, though not directly on the origins, of man, as *Dell'antichità dell'uomo secondo la scienza moderna: Saggio di studi*, first in *La Rassegna nazionale* (as the *Rivista universale* was by then called) in 1879, and then as a book in 1881. That book, which argued that paleontology was not yet capable of

---

56 Teofilo Domenichelli, *Votum*, 1, the note probably being by Marcolino Cicognani (doc. 128, Protocolli 1894–96, CL, ADDF). The image is reproduced in Artigas, *Negotiating Darwin*, 15.

57 Letter to Celestino Orsi, November 20, 1877, reprinted in Pagnini, *Caverni*, 40–41. Indeed, Cecconi's outside reviewer had also remarked, "The stone-throwing at the Jesuits, which seems to be now in fashion, is, at the least, impolite" (Florentine *vota*, 8r). For an example of such phrases, see *Nuovi studi*, 171.

58 Salis Seewis, "De' nuovi studi," 75–76.

59 E.g., Giovanni Giovannozzi, "Un tedesco di Montelupo," 268n1, and Pagnini, *Caverni*, 43.

shedding light on the question, raised no further problems for him. He then set the topic aside in favor of other work, most notably his six-volume *Storia del metodo sperimentale in Italia* (1888), which won him a prize from the Regio istituto veneto di scienze, lettere ed arti, though it also involved him in other (albeit non-theological) controversies.[60]

Artigas and his co-authors called the placement of Caverni's *Nuovi studi* on the *Index* an "ineffective decree,"[61] but that is a mistaken characterization. The intended effect of the decree (the only effect at which the Index was authorized to aim) was the suppression of the book. Its effectiveness can be determined by attempting to find a copy. Very few libraries have it. Further evidence for the effectiveness of the decree is the fact, acknowledged by Artigas, that the book did not figure at all in further public Catholic discussions of evolution.

✳ ✳ ✳ ✳ ✳

The works of two other evolutionist authors, both materialists, were also placed on the *Index* in those first post-Darwinian decades.

The first such author was Niccola Marselli (1832–1899), soldier, historian, politician, and philosopher. His grand *La scienza della storia*, an evolutionistic account of human history somewhat in the style of Herbert Spencer, included five parts, two of which—*L'Origini dell'umanità* (1879) and *Le grandi razze dell'umanità* (1880) were delated to the Index.

The first of those, *L'origini dell'umanità*, devoted chapters to the usual subjects—the place of man in nature, polygenism, and the antiquity of man. It asserted that man differs from animals only in degree, rejected human immortality, and suggested that polygenism was a better explanation of human racial diversity than was monogenism.[62] It ended with a critique of religion:

> I have observed that religions—at least those which we have known so far—do not restrict themselves to admitting the first cause of the universe, do not stop in the face of the unknowable, but . . . try to reveal it, making known to us the particulars of its economy, . . . the causes of natural and social phenomena. I also observed that science, while admitting the Unknown, reveals the falsity of religious superstitions. It tells religion, I do not know the truth, but I know for certain that what you say is not true.[63]

The task of preparing the *votum* was assigned to Capuchin priest Eusebio da Monte Santo, who noted all of the theses just mentioned and concluded by saying, with respect to *L'origini dell'umanità* that:

> Marselli is truly one of those men for whom God, Religion, and Man are nothing other than means to the worship of humanity, which in turn is *Everything*. Immortality is

---

60 For details, see Giuseppe Castagnetti and Michele Camerota, "Raffaello Caverni."

61 Artigas, *Negotiating Darwin*, 51.

62 Marselli, *Origini dell'umanità*, 26, 127–28, and 46.

63 Marselli, *Origini dell'umanità*, 136–37.

a fantasy; in sum, he is one of those men who with a display of indigestible erudition and of ostensible science, teach the most trivial nonsense, the grossest errors, and the most obvious heresies. They destroy in their pupils every feeling of faith.[64]

Le grandi razze, he said, had the same defects as did *L'origini dell'umanità*.[65] Unsurprisingly, the Congregation unanimously recommended that both books be placed on the *Index*, and this was done on June 27, 1881.[66]

The second author was Pietro Siciliani, professor of philosophy and of pedagogy at the Università di Bologna. On June 30, 1881, Lucido Cardinal Parocchi, then archbishop of that city, delated two of Siciliani's books on education to the Index. The books were, the cardinal said, "infected with rationalism from top to bottom."[67] Parocchi's concerns seem to be more about Siciliani's views on religion in general than on evolutionism, and the two books about which he made his complaint—*Sull'insegnamento religioso ai bambini, secondo i dettami della filosofia scientifica* (1881), and *La scienza nell'educazione* (2nd ed., 1881)—are focused on the theory of education rather than on biology *per se*, though the latter is grounded in Siciliani's version of evolutionism.

The Index's consultors met on December 1, 1881. All agreed that both books should be prohibited; most thought that the rest of Siciliani's books should be examined as well and a decree of prohibition published only after that further review was completed. The cardinals, at the general congregation held on December 5, approved the consultors' recommendation.[68]

The Congregation then began the review of the rest of Siciliani's works and on January 23, 1882, the secretary asked Giuseppe Maria Granniello, a Barnabite priest and a consultor at the Index, to write a *votum* on six more of Siciliani's books.[69] Granniello began his review by noting that the fact that Siciliani was an atheist and a materialist would ordinarily be sufficient to condemn all his philosophical works, but since his assignment was to be specific about particular books, he would cite a few relevant passages from each. Included in the passages mentioned was one from *Della psicogenia moderna* which asserted that the transformists were "unexcelled when they undertake to demonstrate the . . . reality of the chain of kinship between different species."[70]

---

64 Eusebio, *Votum*, 4 (doc. 201, Protocolli 1878–81, CL, ADDF).

65 Eusebio, *Votum*, 4–5.

66 Doc. 194 and 209, Protocolli 1878–81, CL, ADDF.

67 Parocchi to the Index (doc. 236, Protocolli 1878–81, CL, ADDF).

68 Decretum, December 5, 1881 (doc. 227, Protocolli 1878–81, CL, ADDF).

69 The books in question were: *Sul rinnovamento della filosofia positiva*; *La critica nella filosofia zoologica*; *Socialismo, Darwinismo e sociologia moderna*, 2nd ed.; *Prolégomènes à la psychogénie moderne*; *Teorie sociali e socialismo*; and *Psicogenia moderna*, 3rd ed.

70 Siciliani, *Psicogenia moderna*, 553; Graniello, *Votum*, March 5, 1882 (doc. 5, Protocolli 1882–84, CL, ADDF).

On March 16, 1882, the preparatory congregation recommended that all six books be prohibited, a recommendation endorsed at the general congregation, and on April 3 the books were placed on the *Index*.[71]

* * * * *

The most important exposition of Catholic evolutionism published during this period, Mivart's *Genesis of Species*, was never evaluated by the Index. There is no indication that Mivart's book was ever delated to the Congregation. For those who wonder why it was not, several factors might be noted.

First, Mivart's contributions to the defense of Catholic doctrine against materialistic scientism were appreciated by the English hierarchy. Both his honorary doctorate and his intended place at the Catholic University College, Kensington, provided public evidence of this.

Second, Mivart was more orthodox in his anthropology and zoology than Caverni had been and had not taken up the hermeneutical questions that had caused problems for Caverni.

Third, books in English tended not to have been delated to the Index until they appeared in Continental translation. This was the case with Erasmus Darwin's *Zoonomia*. William Draper's *History of the Conflict between Religion and Science*, published in English in 1874, first came to the attention of the Index only after publication of its Spanish translation in 1878. John Zahm's *Evolution and Dogma* was published in 1896 with an Italian translation the same year; it was the translation that was delated to the Index.

Finally, some (perhaps most) anti-evolutionists might have thought that works of Catholic evolutionism were wrong without thinking that they should be formally prohibited. Jesuit theologian Joseph Brucker, for example, wrote, shortly after an evolutionist author whose work he had criticized had been subject to official censure: "My conclusions are only as strong as my arguments; . . . I have never, either directly or indirectly, asked for or advised any authority to take action against the authors whom I have criticized."[72]

For whatever reason, although Mivart did not succeed in convincing all of his Catholic readers, his works on evolution were never subject to official disapprobation.

71 Doc. 1 and 9, Protocolli 1882–84, CL, ADDF.

72 Brucker, *Questions actuelles*, ix–x.

CHAPTER 4

NON-OFFICIAL FORA
(1859–1885)

Catholic periodicals, encyclopedias, and textbooks provide a good guide to the broader Catholic reaction to the new evolutionary ideas, but other indications are sometimes also worth noticing, so I will begin this chapter with the reaction of St. John Henry Newman, England's leading nineteenth-century Catholic theologian. Although he never spoke publicly on the issue, in 1868 he wrote to Canon John Walker that:

> It does not seem to me to follow that creation is denied because the Creator, millions of years ago, gave laws to matter. He first created matter and then he created laws for it—laws which should *construct* it into its present wonderful beauty, and accurate adjustment and harmony of parts *gradually*. We do not deny or circumscribe the Creator, because we hold he has created the self-acting originating human mind, which has almost a creative gift; much less then do we deny or circumscribe His power, if we hold that He gave matter such laws as by their blind instrumentality moulded and constructed through innumerable ages the world as we see it. If Mr Darwin in this or that point of his theory comes into collision with revealed truth, that is another matter—but I do not see that the *principle* of development, or what I have called construction, does. As to the Divine *Design*, is it not an instance of incomprehensibly and infinitely marvellous Wisdom and Design to have given certain laws to matter millions of ages ago, which have surely and precisely worked out, in the long course of those ages, those effects which He from the first proposed. Mr Darwin's theory *need* not then to be atheistical, be it true or not; it may simply

be suggesting a larger idea of Divine Prescience and Skill.... At first sight I do not [see] that 'the *accidental* evolution of organic beings' is inconsistent with divine design—It is accidental to *us*, not to *God*.[1]

In his philosophical notebook, he addressed the more sensitive topic of human origins: "It is as strange that monkeys should be so like men, with no *historical* connexion between them, as ... the notion that there was no course of facts by which fossil bones got into rocks.... I will either go the whole hog with Darwin, or, dispensing with time & history altogether, hold, not only the theory of distinct species but that also of the creation of fossil-bearing rocks."[2] In 1870, as Darwin was being proposed for an honorary degree at Oxford, Newman addressed the question in more detail:

> I have not fallen in with Darwin's book. I conceive it to be an advocacy of the theory that the principle of propagation, which we are accustomed to believe began with Adam, and with the patriarchs of the brute species, began in some one common ancestor millions of years before.
>
> 1. Is this against the distinct teaching of the inspired text? If it is, then he advocates an antichristian theory. For myself, speaking under correction, I don't see that it does—contradict it.
>
> 2. Is it against Theism (putting Revelation aside)—I don't see how it can be. Else, the fact of a propagation from Adam is against Theism. If second causes are conceivable at all, an Almighty Agent being supposed, I don't see why the series should not last for millions of years as well as for thousands.
>
> The former question is the more critical. Does Scripture contradict the theory?—was Adam *not* immediately taken from the dust of the earth? "*All* are dust"—Eccles iii, 20—yet *we* never *were* dust—we are from fathers, why may not the same be the case with Adam? I don't say that it *is* so but if the sun does not go round the earth and the earth stand still, as Scripture seems to say, I don't know why Adam needs to be immediately out of dust—Formavit Deus hominem de limo terrae—i.e., out of what was really dust and mud in its nature, before He made it what it was, living. But I speak under correction. Darwin does not *profess* to oppose Religion.[3]

1. THE CATHOLIC PRESS

The first Catholic reactions to the publication of *The Origin of Species* came, naturally enough, in the Catholic press, in reviews of Darwin's book.

England had three intellectually serious Catholic periodicals in 1859, and two of them—Lord Acton's liberal *Rambler* and Cardinal Wiseman's more conservative *Dublin*

---

1 Newman to Walker, May 22, 1868, in Newman, *Letters and Diaries*, 24:77–78, at 77.

2 Newman, *Philosophical Notebook*, 1:158.

3 Letter to Edward Pusey of June 5, 1870, in Newman, *Letters and Diaries*, 25:137–38.

Review—published reviews of *The Origin of Species* in 1860. The reviews were both published anonymously (as was the custom of the day), but their authors have since been identified—Richard Simpson for the *Rambler* and Canon John Morris for the *Dublin Review*.[4] Both reviews objected vociferously to the (few) passages where Darwin (implicitly) extended his theory to the origin of man, commenting with amusement on the fact that "science," which had a few years before had difficulty with the idea of common ancestry for the Chippewa, Hottentot, Chinese, and English now proposed that those same Chippewa and Englishmen shared a common ancestry with plants and animals. Beyond that, however, the reviews differ noticeably.

Morris, a secretary to Cardinal Wiseman, gave the *Origin* a generally sympathetic review:

> The work itself . . . seems to us so valuable, and approves itself to us individually as so genuinely scientific; . . . the reasoning is so dispassionate, and the writer shows himself throughout so keen-sighted to every objection, that we cannot say how grieved we are that the book should be so marred by the introduction of so gratuitous and so repulsive an idea [as the animal origins of man], or that the theory should be carried to so unreasonable lengths.[5]

The review focused on the promise of the idea of natural selection. About common ancestry, apart from its firm rejection of any common ancestry for man and animal, it says only "we do not find ourselves in any position . . . to consider theories as proved which assert even 'that all the existing species of the same group, have descended from one progenitor,' . . . much less any attempt to sketch a still larger genealogical tree."[6]

Simpson's review was more critical. Simpson was a public intellectual, described by Newman as someone who "will always be flicking his whip at Bishops, cutting them in tender places, throwing stones at Sacred Congregations, and, as he rides along the roads, discharging pea-shooters at Cardinals who happen by bad luck to look out of the window."[7] Simpson had addressed the general question of religion and the paleoetiological sciences ten years before in a series of four essays entitled "Religion and Modern Philosophy" published in the *Rambler*. On the basis of those earlier articles, one might have expected him to have been more sympathetic to Darwin's new ideas, for there, he had, after all, imagined Moses characterizing his work as follows:

---

4 For the identification of the authors, see Lyon, "Immediate Reactions to Darwin," 79.

Simpson, editor and co-owner of the *Rambler*, characterized the review's approach in his unpublished history of English Catholicism as follows: "One idea which may be traced throughout its career, is the disposition to exult over the diversity of Catholic thought, and to deny any slavery or even subordination of the laity to the clergy in their opinions on matters of general interest." (Notebook G, "Three Generations of English Catholics," 251, in the Simpson Collection at Downside Archives; quoted from Damian McElrath, *Richard Simpson*, 69).

A. Hilliard Atteridge, "Periodical Literature," 673, characterized the *Dublin Review* as "a record of current thought for educated Catholics and at the same time . . . an exponent of Catholic views to non-Catholic inquirers."

5 Morris, Review, 52.

6 Morris, Review, 80.

7 Simpson to J. D. Acton, July 5, 1861, in Newman, *Letters and Diaries*, 20:4–5, and in Wilfred Ward, *Life of Newman*, 1:529.

> Before the existence of physical science I have given you a description of the genesis of the universe; go, then, form the sciences, inquire as deeply as you please, sift facts to the bottom, believe any thing that you can really prove, and then look into this book, and you shall find the great outlines of your science written here,—in dark mysterious characters, indeed, such as would not assist you in your search, but clearly enough to shew you, when you have found the truth, that I was in possession of it before you or your science were ever thought of; and that, seeing my preternatural knowledge of physical things, you may believe that the moral and religious truths I utter are also supernaturally revealed.[8]

Simpson had gone on to reject the idea that the views about nature expressed by the Fathers of the Church in the course of their interpretation of Holy Scripture bind Catholics of later generations:

> The Church is by no means bound to the scientific theories that have been prevalent among her teachers in past ages. The men of science of those times had come to their own conclusions, and in all their pride of knowledge were as dogmatising and overbearing as their successors of the present day, and refused to listen to the Church till she had shewn that her documents and teaching were not inconsistent with their theories. What could she do? Natural science was out of her province; she had no supernatural guidance in respect to it; she was obliged to trust her defence to such men of science as were devoted to her cause, or else take scientific theories on trust from the philosophers of the day, and adapt her language to the common opinions, which have thus become, to a partial and superficial observer, an integral part of her doctrinal teaching.[9]

Nevertheless, Simpson was hard on Darwin in his review: "Darwin claims the utmost extent for his hypothesis, which he owns he cannot prove, of the infinite variability of the species, but refuses to admit that the law of reversion [sc., the tendency of varieties to revert to earlier type] has one tittle more extent of application than it has already been proved to possess."[10] And, at a more fundamental level: "He has chosen to build, on physical arguments, a metaphysical conclusion that is subversive of psychology, metaphysics, and theology."[11] He characterized Darwin's view of life as "mythological," objecting that Darwin had taken to be true what he had only shown to be useful ("convenient for his classifications and afford[ing] a plausible solution to a number of facts"[12]).

Simpson imputed to Darwin (I think unjustifiably) a "refus[al] to allow that anything which has physical consequences can be the result of metaphysical or divine action" and

---

8 Simpson, "Modern Philosophy," 195.

9 Simpson, "Modern Philosophy," 200.

10 Simpson, Review, 369.

11 Simpson, Review, 365. See also 374.

12 Simpson, Review, 374.

objected (more reasonably) that "the creationist theory does not necessitate the perpetual search after manifestations of miraculous power and perpetual 'catastrophe.'"[13]

Despite his general skepticism about Darwin's ideas, Simpson concluded his review by conceding that religious believers have been guilty of an intellectual fault of their own: "Simply for the benefit of an unauthorized interpretation of certain texts of Scripture, controversialists have exhibited a desire to silence and to crush whole branches of natural investigation,"[14] and it is on that note that he concluded his review.

What was the Catholic reaction to the book elsewhere in Europe?

The Jesuits' new *Civiltà cattolica* was not hostile, but it was skeptical. Jesuit priest-geologist Giovanni Battista Pianciani, in the middle of a long series of articles on natural and theological cosmogony when Darwin's book appeared, took note of the *Origin* in the latter part of an article "Della Origine delle specie organizzate."[15] There, quoting extensively from a review that Swiss zoologist François Jules Pictet de la Rive had published in the *Bibliothèque universelle* (a review about which Darwin said that it was "the single one [of those opposed to his views] which seems to me *perfectly* fair & just & candid"),[16] Pianciani thought that the kind of gradual changes on which Darwin's theory relied could not produce the profound changes that Darwin attributed to them.

A more comprehensive, and more critical, review appeared in the pages of *Natur und Offenbarung*. Shortly after the appearance of Heinrich Georg Bronn's German translation of Darwin's *Origin*, Friedrich Michelis, priest of the diocese of Münster and professor of philosophy, one of the founders of the journal and for many years its editor, published, in *Natur und Offenbarung*, in a style that proves that every unkind word Mark Twain said about German syntax in *A Tramp Abroad* is Gospel-truth, a three-part critique. Michelis acknowledged early on that, as a theologian, he had no fundamental objection to Darwin's ideas themselves ("*dem Wortlaute* nach," he said)[17] and he devoted most of his article to philosophical and scientific reservations about Darwinism. Nevertheless, he saw the new ideas as part of a worrisome direction in science and in the final paragraph of his review he wrote: "I judge the position and the aspiration of science to be atheistic as long as it thinks that it can avoid the recognition of a personal God by reducing natural phenomena to natural laws.[18]

Darwin's publication of *The Descent of Man* in 1871, of course, elicited a new round of reactions. Of particular interest is that of John Cuthbert Hedley, then a Benedictine

---

13 Simpson, Review, 371 and 372.

14 Simpson, Review, 374.

15 Pianciani, "Origine delle specie organizzate." The series was subsequently published as *Cosmogonia naturale comparata col Genesi*.

16 Pictet, "Origine de l'espèce"; Darwin to Pictet, April 1, 1860, in Darwin, *Correspondence*, 8:137.

17 Michelis, "Darwins Theorie," 264.

18 Michelis, "Darwins Theorie," 385–86.

priest, later bishop of Newport (Wales), in *The Dublin Review*.[19] After a careful theological argument, Hedley concluded that:

> It is not contrary to Faith to suppose that all living things, up to man exclusively, were evolved by natural law out of minute life-germs primarily created, or even out of inorganic matter. On the other hand, it is heretical to deny the separate and special creation of the human soul; and to question the immediate and instantaneous (or quasi-instantaneous) formation by God of the bodies of Adam and Eve—the former out of inorganic matter, the latter out of the rib of Adam—is, at least, rash, and, perhaps, proximate to heresy.[20]

* * * * *

Beyond book reviews, the Catholic press found space for a broad range of Catholic views on the general question of the origin of species. It would be impractical to offer a comprehensive review, but a few highlights can be noted. Some Catholics wanted to make a distinction between what was suitable for discussion in professional contexts and what was suitable for discussion in publications intended for a broader audience. Jeremiah Murphy, CC, secretary to the bishop of Cloyne, for example, was willing to participate in an exchange of views on the origin of the human body in *The Irish Ecclesiastical Record*, but objected when the controversy spilled over into *The Tablet*: "I felt all along that the discussion was out of place in a public journal intended for general readers."[21]

Catholic anti-evolutionism, to be sure, found an early stronghold in Italy in the editorial offices of *Civiltà cattolica*, where its most extended exposition was a series of thirty-seven articles published between 1878 and 1880, a series which later appeared in book form. Pietro Caterini's *Dell'origine dell'uomo secondo il trasformismo: Esame scientifico filosofico teologico*, as the subtitle suggests, is divided into three parts. Although the title emphasizes the origin of man, the book in fact offers a more general critique of theories of evolution. The approach of *Civiltà cattolica* was not, however, typical of the Catholic press.

The *Irish Ecclesiastical Record*, established by Paul Cardinal Cullen in 1864 and (according to its cover) "a monthly journal under episcopal sanction," published, between 1866 and 1870, a series of nine numbered articles (one in two parts) on "Geology and Revelation" written by Maynooth theology professor Msgr. Gerald Molloy.[22] Molloy's primary thesis was the compatibility of revelation and nineteenth-century historical geology. He touches only lightly on transformism when, after reviewing the fact of faunal succession wrote: "It may here, very naturally, be asked if these Geological records give

---

19 Hedley, "Evolution and Faith." The review, published anonymously, covered not only Darwin but three other books, including Mivart's *On the Genesis of Species* and Alfred Russel Wallace's *Contributions to the Theory of Natural Selection*.

20 Hedley, "Evolution and Faith," 38.

21 Murphy, "Faith and Evolution," 481.

22 The articles were published unsigned, but Molloy acknowledged his authorship in 1870, when he published a revised version of the articles as a book.

us any information as to the manner in which each period of animal and vegetable life was brought to an end? Did … the new [organic forms] gradually come in to take [the places of the old forms]? Or were [they] suddenly produced?" The task that he had set himself being a "more general outline of Geological theory which is accepted by all," he is unwilling to take a side between the catastrophists and their uniformitarian opponents. Nevertheless, he does conclude by quoting a passage from Charles Lyell's *Principles of Geology* to the effect that "the extinction and creation of species has been … the result of a slow and gradual change in the organic world."[23] Ten years after the publication of Darwin's *Origin*, that sounds evolutionist, but the passage had already appeared in pre-*Origin* versions of Lyell's *Principles*.[24]

Some fifteen years later, the *Irish Ecclesiastical Review* published an exchange between Jeremiah Murphy, a frequent contributor to that journal, and John S. Vaughan, then at St. Bede's College in Manchester and later (from 1909) auxiliary bishop of Salford, on the question of whether it was heretical to accept the evolutionary origin of Adam's body. Murphy argued that it was; Vaughan, though he did not accept the evolutionary account himself, denied that it was heretical to do so,[25] though a few years later Vaughan argued, in the pages of *The Catholic World*, against science's ability to explain major transitions in the history of life, in particular the emergence of rational animals.[26]

In 1877, the Jesuits' *Stimmen aus Maria-Laach* published "Glaube und Descendenz-theorie," a two-part article by the German exegete Joseph Knabenbauer. Knabenbauer found evolutionary phytogenesis and zoogenesis theologically unproblematic.[27] He acknowledged the theological possibility of Mivart's account of anthropogenesis, but argued that a careful reading of the Biblical text strongly favored the formation of Adam's body directly from dust.[28]

In the United States, *The Catholic World*, an influential Paulist monthly, found space for a variety of views on the question. In 1870, for example, it published an anonymous three-part essay in which the author (possibly James Keogh) "den[ied] the very existence of organic evolution," arguing instead for independent origins and the immutability of species.[29] The argument was from nature rather than from Scripture, though the author did occasionally make reference to religion, as when he wrote about the theory and its

---

23 Molloy, "Geology and Revelation," 4:181–82. Molloy quoted the passage from Lyell from *Principles*, 10th ed. (1867–68), 1:313. This was the first edition in which Lyell accepted Darwin's transformism.

24 See, for example, Lyell, *Principles*, 7th ed. (1847), 179.

25 The series of articles began with a pair of articles by Murphy—"Darwinism," a rather intemperate objection to Darwinism asserting the fixity of species and (with slightly more argument) human exceptionalism, and "Evolution and Faith," arguing that the consensus of theologians was against the idea that the human body was the product of evolution. This being Victorian England, the editors of the *Record* made room for four more articles.

26 Vaughan, "What Nature Says of its Creator."

27 Knabenbauer, "Glaube und Descendenztheorie," 72 and 75.

28 Knabenbauer, "Glaube und Descendenztheorie," 123–26.

29 Keogh (?), "Immutability of the Species."

proponents that "its congruity with their atheistic views can alone furnish an adequate explanation of the haste with which they declared themselves its advocates."[30]

In 1884–87, the same monthly published two series (a combined total of slightly over 100 pages) under the head "Scriptural Questions," by Augustine Francis Hewit (1820–1897). Hewit, second superior general of the Institute of St. Paul the Apostle, was for many years the managing editor of *The Catholic World*. He began with a thoughtful prologue in which he reviewed a Catholic ethics of belief and then stated that his intention was merely to distinguish those current scientific ideas that are compatible with Catholic doctrine from those that are not. His topics included the nebular hypothesis (of the formation of the solar system) and the Noachian deluge, as well as biological evolution (including its application to man) and the antiquity of the human race. His general verdict on evolution was this:

> When this theory is pushed to an extreme it is heretical and irreconcilable with some of the fundamental truths of both revealed and natural religion. The extreme is found in the assertion that the complete specific nature of man has been evolved through a series of changes from primordial matter. Those who leave intact the spiritual nature of the human soul, and the doctrine of its immediate creation as a rational and immortal principle which is the form of the body, do not transgress against faith by their theories concerning irrational animals and other genera and species. In respect to these things it is to science and philosophy that they must render a reason for their assertions and conjectures. Prof. Mivart has written so much and so well upon this subject that it suffices to refer the curious reader to his book and articles for information.[31]

Although some of his views will, of course, now seem dated, other of his comments (such as his distinction between reasonable and sentimental orthodoxy—"doctrinal conformity to all authoritative teaching of the church" and "a subjection of the mind to human authorities in the church which exceeds what she prescribes, not founded in sound reasons, but springing from a sentiment of reverence for the great men and the prevalent opinions of antiquity which is exaggerated"[32]) seem as sensible and well-expressed today as they were when they were written.

✳ ✳ ✳ ✳ ✳

Writing of the situation in France, Harry Paul wrote that "Catholic journals opposed nearly all forms of evolution from the appearance of the *Origin* until well into the first decade of the twentieth century,"[33] but the term "opposition" must be qualified, as his book shows. He identified what he called "a pattern followed by most Catholic intellectuals

---

30 Keogh (?), "Immutability," 252. See also 265 and 338.

31 Hewit, "Scriptural Questions, First Series, no. I," 150.

32 Hewit, "Scriptural Questions, Second Series, no, II," 447.

33 Paul, *Edge of Contingency*, 40.

[of] reject[ing] Darwinism [on scientific grounds], although after the appearance of the *Descent* many also thought there was a clash with religious teachings on man."[34]

In 1869, for example, *Études* published an evaluation of the theory written by Jesuit mathematician and Scholastic theologian Ignace Carbonnelle, later one of the founders of the Société scientifique de Bruxelles and of the *Revue des questions scientifiques*. Carbonnelle acknowledged the explanatory reach of Darwin's new theory and its promise as a guide to further research.[35] He even acknowledged that there was a certain consonance between evolutionary biology and better-established scientific ideas:

> Those who have never studied geology find it quite natural to think that long ago the earth came forth from the hands of the Creator in the state in which we see it today, but if one notices the geological events which continually modify it under our very eyes, and if one compares their effects with the current arrangement of the materials that form the earth's crust, one will have to come up with other ideas. It is the same for all the sciences that have the phenomena of inorganic nature as their object. So, it is not surprising that, in a serious study of the facts of biology, one is easily convinced of the possibility, and even of the necessity, of a theory.[36]

Finally, he emphasized that "anyone who studies the idea [sc., biological evolution] itself will be convinced that it has hitherto not taken any anti-religious orientation and that it would probably never have anything to do with dogma."[37] Nevertheless, the theory faced serious difficulties. There were biological facts that it could not explain and there were still prominent scientists who rejected the theory. Carbonnelle was, in the end, an interested, but nevertheless a mere, compatibilist.

A second example can be found in Louvain's *Revue catholique*, which a few years later published "Les Derniers Écrits philosophiques de M. Tyndall," Jesuit Joseph Delsaulx's three-part critique of John Tyndall's 1874 Belfast Address to the British Association for the Advancement of Science. When Delsaulx got to the question of evolution, he wrote that "the doctrine, taken in its general meaning, has always had for me an irresistible attraction. . . . The theory, if it were true, would satisfy, much better than the more straightforward [*facile*] doctrine of successive creations, my idea of the wisdom and the omnipotence of God." "Do we not already," he went on to ask, "have an evolution of worlds in astronomy?" But the truth of the matter, he thought, had to be decided on the basis of geological considerations, and the data there told against the theory.[38]

He returned to his acknowledged "partiality for the theory of evolution"[39] a few pages later, though insisting that the idea was still just a hypothesis.

---

34 Paul, *Edge of Contingency*, 41.

35 Carbonnelle, "Bulletin scientifique," 474–75. See also his *Confins de la science*.

36 Carbonnelle, "Bulletin scientifique," 474.

37 Carbonnelle, "Bulletin scientifique," 473.

38 Delsaulx, "Derniers Écrits," 338–39.

39 Delsaulx, "Derniers Écrits," 348.

As long as the hypothesis coordinates the facts and opens up new avenues for research, I am delighted to follow it. I applaud the efforts of those who support it and who endeavor to increase its probability; but as soon as, handled by clumsy hands, it claims to undermine [*ébranler*] acquired truths, . . . I stop at once.[40]

What truth might Tyndall's evolutionism undermine? "The derivation from matter, by way of evolution or successive transformations, of the powers of intellect and free-will that God has granted to man."[41]

2. ENCYCLOPEDIAS

Several Catholic encyclopedias were published in the first half of the nineteenth century. Although they took some notice of paleoetiological geology,[42] they took practically no notice of evolutionary biology. Materialist anthropology, the existence of human beings before Adam, and polygenesis received some attention,[43] but not in a way that made any connection with an evolutionary origin of species.

The first three post-*Origin* Catholic encyclopedias, in contrast to their pre-Darwinian predecessors, did notice evolutionary biology and all three gave evolutionary ideas a decidedly negative review.

The first of those encyclopedias, product of the Czerwiński publishing house in Warsaw, brought out the first volume of *Encyklopedja Kościelna* in 1873, under the editorship of Michał Nowodworski (later bishop of Płock). The work identified itself on its title pages as "along the lines of [*podług*] Wetzer and Welte's theological encyclopedia with many supplementary articles." The last volume of the encyclopedia appeared only in 1933, but the articles relevant to our story were published much earlier. Nowodworski wrote the article on man in 1874. There he noted that

> Some (such as Mivart in England and A. Tyszyński here in Poland) taking the Darwinian transformationist hypothesis more seriously than it deserves, suggest that one can, without prejudice to the concept of creation, agree to the conjecture that the body of man evolved from lower animal forms, as long as one acknowledges that the body that so arose was meticulously given a soul created by God.

but went on to reject the idea:

> Leaving aside the violence it does to the clear text of Holy Scripture, which speaks of the creation of the human body from *mud* or *earth*, not from *an animal*, there

40 Delsaulx, "Derniers Écrits," 349.

41 Delsaulx, "Derniers Écrits," 350.

42 See, for example, F. Ch. S., "Geologie," in the *Allgemeine Realencyclopädie oder Conversationslexicon für das katholische Deutschland*. The encyclopedia described itself as "prepared by an association of Catholic scholars."

43 For example, Johannes von Kuhn, "Adam," 93 in Wetzer and Welte's *Kirchenlexikon* (1849).

weigh against it: (1) the fixity of animal species, which scientific naturalists have triumphantly demonstrated against the Darwinists, and, what is more important, (2) the unyielding psychological truth that the soul is the essential form of the body.[44]

In his article on the Pentateuch, Aleksander Zaremba, then professor of Scripture at the Płock seminary and later himself editor of the encyclopedia, said that Scripture does not give the age of the universe or of man, but he defended "the fixity of species against the lying utterances of the evolutionists and transformists."[45]

The second edition of Herder's *Conversations-Lexikon* (1877) included a two-column biographical article on Darwin. The author[46] also took a decidedly incompatibilist line about evolutionary biology and Catholic theology: "That Darwin's theory is in direct contradiction with the teachings of Revelation about the creation of the world and all organic beings, especially man . . . is undeniable."[47]

A third post-*Origin* encyclopedia article appeared in 1878–79, when Gaetano Moroni published an annotated index to his *Dizionario di erudizione storico-ecclesiastica* on which he had been working since 1846. Indicative of his views was his one-column entry on Darwin, "oracle of the fanciful system of the *transformation or evolution and derivation* of one species of animal from another." "A profession of *Darwinism* and of *Materialism*," he added, "is one and the same thing."[48]

3. TEXTBOOKS

What would Catholic students (or seminarians as they prepared for the priesthood) have read about the new evolutionary ideas? Catholic textbooks differed on whether some kind of evolutionary process played a rôle in the formation of the world, in the origin of biological species, or in the formation of the human body.

Textbooks had addressed the new developments in the paleoetiological sciences even in the first half of the century. Giovanni Perrone, for example, had addressed them in his *Praelectiones theologicae* (1839). Two questions he left open. The first was the question of whether the days of the Hexaemeron were "natural days" or "indeterminate and indefinite periods of many days or years." The Church has not proscribed that latter view and it would not be rash to defend it. Second, he felt no obligation to make a judgment about "the origin of the world and its formation through the slow and progressive action of the secondary causes which govern the world once it had been constituted."[49] On the

---

44 Nowodworski, "Człowiek," 671.

45 Zaremba, "Pentateuch," 81.

46 All articles in the *Conversations-Lexikon* are unsigned.

47 *Conversations-Lexikon*, "Darwin, Charles," 82.

48 Moroni, *Indice*, 2:437. The italics are Moroni's.

49 Perrone, *Praelectiones*, 3:82–84 (¶¶180–82).

origin of man, by contrast, he was more definite: "Two errors above all are opposed to the Mosaic story of creation [of man]: One of them denies that man was immediately created by God, but says that he was a product of the fecundity of the earth itself.... The other error says that there were men created before Adam (Pre-Adamites)."[50] Perrone attributed the first error to the French naturalist the Comte de Buffon and English Catholic priest John Turberville Needham, according to whom living things came "from organizing particles or essences or from a vegetative force with which God had endowed nature." The doctrine of the direct creation of our first parents applies, Perrone went on to say, not only to their souls but to their bodies. With what degree of certainty? This matter pertains to faith (*ad fidem spectat*).[51] In this judgment, Perrone was followed by many prominent theologians in the second half of the century.

Matthias Scheeben, the Cologne dogmatic theologian whom P. De Letter and W. J. Hill called "the greatest theologian of the [nineteenth] century"[52] and whose influence, and popularity among lay Catholic readers, extended far into the twentieth century, took a different view in his *Handbuch der katholischen Dogmatik* (1873–1903). Scheeben did not, of course, take a literalistic approach to Genesis,[53] but he did propose a generally anti-evolutionist philosophy of nature:

> The species [of material things] . . . originate, on the whole, directly from God [and] not . . . by way of mere natural evolution. . . . Organic beings in particular, which are currently propagated by generation [*Zeugung*], do not have their origin in abiogensis [*Urzeugung*] or in the mere operation of inorganic forces and they did not originate with certain general basic forms. Their origin lies in a divine creative act [*schöpferische Setzung . . . in's Dasein*] as the copy of determinate divine ideas *in all their various species*. This truth is . . . explicitly stated in the creation narrative of Genesis.[54]

What about the origin of the human body? Scheeben took the strongest line here: "It would even be *heretical* if one hypothesized only a bodily 'descent of man from the apes' on the way to a gradual transmutation of forms, even if one added divine creation of the soul on completion of the transmutation." He went on to add that "leaving revelation aside, it is philosophically absurd even to think that it would be *possible* for the fixed laws of nature to bring about the kind of transformation necessary to the production of man

---

50 Perrone, *Praelectiones*, 3:112–13 (¶228).

51 Perrone, *Praelectiones*, 3:113–14 (¶229), citing Lateran IV.

52 De Letter and Hill, "Theology, History of," 912.

53 "One can ask whether, and to what extent, the [Scriptural] depiction is merely a poetic-rhetorical *formulation* of dogmatic truths. . . , or whether it is a *more precise determination and an extension* of the idea. . . . The Church has not decided this question" (emphasis Scheeben's) (Scheeben, *Handbuch*, 2:97. (cf. trans., 1:384)).

54 Scheeben, *Handbuch*, 2:94–95 (cf. trans., 1:383).

or that it would be compatible with Divine Wisdom to allow the organism destined to be the temple of His image to evolve from a lower and different organism."[55]

Similarly, Jesuit theologian Camillo Mazzella, a prominent contributor to the Scholastic revival, later cardinal and prefect of the Congregation of the Index, addressed the question in his *De Deo creante praelectiones scholastico-dogmaticae* (1880), where he cited, in defense of his claim that this was a matter of Catholic doctrine, both Perrone and Suárez. His conclusion was that "even if it were not a doctrine *de fide definita* with which we are concerned (which we by no means concede), it by no means follows that it can licitly be denied."[56] For this he offered both theological and non-theological arguments.

Other authors were less definitive. Dominico Palmieri, SJ, professor of theology at the Collegium Romanum, said in his *Tractatus de Deo creante et elevante* (1878): "We cannot say that the falsity of that opinion [sc., the formation of the human body by the transformation of earlier species] is clear from the narrative of Moses alone. It cannot, however, be denied that that is the obvious sense and, absent some sound reason to the contrary, should be held."[57] That left open, of course, the *possibility* that the paleoetiological sciences might in the end be able to offer some "sound reason to the contrary."

Other books also showed some openness to the new ideas. When Ignaz Schuster died, in 1869, his *Handbuch zur Biblischen Geschichte* (1861), "for teaching in church and school and for self-education," was left an orphan. The task of preparing the next edition of the book was given to Johann Baptist Holzammer, then professor at the episcopal seminary in Mainz. In the "Apologetic Discussion of Biblical Creation-History" which he added as a preface, Holzammer was (at least for the origin of plants and animals) decidedly compatibilist:

> The recent . . . doctrine of a gradual evolution of all living species of plants and animals
> from a few original, extremely simple forms, perhaps even from a proto-form or
> proto-cell (the hypothesis of evolution, or Darwinism) . . . touches Holy Scripture
> hardly at all [*so gut wie gar nicht*]. According to Scripture, every existing species of
> plant and animal can be traced back to God's creative will as its ultimate cause—
> whether that first creation is a matter of God's having put the conditions for their
> origin and existence into nature or of God's bringing it into existence ready-made;
> whether today's species are identical to the original species or whether they evolved
> from the original ones according to laws established by the Lord of Nature.[58]

He added in a footnote that those laws might even have been Darwin's natural selection and struggle for existence, though he also said that scientific considerations made that unlikely. Darwinism, he thought, appealed mostly to people who wanted to use it to

---

55 Scheeben, *Handbuch*, 2:144 (cf. trans., 1:397).

56 Mazzella, *De Deo creante*, 353.

57 Palmieri, *Tractatus de Deo creante et elevante*, 220.

58 Holzammer, *Handbuch*, xxi.

assert the descent of man from animals and to deny the spirituality and immortality of the human soul.

Jesuit philosopher Thomas Harper laid some foundations for the paleoetiological sciences in his *Metaphysics of the School* (1879–1884), particularly in his appendix on "the teaching of St. Thomas touching the genesis of the material world,"[59] which took a generally evolutionary approach to the question. The Thomistic idea of a "progressive development of being" in the embryo, Harper said, "serves to throw light on the perfection of cosmic order": "The truth of the teaching for which we are contending once admitted, [we must] acknowledge a gradual evolution of the whole complex and multiform universe of material substances from a few simple elements created in the beginning."[60] The history of the world began with a primordial act of creation, but that act produced only the *elements* of the material world. The next step was an evolution of those elements "effected by the Creator according to the laws imposed by Himself on nature and through the operation of natural causes."[61] This evolution Harper extended beyond the inorganic world, suggesting an evolutionary origin of life—"there is no apparent reason why it should not have been the result of gradual evolution subject to the ordinary supervision of the Divine Providence"[62]—and an evolutionary origin of species—"Should this inference be legitimate, the appearance of the first pair in any given species can be easily explained without our being obliged to have recourse to any *extraordinary* intervention."[63] In sum, "the Divine Wisdom and Omnipotence superintended the natural evolution of visible things. . . . Compound inanimate substances were first evolved by means of the seminal forces bestowed on nature. Then . . . sprang into being the green life of herb, plant, and tree, gradually unfolding into higher and more complex Forms."[64] But there is a limit to the reach of this process: "Evidently, there must have been a beginning to each higher family of living things. There must have been a first plant, a first fish, a first bird, a first quadruped. . . . God must have been the sole Efficient Cause of the organization requisite and, therefore, in the strictest sense is said to have *formed* such pairs."[65] "A worm cannot generate a fish, or a fish a quadruped."[66] This qualification is particularly true of the human being.[67]

Still, "there is nothing in the *principle* of natural evolution," he concludes, "which is not in strict accordance with the teaching of St. Thomas and of the Fathers of the Church."[68]

59 Harper, *Metaphysics*, 2:730–48.

60 Harper, *Metaphysics*, 2:560.

61 Harper, *Metaphysics*, 2:731.

62 Harper, *Metaphysics*, 2:739. See also 747.

63 Harper, *Metaphysics*, 2:739.

64 Harper, *Metaphysics*, 2:742.

65 Harper, *Metaphysics*, 2:743.

66 Harper, *Metaphysics*, 2:748.

67 Harper, *Metaphysics*, 2:739, 743, and 746.

68 Harper, *Metaphysics*, 2:746.

* * * * *

The orthodoxy of the new ideas, even in Mivart's Catholic version, at best gained a mixed acceptance in the textbooks and encyclopedias, though the views expressed already by Palmieri and Harper became more common as the century came to a close.

* * * * *

PART II

THE ORIGIN OF THE HUMAN BODY I:
EVOLUTION DEFENDED & RESISTED
(1885–1900)

CHAPTER 5

SCIENTISTS & THEOLOGIANS
(1885–1900)

The last years of the nineteenth century saw the emergence of a second version of Catholic evolutionism, as well as the appearance of two books defending Mivartism.

1. ZEFERINO CARDINAL GONZÁLEZ Y DÍAZ TUÑÓN, OP
(1821–94)

Historian Thomas Glick has suggested sorting Spanish Catholic responses to the theory of evolution into three groups. First, there were Catholics who were content to offer a Biblical critique. Second, there were others who tried to develop a scientific refutation of the thesis. And, finally there were Catholics who were at least compatibilist and in some cases were themselves trying to articulate a version of Catholic evolutionism.[1]

An example of that third group was Zeferino González. Born in the Asturian village of Villoria in 1821 into a family of farmworkers that gave a total of three priests to the Church, he entered the Order of Preachers in 1844 and was sent to Manila, where he spent twenty years (1846–66) studying, and then teaching, at the Universidad de Santo

---

1 Glick, "Spain," 334.

Tomás in Manila. After his return to Spain, he was appointed bishop of Córdoba (1875), then archbishop of Seville (1883), cardinal (1884), and finally archbishop of Toledo, the primatial see of Spain (1886). At the end of 1889, he resigned his pastoral responsibilities and devoted the last five years of his life to scholarship.

González had taken an interest in science as early as 1857, when he published articles on earthquakes and on atmospheric electricity.[2] Nevertheless, most of his academic work was in philosophy.[3] He contributed to the Thomistic renewal of his day, beginning with a three-volume *Estudios sobre la Filosofía de Santo Tomás* (1864). In 1868, he published, in Latin, the first edition of his *Philosophia elementaria*, a work that subsequently appeared, over the course of the next three decades, in six more Latin editions and, in a modified form, in six Spanish editions. The first edition did not devote any special attention to Darwin, but by 1873, when he prepared the first (revised) Spanish version of the book, Darwin's books (although as yet available only in French translation) had been a subject of discussion, and controversy, in Spain for five years. So González appended to his discussion of living things a discussion of Darwinism.[4]

✻ ✻ ✻ ✻ ✻

The *Filosofía* begins its treatment of the topic with a brief summary of Darwin's ideas—the gradualism and the common ancestry thesis, the struggle for existence and natural selection, and the animal ancestry of the human race—followed by some scientific objections to the general theory—for example, emphasizing the hypothetical status of the first living things and the lack of direct evidence for transitional forms. He turned next to the questions of the origin of man, to which he also raised scientific and philosophical objections. He repeated Alfred Russel Wallace's doubts that natural selection could be responsible for the loss of body hair in the transition from ape to man[5] and raised other objections at the level of anatomy before turning to the standard Thomistic emphasis on the distinctiveness of the human intellect—the capacity to apprehend universals, the idea of God (and religious sentiment), freedom, and the moral law.

In the first editions of the *Filosofía* (so, from 1873) he concluded his remarks on Darwinism by emphasizing the tension between Darwinism and Catholic doctrine:

> After what we have said, we think it is unnecessary to show that Darwinism contains doctrines and tendencies that are essentially anti-Christian. Leaving other points aside, Darwin's theory on the origin of man is incompatible with the Catholic dogma which teaches us that our first parents, Adam and Eve, were produced immediately by God. Those who claim to reconcile Darwinism with Christianity give reason to suspect that they do not have a thorough knowledge of either one or the other.[6]

---

2 González, "Temblores de tierra" and "Electricidad atmosférica," first published in Manila in 1857.

3 See Gustavo Bueno Sánchez, *Obra filosófica de Fray Zeferino González.*

4 González, *Filosofía elemental,* 1st ed., 2:283–98.

5 Wallace, *Theory of Natural Selection,* 344–49.

6 González, *Filosofía,* 1st ed., 2:298.

That, he pointed out, was just what Clémence Royer had written in the preface to her French translation of the *Origin*. In the third edition (1881), however, in the paragraph immediately following the one just quoted, he adds an important qualification:

> Please note, however, that the dogmatic incompatibility of Darwinism with revelation refers only to Darwinism as explicated and developed in the materialistic and atheistic sense of Vogt, Huxley, Büchner, Haeckel, etc., and principally in its applications to the origin of man.
>
> But prescinding from those essentially atheistic-materialistic developments and applications, if we limit ourselves to the evolution or transformation of plant and animal species, which constitutes the fundamental hypothesis and real characteristic of *Darwin's Darwinism*, if it is permissible to put it that way; if the application to man, an application which science in no way justifies, is excluded from Darwinism, and if we make some reservations about the creation of the world and of the rational soul, it can be fit within Catholic dogma. . . . Here, as in so many other questions, reason and faith both advise us to avoid extremes and exaggerations. We must not let ourselves be seduced by garrulous verbiage of human science, or of what is presented as such, but neither may we deny it its legitimate rights, nor limit its horizons on the pretext of Biblical interpretations or religious ideas which are far from being dogmas. Already in the fifth century, St. Augustine said, "Neither should we be seduced by the loquacity of false philosophy nor should we be frightened by the superstition of false religion." And St. Thomas added in the thirteenth that "since Holy Scripture can be explained in a multiplicity of senses, one should not hold definitively to any particular explanation."[7]

He was, that is to say, if not an evolutionist, at least an explicit compatibilist. His summary and critique of Darwinism in the *Historia* follow the same lines.

He also wrote a multi-volume *Historia de la filosofía* (1878–79, with a second edition published in 1886) in which he devoted two chapters to Darwinism itself, one to the Darwinist movement (Henry Thomas Buckle, Draper, Walter Bagehot, etc.), and one to Haeckel.[8]

✳ ✳ ✳ ✳ ✳

Only in the last years of his life, after his retirement from pastoral work, did he write his two-volume work *La Biblia y la ciencia*.[9] That work begins with chapters on the Bible, on the nature of science, and on the general relations between the Bible and science, and then proceeds to address questions raised by particular sciences (astronomy, physics, geology, and biology) and by particular passages of Scripture or by theological doctrines (the unity and antiquity of the human race and the Flood of Noah). Chapter

---

7 González, *Filosofía*, 3rd ed., 2:305–7. The embedded quotations are from St. Augustine, *De genesi ad litteram*, 1.21.41, and from St. Thomas, *Summa theologiae*, 1a, 68.1.

8 González, *Historia de la filosofía*, 1st ed., 3:403–21; 2nd ed., 4:271–96.

9 I will here cite the second edition. For a summary, see Alberto Colunga Cueto, "Autor de *La Biblia y la ciencia*."

83

11, devoted to "The Biblical Hexaemeron and Biology—Darwinism," consisted of the following articles:

1. The Origin and Nature of Darwinism

2. Darwinism and the Bible

3. Anthropological Darwinism

4. Anthropological Darwinism and the Bible

5. Anthropological Darwinism and the Origin of the Human Soul

6. Retrospective Overview and General Critique of Darwinism

González there articulated (though without explicitly endorsing) a second version of Catholic anthropological evolutionism. He argued that Mivartism, though it could not be said to be contrary to Catholic doctrine, nevertheless had grave drawbacks—philosophical, scientific, and exegetical. He proposed, as an alternative, consideration of what might be called a mixed view:

> These drawbacks disappear, or are at least attenuated, when Mivart's hypothesis is juxtaposed with a possibility, noted by St. Thomas, regarding the possibility that causes or agents other than God intervened in the formation of Adam's body, that is to say, in its preliminary preparation up to an imperfect stage of development, reserving the final stages of its preparation to receive a rational soul to divine action. In this way, the essence of Mivart's hypothesis is preserved, with due regard to the direct and immediate action of God in the formation of the body of the first man, action which traditional Biblical exegesis seems to require.[10]

* * * * *

González also, we should conclude by noting, made a contribution to the development of Catholic hermeneutics. Although a more authoritative response to the challenges of nineteenth-century science and history came shortly thereafter, in Pope Leo XIII's seminal encyclical *Providentissimus Deus* (1893), the issue was also addressed in *La Biblia y la ciencia*. González put the fundamental question of his book as follows:

> What is the route, what is the procedure, which the exegete and Christian theologian must adopt today, in the presence of a scientific movement which expands into every sphere of intellectual life, . . . and against whose background prevail ideas and tendencies opposed to the Bible and to Catholic doctrine? Do those latter have to enclose themselves within the limits of divine revelation, or at least within those of ancient exegesis, content to deny and reject *a priori* the discoveries . . . of modern science just because they appear to be out of harmony with the Bible?[11]

In his answer, he attempted to balance the conservatism that is a constitutive feature of Catholic theology with an openness to the new ideas under development in history and

10 González, *Biblia*, 1:514–15.

11 González, *Biblia*, 1:xix.

in the paleoetiological sciences. Nineteenth-century exegetes had an obligation to know the results of nineteenth-century science or they would not be in a position to accomplish their assigned work, which he characterized as:

> Neither abandoning nor rejecting the wise exegetical maxims taught and practiced by the early Fathers of the Church and by the Doctors of the Schools—neither abandoning nor rejecting, but rather following the principles which those masters formulated—it is necessary to modify the applications of those principles and maxims, putting them in harmonious relation with the new elements of Biblical exegesis later supplied by the sciences, above all in our own day.[12]

That remark he followed with this striking metaphor:

> In intellectual, no less than in material, warfare, one's strategy has to change with the change in weaponry. To insist today on fighting and winning while relying on solutions established by ancient exegesis (on interpretations of certain Biblical texts touching on nature made when no one even suspected the existence and progress of many physical sciences of now-recognized importance) would be the same as insisting on using only the arquebus with which the soldiers of Carvajal won the day at Huarina when our enemy's weapons have the precision of modern rifles.[13]

He also emphasized the importance of distinguishing between established doctrine and "Christian exegesis," of which he said that, "considered in itself, is not necessarily the truth, but is an investigation of the truth."[14]

✳ ✳ ✳ ✳ ✳

González's monumental effort made a great impression on the most outstanding Scripture scholar of the day, Marie-Joseph Lagrange, OP, who concluded the preface to the first issue of his new *Revue biblique* with a four-page extract from González's prologue to *La Biblia y la ciencia*.

Reactions to that extract were, to be sure, not uniformly positive. Lagrange later reported having received a letter from a fellow Dominican, dated October 11, 1891: "Your article, although already printed, did not have the approval of the Master of the Sacred Palace, who does not want any responsibility for the ideas of Cardinal González."[15] Nevertheless, there is a noticeable similarity between the themes of *La Biblia y la ciencia* and those emphasized just a few short years later by Pope Leo XIII in *Providentissimus Deus*.[16]

González had not followed Mivart in the latter's thesis that the human body (though not the human person) was formed by evolutionary processes. Mivart's thesis was, however, endorsed by other Catholics in the final years of the nineteenth century.

---

12 González, *Biblia*, 1:xxxii.

13 González, *Biblia*, 1:xxxii–xxxiii.

14 González, *Biblia*, 1:xxvii.

15 Lagrange, *Loisy*, 76n2.

16 See Victoriano Larrañaga, "González y León XIII."

Two in particular require our attention—the French Dominican Marie-Dalmace Leroy and the American Holy Cross priest John Augustine Zahm.

2. MARIE-DALMACE LEROY, OP (1828–1905)

Marie-Dalmace Leroy was born in Marseille in 1828. In 1851, he joined the French province of the Order of Preachers, which province was just then being reconstituted after having been suppressed at the time of the French Revolution. He had a long-standing interest in philosophy and natural history, but this interest he had to pursue alongside administrative and other responsibilities.

In 1887, Leroy published a book entitled *L'Évolution des espèces organiques* with the approval of his Dominican superiors, and with brief letters affirming its orthodoxy from both Albert Auguste de Lapparent (professor of geology at the Institut Catholique de Paris) and fellow-Dominican Jacques-Marie-Louis Monsabré (preacher at Notre Dame de Paris). The book would, he hoped, "make a contribution towards dissipating the prejudice, unfortunately too widespread, that the theory of evolution, whatever limitations one places on it, should be ruthlessly proscribed as contrary to revealed doctrine." He added that he "would also like to dissuade certain people from giving transformism a cursory treatment, going everywhere repeating that the theory is not based on any scientific fact, but only on the imaginary conjectures of pure fantasy."[17]

The book begins with a chapter addressing the theory of evolution from a religious point of view. There Leroy argued that the fixity of species is clearly not a tenet of Catholic doctrine. Even if fixity did seem to be taken for granted in traditional exegesis, he said (quoting Monsabré), "exegesis has the right to correct superannuated interpretations when experience shows us that they are insufficient or false."[18] The fixity or transformability of species is, he said, a point that is open to free scientific debate. That lays the foundation for the following seven chapters, which address the scientific and philosophical aspects of the question.

Leroy did not give the question of evolutionary anthropogenesis quite the prominence that one might expect, though he did address it:

> As for the simian descent of man, for which some would like to hold the transformist doctrine to account, one can see that it in no way follows. Even if there were not a radical difference between that body of man and that of higher apes,[19] there always remains, in the transcendence of the human soul, an insurmountable barrier separating the human from the animal kingdom. . . . All that one can infer is that the human body can, if absolutely necessary, be derived from animal origins, but

---

17 Leroy, *Évolution*, 198.

18 Leroy, *Évolution*, 19, quoting Jacques-Marie-Louis Monsabré. I have not been able to find a copy of the edition quoted, but the passage can be found in a later edition— Monsabré, *Exposition du dogme catholique*, 9th ed., 34.

19 Leroy had already referred to Wallace on the difference between the body of man and ape at *Évolution*, 32.

nothing proves that it was so derived and I understand perfectly well that some people continue to maintain that the immediate formation of our flesh by the hand of God conforms better to our dignity as well as to the sentiments of the Holy Doctors [of the Church].[20]

Still, he thought, an evolutionary connection between man ("the body of man, but not the total man"[21]) and animal had something (and something theological, not just something scientific) to be said for it. First, it is in better conformity with a traditional understanding of divine action: "God allows secondary causes to act to the extent of their power and following the laws which He created; He gives them all the time necessary to accomplish their task. The tendency to substitute for this slow action of elements the wave of a magic wand seems to me to proceed much more from our ignorance, than from a true understanding of the sacred text."[22] Second,

> Everything in this world tends toward man and man toward God. . . . What relation [on the hypothesis of the fixity of types] could the myriads of extinct species have with man? . . . The hypothesis of a special creation for the modern organic world divides the history of the globe into two parts absolutely irrelevant to one another, leaving the first, the more important both with respect to the number of species and to temporal extent, in an isolation as abnormal as it is inexplicable.
>
> With the theory of evolution, things look quite different, and those innumerable legions of inexplicable beings find their *raison d'être* in the present world of living things, to which they are connected by ties that are as real as they are evident.[23]

This book generated some controversy and was subject to polite, but critical, comment.[24] Reviews of the first edition ("some well-founded, others exaggerated," he said) led him to undertake a second edition, published (with a fresh *imprimatur* from his prior) in 1891. The new edition was longer than the original by half and had a revised title, *L'Évolution restreinte aux espèces organiques*. The "limitation" on evolution made explicit in the revised title is not so much a limitation to *biological* evolution (in contrast to the "universal evolution" being defended by Spencer and others)—that was already made explicit in the last words of the original title. Rather it is a limitation to "species inferior to man,"[25] a point that he developed more explicitly in the final chapter. Many Catholics called this "mitigated evolution," a term that Leroy also sometimes used.[26]

The book was also completely reorganized, as can be seen by a comparison of the tables of contents. In the new edition, he undertook to reduce the controversy to four

---

20 Leroy, *Évolution*, 193–94. The second half of that passage was quoted again in *Évolution restreinte*, 48.

21 Leroy, *Évolution*, 33.

22 Leroy, *Évolution*, 26.

23 Leroy, *Évolution*, 28–9. This point is also presented nicely in *Évolution restreinte*, 65–68.

24 For an example, see Joseph Brucker, SJ, "L'Origine de l'homme," 43.

25 Leroy, *Évolution restreinte*, 10.

26 Leroy, *Évolution restreinte*, 30, 160, 274, 276, and 279.

main topics—universal evolutionism and atheism, evolution limited to organic species, various ways of conceiving transformism, and evolution extended to man.[27]

The most important way in which the second volume differs from the first is in the addition of an entire chapter on "Evolution and the Body of Man." He devoted the first half of that chapter to a defense of the thesis that man's possession of a spiritual soul constitutes a difference in kind between man and animal. Then he asked: "But can one not make a concession to physiology? Can one not divide man in two, attributing the higher part to the immediate action of God and deriving the lower part from the realm of animals? In other words, can the human body not be considered to be a product of evolution?"[28] His answer is negative—"the body of man is the product of a direct intervention by God." This is the teaching of Holy Scripture, of the Fathers, of the Church, and of theology.[29]

There is, however, a further point to be examined:

> The human body is composed of matter and form. And the soul, its substantial form, comes directly from God, of course. But the matter, where does it come from? It comes from the slime of the earth, that is also certain, as the Church and tradition clearly teach. But was the human soul infused immediately into this slime, that is to say, without any preparation? And if it underwent preparation, as Genesis indicates, could it not have been evolution which effected it? That is the question that may still be asked.[30]

There are, he went on to say, two alternative answers to that question. In addition to the idea that God fashioned Adam's body directly from mud (or at least without any intermediate animal form), there is a view that Leroy characterized as follows: "the *substratum* destined to receive the precious treasure of an immortal soul, though it was truly the work of God, was so through the mediation of secondary causes, that is to say by means of evolution."[31] He was not ready to endorse that view. He had said already that it was far from being proven.[32] Here, he added: "I do not absolutely champion that hypothesis, but, as long as it exists, I think that it is good to examine it, in order to know the extent to which one may tolerate or proscribe it."[33] While acknowledging that the question had not been definitively resolved, he concluded the chapter by emphasizing the explanatory power (especially with respect to rudimentary organs) of giving some rôle to evolutionary processes in the formation of a body into which the first human soul would be infused.

27 Leroy, *Évolution restreinte*, 3 and 274.

28 Leroy, *Évolution restreinte*, 256.

29 Leroy, *Évolution restreinte*, 257.

30 Leroy, *Évolution restreinte*, 266–67.

31 Leroy, *Évolution restreinte*, 267.

32 Leroy, *Évolution restreinte*, 240.

33 Leroy, *Évolution restreinte*, 267.

Predictably, publication of this edition led to another exchange of views with his critics. That criticism came particularly from the Jesuits, in their *Études religieuses, historiques et littéraires*. In addition to a mention by Eugène Portalié, there was a full review by Joseph Brucker. Leroy responded to both. The book was also noticed by another Jesuit, François Dierckx, who published a pamphlet critical of Leroy in which, among other things, he raised the question of the origin of the body of Eve.

In 1894, the book was delated to the Congregation of the Index, though not by its Jesuit critics. The resolution of the case will be discussed below.

3. JOHN AUGUSTINE ZAHM, CSC (1851–1921)[34]

John Zahm was born in New Lexington, Ohio, on June 14, 1851, the second of fourteen children of an Alsatian immigrant carpenter and farmer and his wife. In 1867, at the age of fifteen, he left home for the University of Notre Dame, an institution with which he remained associated for most of the rest of his life. Zahm entered the Congregation of Holy Cross in 1871, took a master's degree in 1873, and stayed on at Notre Dame to teach chemistry and physics. His teaching and his administrative responsibilities (e.g., building up the university's science collection and then rebuilding it when that first collection was destroyed by a major fire in 1879) limited the time that he could devote to writing or research. He published only one strictly scientific book, *Sound and Music* (1892), a revised version of a course of lectures he had delivered at the Catholic University of America. The purpose of that book, he wrote, was "to give musicians and general readers an exact knowledge ... of the principles of acoustics, and ... a brief exposition of the physical basis of musical harmony."[35] Although Zahm is often described as a scientist, it would be more accurate to describe him as a science educator. His contributions—to his university, to his religious order, and to Catholic thought—are impressive, but they lay elsewhere than in science itself. By the early 1880s, he began to develop a particular interest in the relationship between science and religion, and it is for his writings in this field—not so much for the originality of his ideas but for his skill at presenting them to a general audience—that he is best known.

Zahm first addressed the question of evolution and theology in a lecture delivered in Denver on March 26, 1883.[36] The general thesis of the lecture was that the conflicts that were alleged to exist between science and religion were always the result of one or another mode of epistemological inflation: either mistaking speculative scientific ideas for demonstrated truths or religious opinions for dogmatically defined doctrines of the

---

34 The major biographies are Patrick J. Carroll, "Mind in Action"; Ralph E. Weber, *Notre Dame's John Zahm*; David B. Burrell, *When Faith and Reason Meet*; and John P. Slattery, *Faith and Science at Notre Dame*. One should, however, also see the chapters on Zahm in Artigas, *Negotiating Darwin*, 124–202, and John L. Morrison, *History*, 190–267.

35 Zahm, *Sound and Music*, 7.

36 Zahm, *Catholic Church and Modern Science*, republished as "Science and the Church" in Zahm's *Catholic Science and Catholic Scientists*, 9–54.

Church. On the topic of evolution, Zahm believed, both mistakes were made. While he did not, in that lecture, commit himself to the truth of evolutionary biology (or to any of the other components of a comprehensively evolutionary account of the world—the nebular hypothesis, historical geology, or spontaneous generation as the origin of life on earth) he argued that there is no conflict between *a theistic version* of that evolutionary story and Catholic doctrine as long as, in the case of the origin of man, evolution is limited to the formation of the human body, with the human soul being directly created by God. On the question of the origin of the human body, he mentions Mivart's account, about which he says: "The hypothesis may be rash, and even dangerous, but I do not think that, considering it simply in its bearing on dogma, any one could pronounce it certainly and positively false."[37] The lecture reached a larger audience than one might at first imagine. It was cited, for example, by Manuel Vélez (discussed in chapter 2), then working in El Salvador. Over the course of the decade or so that followed his Denver lecture, Zahm continued to address these issues, eventually coming to a more positive assessment of the theory of biological evolution, and of Mivartism in particular, than he had presented in that initial lecture.

In 1893, he delivered a series of lectures—on the Hexaemeron and evolution, on the Noachian Deluge, and on the age of the human race—for the Catholic Summer School (a Catholic version of the Chautauqua Institution) held at Plattsburgh (New York). These lectures were later published, first in the *American Ecclesiastical Review* and in the *American Catholic Quarterly Review* and then as a book with the title *Bible, Science, and Faith* (1894). Here Zahm subsumed an evolutionary history of nature under what he presented as an Augustinian theology of nature, namely one that gives prominence to secondary causes (laws of nature) in the formational economy of the world.[38] The origin of the human race, beyond the questions of its age and its unity, he mentioned only in passing, rejecting the animalist genealogy proposed by Ernst Haeckel and others as incapable of bridging the gap between non-rational and rational species.[39] *Bible, Science, and Faith* was generally well-received by Catholics,[40] both in the United States and abroad, where translations were made into French and Italian.

It was at about this time that Zahm requested, and eventually received from Pope Leo XIII, a doctorate in philosophy. That story begins in 1893, when Zahm wrote to Mieczysław Cardinal Ledóchowski, prefect of the Congregation for Propagation of the Faith (which then had responsibility for the Church's affairs in the United States) requesting (or, as Zahm put it, "applying for") a Doctorate of Science.[41] Ledóchowski replied on May 31

---

37 Zahm, *Catholic Science*, 29.

38 Zahm, *Bible, Science and Faith*, 78–84.

39 Zahm, *Bible, Science and Faith*, 222–28.

40 "A veritable god-send . . . , just what intelligent and inquiring Catholics need," said one reviewer (*Catholic World*, 136); "by far the most valuable contribution made by American talent and industry to the cause of Christian apologetics," said another (*American Catholic Quarterly Review*, 893).

41 Zahm to Ledóchowski, June 20, 1893 (fol. 422, Fondo N.S. 33, ASPF).

that his Congregation did not have the power to confer such a doctorate.[42] Zahm then apparently requested a doctorate in theology, for the archives of Propaganda include a letter from Fr. Gilbert Français, superior general of the Congregation of Holy Cross, to Ledóchowski, dated September 3, asking whether any progress has been made in obtaining the degree.[43] Ledóchowski asked Archbishop Francesco Satolli, apostolic delegate to the United States, to look into the matter and to submit his opinion on whether the degree should be awarded.[44] Satolli wrote in reply:

> One finds in Zahm's works, more the philosophical tendencies of the author than a mind formed in profound theological study.... It seems to me that he is too eager to embrace opinions that are somewhat bold.... He defends a partial flood as well as the formation of the various species, except man, by the natural development of seminal forms or powers impressed on matter by God in the act of creation.
>
> For these reasons I do not hide from Your Eminence the fear that conferring the title of Doctor of Theology could be interpreted as at least an indirect approval of exaggerated opinions. So, all things considered, I would be of the opinion that it would be better to confer on Rev. Zahm the degree of Doctor of Philosophy.[45]

Ledóchowski (and Pope Leo) followed the course recommended by Satolli and, on the last day of February, Zahm was awarded his degree at a ceremony at Notre Dame.[46]

At about the same time that he received his doctorate, Zahm began preparing a new series of lectures focused precisely on the origins of man. These lectures he delivered in the summer of 1895 at the Catholic Summer Schools in Madison (Wisconsin) and in Plattsburgh, and then, in January 1896, at the Winter School in New Orleans. The next month, they appeared in book form as the second part of *Evolution and Dogma*.[47] It is this book for which Zahm is best known.

Relying, as had Mivart before him, on St. Augustine and St. Thomas Aquinas, he summarized his theology of nature as follows:

> Theistic Evolution, in the sense in which it is advocated by St. Augustine and St. Thomas, excludes also Divine interference, or constant unnecessary interventions on the part of the Deity, as effectually as it does a low and narrow Anthropomorphism. Both these illustrious Doctors declare explicitly, that "in the institution of nature we do not look for miracles, but for the laws of nature."

---

42 Ledóchowski to Fort Wayne Bishop Joseph Rademacher, May 31, 1894, (fol. 427, Fondo N.S. 33, ASPF) and annotation on the copy of the letter of endorsement sent by Bishop Joseph Rademacher (fol. 424).

43 Français to Ledóchowski, September 3, 1893 (fol. 195–96, rubric 9/1895, Fondo N.S. 55, ASPF).

44 Ledóchowski to Satolli, December 10, 1894 (Posizione 12, Archivio della Delegazione Apostolica negli Stati Uniti, IX, Diocese of Fort Wayne [Indiana], AAV).

45 Satolli to Ledóchowski, January 15, 1895 (fol. 198–99, rubric 9/1895, Fondo N.S. 55, ASPF).

46 Annotation to Satolli's letter (fol. 198–99, rubric 9/1895, Fondo N.S. 55, ASPF) and an untitled news item in Notre Dame's *Scholastic*.

47 The first part of the book consisted of a two-hundred-page scientific introduction to evolutionary biology.

Only the crudest conception of derivative creation would demand that the theist should necessarily, if consistent, have recourse to continued creative fiats to explain the multifold phenomena connected with inorganic or organic Evolution. For, as already explained, derivation or secondary creation is not, properly speaking, a supernatural act. It is merely the indirect action of Deity by and through natural causes. The action of God in the order of nature is concurrent and overruling, indeed, but is not miraculous in the sense in which the word "miraculous" is ordinarily understood. He operates by and through the laws which He instituted in the beginning, and which are still maintained by His Providence. Neither the doctrine of the Angel of the Schools nor that of the Bishop of Hippo, requires the perpetual manifestation of miraculous powers, interventions or catastrophes. They do not necessitate the interference with, or the dispensation from, the laws of nature, but admit and defend their existence and their continuous and regular and natural action. Only a misunderstanding of terms, only a gross misapprehension of the meaning of the word "creation," only, in fine, the "unconscious Anthropomorphisms" of the Agnostic and the Monist, would lead one to find anything irreconcilable between the legitimate inductions of science and the certain and explicit declarations of Dogma.[48]

And a few pages later:

[T]hey did all that was necessary fully to justify my present contention; they laid down principles which are perfectly compatible with theistic Evolution. They asserted, in the most positive and explicit manner, the doctrine of derivative creation as against the theory of a perpetual direct creation of organisms, and turned the weight of their great authority in favor of the doctrine, that God administers the material universe by natural laws, and not by constant miraculous interventions. As far as the present argument is concerned, this distinct enunciation of principles makes for my thesis quite as much as would the promulgation of a more detailed theory of Evolution.[49]

He endorsed Mivart's account of the natural, evolutionary origin of the first human body while, like Mivart, recognizing that a direct act of divine creation is necessary in the case of the human soul.[50]

Evolution and Dogma was quickly translated into Italian and French; nine years later, it was translated into Spanish.

---

48 Zahm, *Evolution and Dogma*, 304–5.

49 Zahm, *Evolution and Dogma*, 313.

50 Zahm, *Evolution and Dogma*, 352–54. Zahm's account of the hostile Catholic reaction to Mivart, presented on those pages, is, in my judgment, somewhat exaggerated. There is, for example, no evidence in the files of the Congregation of the Index that Mivart's book was ever delated to that office despite Zahm's claim that "strenuous efforts" had been made to have the book prohibited. I attribute this exaggeration to the fact that Zahm, while fully committed to doctrinal orthodoxy, seemed to delight in being somewhat of a sensation. See, for example, the letter he wrote to his brother Albert on July 28, 1893, just after the Plattsburgh Summer School: "Didn't I stir up the bears? All enthusiastic over them, but they considered me very daring & ultra liberal. Probably the smoke will have cleared away by the time I return" (Albert Francis Zahm Papers, CAZA 4/07, UNDA).

Reviews of the book were mixed.[51] Herman J. Heuser (professor at Philadelphia's St. Charles Borromeo Seminary) wrote in the *American Ecclesiastical Review*: "There is nothing in this work but what is true or what might be true and be held by a loyal believer in the Catholic doctrine of the Bible. But to say or imply that the theory of immediate creation is less reasonable … is merely a sensational exaggeration."[52] An anonymous reviewer in *Catholic World* gave a similar review, though acknowledging the theological controversy over whether the immediate formation of the human body was *de fide*. The French Catholic anthropologist and paleontologist Jean-François-Albert du Pouget, Marquis de Nadaillac, who reviewed the book in *Revue des questions scientifique*,[53] though not ready to accept an evolutionary account of the origin of species without a better account of the mechanisms underlying evolutionary change, nevertheless thought that *Evolution and Dogma* was a book of "great merit" and endorsed Zahm's compatibilism. On the question of the origin of man, he preferred Zahm's account to that of González—if evolutionary processes played a rôle in the origin of the human body at all, it would be more consistent to extend them to make them entirely responsible for doing so.[54]

Particularly noteworthy was the review by David Fleming, in the *Dublin Review*. Fleming was, from 1896, consultor to the Holy Office and later, in 1903–5, secretary to the Pontifical Biblical Commission.[55] Fleming was more positive about Zahm's scientific claims than de Nadaillac had been, writing, "It seems to us that … the theory of Evolution has passed from the state of being *merely possible* to the state of *probability*." On the theological question, he added that "it is quite evident to us that there is no incompatibility between Evolution and Theism, or between Evolution and Spiritualism [i.e., the spirituality of the soul and its special creation]" and, with respect to Scripture, "the great majority of Catholic theologians hold … that evolution in itself is not excluded by the text of Genesis."[56]

Two bishops also gave Zahm's work a generally sympathetic review, though in each case with qualifications.

Geremia Bonomelli (1831–1914), bishop of Cremona (Italy), was just finishing the first volume of his work of apologetics, *Seguiamo la ragione* (1898), when his friend Antonio Fogazzaro (discussed below) referred him to the Italian translation of *Evolution and Dogma*. It was, by then, too late for Bonomelli to rewrite the mildly rejectionist account of evolution that he had offered when he had written the final draft of his book,

---

51 For more detail on reviews, see Morrison, *History*, 212–19.

52 Heuser, Review, 570. Heuser was no liberal; eleven years later, during the struggle against modernism, he was appointed general censor for all Catholic periodicals in the United States.

53 Nadaillac, Review. This is a review of the English original of the book, not of the French translation, which appeared only the following year.

54 Nadaillac, Review, 234–35.

55 In 1905, Fleming was removed from the latter position, but not from his position as consultor, by Pope Pius X.

56 Fleming, "Evolution and Dogma," 250 (for the first two quotations) and 252 (for the last). For the meaning of the term "probable" in Scholastic philosophy, see John M. Harty, "Probabilism," 441: "an opinion is solidly probable which by reason of intrinsic or extrinsic arguments is able to gain the assent of many prudent men."

but, impressed by what he had read, he added an "Appendice Importante" of about thirteen pages in which he gave an extensive summary of Zahm's work and a qualified endorsement of some of his ideas.

Bonomelli's appendix quickly evoked a critique from Aretine priest Luigi Funghini[57] and Bonomelli felt the need to reply in an open letter in the Milanese newspaper *Lega Lombarda*. There he emphasized, first, that (as he had tried to make clear in the appendix itself) the ideas were Zahm's and not in all cases his own, and, second, that Zahm's ideas had in any case been published with ecclesiastical approbation in Siena. The negative reaction that the appendix evoked in one important Vatican official will be discussed below.

Episcopal openness to Catholic evolutionism came also from John Edward Cuthbert Hedley, OSB. In 1871, while still teaching at Belmont Abbey, Hedley had written for *The Dublin Review* the review of Darwin's *Descent of Man* mentioned in chapter 4. Thirty years later, Hedley, then bishop of Newport (Wales), returned to the topic in "Physical Science and Faith," nominally a review of four of Zahm's recent books, but in fact an article of slightly wider scope (and one that bears reading even today). Hedley was willing to follow Zahm a certain way, saying that "the Catholic student who carefully studies the pages of Dr. Zahm ... will probably conclude that he would be shutting his eyes to scientific truth if he did not admit evolution as a useful and probable explanation and co-ordination of facts."[58] But Zahm had gone further, defending also Mivart's views about the evolutionary origin of the human body, the view that Hedley had, in 1871, thought rash. In 1898, however, while acknowledging that Zahm seems to have done so,[59] Hedley does not seem to place the special formation of the first human body at the same theological level of certainty as the direct creation of the human soul. He wrote that theists "must insist ... that a creative interference of a special nature has intervened, at least in the instance of the rational soul, and also (as seems most probable) when animal life first appeared, and when the body of the first man was formed."[60] "As regards the human soul," he added, "there is no liberty for a Christian,"[61] a point that he did not make about the formation of the body.

✳ ✳ ✳ ✳ ✳

The book, however, had its critics as well. Representative of the more negative reactions was the notice taken of the book in *La Civiltà cattolica*. Francesco Salis Seewis, SJ, in what was more a notice than a review, objected that evolution was both scientifically indefensible and incompatible with Catholic doctrine.[62] There was nothing new in Zahm's book; it was "a tissue of uneducated fallacies, arbitrary suppositions not supported but

---

57 Funghini, *Risposta a Bonomelli*. Funghini also published a book entitled *L'uomo e il trasformismo*. For a brief description of the latter work, see *Civiltà cattolica*, "Bibliografia," 338.

58 Hedley, "Physical Science," 258.

59 Hedley, "Physical Science," 245.

60 Hedley, "Physical Science," 249.

61 Hedley, "Physical Science," 250.

62 Salis Seewis, Review of *Evoluzione e dogma*, 202.

indeed refuted by the facts, fanciful aphorisms, and subterfuges unworthy of the seriousness of scientific work." *La Civiltà cattolica* had already articulated its objections to evolutionary biology[63] and Salis Seewis said that he would not repeat them. A detailed critique of Zahm's book, by Salvatore Brandi, was published in the journal the following year.[64]

Evolution and Dogma was Zahm's last major contribution to the evolution debate. Almost immediately after the book appeared in print, Zahm was called to Rome to serve as his order's procurator-general. Although he found time to deliver a lecture in Malta at the invitation of Alfonso Maria Galea, his Italian translator, and to present some ideas from his book at the Congrès scientifique international des catholiques in Fribourg, he wrote nothing more on the subject of science and religion. No doubt there were several reasons for this. First, on his return from Rome in November 1898, he was made provincial of his congregation, a task that kept him busy until 1906. Second, the Congregation of the Index expressed dissatisfaction with *Evolution and Dogma* and wanted the book withdrawn from sale (a story to be told in chapter 6). Finally, he found other interests, ranging from Dante to the place of women in science.

In 1906, at the end of his tenure as provincial, Zahm left Notre Dame, never to return. He spent his last years in writing and in travel. He traveled up the Paraguay River with former President Theodore Roosevelt in 1913 and wrote several books on Latin America. In October 1921, he set sail for Europe, planning to spend four to five months traveling from Berlin to Baghdad in order to collect material for another book (the notes for which were published posthumously as *From Berlin to Bagdad*). Zahm caught pneumonia before he left Germany and died in Munich on November 10, 1921.

4. OTHER SCIENTISTS AND THEOLOGIANS

Three other works of Catholic evolutionism from the last fifteen years of the nineteenth century are also worthy of brief notice.

a. Denys Cochin (1851–1922)

The first is Catholic chemist (and politician) Baron Denys Cochin's *L'Évolution et la vie* (1886).[65] The central theme of the work is the refutation of what he called "universal evolution," the attempt "to explain the mineral, living, and intellectual world as some kind of great being animated by a single force and producing crystals, plants, man, and

---

63 See Pietro Caterini's 37-part article "Dell'origine dell'uomo," *Civiltà cattolica* (1878–80), series 10–11.

64 Brandi, Review of *Evoluzione e domma*.

65 A third, revised and augmented, edition appeared in 1888, which differs primarily in the inclusion of a preface and of a short report by an M. Caro commending the book to the *Académie des sciences morales et politiques*. (Citations, except as otherwise noted, will be to the first edition.)

societies by the same processes and in accordance with the same laws."[66] It was, that is to say, a rejection of worldviews along the lines of those proposed by Herbert Spencer and Ernst Haeckel. Cochin's alternative was that "ponderable matter, the seed of life, and the intellectual soul, the three elements of our world, could not be derived one from another, but were the product of three distinct acts of creation.... Each of the three elements is subject to its own particular laws, laws which we can know through experiment and observation."[67] Relevant to our topic are two theses.

The first is that the particular laws of the world of life are evolutionary, a thesis to which he was sympathetic, but not fully committed:

> When God created life, he seems, according to Lamarck and Darwin, to have given to living things the general property of adapting to their conditions of existence, of somehow molding themselves to their environment, of bequeathing those changes to their descendants. Species seem to have succeeded one another, the stronger and the more beautiful arising at each generation on the bodies of those which one can well call, since the general law is heredity, the outcasts of fortune [*les déshérités*].[68]

"Seems to have given," Cochin had to say, since "all that one can say about the living world is that the data was still incomplete, that transformism is a mere hypothesis, one on which scientific inquiry continues."[69] He mentions his concerns—how to combine the conservative character of heredity with the variation required by evolution, and the difficulty of experimental testing given the slow pace of evolutionary change and the limits on our ability to modify the environment. Perhaps the inheritance of acquired characteristics will make the combination possible; perhaps experimental work on micro-organisms will facilitate experimental verification. It is, however, in the end, a question for science and experiment to decide.[70]

He emphasized that evolution does not exclude either the existence of a Creator or final causality, two points important to traditional Catholic understanding of the natural world:

> The great fact of the struggle for existence followed by the triumph of the more beautiful and the stronger has its purpose [*finalité*]: the general and indefinite improvement of the forms which life takes. The rôle of a Creator is made certain by the clever progress [*marche intelligente*] assigned to nature. However, just as so many phenomena once attributed to the direct will of the divinity have [now] been recognized to be the effects of laws or secondary causes, it is now necessary to see as the effects of natural laws the appearance and progressive variation of living things.[71]

66 Cochin, *Évolution*, 300.

67 Cochin, *Évolution*, 301.

68 Cochin, *Évolution*, 301.

69 Cochin, *Évolution*, 250–51.

70 Cochin, *Évolution*, 250.

71 Cochin, *Évolution*, 252.

The final cause that he cites here "is not at all for the benefit of the particular individual, but is general, tending to the conservation and constant amelioration of the species."[72]

The difference between evolutionist accounts and the fixist alternative is, in any case, not as great as is sometimes claimed:

> The Creator might have given a separate birth to each species (special creation) or, He might have created a seed and ordained at the same moment, once and for all, the laws of life and of the development of individuals and of species (evolution). Would seeing a radical difference between these two alternatives ascribed to the Creator not be falling into anthropomorphism and subjecting the eternal God to the laws of time?[73]

The second thesis is that, just as the laws of the inorganic material world are not sufficient to account for the origin or behavior of living things, so the laws of the world of living beings are not sufficient to account for the origin or behavior of intellectual beings, i.e., for man. His title warns us that the focus of the book will be precisely on evolution and *life*, not intellect, so, while emphasizing that this second difference is as great as the first, he treats the topic only briefly.

> Nothing fills the gap which separates man from other living things, and the gap is large.... The mind which is aware of itself and has the idea of goodness differs from the mind which lacks that awareness and that idea just as much as ponderable matter differs from empty space and as much as living things differs from brute matter.[74]

The difference is also manifest in human freedom. The existence of that third world requires the creation of rational souls [*âme intelligente*] and "in creating those souls, God gave them a moral law, one that will ensure our happiness and one knowable by reason, but before which our will is free to submit or to revolt."[75]

b. Antonio Fogazzaro (1842–1911)

Antonio Fogazzaro, Italian novelist and poet, Senator and public intellectual, first addressed the question of evolution in 1892–3 in some public lectures that were later collected in his *Ascensioni umane* (1899). Fogazzaro introduced the published collection of those lectures by noting their common origin in "his faith in the Supreme Intelligence's presumed mode of operation in the creation of the Universe and in the governance of human fortunes: the profound conviction that there is a harmony between the evolutionary hypothesis and the religious idea."[76] He emphasized that he was arguing only for the liberty of Catholics to accept biological evolution and certainly not for any formal

---

72 Cochin, *Évolution*, 263. On finality, see also 261.

73 Cochin, *Évolution*, 303.

74 Cochin, *Évolution*, 3rd ed., 298–99.

75 Cochin, *Évolution*, 302.

76 Fogazzaro, *Ascensioni umane*, v.

acceptance of the idea by the Church: "The place of the evolutionist hypothesis in the Church can certainly not be in the pulpit or in the places of honor reserved for known truths. The Church has no reason in the world to subscribe to any scientific hypothesis."[77]

In "Per la bellezza d'un'idea," Fogazzaro offered a sympathetic account of Darwin's ideas about the evolutionary origin of species and of their scientific reception. The point of central interest, of course, was the question of *human* origins: "If we admit that all the lower species have their origin in an evolutionary process, but that man was created by God by molding a statue of clay and animating it with a breath, then it is not worth addressing the conflicts for a theory already stricken in the heart."[78] In "L'origine dell'uomo," he rejected the materialist anthropology being promoted by Haeckel in favor of human exceptionalism: "If the difference between the human body and that of a gorilla does not appear to be large, that between the human soul and that of the most intelligent brute animal appears to be enormous."[79] That difference underlies the human capacity to apprehend concepts and the conscience[80] and it is precisely there that materialism faces problems: "Those men, finding that they could not understand the dogma of an immortal spirit, invented instead another, that of thinking matter, which is even less easy to understand. They removed a big X from the problem of the universe and put an enormous Y in its place, [but] that Y cannot possibly become science."[81] The production of such human souls required "the intervention of the Divine Word"[82] and their sudden creation is "literally an evolutionary fact."[83] In the production of Adam, "the Divine Word, operating as a law of nature, prepared the body and soul together at a lower stage of life and, when the body had become ready, created the soul, operating always as a law of nature."[84] As a conclusion, we might note Fogazzaro's comment that he "did not intend to allow the grand idea of Evolution to be abandoned, almost with contempt, to a philosophical materialism which, not having the least right to it, wields it as a weapon against us."[85]

Unsurprisingly, Fogazzaro came in for his share of criticism on the pages of *La Civiltà cattolica*—for example from Francesco Salis Seewis in "L'origine dell'uomo e il sentimento religioso"—but no action was ever taken against him on account of his evolutionist views.

His novels, by contrast, did not fare so well. Both *Il santo* (1905) and *Leila* (1910) were placed on the *Index of Prohibited Books* shortly after their publication. Given

---

77 Fogazzaro, *Ascensioni umane*, 159; for a more direct reference to liberty, see 63.

78 Fogazzaro, *Ascensioni umane*, 139.

79 Fogazzaro, *Ascensioni umane*, 150.

80 Fogazzaro, *Ascensioni umane*, 166.

81 Fogazzaro, *Ascensioni umane*, 151–52.

82 Fogazzaro, *Ascensioni umane*, 166.

83 Fogazzaro, *Ascensioni umane*, xii.

84 Fogazzaro, *Ascensioni umane*, 168.

85 Fogazzaro, *Ascensioni umane*, 174–75.

the content of the books, this can have had nothing to do with evolutionary biology. Francesco Zanotto, one of the consultors who reviewed *Leila*, explicitly stated that that book "contained no explicitly heretical doctrine."[86] The problem with the books, in the judgment of the Index, was rather their satirical anti-clericalism and their sympathetic depiction of modernism. Pope Pius X wanted *Il santo* placed on the *Index* because of what it said about the necessity of the Church for salvation, about the authority of the Church, about miracles, etc.[87] Laurent Janssens, OSB, the consultor appointed by the Index to review the book, said in his *votum* that the book contained the dangerous idea of "the transformistic evolution *of Catholicism*."[88] "*Il santo* is primarily a novel of ideas," wrote literary historian Robert A. Hall, Jr., "It was [the direct outspokenness of Benedetto, the saint of the title] which (naturally) caused *Il santo* to be regarded with especial disfavor in reactionary ecclesiastical circles. Fogazzaro drew Benedetto principally from George Tyrrell, putting into his mouth even certain specific metaphors which Tyrrell was in the habit of using."[89] Tyrrell's writings were paradigmatically modernist. He had been expelled from the Society of Jesus in 1906 and excommunicated the following year.

c. William Seton (1835–1905)

William Seton, grandson of St. Elizabeth Ann Seton, did not take up the study of biology early in life. He practiced law (briefly), took a commission in the army during the Civil War (and was wounded twice at Antietam), and after the war wrote historical novels. In about 1886, he went to France to study under the Catholic paleontologist Albert Gaudry. Seton returned from France determined to defend a Catholic Darwinism—against both Catholic anti-evolutionists and evolutionist anti-Christians.[90]

To accomplish this, he published about a dozen articles in *The Catholic World* between 1889 and 1904. The articles were generally devoted to particular topics—biogeography, paleontology, mimicry, the evolution of mammals, sea animals—presented from an evolutionary point of view. Only occasionally did he offer a systematic defense of the origin of species[91] or an explicit exposition of a particular theological point.[92]

His general view was that God created at most a few original species, from which all others were descended by small changes that were favored or disfavored in a metaphorical struggle for existence. In other words, he was a Darwinist on four key points that were foci of controversies in the last years of the nineteenth century. First, he defended a relatively comprehensive version of the common ancestry and not merely one that

---

86 Zanotto, *Votum*, 23 (doc. 234, Protocolli 1910–1911, CL, ADDF).

87 Giambattista Lugari (assessor at the Inquisition), Memorandum, February 16, 1906 (doc. 51, Protocolli 1906–1907, CL, ADDF).

88 Janssens, *Votum*, 8 (doc. 52, Protocolli 1906–1907, CL, ADDF) (emphasis mine).

89 Hall, *Fogazzaro*, 81.

90 For a fuller biography, see Morrison, "William Seton."

91 Seton, "Hypothesis of Evolution," "The Century's Progress in Science," and "Darwinism on its Deathbed."

92 Seton, "Divine Action in Natural Selection" and "Plan in the History of Nature."

extended, say, to all rodents, but not to all animals.[93] Second, he emphasized gradual change, the ordinary variation in species, rather than DeVriesian mutations, as the source of new species.[94] Third, he suggested that these variations are "probably largely due to the direct action of the environment,"[95] rather than to factors internal to the organism (an alternative favored by many, less Darwinian, evolutionists). Fourth, he emphasized the rôle of a struggle for existence and natural selection in the process of evolution.[96] About the origin of man, he says only that it was in the Quaternary Period and that "it still remains very mysterious."[97]

Seton was a popularizer, not a research scientist, and most of his effort went into re-presenting to his audience the scientific discoveries and ideas of others. Particularly noteworthy, however, and more or less original, at least in Catholic circles, is his attempt to fit natural selection into a larger providentialist theory of nature. Depending as it did on apparently fortuitous variation among individuals, the central rôle that Darwin gave to natural selection seemed to many Catholics to be somehow inconsistent with the doctrine of Divine Providence. Against this worry, Seton wrote:

> Only for [i.e., without] this God-given tendency in animals and plants to respond in a favorable way to outward changes—and only for [again meaning "without"] such response there could be no selection—the Creator must have been continually working fresh miracles through new creations in order to adapt organic life to new conditions; for vast indeed have been the changes in sea and land and climates; in food and in enemies, since organic life first appeared.[98]

93 Seton, "Hypothesis of Evolution," 198; "Study of Geology," 769; "Highest Problems of Science," 793; and "Museum of the Rocks," 395.

94 Seton, "Disguises of Nature," 773–74.

95 Seton, "Century's Progress," 165.

96 Seton, "Divine Action," 631.

97 Seton, "Study of Geology," 768.

98 Seton, "Divine Action," 626; see also "Disguises of Nature," 774, and "Study of Geology," 769.

CHAPTER 6

THE OFFICIAL CHURCH
(1885–1900)

The last years of the century also saw the first official reaction to Catholic evolutionism from the Vatican.

1. POPE LEO XIII (R. 1878–1903)

To understand the attitude of Pope Leo XIII towards the new evolutionary ideas, it is best to begin by reviewing his thoughts on broader matters.

First, we should note a complaint that he made to Maurice d'Hulst, founder of the Institut catholique de Paris, in 1892:

> There are restless and peevish spirits who press the Roman Congregations to pronounce on matters that are still uncertain. I am opposed to that; I will stop them because it is not necessary to prevent scholars from doing their work. One must give them the time to suspend judgment or even to make a mistake. Religious truth can only gain from that. The Church will always be in time to put them on the right road.[1]

---

1 Baudrillart, "Apostolat intellectuel de Mgr d'Hulst," 390 (retold in *Vie de Mgr d'Hulst*, 3rd ed., 1:456). Pope Leo made the comment to Msgr. d'Hulst, who repeated it to Fr. Joseph Paguelle de Follenay, vice-rector of the Institut catholique de Paris, immediately after his audience with the pope. Paguelle de Follenay wrote the story down and retold it later, which is how the story got to Baudrillart.

Second, we should note the contribution he made to Catholic hermeneutics in his encyclical letter *Providentissimus Deus* (1893). The Vatican Council had not stated as explicitly as it might have done that Scripture was wholly *inerrant* and so, in the years that followed, several Catholic theologians (and one archeologist) attempted to draw a distinction between those parts of Sacred Scripture that were inerrant and those, *obiter dicta* in Newman's phrase,[2] that were not.[3] The goal, of course, was to maintain the doctrine of inerrancy with respect to passages concerned with faith and morals (and, at least in some cases, with "matters of fact" that "bear on faith"[4]) without extending it to those passages that seemed to contradict the results of scientific and historical research. More broadly, could inerrancy, as some suggested, be inapplicable in the case of "unimportant statements of fact" such as whether Tobias had a dog or whether Nebuchadnezzar was King in Nineveh.[5] Questions of natural science and peripheral questions of secular history could then perhaps also be put outside the scope of inerrancy.

One way to do that would be to put the problematic passages outside the scope of *inspiration*: "the doctrinal decisions of the Church extend inspiration only to that which concerns religion (to faith and morals), that is to say, only to the supernatural teachings contained in Scripture. In all other matters, the human character of the Biblical authors is fully present."[6] Another would be to make a distinction between revelation and inspiration: "Everything in the Bible is inspired, but not everything there is revealed."[7] H. J. T. Johnson, building on an example of Newman's, showed us how this might look in practice: "May we not … suppose that when he [sc., St. Paul] asked for the cloak left with Carpus he meant that to the best of his belief he had left it with Carpus, though the request may have been inserted under divine inspiration for the purpose of giving us a more intimate knowledge of St Paul's private life."[8]

All of these attempts were challenged. Some met with a prompt response from more strongly inerrantist critics in Catholic textbooks and reviews. Two books whose account of the relation between inspiration and revelation was deemed unsatisfactory—François Lenormant's three-volume *Les Origines de l'histoire d'après la bible et les traditions des peuples orientaux* (1880–84)[9] and the first edition of Salvatore di Bartolo's *Criteri teologici* (1888)—were placed on the Index of Prohibited Books.[10]

---

2 Newman, "Inspiration of Scripture," 197–99.

3 For an early example, see August Rohling, "'Inspiration der Bibel.'" For more details, see Anthony C. Cotter, "Antecedents of the Encyclical *Providentissimus Deus*."

4 Again, the phrases are Newman's, "Inspiration of Scripture," 190.

5 See Tobit 11:4 (Vulgate 11:9) and Judith 1:1.

6 François Lenormant, *Origines de l'histoire*, 2nd ed., viii (trans., x).

7 Lenormant, *Origines de l'histoire*, 2nd ed., xvi (trans., xv).

8 Johnson, "Leo XIII, Newman, and Inerrancy," 425. For St. Paul's cloak, 2 Timothy 4:13.

9 The relevant material is in the Preface, v–xxii (trans., ix–xviii).

10 Lenormant's book was placed on the Index on December 19, 1887, several years after his death. Di Bartolo's book was placed on the Index on May 14, 1891. Di Bartolo was permitted to revise the book, and a second edition appeared in 1904.

The controversy was reviewed by d'Hulst in his article "Question biblique," which, according to many historians, precipitated the publication of Pope Leo XIII's encyclical on the study of Sacred Scripture, *Providentissimus Deus*.

Leo's verdict on the central question was that "it is absolutely forbidden [*nefas*] to narrow inspiration to only certain parts of Holy Scripture": "All the books which the Church accepts as sacred and canonical, with all their parts, were cowritten under the dictation of the Holy Spirit."[11] The tension that many felt between science and Scripture was to be resolved by careful study and sound interpretation. The encyclical repeated some of St. Augustine's principles—Difficulty of Interpretation, Deference to Science, Theological Relevance, and Accommodated Language (see Appendix II.C).[12] Of particular importance is the encyclical's endorsement of the Accommodated Language Principle:

> the sacred writers, or to speak more accurately, the Holy Spirit who spoke through them, "did not seek to teach man the internal constitution of visible things," but rather ... sometimes described them either figuratively [*translationis modo*] or in terms that were in common use at the time. ... [They wrote] what God Himself had said, speaking to men in a way adapted to human understanding.[13]

It also acknowledged that the deference to the Fathers that is such an important feature of Catholic hermeneutics is presumptive:

> The defense of Holy Scripture ... does not require that all the opinions which individual Fathers or their interpreters have made be equally maintained, since, in passages discussing nature, some of those opinions are merely those of their own times and now seem unlikely. So, one must carefully discern what in their interpretations they pass on [*tradant*] to us as pertaining to faith or closely connected to it, what they pass on with unanimous consent.[14]

And how did Pope Leo handle the question of evolution itself? He did not address the issue directly, but we can draw some conclusions by noting how he handled cases brought to him by the Index, which could not make final disposition of cases without the approval of the pope. Such approval was granted, or not, at a private audience with the secretary of the Index shortly following each general congregation.

He had approved, in 1878, shortly after he became pope, the recommendation that Caverni's *Nuovi studi* be placed on the *Index*. Its hermeneutics were directly inconsistent with those that he would articulate a few years later in *Providentissimus Deus*. The two Mivartist books published later in his pontificate had, as we shall see later in this chapter, a slightly different fate.

---

11 Leo XIII, *Providentissimus Deus*, 288 (trans., ¶20).

12 Leo XIII, *Providentissimus Deus*, 286–89 (trans., ¶18–21).

13 Leo XIII, *Providentissimus Deus*, 286–87 (trans., ¶18). The embedded quotation is from St. Augustine, *De Genesi ad litteram*, 2.9.20.

14 Leo XIII, *Providentissimus Deus*, 287 (trans., ¶19).

Providentissimus Deus, published after Leroy's and González's books, but before Zahm's, made no explicit mention of evolutionary biology. Though he must have had the challenges that the new developments in the paleoetiological sciences were posing in mind, he addressed his topic only in general terms, citing St. Thomas's words of caution: "With respect to matters on which philosophers[15] agree and which are not inconsistent with our faith, it seems to me to be safer neither to assert them as dogmas of faith, even when philosophers present them as such, nor to deny them as contrary to faith, lest that give the wise of this world an occasion to disparage our doctrine."[16] Leo added near the end of the encyclical that:

> If anything [from the physical sciences or from archaeology] appears to be incompatible with Scriptures, the contradiction must be diligently resolved, first by consulting judicious theologians and interpreters as to the true or most probable meaning of the passage in question, and then by carefully evaluating the arguments that are brought against it. The effort must continue, even if some incongruity remains, for truth cannot contradict truth and we can be certain that some mistake has been made, either in the interpretation of the sacred words or in some other part of the dispute. If neither is apparent, then for the time being we must suspend judgment.[17]

2. THE CONGREGATION OF THE INDEX

The Index returned to the matter of evolutionism in the early 1890s, when it was confronted with two cases of materialistic evolutionism. Later in the decade, twenty years after Caverni's *Nuovi studi* was placed on the *Index*, two more books of Catholic evolutionism were referred to it as theologically problematic. Those books differed from the *Nuovi studi* in three respects. They did not adopt his distinction among Biblical passages, they did not distinguish man from animal in the quasi-Cartesian way suggested by Caverni, and finally, both thought that God infused the first human soul into an *evolved* body.

a. The Materialist Cases: Émile Ferrière and Odón de Buen

The first of the materialist cases was that of Émile Ferrière, whom historian Robert Fox characterized as an aggressive champion of scientific naturalism.[18] He had been defending philosophical views incompatible with Catholic doctrine since the publication of his *Essai sur le libre arbitre* in 1865. In 1872, he published a long book entitled *Darwinisme* that presented Huxley and Tyndall (alongside the less confrontational Lyell and Darwin) as "the elite scientists who stand today as the glory of England."[19]

---

15 In St. Thomas's usage, that term would include what we would call "scientists."

16 St. Thomas Aquinas, "Responsio de 43 articulis." Quoted by Leo XIII, *Providentissimus Deus*, 290–91 (trans., ¶19).

17 Leo XIII, *Providentissimus Deus*, 291 (trans., ¶23).

18 Fox, *Savant and the State*, 169.

19 Ferrière, *Darwinisme*, 5–6.

In 1892, six of his books, including an abridged, popular version of *Darwinisme*, were delated to the Index.[20] Ferrière's general philosophy of nature was that everything was reducible to matter and energy. His works, one consultor said, were all "marked by unbelief and materialism."[21]

The task of reviewing *Darwinisme* (along with Ferrière's *Les Erreurs scientifiques de la Bible*) was assigned to Luigi Tripepi. In his relatively brief *votum* on *Darwinisme*, he listed "just a few" examples of passages contrary to Catholic faith. The focus of his concern was on Ferrière's minimization of the difference between man and animal, and his consequent assertion of the common ancestry of man and ape.[22] Consultor Gioacchino Corrado had also noted, and taken exception to, the Darwinian thesis that man and animal differ only in degree in his *votum* on *La Vie et l'âme*.[23]

The preparatory congregation, which met on March 31, 1892, recommended condemnation of all of the books under review, a recommendation that was approved by the cardinals at the general congregation on April 7, 1892, and by Pope Leo. The books were placed on the *Index*.[24]

✳ ✳ ✳ ✳ ✳

The second case came from Spain, where complaints about the philosophical naturalism that dominated the lectures of biologist Odón de Buen y del Cos at the Universidad de Barcelona led Archbishop Jaime Catalá y Albosa, in a letter dated March 15, 1895, to delate the professor's *Tratado Elemental de Zoología* and his *Tratado Elemental de Geología* (both 1890) to the Index.[25]

A review of the books prepared for the archbishop by Jesuits Vincentius Agustí and Aloisius Puiggros objected to the books for theses ranging from pantheism, through spontaneous generation at the origin of life and transformism in the origin of particular (especially higher) species, to the idea that animals had an intellect and will but human beings did not have an immortal soul.[26] The Index turned the books over to another Jesuit, its consultor Michele de Maria, for review. In his *votum*, he raised the same concerns that Agustí and Puiggros had expressed in the reviews that they had written for the archbishop. De Maria mentioned Buen's evolutionism ("the author … embraces the most materialistic and fatalistic version of evolutionism and transformism") in a way that suggests that he might have thought that there were also other (less materialistic) versions

---

20 Foglio informativo, March 31, 1892 (doc. 1, Protocolli 1891–94, CL, ADDF).
It is not clear who delated these books. Although letters of complaint against books are sometimes included among the protocols at the archives, in this case the archives contain no such letter. The other books delated included *Âme est la fonction du cerveau*, *Vie et l'âme*, and *Erreurs scientifiques de la Bible*.

21 Gioacchino Corrado, *Votum* [on *Matière et l'énergie* and *Vie et l'âme*], 1 (fol. 6, Protocolli 1891–94, CL, ADDF).

22 Tripepi, *Votum*, 7–10 (fol. 5, Protocolli 1891–94, CL, ADDF).

23 Corrado, *Votum*, 15–16 (fol. 6, Protocolli 1891–94, CL, ADDF).

24 Decree (doc. 26, Protocolli 1891–94, CL, ADDF).

25 Catalá to the Index, March 15, 1895 (doc. 143, Protocolli 1894–96, CL, ADDF; also diary entry, March 20, 1895, fol. 10r, Diarii XXII).

26 Agustí and Puiggros, *Vota*, October 10, 1894 (doc. 144, Protocolli 1894–96, CL, ADDF).

of those ideas. Whether those versions would still be objectionable, for other reasons, he does not say, though he does cite "the origin of higher living things and especially of man" as something "more connected with dogma and with Catholic morals" than was the origin of lower organisms.[27] In any case, he does not give Buen's evolutionary views special prominence. The books' reductionist anthropology is treated in much greater detail.[28] That, and its materialistic pantheism,[29] would surely by themselves have been quite enough to secure the books' prohibition; the consultors do not vote on the concerns indicated in the *votum* item by item.

The consultors who attended the preparatory congregation (held on June 6, 1895) unanimously recommended condemnation of the books, a recommendation accepted by the cardinals at the general congregation (June 14) and approved by the pope (June 15).[30] The books were placed on the *Index*.

b. The First Mivartist Case: Dalmace Leroy

The decades also brought two complaints about works of Catholic evolutionism. The first was about the work of Leroy. His *L'Évolution des espèces organiques* had been published in 1887, but was delated to the Index only in 1894 (so, several years after the *second* edition of the work had been published, under a revised title). The book was referred to the Index by one Charles Chalmel, an otherwise unknown Frenchman, apparently a teacher, who wrote to the Index to ask whether Leroy's approach to the interpretation of Genesis was acceptable.[31] Chalmel seems to have been something of a crank, for he also asked whether, as he had read (apparently in Hervé Faye's *Sur l'Origine du monde*[32]), the decree against Galileo had been revoked. The Index ignored the second question, but the new prefect, Serafino Cardinal Vannutelli, decided to take up Leroy's book on the question of evolution.

Teofilo Domenichelli, a Franciscan, was given the responsibility of reading the book and preparing a *votum*. Although the inquiry had referred to the first edition, by 1894 the second edition having already been out for several years, Domenichelli reviewed that instead. He did not take Chalmel's letter itself too seriously, saying that most of Chalmel's concerns came from misunderstanding the book or at least from taking what it said in an exaggerated sense.[33] He addressed in detail only Chalmel's idea that the Church required

27 De Maria, *Votum*, October 10, 1894, 13 (doc. 158, Protocolli 1894–96, CL, ADDF).

28 De Maria, *Votum*, 16–20.

29 De Maria, *Votum*, 8–11.

30 Diary entry, June 6 and 14, 1895 (fol. 11r–11v, Diarii XXII, CL, ADDF).

31 Chalmel to the Index, June 20, 1894 (doc. 71, Protocolli 1894–96; and fol. 8r, Diarii XXII, CL, ADDF). The secretary of the Index, in a *pro-memoria*, called him "a certain Mr. [*Signore*] Charles Chamel" (doc. 188, Protocolli 1894–96, CL, ADDF). Chalmel signed his letter as "Officer of the Academy," to which Artigas (*Negotiating Darwin*, 65) pointed as evidence of his profession.

32 Faye, *Origine du monde*, 26.

33 Domenichelli, *Votum*, August 30, 1894, 2, 7, and 14 (doc. 128, Protocolli 1894–96, CL, ADDF).

a kind of literal hermeneutics that would make the early pages of Genesis inconsistent with evolutionism; Domenichelli emphasized that it did not.[34] Then he turned to a more general review of the book, as he had been asked to do by the prefect.

Domenichelli said that he himself was not convinced of the truth of evolutionary phyto- or zoogenesis. Those ideas, he thought, were hypothetical and not well-grounded. Nevertheless, it was not the responsibility of the Index to evaluate theories on any but theological grounds. On that point, he noted that a number of theologically competent Catholics were at least sympathetic to the idea (he mentioned, among others, Newman and Gmeiner) and that it had been taken seriously at the recent Catholic Scientific Congresses.[35] There seemed to be no doctrinal objection to it. If spontaneous generation had never been subjected to theological censure, and it had not, there seemed to him to be no reason to proscribe this weaker version of what was sometimes called heterogenesis. What should the Index do? "If the recommendation to proscribe the theory prevails, it would, it seems to me, have to be based on a study much wider and much more profound than this one [sc., his *votum*], which would be sufficient only for dismissal of the case, or for a suspension of judgment, but not for a condemnation."[36]

And on "evolution and man," the most delicate [*scabroso*] chapter of the book: Domenichelli acknowledged the consensus (of both the Fathers and more recent theologians) in favor of the immediate formation of the body directly from dust, but he was hesitant about letting that consensus determine the action of the Index:

> Saint Thomas, although upholding the immediacy of divine formative action, does not exclude angelic intervention . . . . It does not, therefore, seem to be forbidden to admit a created force in the formation of the human body [*organismo*]; and if one admits the services of angels, it does not seem to be necessary to reject that of material beings, animals.
>
> In such uncertain cases, it is without a doubt more pious and safer to continue to maintain the *sententia communis*. It also seems to me that the evolution of an organism that God will make human touches the limits beyond which daring to hold it becomes a rashness deserving of condemnation. But does it cross those limits in such a way as to merit a theological censure? Although on this point, I do not feel as confident as I did in my preceding conclusions, I must confess that I would not dare to say that it does.[37]

Many distinguished Catholic theologians, he acknowledged, held Leroy's views, the book had already been in circulation for several years without being prohibited, and a condemnation of the book (in particular, singling it out) would unjustifiably bring the author and his Order into some disrepute. So what should the Index do? Domenichelli wrote:

---

34 Domenichelli, *Votum*, 8–14.

35 For more on these congresses, see chapter 7.

36 Domenichelli, *Votum*, 14–19, with the passage quoted on page 16.

37 Domenichelli, *Votum*, 25. The passage from St. Thomas is *Summa theologiae*, 1a, 91.1ad2.

> If this theory seems too dangerous to be tolerated, it would seem to me to be more efficacious and more appropriate to formulate … the errors to be condemned as propositions, with a note of theological censure added, without descending to the condemnation of particular books which contain them, an alternative which, because there are so many of them, would now be impossible.[38]

His recommendation, therefore, was a verdict of *dimittatur*, i.e., dismissal of the complaint without action against the book itself.

The secretary of the Index, Marcolino Cicognani, met with the Master of the Sacred Palace and seven consultors at the next preparatory congregation (held on September 13, 1894) to discuss four books, including Leroy's. Cicognani seems not to have anticipated any particular concern about the book. Indeed he had earlier received a copy directly from the author, as had Cardinal Zigliara. Zigliara, who had written the *votum* critical of Caverni's book some years before, had not brought Leroy's book to the attention of the Index. Indeed in what appears to be a draft of what he would say to the pope during the audience in which he would present the recommendations of the Index to the pope for final approval, Cicognani's summary of the book is positive.[39] The consultors, however, did not see the matter as Cicognani had. They voted unanimously to defer consideration of the book until another *votum* had been prepared.[40] Domenichelli had explicitly said that, although his *votum* might be sufficient basis for refusing to act against the book, the book should not be placed on the *Index* without further consideration of the question.

The general congregation was held the next week (on September 19), with the prefect (Serafino Vannutelli) and four other cardinals in attendance.[41] After serious discussion, in which arguments on all sides were considered, the cardinals agreed with the recommendation of the consultors. They requested a new *votum*, in which three questions were to be addressed:

1. the exegetical criteria that the author thinks are to be used in the interpretation of Genesis;

2. the system of the evolution of organic species proposed by the author; and

3. his doctrine as to the formation of the first man.[42]

Two consultors were assigned the task of preparing *vota*. The first was Luigi Tripepi, who had taken part in the review of Caverni's *Nuovi studi* in 1877–78 and had written the *votum*

---

38 Domenichelli, *Votum*, 26.

39 Cicognani, Pro-memoria on extraordinary audience of September 19, 1894 (but evidently, in light of subsequent events, a draft of what he thought he would need to say, as suggested by Artigas, *Negotiating Darwin*, 74–77) (doc. 88, Protocolli 1894–96, CL, ADDF).

40 Minutes (doc. 82 and 86, Protocolli 1894–96, and fol. 6r–6v, Diarii XXII; both CL, ADDF).

41 Of these, the most important was Camillo Mazzella; the others were Lucido Maria Parocchi (shortly thereafter appointed secretary at the Holy Office), Giuseppe Maria Granniello, and Isidoro Verga. The master of the Sacred Palace was also in attendance.

42 Diary entry, September 19, 1894 (fol. 6r–6v, Diarii XXII, CL, ADDF); also handwritten summary at the end of a copy of Domenichelli's *votum*.

on Ferrière's *Darwinisme* in 1892. The second was Ernesto Fontana who, despite his recent appointment as bishop of Crema, still had an appointment as consultor at the Index.

Fontana submitted a brief *votum* the next month. His summary: "I find nothing contrary to faith or morals to censure here. I agree completely with the two reviewers [sc. Lapparent and Monsabré, whose endorsement had appeared in the book]."[43] He noted that Leroy's thesis was opposed by many naturalists and was contrary to the usual understanding of Scripture, but he would confine himself to answering the three questions put to him by the cardinals. Fontana found nothing to which to object in Leroy's claim that Scriptural passages open to various interpretations may (in the absence of dogma or Patristic consensus to the contrary) be given the interpretation suggested by scientific considerations. He did say that Leroy was being a little too bold [*ardito*] in applying that hermeneutic principle in the case of a scientific idea as hypothetical as evolution. Nor did Fontana think that there was anything to condemn in Leroy's evolutionism, as long as it was restricted to plants and animals. On the third point, the origin of man, Fontana had two concerns. The first was that Leroy should have been more explicit about the annihilation of the animal soul that must have informed the organized matter (i.e., the animal body) into which God would infuse a rational soul. The second was that, although Leroy never said so in so many words, in the end he had endorsed the *animal* origins of the human body, which Fontana thought was repugnant. While these problems were not serious enough to justify placing the book on the *Index*, the author should be strongly cautioned about the boldness [*arditezza*] of his views, "which cannot be accepted by true Catholics."[44]

Tripepi's *votum*, ready by the beginning of December, was much longer, running to fifty-four pages.[45] His evaluation of Leroy's book was more negative than Fontana's had been. He readily acknowledged the strengths of the book, (for example, its critique of atheistic versions of evolutionism), but objected to some of what Leroy had said on each of the three matters on which the consultors had been asked for an opinion. In support of his concerns about the book, Tripepi twice cited Zigliara's *votum* on Caverni's book of some two decades before (which he had read as a consultor officially involved in that case) and the resultant placement of that book on the *Index*.[46]

He began with the question of anthropogenesis, which he regarded as the most important of the three questions and one on the basis of which, by itself, a verdict on the book could be returned. He devoted to it thirty of the *votum*'s fifty-four pages.[47]

43 Fontana, *Votum*, October 24, 1894, 1 (doc. 123, Protocolli 1894–96, CL, ADDF).

44 Fontana, *Votum*, 5.

45 Tripepi, *Votum*, December 8, 1894 (doc. 125, Protocolli 1894–96, CL, ADDF).

46 Tripepi, *Votum*, December 8, 1894, 27–28 and 49 (doc. 125, Protocolli 1894–96, CL, ADDF).

47 Tripepi, *Votum*, 2–31.

The thesis was, he said, demonstrably false, as could be shown on the basis of non-theological grounds alone;[48] it also faced decisive theological objections.[49] That the human body was the product of a "direct and immediate divine action" was the clear teaching of Sacred Scripture and of the Fathers; secondary causes played no rôle. He conceded that Mivart, Gmeiner, and other Catholic authors had defended the contrary thesis and that the Church had not explicitly addressed the question. Nevertheless, he said, even if a thesis could not be adjudged heretical, at least it could be wrong to affirm it (e.g., because it was near to heresy, erroneous, or rash).[50]

Turning to the two remaining questions, Tripepi said that the general idea of an evolutionary origin of plants and animals, no less than the particular question of human origins, was demonstrably false even from a scientific point of view and was in any case vulnerable to theological objections.[51] Leroy's attempt to defend it was the product of an unacceptable hermeneutics. Although the six days of Genesis can safely be interpreted as epochs rather than literal days, Leroy had gone too far in taking a similarly metaphorical interpretation of the origin of plants and animals and denying that Genesis had said anything about the mode in which God produced various species: "It had explained some things, and so those had to be accepted. It had said that some species were produced by the immediate command and the immediate action of God from the matter which he had created. It did not name all the species in particular or their number, but it did name some."[52] In sum, Tripepi thought that the interpretation of Genesis on the origin of species had to be more literal, and less metaphorical, than Leroy's thesis allowed. This, he thought, was what was required by Pope Leo in his then-recent encyclical, *Providentissimus Deus*.[53]

Tripepi did not commit himself on the question of what should be done about the book. Having answered the three questions that had been put to him, he left the further question—of whether the book should be prohibited (i.e., placed on the *Index*) or whether the resolution of the case should be limited to a warning to the author (through his religious superiors) and instructions to do what he could to withdraw the book from circulation—to the wisdom of the cardinals.[54]

The next preparatory congregation was held on January 17, 1895. Whether because evolutionism was to be discussed or whether because of the planned discussion of the novels of Émile Zola, attendance was particularly high. Six of the seven consultors who had met to discuss Leroy's book the previous September were in attendance (as, of course, were Cicognani and Raffaele Pierotti, then Master of the Sacred Palace). They were joined by six other consultors. Its formal conclusion was, as always, briefly stated in the *foglio*

---

48 Tripepi, *Votum*, 8–10.

49 Tripepi, *Votum*, 10–31.

50 Tripepi, *Votum*, 16.

51 Tripepi, *Votum*, 34. His scientific and philosophical critique of transformism is on pages 31–37.

52 Tripepi, *Votum*, 46. His theological objections to transformism are on pages 37–44.

53 Tripepi, *Votum*, 47. Exegesis is addressed on pages 44–49.

54 Tripepi, *Votum*, 54.

informativo prepared for the general congregation to be held the following week: "The doctrine, as it is found in the book, should be proscribed [and] the author be invited through the [Dominican] Master General to retract it publicly, at his own initiative."[55] That was more severe than one might have expected given the views that Domenichelli and then Fontana had expressed in their *vota*. Even Tripepi had suggested that a less serious sanction might be sufficient. What happened? In fact, the archive contains rather more information about the meeting of the consultors than it does in most other cases.

After the meeting, Cicognani wrote a summary for the prefect:

> Discussion of Fr. Leroy's work at the preparatory congregation was vigorous. The consultors' arguments pro and con were evaluated with great care: the consultors [at first] wanted to conclude the case with a warning to the author, but then the resolution finally adopted emerged, in view of the unsustainability of the doctrine of the book, or better, of evolutionism, which is opposed both to science and to faith. Evolutionism is condemned by true ontological and empirical science.... Consequently, the evolutionist system, particularly applied to the body of man, is rash and anti-Christian, since the Fathers and Sacred Scripture present the formation of the body of man in language which proves that it was formed immediately by God.[56]

The view that prevailed in that vigorous discussion is, to all appearances, the one pressed by one of the consultors, Dominican Enrico Buonpensiere.

Buonpensiere had argued that evolutionism is false.[57] Ontology, he said, showed that species had fixed natures, not capable of evolving. Our experience of the world shows that hybridization of the kind that evolution requires does not occur. Although the object of Buonpensiere's critique was evolutionism in general, he did make particular reference to the question of the body of Adam. His conclusion: "Leroy's idea contradicts both science and faith; it is indeed rash."[58]

What relevance did these non-theological arguments have to the exclusively *theological* responsibilities of the Index? The answer can be found in a precise understanding of the theological note of rashness (for a systematic characterization of which, see Appendix II.B). Since the idea of an evolutionary origin of Adam's body was inconsistent with the more traditional idea that God formed his body directly from mud, proposing it would require a strong justification. A solid scientific case for evolutionism could be used as precisely such a plea of justification. The non-theological parts of Buonpensiere's argument were, therefore, an attempt to preclude that plea. He thought that Leroy's book should be place on the *Index*.

---

55 Foglio informativo (doc. 82, Protocolli 1894–96, CL, ADDF; also fol. 8r, Diarii XXII).

56 Cicognani, Pro-memoria (doc.127, Protocolli 1894–6, CL, ADDF). Summaries like this one are not found for most cases at the Index. Whether Cicognani wrote one up in this case on his own initiative or at the request of the prefect is not clear.

57 Buonpensiere summarized the views that he had presented at the preparatory congregation in an extra-ordinary six-page memorandum, prepared after the meeting and addressed to Cicognani. (Buonpensiere, Memorandum for Cicognani, January 21, 1895 [doc. 117–18, Protocolli 1894–96, CL, ADDF]).

58 Buonpensiere, Memorandum, 6.

Nine of the cardinals at the general congregation that met on January 25 agreed that the book should be proscribed, but without publication of the condemnation in the decree of proscription that would announce the results of the meeting and lead to listing the books it had condemned in the next edition of the *Index* itself. Rather, the author should issue a public retraction stating that in the judgment of the Index, "the doctrine contained in the book . . . cannot be taught or maintained."[59] He was also to do what he could to have the book withdrawn from sale. Francesco Cardinal Segna (assessor at the Holy Office and later [in 1908–1911] prefect of the Index) dissented from the condemnation of the book, thinking that a warning to the author would be sufficient. The pope approved the Congregation's decision the following day.[60]

Cicognani sent the decision on Leroy's book to Dominican Master-General Andreas Frühwirth who (in February) summoned Leroy to Rome. Leroy (on two occasions) later said that he was told that "there were two roads open to [him]: either to renounce the work publicly or to rewrite it completely."[61] This does not correspond to the summary of the disposition of the case in the documents of the Index itself.[62] In any case, on February 20, and *perhaps* counting in favor of his claim that he was given the choice just mentioned, is the fact that Leroy got (ultimately from Pope Leo) permission to see Tripepi's *votum*.[63] On February 26, he wrote a letter to *Le Monde*, saying in part:

> my thesis, examined here in Rome by the competent authority, has been judged untenable, above all with respect to the human body, being incompatible both with scriptural texts and with the principles of sound philosophy.
>
> As a docile son of the Church . . . I declare that I disallow, retract, and repudiate [*désavouer, rétracter, et réprouver*] all that I have said, written, and published in favor of this theory.
>
> I also declare that I would like to withdraw from circulation, as far as it is in my power, whatever is left of the edition of my book . . . and to forbid its further sale.[64]

There is no reason to think that Leroy did not follow through in withdrawing the book from sale, though the book probably remained available in many libraries.[65] Leroy did not,

---

59 Diary entry, January 25, 1895 (fol. 9r, Diarii XXII, CL, ADDF).

60 Diary entry, January 26, 1895 (fol. 9v, Diarii XXII, CL, ADDF).

61 Leroy to Andreas Cardinal Steinhuber (the prefect of the Index), February 2, 1897 (doc. 53, Protocolli 1897–99, CL, ADDF), just quoted, and Leroy to the Index, November 21, 1901 (doc. 196, Protocolli 1900–2, CL, ADDF).

62 On January 7, 1902, Thomas Esser, secretary at the Index, wrote to Leroy that "what you assert in your letter to the Congregation of the Index, that is, that you were ordered either to retract or else completely to correct your book on evolution, does not correspond to the documents of this Congregation. The book was specifically and absolutely prohibited" (doc. 198, Protocolli 1900–2; also diary entry, January 7, 1902 (fol. 98, Diarii XXII, CL, ADDF)).

63 Cicognani's note on a copy of the protocol, 1 (doc. 126, Protocolli 1894–96, CL, ADDF).

64 This *Le Monde* was the conservative Catholic newspaper that ceased publication in 1896, not to be confused with the very different newspaper published under that name today. The letter was reprinted by *La Civiltà cattolica* in Brandi's review of Zahm, 49.

65 My personal copy comes from the *Domus studentatus* of a Redemptorist College in Galway. The Saint Paul Seminary in St. Paul, Minnesota, has long had a copy on its shelves. Perhaps access to the book was restricted, though in neither case do the books contain markings suggesting that this was done.

however, give up his evolutionism. This is made clear both by his correspondence (with the Index and with his Dominican superiors) and by several articles that he published during the last years of his life, in particular when he thought that the views that he had already published had been mis-stated by others.

Shortly after his letter appeared in *Le Monde*, while he was still in Rome, he wrote a letter to Vannutelli[66] to get some clarification with respect to the permissibility of defending evolution in general. The question of anthropogenesis he said he would leave completely aside. He emphasized that despite the *philosophical* objections that had been raised against the evolutionary origin of new plant and animal species, science shows it to be possible. That being true, it should be reconcilable with Scripture.

Before the year was out, Leroy wanted to address the issue in print for a more immediate reason. In 1894, Jesuit scientist François Dierckx, professor at the University of Namur, had published a critique of Leroy's ideas about the origin of the human body in the *Revue des questions scientifiques*, and Leroy drafted a reply which he hoped could appear in the *Revue thomiste*.[67] He submitted a draft to Frühwirth on October 17, 1895, saying that he thought that his situation vis-à-vis the Index was no worse than that of an author whose work had been censured "until corrected" (*donec emendetur*).[68]

The initial response (from authorities within the Order) was encouraging. On December 9, after toning down a first draft, Leroy wrote:

> I will be allowed to re-present the thesis of evolution, with the necessary correc-
> tions.... Now, I am puzzled. I do not have to cut out any of my ideas about the
> body of man; I only have to say more explicitly that the human soul, when it arrives,
> absolutely expels or supplants the animal soul which had until then prepared and
> animated the *substratum*.... As for evolution, I was only faulted for one thing,
> namely that I distorted the Scholastic concept of species.... Since evolution is not
> contrary to revelation, then, it is clear that (as long as it does not distort the concept
> of species) it is only a problem of natural history and would no longer be of interest
> to the Congregation of the Index, or so it seems to me.[69]

Although Dominican censors found Leroy's final draft theologically unobjectionable, in the end Frühwirth decided that it was best not to engage the Jesuits in polemics on

---

66 Leroy to Vannutelli, March 7, 1895 (doc. 262, Acta et Documenti 1886–87, CL, ADDF).

67 Dierckx, "L'Homme-Singe en face de la science" and "L'Homme-singe en face de la théologie." The critique of Leroy was in the second of those articles. The articles were subsequently consolidated into a book, with a Spanish translation published the following year.

 Two years later, in his letter to Steinhuber of February 2, 1897 (doc. 53, Protocolli 1897–99, CL, ADDF), Leroy mentioned (in what looks like an account of the events of 1895) that he had wanted to reply to a critique of his work that had appeared in *Études religieuses*, but this seems to me to be a mistake. He had already published replies to two items published in that journal (mentioned above) before the suppression of his book by the Index. Although a third article mentioning his book appeared in *Études* in 1892 (Desideratus Lodiel, "Quelques Appréciations récentes"), Dierckx's articles look more like the kind of work that would evoke a response. Perhaps Leroy confused the two journals two years after the fact; the details do not affect the larger point that I am trying to make.

68 Leroy to Frühwirth, October 17, 1895 (XIII.30134, AGOP). He also mentioned his new article in a letter to Bl. Hyacinthe Cormier, procurator of the Order, November 7, 1895 (XIII.30134, AGOP).

69 Leroy to an unidentified fellow Dominican in Rome, December 9, 1895 (XIII.30134, AGOP).

this subject and ordered that the article not be published. Frühwirth suggested instead that Leroy rewrite his book in light of the comments he had received from the Index.[70]

So, Leroy rewrote his book and, on February 2, 1897, wrote to Steinhuber (the new prefect at the Index) to ask whether the Index would allow him to submit a revised version of his book for their review. The response was affirmative and on March 13 Leroy submitted the revised manuscript.[71] Unfortunately, the consultors at the Index were not satisfied. The proposed revision had been sent first to Angelo Ferrata, who returned an eight-page *relatio* in which he said that he did not think the proposed revisions were sufficient to warrant a change in the verdict.[72] Cicognani thought that Ferrata's *relatio* was not sufficiently impartial and so, with the permission of Steinhuber, he sent the manuscript to Buonpensiere for a second opinion.[73]

Buonpensiere gave a much more thorough response. He thought that the concerns raised in 1895 with respect to the book had not been met and that the revised manuscript should not be published. Philosophically, it was far removed from the ideas of St. Thomas; theologically, "especially with respect to the formation of the Body of Adam, it is erroneous, and cannot be maintained."[74] Although his concluding remarks emphasized Leroy's ideas about anthropogenesis, Buonpensiere's concerns seem not to have been limited to that topic. He thought that there were still problems with Leroy's manuscript even on the question of the origin of plants and animals. The Creed's "maker . . . of all things visible and invisible" "loses its natural force . . . if one restricts it to the divine creation of cosmic matter and to the introduction of the first causes of living things [*germe vitale*] in only one or two copies."[75] The Church, if not with dogmatic precision, then at least persistently, has expressed its repugnance with respect to evolutionism. He thought, incorrectly, that Darwin's work had been put on the *Index*. He remembered, correctly, that the works of two Italian materialists that had been sympathetic to evolutionism, Marselli and Siciliani (both discussed in chapter 3), had been prohibited.[76] In its condemnation of the published version of Leroy's book, the Index had shown its reluctance to accept even the evolution of Adam's body from animal origins. Could the Index revise its judgment? He did not know, but for his part, he was "opposed to any concession towards the evolutionists, under whatever name or guise they might appear in the scientific world."[77] Evolutionism could never be anything more than a hypothesis and "must cede the field to the authority of

---

70 Leroy provided this account in his letter to Steinhuber and again in his letter to Frühwirth, November 2, 1897 (XIII.30136, AGOP).

71 Leroy to Steinhuber; to Cicognani, March 13, 1897 (doc. 51); and to Frühwirth, February 21, 1897 (V.87, AGOP).

72 Ferrata, *Votum* (fol. 54, Protocolli 1897–99, CL, ADDF).

73 Diary entry, June 19, 1897 (fol. 29r, Diarii XXII, CL, ADDF).

74 Buonpensiere, "Sopra il libro *L'Évolution restreinte aux espèces organiques: Nouvelle édition revue et corrigée*, par Le P. M. D. Leroy des Frères Prêcheurs," 55 (doc. 55, Protocolli 1897–99, CL, ADDF).

75 Buonpensiere, "Sopra il libro *L'Évolution restreinte, corrigée*," 5.

76 Buonpensiere, "Sopra il libro *L'Évolution restreinte, corrigée*," 5. With respect to Darwin, perhaps he was confused by the fact that a work by Darwin's grandfather *Erasmus* Darwin *was* on the *Index*.

77 Buonpensiere, "Sopra il libro *L'Évolution restreinte, corrigée*," 6.

revelation."[78] Buonpensiere thought that Leroy had to pay much more attention to the literal sense of Genesis 1 than he had done.[79]

On the particular question of the origin of Adam's body, Buonpensiere conceded that Leroy could only be said to be a sympathizer with the idea that "the human body . . . is the direct product of divine power *by the infusion of the rational soul*."[80] Nevertheless, he emphasized (while acknowledging that Leroy had refused to declare himself to be a champion of the idea), it was, objectively speaking, unorthodox. "It still remains highly probable that the interpretation of Genesis given by the Fathers [sc., one that excludes any secondary causality] belongs *to Catholic Truth and Doctrine*."[81] He cited in support passages from St. Albert the Great, from Suárez, and from the Council of Cologne.[82]

So, on August 14, 1897, the prefect had Cicognani inform Leroy (through the Master-General) "to what extent he should in the future abstain from any publication of this kind of book.[83] Leroy's reaction can be read in a letter he wrote to Frühwirth on hearing of the response:[84] The prohibition was vague and did not point out exactly where the problems lay. It was comprehensive. How could he reply to the critiques of him that the Jesuits were continuing to make? Why could he not write what others were writing? He mentioned Zahm, against whom the Index had not yet acted. "Wouldn't that be a tactic not only useful, but also loyal and quite fair" "to remove our defensive line to uncontested and unshakeable points of revelation and to take from the enemy his best weapons and to put his own inventions to use in the defense of the faith"? Was that not what Pope Leo had invited Catholics to do in taking up the study of science? Why had he been "put out of action and excluded from a phalanx so useful, I dare to say so necessary, in our day to the service of the Church"?

In January 1898, he was subjected to yet another round of criticism on the pages of *Annales de philosophie chrétienne*, this time in an article by Albert Farges, a priest and prominent theologian. In the second part of a two-part article on evolution, Farges had written:

> The hypothesis of the transformation of a simian embryo into a human organism, by an extra-ordinary intervention of God, does not seem to us in any way to surpass the limits of divine omnipotence. . . . But how useless it is; how little it attains the goal sought by the evolutionist system! This system was designed, if not to dispense

---

78 Buonpensiere, "Sopra il libro *L'Évolution restreinte, corrigée*," 7.

79 Buonpensiere, "Sopra il libro *L'Évolution restreinte, corrigée*," 7.

80 Buonpensiere, "Sopra il libro *L'Évolution restreinte, corrigée*," 46, quoting a passage retained from the published edition (*Évolution restreinte*, 273). The emphasis was Buonpensiere's (with a triple underline for the word "by").

81 Buonpensiere, "Sopra il libro *L'Évolution restreinte, corrigée*," 53.

82 Buonpensiere, "Sopra il libro *L'Évolution restreinte, corrigée*," 50–51 and 53. The passages cited are Albertus Magnus, *Summa theologiae*, Pt. 2, Tract. 13, Q. 75; and Suárez, *De opere sex dierum*, Tract. 2, Lib. 3, Cap. 1.

83 Diary entry, August 18, 1897 (fol. 30v, Diarii XXII, CL, ADDF; also doc. 51, Protocolli 1897–99).

84 Leroy to Frühwirth (XIII.30136, AGOP).

with God, at least to replace his immediate action here with secondary causes, the laws of nature.[85]

In a footnote, he cited Mivart and Leroy, "who admit only a natural evolution, by the forces of nature alone, assisted by the *natural* concourse of Providence."

Leroy replied in an eight-page open letter to Farges, with an *imprimatur* from Reginald Monpeurt, his provincial. He began by saying "You have certainly misunderstood, or mis-presented my theory [on the origin of man] and have attributed to me errors of a nature to mislead your readers about me; I think, therefore, that I am not violating the restrictions that have been imposed on me if I offer here an accurate statement of my system."[86] He then restated his view that evolution formed only a substrate; a human body came into existence only with the infusion of a spiritual soul.

Next, in 1899, came a review of the third chapter of Jean Guibert's *Les Origines* in the *Revue thomiste*.[87] (The book itself will be discussed in chapter 7.) Leroy commended, of course, Guibert's acknowledgment that moderated (*modéré*) evolutionism, though still *only* a hypothesis, is a reasonable one, one "containing nothing contrary either to Sacred Scripture or to tradition."[88] Guibert had, however, taken the view that God had infused the first human soul into a lump of clay rather than into the body of a lower animal, and here Leroy expressed his disagreement with Guibert.

> The body of man is said there to be the work of God, proceeding from His hands, but what are the hands of the Creator? Are they not the laws of nature which He had laid down? The natural agents of which he makes use? In a word, secondary causes?
>
> When God acts directly, His action is instantaneous and has no need of any secondary cause; but when it is a question of fashioning pre-existent matter, when it is the question of the work of His hands, do not secondary causes have some rôle in that work?[89]

In conclusion, "The thesis which attributes the preparation of the human body … to evolution, I say, can respond not only to the certain data of revelation, but to all the requirements of the most scrupulous exegesis."[90] That was exactly the thesis that he had defended in his book.

In 1901, he published a reply to Pierre Jousset's pamphlet *L'Homme-singe (Pithecanthropus erectus) et la doctrine évolutionniste*.[91] Jousset had laid out a critique of Catholic evolutionism, to which Leroy replied:

---

85 Farges, "Évolution et les évolutions," 412–13.

86 Leroy, *Lettre*, 3.

87 Leroy, Review of Guibert. It was the practice of the journal to sign book reviews only with initials (here, "D. L."), but (according to Artigas, *Negotiating Darwin*, 114), a later cumulative index identified Leroy as the author.

88 Leroy, Review, 735.

89 Leroy, Review, 739.

90 Leroy, Review, 741.

91 Jousset was a homeopathic physician and president of the Société française d'homéopathie. He had expressed his

Rather than considering the Creator as acting in a human manner, as would a common laborer, personally intervening at each moment throughout the formation of the globe, revising His work, destroying some types in order to substitute for them other types only slightly different; in place of that anthropomorphic conception, the Christian philosophers who are taken to task by Dr. Jousset think of the Creator as proceeding in a completely different way. To limit ourselves to the animal kingdom, they allow at the beginning one single creative act—of a living agent destined to produce all the different species of animals following the ideal plan conceived by His wisdom and according to a law of evolution to which He has subjected it.[92]

In the second part of his paper, Leroy argued that, *pace* Jousset, this view was not refuted by natural history.

In the final part of the paper, Leroy turned to the implications of the recently-discovered Java Man. Christians had no reason to be particularly concerned about these finds:

The distance which separates man from the animal kingdom is principally, if not uniquely, in the spiritual nature of his soul. . . . All that one can infer from this work, strictly speaking, is that lower beings could have formed the *substratum* destined to receive the human soul and thus to serve as an actual link between the globe's past and humanity. There is nothing shocking there; and nothing that cannot be placed in accord with the teachings of the faith about the creation of man.[93]

On November 21, 1901, Leroy wrote back to the Index, again requesting permission from the Index to revise the book:

Many people, both clergy and laïty, expressed their astonishment at the measure taken in my case; even without being supporters of the theory of evolution, they could not quite see how it could be heterodox in itself, especially when it was envisaged as one of the modes by which the Creator could have used for the realization of his work.

With that in mind, I thought that the disavowal demanded of me did not concern the substance of my thesis, but only the inopportuneness of publishing it at that time, as well as the tone of my study and certain passages which would require clarification or correction.

The question having been more fully elucidated and better understood over the course of these last few years, it would seem to me that the danger which was at first feared would tend to disappear and that, it would seem, Catholic authors would be allowed more latitude in choosing between the two rival opinions of creationism and evolutionism.[94]

anti-evolutionism previously at book length in *Évolution et transformisme* (1889).

92 Leroy, "L'Homme-singe," 518.

93 Leroy, "L'Homme-singe," 534.

94 Leroy to the Index (doc. 196, Protocolli 1900–1902, CL, ADDF; also diary entry, November 21, 1891, fol. 93–94, Diarii XXII, CL, ADDF). The request was repeated in a second letter on December 20 (doc. 197) and some of the points made here were repeated in a third letter on January 13, 1902 (doc. 199).

He was again refused permission to do so.[95] Nevertheless, he felt free to re-present a general defense of the evolutionary origins of plant and animal species in "L'Évolution-nisme: Fondé sur une ignorance" in 1902, though without any mention of the origin of the human race. Leroy died in 1905.

c. The Second Mivartist Case: Zahm

Late in 1897, a few months after the Holy Office had dropped its inquiry into the question of Zahm's *Evolution and Dogma* (discussed below), the Index received from Archbishop Otto Zardetti an eight-page letter (dated November 5) detailing his concerns about the book. Zardetti objected both to Zahm's general evolutionism and, more particularly, to his account of the evolutionary origin of the human body.[96]

It is natural to ask why the complaint about Zahm came exactly from Zardetti, an archbishop with no apparent prior interest in evolution and one whose positions at the time—consultor to the Congregation for Bishops and Religious and to the Congregation for Extra-ordinary Ecclesiastical Affairs (in the Secretariat of State)—were far removed from the work of the Index. The obvious answer would be a general concern for the salvation of souls—he thought that the ideas defended in the book were not only false but dangerous. Indeed earlier that very year, Pope Leo had included in the General Decrees with which he had concluded his apostolic constitution *Officiorum ac munerum*, a reminder that "it is the duty of all Catholics, especially the more learned, to delate pernicious books either to the Bishops or to the Holy See."[97] Zardetti had a doctorate of divinity from the University of Innsbruck. I have no reason to doubt that that was the archbishop's motive, but there are a few biographical facts that may shed some light on the case. Of particular relevance are two. First, Zardetti was teaching theology at St. Francis Seminary while John Gmeiner was also teaching there, and indeed was there when Gmeiner published his *Modern Scientific Views and Christian Doctrines Compared* (discussed in chapter 2). Second, during much of Zardetti's time in Rome, he lived in a private apartment at the Holy Cross house there and took meals with its residents. This coincided with Zahm's two years in Rome, so they must have known one another. Despite the risk of exposing the cynical to a near occasion of sin, I should also mention, for the sake of completeness, that one of Zardetti's biographers singled out as two of his "life-long friends"[98] Fr. Daniel Hudson and Archbishop Sebastian Messmer. Hudson was a rival of

---

95 Index to Leroy, January 7, 1902 (doc. 198, Protocolli 1900–1902, CL, ADDF; also diary entry, January 7, 1902, fol. 98, Diarii XXII, CL, ADDF).

96 Zardetti to the Index, November 5, 1897 (fol. 179, Protocolli 1897–99, CL, ADDF). The text of Zardetti's letter (together with a translation) was published in Slattery, *Faith and Science*, 189–99. Unfortunately, Slattery's analysis of the letter (saliently, his complaint that Zardetti's letter "is not a thorough review of Zahm's text and ideas" [*Faith and Science*, 149–51]) is based on a misunderstanding of the details of the process. It was sufficient that a letter delating a book merely bring an apparently objectionable book to the attention of the Index. One does not have to agree with Zardetti to acknowledge that he clearly stated his concerns and his reasons for having them. The Index had its own consultors, who would, regardless of the level of detail in the letter bringing something to its attention, conduct a thorough review of the book.

97 Leo XIII, *Officiorum ac munerum*, 10§27.

98 Yzermans, *Frontier Bishop*, 66.

Zahm in Notre Dame administrative matters;[99] Messmer, a boyhood friend of Zardetti, was opposed to the faction to which Zahm adhered in the struggles that so troubled the American Catholic Church in the 1890s. Zardetti, who had begun his American work at one of the most German of American Catholic seminaries had also committed to one side (not Zahm's) in those controversies. As first bishop of St. Cloud (Minnesota), from 1889 to 1894, he had been, in the words of one historian, "[St. Paul Archbishop John] Ireland's most aggravating suffragan."[100] I see, however, no reason to suggest personal, rather than pastoral, reasons for Zardetti's letter. Against the common charge that the actions against Zahm are entangled with the controversy over "Americanism" I will argue in a moment.

At the Index, Buonpensiere, who had played a leading rôle in persuading his fellow consultors to condemn Leroy's book, was appointed consultor and prepared a report of fifty-three pages, highly critical of Zahm's. Buonpensiere began by remarking that Zahm was "much better versed in the natural sciences (*scienze Fisiche*) than in the profound regions of metaphysics"[101] before turning to the theological issues that were his proper remit. Both Zahm's general evolutionism and his particular account of anthropogenesis, Buonpensiere thought, are offered without proof and are unacceptably at variance with the traditional Catholic interpretation of Genesis.

The evidence that Zahm offered for the evolutionary origins of plants and animals (the usual arguments from geological succession, geographical distribution, and morphological homology) Buonpensiere dismissed as "simple affirmations and arbitrary explanations."[102] Zahm's acknowledgment that the mechanism of change was still in dispute among evolutionists, and thus uncertain, Buonpensiere thought counted against the very occurrence of evolutionary change over the course of time at all.[103] Against Zahm's attempt to ground his theory of evolution in the account of creation and the theology of nature articulated by St. Gregory of Nyssa and St. Augustine, Buonpensiere tried to locate the real difference between evolutionists and anti-evolutionists as follows. Both agreed that God created the material world with powers to become plants and animals present from the start. Anti-evolutionists like Buonpensiere thought that these powers were merely passive (the power to be made into plants or animals); the active power to generate plants and animals was granted only on the "fifth Genesiac day." Evolutionists needed not only active powers from the moment of creation (active powers that are then somehow, inexplicably, not used until sometime later) but they needed powers sufficient to effect the transformation of one species into another.[104] The Fathers, even St. Gregory

---

99 Weber, *Zahm*, 173–74n19.

100 Peter E. Hogan, "Americanism and the Catholic University," 170.

101 Buonpensiere, *Votum*, April 15, 1898, 2 (fol. 180, Protocolli 1897–99, CL, ADDF).

102 Buonpensiere, *Votum*, 8.

103 Zahm, *Evolution and Dogma*, 196; Buonpensiere, *Votum*, 12.

104 Buonpensiere, *Votum*, 15–17. Buonpensiere sounds like he holds to a young earth when he wrote of those who talk nonsense (*farneticare*) about myriads of years (p. 21), but he never says that the "Genesiac days" were twenty-four-hour days or that the world was only a few thousand years old.

and St. Augustine, Buonpensiere thought, admitted only passive powers in the initial creation, and, being fixists about species,[105] never admitted transformational powers at all.

Unsurprisingly, Buonpensiere objected separately to the idea of the evolutionary origin of the human body, citing theologians from St. Augustine through Suárez as well as the canons from two councils against the idea.[106] Focusing on the contradiction that Buonpensiere saw between Aquinas and Zahm over the origin of the human body, he said that even moderate evolutionism could only be a consequence of rashness or of ignorance.[107]

His recommendation was that the book be treated as Leroy's had been, i.e., not by public prohibition but by a personal warning to Zahm, instructing him to issue a retraction and to withdraw the book from sale.[108] He was not sure that the congregation would agree, so he also offered a suggestion about what should be done if the verdict on the book were to be *dimittatur* (i.e., rejection of the complaint)—namely, that Mivartism should be condemned by the Holy Office. He proposed as a formulation of the error to be condemned: "God did not form the body of Adam immediately from the dust of the ground, but out of the body of an anthropomorphic brute, which had been prepared by the forces of natural evolution from inferior matter."[109] The proposed condemnation, one should note, was restricted to evolutionary anthropogenesis; he did not propose a condemnation of evolutionism as applied to the origin of plant and animal species. Nothing in the archives of the Holy Office indicates that it ever took Buonpensiere's proposal under consideration.

Buonpensiere's report was discussed at the preparatory congregation that met on August 5, 1898, with the secretary, the Master of the Sacred Palace, and thirteen consultors in attendance. Six of the thirteen[110] had participated in the examination of Leroy's book three years previously. There are three summaries of the results of the meeting[111] and they do not agree on the exact vote. What is certain is that there were differences of opinion. All the drafts agree that there was one consultor who abstained, explicitly saying that he saw nothing in the book contrary to defined doctrine, and that there were five who

---

105 He cited St. Augustine, *De genesi ad litteram*, 9.17, on page 21.

106 Buonpensiere, *Votum*, 45–52. One of the two councils cited was, of course, Cologne. The other was the sixth-century First Council of Braga, which, in the course of its condemnation of Priscillianism, anathematized anyone who said that all flesh [*universa caro*] was created not by God, but by the bad angels (Canon 13). (This council met in 561, or possibly 563, not in 633 as Buonpensiere [and Artigas (*Negotiating Darwin*, 150) relying on his *votum*] stated. Some historians number it as the *Second* Council of Braga.) Whether that canon is relevant to the controversy over Mivartism depends on whether one reads *universa caro* as "meat" (which the Priscillianists did not eat; see Canon 14) or as "the human body" (the creation of which Priscillianists did attribute to the bad angels; see Canon 12).

107 Buonpensiere, *Votum*, 40. He mentions rashness again on the following page.

108 Buonpensiere, *Votum*, 52–53.

109 Buonpensiere, *Votum*, 53.

110 These were Cicognani, as secretary, and five consultors—Buonpensiere, Domenichelli, Alfons Eschbach, Giuseppe Pennacchi, and Franz Xavier Wernz (whom we will meet again in chapter 9).

111 Two drafts in the protocols and one in the diary of the Congregation (doc. 191–92, Protocolli 1897–99; and diary entry, August 5, 1898 (fol. 39r, Diarii XXII, CL, ADDF)).

thought that the book should be prohibited and the condemnation published. Those who did not want the book prohibited did want the author to be discouraged (by warning or admonition) against promulgating the views contained in the book. Although one thought that the Holy See had, in the Leroy case, already settled the matter, some others thought that the question should be referred to the Holy Office: Did transformism contradict divine revelation? Can it safely be taught?

Six cardinals joined the secretary and the Master of the Sacred Palace at the general congregation on September 1; five[112] had taken some part in the examination of Leroy's book. Their decision was to recommend that "the work of the Reverend Zahm be prohibited; the decree however not be published until such time as the author will be heard out by his Father General as to whether he is willing to submit to this decree and to repudiate his work."[113]

Two days later, Secretary Cicognani met with Pope Leo, who approved the recommendation of the Congregation. This decision was sent to Zahm's superior, Fr. Français, with instructions to communicate it to Zahm.

✳ ✳ ✳ ✳ ✳

Some of the principals in the controversy over Zahm's book saw the condemnation as part of the larger controversy over "Americanism," as some historians also have done. The "Americanist Controversy" was a mare's nest whose stateside components ranged from the personal rivalry between Archbishops John Ireland (of St. Paul) and Michael Corrigan (of New York) to policy questions concerning everything from the Knights of Labor to national parishes, parochial schools, and the Catholic University of America. At its clearest, Americanism was a project that its proponents saw as an American enculturation of Catholicism and its opponents as its Protestantization. But even such enculturation could be understood variously. Alberto Lepidi, as Master of the Sacred Palace, a kind of Vatican official theologian, in the report he prepared for Pope Leo on the meaning of the term, wrote:

> This word has three senses—one political, another religious, and a third politico-religious:
> 1. [a political sense according to which] all those who have chosen America as their homeland, wherever they might have come from, and however numerous they might be, should live as Americans;
> 2. [a religious sense] the substance of which consists in wanting to render more rare the exterior intervention of ecclesiastical authority; and
> 3. [a politico-religious sense recognizing that] it is in practice advantageous for the Church that there be a state of separation between the civil and the ecclesiastical powers; that this state of separation is preferable to any other form of government.[114]

---

112 Lucido Maria Parocchi, Raffaele Pierotti (though he had then been only Master of the Sacred Palace), Francesco Segna, Andreas Steinhuber, and Serafino Vannutelli (diary entry, September 1, 1898 [fol. 39v, Diarii XXII, CL, ADDF]).

113 Cicognani to Français, September 10, 1898 (Congregation of Holy Cross Records, CSCG 1898-IX-10, UNDA).

114 Lepidi, Report to Leo XIII (doc. 157, Protocolli 1897–99, CL, ADDF).

American Americanism was promptly appropriated, and distorted, by some French Catholics in a way that evoked a pointed condemnation from Pope Leo XIII in *Testem benevolentiae* (1899).[115]

Bishop Bonomelli called Americanism and evolutionism "two similar [*affini*] things."[116] Zahm wrote to Denis O'Connell (former rector of the Pontifical North American College) that people like Bishop Hedley (who had written sympathetically about evolutionism) would escape censure because "they are not sufficiently tainted with Americanism."[117] O'Connell wrote to Zahm that "one must consider this maneuver [sc. the condemnation] as a recognition of the part you played in Americanism."[118] Among historians, Morrison called Zahm "to a large extent a victim of the war on Americanism."[119] Artigas entitled his chapter on Zahm "Americanism and Evolutionism." Other historians also suggest or assert a connection.[120]

It is true that many of Zahm's friends were at the heart of the American Americanism that many conservatives disliked, if not of the French Americanism condemned by Pope Leo in *Testem benevolentiae*. These included not only friends from his time in Rome—Keane, O'Connell, and Sefarino Vannutelli—but also Archbishop Ireland in the United States. Zahm himself seems to have been involved enough in such matters that he came to the unfavorable attention of Mieczysław Ledóchowski, prefect of the Congregation for Propagation of the Faith, who complained to Français that Zahm, while he was stationed in Rome, had spent too much time involving himself in "the general affairs of the Church" rather than attending to the affairs of the Congregation of Holy Cross, and indeed had had a tendency to let himself get drawn into church-political intrigues.

It is also true that some of Zahm's prominent opponents had taken the other side in the Americanist controversy. Brandi, who waged a war on Catholic evolutionism from the editorial offices of *La Civiltà cattolica*, was also an ardent opponent even of Archbishop Ireland's version of Americanism and was in frequent correspondence with Corrigan.[121] Zardetti, whose letter to the Index precipitated that Congregation's review of *Evolution and Dogma*, had anti-Americanist connections, as I have already mentioned, and his battles with Archbishop Ireland had been over precisely some of the issues at the heart of the Americanist controversy. His first biographer wrote of him that "we know from reliable sources that he played a notable part in the condemnation of the misguided religious movement called 'Americanism.'"[122]

---

115 For details, see Thomas T. McAvoy, *The Americanist Heresy*.

116 Bonomelli to Sabina Parravicino, October 4, 1898. Cited by Ornella Confessore, *Americanismo cattolico*, 58, from a copy in the Archivio Parravicino, Como.

117 Zahm to O'Connell, October 31, 1898 (John Augustine Zahm Papers, CJZA 2/07, UNDA).

118 O'Connell to Zahm, November 27, 1898 (CJZA 1/12, UNDA).

119 Morrison, *History*, 223.

120 R. Scott Appleby, "Between Americanism and Modernism"; Confessore, *L'americanismo*, 55–66; Francesco Beretta, "Congrès scientifiques internationaux"; and Slattery, *Faith and Science at Notre Dame*, 137–44 and 151.

121 On Brandi, see John Louis Ciani, *Across a Wide Ocean*, especially 256–61.

122 Franz Xaver Wetzel, *Zardetti*, 43.

In the end, however, I think it is not possible to show more than what Morrison called an "alignment of personalities"[123] and perhaps the general idea that both Americanism and Catholic evolutionism showed a kind of "spirit of conciliation"[124] with new ideas that opponents saw as excessive. There are two reasons for thinking that the Americanism crisis was not relevant to the *disposition* of the Zahm case.

First, the disposition of Zahm's case followed the same lines as did the disposition of Leroy's a few years before, a case that had no connection with Americanism. There is, in short, nothing in the Zahm case left in need of explaining, no work for the Americanism connection as an explanatory factor to do.

Second, to suggest that the case was decided under the influence of an Americanist factor is to suggest that the members of the Index, in defiance of their oaths, handled the case prejudicially rather than on its merits. Such a serious charge requires good evidence, though none has ever been produced. Although one may not agree with the reasoning of the consultors and cardinals involved in deciding Zahm's case, there is no reason to doubt that they were sincere in what they said about why they reached the conclusion they did.

✳ ✳ ✳ ✳ ✳

Zahm was notified of the action of the Index by Français, as his superior, on September 16, 1898. *Evolution and Dogma* was prohibited, but the decree would not be published until Zahm had been given an opportunity to submit and to repudiate the book. Zahm was also to notify Alfonso Galea, his Italian translator, of the prohibition of the book. Français was to remind Zahm of his obligation to submit all books on theological matters to prior censorship. The English original, unlike the French and Italian translations, bore no *imprimatur*. Français recommended that Zahm submit.[125]

Zahm's first reaction was to wonder whether he could prevent the publication of the decree altogether. He had influential friends in Rome, including Fleming (at the Holy Office), Serafino Vannutelli (formerly prefect (and still a member) of the Congregation of the Index, and *papabile*), and John Ireland (one of the United States' most prominent bishops). He wrote to Ireland, as well as to two friends in Rome—to O'Connell and to Bishop John Keane, former rector of the Catholic University of America—asking for advice.

Keane seconded Français's advice, writing: "Nothing that you have taught is condemned. You retract nothing and pledge yourself to nothing in quietly and respectfully accepting the prohibition of your book."[126] On October 3, Zahm wrote back to Français, acknowledging receipt of the decree and assuring him of his unreserved submission and promising to comply at once with all its injunctions, but also asking for Français's help also in securing a suppression of the decree.[127] A draft of the letter includes also an

---

123 Morrison, *History*, 227.

124 Salis Seewis used that phrase in his Review of *Evoluzione e dogma*, 204.

125 Cicognani to Français, September 10, 1898, an authenticated copy of which was sent to Zahm, and Français to Zahm, September 16, 1898 (CJZA 1/12, UNDA).

126 Keane to Zahm, September 28, 1898 (CJZA 1/12, UNDA).

127 Zahm to Français, October 3, 1898 (CJZA 1/12, UNDA).

123

explicit promise to notify Galea, his Italian translator, of the prohibition of the book, but this sentence has been crossed out in the draft preserved in the Notre Dame archives and so, presumably, was not part of the letter as sent to Français.

Français went to Rome in October to do what he could. On November 4, he wrote to Andreas Cardinal Steinhuber, prefect of the Index, expressing Zahm's submission, but, on that same November 4, Français wrote a second letter to Steinhuber requesting that he stop the publication of the decree, in part because "Fr. Zahm has ceased to follow bold [*hardie*] and rash ideas" but also to avoid impeding Zahm's administrative work.[128]

In November, Zahm's effort to prevent publication of the decree began to bear fruit. On November 7, Vannutelli spoke about the matter directly with Pope Leo, who agreed not to publish the sentence.[129] Then Ireland, who had written about the matter to Mariano Cardinal Rampolla, secretary of state, heard that the pope had promised not to publish the decree before discussing the matter with him (sc., Ireland).[130] Ireland visited Rome at the beginning of 1899. On February 3, 1899, Pope Leo told Cardinal Steinhuber that "the publication of the decree [should be] suspended . . . until Fr. Zahm, who will soon come to Rome from America, can be heard."[131] Rumors that the matter was not yet closed continued to circulate[132] and they worried Zahm until at least the end of May 1899.[133]

In any case, what exactly did the "suspension of the publication of the decree" mean? Zahm and some of his allies seemed to think that suspension would mean that he would not have to do what the September letter from the Index had required of him, for he had not yet written to his translators. The Index thought otherwise, for on April 25, 1899, almost three months after the notation about the suspension of the decree, Cicognani wrote to Français again. Stéphane Levasseur's brief but favorable review of the French translation of Zahm's book, which had just been published in *Annales de philosophie chrétienne*, drew to the attention of the Index the existence of a French translation about which they had until then known nothing, but which should (in their view) nevertheless have been withdrawn from sale in accordance with their earlier instructions.[134] Français wrote to Zahm on April 29, telling him to take care of the matter promptly.

On May 16, Zahm wrote to both Galea and Flageolet, his two translators, as well as to his French publisher: "I have learned from an irreproachable source that the Holy See is opposed to any further distribution of *Evolution and Dogma*, and therefore I beg you

---

128 Français to Steinhuber, November 4, 1898 (fol. 179, Protocolli 1897–99, CL, ADDF).

129 Letters of Keane to Zahm, November 9 and December 10, 1898 (CJZA 1/12, UNDA). See also Joseph Legrand (procurator general of the Congregation of Holy Cross in Rome) to Français, November 11, 1898 (also CJZA 1/12, UNDA), and O'Connell to Zahm, November 27, 1898 (CJZA 2/07, UNDA).

130 Ireland to Zahm, December 13, 1898 (CJZA 1/12, UNDA).

131 Diary entry, February 3, 1899 (fol. 48r, Diarii XXII, CL, ADDF).

132 O'Connell to Zahm, April 12, 1899, and Ireland to Zahm (by telegram), April 7, 1899 (CJZA 1/12, UNDA). But those who wanted the book condemned seemed confident that *they* would prevail (see Brandi to Corrigan, January 2 and March 28, 1899 [Folders 2 and 10, Box G-34, Archbishop Michael Corrigan Collection (Collection Number 004), AANY]).

133 Entries for April 10, May 3 and 23, Diary of James A. Burns (Holy Cross priest and professor of chemistry at Notre Dame), 28–29 (James A. Burns Papers, CBUR /23, UNDA).

134 Cicognani to Français, April 25, 1899 (CSCG 1898-IX-10, UNDA).

to use all of your influence to withdraw this book from the market."[135] Zahm also wrote to Cicognani, saying that he had not heard anything about the French edition himself after having authorized the translation some three years before. Sad to say, this seems not to have been the truth, for Zahm's papers include several letters from French correspondents noting the appearance of the translation.[136] In addition, the copy of *L'Évolution et le dogme* at St. Mary's College Library (in Notre Dame, Indiana) bears the inscription, "For St. Mary's Library, From the Author, J. A. Zahm, CSC," dated "Rome, Dec. 4, 1897."

The French edition was quickly, and quietly, withdrawn from the market. The fate of the Italian edition was not so quiet. On May 31, Zahm's letter to Galea appeared in the pages of the *Gazzetta di Malta* (at whose initiative is unclear, but clearly not at Zahm's[137]) together with a request from Galea that "my sincere friends neither read nor give any further publicity to my humble translation of the work mentioned." To make certain that even those not in the habit of reading the *Gazzetta di Malta* saw Zahm's statement, the editors of *La Civiltà cattolica* reprinted it in their issue of June 19,[138] and from there the Rome correspondent of the (Catholic) New York *Freeman's Journal* passed it on to the Anglophone press. It was reported, for example, in the *New York Tribune*.

At the beginning of June, O'Connell wrote to Zahm that all danger had passed,[139] but the general impression was that Zahm's book had been placed on the *Index*. That, for example is the way Zahm's friend Fr. James Burns put it in his diary.[140] Nevertheless, the book was never listed in the *Index*.

This brought Zahm's involvement with the question of evolution nearly to a close. Patrick Cardinal Moran, archbishop of Sydney, invited Zahm to prepare a paper on science and religion for an upcoming Australian Catholic Congress to be held in that city, but there is no indication that Zahm ever wrote such a paper. Whether from obedience

---

135 Zahm to Galea, May 16, 1899 (see "Cronaca contemporanea: IV. Cose varie," *Civiltà cattolica* 17th ser., 7, no. 1177 [1899]: 125; Zahm to Flageolet, only slightly different [doc. 274, Protocolli 1897–99, ADDF]; republished in Artigas, *Negotiating Darwin*, 193).

136 In a letter to his brother Albert, August 23, 1896 (CAZA 4/7, UNDA), he had written that "The book will appear in French very shortly." Two French correspondents mentioned to him that they had obtained a copy (Nadaillac to Zahm, October 10, 1897, and Charles de Kirwan to Zahm, October 4, 1897 (both in 1/6 IPA).

137 "My letter to Galea was intended to be confidential, & I cannot imagine why he published it."—Zahm to O'Connell, October 6, 1899 (CJZA 2/17, UNDA).

138 Zahm to Galea, published by the editors of *La Civiltà cattolica*.

139 Zahm to O'Connell, June 21–24, 1899 (CJZA 2/17, UNDA). Some historians, e.g., Weber, *John Zahm*, 121–22, and Artigas, *Negotiating Darwin*, 194–98, emphasize the rôle in this calming of the waters of a visit made by Archbishop Sebastian Martinelli, apostolic delegate from the Holy See to the United States, to Notre Dame on May 10–17, 1899, and a toast made by Zahm (expressing his loyalty to the pope) at a banquet honoring Martinelli. Zahm later wrote of the occasion to O'Connell (October 6, 1899), that "the toast to Martinelli was spontaneous, & intended as a blow to 'our fathers.' No one knew anything about it, not even Martinelli, until it was proposed. It had the desired effect." Français wrote to Zahm on July 22, 1899 that "in Italy, all satisfaction has been given" (all CJZA 1/12, UNDA). (The transcription of the letter in Artigas, *Negotiating Darwin*, 197, incorrectly puts "dissatisfaction.") While it is certainly possible that Martinelli raised the question of the book with Zahm, there is no direct evidence that he did so. The visit and the toast are not, in my judgment, necessary to explain the course of events. More importantly, surely, was the letter to Galea.

140 Entries for May 23 and July 4, 1899, Burns, Diary, 29 and 32.

or from the press of other affairs (Zahm was by then provincial of his order) and the eventual emergence of other interests, Zahm never returned to the topic of evolution.

On the other hand, Zahm never made a public disavowal of his views. To his Italian translator he wrote only that "the Holy See is opposed to any further distribution of [the book]" and even that statement does not seem to have been intended for publication. When he was first notified of the actions of the Index, he did everything he could to have the decree suppressed, and in this he was at least partially successful. His interpretation of what that suppression meant seems to have differed from that of the Index. He acted as though he thought that suppression included the annulment of the instructions that had been given to him. The Index seems to have thought that the suppression extended no farther than a decision not to make the decree public (e.g., in the *Acta Sanctae Sedis*), the condemnation (and the consequent authorial obligations) being still in force, for it objected to the appearance of the French translation as late as May 1899.

The renewed threat of public condemnation did cause Zahm to withdraw the Italian and French translations, but three actions (or omissions) suggest that he continued to take a minimalist interpretation of what he was required to do.

First, Zahm never withdrew the English version of the book from the market. Catholic journalist Arthur Preuss complained about this at the time in his *Review*.[141] That Preuss was correct is clear from Zahm's correspondence with his publisher. He continued to receive royalty checks at least through July 1901. On March 3, 1900, McBride offered to sell Zahm at a discount the fifty-seven copies of *Evolution and Dogma* that it then had on hand. Zahm apparently did not buy those books; the statements from McBride indicate that royalties were paid on fifty-five copies that were sold between January 1900 and July 1901. Perhaps at that point supplies were exhausted.[142]

Second, Galea sent the publisher of *Evoluzione e dogma* £15 to cover the cost of sending the unsold copies to Italian seminaries! It is not clear whose idea that was, but Zahm knew about it, as there is a letter acknowledging the gift among Zahm's papers.[143]

Third, in 1905 the Sociedad Editorial Española published a Spanish translation, *La Evolución y el Dogma*. There no evidence, either in the book or in the Zahm archives, of Zahm's involvement in that translation.[144] It would, of course, be unusual for a translator and publisher to act without the permission of a living author, but perhaps Zahm had approved the translation shortly after the original book was published. Curiously, the book seems to have received no notice in the Spanish Catholic press.

---

141 Preuss wrote ("Dr. Zahm and his Book," 140): "We learn that the American publishers of the original English edition of Rev. Dr. Zahm's book 'Evolution and Dogma' refuse to take back unsold copies of the book from Catholic book-sellers. They declare they have received no notice from the reverend author regarding the withdrawal of his book."

142 McBride to Zahm (Congregation of Holy Cross Indiana Province Records, CUIP 18/08–09, UNDA).

143 Bufalini to Galea, June 23, 1899 (CUIP 18/08, UNDA).

144 However, Thomas T. McAvoy, CSC, then university archivist, wrote to Morrison on February 15, 1950 (Fr. Thomas Steiner: Correspondence M-Mc-N [B-3: 1970/09: 7/8], CUIP 102/, UNDA) that "one of the difficulties about the question of Father Zahm is that he destroyed most of his papers."

d. The Bonomelli Case

As for Bonomelli, the timing of the publication of his book (see chapter 5 above) was unfortunate. Fogazzaro had recommended Zahm's book to Bonomelli at about the same time as Zardetti delated Zahm's book to the Congregation of the Index. As Bonomelli was writing his appendix, Buonpensiere was recommending that the Index prohibit the book. By the beginning of August 1898, Bonomelli had heard that his book, which by then had been published, had evoked an unfavorable reaction in some quarters.[145] Bonomelli turned for advice to his old friend Antonio Cardinal Agliardi, then papal nuncio in Vienna. Agliardi consulted Andreas Cardinal Steinhuber, prefect of the Congregation of the Index, and, on Steinhuber's advice, recommended informally that Bonomelli retract the appendix and publish some notice of the revision.

Bonomelli, in response to the advice that he got from Agliardi (and ultimately from Steinhuber at the Index) published a second letter in the *Liga Lombarda* on October 25, pointing out again that he had advanced these ideas only as a possibility ("non . . . come *tesi*, ma solo come *ipotesi*") and stating that, in light of the concerns expressed to him "by many well-intentioned and knowledgeable friends, both in person and in writing," as to whether the ideas could be made consistent with the Church's usual interpretation, he now wished to retract even that suggestion. In later editions of *Seguiamo la Ragione* Bonomelli included at the end of the eighth lecture (on "Man—His Origin—Transform-ism—His Antiquity—The Unity of the Human Race") the parenthetic remark: "At the end of the volume of the preceding edition I had put an appendix which shed some more light the whole very intricate and grave question of the origin and unity of man; it was a summary of the work of Prof. Zahm. I think it better to omit that appendix, since some people have thought it inappropriate to include it."[146] To his friend Fogazzaro, who had expressed bewilderment at his acquiescence, he wrote simply:

> Let me explain myself. If the theory of evolution had been demonstrated, and so was no longer a hypothesis but a truth, then I too, like you, would say: Be gone, honor! Be gone, life! I will not concede and what I said and affirmed stands. But so far it is not a truth, it is a hypothesis that has all the features of a future thesis. In such a case one can submit to competent authority. The contrary of the evolutionary hypothesis is not heresy and is not even error. The authority which condemns it is not infallible; it is a respectable Congregation, which does not bind absolutely in the internal forum. The time may come in which the hypothesis becomes a thesis as happened with the theory of Galileo; but authority must be respected in the Church and I respect it. Otherwise, it will be good-bye to discipline and order![147]

---

145 Bonomelli to Fogazzaro, August 4, 1898, in Carlo Marcora, *Corrispondenza*, 173.

146 Bonomelli, *Seguiamo la ragione*, 2nd ed., 136 (or 3rd ed., 140).

147 Bonomelli to Fogazzaro, November 6, 1898, in Marcora, *Correspondenza*, 178.

Bonomelli was already at odds with the Vatican, including the pope, over the Roman Question[148] and Artigas has suggested that perhaps Bonomelli, sensibly, wished to limit the number of battles in which he was engaged. Also plausible, of course, is that he did not want to allow the question of evolution to interfere with the larger apologetic project that he had undertaken in writing *Seguiamo la ragione* in the first place. Evolutionism was, after all, he had said, only a hypothesis.

3. THE INQUISITION (THE HOLY OFFICE)

The question of evolution came (or nearly came) to the attention of the Inquisition, whose responsibility it was to clarify points of doctrine, three times during the 1890s, and each time the congregation declined to address it.

The first was in January 1897,[149] several months after publication of the Italian translation of Zahm's *Evolution and Dogma*, when it decided to procure a copy of the book. What had led them to do so is unclear. Artigas pointed out that Francesco Salis Seewis's unfavorable review of the book appeared in *La Civiltà cattolica* at the same time; perhaps that review might have come to the attention of someone at the Holy Office, though there is no direct evidence of this. On May 1, Michele De Maria was assigned to review the book. The Holy Office also asked the Index to send it whatever documents *it* might have on the question of evolution. The Congregation's copy of the book was never read, however, and the Index seems not to have sent anything from its files. The last mention of the matter appears in the files of the Holy Office on May 11, after which the Congregation seems, for reasons that are not clear, to have abandoned the opportunity to consider the question.

The second would have been as a response to Buonpensiere's suggestion (mentioned above), though there is no indication that the idea (apparently approved by the consultors at the Index) was ever forwarded to the Holy Office. In any case, the congregation did not take the matter up then either.

Finally, the Holy Office faced the issue in the case of Manuel Francisco Vélez. Ordinarily, complaints about books would have gone to the Congregation of the Index, but, because Pratolongo's complaint about Vélez had been primarily about the bishop's conduct, the matter was handled by the Inquisition, even with regard to the books implicated in the case. This was unusual, but not irregular.

How did that congregation respond to Vélez's ideas? It began by requesting a report (*relatio*) from Vélez's metropolitan, Ricardo Casanova y Estrada, archbishop of

---

148 Bonomelli had recommended a more conciliatory attitude towards the Kingdom of Italy, in the wake of its conquest of Rome twenty-eight years before, than the Vatican was then willing to adopt (though his proposal was basically that implemented in the Lateran Treaty of 1929 forty years later). For his troubles, his article "Roma e l'Italia e la realtà delle cose" (1889) had been placed on the *Index of Prohibited Books*.

149 Note, January 16, 1897 (doc. 19, SO [Sanctum Officium] CL 1896–97, ADDF). See also Artigas, *Negotiating Darwin*, 141–42.

Guatemala. This Casanova submitted on March 10, 1895. With respect to the question of evolutionism, he reported that, according to a Guatemalan Franciscan then living in San Salvador (where their fellow Guatemalan had been when he had written the items under review): "The Bishop of Comayagua, as shown by the fact that he was 'pleased to support the Darwinian heresy,' has lost the religious spirit. It is quite clear that, because of this, his reputation for learning and piety has been weakened."[150] The *relatio* was discussed at congregations held on July 3 and 10 of the same year. Casanova was then asked to send a copy of Vélez's writings to Rome[151] and, on November 6, 1895, he sent six works, including *Antropogenia* and the article on Darwinism.[152] The Congregation asked Pie de Langogne, one of its qualifiers, for a review of the books, which he submitted on February 20, 1898. His *votum* addressed all six of the texts that had been submitted to him.

He saw no problems in the first twelve chapters of *Antropogenia*, those on the relationship between science and religion and on the creation and physical constitution of man. The problems, he wrote, were in chapters 13–20, which addressed pre-Adamites, monogenism, and Darwinism. Vélez had supported the claim that Darwinism is in no way contrary to faith by distinguishing three versions of evolutionism. Materialistic and atheistic versions were, of course, inconsistent with Catholicism, a point on which de Langogne and Vélez agreed. There was, by contrast, no theological problem with evolutionary accounts of the origin of plant and animal species. That theory the Church had never condemned. The problem with the book was the claim (made by Vélez, but also by other Catholic writers) that the Church was open to the extension of evolutionary theory to the origin of the human race. The suppression of Leroy's book, and, before that, the decree of the Council of Cologne, showed that this idea had already been condemned.[153]

The *votum* was discussed at congregations held the next month, which endorsed de Langogne's concerns about the imprecision of Vélez's catechism. The general congregation added:

> As for the other books, there is much to reproach in those as well, in particular in what is said against the unity of the human species and about transformism as applied to man. Withdraw the catechism, as much as possible, from the hands of the faithful, replacing it with one free of the deplorable defects, and in the future it will be enough that his works are reviewed by the Holy See prior to publication. If

---

150 Casanova to Raffaele Monaco di Valletta (secretary of the Inquisition), March 10, 1895 (fol. 48r, SO CL 1896–99/13, ADDF).

151 Minutes of the congregations of July 3 and 10, 1895, which also records the approval of the Holy Father on July 11 (fol. 52, SO CL 1896–99/13, ADDF).

152 Letter of Casanova to Monaco di Valletta, November 6, 1895, (fol. 56–57, SO CL 1896–99/13, ADDF). The copy of the article was a reprint from the Salvadoran periodical *El católico*, not a copy of the Nicaraguan *Ateneo*, in which the article first appeared.

153 De Langogne, *Votum*, March 1898, 11–20 (doc. 12, SO CL 1896–99/13, ADDF). He also noted that he had not received a copy of *Origen del hombre según la Biblia*, which was mentioned in the works that he did have (*Votum*, 4). That work is quoted in part in *Antropogenia*, 198–209.

he and his writings have not been formally condemned, it is out of consideration for his episcopal dignity.[154]

That would be a strangely restrained verdict if the Inquisition had thought that the ideas were heretical. More likely is that they judged the ideas to be merely rash.

4. THE *STATUS QUESTIONIS* (1900)

The concerns about Leroy's and Zahm's books were known, but only vaguely. What then was the effect of the actions taken against the books? The inaction of the Holy Office meant that there was, in the 1890s and for five decades thereafter, no official church teaching on evolution.[155]

Thus, William Seton, on reading in the *New York Tribune* that Zahm's book had been condemned, wrote to Zahm asking "whether the authorities condemn what is termed the 'Mivartian' thesis in regard to Man's body, or is the general doctrine of organic evolution condemned?"[156] A similar query came to Zahm's Notre Dame colleague Daniel E. Hudson from Harvard's Catholic anatomist, Thomas Dwight, who had seen the report about Zahm in *The Tablet*.[157]

Brandi, to be sure, took the occasion of an inaccurate summary of Hedley's views (published by *The Tablet* and then by *Rassegna nazionale*) to take a swipe at both Hedley and Zahm in *La Civiltà cattolica*.[158] While acknowledging that Hedley had not endorsed Mivartism, he tried to get him to back off the suggestion that that idea should no longer be adjudged rash. As evidence that a stronger note of censure was in fact in order, Brandi republished Leroy's letter of retraction, which had hitherto appeared only in *Le Monde*. Hedley, taking Leroy (wrongly) to have meant that Mivartism had been condemned by the Holy Office, did back off, writing in *The Tablet*, that "if the competent authority has decided in the sense that it appears to have done, the view that the body of Adam was 'evolved' must still be pronounced 'rash'—and something more."[159] But the matter did not end there. About two years later, Spencer Jones, an Anglican clergyman interested in reconciliation between the Church of England and Rome, wrote to Hedley asking for some details of the whole affair. Hedley replied, in a letter he allowed Jones to publish, that "the *Civiltà* quoted no decision of any Roman Congregation, but only spoke vaguely of 'authority.' I have since been informed that the condemnation in question, if it was

---

154 On April 19 and 27, 1898 (with papal approval on April 29)—Minutes of the congregations (fol. 63–65, SO CL 1896–99/13, ADDF).

155 The case that the statements of the Pontifical Biblical Commission did not count as such will be made in chapter 9.

156 Seton to Zahm, July 3, 1899 (CJZA 1/12, UNDA).

157 Dwight to Zahm, July 20, 1899 (CHUD X-4-c, UNDA).

158 Brandi, Review of *Evoluzione e dogma*. The articles that precipitated the controversy were "The Dublin Review," in *The Tablet*, and Theologus's "Le idee di un Vescovo sull'Evoluzione," in *Rassegna nazionale*.

159 Hedley, "Physical Science and Faith: To the Editor," 59.

ever pronounced, emanated merely from [Leroy's] Dominican superior, and not from the Holy See at all."[160] Brandi was not willing to let the matter drop. In a reply to Hedley bearing the subtitle "Erronee informazioni di un inglese," he claimed that the source of the condemnation was the Holy Office, which was incorrect. That congregation, the one with responsibility for defining Catholic doctrine, had in fact made no such condemnation of Mivartism.

Brandi, by publishing the letters of Leroy and Galea in a way that would ensure their permanent accessibility to anyone interested in the matter—*La Civiltà cattolica*, unlike *Le Monde* and the *Gazzetta di Malta*, would be permanently available in Catholic libraries around the world—was able to thwart the efforts of the pope to keep the cases relatively private, efforts that suggest that the pope was trying to put the resolution of the question off to another day.

Without a condemnation of the doctrine by the Holy Office (as suggested by Buonpensiere), however, diocesan censors had no authoritative basis for objecting to books submitted to their judgment. Leroy's book had received a *nihil obstat* and an *imprimatur*. So did the Italian and French translations of Zahm's work several years after Leroy's retraction in *Le Monde*. As long as the books were not listed in the *Index*, there was no formal notice prohibiting libraries to lend out, or readers to read, the books in question. The seminary library in my archdiocese (St. Paul and Minneapolis) had a copy of Zahm's book by 1902 and acquired a copy of Leroy's shortly thereafter. As mentioned above, when Galea, in fulfillment of Zahm's instructions to withdraw the book from sale, wrote to his Italian publisher, he sent the publisher £15 to donate the unsold books to Italian seminaries.[161] That was certainly contrary to the spirit of the instructions given to *him*, but (these books not having been listed in the *Index* itself) seminary librarians had no official or authoritative way of knowing that the books should not be made available to readers. The books had, after all, the *imprimatur* of the bishop of Siena.

Zahm, whose book was published in 1896, cited Leroy with approval despite the fact that Leroy had published his retraction *Le Monde* in 1895. Juan González de Arintero (discussed in chapter 8) also cited both Leroy and Zahm in his *La evolución y la filosofía cristiana* (1898).[162] Jules Souben cited Zahm's "interesting work" in a textbook that he published in 1903 (discussed in chapter 10), though on the general point of the value of an armistice, rather than on the particular point about human evolution that was the focus of the Index's objections.[163] Ludovico Necchi, in an anti-evolutionist review of the Italian translation of Erich Wasmann's *Die moderne Biologie und die Entwicklungstheorie*, writing about "attempts to rehabilitate evolutionistic hypothesis in the eyes of believers," said that they did not turn out well. He cited Zahm and Fogazzaro as examples, but did not

---

160 In Jones, *England and the Holy See*, 298–99.

161 Cavaliere Bufalini (publisher) to Galea, June 23, 1899 (CUIP 18/08, UNDA), first noticed by Artigas, *Negotiating Darwin*, 198.

162 Arintero, *Evolución y la filosofía cristiana*, 93 and 100 (Leroy); 82, 97–98, and 154–56 (Zahm).

163 Souben, *Création*, 2nd ed., 109.

mention any official condemnation of Zahm's book.[164] Bertram Windle, a Catholic scientist who wrote prolifically on the evolution question, put in an early book of his, "I once lent a friend Zahm's very interesting book *Evolution and Dogma*."[165] An unsigned article on Zahm in the first supplementary volume to the *Catholic Encyclopedia* listed *Evolution and Dogma* as among Zahm's published works without mentioning the reservations that the Index had had about the book, though without elaborating on Zahm's ideas on this topic either. A copy of Zahm's book on the shelves of the John Ireland Library of the St. Paul Seminary contained a newspaper clipping of an article, reprinted from *The Catholic World*, with the headline "Tried to Put Father Zahm on the Index." The text emphasized that the book was never in fact placed on the *Index*. A Spanish translation of *Evolution and Dogma* appeared in 1905, though without any indication of ecclesiastical approval.

✻ ✻ ✻ ✻ ✻

What should one make of the fact that the Index took the actions it did against the books of Caverni, Leroy, and Zahm? One might attempt to draw some conclusions by a comparison and contrast with the treatment of other books published in the last decades of the nineteenth century, such as those of Mivart and González. The Index itself, one must recall, did not then have the authority to initiate inquiries against books, but only to make judgments about books referred to it by others. So, Giuseppe Maria Granniello's comment, quoted in Appendix III.B, applies here, too—the other books were not delated; Leroy's and Zahm's were.[166] This reinforces a thesis defended by Artigas, that the Vatican did not have a *policy* about exactly what Catholic evolutionists should or could say about the origin of the human body. For the most part, it responded *ad hoc*. The best evidence for this is the fact that the theses defended by Leroy and Zahm are too similar to that defended by Mivart two decades before to think that there was a reason to condemn the latter two books that would not also apply to the former. Beyond that, one should notice that Caverni's book was something of an outlier, both with respect to its anthropology (or, more precisely, its zoology) and its hermeneutic principles. In both respects it differed from Mivart's only slightly earlier *On the Genesis of Species*. González, unlike Zahm, did not delight in "stirring up the bears." He was both more cautious in his evolutionism and less comprehensive (in his acknowledgment of some rôle for divine action in the formation of the first human body).

---

164 Necchi, Review of *La biologia moderna*.

165 Windle, *Facts & Theories*, 21.

166 Granniello, *Votum* on Salvatore di Bartolo's *Criterii theologici*, ¶50 (doc. 79, Protocolli 1889–91, CL, ADDF).

CHAPTER 7

NON-OFFICIAL FORA
(1885–1900)

1. THE INTERNATIONAL SCIENTIFIC
CONGRESSES OF CATHOLICS

"The future historian of the nineteenth century," a contemporary wrote, "will put down among the novelties of Catholic life the numerous congresses that succeed one another with ever greater frequency."[1] A practice begun locally by German Catholics in Mainz in 1848 was picked up by an international committee for a Catholic congress held in Mechlin in 1863–64. The idea of a precisely *scientific* congress was the brainchild of François Duilhé de Saint-Projet and of Maurice d'Hulst, rectors of the Instituts catholiques de Toulouse and de Paris, respectively;[2] the result was a series of five International Scientific Congresses of Catholics held between 1888 and 1900.

The topical focus of the congresses was "the principal questions of philosophy, the sciences, and history, notably those relevant to Christian truths." Papers concerning "purely theological questions," by contrast, would not be accepted. Also excluded were papers defending "opinions contrary either to decisions of the Councils or of the Holy

---

1 Thomas J. Shahan, "The Scientific Congress at Brussels," 73.

2 Congrès scientifique de 1888, *Compte rendu*, 1:xiii–xxxvii ("Introduction historique"). For a general account of Catholic congresses, see Martin Spahn and Thomas F. Meehan, "Congresses," or John Gilmary Shea, "Catholic Congresses." For a history of the scientific congresses, see Alfred Baudrillart, *Vie de Mgr D'Hulst*, 3rd ed., 1:528–61; Francesco Beretta, "Les Congrès scientifiques" and "Monseigneur d'Hulst;" or Paul, *Edge of Contingency*, 82–93.

See or to common teachings authorized by theology." The congresses would respect the guidelines laid down by Pope Pius IX in *Tuas libenter* (1863).[3]

Also important to note is that the congresses were precisely *scientific* rather than merely or primarily *apologetic*.[4] And so, while they did include papers on evolution and paleoanthropology, they also included papers with no relevance to any "*Christian* truths"—for example, papers on Basque etymology and on conic sections. The first congress divided the papers contributed into sessions on religion, philosophy, law, history, natural science, and anthropology; later congresses used variations on that scheme of division. The organizers of the first congress published a list of some 187 questions as an indication of what they were looking for from contributors. Those relevant to our topic included:

> Transformism from a metaphysical point of view
> Evolution applied to the gradual transformation of egoistic inclinations
>> into altruistic ones, and the possible future disappearance of the
>> former as an effect of social progress
> The origin of species
>> Transformism: Lamarck, Geoffroy Saint-Hilaire, Darwin
>> Evolution: Haeckel (monism)
>> Natural selection and the fixity of species
>>> Arguments for and against the fixity of species on the basis of
>>> morphology, embryology, and paleontology
> The origin of man
>> At what geological epoch did man appear on earth?
>> What evidence is there of the existence of man in the
>> tertiary epoch?
>> What is the geological date of the most ancient human fossils?
>> Was there a gap between the paleolithic and neolithic epochs?[5]

In the end, five congresses were held—in Paris (1888 and 1891), and then in Brussels (1894), Fribourg (1897) and Munich (1900). A record of each congress was subsequently published. Those proceedings include many, but not all, of the papers presented at the congresses, together with a report on the subsequent discussion.

Although attendees included some (but not all) of the more prominent participants in the larger Catholic discussion of evolutionism, the congresses were not, for the most part, the place where major new ideas were introduced. Nevertheless, we can learn from the contents of papers accepted for presentation, and even more from the discussions that followed them, something about the attitudes towards Catholic evolutionism in the larger Catholic scientific community. So what did the participants in the congresses think and say about the paleoetiological sciences?

---

3 Articles 1 and 17–18 of the "Règlement du Congrès," Congrès scientifique de 1888, *Compte rendu*, 1:lviii–lix. See also, Baudrillart, *D'Hulst*, 540–42.

4 On this, see Baudrillart, *D'Hulst*, 531.

5 See the "Program des questions proposées," Congrès scientifique de 1888, *Compte rendu*, 1:xlv–lvii. The list presented above is selective, but the wording is that of the call for papers.

* * * * *

The first congress, held in Paris on April 8–13, 1888, was attended by about two hundred participants and included 79 presentations. Subscriptions, which entitled the subscriber to a copy of the proceedings, numbered about 1600. Both the philosophical and the anthropological sections included papers on evolution; the natural science section, by contrast, did not.[6]

At the philosophical section, John Gmeiner's paper on Herbert Spencer, mentioned in chapter 2, provoked a long and lively discussion. The author of the official summary wrote:

> The assembly appeared to be divided into two fairly distinct camps. Some thought that the concessions which Fr. Gmeiner had made to the theory of evolution went too far; others, while joining the author in maintaining, as a minimum, the restrictions relative to man, were in ready agreement that there is no philosophical impossibility in accepting the doctrine of evolution with respect to plants and animals.[7]

The point of contention, perhaps appropriately for the philosophical section, was the very possibility of the descent of all organisms from one or a few first kinds of living thing. Jean-Marie-Charles Bulliot, for example, doubted that "protoplasma" could have latent powers of a kind sufficient to initiate the evolution of more complex forms of life; Félix Robiou was not willing to insist on such limits to divine power. D'Hulst thought that the theory of evolution could be formulated in a way that would pose no danger for science, philosophy, or the faith, and noted that many scientists already embraced it. Count Domet de Vorges said that it would be dangerous to say that it was metaphysically impossible.[8] No one in the discussion, it seems, thought that the idea had yet been shown to be true.

The papers presented at the anthropological section addressed a wide array of topics. Some focused on topics *within* paleoanthropology (some with more, and some with less, connection to topics of religious interest)—the Canstadt skull, continuity between Paleolithic and Neolithic cultures, the possible religious significance of posthumous trepanation by Neolithic Man. Others addressed the nature of the difference between man and animal. Still others addressed human origins more directly—e.g., monogenesis or the date of man's first appearance on earth. Finally, some addressed the general question of evolutionary biology, without necessarily addressing the question of *human* evolution at all. Here, the organization of the session manifested a certain openness. The open-minded non-evolutionist Marquis de Nadaillac was president of the section; the more evolutionist Adrien Arcelin was vice-president. The papers selected for presentation showed a range of opinion.

The first paper to address the question of evolution directly was from anti-evolutionist Alexandre François Malbranche, botanist at the Académie des sciences, belles-lettres et

---

6 Congrès scientifique de 1888, *Compte rendu*. Attendance figures are at 1:xxiii.

7 Congrès scientifique de 1888, *Compte rendu*, 1:408.

8 Bulliot, a Marist priest, was a professor of Scholastic philosophy at the Institut catholique de Paris. Robiou was a historian and university professor associated with the Université de Rennes and with the Institut catholique de Paris; Domet de Vorges was vice-president of the Société de Saint-Thomas-d'Aquin de Paris.

arts de Rouen.[9] He argued against the very possibility of natural selection or a struggle for existence. His paper was not printed in the proceedings of the congress, but the content of his paper can perhaps be inferred from his earlier essay on "Le Transformisme, ses origines, ses principes, ses impossibilités." A paper at the session (and the remark best fits the views of Malbranche) was later quoted as saying that "it is a duty for Catholics to oppose the theory of evolution, which is manifestly contrary to the faith and to the content of our Holy Books."[10] The paper was criticized by four of the most prominent men at the session—by d'Hulst, Joseph Van den Gheyn,[11] Albert Lapparent, and de Nadaillac.[12]

In sharp contrast to the views of Malbranche were those of Duilhé de Saint-Projet, who had first proposed the idea of holding the congress. He began his presentation on "Le Problème anthropologique et les théories évolutionnistes" (described in the summary of the discussion, however, as having the title "L'Élément psychique dans l'anthropologie") with the remark that "cosmic [i.e., inorganic] evolution includes nothing contrary to spiritualist and Christian doctrine."[13] Animal evolution is "the only evolution relevant to the anthropological problem."

> If it stops at [sc., before offering an account of] man ... it is a scientific hypothesis according to some, an extra-scientific hypothesis according to others, opposed on the basis of very grave objections that have not yet been resolved, but enjoying nevertheless the increasing favor of many. On this matter, the liberty of research and of opinion is complete; no one has the right to appeal to faith in the question of evolution posed in that way.[14]

Duilhé de Saint-Projet then turned to man, who, he said, "was not, and could not be, the final term of a continuous evolution." He had argued elsewhere that reason and free will made man essentially distinct from other animals. Here, he would respond to the most recent attempts to explain the origin of those distinctly human powers by reference to purely material antecedents.[15]

The question of the evolution of the human body alone, Mivartism, came up in the discussion of Duilhé de Saint-Projet's paper. Paul Maisonneuve, scientist and professor at the Université catholique d'Angers, put the question:

> Since Duilhé de Saint-Projet accepts the possibility of evolution, where does he place its limits? Does he stop at man? Does he think, for example, that man, who, *from the*

---

9 His presentation was read by his sometime collaborator Eugène Niel; Malbranche was suffering from his last illness and died the following month.

10 Congrès scientifique de 1888, *Compte rendu*, 2:606.

11 Van den Gheyn, a Jesuit, was a historian and an anthropologist.

12 Congrès scientifique de 1888, *Compte rendu*, 2:774.

13 Duilhé de Saint-Projet, "Problème anthropologique," 2:621.

14 Duilhé de Saint-Projet, "Problème anthropologique," 2:622.

15 Duilhé de Saint-Projet, "Problème anthropologique," 2:622–23. The "elsewhere" is his earlier *Apologie scientifique de la foi spiritualiste et chrétienne* (1885), chapters 17–18.

organic point of view, offers so many points of contact with animal species—composition, chemical constitution, anatomical structure and functions are in reality the same—differs from animals only in his reason, his intellectual and immortal soul, which by itself is sufficient to raise an enormous barrier between him and all the rest of the animal world?[16]

Duilhé de Saint-Projet said that an apologist did not have to resolve the delicate question of the evolutionary origin of man. It was enough to say that man has a soul that was immediately created by God.

Maisonneuve replied that even if the apologist could neglect the question, the Christian scientist could not. More generally, he continued, "A Christian scientist needed to know whether he was permitted to consider this a matter of free debate, yes or no. Without taking up the question of the way in which the soul was united to the body, reserving that to the theologians ... , it is quite natural that the problem of the origin of man be raised."

Duilhé de Saint-Projet replied that, speaking for himself, he considered that the question could be freely discussed. Jean-Marie Bordes (Oratorian priest and teacher of natural science at his order's Collège de Juilly) said that many Catholics accepted evolutionary origin of the human body; he cited Mivart as an example. The next day Arcelin said in his presentation that, "whether one accepts or rejects the transformist hypothesis, one cannot deny that the beings [sc., those found in the fossil record] succeed one another in a logical order in time ...."[17]

Discussion of the theory of evolution continued at the end of the scientific session,[18] even though none of the papers presented there had discussed the topic. Maisonneuve read a note of about two pages that he had composed in response to the assertion, made in a paper delivered at the anthropological session three days before, that Catholics have a duty to fight against the theory of evolution. He wanted to hear discussion on the question of "how far a scientist in other ways firmly attached to the dogmas, and to the spirit, of the Catholic religion could go in adopting transformist ideas." He hoped "to provoke an exchange of ideas that would shed some light on the question, to the benefit of everyone." His own views were these: Although the theory was at first seen by many Catholics as something aimed at the destruction of doctrine, it was now being adopted by some scientists whose acceptance of the authority of the Church could not be questioned. The concern that it denied any place to divine intervention in the formation of creatures [*êtres*], or that it was inconsistent with Scripture, were misplaced. So it is just an ordinary scientific question. He was not asking about the truth of evolutionary theory, about which he had philosophical reservations, or about the animal origins of man, but only whether Catholics should feel free to discuss it.

---

16 Congrès scientifique de 1888, *Compte rendu,* 2:775–76. Paul Maisonneuve ("Dr. Maisonneuve" in the proceedings) must be distinguished from Louis Maisonneuve ("Canon Maisonneuve") who also participated in the congress.

17 Arcelin, "Homme tertiaire," 2:638.

18 Congrès scientifique de 1888, *Compte rendu,* 2:606–9.

Further discussion did not quite answer the question as posed. Fr. Gerard Smets said that he had begun to study the theory three years before, having been asked by his religious superior to do so and had done so with an open mind. The result was a verdict in favor of evolution, though he still, of course, accepted the immediate creation of each human soul and the necessity of divine intervention in human evolution. He proceeded to lay out a scientific case for the theory. Bordes seconded what Smets had said. Fr. Lacouture expressed his dissent. Msgr. Henry Sauvé and Fr. Alfred Vacant expressed the objections that had been made in the philosophical section.[19] D'Hulst brought the discussion to a close with the observation that a collective decision on a point of orthodoxy would turn the scientific congress into a council. A request for participants' individual judgments on the question would yield only contradictory assertions, the arguments in favor of which each person would have to evaluate for himself.[20]

* * * * *

The second congress, held in Paris on April 1–6, 1891, featured 131 presentations and had about 2500 subscribers. Was it Maisonneuve's question at the previous congress—the question about whether Catholics were free to discuss the theory of evolution—that led to a more direct discussion of the question in 1891? Whether that was the cause or was not, de Nadaillac made certain that the general question *was* addressed. He prepared a paper entitled "Les Progrès de l'anthropologie," in which he expressed his reservations about the theory, and invited Maisonneuve to present the other side of the case, which he did in a paper entitled "Création et évolution."[21]

De Nadaillac asked:

> Can one not suppose that the Creator, in the beginning, endowed some of the beings that proceeded from his hand with a power of modification, a plasticity..., a power to develop in the immensity of time, under the rule of a law that we do not know, in circumstances which we cannot describe, by slow and imperceptible changes, ... and continuing generation after generation until the completion of the immutable plan which it is not given to man to know?[22]

The lacunae, de Nadaillac thought, were too significant to accept such a supposition. The progress of anthropology in his title was characterized by the *disfavor* into which evolutionist hypotheses had fallen.

---

19 Smets, who had studied under Louvain paleontologist Pierre-Joseph Van Beneden, taught the natural sciences at the Collège Saint Joseph at Hasselt (Belgium). Later that year, his misidentification of some fossilized wood as dinosaur remains ("*Aachenosaurus*"), quickly corrected by Louis Dollo, has unfortunately secured him, for his mistake, a lasting place in dinosaur lore. Sauvé was the former rector of the Université catholique d'Angers. Vacant was editor of the *Dictionnaire de théologie catholique*.

20 See Baudrillart, *D'Hulst*, 543–44.

21 For the origin of the paired presentations in de Nadaillac's desire to have an exposition of both the pro and the contra, see Maisonneuve, "Création," 8:36, and Congrès scientifique de 1891, 8:211.

22 Maisonneuve, "Création," 8:47.

Maisonneuve quoted de Nadaillac's question but gave a different answer. His paper was a defense of the evolutionary origin of species in general. Despite the fact that the paper was presented to the anthropology section of the congress, however, he chose not to address anthropogenesis:

> Out of deference to the very respectable repugnance of many wise and prudent people, and because of the gravity of the consequences which result from the application of these theories to man, I would like, deliberately and without any prejudgment of the matter, to leave aside the question of the origin of the most perfect terrestrial creature. . . . The introduction of the origin of man into this controversy could raise theological questions which I feel myself incapable of answering and which it is not at all my intention to provoke.[23]

Whatever might be the case with respect to the origin of man, the theory as applied to plants and animals, he said, raised no theological questions: "In agreement with some others, whom I consider to be good and solid thinkers, it does not seem to me that my religious beliefs and my absolute submission to the Church must in any way suffer from what is sometimes called the rashness of the new doctrines, if I think that I should accept them."[24]

One can divide his argument into two parts. The first part addressed the compatibility of the evolutionary origin of species with the idea of God the Creator, the puzzle of why the principle of evolution had remained so long unrecognized, and the idea of a general "organic plasticity." The second part focused on some of the facts about living things standardly cited in favor of evolution. In that part, his argument, like Darwin's, is that positing an evolutionary origins of species allows one to *understand* certain central facts about the biological world while the alternative of *independent* creation leaves those facts at best unexplained and at worst distinctly odd. So, with respect to rudimentary organs:

> While the doctrine of evolution shines a bright light on these various facts, showing us how they can be connected to, or derived from, one another, what interpretation do they get from the creationist doctrine [i.e., the doctrine of *independent* creation]?
>
> Can one think that the Creator was pleased to make something manifestly useless? that he created from scratch, by a special act, organs that will never be used? That hypothesis, you will admit, is hardly satisfying.[25]

And with respect to some facts of embryology: "The similarity of the first phases of development of various organisms is well-explained by evolution, but it is much harder to see why, if each species came fully formed from the hands of the Creator, its descendants would be compelled to go through developmental phases identical to those shown by

---

23 Maisonneuve, "Création," 8:37.

24 Maisonneuve, "Création," 8:37.

25 Maisonneuve, "Création," 8:58.

the species which preceded it."[26] In general, "With the theory of evolution, in place of having only a multiplicity of isolated facts without any real connections among them, we see organic phenomena logically linked one to another by a single law, admirable in its simplicity and in its grandeur." In conclusion, he wrote, "I am singularly hesitant to accept a doctrine which supposes such frequently reiterated acts of creation when there might be a simpler way of offering a rational explanation of the facts. . . . Creationism is a misuse of Creation just as a fallacy is a misuse of reasoning."[27]

There was a long discussion of the two papers on the following day.[28] It was begun by Pierre Jousset, who said that, since the doctrine of creation required the direct creation of each individual species, it was disappointing to see the congress divided on the topic of evolution.[29] This provoked a reply from d'Hulst.[30] The only commitment of the congress was orthodoxy and that required (with respect to biological origins) no more than the immediate creation by God of each individual human soul. Beyond that, any rashness in hypotheses would have to be met by scientific counter-argument. Maisonneuve brought the discussion back to facts and reasoning from those facts and there it remained, focused in particular on the question of the fixity of species. Also noteworthy was the failure, remarked by Augustin Poulain,[31] of the anti-evolutionists to distinguish various versions of evolutionism, differing from one another in whether they included common ancestry or only the transformation of species, in whether they absolutely excluded divine intervention or permitted it only, say, in transition from kingdom to kingdom, and in whether they thought that natural selection was the mechanism of transformation. Without such distinctions, he said, refutations have little value.

Finally, de Nadaillac suggested that, the principal arguments on each side of the question having been articulated, it was time to bring the discussion to a close. Charles Freppel, bishop of Angers and president of the Congress, who was at that point presiding over the debate, remarked that the participants had given an example of the great liberty that science so needed. He added his own thought that the fixists had had the better of the argument.

✳ ✳ ✳ ✳ ✳

The third congress, held in Brussels on September 5–8, 1894, was about the same size as the second, with about 150 presentations and 2518 subscribers. Two papers presented there are of direct relevance to our topic.[32]

---

26 Maisonneuve, "Création," 8:60.

27 Maisonneuve, "Création," 8:41–42.

28 Congrès scientifique de 1891, *Compte rendu*, 8:211–25 ("Procès-Verbaux des Séances").

29 "Procès-Verbaux des Séances," 8:212–13.

30 "Procès-Verbaux des Séances," 8:213.

31 Poulain, a Jesuit, was vice-director of student housing at the Université Catholique d'Angers. His academic specialty was mathematics. The remarks mentioned here are at "Procès-Verbaux des Séances," 8:221.

32 Congrès scientifique de 1894, *Compte rendu*, 1:12, 16–17, and 23.

The first was a paper entitled "La Théorie de l'évolution en botanique," by Nicolas Boulay, a priest and professor of botany at the Université catholique de Lille. Boulay confined himself, as his title indicated that he would, to botany, explicitly avoiding not only anthropology but even zoology. Within the plant kingdom, he acknowledged the possibility of an evolution of species "without doing damage to any dogma or even to any principle of metaphysics."[33] Nevertheless, "the general hypothesis remains vague and indeterminate. It does not have the precision necessary for it to have any scientific value."[34] Beyond that, he had doubts about the unlimited variability of species and was not satisfied that the paleontological record provided as strong a level of support for the theory as he would have liked to see. The theory should be treated "only as an object of research, not as a principle of demonstration."[35] The report of the subsequent discussion says only that the paper led to an interesting exchange between Boulay, Claude Léon Guillemet, and Lapparent on theories of evolution in general, unfortunately without further elaboration.[36]

A more comprehensive defense of Catholic evolutionism, Guillemet's "Pour la Théorie des ancêtres communs," was presented to the anthropological section.[37] A result of an express invitation from de Nadaillac, Guillemet's paper was intended to build on the exchange between de Nadaillac and Dr. Maisonneuve of three years before, responding to some objections of the former and offering some support to the latter. Confusion of evolutionism, taken generically, with its atheistic and materialistic versions may have led many Catholics to remain fixists, Guillemet said, but evolutionism also had a spiritualistic version and, so articulated, had a great advantage over fixism. Guillemet had intended to include a section on human ancestry but, according to Boulay, in an article he wrote on the congress for the *Revue de Lille*, the organizers of the congress refused to allow that part of the paper to be printed, "for reasons which Guillemet called *peremptory*."[38]

As in the case of Boulay's paper, Guillemet's was followed by a general discussion of the theory of evolution. Of this discussion, fortunately, we do have a more detailed record.[39] The sense of the participants is perhaps best revealed by the initial response. Giovanni Giovannozzi, a Piarist priest, attempted to articulate what he thought was the correct attitude for Catholics, namely "praise and encouragement for the study of those who, under the supreme magisterium of the teaching Church, devote themselves to research into the rôle which evolution might have among the array of causes which

33 Boulay, "Botanique," 7:128.

34 Boulay, "Botanique," 7:131.

35 Boulay, "Botanique," 7:137.

36 Congrès scientifique de 1894, *Compte rendu*, 7:341.

37 Guillemet was a biologist, a professor at the Séminaire d'Issy, and a lecturer at the Institut catholique de Paris.

38 Boulay, "Les Sciences naturelles," 622 (italics Boulay's).

39 Congrès scientifique de 1894, *Compte rendu*, 8:298–306 ("Procès-Verbaux: Troisième séance").

have brought the physical world to its current state."[40] The report of the session adds that, "The section ratified Fr. Giovannozzi's proposal by its applause."

De Nadaillac replied at length, re-emphasizing the scientific difficulties that, he thought, evolutionism continued to face. He concluded, however, by saying:

> If I am not at all disposed to accept the conclusions of the evolutionist school, neither can I absolutely reject them. A Scottish Jury, in addition to the usual alternatives, has the right, without giving a verdict with respect to the fact itself, of replying "not proven." That is what I think and what I think it should be for everyone who approaches the question without bias and with a desire to arrive at the truth.[41]

✳ ✳ ✳ ✳ ✳

The fourth congress, held in Fribourg (Switzerland) on August 16–20, 1897, was attended by about 700 participants, featured 200 presentations, and received about 3000 subscriptions.[42]

There was only one paper touching on evolution in the section devoted to the natural sciences. Fernand Meunier, of the Belgian Geological Service, presented a brief paper entitled "Les Insectes paléozoïques et mesozoïques," in which he suggests that the results of paleoentomology seemed entirely inconsistent with evolutionism. By that term, he seems to have meant universal common ancestry, for he does acknowledge the possibility of transformations under the influence of the laws of nature, but only with the various *embranchements* that God created.[43]

As at previous congresses, most of the papers on evolution, even papers of a general nature, were presented to the anthropological section, which was, that year, under the presidency of Zahm, whose *Evolution and Dogma* had appeared the year before.

The first paper on evolutionism was that of Charles de Kirwan, whose "De l'Évolution progressive de la connaissance depuis les organismes primaires jusqu'à l'homme" was a response to Albert Gaudry's *Essai de paléontologie philosophique* (1896). Kirwan conceded the generally evolutionary history of the world that had been one of the central theses of Gaudry's book. He took exception, however, to what that book had said on the precise point of *intelligence*. Of that faculty, Kirwan argued, the origins were not the product of any evolutionary development of animal powers as Gaudry had suggested:

> Has Gaudry ever found any trace, any vague rudiment, of the pursuit of the beautiful, the true, and the good—the characteristic of man—in any class of animals? Has he, or has anyone, ever seriously observed in tertiary, quaternary, or contemporary mammals even the least tendency towards research into the truth, pursuit of the beautiful, or love of the good? There is, therefore, some new element, something

---

40 "Procès-Verbaux," 8:298. Giovannozzi was a Piarist priest, and director of the Osservatorio Ximeniano in Florence.

41 "Procès-Verbaux," 8:305.

42 Congrès scientifique de 1897, *Compte rendu*, with attendance figures at 1:3.

43 Meunier, "Insectes," 7:90.

which had not yet appeared in all that progression of beings and their powers which Gaudry so brilliantly laid out.[44]

The next paper was John Zahm's "Évolution et téléologie." His thesis was that that the evolutionary origin of species, which he said was overwhelmingly favored by the evidence, is in no way inconsistent with teleology. By that term, he meant two distinguishable (but in his view closely related) ideas. The first is that there is purposiveness in nature. Its objects and processes would not be sufficiently understood on the basis of a merely mechanical interaction of parts; understanding required reference to the functions and aims of those objects and processes. The second idea was that one could argue from the existence of purposiveness to the existence of a creator, "a power that intelligently adapts means to ends." The fundamental idea, one which he had articulated in *Evolution and Dogma*, is this:

> To suppose that simple brute matter could, by its own motion or by any power inherent in matter as such, have been the sole efficient cause of the evolution of organic from inorganic matter, of the higher from the lower forms of life, of the rational from the irrational creature, is to suppose that a thing can give what it does not possess, that the greater is contained in the less, the superior in the inferior, the whole in a part.[45]

The third paper was from Boulay. His contribution at Brussels had been limited to botany, but for Fribourg he had prepared a paper entitled "De l'Antiquité de l'homme." His central thesis was that man was much older than would be inferred from exclusive reliance on the historical record, but not as old as certain scientists claimed. He was skeptical, for example, of the 240,000 years proposed by Gabriel Mortillet in 1883.[46] Boulay did not commit to an exact age, but seems to have thought that the order of magnitude is tens of thousands of years. With respect to the origin of man, he thought that what he called the theory of descent was inconsistent with the doctrine of original justice.[47] He added: "One is, therefore, led to admit a direct, immediate creation of the first man, soul and body, or, in the case of a mediate creation of the body, a reorganization and an adaptation more difficult to understand than an immediate and complete creation."[48] He concluded his paper with an expression of a practical concern about religious education: "Many catechisms … aimed at older children contain absolute scientific heresies, positive errors, mixed pell-mell with the teaching of the most essential religious truths."[49] This

---

44 Kirwan, "Évolution de la connaissance," 9:94.

45 Zahm, "Teleology," 821–22, or *Evolution and Dogma*, 431–32.

46 Mortillet, *Préhistorique*, 627.

47 Boulay, "Antiquité," 9:63.

48 Boulay, "Antiquité," 9:64.

49 Boulay, "Antiquité," 9:64.

could only lead to scandal and religious doubt. Such works should be rewritten. His concern was endorsed by those taking part in the discussion of his paper.[50]

The fourth paper, by Louis de Casamajor, a priest, emphasized the importance of greater precision about the concept of species in discussions of fixism and evolutionism.[51]

Finally came de Nadaillac, on "Unité de l'espèce humaine prouvée par la similarité des conceptions et des créations de l'homme," read, however, by Fr. Joseph van den Gheyn, since de Nadaillac was unable to attend the conference.

The report of the discussions also includes a reference to "a letter from M. de Nadaillac to Fr. Guibert on the paper which the latter was supposed to read ("L'Homme primitif au point de vue physique, intellectuel et moral") and a letter from Guibert on the relationship between anthropology and apologetics,"[52] both read by Boulay, as vice-president of the section, in the authors' absence; neither was printed in the proceedings.

* * * * *

The last congress, held in Munich on September 24–28, 1900, was attended by about 700 individuals and had about 3500 subscribers. There were about 250 presentations, five of which (four in the philosophy section and a fifth in the section on natural sciences) addressed our topic. The proceedings of the fifth congress includes only abstracts of the contributed papers.[53]

Victor Cathrein read a paper entitled "Der Entwicklungsgedanke in der Philosophie des 19. Jahrhunderts," an exploration of what Cathrein saw as the dubious logical consequences of a comprehensive philosophical evolutionism rather than an exploration of the empirical evidence for the more modest scientific theory and its compatibility with Catholic doctrine.

In a paper on "The Nature of Species," Walter McDonald of Maynooth College argued that, although there is a clear specific difference between man and other living things, it is not clear that there is a similar difference between animals, plants, and inorganic things. In those cases, there is "no conclusive proof" that the differences in their activities cannot also be explained by a difference of structure. Then he considered whether this "throws any light on the problem of . . . their origin."

On the more scientific side were two other papers. Remigius Stölzle, of the Universität Würzburg, delivered a paper on "Kölliker gegen Darwin" in which he summarized the critique offered by one of Darwin's scientific critics. In his paper "Sur la Genèse évolutionnaire des types zoologiques," Jules Boiteux, at one time department head at the École vétérinaire de Lyon, defended common ancestry, but not natural selection: "the building up of the animal kingdom was not achieved by an imperceptible, progressive sequence of changes: it was *principally* done in distinct steps, of which each one was the

---

50 Congrès scientifique de 1897, *Compte rendu*, 9:12–13 ("Procès-Verbaux des Séances").

51 Casamajor taught at the College de Saint-Louis in Perpignan and published his thoughts on this topic the next year in *Hétérogénie, transformisme et Darwinisme*.

52 Congrès scientifique de 1897, *Compte rendu*, 9:21 ("Procès-Verbaux").

53 Congrès scientifique de 1900, *Akten*, 1 and 9.

effect of an act of creation [*coup de création*]." As for man, "we believed that the species is the result of a separate operation, from scratch corporeally as well as spiritually; but even if it should seem to be connected to an animal stock, there would still be an act of creation between the simple animal and … man, since all of nature would have been built up by the express and voluntary actions of the Author of life."[54]

✳ ✳ ✳ ✳ ✳

The Munich Congress of 1900 was the last to be held. Plans were underway to hold a congress again in 1903, perhaps in Rome, but those plans did not come to fruition. One can only speculate as to why they did not. Attendance at the congresses did not appeal to all Catholic scientists. In a decade characterized by a sharp polarization between irreligious secularists and Catholics, some scientists may have preferred to keep their religious beliefs and commitments to themselves. There were also, however, Catholic scientists who made no secret of their Catholicism but who chose not to attend (e.g., Gaudry). Perhaps they shared the judgment of Pierre Duhem, who did attend the Brussels conference and did not like what he saw as the generally low level of scientific knowledge among the participants:

> If we want to have a competent and fruitful discussion about questions in the common domain of metaphysics and the positive sciences, let us begin by studying those sciences for ten or fifteen years, at first in themselves and for themselves, without trying to bring them into agreement with this or that philosophical claim. … Those who think that I exaggerate should not forget that hasty (and scientifically incorrect) solutions to problems on the border between science and philosophy greatly prejudice our cause.[55]

In a letter of January 28, 1903, Msgr. Louis Duchesne wrote to Georg Hertling (so, the would-be organizer of the sixth congress to the organizer of the fifth): "It is time to take a look at whether it is useful to continue these Congresses, the encyclopedic character of which hardly permits serious scientific work and the religious form of which gives rise to some delicate responsibilities. It is also clear that most Catholic scientists continue to remain outside the grouping."[56] And so, as the new century began, the congresses came to an end.

✳ ✳ ✳ ✳ ✳

What do the papers and discussions at the congresses show us about the attitudes of Catholic scientists with respect to evolutionism? First, there was a genuine divergence of opinion on, and a lively discussion about, the evolutionary origin of plant and animal species. The opposition was on scientific (and philosophical), not on theological, grounds.

---

54 Boiteux, "Genèse évolutionnaire," 441–42.

55 Congrès scientifique de 1894, *Compte rendu*, 3:323–24. See also his letter to his mother printed in Hélène Pierre-Duhem, *Savant français*, 157–58.

56 Quoted in Heinrich Finke, *Görres-Gesellschaft*, 18–19.

145

Second, although there were defenses of human exceptionalism (which were recognized as a critique of the idea of a completely evolutionary origin of man), the question of the evolutionary origin of the human body was only occasionally mentioned and was little discussed. Finally, the topic of evolution seems to have figured more prominently in Paris and Brussels than it did in the later congresses in Fribourg and Berlin. Perhaps no one felt that he had anything to add to what had already been said. It cannot, perhaps, be ruled out that official dissatisfaction with Leroy's, Bonomelli's, and Zahm's books muted discussion on the issue at subsequent congresses, even though what had been at issue in those cases had been evolutionary *anthropogenesis* only, not evolution in general.

2. PERIODICAL LITERATURE

The Catholic press continued to treat the evolutionary origin of species as an open question in the last years of the nineteenth century. Its journals opened their pages both to Catholic evolutionists and to their critics.

The Paulists' *Catholic World* published articles from a number of Catholic evolutionist authors. The work of William Seton, discussed above, appeared in its pages. Though he was a particularly frequent author on this topic, his were not the only articles that they published.

In 1892, the magazine published George M. Searle's "Evolution and Darwinism." Searle was an astronomer, a convert, and a Paulist priest, then teaching mathematics at the Catholic University of America. He later served for six years as superior general of his order. As one might expect from a Paulist, he wrote a number of articles for the Catholic public over the course of his life.[57] In an 1884 article, he had said, in passing, that "the original documents on which the theory of evolution . . . is based . . . are far from being sufficient to establish it."[58] The 1892 article, a reflection written in partial response to the publication of George John Romanes's *Darwin and after Darwin* (1892), presented the theory (both evolutionary change and natural selection, as least as they concerned plants and animals) as better established. First, he acknowledged the scope of the theory—it explains the origin of many species. Next, he acknowledges the superficial reasonableness of generalizing the evolutionary origin to all species, though he says without elaboration that, with respect to the human species, "this is going too far."[59] He concluded the article with a warning against thinking that most evolutionists are "actuated by a desire to injure religion or weaken man's faith in it."[60]

---

57 On the occasion of his death, the editors of *The Catholic World* provided a partial bibliography of his popular writings, along with an account of his conversion.

58 Searle, "Supposed Issue," 581.

59 Searle, "Evolution," 227.

60 Searle, "Evolution," 229. See also, 230–31. This irenicism was a theme of two of his earlier articles, both "The Supposed Issue" and "Scientific Dogmatism."

In 1891, the *American Catholic Quarterly Review* published an article by the Sulpician priest Alexis-Jules Orban entitled "Transformism: Lamarck—Darwin." Orban provided a fair review of transformism and the arguments that were being made in its favor, as well as his own continued purely scientific reservations about whether evolutionists had adequately met the challenges posed by the apparent limits on variation, the absence of gradual transitions in the fossil record, etc. On the question of the theological compatibility of evolution and Christian doctrine, however, he was very clear: "The evolutionist theory of creation is not less glorious to God than the idea generally held among believers."[61] Even with respect to the origin of man, he expressed no *theological* concern about evolution of the human body:

> When it is said of the body of man: "And the Lord formed man of the slime of the earth," it is clear that the expression is anthropomorphic, for we cannot imagine God taking a piece of red clay and giving it the shape of a human body. It means simply that the body of the first man was formed of material elements, which, in the absence of the soul, were no more than clay and dust.[62]

He was, of course, an exceptionalist about human *nature*. By way of conclusion, he wrote:

> There is no reason why transformism in general or Darwinism in particular, as long as it is kept within the limits of scientific research and seeks not to undermine truths of another order with which it has no concern, should not be made the subject of free discussion.[63]

> On the other hand, as the theory is far from being demonstrated, and has not succeeded so far in winning anything beyond a very qualified assent from many of the highest representatives of science (it seems to have lost ground in the last years), we may safely conclude that it is, at most, an open question in which each one may take sides according to his own judgment without being exposed to the reproach of remaining behind his time.[64]

In 1892, the *American Ecclesiastical Review* showed a similar openness to the possibility of an evolutionary origin of species. Early that year, Fr. Joseph Pohle, whom the newly-established Catholic University of America had brought from Europe to teach Thomistic philosophy, had given a public lecture at the university on "Darwinism and Theism;" later in the year, the *Review* published a version of the lecture in its pages.[65]

Although not ready to endorse the *truth* of Darwinian evolution even as it applied to plants and animals,[66] he was emphatic about its orthodoxy and even, in its theistic

---

61 Orban, "Transformism," 292.

62 Orban, "Transformism," 294.

63 Orban, "Transformism," 296.

64 Orban, "Transformism," 297.

65 The lecture itself was reported in the *Washington Post*.

66 Pohle refers to "the process of evolution, if ever it took place" at "Darwinism," 173.

versions, its utility to religion. One must, he emphasized, distinguish the philosophical system sometimes associated with Darwinism, which is inconsistent with Catholicism, from the scientific hypothesis which, "provided only that man be not included, body and soul,"[67] is not. The task that he set for himself is this: "to examine whether Darwinism be in its very nature godless, irreligious and atheistical, or whether its principles when carried to their ultimate logical consequences necessarily and irretrievably lead us to the denial of a personal God, and thus land us on the shores of atheism and agnosticism."[68] He argued that it is not atheistical; indeed he went so far as to say that it is "a principle of scholastic theology" that "God . . . should directly create only those things which but for Him could not possibly come into being, while all other things it is more becoming should have been produced by the secondary causes"[69] and "derivative creation may, if need be, be extended even to the first origin of the first organism."[70]

A few years later, Zahm's *Evolution and Dogma* provoked vigorous discussion in the press. Reviews of the book were cited in chapter 5, but the book also gave rise to articles on some of the particular issues raised by Zahm. And so, in 1899, Philip Burton, CM, wrote, and the *Irish Ecclesiastical Record* published, two articles on evolution—"Was St. Augustine an Evolutionist?" and "St. Augustine & the Missing Link." The first elicited a reply from Patrick F. Coakley, OSA, and, of course, a reply to the reply (also entitled "Was St. Augustine an Evolutionist?"), from Burton.

Burton's article was a reply to claims made by Zahm in *Evolution and Dogma* that "it was [Augustine] who first laid down the principles of theistic evolution essentially as they are known today."[71] Burton argued, contrary to Zahm, that St. Augustine was no evolutionist and could only be thought to be so on the basis of equivocations introduced by Catholic evolutionists. Burton concluded his final article in the exchange by re-emphasizing a point that he had made already in the first two articles: "I am not discussing the merits or demerits of evolution;" he was, as he had said, merely attempting to ascertain St. Augustine's views on the matter.[72]

Coakley insisted on a broad scope for the term "evolutionist." He went on to argue for a difference between St. Augustine and the other early Fathers on the meaning of the relevant passages, a difference, he said, that was noticed by St. Albert the Great, by St. Thomas Aquinas, and by many other respected readers of St. Augustine. "Consequently,

---

67 Pohle, "Darwinism," 164. The exclusive phrase is ambiguous. Was it meant to exclude even the evolution of the human body? The article does not resolve the ambiguity. Pohle addressed the topic again, and with no ambiguity, in his *Lehrbuch der Dogmatik*, ten years later. For details, see chapter 10.

68 Pohle, "Darwinism," 162.

69 Pohle, "Darwinism," 172.

70 Pohle, "Darwinism," 169.

71 John A. Zahm, *Evolution and Dogma*, 71.

72 Burton, "Evolutionist," 530. He had previously made the same point in "Missing Link," 451, and in the first "Evolutionist," 106.

in reply to the question: Was St. Augustine an evolutionist, we answer, emphatically, in the affirmative."[73]

The origin of Adam's body, the question that was of greatest theological concern, was not central to what was at issue between Burton and Coakley. Burton said in his first article (published in January) only that "only very few Catholic evolutionists extend [the present evolutionary theory] even to man's body."[74] Leroy's letter withdrawing his book had appeared in *Le Monde* in 1895, not a particularly accessible place perhaps, but satisfactory to the Index. Bonomelli had retracted his chapter about Zahm on the pages of *La Lega Lombarda* in October 1898. In January 1899, at about the time when the second article appeared in the *Record*, the outcome from the Leroy and Bonomelli cases had reached the Anglophone press. Salvatore Brandi, in the context of a critique of Bishop Hedley's somewhat favorable review of Zahm in the pages of the *Dublin Review*, had published the Leroy and Bonomelli retractions in the much more accessible *Civiltà cattolica*. To this, Bishop Hedley had replied in *The Tablet* that "the 'Mivartian' theory [sc., the evolutionary origin of Adam's body] ... can no longer be sustained."[75] That was in time for Burton to quote Hedley on the untenability of Mivartism in a footnote to his reply.[76]

In 1898, the New York *Freeman's Journal [& Catholic Register]* published a seven-article exchange between Limerick seminary professor Michael O'Riordan and William Seton on whether Darwinism had been discredited.

The series began on July 30, when the newspaper published a few paragraphs from O'Riordan's Draper's *"Conflict between Religion and Science,"* emphasizing a distinction between "the teachings of science and the theories and speculations of the scientists." In elaboration, he wrote that "many scientific theories which seemed conclusive when first propounded were found later on to be only hasty conclusions of imperfect knowledge."[77]

He gave by way of one among several examples "the theory of natural selection as introduced by Darwin," about which he went on to say that "to-day Darwinism, in anything like its once fashionable form, is discredited." The next issue of the paper, on August 6, published a reply from Seton to the effect that O'Riordan was mistaken, that "it is very generally accepted as one of the causes of organic evolution, for Darwin himself did not claim that it was the only cause." The issue being precisely whether Darwinism had been "discredited," the exchange centered on the citation of authorities.

The exchange is important primarily as evidence of the willingness of the popular Catholic press to let the exchange run for over four months, but three things about O'Riordan's contributions to the exchange are worthy of note.[78] First, he said that he was

---

73 Coakley, "St. Augustine," 357.

74 Burton, "Missing Link," 451.

75 Hedley, "Physical Science and Faith: To the Editor," 59; Brandi, "Evoluzione e domma," 46–49.

76 Burton, "Missing Link," 457n1.

77 O'Riordan, "Science and the Scientists."

78 The first two on September 3, in O'Riordan, "Science, Scientists, and Dr. Seton"; the last on October 29, in his "Science and Scientists."

"prepared to admit [natural selection] in the Darwinian sense if its truth is established."[79] Second, he cited Mivart, whom he called "one of the greatest living scientists."[80] Third, he explicitly "refrained from declaring what [he] personally h[e]ld about Natural Selection and Evolution."[81] Theological doctrine, he must have thought, is not, at least not decisively, at issue. His concerns might have been, as a comment in his second article suggests, more philosophical.

Both sides of the evolution controversy were explored in the Francophone press, with the Jesuits' *Études religieuses, historiques et littéraires* generally publishing articles critical of evolution[82] and the Dominicans' *Revue thomiste* publishing articles more sympathetic to the new ideas. The *Revue des questions scientifiques* gradually became more open to evolutionary ideas as the century drew to a close.

In 1889, the *Revue des questions scientifiques* had published Charles de Kirwan (ps. Jean d'Estienne) on "Transformisme et la discussion libre," which said that "though [the evolutionary theories of Darwin and others] can, in many respects, be very seductive, in essence, they are only the product of an imagination brought into play by certain similarities, sequences, and analogies,"[83] even while acknowledging that they did not raise theological questions. In general, "it does not follow that [either natural selection or any debatable effects of the struggle for existence] . . . were not the effect of laws established by the Creator in view of the harmony of his work."[84] And as for Scripture, the point of the passages in question is "to teach that God is the sole author and master of everything that exists" and that it does not really matter whether God brought species into being "suddenly and by an interminable series of direct creative acts or gradually and without special interventions but by virtue of a law laid down *ab initio*."[85] In conclusion:

> Transformism, kept within its natural and legitimate limits, is opposed neither to sound philosophy nor to Christianity [*l'esprit chrétien*] and Catholic tradition, nor to Holy Scripture. No, the theory of evolution, stripped of the materialistic hypotheses which are added to it and which it does not imply, cannot be shown to be false *a priori* as opposed to sound philosophy or to matters of faith.[86]

Kirwan emphasized that he was not alone in his views. Some Catholics, he said, citing as examples Sulpicians Lavaud de Lestrade (professor of science at the Clermont-Ferrand seminary) and Fulcran Vigouroux (a Biblicist, later professor at the Institut catholique de Paris), emphasized that God could have created the kind of world the transformists

79 The non-Darwinian sense is one that "every peasant who feeds poultry and pigs or plants cabbages knows and recognizes."

80 Mivart, one might note, gave natural selection only a minor rôle in the evolutionary origin of species.

81 O'Riordan, "Science and Scientists."

82 E.g., Joseph de Bonniot, "Essai philosophique"; and Joseph Brucker, "Jours de la création" and "Origine de l'homme."

83 Kirwan, "Transformisme," 413–14.

84 Kirwan, "Transformisme," 127.

85 Kirwan, "Transformisme," 135.

86 Kirwan, "Transformisme," 142.

described but thought that Scriptures told against his having done so. Others, even some who doubted the truth of transformism for scientific reasons, insisted that the idea was compatible both with Scripture and with Catholic doctrine. Here he cited, among others, Antoine Ducrost (parish priest and professor of geology at the Facultés catholiques de Lyon), Hyacinth de Valroger (an Oratorian priest), and Alexis Arduin.[87]

In 1896, the journal chose the generally evolution-skeptical Marquis de Nadaillac to review John Zahm's *Evolution and Dogma*, as mentioned in chapter 5. That article too was explicitly compatibilist:

> I hasten to add, with Fr. Zahm, that the ideas contain nothing contrary to the funda-mental dogma of our faith. Can one not suppose that the Creator, at the beginning of His work, endowed all the beings that came forth from his hand and created from His will, or at least some of them, with the power of modification? ... That is a solution more satisfactory to the human mind, even more religious, than that of a Creator proceeding by successive creations and modifying His work over the course of time and space the way a sculptor kneads his clay and drafts the contours of the statue that he has in mind.[88]

The next year, the journal published Zahm's Congress lecture on evolution and teleology, but with a prefatory remark to the effect that "the editorial committee leaves entirely to the author the responsibility for the ideas which are defended here and which differ significantly from those which have appeared in this journal many times." After mentioning scholarly differences in the interpretation of relevant passages in SS. Augustine and Thomas, it went on to emphasize the importance of "distinguishing more than just two systems (the literal and the non-literal) in Biblical exegesis and more than just two hypotheses (creationist and evolutionist) in biological philosophy."[89] In 1898, the *Revue* published Kirwan's particularly severe critique of Louis de Casamajor's *Hétérogénie, transformisme et Darwinisme: Problème de l'espèce*, emphasizing both that "the time is long past when one could look to the Genesis narratives for arguments for or against evolution" and that it is everyone's right, having recognized that God is the Creator of everything that exists, either to be "exclusively creationist" or "to conceive and accept some other way in which the Almighty effected and directed the formation of things."[90]

Of particular note in the *Revue thomiste* was an eight-part article by Ambroise Gardeil under the general title "L'Évolutionnisme et les principes de S. Thomas" between 1893 and 1896. Gardeil, a professor at the house of formation for the French Dominican Province from 1884 to 1911 and co-founder of the *Revue thomiste*, was decidedly open to the new evolutionary ideas. His goal in those articles was to disassociate evolutionism, to which he was sympathetic, from materialism, which had "monopolized" it, and to show

---

87 Ducrost, *Évolution*; De Valroger, *Genèse des espèces*; and Arduin, *Religion en face de la science.*

88 Nadaillac, Review, 238–39.

89 Editorial note to Zahm, "Évolution et téléologie," 403–4.

90 Kirwan, Review, 296–97.

that Thomism offered more philosophical advantages to the scientific hypothesis of evolution than did materialism. Indeed he hoped to "show the possibility of a reconciliation, and to discuss the conditions of an alliance, between the theory of evolution and Thomistic philosophy."[91] The evolutionism that he had in mind was not just a transformist account of the origin of species, but a broad history of nature including also the nebular hypothesis (of the origin of solar systems) and an account of the origin of life. In general, "Any rational system of evolution must subscribe to two conditions. First, it must recognize a mover extrinsic to the world which gives each being the *complément d'activité* necessary for it to evolve. Second, it must admit, in its primitive nature, one or several forms which determine the direction of evolution and which are like a seed of the future world."[92] Gardeil proposed, as an alternative to the materialistic versions of evolution incompatible with Catholic doctrine, "an evolution of stable dispositions" [*habitudes*, ἕξεις], adding that "species are, for us, a disposition. Different from dispositions in their substantial character, they resemble them in their formal concept, by their principles and the laws of their genesis." Such a version of evolutionism, he thought, "responds to all the requirements of the Catholic *credo* provided that, in the production of first types, it avoids the intervention of intermediate causes and provided that one remembers that a disposition can be educed instantaneously by an infinitely powerful agent."[93]

3. ENCYCLOPEDIAS

The two encyclopedia articles that appeared in the last decade and a half of the nineteenth century were not only much longer than were those that had been published in earlier encyclopedias, but were much less negative about evolutionary biology. They were, though not evolutionist, explicitly compatibilist.

First off the presses, and perhaps the most important Catholic encyclopedia of the nineteenth century, was the second edition of *Wetzer und Welte's Kirchenlexikon*. It assigned the article on evolution to Georg von Hertling (1843–1919), philosopher and political leader in the (Catholic) Center Party. In the 1880s, when he wrote his article on evolution, he was an extra-ordinary professor at the Universität München. One of his major philosophical interests was the relationship between Aristotelianism and modern science, recognizing the genuine progress of the latter and the fundamental soundness of the former.[94] He had written previously on evolution—the 75-page booklet *Die Hypothese Darwins mit Berücksichtigung neuerer Darstellungen geprüft* (1876). His treatment of the topic in the *Kirchenlexikon*, which ran to twenty columns, appeared ten years later.

---

91 Gardeil, "Évolutionnisme," 1:30–31.

92 Gardeil, "Évolutionnisme," 1:327.

93 Gardeil, "Évolutionnisme," 4:245–46.

94 For more on Hertling, see Hans Weinzierl, *Entwicklungsgeschichte der neueren katholischen Philosophie*, or Adolf Dyroff, "Hertling."

He presented the main points of the theory (on his view, its contributions to taxonomy, to increasing complexity, and to adaptation) in some detail before turning to a discussion of the implications of the theory for a comprehensive worldview.[95] Von Hertling's article included a long scientific critique of the evolution of species, but he was not an incompatibilist: "The importance and range of the theory lie, in the final analysis, exclusively within the boundaries of natural explanation. There is no friendly or hostile relationship to this or that world-view—neither to materialism, nor to theism or pantheism."[96] He acknowledged the existence of a line of thought that is "inclined to make extensive concessions to the hypothesis [viz., the abandonment of the fixity of species, and the acceptance of both common ancestry and natural selection] in order better to defend the fundamental theses of the opposite world-view from the aggressive onslaught of materialism."[97] Those concessions made, he said, the conceders rightly go on to emphasize that none of that puts into any question two other theses—the existence of a first creative cause and the operation of divine action in the world.[98]

Some Christian apologists, he noted, accept even the animal origin of the human body, "into which, according to the Biblical creation story, God breathed the breath of life." In this, von Hertling said, "they go without a doubt too far, and force one to ask whether the whole theory is really so solid as to make such concessions unavoidable." Part of the problem was that natural selection faced special objections when it came to the origin of man:

> If man, including his intellectual [*geistig*] powers, is only the latest product of the process of natural selection, then he would show only what has some connection to the struggle for existence and it would be only his greater guile and curiosity that would distinguish him from the next-highest animal. His disposition for science and art, his consciousness of duty and sense of justice, and finally his religion would have had no claim to preservation in the face of the inexorable process of natural selection.[99]

So, he concluded, "even if someone wanted to retain the theory of evolution for the rest of the organic world, man would still have to be excluded from the evolutionary series; the distinctive properties of his nature require a different origin."

Von Hertling ended his article by commenting that "the theory of evolution is not a system, . . . but a conglomerate of assertions—more or less cohering, more or less susceptible to varying interpretation—about the origins of living things."[100] This pointed, he concluded, to a more general issue: "It makes hopeless the attempt to use the theory

---

95 Hertling, "Entwicklungslehre," 643–51 and 651–61, respectively.

96 Hertling, "Entwicklungslehre," 646.

97 Hertling, "Entwicklungslehre," 651.

98 Hertling, "Entwicklungslehre," 652.

99 Hertling, "Entwicklungslehre," 659.

100 Hertling, "Entwicklungslehre," 661.

of evolution to remove from the world all traces of purposiveness ... and thus leaves the teleological world-view triumphant."[101]

* * * * *

A second Catholic encyclopedia published during this period, the first edition of the *Dictionnaire apologétique de la foi catholique*, appeared in 1889.[102] Shortly after its publication, it was translated into Spanish and Polish. This work contains four articles relevant to our topic, all by Pierre-Julien Hamard (1847–1918), an Oratorian priest with a special interest in the relations between science and the faith.[103] In his *L'Âge de la pierre et l'homme primitif* (1883), he had argued that the succession of cultural ages (stone, bronze and iron) could be placed within the one to three millennia of human history suggested by a traditional interpretation of the Biblical chronology.

Hamard began his article by observing, "The fact that transformism has been received with enthusiasm by materialists and atheists has given rise to a suspicion [*défiance*] of the doctrine among believers. It should not, however, lead them to evaluate the theory unfairly."[104] He said that it "rests entirely on conjecture and hypothesis" and that its success is due to the fact that rationalists need it to avoid miracles in the history of life.[105] Nevertheless, about transformism (even in its Darwinist form) he was emphatically compatibilist:

> The Bible grants equal freedom to transformists and to the defenders of successive creations.... Whenever it is not absolutely explicit, ... anyone who invokes its authority puts at risk both the Bible itself and the religious cause of which it is the support.[106]

> It would be superfluous and irrelevant to say any more about a question which concerns religion only indirectly.... The teaching of evolution is in no way incompatible with Christian dogma.... What aggravates the debate is the making what is, in itself, a purely scientific question, into a question of orthodoxy, as if the evolutionist principle were absolutely irreconcilable and incompatible with religious faith.[107]

He did not, however, extend this to anthropogenesis. His anthropology began with a thesis that he might have held on purely philosophical grounds: "An abyss separates man from animals, an abyss as insuperable as that which separates animals from plants and plants from inorganic beings."[108] To this he added the theological observation that "as for the

---

101 Hertling, "Entwicklungslehre," 659–60.

102 Second and third editions were published in the 1890s, but were little changed from the first edition.

103 For biographical information, see François Laplanche, *Sciences religieuses*, 316.

104 Hamard, "Transformisme," 3090. See also 3089 and 3103–4. See also "Darwinisme," 783, where he acknowledges the judgment of Catholic scientists on these matters.

105 Hamard, "Transformisme," 3088. See also "Darwinisme," 723.

106 Hamard, "Transformisme," 3093.

107 Hamard, "Transformisme," 3103–4.

108 Hamard, "Homme: II. Origine de l'homme," 1412.

creation of Adam and Eve itself, it is presented in quite explicit terms at the beginning of our Holy Books in such a way that it is impossible to exclude the direct intervention of the creator."[109] That is, strictly speaking, compatible with Mivart's view, since the creation of the human soul, without which there would be no first human being, would also count as a "direct intervention." The fact that Hamard's statement is compatible with two competing views might be a sign that the controversy over the origin precisely of the human *body* was not as prominent in 1889 as it was soon to become.

4. TEXTBOOKS

By 1890, an openness even to Mivartism had begun to make its way into Catholic textbooks, both scientific and theological, though not, apparently, without meeting some resistance from the thesis's opponents. Michael Maher, SJ, addressed the issue in his well-regarded neo-Scholastic textbook, *Psychology: Empirical and Rational* (1890). He devoted some five pages to the question of the origin of the human body, writing:

> Whatever real dignity man has got comes from the soul, not from the body; and in any case it is not easy to see that an animal organism, developed to as high a state of perfection as physical laws can bring it, is baser material to form the body of man than the "slime" of the earth. . . . On the grounds of reason alone there can, it seems to us, be no cogent argument framed against such a hypothesis when carefully stated. It is indisputable that God *could* form the body of the first man as easily out of a living organism as out of dead matter. And were the general doctrine of evolution *demonstrated* as regards all other animal organisms there would in the light of pure reason be obviously—from the likeness of the life history of the individual human body to that of the brute—a fair presumption in favor of a similar origin.[110]

The book was reviewed favorably in the Jesuit *Month*. The passage can still be found in the third (1895) edition, but in the fourth (1900), those four pages were gone, replaced only with the brief comment that "the business of the rational psychologist, fortunately for us, is neither the Theology nor the Philosophy of the Evolution hypothesis, as applied to the animal species or even to the body of man: our official concern is with the *Soul*."[111]

＊　＊　＊　＊　＊

In 1894, the French-American Sulpician priest Adolphe Tanquerey (1854–1932), then teaching at St. Mary's Seminary and University in Baltimore, published his *Synopsis theologiae dogmaticae specialis* and addressed, among many other topics, the question of evolution. His verdict on the evolutionary origins of non-human species was that:

---

109 Hamard, "Homme: II. Origine de l'homme," 1397.

110 Maher, *Psychology*, 1st ed., 542–43 (emphasis Maher's); and, more broadly, 540–44.

111 Maher, *Psychology*, 4th ed., 578.

Mitigated Transformism [sc. the version of transformism that, "recognizing the existence of the First Cause, holds that the first living thing (or living things) was created by God, and even that animal life cannot evolve from plant life without the intervention of God; likewise, that God intervened in the formation of the human body"], although at first sight seemingly opposed to the obvious sense of Scripture, is nevertheless not evidently contrary to faith, but can be maintained as a probable hypothesis, until the church has pronounced a judgment on the matter.[112]

About the origin of the first human beings he wrote: "That the body [of our first parents] was immediately created by God is a *sententia communis*, but the contrary opinion cannot be declared heretical."[113] Mivart's view, he went on to say, is philosophically possible, but is scientifically a mere hypothesis. Augustine, in his review of Tanquerey's text (which included explicit mention of the passages just quoted) said:

It is manifest that the author keeps carefully within the limits of the doctrine prescribed or permitted by ecclesiastical authority. Moreover that he is very sober and moderate in his own private judgment upon disputed questions, and not addicted to novel and singular theories. His work is, therefore, eminently safe, is in general a reflex of the common teaching of theologians and even where it advances beyond the beaten path into ground where the road is not yet so accurately surveyed and laid out, he is careful to avoid any temerarious excursions into bypaths and across lots.[114]

* * * * *

Another textbook worth noting was published by another Sulpician, Jean Guibert (1857–1914), who taught the natural sciences at the Séminaire d'Issy (1887–97) and then was appointed superior at the seminary of the Institut catholique de Paris (1897–1912). The first edition of his *Les Origines: Questions d'apologétique* appeared in 1896. A second, much longer, edition was published in 1898 and was translated into English, as well as going through three more editions before a final revision in 1910.[115]

Guibert wrote the first edition of his book with his seminarians in mind: "Speaking to young ecclesiastics, whose mission would be to spread and to defend the faith, I had to clarify those points where free-thought, apparently founded on the Natural Sciences, claims to find Christian revelation wanting."[116] He devoted a chapter each to the origin of the universe, of life, of species, and of man, followed by additional chapters on the unity of the human species, the antiquity of man, and the condition of primitive man.

The origin of life itself, he argued, began by a divine act of creation, but he added, "we do not have as much at stake in this controversy as does materialism. Even if life

---

112 Tanquerey, *Synopsis*, 1:272, with the definition in brackets on page 269.

113 Tanquerey, *Synopsis*, 1:313–14.

114 Hewit, Review of Tanquerey, 620.

115 I will cite here the second edition; the English pagination is almost the same as the French.

116 Guibert, *Origines*, v.

had begun spontaneously, we would still have a scientific demonstration of God as first and supreme cause."[117]

On the question of the origin of species, he saw even less need for direct divine action in the origin of individual species. He focused his discussion on evolutionism in general (transformism and common ancestry), rather than on particular mechanisms of evolutionary change. Catholic scientists, he said, favor an evolutionism that is both spiritualist (recognizing not just physical forces, but God and human souls) and moderate (avoiding four excesses of versions of evolutionism that took the theory beyond Darwin's *Origin* itself).[118] Two of those excesses were the extension of the theory to man as an intelligent and free being (to be discussed below) and to the origin of life. The third was the idea that the theory of evolution somehow validates the idea, of Herbert Spencer and others, that "the same mechanical laws that govern the physical world also govern the intellectual and moral world."[119] The fourth excess was the idea that the evolution of species, if it occurred, could be considered a pure effect of chance, rather than "following a preconceived plan, a law of order … laid down by God."[120] He explicitly rejected the rôle of blind mechanical forces, but did not seem explicitly committed to the kind of internal, orthogenetic drive that had some currency in the 1890s.

A moderate, spiritualistic evolutionism, he thought, not only takes scientific knowledge seriously, but has theological advantages over theories that make God the immediate cause of the formation of new species. First, he cited the Scholastic adage, *Melior est causa causæ, quam causa causati*. He offered an additional consideration:

> With moderate [*modéré*] evolutionism, the long succession of living creatures which existed before man appeared makes sense; even if no one knew them and even if most of them perished without leaving any trace of their existence, still they were indispensable links in that long chain that reaches down to the present day.… Over the course of the thousands of years in which life throve under the fructifying blessing of God, its forms gradually ascended, blossomed, and prepared the natural environment into which man would be placed.[121]

Such a moderate evolutionism is not inconsistent either with Holy Scripture or with Catholic tradition. Can it be reconciled with the Scholastic doctrine that essences, being invariable, cannot be transformed? He thought that it could. First, he pointed out, the transformations in question might better be characterized as a "substitution of essence" (as in the case of oxygen and hydrogen combining to form water), with "the new substantial forms appearing as new morphological states are produced by the environment."[122] In

---

117 Guibert, *Origines*, 87–88.

118 Guibert, *Origines*, 135–45.

119 Guibert, *Origines*, 140.

120 Guibert, *Origines*, 142.

121 Guibert, *Origines*, 147–48.

122 Guibert, *Origines*, 152.

any case, he went on to ask, "is it really certain that there are as many essences as there are species in natural history?" Some Scholastics, he pointed out, think that, within kingdoms, "essential differences between species cannot be demonstrated philosophically" and "distinctive characteristics of species cannot appear to be more than accidental."[123]

Two additional points are worthy of note. First, he devoted relatively little attention to Natural Selection, which he reported "now to be considered as only one of the thousands of factors brought into action by nature for the differentiation of species."[124] Second, on the number of primitive forms, he thought that it was more likely that there were many than that there was only one.[125]

What about man, and in particular the origin of the human body? There are two possibilities, he said—that God fashioned it in all its parts from inorganic elements, or that He raised the most perfect of evolved animals to human dignity. He acknowledged the existence of Catholic evolutionism by reference to a range of authors—Mivart and González, Leroy and Zahm.[126] He reported of Leroy's book that "it had not been put on the *Index*, as several authors had wrongly said, but it had been disapproved to the point of being publicly disavowed by its author and withdrawn from sale. But some correspondence which has been communicated to us shows that the concern about the work was that the author had not taught explicitly enough [*assez formellement*] the immediate creation of the human soul."[127] Zahm's *Evolution and Dogma* was, as the second edition of Guibert's book was published, still under review at the Index, and, such reviews being conducted in secret, Guibert would not have known this. About Zahm's book, he said only that Zahm "claimed that 'the derivative origin of Adam's body, is also quite in harmony with other principles laid down both by the great Bishop of Hippo and the Angel of the Schools.'"[128]

Guibert summarized some of the points that particularly appealed to Catholic evolutionists. For example:

> On this hypothesis there would be a certain grandeur in considering the human body, which is the most perfect of organisms, as the final product of the evolution of living beings, as the final stage, which the Creator had awaited in order to give to nature its intelligent master. One better understands man's physical relations with the rest of nature. One sees all those species united into a harmonious whole. The millions of species which disappeared before the advent of man would have a reason for their existence if one considers them as the elements of a great tree at the summit of which God would harvest a human organism.[129]

---

123 Guibert, *Origines*, 153 and 153n1.

124 Guibert, *Origines*, 156.

125 Guibert, *Origines*, 169–70.

126 See the bibliographies at Guibert, *Origines*, 170–71 and 214.

127 Guibert, *Origines*, 202–3n1.

128 Guibert, *Origines*, 202–3n1, at 203. Although the book underwent revisions between the second and the fifth (1910) edition, the Index's concerns about Zahm's book were never mentioned; Zahm retained a place in the bibliographies cited above.

129 Guibert, *Origines*, 202–3.

Nevertheless, Guibert had his doubts about the fully evolutionary origin of the human body. He reviewed the objections raised by Wallace and by Jean Louis Armand de Quatrefages as well as the paucity of fossil evidence. In the end, he wrote that "science itself inclines us to believe that the Creator, at the moment in which He decided to form man, fashioned, or at least completed, the organism that He was about to vivify by means of a spiritual soul."[130] "In the end, the only conclusion that it is important to establish is that man is the work of God, and not of nature."[131]

The work got a favorable review from one of the day's most prominent secular paleoanthropologists, Marcellin Boule, who called it "a very trustworthy, very strong, and very likeable work."[132]

* * * * *

Finally, though at a lower educational level, William Seton published a high-school textbook entitled *A Glimpse of Organic Life, Past and Present* (1897), which is organized as an introduction to the successive ages of earth history. On Seton's account, the ages, and the living things that characterize them, are not merely successive: the book is explicitly transformist, presenting "an unfolding, a progressive development of organic life from the simple to the complex, from low to higher forms."[133] Indeed, "it was vitally necessary for animated nature to vary as surrounding conditions varied"[134] and that variation is, to a significant extent, caused by natural selection.[135] He did not address the question of the origin of man except in referring to the Reindeer Age (i.e., the Late Paleolithic), about which he said, "by this time God had created Man."[136]

130 Guibert, *Origines*, 213.

131 Guibert, *Origines*, 214.

132 Boule, Review of Guibert, 331.

133 Seton, *Glimpse*, 93.

134 Seton, *Glimpse*, 90.

135 Seton, *Glimpse*, 23–24, 129.

136 Seton, *Glimpse*, 82.

PART III

THE ORIGIN OF THE HUMAN BODY II:
DIVINE FORMATION FROM AN EVOLVED ANIMAL BODY
(1898–1909)

CHAPTER 8

SCIENTISTS &
THEOLOGIANS
(1898–1909)

It is important not to see more anti-evolutionism in the restrictions placed on Leroy and Zahm than there was. First, although Luigi Tripepi had included in his *votum* precisely theological reasons to reject even the evolutionary origin of plants and animals, the concern of the Index (as indicated in Leroy's letter of retraction) seems to have been focused on the application of the theory to the origin of the human body. Second, the actions of the Index did not require as their basis a judgment that Mivartism was heretical. It would be sufficient that, given the knowledge available at the time, it seemed to be rash.

It is therefore important to keep in mind that, until 1929, the fossil evidence for human evolution rested almost entirely on two fragmentary and scientifically controversial finds—Java Man and Piltdown Man. Smithsonian Institution biologist Garrit Miller, however, commented that

> Superficial or prejudiced readers might regard this [paucity of human fossils] . . . as having an important bearing on the subject of organic evolution in general and of man's origin in particular; but no conclusion could be more unjustified. The idea that all existing plants and animals are derived through some process of orderly change from kinds now extinct is supported by an array of facts too great and too

well established to be weakened by doubts cast on alleged family records of any one creature.[1]

Still, that verdict, however much weight it might have for a committed naturalist, would have less weight in the context of the Catholic question of whether the (allegedly) traditional view of the immediate formation of the first human body by God would have to be given up in the face of scientific generalizations to the contrary (any more than would beliefs about what happened at Cana have to be given up in the face of generalizations about wine production).

And so we find some prominent Catholic authors at the beginning of the twentieth century ready to accept the evolutionary origins of plant and animal species but not ready to accept the same for the origin of man. Most Catholics, evolutionist about human origins or not, acknowledged that theological considerations were relevant to resolution of the question.

1. ERICH WASMANN, SJ (1859–1931)

Of all the Catholics who took part in the discussion of evolution and theology, surely one of the two with the most impressive scientific credentials was Erich Wasmann.[2] Wasmann was born in the South Tyrol (then in Austria-Hungary, now in Italy) and entered the Society of Jesus in 1875. He subsequently studied zoology in Vienna and Prague and, over the course of many years of work, made important contributions to the study of ants and termites, his specialty. His work finds a prominent place even in such more recent work as E. O. Wilson's *Insect Societies*, where he is recognized as initiating the study of arthropod symbionts.[3] In addition to his purely scientific work, he wrote on the philosophical implications of his studies of animal behavior (*Instinkt und Intelligenz im Thierreich* and *Vergleichende Studien über das Seelenleben der Ameisen und der höheren Thiere*) and on the theory of evolution as a mixed question involving philosophy and theology as well as science (in the works discussed below).

Wasmann first addressed the question of evolution in 1883–1884, in a study of the peculiar behavior of the hazel leaf-roller.[4] These beetles make cuts in birch leaves in such a way that the wilting leaves curl up into a cone in which the beetle could lay its eggs, a cone which would also protect the larvae when they emerged. "A newborn leafroller," Wasmann pointed out, "solves with surprising universality mechanical-technical problems

---

1 Miller, "Controversy over Human 'Missing Links,'" 446.

2 For a more detailed biography, see Heike Baranzke, "Wasmann." For historical overviews of his work, see Robert J. Richards, *Tragic Sense of Life*, 356–71, and A. J. Lustig, "Ants."

3 Wilson, *Insect Societies*, 390.

4 Wasmann, *Trichterwickler*. The species in question was called *Rhynchites betulae* when Wasmann wrote, but has since been renamed *Byctiscus betulae* (Linnaeus, 1758).

which the human mind was able to understand only after six millennia of research."[5] Such an instinct, he argued, was beyond the reach of Darwinian explanation[6] and must be attributed more directly to the Creator.[7] Wasmann's doubts about the power of natural selection did not, however, prevent him from making a more positive assessment of the explanatory power of common ancestry, at least within limits. Seventeen years later, he published an article entitled "Giebt es tatsächlich Arten, die heute noch in der Stammesentwicklung begriffen sind?," in which he acknowledged that the pattern of morphological variation and geological distribution of various species of the *Dinarda* beetles in which he was interested was just what one would expect if those species originated by descent with modification from a common ancestor. His new views, presented in the Jesuits' *Stimmen aus Maria-Laach* over the course of two years (1901–1903) and then published as *Die moderne Biologie und die Entwicklungstheorie* ("2nd ed.," 1904; 3rd ed., 1906),[8] can be summarized in four points.

First, there was no conflict between an evolutionary account of the origin of species and Catholic doctrine: "It is absolutely not 'dogma' that every species owes its existence to a particular act of creation."[9] He later asked, "What has it to do with theistic conception of the world whether a hare, a rabbit, a horse, and an ass are phylogenetically related or not?"[10] Indeed it is, he said, a general principle of "the Christian account of nature" that "God does not directly intervene in the natural order where He can work through natural causes."[11] Wasmann went on to say that "God's power and wisdom manifest themselves in a much brighter light for having produced the extremely varied morphological and biological relationships just mentioned through natural causes (phylogenetic evolution) than it would have by the direct creation of the respective systematic species."[12] He summarized this point by citing a simile of Fr. Ludwig von Hammerstein, in a line of thought that goes back to the closing sentence of the first edition of *On the Origin of Species*: "A billiard player wants to send a hundred balls to their respective goals. Which will require greater skill—hitting each of the hundred balls separately or hitting one ball and thereby sending the other 99 to their intended goals as well?"[13] All this would be

---

5 Wasmann, *Trichterwickler*, 160.

6 Wasmann, *Trichterwickler*, 19–40.

7 Wasmann, *Trichterwickler*, 166–67.

8 Herder published the 1904 edition as the "second, expanded edition," counting the *Maria-Laach* articles as the first. Two years later, Wasmann published a third, "greatly expanded," edition. The book's ideas are repeated in Wasmann, *Kampf*.

9 Wasmann, *Moderne Biologie*, 167–68n1 (cf. trans., 251n1). Citations here are to the second, 1904, edition unless otherwise noted, with parenthetical reference to the corresponding passage in the English translation of the third edition, when there is one.

10 Wasmann, *Moderne Biologie*, 199 (cf. trans., 299).

11 Wasmann, *Moderne Biologie*, 180 (cf. trans., 274). He cited in support both St. Thomas Aquinas (*Summa contra Gentiles*, III.77) and Francisco Suárez (*De opere sex dierum*, 2.10.12).

12 Wasmann, *Moderne Biologie*, 272 (cf. trans., 429).

13 Hammerstein, *Gottesbeweise und moderner Atheismus*, 6th ed., 150 (quoted at *Moderne Biologie*, 272 (cf. trans., 429)).

easier to see, Wasmann added, if Monists were not so determined to drag evolutionary biology into their philosophical war against the Christian religion.[14]

Second, his own entomological work led Wasmann to accept the common ancestry of certain species: "If we compare the ants and *Paussidae* [a kind of ant-nest beetle] of today with those found in Baltic amber from the Tertiary period, we would not explain the former as new creations, but as true descendants of the Tertiary forms, even though they differ from those earlier forms specifically and sometimes even generically."[15] Wasmann was not, however, willing to extend the idea to the common ancestry of *all* species:

> For the species of a genus, one often has a very great, indeed an almost irrefutable, probability [of a phylogenetic relationship]. In many cases, this is also true for the genera of a family; in some, also for the families of an order; but seldom for the orders of a class. The scientific evidence for the theory of common descent becomes weaker the higher we go in taxonomic rank as well as the deeper we go into the palaeontological history of the earth in the search for common ancestors of the more recently separated systemic taxa.[16]

Developing an idea of Tilmann Pesch, SJ, whose *Institutiones philosophiae naturalis* was one of the new textbooks being published in response to *Aeterni Patris*,[17] he distinguished the *systematic* species identified in ordinary taxonomic practice from *natural* species, a taxonomic group "whose members are phylogenetically related to one another and each of which leads back to the same original ancestral form as their starting point." Systematic species are the products of evolution from the "originally created forms"[18] that lie at the root of natural species. How many distinct natural species there were, he was not prepared to say, insisting only that, although "many hundreds of thousands of systematic species may have to be united into a single phylogenetic tree of a single 'natural species'" "the boundary of natural species becomes more uncertain the higher the systemic rank under consideration and the further we go into the dark prehistory of the organic world of today."[19]

Wasmann distinguished two versions of evolutionary history—a monophyletic theory according to which "all organisms have originated in one primitive cell, or at least there is one phylogenetic tree for all animals and another for all plants," and a polyphyletic theory which assumes several different, independent phylogenetic series both *within* the

---

14 Wasmann, *Moderne Biologie*, 184 (cf. trans., 277–78).

15 Wasmann, *Moderne Biologie*, 182–83 (cf. trans., 276).

16 Wasmann, *Moderne Biologie*, 3rd ed., 299 (trans., 292).

17 It was the second volume of *Philosophia lacensis*. On this point, see Pesch, *Institutiones philosophiae naturalis*, 2nd ed., 2:333–34.

18 Wasmann, *Moderne Biologie*, 197 and, more broadly, 197–201 (cf. trans., 296–302). For more on this, see James R. Hofmann, "Erich Wasmann."

19 Wasmann, *Moderne Biologie*, 3rd ed., 305–6 (cf. trans., 298).

plant and *within* the animal kingdom, each series going back to its own original form as a starting point."[20] His own account of the history of life was of the latter type.

Third, like many of his scientific contemporaries in the first decade of the twentieth century, he thought that Darwin had overemphasized the importance of natural selection. He saw evidence of the insufficiency of natural selection as a mechanism of evolutionary change in the host-guest relationship between some species of ants and the *Lomechusini* beetles, whose larvae the ants raise despite the fact that those beetle larvae prey on the ant larvae, eventually destroying their nests: "Natural selection could never to go so far as to allow the ants themselves to raise their worst enemies as 'guests.' It would always have to give preference to those female Formica in which that disastrous instinct of the worker ants was either absent or was present only in a weaker degree."[21] He gave a greater rôle than did Darwinians, in the transformations that constituted evolution, to interior factors and saltational changes.[22] Still, he did recognize that natural selection played some rôle in evolution: "A goal-directedness internal to the organism [*immanente Zweckmäßigkeit*] and the principle of selection are not related to one another as fire and water, but complement one another."[23]

Fourth, Wasmann, unlike such earlier Catholic evolutionists as Mivart, Leroy, and Zahm, expressed reservations about the descent of man from animals even with respect to the body. Wasmann organized his discussion of this subject around two questions:

1. Is zoology really the only science entitled to form an opinion regarding the origin of man?

2. What actual evidence is supplied by zoology in support of the descent of man from beasts?

The first question he answered in the negative. This was rather a "mixed" question, the answer to which was not purely zoological. Philosophical psychology has something to contribute to the question as well, and so does theology.

The former discipline shows that human beings have an intellectual power that no other animal possesses.[24] Wasmann had made this point in earlier work, in particular in *Instinkt und Intelligenz im Thierreich* and in *Vergleichende Studien*. That fact brings us to a theological conclusion: "Because the soul of man is *intellectual* [*geistig*[25]] and therefore different *essentially*, and not only in degree, from the soul of an animal, it can come to

---

20 Wasmann, *Moderne Biologie*, 3rd ed., 261 (cf. trans., 255–56).

21 Wasmann, *Moderne Biologie*, 230 (cf. trans., 339). The original research was reported in Wasmann, "Giebt es tatsächlich Arten?," 738–40.

22 Wasmann, *Moderne Biologie*, 172–74 and 181n3 (cf. trans., 260–65 and 275n2), among other places. See also his *Entwicklungstheorie und Monismus*, 15: "As one auxiliary factor among other, much more important factors, Darwin's natural selection also has its place, and will continue to do so."

23 Wasmann, *Kampf*, 69 (cf. trans., 106).

24 Wasmann, *Moderne Biologie*, 276 (cf. trans., 433).

25 In these contexts the German word *geistig* hovers uneasily between *spiritual* and *mental* or *intellectual*.

be only by *creation*, and not by *evolution*."[26] More generally, revealed theology also has something to say on the question: "It is a mixed question.... The creation of man is a doctrine of faith.... One can therefore by no means blame the dogmatic theologians and the exegetes if, in view of the obvious meaning of the creation story and with regard to decisions such as those of the Provincial Council of Cologne in 1860, they proceed with great caution and restraint with regard to the doctrine of descent."[27]

So what about the origin of the human body? Wasmann acknowledged two possibilities.[28] First, "God [could have] created the whole man directly, in finished condition, even making use of already existing atoms for the production of the [first] human body." Or second, "In the production of the first man, just as in the production of the rest of nature, God [could have] made use of natural causes to the extent that they were capable of co-operating in the origin of the first man." On the first alternative, God formed the first human body directly from the slime of the earth; on the second, He allowed the natural processes which He had created to do some of the preliminary work.

What was Wasmann's view? When a critic of Wasmann's articles in *Stimmen aus Maria-Laach* (Eugen Rolfes) objected that God's use of "prepared matter" (as opposed to using mere slime) was contrary to Scripture, Wasmann disagreed. This was, he said, a mixed question, one with a scientific as well as a theological side.[29] There are several ways in which natural processes could have played a rôle.

First, there was Mivartism. God could have infused the first human soul into an evolved animal. Wasmann, however, did not think that the prepared matter that God had used was an *animal* body. In that same reply to Rolfes, he denied that he held to "the animal descent of the human body" since "a critical examination of all the aspects of the evidence" showed the idea to be "insufficiently grounded."[30]

What reasons did Wasmann give for his doubts that human beings actually had an animal ancestry? Proponents of evolutionary anthropogenesis were advancing three lines of argument—comparative morphology, embryology, and paleontology—each of which Wasmann thought insufficient to overcome the theological presumption against the thesis.

About comparative morphology, Wasmann acknowledged that "it would not occur to any scientist to deny that these facts [sc., the many resemblances between man and other mammals in the formation of the skeleton, of certain organs and of the nervous system] provide the theory of man's descent from animals with a certain general probability."[31] He denied, however, that that evidence went beyond probability.[32] He was not

---

26 Wasmann, *Moderne Biologie*, 279 (cf. trans., 436).

27 Wasmann, *Moderne Biologie*, 284n1 (cf. trans., 442n1).

28 Wasmann, *Moderne Biologie*, 282 (cf. trans., 439–40).

29 Wasmann, *Moderne Biologie*, 2nd ed., 279–80n2. This footnote was dropped from the third edition.

30 Wasmann, *Moderne Biologie*, 2nd ed., 279–80n2.

31 Wasmann, *Kampf*, 36 (cf. trans., 55).

32 Wasmann, *Moderne Biologie*, 3rd ed., 453 (cf. trans., 445).

ready to rule out the possibility that the resemblances were "convergent phenomena, which, independent of a common ancestry, were brought about by adaptation to similar conditions of life and development.[33]

The embryological evidence was typically presented in terms of Haeckel's biogenetic law—that ontogeny recapitulates phylogeny—which had been controversial from its inception and was not taken as good evidence by Wasmann.

The paleontological evidence for human evolution was, in the first decade of the twentieth century, as I said above, still weak. Neanderthalers were too close to modern man; the nature of Java Man had not yet been established.[34]

He did not find, in the case of human beings, the kind of adaptive radiation that had convinced him of the evolutionary origins of the various species of the insects that were his specialty. This answered the second of the two questions. Combined with the theological caution that he mentioned in passages cited above, it made him unwilling to go as far as Mivart and others had done at the end of the previous century.

What alternative to animal ancestry could he have had in mind?

> Someone could assume as a possible starting point for the origin of the human body a *primordial cell* created by God and say something like this: The oldest ancestors of man were organisms which first possessed *a simple cellular life*. Later, with a differentiation of organic life, a nervous system was formed and the emergence of a sensitive soul, and they became *animals*. That soul, through gradual perfection of the organism (namely, further development of the brain) finally prepared a human body, suitable for being informed by an intellectual [*geistig*] soul. Man, to be sure, first *became man*, even in this scenario, only at the moment of the creation of the intellectual soul. In the earlier stages he was nevertheless not simply a plant or an animal, but already a *man in the process of becoming* [*ein im Werden begriffener Mensch*]. The whole evolution of man would therefore have happened *within one and the same natural species, "man."*[35]

This does, Wasmann pointed out, give natural processes a greater rôle in the formation of the first human body than does the alternative of direct formation by God. He compared it to the idea of *some* Thomistic embryologists of the succession of vegetative, sensitive, and intellectual being in human ontogenesis. Without endorsing that idea, he pointed to its relevance with the remark that "if such succession of life forms in in the course of the individual [ontogenetic, i.e., embryological] development [*Entwicklung*] does not preclude the later infusion of a rational soul, then there should be no contradiction in assuming the hypothetical phylogenetic evolution [*Entwicklung*] of the body of man."[36]

---

33 Wasmann, *Moderne Biologie*, 291 (cf. trans., 456).

34 See, for example, Hugo Obermaier, *Der Mensch der Vorzeit*, 370–72, or Marcellin Boule, *Hommes fossiles*, 93–110. Wasmann's account is in *Moderne Biologie*, 296–304 (cf. trans., 464–80).

35 Wasmann, *Moderne Biologie*, 283 (cf. trans., 441). Wasmann also mentioned this in his "Vorbemerkungen," 128–29.

36 Wasmann, *Moderne Biologie*, 282–83 (cf. trans., 441).

Wasmann's imagined scenario does not seem to do anything to explain the similarities between human and animal bodies, but he did emphasize that the scenario had only "purely speculative importance," a "theoretical possibility," not a "factual reality."[37]

He did not mention Cardinal González's own speculative scenario, which was to be promoted a few years later by Juan González Arintero (to be discussed below).

Wasmann's evaluation of the possibility of God having used prepared matter in the formation of the first human body varied (at least in its formulation) over the course of the decade.

In *Stimmen aus Maria-Laach* (1903), he wrote that, from a theological standpoint, the question "could calmly be left open [*ruhig offen lassen*]."[38] In the slightly expanded version of the article that became chapter 10 of the second edition of *Moderne Biologie* (1904), Wasmann changed *ruhig offen lassen* to *ruhig annehmen* [calmly be accepted].[39] That may sound like an endorsement of Mivartism, but that it is no more than an assertion of compatibilism[40] is shown by two facts. The first is a clarification that he sent to Agostino Gemelli, his Italian translator: "The passage speaks only of the *possibility*, not of the *factuality*, of a formation of the human body from already prepared matter."[41] The second is the fact that he ended his discussion of the topic with the remark that "*science knows nothing about the origin of man*."[42]

Two years later, in the third edition, he revised the sentence again. He clarified the imprecise verb by adding the phrase "as *possible*" [*annehmen als möglich*][43] and changed its object (the possibility) from "God used" to "God could have used." He also added, in a long footnote, that

> A great majority of theologians hold that the matter which God united with the intellectual soul in the creation of man should be regarded as inorganic matter. Since the creation of man is, in the first place, a point of doctrine, one cannot blame the theologians who, keeping in mind the constant tradition and the statements of the ordinary magisterium, hold on to the literal interpretation of the relevant texts until there is solid evidence that the text should be understood differently.[44]

These revisions were, in part at least, a response to concerns expressed by the Jesuit curia in Rome (discussed in chapter 9).

✳ ✳ ✳ ✳ ✳

---

37 Wasmann, *Moderne Biologie*, 283 (trans., 442).

38 Wasmann, "Anwendung der Deszendenztheorie auf den Menschen," 392.

39 Wasmann, *Moderne Biologie*, 279.

40 One could, to be sure, think that an idea was *compatible* with Catholic doctrine without thinking that its truth was an *open question*, as attention to the distinction between the censures of rashness and heresy shows (see Appendix II.B).

41 Wasmann, "Vorbemerkungen," 128–29. Wasmann's clarification was also published in a foreword to *Biologia moderna*, xi.

42 Wasmann, *Moderne Biologie*, 304 (trans., 480) (emphasis Wasmann's).

43 Wasmann, *Moderne Biologie*, 3rd ed., 444, emphasis Wasmann's (trans., 436).

44 Wasmann, *Moderne Biologie*, 3rd ed., 444n2 (trans., 437n1).

All three editions appealed to St. Augustine about the possibility of prepared matter.[45] In the first, he added that St. Augustine "shows us by his example that Catholics need not be too anxious about this."[46] In the second, he said that "St. Augustine seems to have hypothesized [prepared matter]."[47] He added in that second edition, by way of clarification:

> The main ideas of St. Augustine seem to be the following: The difference between the mode of creation of man and that of the animal world is primarily in the fact that God gave man an intellectual [*geistig*] soul. The human body, by contrast, was derived from the *rationes seminales* by primordial causes, just as were those of other corporeal beings. How far the primordial causes and the *rationes seminales* went in preparing the matter, however, St. Augustine does not say. He does not go further into the question of whence the matter with which God united the soul came, saying only, "it is superfluous to ask from what it was that God made the human body."[48]

The third edition dropped the claim about what St. Augustine had hypothesized, but kept the summary of St. Augustine's views just quoted.

Wasmann's conclusion was that "the mental [*geistig*] evolution of man from out of the animal kingdom is unacceptable, and his bodily descent from brute ancestors presents, from the scientific standpoint, difficulties that have hitherto not been solved."[49] Although Wasmann intended his work to be primarily scientific, rather than theological, he added, in the third edition, the remark that "the Church has not given a definitive answer to the question of the composition of the matter which God used in the creation of the first man. In any case the point of the Biblical creation story was not to provide us with a scientific account of the origin of man."[50] He also quoted from Leo XIII's then-recent encyclical *Providentissimus Deus*, which he read as saying that "natural science remains perfectly free to investigate the origin of man."[51]

Wasmann's *Moderne Biologie* evoked a fierce response from German Monists, and in particular from Ernst Haeckel.[52] Haeckel attacked Wasmann's ideas in a series of lectures delivered in Jena and Wasmann was invited to reply in three public lectures delivered in Berlin on February 13–17, 1907, with responses from his critics scheduled for the following evening. Wasmann's lectures—"The Theory of Evolution as Scientific Hypothesis and Theory," "Theistic and Atheistic Evolutionary Theory: Evolutionary

---

45 He cited in particular Augustine, *De Genesi ad litteram*, 6.11–12 and 15.

46 Wasmann, "Anwendung," 392.

47 Wasmann, *Moderne Biologie*, 279–80. This remark, I think, further justifies taking *annehmen* to mean "hypothesize," rather than "accept" or "believe"; otherwise it would not quite correspond to St. Augustine's view.

48 *Moderne Biologie*, 280–81n2 (cf. trans., 438–39n2). The embedded quotation is from *De Genesi contra Manichaeos*, 2.7.9.

49 Wasmann, *Moderne Biologie*, 3rd ed., vii (trans., viii).

50 Wasmann, *Moderne Biologie*, 3rd ed., 446 (trans., 438).

51 Wasmann, *Moderne Biologie*, 3rd ed., 447, note continued from 446n1 (trans., 439n continued from 437n1).

52 Wasmann outlined this in the short essay entitled "A Few Words to My Critics," which he included in the third edition of his *Moderne Biologie*, ix–xxi (trans., xi–xxiii).

Theory and Darwinism," and "The Application of the Theory of Descent to Man"—(and Wasmann's summary of, and comments on, the discussion that followed) were published later that year as *Der Kampf um das Entwicklungsproblem in Berlin*, with an English translation following two years later.[53]

Catholic reaction to the two books was generally favorable. The American Paulist monthly *Catholic World* said of the *Berlin Discussion* that it "may well be accepted as the most authoritative non-official definition of the Catholic position to-day regarding the question."[54] Favorable reviews of *Moderne Biologie* appeared in the American *Fortnightly Review*, the Spanish *Razón y Fe*, and the Belgian *Revue des questions scientifiques*.[55] Wasmann was invited, at about the same time, to write part of the article on evolution for the American *Catholic Encyclopedia*, work on which began only in 1905. When the *American Catholic Quarterly Review* published a long, critical review of *The Berlin Discussion* by Fr. Simon Fitzsimons, the *Catholic Fortnightly Review* allowed Wasmann space for an extended response. About that exchange, Notre Dame's *Ave Maria*, a popular magazine with very broad circulation, reported that "Father Wasmann puts his opponent to utter and ignominious rout."[56]

The reaction at the Jesuit Curia to Wasmann's ideas about the applicability of the theory of the evolution to the human body were decidedly less favorable and will be discussed in chapter 9. Wasmann's Jesuit colleague Karl Frank mentioned in print that Wasmann would be publishing a fourth edition,[57] but, as a result of the concerns of his superiors, Wasmann decided in the end not to do so.

The concerns of the Jesuit Curia, and Wasmann's willingness to act in accordance with them, did not put an end either to his scientific work or to his work on the relation between science and theology. On the former front, he continued to publish on myrmecology (*Das Gesellschaftsleben der Ameisen*; *Die Gastpflege der Ameisen*; *Die Ameisen, die Termiten und ihre Gäste*; and *Ameisenmimikry*) and on the difference between human and animal psychology (*Menschen- und Tierseele*). On the latter, he kept up his attacks on Haeckel's monism and his defense (in public lectures) of evolutionary biology (e.g., in his *Innsbrucker Vorträge*), at least as it applied to plants and animals. He also published two books on philosophy and religion (e.g., *Der christliche Monismus*), though without any discussion of evolutionary biology.

When the Pontifical Biblical Commission published its decree on the first chapters of *Genesis* (in 1909),[58] Wasmann wrote out, as a guide for pastors on how to address questions that might be posed by scientifically educated Catholics, his own thoughts on the document's content and its bindingness.[59]

---

53 The full text of the critics' remarks was published by Ludwig Plate in *Ultramontane Weltanschauung*.

54 *Catholic World*, Review of *The Berlin Discussion*, 116.

55 The authors were H. M. (probably Hermann Muckermann, SJ), J. Pujuila, and Robert de Sinéty, SJ.

56 *Ave Maria*, "With Authors and Publishers," 351.

57 Karl Frank, *Entwicklungstheorie im Lichte der Tatsachen*, v (trans., vi).

58 For details, see chapter 9.

59 Wasmann, "Bemerkungen," 123n1.

With respect to content, he emphasized the Commission's own declaration (in Dubium 7) that "the inspired author did not intend to instruct us about the details of the process of creation scientifically [*scientificio more*] but rather popularly [*vulgari more*], and that therefore we do not have to apply the exactness of scientific language [*scientifici sermonis proprietas*] as a standard to that account."[60] That covers not only the evolutionary explanation of plants and animals, but anthropology as well:

> God revealed nothing in Holy Scripture about the scientific aspect of the origin of man. Science, for its part, offers us only more or less probable hypotheses, which can never lead us to certain scientific knowledge about these processes, even though the general probability of a phylogenetic connection of the human body to the higher animals must in no way be underestimated.[61]

He added a comment about the exact wording of the key passage on anthropogenesis:

> It says "the distinctive creation of man" (*peculiaris creatio hominis*), not "the formation of Adam from the slime of the earth" and not even "the distinctive creation of the human body." ... The Biblical Commission surely did not express itself here so carefully without a reason....

> There would also be a distinctive creation of man if, at the creation of man, God had used organized matter [i.e., a living being], which He had predisposed [to exercise human powers] by means of the natural laws of evolution.[62]

How authoritative is the decree? On the one hand, it is not irreformable; on the other, it requires not merely external, but also internal submission. The assent that it requires has, however, two limitations. First, one is bound only "until the magisterium decides otherwise." Second, experts in the subject matter who have good reason to think that the decree is in error are bound only to obedient silence (*silentium obsequiosum*). Such experts are also permitted, of course, to propose reforms of the decree to the competent authorities.[63]

Wasmann died in 1931.

2. AGOSTINO GEMELLI, OFM (1878–1959)

Agostino Gemelli, whom historian D. A. Binchy called "the outstanding figure in the intellectual life of Catholic Italy,"[64] was a physician by academic training, a Franciscan priest, and founder of the Università cattolica del Sacro Cuore in Milan.

---

60 Wasmann, "Bemerkungen," ¶7.

61 Wasmann, "Bemerkungen," ¶10.

62 Wasmann, "Bemerkungen," ¶11–12.

63 Wasmann, "Bemerkungen," ¶1–3.

64 Binchy, *Church and State in Fascist Italy*, 482.

Born in Milan in 1878 and raised in an anti-clerical family, he took his degree in medicine at Pavia in 1902 and showed great promise in that field. Indeed he did research work under Camillo Golgi as that scientist was doing the work for which he won (in 1906) the Nobel Prize. His intellectual interests during his student years were broad and he managed to exemplify the adage that students entered the university as republicans and left as socialists. He underwent another intellectual conversion during his year of mandatory military service (1902–1903). A year of intense discussion with some Catholic intellectuals with whom he served—in particular his pre-service friend Ludovico Necchi, but also others—led Gemelli not only to an intellectual stance of committed Catholicism but to the discernment of a vocation to religious life. Immediately on his release from military service, he joined the Franciscans. The story of his family's reaction to this—the attempted kidnapping, the petition to have him declared legally insane—will have to be left to other authors.[65] So will his rôle in the establishment of the Università del Sacro Cuore in 1921 and his academic work in the field of psychology, which continued over many years. Here I will take up only his rôle in the controversies associated with the emergence of Catholic evolutionism. This began when, after his year-long novitiate, his superior allowed him to return to scientific research. He not only completed a number of papers in physiology and histology, but began to address the matter of evolutionary biology.

He translated Wasmann's *Moderne Biologie* into Italian, but in that task did more than merely make a translation. He added his own thoughts on the question in a hundred-page introduction and added more comments in (signed) footnotes. Wasmann later wrote, "The Italian edition, for which Gemelli alone is responsible, is in many respects a totally new work," though he hoped that it would receive a friendly reception.[66]

Gemelli's introduction to his translation of Wasmann's *Moderne Biologie* began with his assessment of various theories of evolution (including his critique of monism) and ended with a systematic review of central themes (chance and finality, monophyletism, the nature of species, the causes of evolutionary processes). Although he accepted a transformist account of the origin of some (namely "systematic") species, he rejected the central components of Darwinian evolutionism.

First, the original species, of which there were more than one, "were immediately formed by the same number of acts of creation."[67] These "natural species" were immutable in the sense that all of their descendants would be members of that same natural species. Nevertheless, *within* the species there was a differentiation into various systematic species. His was, therefore, a limited transformism.

Second, "the causes of this polyphyletic development are both internal factors, placed by the Creator Himself in the species which He had created, and external factors."[68] He

---

65 For example, Maria Sticco, *Father Gemelli*. See also Giorgio Cosmacini, *Gemelli*.

66 Wasmann, *Moderne Biologie*, 3rd ed., vii–viii (trans., viii).

67 Gemelli, "Problema dell'origine delle specie," xiii–cvii.

68 Gemelli, "Problema," civ. Gemelli preferred the term *polifilogenesi*.

minimized the relevance of natural selection[69] and emphasized that "in nature everything speaks in favor of teleological discourse: there is in it something that constantly shows a harmony and, what is more significant, a harmony coordinated to an end."[70] That finalism led in turn to a recognition of a first, intelligent, cause.[71]

Finally, "with regard to the origin of man, it is necessary to recognize, even from the scientific point of view, and even just for the body, that it was the result of an immediate act of creation."[72]

His (and Wasmann's) version of the theory of evolution, he said, "does not contradict any of the statements revealed to us by Sacred Scripture and taught to us by dogma. In showing the beauty of the Christian cosmogony narrated in the Genesis of Moses, it exalts the wisdom and omnipotence of the Creator."[73]

Gemelli also wrote two series of articles on the topic for *La Scuola cattolica*. Gemelli there described himself as a "tepid evolutionist"—"tepid,' but in the sense of giving hypotheses their due value, but for all that no less an evolutionist and no less averse to the old formulae accepted by those who, even today, insist on the absolute fixity of organic species."[74] The scientific method, he thought, yielded a polyphyletic evolutionism which, he thought "lives up to the need for scientific research [while] allowing us to move easily within the limits set down by dogma and sound philosophy."[75]

In the 1906 articles, Gemelli said that the theory did not extend to the origin of man: "The natural sciences cannot tell us anything about the origin of man's body. So, they are forced, negatively, to recognize that it is necessary to posit an immediate act of creation in order to explain its origin."[76] This topic, he said, he would leave for another series of articles, but when he published his "Teorie recenti sull'origine dell'uomo" in *Rassegna nazionale* in 1909 he seems to have modified his views. The question of the origin of man, he there wrote, would be easy to resolve on the basis of theology, but he would limit himself to some philosophical considerations. Following Wasmann, he said, the most important of those is, of course, that "zoology and its auxiliary sciences cannot determine the exact nature of man's intellectual (*spirituale*) life":

> From that it follows that zoology is not competent to determine the phylogenetic evolution of man *as such*. Its competence is limited to the part of the question which concerns the body and even there it cannot make a definitive determination since the soul and body of man are so connected as to form a substantial whole. So, the question of the derivation of man is a mixed one in the solution of which psychology

---

69 Gemelli, "Problema," xxx.

70 Gemelli, "Problema," lix.

71 Gemelli, "Problema," lx.

72 Gemelli, "Problema," cv.

73 Gemelli, "Problema," civ.

74 Gemelli, "Conflitto di tendenze," 56.

75 Gemelli, "Conflitto di tendenze," 56.

76 Gemelli, "Nuovo indirizzo," 545.

has the most important part.... Zoology can make a determination only on the lower part of man: the body.[77]

Evolution could not even be fully responsible for the origin of the human body:

Give it all the capacity for progress that you want, you would never be able to give it the potential for receiving an intellectual [*spirituale*] soul.... Evolution could, to be sure, prepare a human body, but on what it produced, the Creator would still have to act in order to adapt it and make it able to be informed by an intellectual soul. There is thus, between the end-point of evolution and the organism which receives from God the breath of life, a difference, a hiatus, of which evolution cannot account to us.[78]

The Mivartist alternative fails to appreciate the *unity* of the body-soul composite that is man; it sees the relation only like that of a pilot to his ship.

3. JACQUES-JOSEPH LAMINNE (1864–1924)

Jacques Laminne, born in Aerschot (Belgium) on May 18, 1864, completed his doctoral studies in philosophy and theology under Camillo Mazzella at the Gregorian University in Rome before returning to Belgium to study physics at the Université catholique de Louvain. He was ordained a priest in 1886 and, after several years of teaching elsewhere, in 1904 joined the faculty of Louvain's Institut supérieur de philosophie.[79]

That Institute had been established by Désiré Joseph Mercier in 1889, with the explicit support of Pope Leo XIII, for the purpose of contributing to the implementation of the Neo-Scholastic revival proposed in *Aeterni patris* (1879). Mercier placed particular emphasis on the articulation of a Catholic philosophical response to developments in the natural sciences. That emphasis is responsible for the presence on the Louvain faculty of three priests with a particular interest in the question of evolution—theologian Jacques Laminne, geneticist Victor Grégoire, and geologist Henry de Dorlodot.

Laminne was generally conservative in his theological views, though not on the topic of evolution. He published a number of books and articles on the topic over the course of the first decade of the twentieth century and covered it in his lectures when he taught the course "De Deo creante et elevante" at Louvain.

We can divide his work on evolution into two parts. The first, more theological, part began with an article on the Hexaemeron, in which he rejected several interpretive approaches popular in his day—the concordist attempt to align the six days of the text with particular successive geological periods, Bishop William Clifford's suggestion that

---

77 Gemelli, "Teorie recenti," 491.

78 Gemelli, "Teorie recenti," 493–94.

79 For more on Laminne, see A. Collard, "Laminne"; Joseph Schryrgens, "Laminne"; or de Bont, "'Peut-être pas bien vu à Rome.'"

the text is a liturgical poem, and von Hummelauer's idea that it was a vision revealed to Adam by God. Instead, Laminne proposed that it be understood in light of its Mesopotamian cultural background. Laminne suggested that "Moses proposed to bring analogous popular stories over into his work, not with the intention of attributing to them the status of an exact historical narrative, but because they seemed to him suitable for teaching the people very important religious truths."[80] And later:

> The puerile and confused mythology of Chaldea was replaced by a grand and confident monotheism. These important divergences will not prevent us from admitting a certain kinship between the two accounts which is impossible to specify and which will incline us not to consider the Genesis narrative as history properly so called, but rather as a popular account intended to represent granules of [theological] truths in concrete form.[81]

In a later article, entitled "L'Idée d'évolution chez Saint Augustin," he presented St. Augustine as laying the foundations of Catholic evolutionism, not in the sense of having anticipated any of the details of modern evolutionary theory, but of having endorsed its essential ideas: a simultaneous creation of the world followed by "the origin of material things by the forces inherent in matter," and "the progressive deployment of a natural order implicitly contained in the original state of affairs."[82]

Finally, in a lecture delivered at Liège on December 2, 1908, (*La Situation actuelle du catholicisme en face de la science*) he discussed his view of evolution in the context of a larger account of Catholicism and science. In that lecture, he made four points.

The first was that "the idea of evolution, well understood and within necessary limits, is not at all incompatible with Catholic doctrine."[83] It can be extended from biology to the other natural sciences; the problem arises only when it crosses over into metaphysics, claiming to explain the origin of matter, of life, or of intelligence.

A second was that "the Universe did not leave the hands of the Creator just as we see it now; the idea that it did so is not one that the Faith requires us to accept."[84] The idea is found in St. Gregory of Nyssa and in St. Augustine.

A third was that the idea of evolution fits particularly nicely together with the idea that the universe had a beginning in time, an idea that, if not necessary to the idea of creation itself, is at least for other reasons a matter of Catholic doctrine.

Fourth, a point more Spencerian than Darwinian, "the idea of evolution implies the idea of a perfection towards which the Universe tends and which, consequently, if we do not want to renounce the principle of causality, must be at its origin."[85]

---

80 Laminne, "Que nous enseigne le Ier chapitre de la Genèse?," 339.

81 Laminne, "Que nous enseigne le Ier chapitre de la Genèse?," 341.

82 Laminne, "Saint Augustin," 506.

83 Laminne, *Situation actuelle*, 26; see also 24–25.

84 Laminne, *Situation actuelle*, 25.

85 Laminne, *Situation actuelle*, 28.

✳ ✳ ✳ ✳ ✳

At the same time that he was addressing more strictly theological questions about the compatibility of evolutionism and Catholic thought, he devoted some attention to the philosophical versions of evolutionism then being advanced by Haeckel, Spencer, and Bergson.

His critique of Haeckel[86] is of less importance to our story than is his much more detailed, and more sympathetic, book on Spencer. Spencer had died in 1903 and the next year the Moral and Political Science Section of the Académie royale de Belgique had included among the five topics posed for its annual prize competition for 1907, "a critical study of Spencer's *First Principles*, taking into account the applications that he had made of it in his other works."[87] Laminne took the occasion to articulate his thoughts on Spencer's work and submitted a manuscript of nearly 800 pages. The Académie's procedure was to invite three reviewers to prepare a report on each submission before putting the award to a vote of the larger body.

The reviewers whom they selected to report on Laminne's work—philosopher and vicar-general of the diocese of Liège Georges Monchamp, sociologist Gillaume De Greef, and Archbishop Désiré Mercier—differed in their appraisal of the work. Monchamp liked it and voted for awarding it the prize. De Greef, however, did not and wrote an extremely harsh critique. Laminne, he complained, "was preoccupied with leaving the door open not only to hypotheses, which would be legitimate as long as they are subject to scientific verification, but also to the purely dialectical and syllogistic procedures of theology and metaphysics." He concluded by remarking that "the memoir does not contain any original observations, not even any original errors. All of his criticisms have appeared before and were better expressed elsewhere."[88] Mercier expressed some reservations—Laminne was right to address philosophical questions and had made some original contributions to the discussion of Spencer's work, but could have done better at clarifying the guiding ideas of Spencer's system.[89] In the end, however, Mercier also recommended granting Laminne the prize. Nevertheless, after a vote, the Académie decided not to do so.

Laminne published his submission as a book that same year. The book began with an analogy: Spencer's system was like a building with a well-designed superstructure but with flawed, but reparable, foundations.[90] One could reject the foundations laid in Part I of Spencer's *First Principles* ("The Unknowable") without having to give up the guiding idea (*l'idée maîtresse*), the idea of evolution, articulated in Part II ("The Knowable") and then in *The Philosophy of Biology* and elsewhere. Laminne rejected "from one end to the other" the ideas contained in Part I of *First Principles*. Those he regarded as merely a

---

86 Made first in short articles in *La Revue apologétique* (1903–1904)—"Cosmologie matérialiste," "Psychologie matérialiste," and "Morale matérialiste"—and in two pamphlets of about sixty pages each (both in 1905)—*L'Homme d'après Haeckel* and *L'Univers d'après Haeckel*.

87 Académie royale de Belgique, "Programme du concours," 195.

88 De Greef, "Rapport," 220 and 261.

89 Mercier, "Rapport," 264.

90 Laminne, *Évolution*, 5–6.

"disguised form of skepticism."[91] Relevant to our topic, however, is only his appraisal of what Spencer had to say (in Part II and elsewhere) about biological species.

First, Spencer had attempted to describe a process that he applied to all corporeal existence:

> The law of Evolution has been thus far contemplated as holding true of each order of existences, considered as a separate order. . . . While we think of Evolution as divided into astronomic, geologic, biologic, psychologic, sociologic, &c. it may seem to some extent a coincidence that the same law of metamorphosis holds throughout all its divisions. But when we recognize these divisions as mere conventional groupings, made to facilitate the arrangement and acquisition of knowledge—when we regard the different existences with which they severally deal as component parts of one Cosmos; we see at once that there are not several kinds of Evolution having certain traits in common, but one Evolution going on everywhere after the same manner. . . . Evolution becomes not one in principle only, but one in fact. There are not many metamorphoses similarly carried on; but there is a single metamorphosis universally progressing, wherever the reverse metamorphosis has not set in.[92]

In this idea of a "Universe carrying out a single evolution of which all particular [evolutions] are only episodes" (Laminne's characterization),[93] however much Spencer's system was "a body of doctrines of great scope and largely supported by the facts," Laminne thought that Spencer had gone too far, presenting evolution as more unified and more continuous than can be justified—"an aggregate of evolutions does not necessarily make up an evolutionary whole." With respect to unity, he went on to say:

> It is easy to see that the evolution of the earth and that, for example, of living beings are two entirely distinct processes and that one cannot reasonably think of the latter as being a part of the former.
>
> That the earth has become more heterogeneous in virtue of the differentiation of a society that lives on its surface in no way implies that that differentiation had anything to do with the evolution of the globe itself.[94]

Or, with a particular focus on continuity and living things:

> Evolution, in which each phase has its reason for being in the preceding phase, cannot explain the origin of radically new things. If, as we have admitted, organic life is not reducible to physical-chemical forces, then the evolution of inorganic bodies is incapable of producing life. In the same way, since sensation [*sensibilité*]

---

91 Laminne, *Évolution*, 472.

92 Spencer, *First Principles*, 6th ed. (1900), §188. The passage is quoted in part in Laminne, *Évolution*, 443–44.

93 Laminne, *Évolution*, 446. Laminne had written "*existences* particulières" (my italics) here, but he had referred to "évolutions particulières" on pages 443 and 444 and did so again on pages 447 and 459; I have not been able to find any other occurrence of the phrase "existences particulières" in the book. I think that this must be a typographical error and have made the correction, in brackets, in the translation above.

94 Laminne, *Évolution*, 445. The qualification "not necessarily" is important. Earlier Laminne had said that "the evolution of the entire realm of living things *is* the sum of particular evolutions" (*Évolution*, 352, emphasis mine).

obviously cannot be reduced to the displacement of atoms, an evolution that does not include anything more than that cannot explain the origin of sensory life. And since sensory life is limited to the concrete knowledge of material things and to the movements that that knowledge determines, the evolution of sense powers cannot be the sufficient reason for the appearance of general ideas, of morality [*conscience*], or of freedom.[95]

Second is the matter of the cause of evolutionary change. Spencer had placed heavy emphasis on the inheritance of acquired characteristics. Laminne pointed out that the operation of such a process was "far from being established,"[96] though he also had reservations about the sufficiency of natural selection, then being emphasized by August Weismann.[97] Laminne suggested a rôle for internal spontaneous factors, a cause distinct both from Spencer's acquired characteristics and from Weismann's selection. At a minimum, it would supplement selection (narrowly understood): "Let us note with Hugo De Vries that selection does not produce forms, but only conserves some, at the expense of others, and so is of no use in explaining their origin."[98] He recognized that the idea of "internal evolutionary tendencies" was still too vague to be definitive. The most that he thought he could do was to point to the work of Carl Nägeli and Theodor Eimer. Laminne thought that such internal factors could be associated with an element of teleology, as had been proposed by James Ward.[99]

Laminne was not committed to an entirely natural account of the origin of biological species. He wrote that "It is a prejudice to believe that there cannot be natural forces other than those manifested by inorganic matter. If vital forces are irreducible to physico-chemical forces, something that it is in any case necessary to admit for psychic life, then it is necessary to acknowledge a Creator at its origin, as well as at the origin of the material universe."[100]

Third, with respect to phylogeny, Laminne followed Spencer's general acceptance of a law of divergence and a generally monophyletic account of the history of life:

> It is certain that phylogeny [i.e., the origin of new species] takes place by divergence, that is to say that as one traces back the line of ancestors in groups that are very different today one encounters groups that are less and less different, sometimes ending in a single group.... One must also recognize that ancestral lines, in converging as one goes back into the past, always finally end in a single group of individuals so similar to one another that there is no need to distinguish systematic groups. In

---

95 Laminne, *Évolution*, 473.

96 Laminne, *Évolution*, 366.

97 *The Contemporary Review*, as Laminne pointed out (*Évolution*, 378), had run a nine-article exchange between Spencer and Weismann on the question in 1893–1895. See Laminne, *Évolution*, 381.

98 Laminne, *Évolution*, 384. He cited De Vries, *Species and Varieties*.

99 Laminne, *Évolution*, 386. James Ward, professor of mental philosophy and logic at Cambridge, wrote *Naturalism and Agnosticism* as his Gifford Lectures for 1896–1898.

100 Laminne, *Évolution*, 383–84.

addition, in a general way, when one begins with present groups that are less different from one another, the ancestral lines meet in a more recent past.[101]

What does Laminne's book have to say about the two questions of greatest *theological* concern—the origin of Adam's body and monogenesis? It touches only indirectly on the former; it makes no mention of the idea advanced by Mivart, Leroy, and Zahm, or of the alternative suggested by González. The second (monogenesis) it addresses not at all.

❋　❋　❋　❋　❋

Laminne addressed evolution and the origin of man in the classroom in 1907–8, when he was assigned for the first time to teach the course "De Deo creante" at Louvain.[102] He taught that intervention of the Creator was necessary for the origin of life, of animals, and of rational beings.[103] The theologically important point was the last, so it is worth reviewing his ideas on that point in more detail:

1. ... Man owes his origin to the direct intervention of the Creator. This is theologically certain and can be demonstrated philosophically.

2. ... Man was created by God in a supernatural state, not only with respect to his soul, but also with respect to his body; consequently the production of the body of man did not take place without the direct intervention of the Creator.

3. If one distinguishes between the natural and the supernatural aspects of the body of the first man and asks whether at least the natural aspects were not produced by evolution, we reply that (1) one can cite arguments for an affirmative answer and for a negative one, neither the one nor the other being demonstrative (or peremptory); (2) one can propose a third hypothesis according to which some of the natural aspects of the human body (those which are found, or closely resemble, those of lower species) would have been produced in man by evolution while others were determined directly by God; and (3) this third hypothesis, while less in keeping with transformist ideas, would make it possible to resolve certain arguments that have been put forward against the two previous solutions.[104]

His third hypothesis, of course, is similar to that articulated by González nearly twenty years before.

---

101 Laminne, *Évolution*, 353–54.

102 There are two sources for what he said there on the topic of evolution.

    The first is some undated notes evidently written after the fact and entitled by an archivist "Notes du chan. Laminne sur la question de l'évolution et de la création" (Faculté de théologie 1914–1918, 26 I/21, AKUL).

    The second is a letter from Laminne to Ladeuze, June 17, 1911 ("Au mois d'octobre"), in which he summarizes what he had said to Cardinal Mercier, on the basis of a review of his notes, in 1908. (Laminne wrote two letters to Ladeuze on that date, which, their not having distinct archival numbers, I will distinguish by *incipit* ("Au mois d'octobre" and "Je joins ici," Faculté de théologie 1914–1918, 26 I/28, AKUL).

103 Laminne, "Notes," 1.

104 Laminne to Ladeuze, June 17, 1911 ("Au mois d'octobre").

181

Some of what Laminne had said, or was reported to have said, in the classroom gave rise to some concerns among the Belgian bishops and in October 1908 Laminne was summoned to see Cardinal Mercier. Part of the problem was a report that Laminne had denied that the human soul is the substantial form of the human body. Laminne said that he had taught just the opposite. More directly related to our question is whether he had taught that the origin of the human body was a theologically open question. Laminne acknowledged that he thought that arguments for the direct formation of the human body by God, without any rôle for secondary causes, were not decisive.

The cardinal said that he did not have any objection [*ne voyait pas d'inconvénient*] to treating the evolutionary view hypothetically, but suggested that that view would perhaps not be well-received in Rome. Laminne would in any case not have to say anything about the matter in the upcoming year, since he was not scheduled to teach the course; perhaps the ecclesiastical authorities would address it before he would have to take it up again.[105]

In 1911, the question of evolutionism at Louvain came up again, as several documents in the university archives at Louvain make clear. It arose at least partially in connection with the plan to have Laminne teach "De Deo creante" again in the fall of that year.

The first document comes from university rector Paulin Ladeuze. In March, he had made a visit to Rome on other business, but had taken the occasion to make some inquiries about how much openness there was on the evolution questions. He discussed the matter with two men, David Fleming, OFM, formerly (but no longer in 1911) secretary of the Pontifical Biblical Commission, and Leopold Fonck, SJ, first rector of the Pontifical Biblical Institute in Rome. Their assessments of the situation differed:

> [Fr. Fleming said that] the q[uestion] of transformism, from the perspective of dogma and of the Bible, no longer provokes misgivings [*ne provoque plus de défiance*] in Rome. [Father Fleming] had had, under Leo XIII, the occasion to write for the Pope two papers [*dissertations*] on the question, concerning Fr. Leroy and Fr. Zahm. Since then, the matter has become better understood; it is no longer of concern [*on ne s'en préoccupe plus*] to the Congregations. According to Fr. Fleming, one may now cautiously [*prudemment*], given the current state of things, teach Catholic transformism.
>
> Fr. Fonck is much more reserved on this question. The response of the Biblical Commission on the Pentateuch had avoided a condemnation of transformism, but that does not mean that they intentionally chose vague expressions.[106]

✳ ✳ ✳ ✳ ✳

---

105 Laminne to Ladeuze, June 17, 1911 ("Au mois d'octobre").

106 "Visite du Recteur à Rome en 1911" (Archives spéciales, Affaire de Dorlodot, T73 XXXIII, AKUL). This small memorandum, a copy of an apparently lost original, is labeled "notes taken in Rome itself, copied word for word." It does not indicate exactly why Ladeuze had raised the question.

In June 1911, as Laminne began to think about how he should handle the question of evolution in the lectures of his upcoming course, he wrote Ladeuze three letters on the question.[107]

He began one letter with a summary of his 1908 meeting with Mercier.[108] He thought that his treatment of the topic had been perfectly orthodox and was entirely consistent with the decisions that the Biblical Commission had published the following year. If his superiors had any concerns about his approach to the topic, he would omit it from his courses, but he did think that the topic was not only one of current interest, but one on which some other Catholic writers were approaching in a way that was both theologically and scientifically problematic.[109] He concluded by asking what he should do.

The other letter written the same day went into some detail about the approach that he took to the general question of evolution.[110] Arguments based on the texts of the Fathers or on the Council of Cologne could be answered. Evolutionary explanations did not have the theologically problematic consequences sometimes attributed to them (e.g., polygenesis) since they depended in any case not just on the intrinsic powers of nature, but on extrinsic circumstances. If God wanted a monogenetically unified human race, then He could arrange circumstances in such a way as to produce only a single individual human being. However much the human body might have certain features in common with (and so be the product of) animal ancestors, "nevertheless, some features, including natural ones, especially essential elements of the brain were received immediately from the Creator." This, he pointed out, was also the view of Alfred Russel Wallace. He added that "Revelation tells us with certainty that the body of the first man was, at least with respect to the supernatural gifts, formed by God without the participation of natural causes, and man, with respect to his psychological gifts, is the work of God, not of nature." By "psychological gifts" Laminne surely meant the power of intellectual thought and free choice; by "supernatural gifts," given the focus on the body, perhaps the "relatively supernatural" (or preternatural) gifts that "elevate human nature to [a] state of higher perfection," e.g., impassibility and freedom from concupiscence.[111]

Ladeuze met with Mercier on June 25.[112] Mercier complained that Laminne had, a few years before, given the impression that the question of an even partially evolutionary anthropogenesis was more open than it in fact was. Laminne, de Dorlodot, and others should be more cautious "not to let any rumors about orthodoxy spread around," not least

---

107 Two were written on June 17, 1911 (cited above) and a third on June 20 (also Faculté de théologie 1914–1918, 26 I/28, AKUL).

108 Laminne to Ladeuze, June 17 ("Au mois d'octobre").

109 In his letter of June 20, Laminne cited Hector Lebrun, biologist at the University of Ghent, as an example of a Catholic whose views he thought were unsatisfactory.

110 Laminne to Ladeuze, June 17 ("Je joins ici"). This three-page letter is followed by four unlabeled and unnumbered notes about how the topic should be treated.

111 See T. B. Scannell, "Gift, Supernatural," 553.

112 Ladeuze, "Parlé au Cardinal le 25 juin 1911," a hand-written note (Faculté de théologie 1914–1918, 26 I/28, AKUL).

in order to avoid any unfavorable notice from the "punctilious and inquisitive" nuncio (Giovanni Tacci Porcelli).

On December 19, 1911 Laminne wrote to Ladeuze again, sending an account of what he proposed to say about evolutionary anthropogenesis.[113] He began, of course, by emphasizing the idea that every human soul was directly created by God. The question of the origin of the first human body, by contrast, was more complex. On that topic, he proposed to teach as follows:

> Do some arguments of the evolutionists, even if they in no way prove the natural origin of man, nevertheless seem not to be completely without cogency with respect to affirming a causal connection between man and lower forms of life?
>
> Could God, when He constituted the first human body, have taken a preëxisting organism, *furnished with the dispositions necessary* for the infusion of a rational soul which would take the place of the brute-animal soul just as the ancients thought happened in the case of embryological development?
>
> If this is only a matter of possibility, and the question of fact is put aside, then the answer is undoubtedly affirmative.
>
> Is it *possible*, supposing general laws of the organic evolution of animal forms, for a human organism of the kind required for the infusion of a rational soul to be produced by natural evolution? If it is, then the origin of man, even though it is from God, nevertheless can in some sense be said to be natural, positing, to be sure, that it is by divine ordination that the rational soul is imparted to matter when phylogenetic forces produce a suitable organization.
>
> The answer to this question is much less clear because of our ignorance both of the forces which direct the evolution of living forms and of the dispositions necessary for the infusion of a rational soul, sc. the organization required for the activity of a rational soul.
>
> We do not know whether human [bodily] organization requires rational life by its very nature or whether rational life is conferred on a body so organized only by divine arrangement.
>
> Clearly what is more needed are arguments which, given especially that neither the necessity nor the impossibility can be demonstrated *a priori*, show with more or less probability *what actually happened*. There are two kinds: (1) those which can be deduced through our knowledge of general laws from inspection of the human organism and from its comparison with other organisms, and (2) those which we learn from revelation about the origin of man.
>
> To begin with the latter: It is theologically certain that the first human being was raised to the supernatural order not only with respect to the soul, but also with respect to the body—So it is certain that the body of the first man was not simply the effect of a natural evolution, but was made by the particular action of divine omnipotence.

113 Laminne, letter to Ladeuze, December 19, 1911 (Faculté de théologie 1914–1918, 26 I/28, AKUL).

There still remains the question whether the human body is a product of lower beings at least with regards to its natural endowments.[114]

Ladeuze told Laminne that his proposed approach was certainly orthodox, but emphasized that he should pay particular attention to several points. First, he should categorically affirm the creation of the soul and direct divine intervention with respect to the supernatural gifts. Second, he should be quite explicit that he was providing a critical summary of the controversy, without directly taking the side of evolution. Third, he should emphasize the way in which the idea of evolution is in accord with the unity of the human race (without having to reject the origin of the body of the first woman from that of the first man) and the way in which it confirms the idea of an intelligent God and of Providence.[115]

Laminne taught philosophy and dogmatic theology at Mercier's Institute in Louvain until 1915. In 1919 he was made auxiliary bishop of Liège. He died in 1924.

4. JUAN GONZÁLEZ DE ARINTERO, OP (1860–1928)[116]

Juan González de Arintero was born in Lugueros (Spain) on June 24, 1860, and entered the Order of Preachers in 1875. In 1881, before he had even completed his course in theology, his order decided to send him to the Universidad de Salamanca to study the natural sciences. The intellectual climate there being heavily influenced by evolutionism and somewhat hostile to Catholic ideas, he resolved to undertake a project of apologetics emphasizing the compatibility of science and religion. On the completion of his university studies in 1886, he was assigned to teach science at Dominican schools, first at Vergara and then, from 1892, at Corias, an assignment that left him time for writing.[117]

After addressing questions concerning the Garden of Eden and the Flood of Noah, he decided to undertake a discussion of biological evolutionism. He later wrote that, when he first approached the topic, he had rather unreflectively adopted the anti-Darwinism of his intellectual environment and intended to subject transformism to a thorough rebuttal, but the careful study of the topic that he undertook as a necessary preparation for this work forced him to acknowledge that the theory was at least partially correct, even if some of its proponents exaggerated the extent to which this is so.[118]

One of the impediments to his conversion to transformism fell quickly. The materialism and atheism that its critics associated with the idea he quickly recognized to be associable only with its misuse. The transformist view of the world, he concluded,

---

114 Laminne to Ladeuze, December 19, 1911.

115 Ladeuze, "Dit oralement à M. Laminne," an annotation to Laminne's letter of December 19, 1911.

116 On Arintero, see Ricardo Alba Sánchez, *Evolución de las especies*; Ctirad V. Pospíšil, *Průkopníci*, 292–309; and Alvaro Huerga, "La evolución."

117 For a more detailed survey of his writing on science and religion, see Antonio Gutierrez, "El Padre Arintero."

118 Arintero, *Evolución: Introducción general*, 88–91.

provides an even grander conception of the Creator than does its fixist alternative.[119] The second, and more difficult, impediment was the apparent contradiction between the Thomistic philosophical principle of the immutability of species and the transformist principle of mutability, his discussion of which will be presented shortly.

He laid out a plan for an ambitious, eight-volume work entitled *La evolución y la filosofía cristiana*, which would begin with the mutability of species, move through evolution and the Christian tradition, the philosophy of evolution, paleontology, life, the sensitive powers, and irreducible types, and end with the origin of man. Of this, he published only an introduction and the first volume (on mutability), in 1898. We know something of what he intended to do from the prospectus he provided in the introduction, more from nearly two thousand unpublished draft pages still in the archive at the convent of San Esteban in Salamanca. Some of his ideas are also found in a few of his other works, the first of which was a series of articles entitled "La Evolución ante la fe y la ciencia," written (or at least begun) while he was still in Corias.

In 1900 Arintero was sent to Valladolid to establish the Academía de Santo Tomás, dedicated to the study of the relationship between natural science and philosophy and theology. There he published another series of articles, on "La Creación y la evolución" and a book, *El hexámeron y la ciencia moderna*, both in 1901. In 1904 he published a two-volume work entitled *La providencia y la evolución*.

* * * * *

Arintero's review of the history of evolutionary ideas included three points of particular interest.

The first is his emphasis on the fact that many evolutionists defended only a polyphyletic theory of descent.

The second is his insistence on the importance of distinguishing the theory of descent from natural selection. The latter, quoting Eduard von Hartmann, he called a "a complex set of hypotheses based on nothing more than a general tendency to replace the idea of an organic evolution—internally driven and carried out in accordance with a determinate plan—with the sum of mechanical actions—external and fortuitous."[120] Failure to make that distinction led anti-evolutionists to take arguments against selection as arguments against the theory of descent and some defenders of the theory of descent to accept selection and "the cosmico-mechanical concept that is deduced from it."[121]

The third (quoting Hartmann again) is that "the theory of descent can equally well be adapted to mechanistic or to organic cosmogonies, and to materialistic, to pantheistic, or to theistic ones,"[122] a point on which he cited in support three Catholic authors—Zahm, Guibert, and Duilhé. Near the end of his historical review, Arintero also emphasized that,

---

119 Arintero, *Evolución: Introducción*, 92–94.

120 Arintero, *Evolución: Introducción*, 137. The passage is from Hartmann, *Darwinismus*, 4.

121 Arintero, *Evolución: Introducción*, 138.

122 Arintero, *Evolución: Introducción*, 139; Hartmann, *Darwinismus*, 4. Hartmann put *theistisch*; Arintero, citing Georges Guéroult's French translation (p. 5), put *deistico*.

the questions at issue not being purely scientific, philosophy has not only the right, but the duty, to take part in their discussion.

* * * * *

Arintero recognized, of course, that he was not the first Catholic to defend a version of evolutionism. In addition to the Spanish authors González and Ramón Martínez Vigil (bishop of Orviedo), he cited Mivart, Leroy, and Zahm.

González I have already discussed. Martínez Vigil, in his *La creación, la redención y la Iglesia ante la ciencia* (1892), had expressed the usual scientific reservations about transformism, such as the fixity of species and the limitation of any natural selection by the tendency of reversion to the original type, but did not think that the theory was philosophically or inherently problematic. Martínez Vigil wrote that "transformism does not necessarily include either materialism or atheism, both because the production of the first organism peremptorily calls for the intervention of a personal God, and also because the Lord was capable of infusing the soul of the first man into an ape, just as He infused it in a piece of kneaded clay, and as He does into a human fetus every day."[123] Nevertheless, he had Scriptural concerns about the origin of man, for he thought that the immediate divine formation of the first human bodies was "the obvious and natural sense of Holy Scripture"[124] and "abandonment of the literal sense commonly accepted over the centuries and by the most eminent experts requires, if not scientific demonstrations, at least rational and well-founded hypotheses, which have survived testing and have made their solemn entry into the domain of science, and, as we shall see, the transformist hypothesis does not meet those conditions."[125] Still, he added that he would "abstain from characterizing the opinions of the erudite Mivart as heretical, impious, or even just materialistic."[126] In sum, "Transformism is an hypothesis that is still in its novitiate and cannot yet be classified as scientific. Other than Church teaching about the rational soul, against which it presents no arguments, it cannot be described as irreligious, and even less as materialistic. There is no reason for conflict between faith and science."[127]

Like earlier Catholic authors, Arintero thought that the ideas of St. Gregory of Nyssa and St. Augustine of Hippo—that God created things "in potentiality," allowing them to develop over time—made it reasonable to consider them to be the founders of a theological evolutionism. He also pointed to St. Albert the Great's defense of the mutability of species in his *Parva naturalia*.[128]

Nevertheless, he thought that earlier attempts to articulate a Catholic evolutionism were either "too brief, and therefore confused or incomplete (when they were not somewhat

---

123 Martínez Vigil, *Creación*, 1:158.

124 Martínez Vigil, *Creación*, 1:142.

125 Martínez Vigil, *Creación*, 1:158.

126 Martínez Vigil, *Creación*, 1:142–43.

127 Martínez Vigil, *Creación*, 1:174.

128 Albertus Magnus, "De quinque modis transmutationis unius plantae in aliam," *De vegetalibus*, bk. 5, tr. 1, ch .7 (Jammy ed., 5:422–24).

bold [*atrevido*] or perhaps dangerous)."[129] He took exception to the views of Mivart, Leroy, and Zahm, both for their monophyletism (at least within the plant and animal kingdoms, if not for life itself) and for their view that the human body was a product of evolutionary processes rather than of direct divine action. He knew that something Mivart had written had been placed on the *Index*, but he did not know what and thought, incorrectly, that it was something about evolution;[130] he did not know anything about the Leroy case.[131] He contrasted those authors' views with those of Gaudry (on monophyletism) and Zeferino González (on God's rôle in the formation of the first human body).

Central to his own theory, which he called a *transformismo restringido*, was his treatment of the species question, in particular his attempt to resolve the apparent contradiction between the Thomistic philosophical principle of the immutability of species and the transformist principle of mutability. He argued that the word "species" did not have the same sense in natural history and in metaphysics, distinguishing *ontological* species, to which the Thomistic principle of immutability applied, from *organic* species, to which it did not.[132]

The "ontological species" that were the concern of metaphysics were immutable in the sense that one could not give rise to another. Such a change would be a change of essence and a violation of a philosophical principle.[133] Natural history (and transformism), by contrast, was interested in organic species, of which there could be many within a single ontological species, varying from one another only accidentally. Since the transformation of one such species into another was merely a change in these accidents, the transformation of one into another was not philosophically problematic.

✳ ✳ ✳ ✳ ✳

On the question of the *cause* of such transformation as he thought existed, however, he differed from the earlier evolutionary theories of Darwin, Geoffroy Saint-Hilaire, and Lamarck. That cause, he said, was not natural selection, or environmental influence, or emergent needs, but an "interior teleological impulse initially implanted (*comunicado*) by God in order to realize His divine plan." Arintero compared it to Claude Bernard's *idée directrice*.[134] The impulse that effected the embryological development of a single organism, could, in the appropriate circumstances, also lead to the evolution of new species.

And what exactly did he identify as the ontological species that were beyond the reach of evolutionary processes? Arintero rejected the view of Zigliara and Leroy that animals constitute a single sensitive species, and plants a single vegetative one, on the

---

129 Arintero, *Evolución: Introducción*, 98.

130 Arintero, *Hexámeron*, 193.

131 The case for this is an argument *ex silentio*. If Arintero had known about the condemnation of Leroy, he would surely have mentioned it in his discussion of Leroy's views at *Evolución: Introducción*, 160–61. When he wrote *Evolución*, the Zahm case still lay in the future.

132 Arintero, *Evolución: Introducción*, 168. See also 94 and 170.

133 Arintero, *Evolución: Introducción*, 94–96.

134 Arintero, *Evolución: Introducción*, 174. He cited Bernard, *La Science expérimentale*, 52, 134, and 207 ff.

188

grounds that there was simply too much variation in vital expression between, say, a polyp and a horse. Ontological species were not so general, corresponding rather, he thought, to the biological taxon of class (so, fish, birds, or mammals).

So, though evolutionary processes could give rise to distinct (organic) species such as foxes and wolves, or even foxes and elephants, the proto-mammal, from which they all evolved, could not itself have evolved (along with the proto-bird or proto-fish) from some kind of proto-vertebrate. Ontological species had to be the product of an immediate intervention by God.[135] Divine production of these new species did not, however, mean that the species were completely unrelated, nor did it completely exclude a contribution from secondary causes: "In producing [a new] organism, God did not begin with mud. . . . Rather, He began with the pre-existing organisms most similar to the new one and merely adapted it sufficiently to make it suited to the new vital principle."[136]

✳ ✳ ✳ ✳ ✳

Theologically most important, of course, was the question of the origin of man, whom he placed in a kingdom distinct from plants and animals. Given the views summarized above, he thought that the origin of man "requires, even more than that of other species, a very special intervention on the part of the Creator, not only for the creation of the immortal soul, but even for the formation or immediate preparation of the body."[137] So the efficient cause of the formation of the first human body was God; Mivart's alternative view is "scientifically false, and dogmatically, if not dangerous (*peligroso*), as we think, is extremely bold (*atrevido*)."[138] The question of the matter *from which* the first human body was made, however, is completely open. "Reason leads us to believe that God took the matter most adequate or best prepared; that he did not take unprepared mud, but a special mud or *limus*, prepared, *organized* [i.e., with biological organs]."[139] Indeed this account also has explanatory value:

> The analogies between our organism and that of the higher mammals is clear. There is no reason to deny that they are there or to think that God did not make them for that. . . . Without . . . being able to be the product of a continuous evolution, man is, for all that, much more closely related to the higher mammals than is commonly thought. The identity of fundamental plan, both anatomical and embryological, . . . and the various rudimentary organs, useless in man but more or less developed and active in the higher mammals, show that they really have something in common. That commonality can very well be explained as one of *material origin* without the necessity of appealing, with the ultra-evolutionists, to a humiliating *kinship* founded in an imagined evolution or descent.—For God to form the body of the first man

---

135 Arintero, *Evolución: Introducción*, 170–75.

136 Arintero, *Evolución: Introducción*, 175. See also the passage from Arintero's unpublished *Nachlaß* quoted in Sánchez, *Arintero*, 270–72.

137 Arintero, *Evolución: Introducción*, 188.

138 Arintero, *Evolución: Introducción*, 189. See also, *Hexámeron*, 192–95.

139 Arintero, *Evolución: Introducción*, 189. See also, *Hexámeron*, 196–98.

189

from another organism or from pre-existent organic matter, acting as always with wisdom and economy, he did not form it using a totally new plan, but an old one modified solely in accordance with the requirements of the soul for which it was destined. Organs which, though not serving that destiny, were nevertheless not opposed to it, did not have to be suppressed by some kind of useless miracle. That is why there are so may rudimentary organs, which are only good for pointing to a common material background.[140]

* * * * *

Arintero concluded the introduction to his intended eight-volume work on evolution with the following remarks:

> All that remains is to know whether evolution is an undeniable truth. We think that it is, even though that is certainly not the general opinion. The only doubt that remains, in our opinion, is over the mode in which evolution is effected, over how far it reaches, over the various causes which play a rôle in it, etc., but not over its reality. The theory would already have been generally accepted without reservation if it were not for the entrenched prejudices which oppose it, prejudices which have been greatly strengthened by the exaggerations of its first supporters.[141]

And

> Mutability and evolution are, up to certain limits, demonstrated facts. Reason tells us that, when a known cause is sufficient to explain an effect, we should not attribute that, or analogous, effects to mysterious and unknown causes unless the absolute necessity of doing so has been demonstrated. What the insuperable limits to evolution are, however, and what are the causes and circumstances which favor it, these are where there is room for much discussion. As for the principal cause of evolution, we certainly believe that it cannot be anything other than that which, in our view, produces individual development [*evolución*], i.e., the immanent, teleological, developmental [*evolutivo*] principle which we call *the vital principle*.[142]

* * * * *

As he finished writing the books just discussed, his interest shifted away from questions of science and religion in the direction of ecclesiology and mysticism. It was on those topics that he published the work for which he is best known, *La evolución mística en el desenvolvimiento y vitalidad de la Iglesia* (1908–11). One can see only a faint connection between his old interests and his new ones, for example in a line from his inaugural talk given at the College of Valladolid in 1900, where he said: "The Church is a living organism, and as such develops and always maintains itself in harmony with and in perfect adaptation to its circumstances."[143]

140 Arintero, *Hexámeron*, 199–200.

141 Arintero, *Evolución: Introducción*, 191–92.

142 Arintero, *Evolución: Introducción*, 193–94.

143 Arintero, *Crisis científico-religiosa*, 23.

190

In 1912, Arintero returned to Salamanca, where he remained until his death in 1928.

5. OTTOKÁR PROHÁSZKA (1858–1927)

Ottokár Prohászka, appointed in 1903 as university professor at Budapesti Tudományegyetem [the University of Budapest] and then, in 1905, as bishop of Székesfehérvár, was one of the most influential theologians in the history of the Hungarian church. A posthumous collection of his writings ran to twenty-five volumes. John A. Hardon, SJ, who included Prohászka's three-volume *Meditations on the Gospel* in his *Catholic Lifetime Reading Plan*, said of him that "it is almost impossible to exaggerate the intellectual greatness of the man."[144] He is perhaps best remembered for the more political side of his theological work—for the defense of the rights of workers and peasants (on the positive side) and for his stridently hostile remarks about Hungarian Jews (on the negative side)—but he also tried to articulate a Catholic perspective on developments in the natural sciences. These two themes can be seen as parts of a larger project. His biographer Ferenc Szabó, SJ, characterized "the whole axis of [his] apologetic and apostolic activity" as constituted by a twofold modernization—"openness to science" and "the ethical application of theology to the national economy and social problems."[145]

In his writings on science, he attempted to lay out a middle way between embracing scientism and "looking at modern science with anathematizing eyes."[146] "Those who do not read new authors and are not aware of advanced science," he wrote, "cannot reserve the Christian worldview for themselves to the exclusion of us."[147] He addressed the emerging paleoetiological sciences in their relation to theology in two books and in one academic lecture, all written during his academic years.

The first of these was *Isten és a világ: Különös tekintettel a természettudományokra* [*God and the World: Especially in Light of Science*] (1890),[148] which offered a general critique of Darwinian versions of evolutionary biology, i.e., of versions that rely on random variation and external circumstances rather than on an internal principle to explain evolutionary change. He did not address the question of human evolution.

Prohászka next addressed the topic of science and religion in an 1899 lecture entitled "Mire kell ma a theológiában súlyt fektetni?" ["What Should be Emphasized in Today's Theology?"] His answer, of course, is modern science, even the new paleoetiological sciences: "The whole world is potentially contained within a single divine thought and now it evolves [from a primordial world into the world with all of its creatures]. . . . Is

---

144 Hardon, *Reading Plan*, 144.

145 Szabó, *Prohászka*, 70.

146 Prohászka, "Mire kell ma?," 179.

147 Prohászka, Föld és ég, 5th ed., 1:4–5.

148 A second edition was published in 1892. It was included in the edition of his collected works published in 1928.

there any exegete who has illustrated the greatness of God as well as the natural sciences have done?"[149]

Prohászka elaborated the themes of that lecture in a series of articles first published in *Magyar Sion* and then, extensively supplemented by new material, issued in book form as *Föld és ég: Kutatások a geologia és theologia érintkezö pontjai kórúl* [*Earth and Heaven: Studies on the Connection between Geology and Theology*] (1902).[150] *Föld és ég* had a broad range, running from the origin of the solar system through the origin of life to the origin of man. On the question of *biological* evolution, it made three main points.

First came a general point:

> If evolution is used only to explain the origin of the animal world, then it will not collide with theology. There are no dogmatic challenges from theology to the evolution of animal life; dogmatics only concerns the origin of man. The first chapter of Scripture (with its six days of the creation of the world) ... raises no objections against evolution; in fact, it seems strongly to suggest that the world was built by its inherent power and not by repeated introduction of new creatures.[151]

Second, on the question of the origin of man, he wrote that "human dignity should be the indubitable thesis and not evolution; man should be the Archimedean Point from which our understanding of evolution can be extrapolated," but "evolution does not deny the dignity of man, nor does it reject the distinctiveness of our intellectual, moral, and religious life."[152] Does Scripture require direct divine action in the formation of the first human body, as the opponents of Mivartism insisted that it did?

> The real objection to Darwinism is that man is not an animal, that there is an essential difference between them, an ontological difference, which creates in man a world of intellect, morality, and religion. Let us not say anything more than that. Let us not say that the anatomical differences are so great that evolution could not have created the body of man. What if it did create it? What if the human body was not directly created by God, but was the product of evolutionary development?! Our thesis is not that there is an essentially different constitution in man and ape, but rather that there is an essentially different nature.[153]

> And if the [human] soul has not evolved from an animal, could the human body have evolved? If that is ever proven, we will accept it. At present, there is nothing beyond the unifying demands of the theory of evolution in support of that proposal.

---

149 First published in *Magyar Sion* (1899), the text of the lecture is most conveniently available in the posthumous edition of Prohászka's collected works (*Összegyüjtött munkái*, 15:179–235), to which my citations refer. Here, "Mire kell ma?," 196.

150 A third edition was published in 1906. The first three editions are substantially identical. Changes in the fourth (1912) will be discussed below. A fifth edition, substantially equivalent to the third, but with some notes added by Antal Schütz, the editor, was published as the third volume of Prohászka's collected works at the time of Prohászka's death. Citations here will be to that more conveniently available fifth edition, but in all cases the passages cited are substantially equivalent to those in the third edition.

151 Prohászka, Föld és ég, 3rd ed., 315; 5th ed., 2:69.

152 Prohászka, Föld és ég, 3rd ed., 308; 5th ed., 2:61–62.

153 Prohászka, Föld és ég, 3rd ed., 313; 5th ed., 2:67.

Let us summarize our view briefly: With the human soul begins a higher, separate world. The body, by contrast, the physical man, is just the foundation. The human soul is created by a special act of God. It is not possible at present to be certain where the body came from.[154]

Third, on the first woman:

The most challenging part of Scripture is the creation of woman. Symbolism is evident throughout the narrative and there will hardly be an intelligent reader who would understand the narrative literally.

It would be tasteless to keep asking whether God really removed Adam's ribs and would only lead to childish explanations.[155]

In conclusion, he wrote:

Nothing is certain here. Evolution is beautiful; it is a plausible [*valószínű*] hypothesis, but there will be differences about how far it extends. Those who think that our explanations are too tolerant and recommend that we keep our distance [from evolution], should not just keep repeating that God *would* have created each species separately, for here we are not talking about "what-if" but about fact, and evolution is not contrary to Scripture.[156]

Is his interpretation of Scripture consistent with the Fathers? His answer was "yes":

The interpretations of Genesis offered by the Fathers do not preclude evolution. Even if all the Fathers had offered a literal interpretation of the first chapter of Holy Scripture, we may deviate from their interpretation, because they themselves assert the principle that unanimity of interpretation does not bind subsequent interpreters to the Fathers' views on scientific matters once we have a clearer view of the scientific facts.[157]

✳ ✳ ✳ ✳ ✳

The chapter on man and evolution was omitted from the fourth edition, published in 1912. That edition offered no explanation for the omission, but two events that occurred between 1906 and 1912 surely shed light on the decision (whether his or that of ecclesiastical censors) to omit the chapter.

The first was the 1909 decree of the Pontifical Biblical Commission on the first three chapters of Genesis.[158] That decree forbade Catholics from calling into doubt the

---

154 Prohászka, *Föld és ég*, 3rd ed., 320; 5th ed., 2:74.

155 Prohászka, *Föld és ég*, 3rd ed., 321–22. The fifth edition (at 2:75) differs from the third here in two phrases: It begins with the phrase "The most naïve" and is harsher in the second sentence where it has "there would hardly be any intelligent readers." The fifth edition being posthumous, the change was probably not made by Prohászka; perhaps the language of the fifth edition comes from the second edition and was toned down in the third. I have not been able to confirm this hypothesis.

156 Prohászka, *Föld és ég*, 3rd ed., 323; 5th ed., 2:77.

157 Prohászka, *Föld és ég*, 3rd ed., 323–24; 5th ed., 2:77.

158 Details of the decree are discussed in chapter 9.

193

"literal historical sense" of, among other things, "the distinctive creation of man" and "the formation of the first woman from the first man." Whether the decree condemned Mivartism, to which Prohászka had explicitly left the door open, was a matter of some debate in the years that followed the promulgation of the decree. There is no doubt, however, that Prohászka's chapter, calling into doubt as it did the literal historical sense of the Scriptural passage on the origin of Eve, was one of the ideas that the decree did not allow.

A second relevant event occurred on June 12, 1911, when three of his other works were placed on the *Index*.[159] This, he wrote in his diary, struck as if lightning from a clear sky.[160] The first was a Christmas article entitled "Több békességet!" ["More Peace!"] (1910).[161] Critics objected to Prohászka's remarks about the wealth of the Church (that historical claims alone were not sufficient moral justification for landholdings as extensive as those the Church possessed in Hungary) and about the Russian Orthodox Church (namely, that it had "the charism of holiness").[162] The other two works were a short book on *Modern katholicizmus* (1907) and his inaugural lecture to the Hungarian Academy, "Az intellektualizmus túlhajtásai" ["The Exaggerations of Intellectualism"] (1910). Here the objection was rather to the works' perceived modernism. In the lecture, the concern was Prohászka's account of notion of truth and the value of concepts.[163] Prohászka's evolutionism did not feature in these texts and was not raised as a concern by his critics. Prohászka immediately submitted.

Did Prohászka's views on evolution play any rôle in the condemnation of his writings? One would think that, if the Budapest Vigilance Committee that initiated the action against him had been concerned about evolutionism, they would have reviewed *Föld és ég* and the other works mentioned above, which they did not do.

Traces of evolutionism in *Modern katholicizmus* were noted, but not emphasized, in the *votum* submitted by Szádok Szabó, a Dominican theologian then on the faculty at the Angelicum: "The author's statement that God gave formative powers to matter is ambiguous. For from what he says, it would seem to follow that the author is open to materialistic evolution, although he accepts the special action of God when it is a matter of the transition of inorganic to organic and to the higher species of life."[164] In the summary of his *votum*, he wrote that the author had "spoken of the relation of God to the course of the laws of the universe as if today the 'intervention' of God is no longer appropriate

---

159 Details of the case are provided by Szabó, *Prohászka*, 177–89.

160 Prohászka, *Naplójegyzetek*, 1:297ff., quoted in Szabó, *Prohászka*, 183.

161 Published in *Egyházi közlöny* [*The Church Gazette*] on December 23, 1910.

162 For more details, see Szabó, *Prohászka*, especially 181–83.

163 See the report of the Vigilance Committee, submitted to the Vatican Secretariat of State (doc. 269, Protocolli 1910–1911/140, CL, ADDF).

164 Szabó, *Votum* on *Modern katholizismus*, §60c (doc. 318, Protocolli 1910–1911/140, CL, ADDF; reprinted as an appendix to F. Szabó's *Prohászka*). Szabó did not have a regular appointment as a consultor to the Index. Thomas Esser, secretary of the Index, requested him to submit a *votum* because of the difference of opinion between the two *vota* that the Index received from the Budapest Vigilance Committee.

[*non conveniens*],"[165] but this was grouped with an unrelated concern (about asceticism) in one of eight points of objection.

Nevertheless, the unexpected blow of the placement of two of his works on the *Index* might well have made him cautious about any attempt to retain his chapter on evolution and man, even in revised form, when *Föld és ég* was reissued the following year. Safer would just be to omit the chapter altogether. (The book's more general evolutionism, one should note, is still there.)

When, at the time of Prohászka's death in 1927, the Szent István Society decided to issue a collected edition of his works, it restored the chapter on the evolution of man to *Föld és ég*, with several explanatory notes, presumably written by the collection's editor, Antal Schütz. One note concerned Prohászka's comment that whether God had a direct rôle in the formation of the human body could not yet be decided. There Schütz added in a footnote: "One cannot be certain on the basis of the natural sciences or humanities. On the basis of theology, one can be almost certain: The various statements of Holy Scripture and the almost unanimous statements of the Fathers can hardly be interpreted differently than that the first pair of human beings, even with respect to the body, came directly from the hand of God."[166] And on the origin of Eve that "It is not dogma, but theologically it is almost certain, that the story of the creation of woman must be understood literally. . . . Today, therefore, theologically, the view expressed in the author's text cannot safely be maintained."[167] The publishing house received ecclesiastical permission for the collected works.

---

165 Szabó, *Votum* on *Modern katholizismus*, §65e. See also §13.

166 Schütz, "A kiadó jegyzetei" [Publisher's Note], *Föld és ég*, 5th ed., 2:257.

167 Schütz, "A kiadó jegyzetei," 2:258.

CHAPTER 9

THE OFFICIAL CHURCH
(1898–1909)

1. POPE ST. PIUS X (R. 1903–1914)

Pope Pius X never addressed the question of evolution directly. He was, of course, very concerned about certain new ideas in theology, ideas that he condemned under the name "modernism." These concerns were laid out in his encyclical letter *Pascendi Dominici gregis* along with the associated decree *Lamentabili sane* (both 1907), and in the Oath against Modernism (1910),[1] subscription to which was required of all clergy, including seminary professors.

The "modernism" that so concerned Pope Pius was fundamentally the practice of exegesis detached from any dogmatic guidance. Ideas about the origin of the Church and of the sacraments, and the idea of an evolution of doctrine, figure prominently on the syllabus of errors that was *Lamentabili sane*;[2] scientific ideas like the evolution of biological species, by contrast, do not. Because there continues to be a certain tendency to suggest a connection between Pius's rejection of modernism and Catholic reservations about the evolutionary origin of biological species, it is worth looking at the matter a little more closely.

---

1 Pius X, *Sacrorum antistitum* (*motu proprio*).

2 See in particular *Lamentabili sane*, ¶¶ 53 and 58–60, and the explicit mention, in the Oath against Modernism, of the ideas that "dogmas evolve and change from one meaning to another, different from the one which the Church held previously," and of objectionable approaches to the "history of dogmas."

Only four of the propositions condemned as erroneous in *Lamentabili sane* have anything to do with the natural sciences.

5.   Since the deposit of Faith contains only revealed truths, the Church has no right to pass judgment on the assertions of the human sciences [*disciplinarum*].

57. The Church has shown that she is hostile to the progress of the natural and theological sciences.

64. Scientific progress demands that the concepts of Christian doctrine concerning God, Creation, Revelation, the Person of the Incarnate Word, and Redemption be revised [*reformentur*].

65. Modern Catholicism can be reconciled with true science only if it is transformed into a non-dogmatic Christianity; that is to say, into a broad and liberal Protestantism.

To what extent could this list make problems for the development of a Catholic evolutionism? Let us set to one side the question of authors whose work clearly exemplified modernism in ways that had nothing to do with science and who *also* defended some form of scientific evolutionism. Of the four theses just quoted, two in particular laid foundations for disputes over whether a particular articulation of a Catholic version of *scientific* evolutionism ran afoul of one of the errors listed on the syllabus.

The first is proposition 5. One way to avoid a conflict between science and the Church over evolutionary theories would be to place limits on the matter about which the Church, and science, can teach with authority.

The second, more distinctively *scientific*, is proposition 64. Here, the issue is particularly complex because the exact *content* of the doctrine of creation is not specified. Some ideas—that God only *formed* the world out of eternally existing matter, which itself was not also dependent on God for its existence, or (probably) that individual human souls were not directly created by God, for example—would fairly clearly call for a "revision" of the doctrine of creation. Others—for example that the days of Genesis were not the twenty-four-hour periods of our own experience—would equally clearly not do so. But what about the idea that the human body was formed, not by direct divine action, but by evolutionary processes or the idea that there was more than one first human couple at the root of the human phylogenetic tree? On these last propositions, there was room for disagreement between those who took a more expansive and those who took a more restrictive view of exactly what was immune from revision.

These issues were fought out, but in the end they were fought out on their own terms. However much the *term* may have been deployed by Catholic anti-evolutionists, the *concept* of "modernism" *per se* did not play a *mediating* rôle in the resolution of the question of whether Catholic thought could or could not accommodate, say, the evolutionary origin of the human body.

2. THE INDEX: THE MARTINELLI & MARTEL CASES (1906–1907)

After the two prominent evolution cases of the 1890s, that front was relatively quiet during the first decade of the twentieth century. Still, two books espousing Catholic evolutionism in one way or another came to the attention of the Congregation of the Index during the first decade of the twentieth century.

The first of those books was Pietro Martinelli's *I primi tre capitoli della Sacra Bibbia annotati secondo il sistema delle apparenze*, published in 1906, so three years before the key decree of the Biblical Commission. Martinelli was a priest of the diocese of Montalcino (Italy). He had previously published an Italian translation of Pierre Bouvier's short *L'Exégèse de M. Loisy*, a book highly critical of Loisy's modernist attack on Catholic orthodoxy. In Martinelli's book on Genesis, he argued that the chapters that were his subject were a poetical account of the origin of the world rather than a historical narrative. ("Martinelli finds in Genesis 1–3 only religious and social doctrines," said one reviewer, "all the rest is allegory."[3]) Martinelli had written:

> The system "of appearances" consists in holding that God inspired the sacred writer in his choice of a subject and in the noble attainment of the end at which he aimed. One could almost say that the sacred writer receives assistance in the same way as does the Supreme Pontiff, to ensure that he does not say anything contrary to faith or morals (with exception made for the revelation of supernatural truths or truths about the future). Facts about nature (*fatti cosmici*), then, the sacred writer describes as they appeared to be or as he knew them (on the basis of his own knowledge).[4]

So, details about nature the reader would have to learn from geology or astronomy. Martinelli saw evolution in the verses that describe the appearance "of the *material* parts of the animals and of man himself."[5] Original sin, the book added, brought only the death of the soul; nothing more.[6]

Martinelli sought permission from diocesan authorities to publish the book (as he was required to do). When he did not get it, he published the book anyway. Shortly after it appeared, his bishop, Iader Bertini, a vigilant anti-modernist[7] though one who, as vicar-general in Siena, had signed the *imprimatur* for the Italian translation of Zahm's *Evolution and Dogma* ten years before, reported the case to the Holy Office, which referred the book to the Index.[8] The task of examining the book was given to Enrico Gismondi, SJ, who thought that the author relied too much on evolutionism, "a theory completely foreign

---

3 *Biblische Zeitschrift*, Notice, 322.

4 Martinelli, *Primi tre capitoli*, xv.

5 Martinelli, *Primi tre capitoli*, 47.

6 Martinelli, *Primi tre capitoli*, 85–96, noted in Gismondi, *Votum*, 5 and 9 (doc. 193, Protocolli 1906–7, CL, ADDF).

7 See the favorable mention of him in this regard in the "Cronica contemporanea," *Civiltà cattolica*, 107.

8 On November 20, 1906 (doc. 192, Protocolli 1906–7, CL, ADDF).

to the Bible, even in the very mild form in which the author envisions it."[9] Gismondi's concerns were seconded by the consultors and by the cardinals of the Index at their respective congregations.[10] Nevertheless, the cardinals decided not to place the book on the *Index*. As Thomas Esser, secretary at the Index, explained to Bishop Bertini: "In view of the many blunders contained in this book, their Eminences would have condemned it and placed it on the *Index* if, on the other hand, they had not thought that that would give too much importance to a book so bad in all respects that it will probably not spread much beyond the author's own community."[11] The Index suggested that the bishop prohibit it in his own diocese and have Martinelli destroy all the remaining copies.[12] The bishop, however, was reluctant to promulgate a local prohibition. Martinelli was a good priest; a local prohibition could do more harm than good, among other things making people inclined to read a book that they might otherwise ignore. He requested that that point be reconsidered and the pope (St. Pius X) lifted the instruction to implement a local prohibition.[13] The author was still, of course, expected to do what he could to withdraw the book from circulation[14] and this he seems largely to have succeeded in doing. The book is not widely available.

✳ ✳ ✳ ✳ ✳

The second of those books was *Les Conflits de la science et de la Bible* published pseudonymously under the name "l'Abbé E. Lefranc" in 1906. It had in fact been written by Louis-Charles Martel, curate of the parish of Saintines in the diocese of Beauvais.[15] Like Martinelli, the author had published his book without an *imprimatur*.

Martel distinguished two approaches to the appearance of conflict between science and the Bible. One approach simply denied the truth of even the best-established scientific ideas—heliocentrism, historical geology, the decipherment of hieroglyphics. This was quixotic. The other (concordism) erased the conflict by offering new (and forced) interpretations of the offending passages of the Bible. This, Martel thought, would not work either. Scripture leans rather towards a non-transformist origin of species; Catholic transformists (he cites Leroy and Zahm) would not succeed in making the sacred text

---

9 Gismondi, *Votum*, 4 (doc. 193, Protocolli 1906–7, CL, ADDF).

10 The preparatory congregation was held on March 26 and the general congregation on April 12, both in 1907.

11 Esser to Bertini, April 22, 1907 (doc. 201, Protocolli 1906–7, CL, ADDF). In this prediction, Esser seems not to have been entirely correct. The book had been announced in *La Civiltà Cattolica* and had been, or was soon to be, reviewed in six other journals—by M. Federici in both *Rivista bibliografia italiana* and *Rivista storico-critica delle scienze teologiche*, and anonymously by others in *Rivista internazionale di scienze sociali e discipline ausiliarie*, in *Rivista di studi religiosi*, in *La Scuola cattolica*, and in *Revue biblique internationale*. It had also been noticed in the *Orientalistische Literaturzeitung* and in the *Biblische Zeitschrift*. It eventually reached libraries as far afield as Berlin and Jerusalem. Nevertheless, the reviews were not particularly favorable. The *Revue biblique* had said that the author was poorly equipped for the task and not familiar enough with technical aspects of the subject. Perhaps that is all that the cardinals meant.

12 Esser to Bertini, April 22, 1907 (doc. 201, Protocolli 1906–7, CL, ADDF).

13 Bertini to Pius X, June 19, 1907 (doc. 232, Protocolli 1906–7, CL, ADDF); and Esser to Bertini, June 26, 1907 (doc. 233).

14 Esser to Bertini, June 26, 1907.

15 Jean-Célestin Douais, bishop of Beauvais, to the Holy Father, June 20, 1908 (doc. 109, Protocolli 1908–9, CL, ADDF).

199

say what they wanted it to say.[16] The two approaches failed for the same reason—the commitment of each to Biblical inerrancy even on scientific matters. This principle, Martel thought, would have to be abandoned. God did not intend revelation to include "the secrets of nature," but left the resolution of such matters to free human discussion and did not correct the erroneous ideas of his "secretaries."[17] "One must," Martel said, "distinguish in the text between the symbolic and religious element and the traditional story."[18]

So, with respect to scientific matters, the Bible was capable of error. His introduction described the book as a popularization of the *école-large* approach to hermeneutics then being developed by some Scripture scholars, but strongly rejected by more conservative theologians.[19]

He denied that this contradicted the doctrine of Trent, which, at most, taught the inerrancy of Scripture only with respect to faith and morals. Neither, he thought, had he gone beyond what was allowed by *Providentissimus Deus*. Pope Leo XIII had acknowledged that Scripture sometimes uses language accommodated to its first audience, reporting things as they appeared to the senses. In any case, however wise the principles of that encyclical were, it was not an infallible document.[20]

Martel's book is divided into three parts—one on the universe (cosmogony and cosmography), one on the plant and animal kingdoms, and one on man. It defends (in addition to an evolutionary cosmology) the evolutionary origin of species and of the human body, and the antiquity of man.[21] He (at least implicitly) accepted the creation of human souls. On monogenesis, he wrote: "Science is here reduced to uncertainty and silence. So nothing prevents us from rallying around a rigorous monogenism, which is in any case a truth of faith. . . . The explicit teachings of St. Paul on original sin, as well as the infallible teachings of the Church [make this a matter of] revealed dogma."[22]

Three passages indicate both the direction of argument and the tone of the book. Two are his own:

> Darwinism is no more contrary to the sacred texts than are the theories of Faye or Laplace on the origin of the world, or than is the doctrine of all the geologists, and those are accepted without any difficulty by apologists.[23]

> Transformism, far from suppressing the First Cause, increases our respect for the Divine Engineer [*le Génie divin*] who traced out the plan of the Universe, who

---

16 Martel, *Conflits*, 161.

17 Martel, *Conflits*, 13.

18 Martel, *Conflits*, 248.

19 Martel, *Conflits*, 12.

20 Martel, *Conflits*, 24–25.

21 It also takes up a few other matters, such as the Flood of Noah.

22 Martel, *Conflits*, 249.

23 Martel, *Conflits*, 163 (see also 147). The references in the passage are to Hervé Faye, *Sur l'Origine du monde* and to Pierre-Simon Laplace's *Système du monde* (1795, with five subsequent editions), Book V, chapter 6, both of whom suggest an evolutionary origin of the solar system.

designed the progressive development of life, put into an initially uniform matter the eternal forces which, little by little, by a constant evolution, transformed it into a world of an infinite variety of substances and organisms, grouped and arranged in magnificent harmony.[24]

The third he took from Jean Guibert:

In this hypothesis there would be a certain grandeur in considering the human body, which is the most perfect of organizations, as the terminal shoot produced by the evolution of living beings, the final result intended by the Creator to furnish an intelligent master of all nature. The physical relations of man with regard to the rest of nature are most readily comprehended—all creation is seen to make one harmonious whole; those millions of species which disappeared before man's arrival would have a "raison d'être," if they are considered as the component parts of a mighty tree from the topmost branches of which God would gather the human organism.[25]

Despite the book's generally Catholic tone, Pius X had a copy sent to the Index for examination on March 26, 1906.[26] It was discussed at the congregations held on November 29 and December 11, 1906.[27] The decree placing this book on the *Index* was published on December 14, 1906.[28]

Two years later, Célestin Douais, bishop of Beauvais, was able to identify the author of *Les Conflits* as one of the priests of his diocese. In a letter dated June 19, 1908, Martel wrote to Douais: "I regret having written on that subject without asking for the approval of my bishop, for scandalizing the faithful, and for undermining in certain souls their faith in Sacred Scripture. I absolutely retract anything in my book which could be contrary to Catholic doctrine."[29] The next day Douais sent the letter to the Holy Father.

3. THE HOLY OFFICE:
THE ARINTERO CASE (1908–1911)

In 1908, so the year after Pope St. Pius X published the two anti-modernist documents mentioned above, Juan González de Arintero was at the margins of a more broadly targeted local anti-modernist campaign launched by two diocesan priests in Salamanca.[30] The case began on January 24, 1908, when Manuel Antonio Rodríguez García (of St.

---

24 Martel, *Conflits*, 144–45.

25 Martel, *Conflits*, 246, from Guibert, *Origines*, 2nd ed., 202–3 (trans., 200).

26 Pius X to the Index, March 26, 1906 (doc. 154, Protocolli, 1906–7, CL, ADDF).

27 Gismondi, *Votum* (doc. 155, Protocolli, 1908–1909, CL, ADDF).

28 Decree, December 11, 1906 (doc. 147–49, Protocolli 1908–1909, CL, ADDF).

29 Martel to Douais and Douais to Pius X, June 19 and 20, 1908 (doc. 109–10, Protocolli, 1908–9, CL, ADDF).

30 Evidence for the events related below can be found in RV [Rerum Variorum] 1911/7, ADDF (or, equivalently, SO 387/09). The documents contained in this file are not numbered. Citations will be made in the footnotes when a further description of the source document would add to what is contained in the text, but not otherwise.

Martin's Parish) and Laurenzo Domingo García (of St. Paul's Parish) made a complaint (*ricorso*) to the Holy Office against their bishop (Francisco Javier Valdés y Noriega) and various local priests. Although Arintero was not directly mentioned in the original *ricorso*, he was mentioned in the first episcopal response to the inquiries of the Holy Office, as one of "three Salamanca priests more or less suspected of modernism."

Investigation into the case by the Holy Office was begun promptly, and lasted about three years. It is important to keep in mind that Arintero was only a small part of the larger affair; comments about him generally take up only a paragraph or two in documents of ten or twenty pages. That larger question of modernism in the diocese of Salamanca falls, of course, outside our story. Relevant to our story are only the answers to three questions:

1. To what extent were Arintero's views about scientific theories of evolution (as opposed to, for example, the evolution of theological doctrine) the cause of concern?

2. What did Church authorities *say* about those views?

3. What did they *do* about them?

The Holy Office began its inquiry into the larger case by writing to José María Cos y Macho, archbishop of Valladolid and, as such, the metropolitan responsible for Salamanca.[31] The archbishop, in his reply, characterized Arintero as follows:

> Fr. Juan González Arintero published two treatises in Spanish. In the first one, entitled *La evolución y la filosofía cristiana*, he introduces and defends a kind of mitigated transformism. The other, *El Diluvio*, was fiercely attacked when it came out by Don Ramirio Fernández Valbuena, Canon Penitentiary of Toledo. . . . One important person, endowed with virtue and knowledge, has again and again said that, in a disputation he had about modernism (privately, I think), Fr. Juan said many things that border on heresy. So one cannot say that he is above suspicion.

Near the end of his letter, the archbishop thought that it would be sufficient for Arintero to be gravely warned by his superior.[32]

The Holy Office, having heard back from the archbishop, on July 25, 1908, instructed Vicente Fernández y Villa, OSA, a professor of philosophy at his order's College of St. Monica in Rome and one of the Congregation's consultors, to write a *relatio* and *votum*. In his report, submitted on October 28 of that year, Fernández emphasized the Spanish context of the complaint, the infighting between Carlists and Integralists in the course of which the latter were quick to label as "liberals" or "modernists" anyone who was not of their party. The accusers, he went on to say, were priests "whose accusations of

---

31 Memoranda, January 28 and February 1, with a letter going out on February 7 or 8. The bishop's reply was dated July 11, 1907, but this must be a mistake, as the letter cites articles that appeared in November and December of 1907 (p. 36).

32 Cos, Response (reprinted in Fernández, *Relatio altera et votum*, July 1910, passage quoted on 38–39).

liberalism or modernism against other Catholics made these accusations suspect, unless they provided some evidence."[33] About Arintero in particular, he wrote:

> With respect to the accusation of modernism, made against Fr. Arintero …, it seems to me not to amount to much. … It is true that a few years ago, before these modernist questions were raging so feverishly and long before the publication of *Pascendi*, he wrote two books in Spanish *La evolución y la filosofía cristiana* and *El diluvio*. The latter I have seen warmly praised in Catholic periodicals even though other writers, such as those mentioned by the Archbishop, disagreed with it. In the former, it is true that Fr. Arintero, like a few other Catholic writers in those days, was too ready to make unnecessary concessions to modern scientists and had defended, with respect to transformism, opinions that are a bit incautious [*arrischiate*] (or so I have heard, though I have not read the book). As the Archbishop said, he "introduces and defends a kind of mitigated transformism." Anyway, the works were, as far as I remember, published with the approval of ecclesiastical authority, and I know of no one who before now found in them anything contrary to faith. With respect to modernism, there is nothing else about Fr. Arintero; it does not seem to me to be possible to consider him to be a modernist, at least not until there is proof to the contrary.[34]

Fernández concluded: "It does not seem to me to be just to transfer Fr. Arintero … and to suspend [him] from teaching, as the Archbishop would do. In my opinion, that would be a real and grave public punishment, and it does not seem to me, at least not on the basis of what we have been told, that [he] deserves such a punishment."[35] But, the *votum* continued, he should be "charitably advised by [his] superiors not to allow [himself] to be dominated by the spirit or the tendencies of modernism."

The larger case was taken up again on April 28, 1909, but action was postponed in the expectation that the Papal nuncio in Spain, Antonio Vico, would be able to submit to the Holy Office a fuller report, including copies of relevant publications.[36] On June 9–10, 1909, the cardinals postponed the case again, with a request for further investigation. The nuncio solicited some opinions from priests he respected and submitted a report on November 6, 1909. Neither his correspondents nor he made any mention of Arintero.

Fernández was then asked for a second *relatio*, which was printed in July 1910. On November 23, 1910, the Holy Office had the accusations against Arintero forwarded to the general of the Order "so that he can verify them, and make a decision and a referral." Hyacinthe Cormier, Dominican master-general, replied on December 6, 1910, writing:

> In order better to carry out the inquiries which the Holy Office has requested that I make, it would be important and useful to have some indication of the charges in question. There is no lack of men who, either from envy or zeal, but without any

---

33 Fernández, (first) *Votum*, (printed) December 1908, 6–7.

34 Fernández, (first) *Votum*, 4–5. Arintero's case was handled along with that of his fellow-Dominican Matthia García.

35 Fernández, (first) *Votum*, 7.

36 This was approved by the pope the following day, with a letter sent to the nuncio on May 11.

knowledge, or to distinguish themselves or to earn someone's gratitude, scream about modernism without any real solid foundation.

As the case developed, the focus was on his later, mystical writings and not on questions of science and religion.[37] On May 17, 1911, the Congregation decided to take no action in the case (verdict: *reponatur*), a decision approved by the pope on the following day.

4. THE PONTIFICAL BIBLICAL COMMISSION: DECREE ON GENESIS (1909)

On June 30, 1909, the Pontifical Biblical Commission, established by Pope Leo XIII in 1902 to implement the directives of *Providentissimus Deus*,[38] answered eight *dubia* on the historical character of the first three chapters of *Genesis*. The Commission said that Catholics may not teach that

> the chapters contain not accounts of actual events, accounts, that is, which correspond to objective reality and historical truth, but, either fables derived from the mythologies and cosmogonies of ancient peoples and accommodated by the sacred writer to monotheistic doctrine after the expurgation of any polytheistic error; or allegories and symbols without any foundation in objective reality proposed under the form of history to inculcate religious and philosophical truths; or finally legends in part historical and in part fictitious freely composed with a view to instruction and edification.

More specifically, it said that

> the literal historical sense [*sensus litteralis historicus*] [may not] be called into doubt in the case of ... the creation of all things by God in the beginning of time; the distinctive [*peculiaris*] creation of man;[39] the formation of the first woman from the first man; the unity of the human race; the original felicity of our first parents in the state of justice, integrity, and immortality; the command given by God to man to test his obedience; the transgression of the divine command at the instigation of the devil under the form of a serpent; [and] the degradation of our first parents from that primeval state of innocence.

The exact sense in which the creation of man was distinctive later became a focus of controversy (in particular in the de Dorlodot Affair, which will be discussed in chapter 12).

The document also said that "it is not always necessary to understand each and every word and phrase occurring in the aforesaid chapters in its proper sense [*sensus*

---

37 A report dated March 13, 1911, indicates that it was *Evolución Mística* and *Mecanismo divino de los factores de la evolución eclesiástica* that were reviewed.

38 Leo XIII, *Vigilantiae studiique*.

39 *Peculiaris* is hard to render concisely and precisely into English. Charlton T. Lewis and Charles Short, *Latin Dictionary*, put "not held in common with others," so I have put "distinctive" rather than the more common (but, in my view, less accurate) translation, "special."

proprius] . . . when either reason forbids the retention or necessity imposes the abandonment of the proper sense."[40] This explicitly includes the word יום *yom* (day). Nor,

> as it was not the mind of the sacred author in the composition of the first chapter of Genesis to give scientific teaching about the internal Constitution of visible things and the entire order of creation, but rather to communicate to his people a popular notion in accord with the current speech of the time and suited to the understanding and capacity of men, must the exactness of scientific language be always meticulously sought for in the interpretation of these matters.

Although the decisions of the Commission are published with the approval of the pope, they remain decisions of the Commission itself. They are not infallible, but they are official norms requiring not only obedience, but interior assent. To reject them would be rash.[41]

Some have seen in these statements an official rejection of the evolutionary origin of the first human body, but this does not seem to be correct. That the decree did not constitute such a rejection is clear from some informal remarks that Laurent Janssens, secretary to the Commission (and in that capacity also signatory of the published decree), made to Jules de Becker, rector of the American College of Louvain, later that year. Henry de Dorlodot wrote an account of those remarks in a letter to Paulin Ladeuze, rector of the Catholic University of Louvain, in 1925:

> At a reunion of the former students of the Belgian College in Rome, held at Louvain in 1909, two or three months after the decree of the Biblical Commission on the historical character of the three first chapters of Genesis, Msgr. [Charles] de T'Serclaes [Rector of the Belgian College] expressed the opinion that the expression *peculiaris creatio hominis* was aimed at the hypothesis of the production of the body of the first man by way of organic evolution. All of the assistants who spoke challenged that idea on the basis of the rules of interpretation and of the fact that, if that had been the intention of the Biblical Commission, they would have expressed themselves more clearly. M. Jacques Laminne, then professor of dogmatics at the Catholic University (and later auxiliary Bishop of Liège), who was among the opponents and whom the matter especially interested because he had to discuss the subject in his courses, asked Msgr. de Becker, who would run into Dom Laurent Janssens at the benediction of the new abbot of Maredsous, to ask the secretary of the Biblical Commission about the matter.
>
> Msgr. de Becker put the question as follows: "Is it true that the Biblical Commission had the intention to condemn [*réprouver*] application of the transformist theory to the origin of the body of the first man?" "Not at all," replied Msgr. Janssens. "Quite the contrary, it avoided doing that. It is true that certain Cardinals were not exactly proponents of that theory. But we chose the wording precisely so as not to touch on that question, and in order not to exclude that theory."

40 Dubia V and VII–VIII.

41 Pope Pius X, *Praestantia Scripturae*, and John Corbett, "The Biblical Commission."

Then, after a moment of silence, he added, "It was not the same for the origin of woman. Because, in short, once one acknowledges that the soul was created by God and that God is the creator of everything, the precise way in which the human body came to be has no theological importance, while, both in the New Testament and in Tradition, the origin of Eve, as coming from Adam, is placed in relation to theological and moral doctrines of great importance. That's why we judged that it is necessary to be rigorous about the question of woman and more open [*large*] on the question of man.[42]

5. THE JESUIT CURIA: THE WASMANN CASE

The first decade of the new century saw growing concerns at the Jesuit Curia in Rome about some of what was being written by Jesuit scholars, not least at the Writers Home in Bellevue (Luxembourg), where Wasmann then lived. On August 6, 1902, for example, Luis Martín, then superior-general, had written to German provincial Karl Schäffer expressing grave dissatisfaction with the work of Franz von Hummelauer and requiring the names and opinions of the censors be sent to him before publication of anything concerning the inspiration of Sacred Scripture.[43] That concerns about some of that scholarly work were still present in 1906 is shown both by a consultors' report of that year and by correspondence between Karl Frick, rector at the Writers Home, and Ruggero Freddi, vicar-general after the death of Martín on April 30, 1906.[44] Among those whose work caused the concern was Wasmann.[45]

The exact point of concern was what Wasmann had said about the extent to which the animal origin of the human body was a theologically open question. At some point Martín (who died in April 1906) had told him to be more cautious in what he said on

42 De Dorlodot's draft reply to the Commission, submitted to Ladeuze and attached to a letter from Ladeuze to Mercier, April 14, 1925, III.1–3 (Archives spéciales, Affaire de Dorlodot, T73 XXXIII, AKUL). (Again, the larger context will be discussed in chapter 12). There is, to be sure, a gap of some sixteen years between the conversation and the record of it in light of its relevance to later controversy, but, de Dorlodot added:

> Janssen's response is of the greatest importance. De Becker's memories were quite fresh and Janssens knew that the question was put to him in the name of the professor of dogmatics at the Catholic University.
>
> A couple of years ago, I asked Msgr. Laminne if he remembered the details of the conversation exactly as they had been reported to us by Msgr. de Becker. Msgr. Laminne replied that he could not recount all the details, but that he was certain that he had put into some handwritten notes the very words of Msgr. Janssens. For his part, Msgr. de Becker says that he is certain that he reported the words and the whole conversation very exactly. He could not have any doubt on the subject.
>
> For my part, I believe that I remember the whole conversation very well, at least as to the substance.

Messenger covered this in brief in 1930 in *Evolution and Theology*, 227–31.

43 Martín to Schäffer, August 6, 1904 (Registro Lettere dei General Germania, VI, 353, ARSI). For more on this, see Klaus Schatz, SJ, "'Modernismo' tra i Gesuiti."

44 Excerpta ex litteris Consultorum, May 23, 1906, 33 (33–46, Prov.Germ. VII, ARSI), and Freddi to Frick, May 20, 1906 (31–33, Prov.Germ. VII, ARSI).

45 See Schatz, "Modernismo," or his "Wasmann."

that point,[46] but the revisions he had made in the problematic passage between the first edition and the third (discussed above), despite the fact that they had all passed censorship, had not allayed everyone's concerns.

Wasmann again came to the notice of the Jesuit Curia shortly after Franz Xavier Wernz was elected superior-general. Wernz, canon lawyer and rector of the Gregorian University, had been a consultor at the Congregation of the Index in the 1890s, and as such had participated in the preparatory congregations that had reviewed the works of Leroy and Zahm. It is not clear what exactly drew Wernz's attention to Wasmann's work. The most likely possibility is the publication, on January 25, 1907, of the syllabus for Wasmann's upcoming Berlin lectures, the third of which would address precisely "the application of the theory of evolution to man." Another possibility is the harsh criticism of Wasmann's work made by Gregorian University professor Bellino Carrara, SJ, in his *La biologia a suo posto* (1907). Whatever might have been the precipitating cause, Wernz asked Jesuit theologian Hermann van Laak for his opinion on what Wasmann had said about the animal origins of the human body early enough for van Laak to have prepared a fifteen-page reply by February 22, 1907.

Van Laak's reply addressed three questions—the factual question (what Wasmann had said), the legal question (of what it was permitted to say on the question), and the practical question of what Wernz should do.[47] Van Laak first addressed the question of fact. Did Wasmann think that Catholics were free to accept the animal origin of the human body? Van Laak acknowledged that Wasmann had softened the way he had expressed his views in the third edition of the book, but thought that the book still presented the question itself as theologically open. That raised the legal question, on which van Laak argued that Wasmann's case for openness was too weak to make publication of his view permissible. So what should Wernz do? Van Laak recommended that any new edition of the book should be permitted only after changes. It should either omit the theological aspect of the question[48] altogether or at least modify it by, among other things, omitting the citation of St. Augustine and the idea of human ancestors that were neither plant nor animal. This constituted, of course, a critique of the censors who had approved publication of the book.

That report was passed on to Frick, as rector at Bellevue. On July 8, Frick wrote back to Ernst Thill, by then Wasmann's newly-appointed provincial, objecting to most of what van Laak had said. [49] He conceded that *Moderne Biologie* was in some places insufficiently clear and could "give rise to the *appearance* or *suspicion* that Fr. Wasmann still wanted to give implicit support to the view to which his superiors, and the censors, had objected." Nevertheless, van Laak had (according to Frick) misstated Wasmann's

---

46 Wasmann mentioned the fact that he was adhering to such instructions in a letter to Martín's successor, Franz Xavier Wernz, July 17, 1907 (Censurae (U–Z), ARSI).

47 Van Laak to Wernz, February 22, 1907 (Censurae (U–Z), ARSI).

48 I.e., Wasmann, *Moderne Biologie*, 3rd ed., 444–51 (trans., 436–43).

49 Frick to Thill, July 8, 1907 (Censurae (U–Z), ARSI). Van Laak was not named in the copy of the report sent to Frick.

views: Wasmann had not defended theological liberty on the question of the evolutionary origin of the human body.

Wernz's request came just as Wasmann was preparing to give his Berlin lectures (delivered on February 13–18), part of a very public controversy between Wasmann and Haeckel. Wasmann's critics had been quick to get their evaluation of the lectures into the press. The *Vossische Zeitung* published articles on the lectures for three months running. There, in what might fairly be called Prussia's newspaper of record, and elsewhere in the secular press, the discussion following the lectures was characterized as a "brilliant triumph of free research over ecclesiastical constraint."[50] Wasmann called the reporting an "undignified smear campaign [*Hetze*]."[51] Wasmann was, therefore, eager to publish the lectures themselves,[52] but these would have to be cleared by the Jesuit curia prior to publication.

Wernz's view on the animal origin of the human body was clear. On May 13, 1907, he wrote to Thill that "the real and immediate creation of the body of the first man by God is a fact, as coming to us from Sacred Scripture, as the *communis et certa sententia theologorum* proposes it, and as already emphasized in three cases by the Roman congregations. To speak about 'liberty' in this case does not make any sense."[53] Two of the "three cases" were surely Leroy and Zahm; what he meant by the third is not clear.[54] No congregation other than the Index had taken up the question. That immediate formation should be regarded as a *sententia certa*, or at least *communis*, in a way that explicitly excluded evolutionary processes continued to have much currency at least for some three more decades.[55] Wernz went on to say:

> What Fr. Wasmann (1) philosophizes about a "possibility" and (2) says about theological "freedom" on this question, must absolutely be omitted. Because this philosophizing about the possibility is, first, completely impractical craziness, based in insufficient evidence and at risk of a very worrisome misunderstanding; because this "possibility" would often as a matter of fact be interpreted as meaning that it is possible that things really were so. That would be a claim about where theological "freedom" ends; because it doesn't end only once there is a *definitio ex cathedra*.[56]

By July 14, the censor's reports on the Berlin lectures were ready, and Wernz passed them on to Frick. Publication was approved, but with conditions: "The cardinal point of

---

50 Wasmann, *Kampf*, 146–47 (trans., 242), with the quotation from the press apparently from the *Vossische Zeitung*.

51 Wasmann, *Kampf*, 151 (trans., 249).

52 Wasmann, *Kampf*, viii (trans., v–vii).

53 Wernz to Thill, May 13, 1907 (2/20, APG; quoted from Schatz, "Modernismo," 356).

54 Possibly Martel, though the case does not seem to have received much notice. Bonomelli's "case" was surely better known, but it was not really a formal act of the Congregation; it was only informal advice. Caverni had not defended the evolutionary origin of the human body, though of course Wernz might have had the details of that case wrong.

55 See, for example, J. M. Hervé, *Manuale theologiae dogmaticae*, 12th ed., 2:325; John Moran, *Alpha et omega*, 98; and Gabriel Huarte, *De Deo creante*, 155. All three agreed that defense of the evolutionary formation of the human body was rash.

56 Wernz to Thill, May 13, 1907 (2/20, APG; quoted from Schatz, "Modernismo," 356n49).

the whole question is that the author may not teach, either directly *or indirectly*, that the opinion that the body descends from an animal is permissible [*libera*] for Catholics."[57] Later correspondence suggests that two other conditions were that Wasmann be less extensive in his acknowledgment of "possibilities" and that he omit his references to St. Augustine.[58]

On July 17, Wasmann wrote back to Wernz:

> No one will be able to think that I here said that there was "theological freedom" of opinion about the animal ancestry of man with respect to the human body. I did not even say that there was "theological freedom" of opinion about the idea that God used already organized matter [i.e., a living being], although that idea would be completely different from that of animal ancestry, since man could have had his own phylogenetic history, one which had no genetic relationship to that of the animal world. I characterized that last idea in *Moderne Biologie* (3rd ed., 449) *explicitly* as a purely *philosophical, abstract* possibility, but not as a *theological* possibility.[59]

That philosophical possibility was also raised in the published version of the discussion following the Berlin lectures: "If man has a phylogenetic history, it does not at all have to be identical to that of the higher animals; it could have begun with similar, but nevertheless essentially different original cells. That would be entirely sufficient to explain all the similarities of man and animal without our having to suppose that man has an animal ancestry."[60] But Wasmann also said: "I have not disputed the possibility of the animal ancestry of man with respect to the body—I explicitly say 'the possibility'—and thereby abstain completely from saying anything about the theological question, with which we are here not at all concerned."[61] As for the third condition, the Berlin lecture made no mention of St. Augustine.

On July 22, Wernz wrote to Thill again.[62] That same day, Thill gave permission for the lectures to be published.

Nevertheless, Wernz's concerns about *Moderne Biologie* remained, and, in March of the following year, he told both Frick and Wasmann that any fourth edition of *Moderne Biologie* would have to omit the earlier discussions of the philosophical and theological side of the question and to treat only the scientific side. That, he added, "seems to correspond most fully to the clear directives of the Holy See."[63]

Wasmann had defended ecclesiastical censorship in Berlin. It was not, he said, any different from any editor's decisions about what a contributor was allowed to publish in

---

57 Wernz to Frick, July 14, 1907 (78–79, Prov.Germ. VII, ARSI).

58 Wernz to Frick, December 12, 1907 (101, Prov.Germ. VII, ARSI).

59 Wasmann to Wernz, July 17, 1907 (Censurae (U–Z), ARSI).

60 *Kampf*, 81 (trans., 128).

61 *Kampf*, 138 (trans., 229–30).

62 Wernz to Thill, July 22, 1907 (2/20, APG; quoted from Schatz, "Modernismo," 355n44).

63 Wernz to Wasmann, March 18, 1908 (121–22, Prov.Germ. VII, ARSI).

a scientific journal, or even in a popular newspaper.[64] "When I show someone something and have them check whether it is right or not, it is fair to say, 'Four eyes see more than two.'"[65] In the end, he chose not to prepare a fourth edition.

64 *Kampf*, 135n3 (trans., 225–26n2).

65 *Kampf*, 136 (trans., 226).

CHAPTER 10

NON-OFFICIAL FORA
(1898–1909)

1. PERIODICAL LITERATURE

As the new century began, the Catholic press continued to find space for a discussion of evolutionism.

* * * * *

In France, the *Revue thomiste* published Charles de Kirwan's "Où en est l'Évolutionnisme?," a long, two-part appraisal of transformism, in 1901. He began by saying that "The theory of evolution in the organic kingdoms has, nowadays, the right to be cited in science whether we like it or not."[1] The evolution that he wanted to discuss "is situated between two extremes: at the beginning, the action of a Creator and Legislator for all of living nature; at the other extreme, the appearance of Man, endowed with intelligence, i.e., with an idea of the universal; of truth, beauty, and goodness; as well as with a free will."[2]

Kirwan was doubtful about the *truth* of transformism, but argued that the metaphysical objection—that it depended on effects being greater than their causes—was unsound.

1 Kirwan, "Évolutionnisme," 379.

2 Kirwan, "Évolutionnisme," 381.

> Is it not permitted to conclude that the whole animal kingdom *could* include only
> one essence, one nature, one species in the metaphysical sense—the animal *species*,
> as opposed to the human *species* and the plant *species*—all three of them included,
> with the inorganic kingdom, in the *genus* creature. . . . On this hypothesis, one can
> conceive of divine action as divided into four principal acts: creation of the inorganic
> world (including light) *ex nihilo*; creation of a principle of vegetative life added to
> certain elements of the inorganic world, [etc.].[3]

The differences among the various types of plants and animals would, that is, be only
accidental differences. That may be only a hypothesis, but it does not violate any metaphysical principle.[4]

Did evolutionary processes play any rôle in the formation of the human body? He
thought that it was at least a discussable question "whether it would be more difficult
for a spiritual soul created for that purpose to inform, in order to make a mechanism as
complicated and as perfect as the human body, an inert mineral mass, than it would be
to inform, for its own ends, a similar body already organized although for other, lesser
purposes."[5] Catholic evolutionism is committed to "an evolution directed by Providence
[rather than a spontaneous one], and developing not blindly or inevitably, but following
the plan preconceived and willed by God Himself."[6]

His overall verdict was that

> Spiritualist evolutionism . . . faces no objection in principle and very ingeniously
> explains a great number facts, leaves a great number of others unexplained, and faces
> many difficulties on points of detail. . . . Nevertheless, as an hypothesis about the
> mode which God could have used to effect creation, it is a plausible system, in some
> respects even an appealing [*séduisant*] one, and one that can satisfy the mind with
> a quite comprehensible conception of the divine plan and of the sovereign wisdom
> of a legislative and governing Providence. . . . The evolutionary theory remains,
> undoubtedly, a possibility that one does not have the right to take as an established
> fact, much less to impose, but one that one also has no right to dismiss in the name
> of metaphysics or especially in the name of spiritualist or Christian beliefs.[7]

The *Revue du clergé français* gave space to both sides of the issue. In 1902, It published an article by Elie Blanc arguing that "metaphysics has the right to intervene on
the question of transformism" and that, it being metaphysically impossible for a lower
being to produce a higher being by means of generation, to accept transformism is to
maintain an absurdity.[8] After publishing Blanc's metaphysical critique of transformism,

---

3 Kirwan, "Évolutionnisme," 553.

4 Kirwan, "Évolutionnisme," 555.

5 Kirwan, "Évolutionnisme," 561.

6 Kirwan, "Évolutionnisme," 560.

7 Kirwan, "Évolutionnisme," 567–68.

8 Blanc, "Le Transformisme," 52.

it made room for replies. Priest-philosopher Camille Mano accepted the principle about the connection between metaphysics and science, but rejected its deployment against transformism.

> The crux of the question is to know whether the complexity of the antecedent causes (principal and secondary) can ground the appearance of a new, *dissimilar,* and perhaps superior, being. The appearance of new beings is determined, not by a principal cause (the generator) alone, but also by a whole set of concomitant circumstances, an entire complex of facts and laws. The *complexity* of causes will explain the apparent superiority of the effect.[9]

The same physiological laws, he went on to say, explain the behavior of both amoebae and elephants. "The animal scale reveals rather complexity than absolute transcendence with respect to species. It is difficult to explain life on the basis of physico-chemical laws, but it is easy to reduce all animal phenomena to the great laws of biology."[10] Mano did not want to appear as a champion of transformism, but, he concluded, it should not be opposed on the basis of ontological principles alone. "If science is not exempt from metaphysical critique, all the more should metaphysics not isolate itself from the scientific and *bona fide* observation of facts."[11]

Mano's article was seconded by Georges Surbled (physician and professor at the École hospitalière de San Salvadour) in the next volume of the journal. Surbled was skeptical about the scientific evidence for transformism, but "it is a controverted question which can only be answered by an appeal to facts." "It is susceptible to a reasonable interpretation [and] is defended by men of unquestioned science and faith.... It is dangerous—and extremely unjust—to confuse a perfectly scientific idea with the aberrations of materialism."[12]

＊ ＊ ＊ ＊ ＊

Other European Catholic periodicals also found room for the presentation of evolutionist views. I have already mentioned several—*Stimmen aus Maria-Laach* published an early version of Wasmann's *Moderne Biologie* in 1901–1903, and *Soluciones católicas* published Arintero's "La Evolución ante la fe y la ciencia" in 1899–1900.

In 1906, *La Scuola cattolica,* a monthly then put out under the auspices of the Pontificia Facoltà Teologica of the Seminario di Milano, published Agostino Gemelli's multi-part article "Su di un nuovo indirizzo della teoria dell'evoluzione," followed later in the year by another multi-part response to his critics[13] (discussed in chapter 8). This was followed in 1909 by a multi-part article by Guido Mattiussi, SJ, taking the other side of

---

9 Mano, "Métaphysique," 208.

10 Mano, "Métaphysique," 209.

11 Mano, "Métaphysique," 210.

12 Surbled, "Chronique scientifique," 87.

13 Gemelli, "Conflitto di tendenze (A proposito di alcune critiche mosse alle mie idee sulla teoria dell'evoluzione)." The critics whom he had in mind were, in particular, Giuseppe Tuccimei and L. Necchi, "Nuovo libro sull'evoluzione."

213

the evolution question, "Le speranze svanite del Darwinismo."[14] To the third installment of Mattiussi's article, the editors added a curious explanatory preface:

> The editors of *La Scuola Cattolica*, in publishing this article, which reaches conclusions different from that defended in our journal by Fr. Gemelli, do not intend to take a position on the merits of the question. It only wishes to make known to its readers, by means of articles from scholars with opposite points of view, the present state of the question of evolution, a question which, within certain limits, is still being discussed by Catholic scholars.[15]

In the United States, William Seton wrote for *The Catholic World* a critique of Eberhard Dennert's *Vom Sterbelager des Darwinismus* (1902), an English translation of which had just appeared. Dennert, a botanist and a Lutheran, accepted some kind of evolution as a working hypothesis, but emphatically rejected Darwin's mechanism of evolutionary change. Seton's "Darwinism on its Deathbed" replied by quoting some twenty-four authors in defense of the idea that the natural-selection thesis was by no means on its deathbed. This evoked, in turn, two replies. The first, James J. Walsh's "The Present Position of Darwinism," appeared in *The Catholic World* the following month. Walsh expressed reservations about natural selection, "not with any idea that [it] … contains any dangers overt or covert for orthodox thinking, but entirely because of the scientific interest of the question."[16] The second, appearing at about the same time in the *Catholic Fortnightly Review*, was entitled "Natural Selection or Organic Evolution?" and signed only "H. M." (probably Hermann Muckermann).[17] The author was himself an evolutionist, but one unwilling to give natural selection the prominence that Darwin had given it.

If not quite literally a periodical publication, then at least similar in also being evidence of Catholic thought about evolution, was another project of the American Paulist Fathers, a book of short "replies to questions received on missions to non-Catholics" entitled *The Question Box*. Its author, Bertrand Conway, CSP, addressed the question of evolution twice.

First, in response to the idea that the general orderliness of the natural world, including "the special adaptation of the various organs and senses of the human body" "declare an Intelligent Lawmaker by whose wisdom all has been established," he replied that "all that evolution has accomplished 'is to throw back the question of design from the facts immediately observed to the causes subsequently discovered. And there the question must be left by science, to be taken up by philosophy.' As the evidence of design points

14 Mattiussi had addressed the question previously in "L'evoluzione è possibile?"

15 Editors' note to Mattiussi, "Speranze svanite," 441.

16 Walsh, "Present Position," 499.

17 Identification of the author is based on the fact that Muckermann is referred to in a review of his own book in that same periodical a few years later as "an occasional contributor" (*Catholic Fortnightly Review*, Review, 73). The identification is also made by Morrison, *History*, 155n7.

to a Designer, so evolution points to an Intelligence who is the origin of the universal law of progress."[18]

About the particular question of *human* evolution, he wrote only that:

> If men in the name of science, although without its warrant, deny … the unity of the human race, or maintain the evolution of man, body and soul, from the monkey, the infallible Church of God in the name of truth denounces them as false teachers. But if, for example, men declare the six days of Genesis to be long epochs, and not days of twenty-four hours each, the Church has no quarrel with them. They have contradicted none of her dogmas.[19]

✳ ✳ ✳ ✳ ✳

In 1906, the Czech Catholic theological journal *Museum: Časopis Bohoslovců Českoslovanských* published a four-part article by Br. Jan Mejzlík, an article that won for the author a prize from the editors. Three points that he made should be noted.

First, on the question of whether it is possible "to admit the evolution of an organism from the Biblical point of view," asked at the beginning of the final part of the series, Mejzlík wrote:

> The Bible is not a handbook of natural science. … One must also keep in mind the great difference between dogma, on the one hand, and the application of revealed truths or the opinion of Biblical times on the other. The former never loses its validity, being absolute truth; the latter can be corrected or supplemented as time goes on. … There can, therefore, be no mention of any fundamental dispute between the theory of evolution and the Bible, all the less because natural science has no clear certainty on that question of the origin of organic life, but admits various hypotheses.[20]

Second, with respect to the transformation of plant and animal species, "evolutionary theory [as long as it] … recognizes evolutionary progress as one of the main features of a world plan outlined [*naznačený*] by the Creator Himself, generates no controversy and no clash with Biblical views."[21]

Third, he thought that there were scientific as well as theological reasons for rejecting evolutionary anthropogenesis.[22]

Fourth, the summary verdict on evolution with which he concluded the article was this:

---

18 Conway, *Question Box*, 1st ed., 2–3. Conway attributed the embedded quotation to George Romanes, but his citation is incorrect and I have not been able to verify the quotation.

19 Conway, *Question Box*, 1st ed., 142.

20 Mejzlík, "Jak pohlížíme?," 173–74. For the fuller account of Catholic evolutionary thought in Bohemia and Moravia, see Pospíšil, "Czech Thinkers," and *Průkopníci*, 75–90.

21 Mejzlík, "Jak pohlížíme?," 117–18.

22 Mejzlík, "Jak pohlížíme?," 176–80.

We are not yet in a position to decide the question definitively; nevertheless, we have the diligent research of the last four decades to thank for the building blocks of a future theory, one which will differ from Darwinism on five essential points:

1. Evolution proceeds according to a definite plan and aims at a predetermined end.
2. Nature knows no chance or confusion [*zmatek*]; each stage of development is the result of law-like factors.
3. The harmonious union of all creatures puts egoism and struggle in the background.
4. The human soul has no equal in the whole organic world and cannot be understood as a higher stage in the evolution of an animal instinct.
5. The Creator put into organisms internal evolutionary [*vývojný*] powers, and a life principle, and these are the primary agents of evolution.[23]

He ended by quoting from Joseph Delsaulx both the claim that "the theory of evolution should be neither over- nor underestimated" and that

> the doctrine of evolution, which I defend as a philosopher and as a natural scientist, rests on the foundations of a Christian world view, which I hold to be the only correct one. On an evolutionary worldview built on a Christian foundation, the history of the animal and vegetable kingdoms on our earth becomes a short line in a million-page book of the natural evolution of the whole universe, on the title page of which is written, in indelible letters, "In the beginning God created the heavens and the earth."[24]

2. ENCYCLOPEDIAS

The first decade of the twentieth century also saw the appearance of three new Catholic encyclopedias.[25] Neither the Leroy and Zahm cases nor the war against modernism seems to have had any effect on the range of views about evolution that those encyclopedias expressed. I will focus here on two.[26]

The first, appearing in 1907, was the two-volume *Kirchliches Handlexikon*.[27] The two articles on evolution were assigned to Fr. Ludwig Baur, a philosopher, then at the Universität Tübingen, interested in the synthesis of Aristotelian-Thomistic philosophy and modern science. He wrote that "a limited transformation, one which does not cross species boundaries, must be conceded, [though] the boundaries between species were

23 Mejzlík, "Jak pohlížíme?," 180.

24 Mejzlík, "Jak pohlížíme?," 180. He does not indicate the source of the quotation.

25 A number of encyclopedias were published gradually over the course of the decade. In this chapter, I will discuss only those whose articles were published before 1909. Encyclopedias that began publishing before 1909 but reached our topic only after that date will be discussed in later chapters.

26 The third is *Herders Konversations-Lexikon*, 3rd ed. (1902–1903), which contained two unsigned articles—"Abstammungslehre" and "Darwin."

27 Published in Munich under the general editorship of Michael Buchberger, professor of canon law at the Philosophisch-Theologische Hochschule in Regensburg and later bishop of that city, it bore an *imprimatur* from the vicar general of the Archdiocese of Freising-Munich.

previously drawn too narrowly."[28] More generally, "creation could have taken place either in such a way that God created living things already differentiated into genera and species by invariable essential differences or in such a way that he created one or several original types from which the currently existing differentiated species then arose by generation."[29] How should one decide between possibilities? He went on to say that "The wording of Holy Scripture . . . and the preference of exegetes and theologians is decidedly in favor of the first interpretation [sc., that God directly differentiated living things into genera and species with fixed essential differences], even if these considerations do not positively require it."[30]

✳ ✳ ✳ ✳ ✳

Second came the American *Catholic Encyclopedia* (1907–1912), published with the *imprimatur* of John Cardinal Farley, archbishop of New York, which first addressed the topic in a two-part article. The first part, "Catholics and Evolution," was written by Wasmann; the second, "History and Scientific Foundation of Evolution," by Hermann Muckermann.

Like Wasmann, Muckermann (1877–1962) was a Jesuit, and a biologist. After having spent several years teaching mathematics and science in the United States, he returned to Europe (in 1908), to the German Jesuit expatriate community at the Ignatiuskolleg, in Valkenburg (the Netherlands). In 1906, he published a book entitled *Attitude of Catholics towards Darwinism and Evolution* and another entitled *The Humanizing of the Brute.* Later, in 1916, he developed a strong interest in eugenics and by the 1930s even endorsed voluntary sterilization despite Pius XI's clear condemnation of the procedure in *Casti conubii.* Despite his rejection of Catholic teaching on this particular point, he remained sufficiently Catholic to be ejected from his position at the Kaiser-Wilhelm Institute by the new National Socialist government in 1933.

Wasmann's part of the article ran to just over a page. It emphasized the importance of distinguishing scientific hypothesis from philosophical speculation, theistic evolution from atheistic, evolution in general from Darwinism, and the evolution of plants and animals from the origin of man. About evolution in general, he wrote that "the theory of evolution as a scientific hypothesis . . . is in perfect agreement with the Christian conception of the universe; for Scripture does not tell us in what form the present species of plants and of animals were originally created by God."[31] And about human evolution, he acknowledged that there was no intrinsic *theological* problem with a partially evolutionary anthropogenesis: "That God should have made use of natural, evolutionary, original causes in the production of man's body, is *per se* not improbable."[32]

---

28 Baur, "Abstammungslehre," 31.

29 Baur, "Abstammungslehre," 30.

30 Baur, "Abstammungslehre," 30.

31 Wasmann, "Catholics and Evolution," 5:654.

32 Wasmann, "Catholics and Evolution," 5:655.

217

Muckermann's part of the article is much longer, running fifteen pages and covering the more substantive aspects of the subject. He summarized *his* conclusions in six points:

1. The origin of life is unknown to science.

2. The origin of the main organic types and their principal subdivisions are likewise unknown to science.

3. There is no evidence in favour of an ascending evolution of organic forms.

4. There is no trace of even a merely probable argument in favour of the animal origin of man.

5. Most of the so-called systematic species and genera were certainly not created as such, but originated by a process of either gradual or saltatory evolution.[33]

The whole question of the transformation of one species into another was complicated by the fact that different disciplines use the term "species" differently. The distinction was sometimes maintained by using the term "natural species" for the philosophical concept and the term "systematic species" for the biological. Muckermann emphasized this in the passage quoted above as well as in another passage, in which he wrote: "We must strongly emphasize the fact that the biological idea of species has nothing whatever in common with the Scriptural conception or with that of Scholastic philosophy."[34]

6. There is very little known as to the causes of evolution. . . . In our opinion the principle of "Mendelian segregation," together with Darwin's natural selection and the moulding influence of environment, will probably be some of the chief constituents of future evolutionary theories.

The topic was discussed again in a later volume, in Austrian geologist Lukas Waagen's article on paleontology. After discussing the origin of fossils, and fossilization, he turned to the theory of evolution (or development, as he generally called it under the influence of the German *Entwicklung*).

He readily distinguished "progressive" evolution, a "strong differentiation and specialization of peculiarities" that produced new genera or families, from an "ascending" evolution. Paleontology, he thought offered "probable arguments" for the former but the absence of a "series of intermediate forms" meant that proofs of ascending evolution, and in particular of its extreme (i.e., monophyletic) form, were lacking. In sum:

> We may . . . say that the organisms of the geological ages are connected by descent, and that there is good reason for accepting progressive development [i.e., evolution] in the several lines of descent down to the present time. But if we go beyond this and set up a divergent line of descent for the whole world of organisms, or seek to trace all organisms back to a single cell, we abandon the foundation of fact. If, therefore, we infer that a general development [i.e., evolution] cannot be established by the

---

33 Muckermann, "Evolution," 5:670, for these and the sixth point, below.

34 Muckermann, "Evolution," 5:660.

facts, we are still within the lines of the theory of descent, for the essential conception of this theory is that the systematic species of zoology and botany are not rigid and unchangeable, but have developed [i.e., evolved] from ancestors unlike themselves, and may likewise develop [i.e., evolve] into differently formed descendants. It is the business of the theory of development [i.e., evolution] to investigate the facts and causes which underlie the series of organic forms, at the head of which stand existing species. Consequently, it is no essential part of its aim to prove that development [i.e., evolution] is ascending or that it supposes a single original progenitor.[35]

On the question of the *cause* of evolutionary change, he acknowledged the increasing acceptance among paleontologists of Edward Drinker Cope's Neo-Lamarckism—that "the development of organisms rests mainly on hereditary changes, produced by the use or the non-use of the organs, as well as by correlation and direct transforming influences, while selection has only a slight, if any, importance."[36]

His article included two paragraphs on paleontology and the origin of man, mentioning Neanderthalers and Java Man, but citing Freiburg zoologist Ludwig Kathariner to the effect that

> it is impossible to reach a completely satisfactory conclusion on the origin of mankind if we base it solely of morphology and ignore man's spiritual side. A discussion of this question based on palæontological data is fruitless, as the decision is too greatly influenced by the conception which men have of creation as a whole and of its need of a first cause, of their views on the theory of cognition, and of other subjective considerations.[37]

The evolutionary origin of man is also addressed briefly in another volume, in which Francis Aveling wrote that

> As to the mode of creation [of man], there would seem to be two possible alternatives. Either the individual composite was created *ex nihilo*, or a created soul became the informing principle of matter already pre-existing in another determination. Either mode would be philosophically tenable, but the Thomistic principle of the successive and graded evolution of forms in matter is in favour of the latter view.[38]

35 Waagen, "Palæontology," 11:413. The preceding phrases are found on 11:413–14.

36 Waagen, "Palæontology," 11:414.

37 Waagen, "Palæontology," 11:414.

38 Aveling, "Man," 5:582.

3. TEXTBOOKS

Many textbooks also were compatibilist about the evolutionary origins of plants and animals, though many still had reservations about what, if any, contribution evolutionary processes had made to the origin of the human race.

Let us begin a review of some early twentieth-century textbooks with Joseph Pohle's *Lehrbuch der Dogmatik* (1902).[39] Pohle's teaching career stretched from Washington to Breslau. His *Lehrbuch* ran through many German editions and was translated into English. In that book, read by so many seminarians, he emphasized that:

> The Bible is not a scientific textbook.... Its language with respect to natural-scientific matters is always that of the ordinary man ..., grounded in external appearances.
>
> The Mosaic account of creation provides scientific research only with negative norms, not with positive ones.... In questions such as the Kant-Laplace hypothesis and evolutionary accounts of the surface of the earth or of plant and animal species, the scientist has a free hand.[40]

That free hand, however, did not extend to the origin of man. After rejecting *atheistic* Darwinism, according to which "the whole man, i.e., body and soul, evolved, from the animal kingdom," Pohle added that "the view of the Catholic zoölogist St.-George Mivart, hitherto tolerated by the Church, ... also requires the most decided rejection, even though it has not yet been subject to theological censure. Even if it is not heretical, it at least certainly contradicts the natural meaning of the words of the Bible as well as Christian opinion."[41] His own assessment was that the direct formation of the body of the first man by God was theologically certain (*sententia certa*).

✳ ✳ ✳ ✳ ✳

Nikolaus Gottesleben and Johann Baptist Schiltknecht published another German-language textbook, *Die Biblische Geschichte auf der Oberstufe der katholischen Volksschule*, three years later. They first addressed the topic in a section entitled "The Relation of the Biblical Story of Creation to the Results of the Natural Sciences,"[42] where they acknowledged as basic principles both that Holy Scripture is a religious text, from which one should not expect answers to scientific questions, and that when it does address such questions, it, being the work of the Holy Spirit, will do so without error. In any case, nature is also God's book and so also reveals the Creator. Any apparent contradiction

---

39 On Pohle, see J. Sickenberger, "Joseph Pohle zum Gedächtnis."

40 Pohle, *Lehrbuch der Dogmatik*, 401 and 402 (cf. trans., 105 and 107–8).

41 Pohle, *Lehrbuch*, 412–13. Pohle had been a student in Trier, in the Archdiocese of Cologne, in the 1860s. Perhaps in this view he consciously continued to follow the teaching of the Council of Cologne, though he is surely not unique in holding this opinion. His wording here is noteworthy in light of the fact that Salvatore Brandi had seemed to suggest otherwise in his exchange with Bishop John Cuthbert Hedley a few years before, though of course neither Brandi's article nor the evidence he cited constitute, in the formal sense, a theological censure.

42 Gottesleben and Schiltknecht, *Geschichte*, 42–49.

indicates either a misunderstanding of Scripture or insufficiently understood scientific research.

The authors went on to canvas the paleoetiological sciences, addressing in turn the origin of the cosmos (i.e., of solar systems), of the earth, of life, and of the diversity of biological species. They point out that paleontology, which they quickly reviewed, provides good evidence of a generally progressive faunal succession. In their judgment, however, acceptance of the *transformation* of the earlier, lower, animals into the higher, later, ones would have to await the appearance of a more complete series of transitional forms than had yet been found. The question of the origin of biological diversity was not, however, (the origin of man excepted) an important theological question. They cited anti-evolutionist scientists such as Virchow in support of their skepticism, but also quoted the compatibilist remarks of Johann Baptist Holzammer cited in chapter 4.[43]

Gottesleben and Schiltknecht returned to the questions of the origin, the unity, and the age of the human race a few pages later, in a section on "The Relation of the [Scriptural] Narrative to the Results of Human Research."[44] While acknowledging the similarities between man and higher mammals, they nevertheless emphasized the anatomical and paleontological gaps [*Klüfte*] between them. Common ancestry of man and ape, they said, "abandons a basis in fact for the realm of speculation."[45] Whatever one makes of those arguments, they went on to say, the essential difference between animal and man—the uniquely human capacity for abstract thought, morality, and religion—makes animal ancestry for man impossible. Science, they concluded, tells against an evolutionary origin of the human body; reason tells us that the origin of the essential difference (the difference in capacities) must lie in the action of a supernatural creator.

In presenting this case for the direct formation of the human body, the authors limited themselves to scientific and philosophical arguments, without any citation of Scripture. Their treatment of the second of the anthropological questions, by contrast, began with the remark that "Holy Scripture explicitly teaches the unity of the human race." Perhaps they believed that Scripture had taught on both issues; the motivation for silence is not always easy to identify. Still, it is interesting that, although Paderborn (where the book received its *imprimatur*) was then within the archdiocese of Cologne, the authors did not repeat the anti-evolutionary thesis about the origin of the human body promulgated by the provincial council forty-five years before.

By 1906, a revision of Schuster's *Handbuch* was in the hands of Joseph Selbst, like Holzammer on the faculty of the Mainz seminary. Holzammer's prefatory "Discussion" was now gone; Selbst put his own, perhaps slightly more evolutionist, thoughts into a long footnote that "all living things, and all evolution, presupposes a creator and a law-giver, whose power and wisdom appear all the greater if He allowed the many forms of living beings and their perfected forms to evolve in accordance with natural laws. So

43 Gottesleben and Schiltknecht, *Geschichte*, 46.

44 Gottesleben and Schiltknecht, *Geschichte*, 59–63.

45 Gottesleben and Schiltknecht, *Geschichte*, 60.

the mitigated evolutionary theory ... is surely consistent with the faith."[46] He rejected, however, extension of the theory to the origin of the human race.

＊ ＊ ＊ ＊ ＊

France during the same years saw the publication of Jules Souben's nine-volume *Nouvelle théologie dogmatique*, in the eyes of at least two reviewers more a work of popularization than a textbook, though one that could be expected to find its way into the classroom as well.[47] The third volume, *La Création selon la foi et la science*, included a second part, on the work of the six days, itself divided in two—one section focused on natural science and the other on the Biblical narrative. Two points are of particular interest.

First, on evolution in general, Souben reviewed the evidence and acknowledged the controversy between its defenders and its opponents. He rejected, of course, the monistic evolutionism of Haeckel and others, but about more strictly scientific theories of evolution he wrote:

> If the transformists content themselves with proposing their hypotheses modestly, as a possible or probable explanation of the production of species, if they do not try to convince us that all organisms are descended from a cell organized by chance and animated by a universal *nisus*, then it would be unseemly of theologians to be too severe. Without giving up any essential truths, they can allow evolutionists to develop their system and to support it with solid evidence if they are able to do so.[48]

He cited Zahm's *L'Évolution et le dogme* and added his hope for "a peace treaty which would not in any way stop research or even discussion, but which would put an end to reciprocal recriminations and unjustified accusations." That would, he thought, conform to Pope Leo XIII's recommendation "that scientists be left free to do their research, or even to make mistakes, as long, of course, as their errors did not compromise articles of faith."

Second, on the origin of man, Souben argued for the original unity of the human race against those polygenists who thought that human racial diversity pointed to a diversity of origin.[49] His answer to the question of the rôle of evolutionary processes in forming the first human body is, by contrast, not entirely clear. He began by saying that "the intervention of God in the act of the creation of man is too clearly underlined in the two narratives to allow one to treat it lightly or to pass over it in silence."[50] Although "the transformists are correct when they refuse to separate man from animal, for that is indeed the place which he occupies in nature—by his power of sensation, by his mode of propagation," still "he is not an animal like the others,"[51] and that forces a different

---

46 Selbst, *Handbuch*, 103–4.

47 As a popularization: anonymously in *The Month*, and by Léon Noël in *Revue philosophique de Louvain*. On expected classroom use: Martin Jugie in *Échos d'Orient*.

48 Souben, *Création*, 109.

49 Souben, *Création*, 89–98.

50 Souben, *Création*, 131.

51 Souben, *Création*, 132–33.

account with respect to human origins: "Left to themselves, natural forces are unable to lift an anthropoid ape little by little to the dignity of human being. . . . Secondary causes by themselves do not have the magical power to endow a brute animal with intelligence and will."[52] How exactly *did* the first man come into being? "He came as an adult from the hands of God."[53] Does that mean direct formation of an adult body or the infusion of a human soul into an adult animal body? Souben did not say.

52 Souben, *Création*, 131.

53 Souben, *Création*, 133.

PART IV

OLD CONTROVERSIES & NEW:

EXTENSIVE CHRISTIAN NATURALISM TOLERATED; BERGSONISM & POLYGENISM REJECTED

(1909–1931)

CHAPTER 11

SCIENTISTS & THEOLOGIANS
(1909–1931)

1. WILHELM SCHMIDT, SVD (1868–1954)

Wilhelm Schmidt was born in the Westphalian city of Hörde in 1868. His youthful desire to become a missionary led him to join the Society of the Divine Word, into which he was ordained in 1892. After two years of study at the University of Berlin (1893–1895), he did important academic work in both linguistics and ethnology, with a particular focus on the history of religion. In 1918, he was appointed professor at the University of Vienna. In 1923, at the request of Pope Pius XI, he began work on an exhibit in Rome that later (while still under his direction) developed into the Pontificio Museo Missionario-Etnologico in the Lateran Palace. He also played an important rôle in the foundation of the Museum für Völkerkunde in Vienna. In the wake of the *Anschluß*, he took refuge in Switzerland, where he received a teaching appointment at the University of Fribourg.[1]

He devoted some pages to our topic in his "Die Uroffenbarung als Anfang der Offenbarungen Gottes" (1911)[2] as part of a more general attempt to establish the capacity

---

1 For more on Schmidt, see Joseph Henninger, "Schmidt," or one of the books by Ernest Brandewie, *When Giants Walked the Earth* or *Wilhelm Schmidt and the Origin of the Idea of God*.

2 Schmidt, *Uroffenbarung*, chap. 2, §2, "Ursprung des Leibes des Menschen," 519–40 (trans., *Primitive Revelation* [Herder, 1939], 49–84). The section that follows takes up the question of the origin of the human soul. Joseph J. Baierl's adapted

of early man to receive Divine revelation. After a review of various attempts that had been made to reconstruct the phylogenetic history of man, he wrote:

> It is a matter of certainty that there is today not a single anthropologist or paleontologist of any note, Catholics not excluded, who rejects evolutionary ideas, even as applied to man. They are also of the opinion that the circumstantial evidence for the actual descent of man from earlier, lower forms has, in the last decades become, not more limited, but more extensive and more significant.[3]

He does go on to acknowledge that the force of the argument from authority is somewhat diminished by the fact that those scientists do differ among themselves about important points of detail.

Did theological considerations count against evolutionary anthropogenesis? Schmidt cited the Biblical Commission's acknowledgment that "it is not always necessary to seek in the text of Genesis 1 the precision of scientific language" and applied the principle to Genesis 2 as well. The text did not have to mean that God used His hands, and did not have to mean that He started with slime either. If the idea of the transformation of a prehuman species is not even suggested by the text, that was only because the Darwinian idea would have been, for his audience, unimaginable (*unfaßbar*).[4] The fact that St. Thomas did not read the text as requiring the creation of the soul to be temporally subsequent to the formation of the body shows that the text does not have to be read as literally as possible. Nor does anything in the Commission's *responsa* rule out the evolutionary origin of Adam's body, though it does seem to do so with respect to Eve's.

Schmidt concluded by counseling against imposing on the text of Scripture an anti-evolutionary sense which seemed inconsistent with the scientific consensus and which the text itself does not require.

2. BERTRAM WINDLE (1858–1929)[5]

Bertram Windle was born in 1858 to the Anglican vicar of the village of Mayfield (Staffordshire). He grew up, however, in Ireland and took his degrees at Trinity College, Dublin. Having completed his education, he went to Cardinal Newman's Birmingham to teach anatomy at Mason College. After the college was merged into the new University of Birmingham, he became dean of the university medical faculty. While in Birmingham, he began to visit St. Chad's Cathedral, which stood directly across from the hospital in which he worked. First attracted by the beauty of the Gregorian chant that was sung there,

---

translation of the 5th (1923) edition of this book includes notes that are sometimes useful, but unfortunately suffers from defects in translation. Since in any case what I want to show here is the *status questionis* in 1911, not that ten or thirty-five years later, I will here cite only the 1911 edition.

3 Schmidt, *Uroffenbarung*, 529–30 (cf. trans., 69).

4 Schmidt, *Uroffenbarung*, 532–33 (cf. trans., 71–73).

5 For biographical material, see E. J. McCorkell, "Windle"; Denis Gwynn, "Windle"; and Monica Taylor, *Windle*.

he proceeded to read himself into the Catholic Church. In 1904, he left Birmingham to accept the presidency of Queen's College, Cork, where he remained for fifteen years. In 1909, impressed by his *The Church and Science*, the president of St. Michael's College at the University of Toronto invited him to take a position there as professor of anthropology. His scientific work earned him a fellowship in the Royal Society, and his administrative work gave him a lasting place in the historics of the University of Birmingham and of University College, Cork. His skill at writing for general audiences led to his rôle in our story.

Windle began writing on evolutionary biology in 1906, in the pages of the *Dublin Review* and, slightly later, in *The Catholic World* and *Studies*. These articles were republished—in their original form in *A Century of Scientific Thought and Other Essays*, and then with some supplementary material in *Facts and Theories: Being a Consideration of Some Biological Conceptions of Today*. These works were followed by *The Church and Science*, half of which is devoted to evolution and closely related topics. He returned to the topic for the last time in 1927, in a short book entitled *The Evolutionary Problem as it is Today*.

Facts and Theories is centered on evolutionary biology, though it begins with some general remarks on science and takes up also such other topics as the nature and origin of life. Windle summed up his views about the origin of one species from another by saying that "transformism, though widely accepted, is not proved to a demonstration. It is an excellent working hypothesis, and, as such, need not disturb the mind of a Catholic in the smallest possible degree."[6]

Windle's discussion of the origin of man (in chapter VIII) begins with a reference to the famous passage from Darwin's correspondence in which he wrote, that "with me the horrid doubt always arises whether the convictions of man's mind, which has been developed from the mind of the lower animals, are of any value or at all trustworthy."[7] "This result," Windle added, "should have led him to doubt the certainty of his own conclusions as to the spiritual relationship of man and apes, rather than to doubt the dependability of human reasoning."[8] About the origin of the human body he was determinedly agnostic. There was as yet little paleontological evidence.[9] In addition, selectionists faced the problem that the variations that would lead to man would seem to be piecemeal—more disadvantageous than advantageous.[10] In sum, he wondered whether this is a question "on which science has . . . any right to express anything but the most guarded hypothesis."[11] About the human soul, he added: "We Catholics believe in the existence of an immortal soul, created by God Almighty Himself and temporarily occupying a human body. In

---

6 Windle, *Facts*, 135. See also his *Evolutionary Problem*, 12 (on the former point) and 65 (on the latter).

7 Darwin to William Graham, July 3, 1881 (Darwin, *Life and Letters*, 1:316), quoted by Windle, *Facts*, 101, and referred to again on page 118.

8 Windle, *Facts*, 118.

9 Windle, *Facts*, 123–25.

10 Windle, *Facts*, 128–29. This argument he credited to fellow-Catholic Thomas Dwight, *Thoughts of a Catholic Anatomist*, 158.

11 Windle, *Facts*, 129–30.

connection with this view we can bring forward psychological arguments, not unworthy of attention."[12] He cited several non-Catholic scientists who had emphasized the difference between man and animal as a difference in kind.

The Church and Science, as the title suggests, has a broader range—"to show how very few of these problems [sc., of physics and biology] come in any way in contact with dogmatic religion"[13]—than do his earlier books. Despite that greater range (extending from cosmology to prayer and miracles), the book presents a more detailed discussion of the origin of species and of man than do any of his other books.

Windle's general epistemological approach to the relationship between science and religion, articulated in his chapter V, emphasized that the kind of practical certainty that comes with observations ("facts") does not extend to the hypotheses or theories that scientists advance to explain those facts. Such theories can be so well-established as to be unreasonable to doubt (and useful as working hypotheses even before that point), but can, perhaps, never be "definitely or irrefutably proved."[14] For that reason "[a person] can be pardoned if he suspends his opinion on any theory of science, and particularly if he suspends it when that theory appears to conflict with anything which he believes on higher grounds."[15]

Near the end of his life, in an article occasioned by the Scopes Trial, he emphasized that Catholic positions on evolution ranged from George Barry O'Toole's compatibilist anti-evolutionism to Henry de Dorlodot's judgment that the theory of evolution has been proved.[16] As for his own view, he agreed with Wasmann that "evolution is by far the most plausible hypothesis, indeed at the moment the only conceivable hypothesis and that—with the limitation [that the spiritual side of man cannot be brought into any relation with the theory of evolution]— it is quite innocuous from the religious point of view."[17] When the Paulist Fathers opened WLWL radio station in New York in 1925 and wanted to launch the station with a series of four talks on evolution and Catholicism, Patrick Cardinal Hayes insisted that they invite Windle to give these lectures.[18]

Windle returned to the topic for the last time in 1927, in his short *The Evolutionary Problem as it is Today*. He stood by the positions that he had adopted in 1911—with regard to the central Catholic question of the origin of man's body, "the facts are strongly suggestive, [but] they do not amount in any way to a demonstration."[19]

---

12 Windle, *Facts*, 133–34.

13 Windle, *Church and Science*, 3rd ed., vii. (All quotations will come from the third edition (1924), which Windle described as a "thorough overhaul" of the first two editions.)

14 Windle, *Church and Science*, 3rd ed., 48.

15 Windle, *Church and Science*, 3rd ed., 51.

16 De Dorlodot's work is discussed below. The other reference is to George Barry O'Toole, *Case against Evolution*.

17 Windle, "Roman Catholic View," 337 and, for the limitation specified in brackets, 339.

18 They were subsequently published as *Evolution and Catholicity*.

19 Windle, *Evolutionary Problem*, 61.

3. HENRY DE DORLODOT (1855–1929)[20]

Henry de Dorlodot, born in Marchienne-au-Pont (Belgium) on July 15, 1855, studied the natural sciences at the Université catholique de Louvain—zoology under a former student of Étienne Geoffroy Saint-Hilaire and geology under a former student of Jean Baptiste Julien d'Omalius d'Halloy. He had, that is to say, two lines of evolutionist intellectual ancestry, though his own zoology teacher (Geoffroy Saint-Hilaire's student), Pierre-Joseph van Beneden, was not an evolutionist.[21] Those studies completed, he took up the study of theology at the Gregorian University in Rome, where he came to see, in certain of the Fathers in particular, a theology of nature that struck him as consonant with some of the results of evolutionary biology. He was ordained to the priesthood in 1882.

On his return to Belgium, de Dorlodot taught theology at Namur, and then philosophical cosmology at Désiré Mercier's newly established Institut St. Thomas at Louvain. In 1892, after philosophical disagreements with Mercier, he was transferred to the Faculté des Sciences, where he was responsible for teaching geology. De Dorlodot's work in geology did not, however, keep him from thinking about theology.

In 1909, when Cambridge University organized a celebration of the centennial of the birth of Charles Darwin (and the semicentennial of the first publication of *On the Origin of Species*), Louvain's rectoral council sent de Dorlodot to represent the university at the celebration. He did not, to be sure, represent the views of the entire faculty. Mercier, to cite a prominent example, was anti-evolutionist. De Dorlodot was not, however, the only evolutionist at Louvain. The work of Jacques Laminne, who also taught there, was discussed in chapter 8. Another Louvain evolutionist, botanist Victor Grégoire, accompanied de Dorlodot to Cambridge.[22] De Dorlodot's remarks at the celebration itself were, of course, brief—ceremonial rather than analytic or argumentative. Darwin should be honored for his place in "establishing the truth, foreseen by the genius of St. Augustine, that God, in making the world, had put in it all the forces necessary to its development (*épanouissement*)."[23]

The circumstances of the German occupation of Belgium during World War I not being conducive to academic research—the university library, for example, having been deliberately burned by the German Army—Paulin Ladeuze, then rector, organized a series of lectures which faculty who had remained at the university during the war would present to each other. De Dorlodot gave his on the topic of evolution and, before the war

---

20 For more on de Dorlodot, see Marie Claire Groessens-Van Dyck and Dominique Lambert, "Darwinisme d'un chanoine"; Marie Claire Groessens-Van Dyck, "Théorie iconoclaste"; and Dominique Lambert, "Acteur majeur." See also De Bont, "Rome and Theistic Evolutionism" and *Darwins kleinkinderen*, 283–93.

21 D'Omalius, of course, was discussed in chapter 1. For more on Geoffroy St. Hilaire, see Toby A. Appel, *The Cuvier-Geoffroy Debate.*

22 See P. Martens, "Grégoire."

23 Reprinted (in the French original) in *Darwinism*, 177.

was over, published them as *Le Darwinisme au point de vue de l'orthodoxie catholique. 1. L'Origine des espèces.*[24]

De Dorlodot's book was devoted to "the Darwinian theory in general," i.e., the origin of species "apart from the special question of the origin of man."[25] Unlike Mivart's and Zahm's, it did not take up scientific questions at all, being devoted solely to the theological aspects of the topic. De Dorlodot summarized Darwinism as containing two theses:

> (1) The first origin of living beings is the result of the special influence on the part of the Creator, who infused life into one or a small number of elementary organisms.

> (2) These organisms, by evolving over the course of ages, gave rise to all the organic species that now exist, or of which vestiges have been preserved in the fossil record.[26]

His first point does follow the letter of Darwin's text—"There is grandeur in this view of life, with its several powers, having been originally breathed by the Creator into a few forms or into one."[27] Still, it is important to note, as de Dorlodot did not, two things. First, Darwin was more agnostic than creationist about the origin of life.[28] Second, he thought that the question was entirely separable from the theory he was trying to articulate: "It is no valid objection [to my theory] that science as yet throws no light on the far higher problem of the essence or origin of life."[29]

De Dorlodot contrasted the view he called Darwinism with two extreme views:

> Absolute evolutionism denies the special intervention of God, even at the origin of life.

> Fixism, or Creationism, admits a special intervention of God at the origination of each one of the groups we now call species.[30]

He also distinguished an array of intermediate views ("mitigated creationism" or "mitigated evolution") ranging from direct creation of each genus to interventions only in a very few cases (perhaps the origin of life, the origin of animals, and the origin of man).

His own theses about evolution are four.[31] The first is negative:

---

24 Belgium being still under occupation, the book was printed with the false date of 1913 to avoid the shame of submitting it to German censorship. It was reprinted in a more generally available edition in 1921, and then in translation as *Darwinism and Catholic Thought*, with some supplementary material.

25 He makes this exclusion four times in the first few pages (*Darwinisme*, 9 and 11; trans., 3 and 5).

26 De Dorlodot, *Darwinisme*, 10 (trans., 4).

27 Darwin, *Origin of Species*, 2nd ed., 490. The phrase "by the Creator" was new to the second edition and remained in all subsequent editions.

28 In his correspondence, he later wrote that the phrase quoted above did not express his meaning well: "I have long regretted that I truckled to public opinion, and used the Pentateuchal term of creation, by which I really meant 'appeared' by some wholly unknown process. It is mere rubbish, thinking at present of the origin of life; one might as well think of the origin of matter" (Darwin to J. D. Hooker, March 29, 1863, in Darwin, *Life and Letters*, 3:17–18.

29 Darwin, *Origin of Species*, 3rd ed., 514.

30 De Dorlodot, *Darwinisme*, 10 (trans., 4).

31 De Dorlodot, *Darwinisme*, 11–12 (trans., 5–6) (italics de Dorlodot's).

(1) Holy Scripture, interpreted according to the rules of Catholic exegesis, [provides no] convincing argument against the theory of natural evolution, not even of *absolute evolution.*

This he defended in the first lecture,[32] "Darwinism and the Work of the Six Days." The other three, defended in the second lecture, on "Darwinism in the Light of Tradition and Catholic Philosophy," are positive:

(2) The teaching of the Fathers of the Church is *very favorable* to the theory of Absolute Evolution. However, the example of the great Doctors [of the Church] authorizes us simply to accept, in this matter, the solution indicated by *the present state of science.*

(3) The application of certain principles of Catholic theology and philosophy to the concrete data of the empirical sciences transforms the simple naturalist's conviction in favor of a very advanced system of transformism into an *absolute certainty*; at least it leads us to accept, *as eminently probable,* the theory that derives all living beings from one or a few very simple types of organisms....

(4) The Catholic theory concerning the natural activity of secondary causes is capable of explaining *a natural transformist evolution* ... and entitles us to reject *as entirely superfluous* the additional special interventions postulated by fixists and moderate creationists.[33]

De Dorlodot argued that many Catholic theologians of the first eight centuries—SS. Gregory of Nyssa and Augustine of Hippo in particular—themselves accepted an account that attributed the origin of life and of biological species to "the sole exercise of the active powers with which God endowed the world when He created it,"[34] a view that "formally denies any special intervention on the part of God other than the unique impulse ... of the original creation at the beginning of time, which produced as its immediate result a formless and homogeneous whole."[35] He later summarized the point in a letter to Notre Dame professor John A. O'Brien as follows:

It is permissible to conclude that the Hexaemeron, *at least understood in its obvious sense,* affirms that all the plants, and all the [non-rational] animals, ... were produced by God without doubt, but at the same time *through the active causality of inorganic, terrestrial elements.* ... All Tradition, up to the thirteenth century, understood that such was also the *literal historical sense,* with this shade of meaning, however, that certain species were not produced by the earth and by its waters. In other words, Tradition believed in *spontaneous generation* (a term used by St. Ambrose) at the beginning, but a *certain phylogenetic evolution* was admitted for a great number of species.[36]

---

32 "Conference" in the words of his translator.

33 De Dorlodot, *Darwinisme,* 12 (trans., 5–6) (emphasis de Dorlodot's).

34 De Dorlodot, *Darwinisme,* 95 (trans., 76).

35 De Dorlodot, *Darwinisme,* 98 (trans., 79).

36 De Dorlodot to John A. O'Brien (professor at the University of Notre Dame, about whom more in chapter 16), October

This hypothesis, de Dorlodot concluded in that letter, was surely *tutior*, the safer one. De Dorlodot was certainly frustrated by the resistance his book had received by the time he wrote the letter, for he added that "*tutior* does not mean in *theology* that the opinion upheld is very pleasing to such and such a cardinal, were he even Grand Inquisitor."

De Dorlodot called this general theology of nature "Christian naturalism," and defined it as "the tendency to attribute to the natural action of secondary causes all that reason and the positive data of the natural sciences allow us to attribute to them, and to have recourse to a special Divine intervention distinct from God's general governing activity only in cases in which it is absolutely necessary to do so."[37] Such Christian naturalism is "the constant doctrine of the Fathers and Doctors" and it would be rash to deny it.

The Scholastics, he argued, though in general committed to Christian naturalism, had mistakenly thought that the origin of life and of new species were cases where Divine intervention was in fact absolutely necessary.[38] More recent scientific work, he went on to say, had shown that such intervention was not necessary for the origin of species after all. The Scholastic attempt to defend divine intervention by appeal to the Principle of Causality would prove too much, requiring such intervention even in the embryological development of individual organisms. "We do not see by what right we could deny *a priori* that God was able to produce primitive organisms possessing an instrumental power sufficient to give rise to the most widely differing organisms over the course of centuries."[39]

Modern science did, he said by contrast, show that natural causes were incapable of generating living things from non-living matter. The origin of life, therefore, required divine intervention. His own version of evolutionism (and Darwin's, he said) was therefore less comprehensive (less "absolute") than that allowed by Scripture and than that supported by some of the Fathers.

Although well-received in some Catholic quarters,[40] particularly in the United Kingdom and the United States, the book met with opposition from officials at the Pontifical Biblical Commission, to be discussed in chapter 12.

✳ ✳ ✳ ✳ ✳

De Dorlodot had said that he was leaving the topic of the origin of man for a second volume, but had not gotten to it when the Armistice brought the university lecture series

---

26, 1926, 6 (emphasis de Dorlodot's). I have not seen the copy of De Dorlodot's letter, which was written in French; I have slightly polished the translation found in the files of UNDA.

37 De Dorlodot, *Darwinisme*, 115 (trans., 94).

38 De Dorlodot, *Darwinisme*, 178–90 (trans., 152–75).

39 De Dorlodot, *Darwinisme*, 150 (trans., 125).

40 Book reviews included Frances J. Wenninger in *American Midland Naturalist*, an anonymous review in *The Tablet*, P. Synave in *Revue des sciences philosophiques et théologiques*, and Lucien Roure, in *Études*.

De Bont said that the French reviews are "positive, *but cautious*" (my emphasis). I do not agree. He cites as evidence of this "caution" Synave's decision (which he incorrectly attributes to Antoine Lemonnyer) not to discuss de Dorlodot's evolutionism: "Si je m'interdis de prononcer quelque jugement sur la partie positive de la thèse,..." (Synave, Review, 133). De Bont translated this as saying that "he 'forbade himself' from treating the 'positive part' of the book" (De Bont, "Rome," 469). The phrase could, however, at least as well be translated "I refrain from," and the reason be that he was writing the review for a section of his journal devoted to books on the bible ("Bulletin de théologie biblique").

234

of which it was to be a part to an end. He was, for the next four years, too occupied with other university duties to continue his research.[41] That means that he probably began work on the topic at the end of 1922; in October 1926, he wrote to O'Brien that "without having finished, [he was] far advanced in this study."[42] He never did publish his thoughts on this topic, partly as a consequence of the troubles over the first book. In his letter to O'Brien, who had urged him to do so, he replied: "I must tell you, very confidentially, that those who urged me most to undertake this now believe that the time is not opportune, and that it is first necessary to allow the passions to subside which my little book on the 'origin of species' aroused in certain persons who are as incompetent as they are high-placed."[43] He turned down invitations to speak in Germany in 1925 and in France in 1927 (details of both incidents are in chapter 12). We know what he thought directly from two sources, and indirectly from a third. The first is his letter to O'Brien; the second is his manuscript, long presumed lost, but found in the spring of 2006 when members of de Dorlodot's family found a draft in the family archives.[44] The indirect source is his translator, Ernest C. Messenger, former student at Louvain and English diocesan priest, to whom he sent a copy of the manuscript and who, with de Dorlodot's permission, worked much of the material (often translated directly from de Dorlodot's text) into his own *Evolution and Theology* (1931).

The summary of what de Dorlodot intended to write, which he sent to O'Brien in 1926, emphasized "the *great* error that I committed in the pamphlet," one which, of course, would have to be abandoned. The error contained two parts.

First, "it is necessary to separate clearly the question of the origin of Eve from the question of the origin of Adam."[45] Some theologians, e.g., Gerard Van Noort,[46] had tried to use the thesis of divine action in the formation of the body of Eve as a kind of Archimedean point against the hypothesis of the evolutionary origin of the body even of Adam. De Dorlodot, however, was willing to attempt just what Van Noort had said that no thoughtful person would do,[47] since the origin of Eve from the body of Adam is theologically important in a way that the formation of the body of Adam directly from non-living matter is not. In any case "*God could not have made a companion worthy of Adam except by having her brought forth from him.*"[48] The mode of production is

---

41 De Dorlodot to O'Brien, 1 (COBR 1/21, UNDA). Lambert and Groessens-Van Dyck suggest that de Dorlodot began work on the second volume of *Darwinisme* by 1918 and that he may have continued work on it until about 1925 (Groessens-Van Dyck and Lambert in their commentary and notes in De Dorlodot, *Origine de l'homme*, 159n83 and 67–68). The letter to O'Brien indicates slightly later dates.

42 De Dorlodot to O'Brien, 2.

43 De Dorlodot to O'Brien, 1.

44 Groessens-Van Dyck and Lambert, "Darwinisme d'un chanoine," 67–68.

45 De Dorlodot to O'Brien, 6–7.

46 "No thoughtful person thinks that, the body of Adam having been formed by evolution, the body of Eve was not" (Van Noort, *De Deo creante*, 2nd ed., 115; cited by de Dorlodot, *Origine de l'homme*, 161).

47 De Dorlodot, *Origine de l'homme*, 159–78.

48 De Dorlodot to O'Brien, 6–7.

extraordinary and certainly involved Divine Omnipotence; we cannot understand exactly how it took place: "Other than being a mode extraordinary for the human species, it is entirely analogous to the phenomena of asexual generation that is so frequent in the animal kingdom. Modern science, far from creating new difficulties, makes the matter less difficult to understand."[49] He concluded by saying that, although there is something supernatural in the origin of Eve, "all things considered, there is nothing here that should dismay a Christian *naturalist*."

Second was his renunciation of the more Mivartian position he had taken in *Darwinisme* in favor of the kind of mitigated Mivartism first suggested by González.

His discussion of the origin of Adam's body began with a defense of the rôle of evolutionary processes in anthropogenesis based on a close analysis of Genesis 2:7.[50] The grammatical construction of the first part of the relevant verse is peculiar.

Septuagint: ἔπλασεν ὁ θεὸς τὸν ἄνθρωπον χοῦν ἀπὸ τῆς γῆς.

Masoretic Text: וַיִּיצֶר יְהוָה אֱלֹהִים אֶת-הָאָדָם עָפָר מִן-הָאֲדָמָה.

Vetus Latina: *finxit Deus hominem pulverem de terra.*

Literally, God made "the man dust from the earth." How are the words "man" and "dust" related? Some codices of the Septuagint include a participle—. . . χοῦν λαβὼν ἀπὸ τῆς γῆς, "*taking* dust from the earth;" St. Jerome, in the *Vulgate*, added a preposition—*formavit . . . hominem de limo terrae,* "formed . . . *from* the slime of the earth." These emendations of the text were particularly congenial for those defending a non-evolutionary anthropogenesis, but they do not re-present the Hebrew or Greek text itself. De Dorlodot argued for an alternative. Following Franz von Hummelauer,[51] he argued that the two nouns stood in apposition, so "God formed "the man-dust from earth."

This reading recognizes the parallelism between v. 7 and v. 19:

So out of the ground the LORD God formed every beast of the field and every
bird of the air

Septuagint: ἔπλασεν ὁ θεὸς ἔτι ἐκ τῆς γῆς πάντα τὰ θηρία τοῦ ἀγροῦ καὶ πάντα
τὰ πετεινὰ τοῦ οὐρανοῦ

Masoretic Text: וַיִּצֶר יְהוָה אֱלֹהִים מִן-הָאֲדָמָה כָּל-חַיַּת הַשָּׂדֶה וְאֵת כָּל-עוֹף הַשָּׁמַיִם

Vetus Latina: Et finxit Deus adhuc de terra omnes bestias agri, et omnia volatilia cœli.

---

49 De Dorlodot, *Origine de l'homme*, 178. Messenger presented a slightly adapted version of this conclusion in *Evolution and Theology*, 273.

50 De Dorlodot, *Origine de l'homme*, 124–36. For an English version of this argument, see Ernest C. Messenger, *Evolution and Theology*, 100–116, especially 107–16. The relation between de Dorlodot's manuscript and Messenger's book will be discussed in chapter 14.

51 Hummelauer, *Commentarius in Genesim*, 126–27.

God made "from the earth" two things—animals ("every beast of the field and every bird of the air") and the human body.[52] God's making something "from the earth" did not rule out the participation of secondary causes, de Dorlodot said, and that point was generally conceded by Catholic authors, who raised no theological objections to an evolutionary origin for animals.[53] The point of Genesis 2:7a is not that God made man immediately *from* dust—the preposition is just not in the text and dust, in any case, is not a material *from which* things can be made. The point is rather that it was not *man* that was made "from the earth," but only the human body, "man-dust." The making of *man also* required "the breath of life" (the soul) mentioned in the second part of the verse. The choice of the word "dust" made a second theological point: "In general, the term הפר (dust), when employed without qualification ..., always means something to be despised, good for nothing.... Its figurative sense is derived from ... the disdain associated with dust. But the term also expresses something else.... [that] the human body, when it has been abandoned by the soul, is destroyed and leaves nothing but a residue of dust."[54]

Was the idea of the natural origin of Adam's body, if not inconsistent with Scripture itself, at least inconsistent with authoritative traditional Patristic and Scholastic interpretation of the passages in question, as some of his contemporaries thought?[55] De Dorlodot argued that it was not. Two points only, he said, constituted doctrine—that the angels played no rôle in the formation of Adam's body and that the principal cause of the formation was God.[56] The articulation, by some of the Fathers (SS. Gregory of Nyssa and Augustine, in particular, though not exclusively[57]), of a theory of *rationes seminales*, was sufficient to allow natural processes to play an intermediate rôle. The rejection of this idea by the Scholastics relied on Aristotelian scientific theories that we now know must be abandoned.[58]

That thesis had been defended in *Darwinisme*. What was new is found in brief in his letter to O'Brien, to whom he wrote that "as for Adam, it was necessary ... to admit, in the present state of theology, *a special and supernatural intervention of God*, for its elevation to the supernatural order." St. Augustine may have "admitted no intervention on the part of God to *modify* the normal course of nature, [but merely] conceded that *perhaps* [with double emphasis] *the manner according to which man was to originate from his causes*

---

52 De Dorlodot argued that this phrase does not indicate the matter from which the things named were made, but that from which they were separated, as in v. 9: "out of the ground the LORD God made to grow every tree that is pleasant to the sight" (מִן-הָאֲדָמָה, though the Greek says ἐκ τῆς γῆς). See De Dorlodot, *Origine de l'homme*, 132–34.

53 The beasts that (he might have added) Genesis 1:24 had said were brought forth from the earth.

54 De Dorlodot, *Origine de l'homme*, 128–29.

55 De Dorlodot said (*Origine de l'homme*, 136), without identifying an example, that some anti-evolutionists had based their opposition solely on the authority of the Fathers. Groessens-Van Dyck and Lambert (136n51) said that he had Laurens Janssens in mind. For more on Janssens, see below.

56 De Dorlodot, *Origine de l'homme*, 155.

57 "The 'ratio seminalis' is by no means a theory unique to St. Augustine. St. Augustine only presented ... the common sentiment."—De Dorlodot to O'Brien, 4. (Here I have polished the translation—"unique" for "proper" and "presented" for "exposed.")

58 De Dorlodot, *Origine de l'homme*, 155.

had not been determined in these causes as they had been created at the beginning." De Dorlodot, however, said that "a Catholic evolutionist could grant a special intervention, were it judged necessary, on condition of maintaining that the active virtuality pre-existed in the creature." God, might have "accelerated evolution and forced the production of the superior man at one stroke," for example by "a great mutation, equivalent to the sum of a great number of successive mutations, which should have been produced naturally," even though "we do not know what, in the organization of the human body and especially of his brain, cause this organization to *demand* (according to the Scholastic expression) animation by an intellectual or *rational* soul."[59] In the unpublished draft, he put it as follows:

> I do not see, either in Holy Scripture, or in the Fathers, in the authoritative Doctors of the Middle Ages, or in more recent theologians, any decisive reason to oppose the hypothesis of the origin of the body of Adam by way of organic evolution, provided that one admits that the ultimate state [*disposition*] [of that body], requiring to receive as its form a rational soul, is the result of the *immediate* action of God (I have become a bit broader [*plus large*] on that last point).[60]

✳ ✳ ✳ ✳ ✳

De Dorlodot concluded his work with a few pages on pre- and co-Adamitism.[61] He recognized, of course, that "any hypothesis which tends to say that there exist, *among the natural races*, men who are not descended from Adam" would be contrary to Catholic doctrine.[62] Catholics could accept such a hypothesis only to the extent that it was limited to "ancient races which had disappeared long ago." The appeal of pre-Adamitism for Catholics, he wrote, would be to reconcile the antiquity of man according to science with the chronology presented in Holy Scripture, but de Dorlodot thought that the literary form of the scriptural passages in question show that they do not constitute a historical chronology.

De Dorlodot began his discussion of *pre*-Adamites by acknowledging that there could have been early, non-rational species of the genus *Homo*. He saw nothing in orthodox doctrine inconsistent with the idea that Adam had ancestors that were zoologically, but not philosophically, human (i.e., that were non-rational members of the genus *Homo*).[63]

What about another idea—that Adam had *philosophically* human ancestors? Perhaps there were once beings endowed with an intellectual soul [*âme spirituelle*] but whose intellectual acts remained at the rudimentary level. Perhaps their intellects

---

59 De Dorlodot to O'Brien, 8–9.

60 De Dorlodot, *Origine de l'homme*, 160 (emphasis de Dorlodot's).

61 Because Louis Agassiz (in his "Natural Provinces"), Alexander Winchell (in *Adamites and Preadamites*), and others used the ideas of pre- and co-Adamitism to make invidious distinctions among human races, the theories have been thought by some recent writers to be essentially or logically connected to those authors' views on the superiority of some races over others. It is, therefore, important to note that pre- and co-Adamitism had no such racial significance either in their origin (in Isaac La Peyrère's *Prae-Adamitae* [1655]) or in de Dorlodot's discussion of the theory.

62 De Dorlodot, *Origine de l'homme*, 179 (emphasis de Dorlodot's).

63 De Dorlodot, *Origine de l'homme*, 191.

238

developed until, after the passage of centuries, God raised one of them ("Adam") to the supernatural level while all of the races not descended from Adam became extinct. De Dorlodot said that he "did not know of any Catholic author who had published such an idea, but that there were some who, in their desire to reconcile Catholic orthodoxy with integral Darwinism, were not far from it." Such a hypothesis could not, he thought, be declared to be heretical. Nevertheless, he continued, that did not mean that it was an open question. The idea is too much in tension with "common and constant belief and with the text of Holy Scripture … and if we add that it does not seem to be supported by any truly scientific evidence, we can conclude that it is *at least rash*; though perhaps it merits an even more severe note of censure."[64]

De Dorlodot's own view was that it would not really be correct to say that man was the product of *natural* evolution since "Adam, *as he was before he had sinned,* was a supernatural being."[65]

De Dorlodot died in 1929.

4. PIERRE TEILHARD DE CHARDIN, SJ (1881–1955)[66]

Teilhard was born in France in Sarcenat (Auvergne) in 1881; he entered the Jesuit novitiate in 1899. Three years later, when the anti-clerical measures implemented by the government of Prime Minister Émile Combes forced the French Jesuits into exile, Teilhard went with them. His preparation for the priesthood took him first to the Jesuit philosophate in Jersey (1902–5), then to teach physics at the Jesuit high school in Cairo (1905–8), and finally (1908–12) to the Ore Place theologate in Hastings (England), where he was ordained in 1911.

Given his scientific interests, it was only natural that, on the completion of his theological studies in 1912, Teilhard took up the study of paleontology, which he did under the direction of Marcellin Boule, one of France's leading paleoanthropologists. Differences between Boule's views and Catholic doctrine did not prevent him from accepting Teilhard as a student, nor did it prevent the Jesuits from allowing Teilhard to study under him, though it was sometimes a cause of concern. Interrupted by the First World War, in which he distinguished himself as a stretcher-bearer, Teilhard completed his studies only in 1922. In 1920, as he was finishing his scientific education, he accepted a position teaching geology at the Institut catholique de Paris.

In 1923, his fellow-Jesuit Émile Licent, whose finds Teilhard had been cataloging at the Muséum national in Paris, invited him to spend a year in China at Licent's Musée Hoangho Paiho in Tientsin [Pinyin: Tiānjīn]. After his year of field research, he returned to

---

64 De Dorlodot, *Origine de l'homme*, 192–93 (emphasis de Dorlodot's).

65 De Dorlodot, *Origine de l'homme*, 193 (emphasis de Dorlodot's).

66 The standard biography of Teilhard is Claude Cuénot's *Teilhard*. An excellent shorter account of his life can be found in Paul Grenet, *Teilhard*. For a short biography focused on Teilhard's *scientific* work, see Jean Piveteau, *Teilhard, savant,* or, for a still shorter account of Teilhard's scientific work, Marc Godinot, "De la Géologie à l'évolution."

France, but not for long. His unorthodox ideas about original sin, which he had expressed (in some unpublished notes) even before his departure for China, eventually came to the attention of the Jesuit superior general, Włodzimierz Ledóchowski. In the end, he was sent back to China to continue his scientific work and his teaching appointment at the Institut catholique was terminated. He was associated first with Licent's museum and then, from 1929, with the Geological Survey of China in Beijing. China remained his base of operations until 1946, though he made research trips to Kashmir, Burma, Java, and Abyssinia. He published just over one hundred scientific papers during this period, of which about a quarter concerned paleoanthropology, the rest discussing other questions in paleontology or geology.[67]

The outbreak of the Second World War, and the resultant restrictions on travel during the years of Japanese occupation, brought his opportunity to do field work, even in China, to an end. He was able to work a little longer on material he had already found, but by war's end he had written it all up.[68] Further professional work would have to await the emergence of new opportunities.

At the end of the war, Teilhard returned to France. Denied by his order permission to take up the chair in paleontology at the Collège de France, from which Henri Breuil was retiring (in 1948), he accepted a research position at the Viking Fund (now the Wenner-Gren Foundation for Anthropological Research) in New York. His age and health allowed him to do technical scientific work only sporadically during these final years of his life, but he remained active, and affiliated with that institution, until his death in 1955.

I will organize my summary of Teilhard's work and thought thematically, beginning with his purely scientific work, the high quality of which won for him a worldwide recognition in his field.[69] Much of it, of course, is highly technical. Sufficient for our purpose is a quick review of its general direction, with some more detail on paleoanthropology.

✳ ✳ ✳ ✳ ✳

The geology and mineralogy of Jersey, the fossil beds at el-Faiyum and Minieh in the Egyptian desert, and the fossils and plants of Sussex served to intensify an interest in nature, which Teilhard had begun to experience even as a child.[70] On Jersey, he did his first work in geology. In Egypt he published a paper, "L'Éocène des environs de Minieh," and discovered new fossil species of echinoids, the scientific descriptions of

---

67 Cuénot, *Teilhard*, i–xlix (trans., 409–84), contains a chronological bibliography of Teilhard's publications (as does Teilhard, *Cœur* [1976], 211–22 [trans., 241–62]); an alphabetical version is available in Joseph M. McCarthy, *Teilhard: A Comprehensive Bibliography*.

68 Teilhard to an unnamed friend, October 10, 1945, in *Letters to Two Friends*, 162–63. The two friends are described by René d'Ouince, author of the book's Prologue, only as "two of the Father's correspondents presently living in America . . . [who] 'have wished to remain anonymous,'" *Letters to Two Friends*, 3.

69 See, for example, Thomas F. Glick's article on Teilhard. Teilhard's technical scientific work has been collected in the ten volumes of Nicole and Karl Schmitz-Moormann, *Teilhard: L'Œuvre scientifique*. For Teilhard's own summary of this work, see his *Titres et Travaux* (1948), a document prepared in typescript and distributed by Teilhard when the Collège de France offered him the chair of paleontology.

70 For details, see Teilhard, *Cœur* (1976), 25–35 (trans., 16–24).

240

which were prepared by his colleagues.[71] He also discovered a species of moth, which was subsequently named *Autoba (eublemma) teilhardi*.[72] He found time for scientific exploration in England as well and was able to discover a new species of fossilized club moss, *Lycopodites teilhardi*.[73]

His stay in England also involved him in one of the most famous (and strangest) events in the history of paleontology. Looking back some thirty-five years later, he wrote: "My first stroke of good luck in the area of ancient human paleontology, was to be included, when still young, in the excavation of *Eoanthropus dawsoni* [popularly, Piltdown Man] in England."[74] But of course it was not such *good* luck after all, for a few years after he made that remark, much to his distress, the "find" was proven to be a forgery. Worse, though fortunately after his death, Teilhard himself was suspected, unjustifiably in the judgment of most historians, to have been partially responsible for the forgery.[75]

What did Teilhard think about Piltdown Man?

Although he had been present when Arthur Smith Woodward, Keeper of Geology at the British Museum, discovered a part of the jaw and had himself discovered a tooth, he took no part in the scientific description of the find. Still, first as an advanced student of paleontology and then as a professional paleoanthropologist who was also interested in presenting the results of science to the broader public, he did have occasion to mention the fossil. Teilhard, like Boule, had his doubts about Piltdown Man for obvious scientific reasons that both he and others clearly articulated.

Teilhard's only extended treatment of the subject was a popular article he wrote for *Revue des questions scientifiques*.[76] Like Boule, under whom he was then studying, he emphasized the tension between topography and osteology. How could such a simian

---

71 An extinct sea star (*Metopaster teilhardi*) was described by P. de Loriol in "Note sur quelques stellérides." Another eight fossil echinoid species, one of which (*Gisopygus teilhardi*) was named after him, were described by René Fourtau in "Échinides fossiles."

72 J. de Joannis, "Trois nouvelles espèces."

73 Albert Charles Seward, "Knowledge of Wealden Floras," 86. See also the letter to his parents (no. 20), May 16, 1913, in *Letters from Paris*, 75.

74 Teilhard, *Titres et Travaux* (1948), 8. When this autobiographical sketch was republished in 1976, the reference to Piltdown was, for reasons to be explained in a moment, omitted and his "second" stroke of luck (his discovery, with Licent, of Paleolithic Man in northern China) was elevated to first place (*Cœur*, 178 [trans., 162]).

75 For an account of Piltdown Man in the context of the history of science, see Appendix I.B.

The charge against Teilhard was first made by Stephen Jay Gould, without yet accepting it as the best explanation of the fraud, in "Piltdown Revisited." After Gould made his initial charge, Ashley Montagu wrote to Gould (December 3, 1979): "I feel sure that you are wrong about Teilhard. I knew him well, and, in fact, was the first to tell him, the day after it was announced in the *New York Times*, of the hoax. His reaction could hardly have been faked." Despite Montagu's testimony, other points led Gould to dig in on the plausibility of the charge and he defended it in "Piltdown Conspiracy" and "Reply to Critics." For a defense of Teilhard against this charge, see Walsh, *Unraveling Piltdown*, 128–48, or Thomas M. King, "Appendix: Teilhard and Piltdown."

Michał Chaberek is thus completely wrong in suggesting that Teilhard was one of the researchers involved in Piltdown, in saying that the discovery was "popularized by Teilhard" (*Catholicism & Evolution*, 38), and in implying that the find played some rôle in the growth of Teilhard's reputation (pp. 198–99).

76 Teilhard, "Piltdown" (1920). Teilhard had mentioned the find twice previously, in book reviews of Hugo Obermaier's *Mensch der Vorzeit* ("Préhistoire et ses progrès" [1913], 48) just months after the find was publicly reported, and of Boule's *Hommes fossiles* ("Les Hommes fossiles" [1921], 572).

jaw and such a human skull be part of a single individual? How could there have been just two primates, from one of which we have only a skull and from the other only a jaw? He concluded with what he called a "minimalist, but very safe, hypothesis:" namely that "Without forgetting the possibility, or even a certain probability, of the contrary hypothesis, we should proceed, *until further notice*, as if the Piltdown skull and the mandible pertain to two different subjects."[77]

In later survey articles, he conformed to the scientific consensus (as to the unity of the find), e.g., by citing both Piltdown and Heidelberg Man as representatives of Chellean Man, but continued to express reservations. In one article, he added, "supposing the jaw really belonged to him."[78] In a 1943 lecture at the Catholic University of Peking, he was even more skeptical:

> Here has to be mentioned the enigmatic *Eoanthropus* .... Should the two series of bones [sc., skull and jaw] really belong to the same individual, we should be in the presence of a most remarkable type of Prehominian. Unfortunately, most of the anthropologists (although unable to explain the presence of a Chimpanzee in Pleistocene England!) regard the association of the skull and of the jaw as anatomically impossible.[79]

Still, he, "tentatively," accorded the fossil a place on his summary diagram.

N. M. Wildiers, in the preface to *L'Apparition de l'homme*, reported that Teilhard (after the exposure of the forgery) requested that references to Piltdown Man be suppressed in a planned collection of his writings: "The question could be considered as settled. The *Eoanthropus* posing (and for good reason!) an insoluble problem of classification, Teilhard was glad not to have to mention it further."[80] Wildiers went on to quote a letter of Teilhard: "The matter of the Piltdown *Eoanthropus* spoiled for me some happy memories from my youth. But it is so much more satisfying that way!—Only I cannot bring myself to believe in a hoax on the part of dear, poor Dawson. And as fantastic as it appears, I would prefer the hypothesis that it was rubbish thrown into the open hole by the workmen digging for gravel."[81]

The early phase of his fully professional scientific work was focused on the study of European Tertiary mammals. His first major work, "Les Carnassiers des phosphorites du Quercy," established evolutionary series for some Eocene and Oligocene fossils that had been collected by others at the end of the nineteenth century. His doctoral dissertation, *Les Mammifères de l'éocène inférieur français et leurs gisements*, similarly, fleshed out the details of several successive, previously poorly known fauna, demonstrating evolutionary

---

77 Teilhard, "Piltdown" (1920), 155 (emphasis Teilhard's).

78 Teilhard, "Paléontologie et l'apparition de l'homme" (1923), 162–63. See also "Importante Découverte" (1930), 12 and 15.

79 Teilhard, *Fossil Men* (1929), 12–13n.

80 Wildiers, in Teilhard, *Apparition*, 17. Contrast the passages cited above: "Paléontologie et l'apparition de l'homme" (1923), 162–63, and "Importante Découverte," 12 and 15, with the corresponding passages in the published translations, "Paleontology," 47–48, and "Important Discovery," 64 and 66.

81 Teilhard to an unidentified addressee, December 8, 1953 (*Apparition*, 17).

connections among the French species and comparing them to similar species then being found in America.[82]

His assignment to China, however, returned him to questions of paleoanthropology, in which his first major contribution was his discovery (together with Licent) of the first evidence of Paleolithic culture in China.[83]

His most famous piece of scientific work came next. Over the course of the latter half of 1929, he took on an increasing important rôle at the Chinese Geological Survey, with special responsibility for directing the geological and paleontological aspects of the work at Choukoutien [Pinyin: Zhōukǒudiàn], where two fragments of the jawbone of Peking Man (originally designated *Sinanthropus*, now *Homo erectus*) had been found the previous year. By the end of 1929, a nearly complete skull had been found. Like Java Man, the new finds were morphologically intermediate between man and some kind of prehuman ancestor. A second specimen was found the next year. The year after that (1931) turned up evidence of culture—both firemaking and toolmaking. "The chances are," Teilhard concluded, "that *Sinanthropus* was intelligent."[84]

Teilhard was not personally the discoverer of these skulls. Cuénot wrote: "Teilhard's great value [at Choukoutien] was in the rôle of geologist and the way in which he coordinated both the work and the publications.... And it was he who, thanks to an ever-expanding knowledge base and to his ability to synthesize ideas, placed the very complex geology of Choukoutien within the vast geological context of Northern China and of Eastern Asia generally."[85] Although the technical description of the skull was done by others, Teilhard did write some technical articles on Peking Man.[86]

✳ ✳ ✳ ✳ ✳

A second tranche of his written work was aimed at a wider audience—the educated Catholic world.[87] Even before he had left Hastings, Teilhard had begun what became a lifelong effort to present the results of scientific work to the general public and to reassure that public that there was no conflict between those scientific results and any definitive Catholic doctrine. That project was not, as he saw it, wholly conservative. Publicly, Teilhard generally emphasized the ultimate compatibility of the insights of science and the doctrines of faith; privately (but not, in the judgment of his critics, privately enough), he gave expression to what he saw as the necessity of moving beyond some of the traditional

---

82 Other major works from this period were "Quelques Primates" and "Mammifères de l'Éocène inférieur" (both 1916–21).

83 Teilhard and Licent, "Discovery of a Palaeolithic Industry."

84 Teilhard, "Fouilles préhistorique de Péking" (1934), 187 (trans., 74).

85 Cuénot, *Teilhard*, 215–16 (trans., 176–77).

86 E.g., Teilhard and Pei W. C., "Lithic Industry in Chou-Kou-Tien."

87 Many, but not all, of these articles were collected and published after Teilhard's death as volumes II (*L'Apparition de l'homme*), III (*La Vision du Passé*), and X (*Comment je crois*) of *Œuvres de Pierre Teilhard de Chardin*, available in English translation as *The Appearance of Man*, *The Vision of the Past*, and *Christianity and Evolution*. Although these volumes are conveniently available, they cannot be used as the basis for historical research—first because they suppress all references to Piltdown Man at Teilhard's request and, second, in the case of the translations, because they are sometimes inaccurate.

formulations of those doctrines. As early as 1922, he had written in a letter to his friend Paul Valensin:

> If you ever find the first volume of the great Venice Bible, read Calmet's critique of Vossius, who did not admit the universality of the flood. You will be struck by the dogmatic place which this idea (now abandoned) held in the eighteenth century. Once we have gotten beyond it, we forget how difficult it was to overcome!—We have many more "Floods" to expel from the essence of our faith.[88]

Teilhard's first published comments on religion and anthropology appeared in his contribution to a four-part article in the revised edition of the *Dictionnaire apologétique de la foi catholique*, one that also included sections on man in Genesis (by Adhémar d'Alès), on prehistoric man according to paleontology (written by Amédée and Jean Bouyssonie, with the help of Breuil), and on the unity of the human species (by Jean Guibert). Teilhard's assignment was to address "man according to the teachings of the Church and according to spiritualist philosophy."[89] As such, it was focused more on human nature than on human origins. Nevertheless, he did not pass the question of evolutionary anthropogenesis completely by. In the first part of his contribution, on "man and the rest of the world," he wrote that

> Catholic thought must isolate the human race itself from the general advance of life and matter. . . . This separation should be prominent in the history of its appearance. Because *a priori* deductions are so often risky, but also because of the documents that constitute Scripture, the Christian is not free to represent the origin of Humanity whatever way he likes. Without a doubt, these points are only half-illuminated. Genesis is a genre of history so unique that there will long remain doubts about the precise meaning of many of the details which it has conserved for us.[90]

Nevertheless, he went on to say, there are several truths of which we can be certain, including "that God created the first soul of the first man immediately, and probably completely recast [*remanié*] the matter destined to form his body" and "that the human race is entirely descended from a single couple (the monogenism required by the doctrine of original sin)." This requires "the necessary rejection of an evolutionism which, joining man . . . with lower forms of life and matter, sees in him only a product of a transformation, . . . but that falls short of a sudden and profound alteration [*remaniement*] . . . which would place man in a position of transcendence and stability."[91] But that, as he went on to say as he turned to "man according to the conclusions of philosophy and the sciences," does not require the rejection of every form of evolutionism: "It is possible to

---

88 Teilhard to Valensin, May 14, 1922, in *Lettres intimes*, 84. The reference is to French Benedictine Antoine Augustin Calmet, one of the leading exegetes of the eighteenth century, and Protestant Isaac Vossius. Calmet's views on the question can be found in his *Commentarius literalis*, 1: 1: 64–67 (trans., 341–44).

89 Teilhard, "Homme: IV. L'Homme devant les enseignements de l'Église et devant la philosophie spiritualiste" (1911).

90 Teilhard, "Homme," 504–5.

91 Teilhard, "Homme," 505, for both passages.

agree with many of the postulates of an evolutionism which brings man forth by means of a generative force immanent in the world. . . . Man 'grew' in the world more than he was grafted onto it. . . . What follows from that that contradicts the spirituality of the soul and our transcendence relative to other living things? Nothing."[92] His final remarks on this subject brought him back to revelation:

> From a strictly philosophical point of view, the probability (whatever it is) of evolution extending to man is not at all a problem. Only Biblical data could create an obstacle, imposing as they do theoretically verifiable determinations on human history: some requiring a certain degree of discontinuity between animals and the first man, others (such as monogenesis) implying the quasi-artificial intervention of free activity.—In practice, the difficulty which we will always have in putting the facts reported in Genesis into a concrete and scientific form, together with the uncertainty and approximation that will always be a part of paleontology and prehistory, make a collision between dogma and the sciences unlikely. Even for points as close to the domain of verifiable facts as are the origin of the human body and our descent from a single couple, it is necessary to say, once more, that from the study of mere appearances, dogma has nothing to fear and nothing to hope for.[93]

✳ ✳ ✳ ✳ ✳

Teilhard developed his ideas about the connection between paleoanthropology and theology in popular-science articles for the educated non-scientific audience and published, for example, in *Études* or in the *Revue des questions scientifiques*, in book reviews, and in unpublished lectures. These articles were sometimes of a purely scientific character, but they also served as a natural place for Teilhard to address questions of the compatibility of science and religion.

Two of the book reviews he published in *Études* while still a student at the Sorbonne—one on Hugo Obermaier's *Mensch der Vorzeit* and one on Boule's *Les Hommes fossiles*[94]—include brief reassurances to the reader that, as he put it in the earlier review, "now that a calmer view of the relations between science and faith shows that religious truth is well-protected against any possible sudden shocks that the empirical science of Man may undergo, it would be unpardonable to ignore the work of the prehistorians or to anathematize it."[95] The review of Boule's book, which, Teilhard acknowledged, contained "expressions unacceptable as they stand to Christian thought," concluded with the remark that:

> The letter of the Bible shows us the Creator forming the body of man from earth. Conscientious observation of the world tends to make us perceive today that by

---

92 Teilhard, "Homme," 512.

93 Teilhard, "Homme," 512–13.

94 Teilhard, "Préhistoire et ses progrès" (1913) and "Les Hommes fossiles" (1921).

95 Teilhard, "Préhistoire et ses progrès," 40 (trans., 11, which incorrectly put "experimental" rather than "empirical" for the French "expérimentale").

245

this "earth" we must understand a substance slowly elaborated by the totality of things, so that man has been drawn not precisely from a bit of amorphous matter, but by a prolonged effort from the "Earth" as a whole. Despite the serious difficulties which still prevent us from fully reconciling them with certain more commonly accepted representations of creation, these ideas (familiar to SS. Gregory of Nyssa and Augustine) should not upset us. Gradually (though we cannot yet say exactly in what terms but without the loss of a single fact, whether revealed or definitely proved) agreement will be reached, quite naturally, between science and dogma on the burning issue of human origins. In the meantime, let us take care not to reject the least ray of light from any side. Faith needs all truth.[96]

Teilhard also reviewed a work by saltationist, and finalist, Louis Vialleton—*Membres et ceintures des vertèbres tétrapodes: Critique morphologique du transformisme* (1924). Near the end of the review, Teilhard added in a footnote that "in Christian transformism, God's creative action is no longer conceived as pushing his works intrusively into the milieu of pre-existing beings, but as *bringing* the successive stages of His work *to birth* within the womb of things. It is, for all that, no less essential, no less universal, and above all no less intimate."[97]

✳ ✳ ✳ ✳ ✳

Teilhard's general compatibilism is most systematically developed in three articles he published in 1921–30. "Comment se pose aujourd'hui la Question du transformisme" and "Que faut-il penser du Transformisme?" were addressed to a theologically-minded Catholic audience; "La Paléontologie et l'apparition de l'homme" was intended to provide an introduction to paleoanthropology to a philosophical audience.[98]

In these articles, he emphasized that:

> Fundamentally, and more than ever in the eye of the immense majority of natural scientists, Man is coming back (and increasingly so) into the general transformist perspective. The more one examines our zoological type scientifically, the more irresistibly one is led to admit that neither the coincidence of its appearance with that of the other great anthropoids, nor the most minute details of its anatomical conformity with them, nor the characteristics of the fossil remains (still rare but significant) which we possess, can reasonably be explained without some historical (that is to say empirically detectable) connection between Man and the primates.[99]

This does not raise the theological problems that it was sometimes thought to raise:

---

96 Teilhard, "Hommes fossiles," 577 (trans., 32).

97 Teilhard, "Paradoxe transformiste" (1925), 80n1 (trans., 102n1). Vialleton was a professor of medicine at the University of Montpellier.

98 Two other articles published during this period round out Teilhard's views, but are less relevant to our current topic—"Face de la Terre" (1921) and "Phénomène humain" (1930). They elaborate his views on geology and anthropology, respectively.

99 Teilhard, "Que faut-il penser?," (1929), 94–95 (trans., 155–56). In the French text printed in the posthumous collection *La Vision du passé*, the "décelable" ("detectable") of the original was miscopied as "décevable" ("fallible"), which the English then incorrectly translated as "disappointing" ("décevant").

> Even if the transformist theory is accepted, there is room (more open than ever) for a first creative Power. And even, better, for creation of an evolutionary type (God *making things make themselves*) which has long seemed, to some very great minds, the most beautiful form that we can imagine for divine action in the Universe.
>
> From the philosophical point of view, the Christian, as such, can have no reason to deny, in principle, an extension of scientific evolutionism to Man, nor to be afraid if this extension were one day to become necessary.[100]

He did draw attention to the disagreement between science and faith on the question of monogenesis, suggesting that "monogenesis will gradually, without losing any of its theological 'effectiveness,' assume a form fully satisfying our scientific requirements."[101] As a conclusion, we can cite one of the last lines from the earliest of these articles:

> What must appear astonishing [is that believers] do not recognize more easily, beneath the sometimes unacceptable language of the evolutionists, the Catholic and traditional tendency to safeguard the efficacy [*vertu*] of second causes, to which, very recently, a very informed theologian, who is also a true scholar [sc. Henry de Dorlodot], was able to give the beautiful name of "Christian naturalism."[102]

In his work on Peking Man, Teilhard had begun to touch on a question of particular theological interest, the question of the origin of the first human body. As he wrote to a friend: "If that last point [sc., the cranial dimensions being completely human] is confirmed, ... it will be the conclusive answer to the opponents of transformism as extended to man."[103] So, in addition to pursuing his strictly scientific tasks, Teilhard undertook to introduce these scientific results to a broader Catholic audience.[104] *Sinanthropus* was probably, Teilhard wrote, "a true and new link in the series of morphological stages leading to the modern human type."[105] "To the very loose degree of precision that is all our paleontological series can ordinarily attain, only one place below Peking Man theoretically remains to be filled for the chain from the anthropoid to the human type to be made practically complete."[106] Teilhard's popular summaries of this work also emphasized the compatibility of the new finds with Catholic doctrine. In his articles on Peking Man, he emphasized that "these results ... in no way threaten (quite the opposite) a spiritualist conception of humanity.... Thought would not be queen of the world if it were not connected to it by all the fibres of matter, even the most humble ones."[107]

✳ ✳ ✳ ✳ ✳

100 Teilhard, "Que faut-il penser?," 93 and 95 (trans., 154 and 156).

101 Teilhard, "Que faut-il penser?," 96 (trans., 157).

102 Teilhard, "Comment se pose?" (1921), 544 (trans., 25).

103 Teilhard to a friend, September 16, 1929, in *Letters from a Traveller*, 160.

104 See Teilhard, "Une Importante Découverte" (1930); "Fouilles" (1934); and "La Découverte du Sinanthrope" (1937).

105 Teilhard, "Fouilles," 183 (trans., 70).

106 Teilhard, "Découverte du Sinanthrope," 11 (trans., 90).

107 Teilhard, "Découverte du Sinanthrope," 13 (trans., 92).

It is not surprising that, being the geologist on staff at the Institut catholique, and having discussed the theory of evolution in print, Teilhard received numerous invitations to speak on the connection between science and religion. During the last weeks of Lent in 1922, Teilhard received from Fr. Joseph Subtil of the Jesuit scholasticate in Enghien (Belgium) an invitation to address his students on the topic of transformism (to include a discussion of primates). In the course of the discussion that followed the lecture, Teilhard stated his views on the doctrine of original sin and then was asked (by Fr. Louis Riedinger, a theologian on the Enghien faculty) to make a written summary of his views on this question. He wrote up about ten pages, a "first approximation" of his views, and sent them to Riedinger, and to some other friends as well.[108]

Teilhard began his Note with a distinction between "the dogmatic attributes of the first transgression [*faute*] (the universal necessity of Redemption, *fomes peccati*, etc.)" and "the external circumstances in which this transgression was committed."[109] There is, Teilhard went on to say, "no acceptable place for Adam" and "still less . . . , in our historical picture, for the earthly paradise": "If one tries to concentrate in one single individual (or one single couple) all the primitive characteristics that can be recognized in Heidelberg Man, the Neanderthaler, the Tasmanians, Australians, etc., one arrives at an extremely dehumanized being, maybe a monstrous one"[110] and "we see now that everything fits together—physically, chemically, and zoologically—too well to allow the permanent absence of death, suffering and evil . . . to be conceivable apart from a *general state* of the World different from our own."[111] He suggested, in place of the traditional account, that

> We must so enlarge our ideas of original sin that we can no longer situate it anywhere around us, but know only that it is everywhere, as blended into the being of the World as is the God who creates us and the Incarnate Word who redeems us.[112]

> Original sin expresses, translates, personifies, in an instantaneous and localized act, the perennial and universal law of imperfection [*faute*] which is in Humanity *by virtue of* its being "*in fieri.*"[113]

---

108 Teilhard to Auguste Valensin, SJ, April 15, 1922, in Teilhard, *Lettres intimes* (1972), 81–83. Teilhard himself seems not to have had kept a copy of this text. The editors of his collected works found copies, under the title "Note sur quelques représentations historiques possibles du Péché originel" (1922), in the possession of both his cousin Marguerite Teilhard-Chambon and of Breuil. Although it is listed as included in Censurae 27–I at ARSI, it is not there; a note filed as OPP. NN. [Opera Nostrorum] 1432/2 says that "the two articles on original sin, along with another, were destroyed in August 1931, on order of T. R. P. L. [sc., Ledóchowski]."

Teilhard had touched on the topic of original sin earlier in his unpublished "Chute, rédemption et géocentrie" (1920). For further expressions of his views on this subject, see his letters to Valensin, October 20, 1919 and May 14, 1922 (in *Lettres intimes*, 18 and 84–85), as well as to Louis Richard, October 20, 1924, and to C. Gaudefroy, Easter 1927 (both quoted in *Lettres intimes*, 112–13n3).

109 Teilhard, "Note" (1922), 61 (trans., 45).

110 Teilhard, "Note," 62 (trans., 46).

111 Teilhard, "Note," 62 (trans., 46).

112 Teilhard, "Note," 70 (trans., 54).

113 Teilhard, "Note," 67–68 (trans., 51).

What Teilhard said, there and later elsewhere, about original sin and monogenesis provoked concern about the orthodoxy of his views on these related questions. I will discuss this further in chapter 12. It was perhaps as a result of that reaction at Rome that when he mentioned the topic again (in his "Que faut-il penser du Transformisme?" in 1930), he treated the topic with more caution, writing:

> If there is anything in modern science that still disturbs (and greatly so) Catholic thought, it is . . . the difficulty of finding a plausible way of harmonizing Transformism (once accepted) and a *strict monogenism*, that is to say our common descent from a single couple. On the one hand, for reasons which are not definitely philosophical or exegetic but essentially *theological* (the Pauline conception of the Fall and of Redemption), the Church holds to the historical reality of Adam and Eve. On the other, for reasons of probability and also of comparative anatomy, Science, left to itself, would never (that is the least that one can say) dream of attributing so narrow a basis as two individuals to the enormous edifice of humankind. . . .
>
> What will the solution be? It is impossible to say yet. . . . On the subject of human origins Science has certainly much more to discover, and Catholics much more thinking to do. All that can be foreseen is that the Church will increasingly recognize the scientific validity of an evolutionary form of creation;—and Science will in the end give a larger place to the powers of the mind, of liberty, and therefore of "improbability," in the historical evolution of the world. Monogenism will then without losing any of its theological "efficiency," gradually assume a form fully satisfying the requirements of Science.
>
> In the meantime the proper attitude for the believer cannot be in doubt. It is nothing other than to try, with patience and confidence, to understand *each side*. Faith guarantees that there can be no contradiction between his Credo and his human knowledge.[114]

✳ ✳ ✳ ✳ ✳

The third theme of Teilhard's work was a larger theology of nature. These are the ideas for which he is best known. However much they were adumbrated in earlier work, they came to full fruition, and the official reaction to them came, only after 1937. Consequently, discussion of them will be deferred to chapter 14.

5. ÉDOUARD LE ROY (1870–1954)

The final Catholic evolutionist from this period at whom we must have a look is philosopher Édouard Le Roy, whose work was focused not so much on any particular scientific finding or theory as on the development of a general cosmology that rejected the mechanistic philosophy of nature so widely associated with science, but accepted an

---

114 Teilhard, "Que faut-il penser?," 95–96 (trans., 156–57).

evolutionary account of the history of the universe. In this, he followed in the tradition of Henri Bergson (1859–1941).

Bergson, whom T. A. Goudge began an encyclopedia article by describing simply as "French philosopher of evolution,"[115] was one of the most prominent and widely read philosophers of the early twentieth century (though one not focused exclusively on the subject of evolution). He was born to Jewish parents, but was not given a religious upbringing. By the late 1880s, Bergson began to reject the mechanism that had at first appealed to him and to develop a philosophy of time and of human conscious experience that stood in some tension with the standard scientific interpretation of time. He published *Essai sur les données immédiates de la conscience* in 1889, and then *Matière et mémoire: Essai sur la relation du corps à l'esprit* in 1896. In 1900, he was appointed chair in the history of philosophy at the prestigious Collège de France, and in 1907 he published his *L'Évolution créatrice*. Le Roy said of Bergson's work that "it investigates and perfects [the contemporary idea of evolution], sifting it from its ore of materialism and turning it into genuine metaphysics."[116] In Bergson's judgment, he was moving closer and closer to Catholicism. In a letter to Joseph de Tonquédec, SJ, he wrote:

> The considerations set forth in my *Essai sur les données immédiates de la conscience* shed light on the fact of liberty; those set forth in *Matière et mémoire* give us, I hope, an intuitive understanding of the reality of spirit; those in *L'Évolution créatrice* present creation as a fact. From all that, the following become clear: the idea of a free creator God generator of both matter and life, and from that the effort of creation continues, on the side of life, by the evolution of species.[117]

Many Catholic critics disagreed and, for reasons that will be discussed in chapter 12, on June 1, 1914, the books mentioned above were placed on the *Index*.[118]

In 1927, Bergson was awarded the Nobel Prize for Literature. He never converted to Catholicism, but he refrained, he later said, only out of solidarity with Jewish populations then suffering persecution under National Socialism. Nevertheless, his philosophical ideas had a great influence on Catholic thinkers from Jacques Maritain and Étienne Gilson to Gabriel Marcel.[119] Of greater importance to our topic, is, of course, his influence on Teilhard de Chardin (already mentioned) and on Le Roy.

✱ ✱ ✱ ✱ ✱

Le Roy, mathematician and philosopher, took Bergson's chair at the Collège de France when ill health forced Bergson to step down in 1921. Le Roy was Catholic, not just in family background but in religious practice. In 1905, he published an article

---

115 Goudge, "Bergson," 1:287.

116 Le Roy, "Quelques objections," 294.

117 Joseph De Tonquédec, *Dieu dans "L'Évolution Créatrice,"* 34.

118 See Bruno Neveu, "Bergson et l'Index."

119 See Étienne Gilson, *The Philosopher and Theology*, and Jacques Maritain, *Bergsonian Philosophy and Thomism*. See also: Robert C. Grogin, "Catholic Revival," and Idella Jane Gallagher and Thomas M. King, "Bergson."

250

entitled "Qu'est-ce qu'un Dogme?" in the pages of *Quinzaine*. When he republished it as a booklet (with the title *Dogme et critique* in 1907), it was delated to Rome and placed on the *Index*.[120] In the late 1920s, he gave at the Collège de France two series of lectures in which he tried to develop Bergsonian evolutionism in what seemed to him to be a more Catholic direction. These lectures he subsequently published as *L'Exigence idéaliste et le fait de l'évolution* (1927) and *Les Origines humaines et l'évolution de l'intelligence* (1928). Over the course of the next two years, he published two more books—*La Pensée intuitive* (1929–30) and *Le Problème de Dieu* (1930).

The first two, more than the latter two, have a close connection to the Catholic evolutionism that is our topic. Le Roy said that *L'Exigence idéaliste* should have had as a subtitle, "In the margin of *L'Évolution créatrice*." Both books are fundamentally philosophical,[121] making connections to science and to theology without being either exactly theological or exactly scientific. They offer a general philosophy of nature and draw conclusions from that philosophy even on matters (saliently, the natural origin of life) for which there was then (as now, for that matter) no good *scientific* argument. They take up some scientific questions (such as the paleontological evidence for human evolution), but set aside those scientific controversies that are irrelevant to their larger purpose. They touch on the questions of God and creation, but discuss them very little. They do not take up Scriptural questions or questions of the Catholic tradition as had de Dorlodot's *Darwinisme*.

L'Exigence idéaliste is focused on effecting a reconciliation between idealism and evolution. Idealism, of course, in some sense reduces the world to thought: "The great fact, prior to any other, which is manifested to us by the demands of idealism consists of a formula without a subject: 'it is thinking,' analogous to 'it is raining.'"[122] Evolution, by apparent contrast, "shows thought emerging from matter, stepping out of the night."[123] So, "the history of the cosmic phenomenon appears as a genuine enigma, paradoxical and almost scandalous from the idealist point of view, because it forces us to acknowledge an origin that is completely material. That will be precisely what we will try to puzzle out: it will bring us to the problem of biological evolution, as characterized in the title of this book."[124] The book begins with an account of the natural history of the planet (matter and life; bacteria, insects, and dinosaurs) and proceeds through an analysis of competing scientific theories of evolution (Darwinism, mutationism, and Lamarckism; orthogenesis), concluding with a discussion of more philosophical concepts (vitalism,

---

120 For a history of that controversy, see Guy Mansini, *"What is a Dogma?"*

121 In the introduction to *Origines humaines*, Le Roy wrote, "My final goal is metaphysical; but before attaining it (even in order to aim at it directly), it is necessary to establish with care a basis of facts. I cannot approve a philosopher who speculates without a foundation in science any more than I can a scientist who blinds himself with the vanity of a science destitute of philosophy" (pp. v–vi).

122 Le Roy, *Exigence*, 266.

123 Le Roy, *Exigence*, 1.

124 Le Roy, *Exigence*, xiii.

finality, and creation). It takes us as far as the appearance of man—the transformation of the biosphere into the noosphere.[125]

Les Origines humaines, of course, focused on anthropological questions—human exceptionalism and its importance in a comprehensive cosmology (so, the very concept of a noosphere), thought and language, tools and fire, paleontology and prehistory.

On two points of major importance, the books conform to Catholic doctrines—the distinctiveness of creation (in contrast to natural processes) and human exceptionalism. On the first point, Le Roy wrote:

> Science, as such, is incapable of reaching the creative act, . . . in the course of, or even at the start of, the series of phenomena. . . . It is by its nature dedicated—when going back through the course of time or a chain of causes—to acts of analysis (*morcelage*) that always leave a residue, and can thus never get to an absolute "beginning." It is by different routes and by following another perspective that philosophy gets to the idea of creation.[126]

On the second:

> The difference [between a human infant and a young chimpanzee] is a difference of nature and not simply one of degree. The characteristic proper to human intelligence . . . consists in that capacity of reflection which opens fields of rationality beyond the senses, the common source of language, which transforms social life, and of artifact—tool and fire—which have permitted Man to conquer the world.[127]

On one point, Le Roy took a position that was still quite controversial among Catholics—the evolutionary origin of the human body. His general view was that evolution was simply a fact. The paleontological evidence for the evolution of man still being rather sparse, he relied rather on both the general morphological evidence that had been the foundation of the view since Darwin published *The Descent of Man*, and the new biochemical evidence that had been emerging since the turn of the century.[128] He cited in particular the work of Teilhard, with whom he was in close contact as he was thinking through the questions that were the subject of these lectures.

Some Catholics found the books helpful on various particular points, but that was not the judgment of everyone. In any case, the institutional prohibition of books operated on the Dionysian Principle—*malum ex quocumque defectu*; helpful insights on some points would not outweigh defects on others. Complaints about the books soon made their way to the Holy Office, so the story will resume in chapter 12.

---

125 The term is widely credited to Pierre Teilhard de Chardin, but it must be equally associated with Le Roy, and perhaps also with Vladimir Ivanovich Vernadsky, all three of whom were in Paris in the mid-1920s (Teilhard, "Antiquity and World Expansion of Human Culture" [1956], 103). Teilhard later said of the word, "I think that the word 'noosphere' was my invention (but who knows?); it was Le Roy who began to use it" (letter of December 3, 1954, quoted in Cuénot, *Teilhard*, 81–82 [trans., 59]).

126 Le Roy, *Origines*, 368–69. See also Le Roy, *Exigence*, xv.

127 Le Roy, *Origines*, 147.

128 Le Roy, *Origines*, 142–43, quoting, on that last-mentioned point, Boule, *Hommes fossiles*, 450.

CHAPTER 12

THE OFFICIAL CHURCH
(1909–1931)

1. THE POPES

a. Benedict XV (r. 1914–22)

Benedict XV never directly addressed the question of evolution. We should, however, note the several passages from his first encyclical letter, *Ad beatissimi Apostolorum* (1914). On the one hand, he commended his predecessor (St. Pius X) for removing "the danger of rash innovations ... from the teaching of the sacred sciences" and renewed Pius's condemnation of modernism, warning against "the modernistic spirit, a spirit that fastidiously rejects what is ancient, and is ever on the search for novelties." [1] Nevertheless, he also wrote that "in matters about which the Holy See has not given a decision, and in which, without injury to faith and ecclesiastical discipline, there may be differences of opinion, each may lawfully defend his own. ... Each is free to maintain his own opinion ... and if others do not accept his view, he must not cast suspicion on their faith or spirit of discipline." [2]

---

1 Benedict XV, *Ad beatissimi Apostolorum*, 575 and 578 (trans., 655 and 657).

2 Benedict XV, *Ad beatissimi Apostolorum*, 576–77 (trans., 656).

b. Pius XI (r. 1922–39)

Pius XI is among the scholars who have, intermittently, worn the papal tiara. Historian Harry Paul characterized him as "the type of pope most likely to be impressed by scientific arguments."[3] As Achille Ratti, he had been on the staff of, and finally director of, the Biblioteca Ambrosiana in Milan (1888–1911) and then took a position at the Biblioteca Apostolica Vaticana (1911–18), where, during his last years at that institution, he was prefect. He published, during that time, over sixty scholarly articles.[4] Despite the emphasis on the historical and paleographical topics that characterized his scholarly work, Ratti had, from his early years, taken an interest in geology under the influence of two priest-geologists, Antonio Stoppani and Giuseppe Mercalli.

Stoppani had played a major rôle in the development of Italian geology and paleontology, writing both professional and popular works on the subject. He also devoted some attention to questions of the relationship between science and religion, with a long book entitled *Il Dogma e le scienze positive, ossia La missione apologetica del clero nel moderno conflitto tra la ragione e la fede* (1884). Mercalli, perhaps best-known for his invention of the Mercalli Intensity Scale for the measurement of earthquakes, entrusted to the young Ratti the preparation of a chronology of Italian earthquakes for his *Vulcani e fenomeni vulcanici in Italia* (1883).[5]

Perhaps because of those connections and interests, Friderico Sala, Ratti's former colleague at the Milan seminary (where Ratti had taught from 1882 to 1888), asked him to prepare a discussion of the origin of the first human body for the fifth edition of Sala's *Institutiones positivo-scholasticae theologiae dogmaticae* (1899–1900). There is no other discernible reason why Sala should have turned exactly to Ratti for a discussion of this topic. Whatever the reason, Ratti's "De hominis origine quoad corpus" appeared as a scholium in Sala's *Institutiones*.[6] The scholium was a fairly standard presentation of the anti-evolutionist answer to the question, citing Camillo Mazzella and Tilmann Pesch on theology and philosophy, and Stoppani and Joachim Barrande on science.[7] Catholic evaluation of the thesis that the bodies of our first parents were directly formed by God, he said (citing Mazzella), ranged from "Catholic doctrine" to "nearly a matter of faith" (*ad fidem spectare*).[8] Theologically, he emphasized a literal reading of the relevant scriptural passage (sc., Genesis 2:7, not Genesis 1). Scientifically, he raised the usual questions about whether morphological similarity provides evidence for common ancestry.

---

3 Paul, *Edge of Contingency*, 105.

4 For a list, see "Werken en geschriften van Z. H. Paus Pius XI" in *De Tijd*.

5 Ratti, "Terremoti storici italiani." The book in which it was published was the third volume of Stoppani's *Geologia d'Italia*. Ratti's contribution is not acknowledged in the book itself, and for that reason, perhaps, is not included in some lists of Ratti's work. For the attribution, see Cristoforo Allievi, "Un contributo poco noto." My thanks to Luca Jaselli for drawing this article to my attention.

6 Sala, *Institutiones*, 5th ed., 2:197–211.

7 Mazzella, *De Deo creante*; Pesch, *Große Welträthsel*; Stoppani, *Note ad un corso annuale di geologia*; and Barrande, *Système silurien*.

8 Ratti, "De hominis origine," 198; Mazzella, *De Deo creante*, ¶ 512.

Philosophically, he appealed to principles of causality and teleology. In discussing these latter two aspects of the question, of course, he raised objections that would, if sound, tell against the evolutionary origins of plants and animals, not just of the human body.

In 1922, Ratti became Pope Pius XI. His continued interest in science was manifest on the institutional level. He reconstituted, for example, the Pontifical Academy of Sciences in 1936. He also maintained a more personal interest. Breuil, on his return from a visit to China to study the newly discovered remains of Peking Man, is reported to have intended to make a presentation directly to the pope.[9]

The incidents mentioned below suggest that he was more open to the possibility of evolutionary origins in the 1920s and 1930s than he had been in 1900. As pope, he prevented the Index from suppressing the work of de Dorlodot, Messenger, and Paquier, though he did not address the issue directly.

2. THE CONGREGATION OF THE INDEX & THE HOLY OFFICE

Two institutional changes need to be noted here. First, in 1908, the Index was granted the authority to initiate inquiries into books itself, without waiting for books to be referred to it by others. It does not, however, seem to have exercised this authority in the case of books on evolutionism.

Second, in 1917, the Index ceased to exist as an independent congregation. It was, in that year, subordinated to the Holy Office, though without any change in its responsibilities or in its procedures.

Two kinds of cases came to the Vatican for resolution. The former concerned what might be called cosmic evolutionism; the latter, anthropogenesis.

a. The Bergson & Le Roy Cases

Henri Bergson had been writing for some twenty-five years when his works first came to the attention of the Index. On March 8, 1913, Édouard Hugon, an influential Dominican philosopher and theologian then teaching at the newly-formed Pontificium collegium internationale Angelicum, delated three of Bergson's books—*L'Évolution créatrice* (1907), *Matière et mémoire: Essai sur la relation du corps à l'esprit* (1896), and *Essai sur les données immédiates de la conscience* (1889). "The books," Hugon charged, "attack three fundamental doctrines of our faith: (1) the *personality* of God, (2) the *substantial union* of the soul with the body, and (3) human *freedom*."[10]

---

9 Felix Rüschkamp, "*Sinanthropus*," 54.

10 Hugon, *Votum* (doc. 71, Protocolli 1913, CL, ADDF). Hugon recommended, in support of his critique, the following works: Albert Farge, *Philosophie de M. Bergson*; Jacques Maritain, "*Évolutionnisme de M. Bergson*"; Joseph de Tonquédec, *Notion de vérité dans la "philosophie nouvelle"*; Réginald Garrigou-Lagrange, *Sens commun*; and Thomas-M. Pègues, "*Évolution créatrice*." For an article on this case, see Bruno Neveu, "Bergson et l'Index."

The task of reviewing *L'Évolution créatrice*, the book most relevant to our subject, was given to Henri Laurent Janssens, OSB, who wrote that "the title alone would be sufficient reason for the Congregation of the Index to condemn the book": "*L'Évolution créatrice* is a work of atheistic thought aimed at explaining the origin of the world, the mystery of the universe, and the human species without resort to a wise and powerful God, creator, organizer, and governor of things." He summarized his estimation of the book by saying "the grave error of the first chapter forms the foundation. It is evolutionism without God."[11]

The verdict at the preparatory congregation went against the book:

> The teaching of this philosopher is diametrically opposed to the perennial Christian philosophy, indeed it is the destruction of all philosophy, and especially of metaphysics. It is subversive of many revealed doctrines. However much it seems to assert the immortality of the soul, the freedom of the will, the personality of God, the creation of the universe, etc., in words, in fact it overturns all dogmas.[12]

The vote was unanimous, though one consultor (Alberto Lepidi, Master of the Sacred Palace) said that he would have been content to leave the books to their fate. The general congregation concurred with the vote, and the three books were placed on the *Index* on June 1, 1914.[13]

Bergson, who was not Catholic, accepted the condemnation with serenity: "Condemnations leave me indifferent, just as does unmerited praise. . . . What is strange in the whole affair is that many people denounce my philosophy as 'reactionary,' Catholic, and even (they have used the word) clerical!"[14] It is important to note that Bergson's ideas constituted a theology, or a philosophy, of nature; they did not make direct contact with the paleoetiological sciences.

That topic returned to the docket of the Index only in the 1930s, seventeen years after Bergson's books were placed on the *Index*, when the work of a second author in the Bergsonian tradition was delated to Rome. On April 19, 1931, Agostino Gemelli wrote to Pope Pius XI to draw to his attention "the growth, in France, of a scholarly movement which seems to me to be rather dangerous from the point of view of sound Catholic doctrine. I allude to the spread of evolutionist doctrines even among Catholics. The promoter of this movement is a professor, a student of H. Bergson and his successor at the Collège de France, Le Roy."[15] Although Gemelli was not an anti-evolutionist, as his

---

11 Janssens, *Votum*, January 17, 1914, 1–2 (fol. 93, Protocolli 1914–17, CL, ADDF).

12 The preparatory congregation was held on May 22, 1914; the general congregation on June 1 (fol. 88, Protocolli 1914–17, CL, ADDF).

13 Decree (fol. 101, Protocolli 1914–17, CL, ADDF).

14 Bergson to the Countess Thérèse Murat, June 21, 1914, in Bergson, *Correspondances*, 586.

15 Gemelli to Pius XI, April 19, 1931 (fol. 19–22, doc. 3, CL 1930/461, ADDF). Pope Pius, then still Achille Ratti, was archbishop of Milan when Gemelli founded that city's Catholic university. It must have been as a consequence of personal acquaintance that Gemelli addressed his letter directly to the pope.

translation of Wasmann's *Moderne Biologie* shows,[16] he was a determined anti-Bergsonian and rejected evolutionary explanations of the origin of the human body.

In his letter, Gemelli objected to all four of books mentioned in the earlier discussion of Le Roy (in chapter 11)—*L'Exigence idéaliste* (1927), *Les Origines humaines* (1928), *La Pensée intuitive* (1929), and *Le Problème de Dieu* (1930). These books, Gemelli said, presented an idealistic evolutionism destructive of all religious faith. Gemelli added that "Le Roy is an old modernist fox and unfortunately has that French refined art of only half-saying things so that he can later excuse himself with an 'I didn't say that.' It seems to me that a word from the Church in condemnation of Le Roy's works would respond to an urgent need."[17] The letter also took exception to the recent work of Teilhard de Chardin, as will be discussed below, as well to that of several other theologians whose work he saw as in a loose sense analogous to Teilhard's—Maurice Blondel, Auguste Valensin, Erich Przywara, and Karl Adam.[18]

On April 29, 1931, the Holy Office asked Gemelli and Marco Sales, OP, Master of the Sacred Palace, for *vota* on Le Roy's four books. It said it would also look into the cases of the other authors named, but not much seems to have come of that inquiry.[19]

Sales limited his *votum* to *Le Problème de Dieu*, about which he wrote that "the philosophical foundation of the author's whole argument is Bergson's philosophy of becoming and his creative evolution." "The book retains," he said," the usual Christian terms, but empties them of their real content." He recommended that the book be placed on the *Index* on account of its modernism.[20]

Gemelli wrote a short *votum* (of seven pages) on all four books. It began with a general critique of Le Roy, "the well-known modernist," whose earlier work had already been placed on the *Index* and whose errors had been on the list of propositions condemned by Pius X in his encyclical *Lamentabili*. He was "an ardent disciple and passionate popularizer of the philosophy of Henri Bergson." The works under review were just a repetition of ideas that had already been condemned.[21]

Le Problème de Dieu, and the objections to it, fall outside our topic. *La Pensée intuitive* touches it only slightly. *L'Exigence idéaliste*, Gemelli said, defends a "Bergsonian

---

16 That he did not change his mind about this is clear from the memorial note he wrote on the occasion of Wasmann's death in 1931 (Gemelli, "Wasmann").

17 Gemelli to Pius XI (fol. 20).

18 Gemelli to Pius XI (fol. 20–21). Blondel, Valensin, and Przywara were Catholic philosophers who offered alternatives to the more traditionally Thomistic approach to philosophy valued by Gemelli (and many other Catholics) and officially recommended by the Church. Valensin and Przywara were transcendental Thomists, who gave Immanuel Kant a place in philosophy more favorable than did most Thomists. Blondel rejected the standard Thomistic approach to apologetics—through natural religion—and offered an entirely different approach to the philosophy of religion in its place. Adam was a historian of dogma and a dogmatic theologian. None of them said much about evolution. Although the Index asked Gemelli to take a closer look at two of Adam's books (*Das Wesen des Katholizismus* and *Christus unser Bruder*), and Gemelli wrote a *votum* on them (fol. 23, doc. 4, and fol. 32–33, doc. 7–8, CL 1930/461, ADDF), no work of Adam, or of any of the other authors, was ever placed on the *Index*.

19 Minutes of the preparatory congregation, April 23, 1931 (fol. 23, doc. 4, CL 1930/461, ADDF).

20 Sales, *Votum*, May 8, 1931, 7 (for the passage quoted) and 8 (for the verdict) (fol. 26, doc. 6, CL 1930/461, ADDF).

21 Gemelli, *Votum*, May 21, 1931, 2 (fol. 36, doc. 8, CL 1930/461, ADDF).

ultratransformism" according to which "the First Reality is the élan-creator [*slancio creatore*] which produces matter and (in divergent lines) plants, animals, and man." *Les Origines humaines*, he said, defends the idea that "an integral transformism, which includes both man and intelligence, is 'literally a fact which emerges just as does a fact of history . . . .'"[22] Man, Gemelli quoted Le Roy as saying, is "just a particular case in the history of other animal forms."[23] Gemelli mentioned Le Roy's reliance on Teilhard here, but reserved his comments on Teilhard for a separate *votum*.

Gemelli concluded by arguing against a condemnation of just one book. That, he objected, would be construed as a recognition of the permissibility of reading the others.

❋ ❋ ❋ ❋ ❋

The preparatory congregation met on June 15, 1931. The consultors in attendance recommended that the books be put on the *Index* with the formula "already condemned (per c. 1399, 2°)" and emphasized the importance of reminding Catholics of the teachings of the [First] Vatican Council, particularly regarding the proofs for the existence of God. Le Roy was to give to his archbishop, Jean Cardinal Verdier, a letter retracting all his errors. If he did not, he was to be denied the sacraments.[24] The cardinals in attendance at the general congregation on June 24 unanimously agreed that the books "denied the objective and extrinsic reality of the traditional proofs" and in general "contained an accumulation of heresies, as the passages cited by Fr. Sales and Fr. Gemelli suffice to show." Exceptionally, in this case, the cardinals also suggested that the condemnation be accompanied by a brief statement of the reason for the condemnation.[25]

The condemnation of the books was approved by the pope and on June 27 all four books were placed on the *Index*. The disposition of the case was to be made public in *L'Osservatore Romano* (as well as in the *Acta Apostolicae Sedis*, where such matters always appeared), but, the pope specified, was to be announced "without further comment."[26]

Le Roy promptly wrote to Verdier, saying that he "faithfully and straightforwardly accepted the decree of the Holy Office."[27] Later that same day, he wrote again: "In light of certain comments in the press, will you permit me to add that I believe, in the same sense as does the Church, in the possibility of an objective demonstration of the existence of God, in the distinction between Creator and creature, in the creation of the world in general and in particular of the soul by God, and in the objective value of human

---

22 Gemelli, *Votum*, 5.

23 Gemelli, *Votum*, 6. The Le Roy passages are in *Origines humaines*, 81 and 130. It is perhaps important to note that Le Roy had qualified the latter remark: "*In the eyes of the pure zoologist,* the natural of history of man is just a particular case . . . ." (emphasis mine). At the end of the chapter, he said that the difference between chimpanzee and man is "one of nature, not of degree" (*Origines humaines*, 147).

24 Minutes from the preparatory congregation of June 15, 1931 (fol. 45, doc. 9, CL 1930/461, ADDF).

25 Minutes from the general congregation of June 24, 1931 (fol. 47, doc. 10, CL 1930/461, ADDF).

26 Minutes, June 24–25, 1931 (fol. 49, doc. 11, CL 1930/461, ADDF). See *Acta Apostolicae Sedis* 23 , no. 9 (1931): 330, and *L'Osservatore Romano,* June 28, 1931.

27 Le Roy to Verdier, July 3, 1931 (fol. 56, doc. 15, CL 1930/461, ADDF).

knowledge."[28] Le Roy's letters did not satisfy his critics (or the Holy Office), because, they said, he had only written a letter of submission, and not the required letter of *retraction*. The correction of two documents on the case in the files of the Holy Office—"Sur la ~~ritrazzione~~ sottomissione del Prof. Le Roy"[29]—illustrates the concern. Le Roy wrote to Verdier again, explicitly using the word "retract," on November 19, 1931.[30]

✳ ✳ ✳ ✳ ✳

While it is true that two of Le Roy's books had a connection with the paleoetiological sciences, and that fact was noted by Gemelli in his *votum*, the documents associated with the case suggest that that was not an important consideration in the books' condemnation. First, the secretary's notes about the concerns expressed at the preparatory and general congregations emphasize other matters, as was reported above. The books, they said, "champion and apply to religious dogmas a system of modernistic evolutionism which leads to pantheism, a system which has already been condemned."[31] And in another note, Ernesto Ruffini referred to the importance of calling to the minds of Catholics "the fundamental doctrines defined by the [First] Vatican Council, especially in regard to proofs for the existence of God."[32]

That this was the focus of the Congregation's concern is clear from correspondence associated with the subsequent controversy over whether Le Roy's submission had addressed all that it was supposed to address. The issues central to *that* controversy were those that Le Roy had mentioned in the two letters to Verdier quoted above.

The condemnation of Le Roy's books (like that of Bergson's fourteen years before) seems, therefore, despite Gemelli's attempts to connect them with Teilhard's views on the origin of man,[33] to have been directed at the authors' general philosophical and theological views rather than at any view connectable to the paleoetiological sciences. Nevertheless, since the *Index* only *lists* books Catholics were prohibited from reading, without anything by way of explanation or critique, the general public could not know the reason for a particular book's condemnation.[34] That did not, however, keep Le Roy's anti-evolutionist Catholic critics from speculating in the press as to *why* his books might have been condemned. And so the fate of Le Roy's books, especially in light of press comments from his detractors, elicited a response from Henri Count Bégouën, a Catholic and one of France's leading paleoanthropologists.

28 Le Roy to Verdier, July 3, 1931 (fol. 57, doc. 16, CL 1930/461, ADDF).

29 Fol. 58–61, doc. 17a–b.

30 Le Roy to Verdier, November 19, 1931 (fol. 63–65, doc. 19–20).

31 Summary of Congregation of Consultors, June 8, 1931 (Acta C[ongregationis] G[eneralis] 1931, ADDF).

32 Note of June 15, 1931 (fol. 45, doc. 9, CL 1930/461, ADDF).

33 Sales, *Votum*, 6; Gemelli to Pius XI (fol. 19–20).

34 Exceptionally, in this case, the cardinals at the general congregation suggested that the condemnation be accompanied by a brief statement of the reason (fol. 47, doc. 10, CL 1930/461, ADDF), but Pope Pius, in the audience of the following day, instructed that the resolution of the case be announced "without further comment" (fol. 49, doc. 11). (See *Acta Apostolicae Sedis* 23, no. 9 (1931): 330) or *L'Osservatore Romano*, June 28, 1931.

Some six weeks after the publication of the condemnation, on August 17, 1931, Bégouën wrote a "strictly confidential" letter to Bonaventura Cardinal Cerretti, former Apostolic Nuncio to France but in 1931 in Rome as a member of the Supreme Tribunal of the Apostolic Signatura, expressing his concern about the condemnation of Le Roy's works. On September 2, on Cerretti's advice, he wrote to Donato Cardinal Sbaretti, then prefect of the Holy Office, enclosing a copy of the earlier letter.[35] Bégouën thought that the fears of the Holy Office were mistaken. Le Roy's work could actually draw readers closer to the faith and to God. The condemnation, by contrast, would alienate Catholic intellectuals, create institutional tensions between universities and the Church, and in general become a tool in the hands of the Church's enemies. Bégouën's substantive concerns were two. The first was the compatibility of the concepts of creation and evolution. This was, he wrote, the same point that his father had made fifty years before. His second concern was that the recent discoveries in China (*Sinanthropus*) could only be seen as the undeniable foundation for a new argument in favor of the evolutionary origins of man.

b. The de Dorlodot Case (1923–25)[36]

De Dorlodot's troubles (centered on a dimension of Catholic evolutionism quite distinct from the cosmic evolution of Bergson and others) began in early 1923, at the Pontifical Biblical Commission, when its secretary, Laurent Janssens, brought de Dorlodot's *Darwinisme* to the attention of Willem Cardinal van Rossum, the Commission's president. The book, in their judgment, was inconsistent with the *responsa* that the Commission had given in 1909 to some questions that had been put to it concerning the historicity of the first three chapters of Genesis. Janssens, as it happens, had been secretary when those *responsa* were prepared and they had been published over his signature.[37]

Being sympathetic with de Dorlodot's central thesis, Catholic evolutionists have tended to overlook some of his book's defects, defects that were sure to provoke a reaction from readers apprehensive about modernism and disposed to see in evolutionism just what so many atheists and materialists said was there.

One defect was that de Dorlodot seemed to take a rather minimalist approach to the decrees of the Pontifical Biblical Commission. He began by pointing out, correctly, that "*in accordance with canonical rules*, these decisions, since they place a limitation on freedom, are of *strict interpretation*."[38] As an example, however, he wrote: "When the Commission declares that one cannot *affirm* an opinion, it does not follow that one cannot

35 Bégouën to Sbaretti, September 2, 1931 (fol. 80r–82, CL 1930/461, ADDF).

36 The work of Raf De Bont ("Rom" and *Darwins kleinkinderen*) is useful, though I am not in complete agreement with his interpretation of the case.

37 Van Rossum to the Holy Office, November 6, 1923 (fol. 1 and 3, doc. [red] 1, CL 1922–23/904, ADDF). See also the note labeled "du P. Placide—très confidentiel," May 28, 1923 (Archives spéciales, Affaire de Dorlodot, T73 XXXIII, AKUL [hereafter, "De Dorlodot Papers"]).

38 De Dorlodot, *Darwinisme*, 25 (trans., 18) (italics de Dorlodot's).

regard that opinion *as probable*."[39] So one may still "regard as probable" something that the Commission said that one may not "affirm." Is that correct? He needs a distinction somewhere within this spectrum:

affirming	affirming	regarding	regarding
as certain	as true	as probable	as possible

E. C. Messenger, in his English translation of *Darwinisme*, chose from the extremes, which minimizes the problem—"we may not affirm [a proposition] *with certainty*" does not preclude "regard[ing] it as a possible view."[40] De Dorlodot's original text, however needs a difference between "affirm" and "regard as probable," where the difference is not quite so clear.

To affirm an opinion is merely to maintain that it is true[41] and that is how the word was used the only time that the Commission used it.[42] As for how such opinions may be regarded, de Dorlodot could have said "as possible," but he said "as probable," which is stronger. In ordinary usage, probability would mean "having a great appearance of truth,"[43] but the word also has a precise technical meaning in Catholic epistemology—"A probable proposition is one supported by reasons which are fallible, but nevertheless fairly weighty."[44] Two consequences of this definition are worth noting. First, "two contradictory propositions can be probable at the same time." Camillo Mazzella applied this consequence in evaluating older and more recent views about the Hexaemeron. Both views—that the days were and were not twenty-four hours long—he calls probable.[45] Second, "one can think that a proposition is true and at the same time think that the opposite proposition is probable."[46]

Can one say that an opinion "has a great appearance of truth" or that "by reason of intrinsic or extrinsic arguments it is able to gain the assent of many prudent men" without "maintaining that it is true"? Can one say those things without putting the alternative in doubt? The distinction is slight enough to create a controversy between a commission jealous of the authority of its official statements and a professor jealous of his freedom in scholarly inquiry.

---

39 De Dorlodot, *Darwinisme*, 26: "Lorsque la Commission Biblique déclare que l'on ne peut *affirmer* une opinion, il ne s'ensuit pas que l'on ne puisse considérer cette opinion *comme probable*" (de Dorlodot's italics). Messenger's published translation is inaccurate in ways that I will make clear below.

40 De Dorlodot, *Darwinism*, 18.

41 See Claude Augé, *Petit Larousse Illustré*, 19: "soutenir qu'une chose est vraie."

42 This was in its (earlier) response to the question of whether arguments impugning the Mosaic authorship of the Pentateuch were weighty enough to justify *affirming* that Moses was not the author of the Pentateuch ("ius tribuant affirmandi hos libros non Moysen habere auctorem"). Their answer was that they were not strong enough to permit such an affirmation (Pontifical Biblical Commission. "De Mosaica authentia Pentateuchi").

43 Augé, *Petit Larousse illustré*, 797.

44 Cartechini, *De valore notarum theologicarum*, 104.

45 Mazzella, *De Deo creante*, 166–67.

46 Cartechini, *De valore notarum theologicarum*, 106.

De Dorlodot was on somewhat firmer ground when he took up the Commission's response on the matter most directly connected to his thesis. There, the prohibition was not against affirmations, but against "putting [certain points] in doubt."[47] He emphasized that "if the Commission has abstained from including in its enumeration a point the historical and doctrinal character of which has led to great discussions in modern times, it is clear that the silence of the Commission on that matter is voluntary."[48] Anyone who attempted to *censure* views not explicitly listed (other than those that "were regarded by the general opinion of the Fathers as taught in the first chapters of Genesis") would be guilty of calumny and rashness.

Were de Dorlodot's ideas among those inconsistent with the general opinion of the Fathers? Or, on the other hand, had the Commission, as de Dorlodot claimed, given its approval to "the opinion which considers the Hexaemeron as belonging to the literary genre of *figurative and popular history*"?[49] It is easy to see why de Dorlodot would think that the Commission was, in 1923, guilty of prohibition creep. It is equally easy to see why anti-evolutionists would think that de Dorlodot's ideas were rash or at least that he had interpreted the responses of the Biblical Commission in a way that would lead to theological error.

The idea that de Dorlodot was not inclined to take the decisions of the Commission with sufficient seriousness could only gain force from consideration of a second passage. About the Mosaic authorship of the Pentateuch, de Dorlodot had said, "The part of Genesis which specially interests us is . . . the work of a compiler, whom we will call Moses if you wish,"[50] which rather obtusely mistook what the Commission had said.

Another defect in de Dorlodot's book is a certain lack of clarity with respect to two key terms. The heart of the problem is that the broad subject of discussion includes three questions—the origin of life, the origin (i.e., transformation) of species, and the origin of man. De Dorlodot defined "absolute evolution" as explicitly including the first and the second and implicitly including the third as well (since he says "all living species"). "Darwinism" he defined as excluding the first, but including the second and (implicitly) the third.[51] He said that empirical evidence favors Darwinian over absolute evolution on the point with respect to which they differ.[52] He went on to say, four times in the first five pages, that *his topic* was the Darwinian theory "apart from" or "leaving out" (*faisant abstraction de*) the question of the origin of man. That question would be left for future lectures.[53]

47 Pontifical Biblical Commission, "De charactere historico," 568; de Dorlodot cited this wording (*Darwinisme*, 29; cf. "calling [them] in question," trans., 21).

48 De Dorlodot, *Darwinisme*, 30 (trans., 21).

49 De Dorlodot, *Darwinisme*, 33 (trans., 24) (italics de Dorlodot's).

50 De Dorlodot, *Darwinisme*, 29 (trans., 20–21).

51 De Dorlodot, *Darwinisme*, 10–12 (trans., 4–6).

52 De Dorlodot, *Darwinisme*, 151 (trans., 126).

53 De Dorlodot, *Darwinisme*, 9 and 11 (trans., 3 and 5) (twice on each page).

So when he said that "one cannot find in Holy Scripture . . . any convincing argument against the theory of . . . absolute evolution"[54] or when he complained about "those who . . . seek to hinder Catholics from professing [Darwinism] openly,"[55] did he mean those terms as he had just defined them, or did he mean only that *part* of the meaning that he had identified as his subject? Did he mean that nothing in Scripture tells against a purely natural origin of man (without any special divine intervention)? Was he concerned that someone was hindering Catholics from professing *that* openly? How is "absolute evolutionism leaving aside the question of the origin of man" not just another form of the "moderate evolutionism" with which he explicitly contrasted it?

A final defect is this: In justification of his participation in Cambridge's Darwin Celebration, he said that "if the thesis of the origin of man by way of [*par voie de*] evolution had been regarded as in substance worthy of condemnation—if Darwin were a heretic on this point, as certain people have declared . . . ,"[56] but surely Darwin's own account did not include the special creation of the human soul and, on *that* point, it was heretical (as everyone agreed). It is clear enough what de Dorlodot *means*, as long as one does not pay too close attention to the words he uses to say it.

The charitable reader can perhaps adjust for de Dorlodot's imprecision of expression, but, unfortunately for the author, the struggle against modernism had taken its toll and charity among Catholic anti-evolutionists was, in the early 1920s, still in short supply.

✳ ✳ ✳ ✳ ✳

It is perhaps worth keeping in mind that de Dorlodot's book came to the attention of the authorities in Rome in the same year that the Holy Office decided another major case. On December 15, 1923, Augustin Brassac's revision of Fulcran Vigouroux's *Manuel Biblique* had been placed on the *Index*. This book had not said much about evolution, but, in the minds of its critics, de Dorlodot's book had relied on the approach to exegesis that had led to the condemnation of Brassac's *Manuel*.

In early May 1923, van Rossum wrote to Louvain rector Paulin Ladeuze asking for some clarification of points that de Dorlodot had made in *Darwinisme*.[57] Van Rossum's primary concern seems to have been that de Dorlodot had (he thought) appealed to the authority of the Commission in a way that suggested that the Commission had pronounced in favor of his opinion, though no particular passages were indicated as the locus of the problem.[58] The only passage mentioned explicitly was the one in which

---

54 De Dorlodot, *Darwinisme*, 11 (trans., 6).

55 De Dorlodot, *Darwinisme*, 79 (trans., 62).

56 De Dorlodot, *Darwinisme*, 8 (trans., 2).

57 I have not been able to find a copy of this letter. It is not in the archive of the Katholieke Universiteit Leuven or of the DDF. Rumor has it that the archive of the old Pontifical Biblical Commission still exists somewhere in Rome (see Vefie Poels and Hans de Valk, "A Stranger in the Sacred College of Cardinals," ¶45), but no one seems to know where it is. Some idea of the content of the letter can be gathered from subsequent correspondence.

58 For both the Commission's concern about unjustifiable reliance on its statements and de Dorlodot's complaint about the lack of specificity on the part of the Commission, see the first draft of de Dorlodot's proposed reply to the Commission, attached to his first letter to Ladeuze, May 13, 1923, p. 1 (Letter I, De Dorlodot Papers, AKUL). Ladeuze also mentioned, in

de Dorlodot had said that the Commission's prohibition against affirming a proposition did not prohibit saying that the proposition was probable.[59] Van Rossum must also have mentioned Janssens as the source of the complaint,[60] because de Dorlodot's first reply to Ladeuze made a point of emphasizing that relations between de Dorlodot and Janssens were not good.[61]

Whatever personal animosities there might have been, it is only natural that the Biblical Commission, whose mission, according to its charter, was to shield the divine text "not only from every breath of error but also *from every rash opinion*,"[62] would have taken an interest in a book the first third of which was devoted precisely to the first chapters of Genesis.[63] It is perhaps even more natural given that the book had devoted a section to the question of how certain decrees of the Commission were to be understood. Both van Rossum and Janssens were distinctly conservative on these questions. In the 1920s, that still meant understanding inerrancy extensively by reference to the Author of Scripture (*l'école étroite*), rather than limiting inerrancy by reference to its end, the salvation of

his reply to van Rossum of May 21, 1923 (De Dorlodot Papers, AKUL), the Commission's failure to indicate the particular passages to which it took exception.

59 De Dorlodot, *Darwinisme*, 25–26 (trans., 18).

60 Janssens is mentioned explicitly by Ladeuze ("the sole passage cited to me by Msgr. Janssens") in his reply to van Rossum of May 21, 1923 (De Dorlodot Papers, AKUL).

61 De Dorlodot said that Janssens did not like him (postscript to Letter I). He may, of course, have been right, but we have only de Dorlodot's word on that. The direct evidence that I have seen points only to de Dorlodot's strong dislike of Janssens.

De Dorlodot thought that Janssens's dislike of him dated back to de Dorlodot's refusal to contribute, some years before, to the making of a bust. On hearing that the Commission was unhappy with his book, de Dorlodot mentioned to Ladeuze that that "Pius X, whose favorite Janssens had for a while been, later said of him, 'He's a *fanciullo*!'" (Both in the postscript to Letter I). Without a context, Pius's comment sounds more negative than it may in fact be. Although the literal meaning of *fanciullo* is "child" (and de Bont ["Rome," 470] makes this sound worse by putting "big child"), it can also mean "someone who is naïve or lacking in judgment" (see Policarpo Petròcchi, *Nòvo dizionàrio*, 1:876). What could have been the context for this remark? Perhaps the remark about Janssens being "once a favorite" provides a clue. Could it be fallout from Janssens's well-intentioned but clumsy attempt to smooth the waters in the wake of former President Theodore Roosevelt's unsuccessful request for an audience with Pope Pius X in 1910? (For details on the incident, see *Current Literature*, "Review of the World."). The Vatican said that Janssens's action "lends itself to an interpretation offensive to the Holy Father" and Janssens lost his position as secretary of the Congregation for the Affairs of Religious Rites as a result. *If* Pius called him a *fanciullo* in *that* context, then he probably meant not that he was immature (as one might otherwise think), but just that he was a bit naïve or lacking in judgment.

That evening, in another letter to Ladeuze (Letter II), De Dorlodot said of Janssens, "the troublemaker, the Bishop of the defunct St. Peter's Abbey, wanted to manipulate things." By 1923, Janssens was a bishop (titular bishop of Bethsaida), but his relation to the abbey (St.-Pierre au mont Blandin in Ghent, closed at the time of the French Revolution), was that of titular abbot (to which honor he was appointed in 1909).

There is no reason to doubt that, at the heart of this affair, lay real, and honest, differences of opinion between de Dorlodot and Janssens on the two important matters on which they disagreed. As a historical matter, it is important also to note the presence of personal antagonisms in this case, though without drawing an unduly negative portrait of Janssens.

62 Leo XIII, *Vigilantiae Studiique*, 235 (emphasis mine).

63 Dominique Lambert ("Acteur majeur," 516–17, and, with Marie Claire Groessens-Van Dyck, in "Darwinisme d'un chanoine," 47–51) blamed the appearance of the English translation for the problem, but I am not convinced that the problem lay exactly there. I do not see why the translation should have precipitated, or in any way affected, the concerns of the Pontifical Biblical Commission, the president of which was Dutch and the secretary Belgian. In addition, Gemelli wrote in his *votum* on the book, p. 9, (fol. 12, CL 1922–23/904, ADDF) that the English translation had passed unnoticed. Gemelli might not have been correct, of course, but his remark reinforces (even if it does not prove) my doubts about the significance of the English translation in the whole affair.

souls (*l'école large*). It was concerns about the lengths to which *l'école large* had gone that had led Pope Leo to write *Providentissimus Deus* in the first place. De Dorlodot was certainly not a partisan of that latter school and whether the Commission was applying the principles of the encyclical exactly as Pope Leo had intended is a legitimate subject of debate. But one can only understand the position of the Commission by placing it against that background.

Ladeuze, of course, passed van Rossum's concerns on to de Dorlodot and asked him to draft a reply, suggesting to de Dorlodot three passages that he thought might have been the source of the trouble.[64] On May 13, de Dorlodot sent to Ladeuze his first draft of a defense of his book. That reply focused on the passages Ladeuze had marked, but over the course of the next couple of days de Dorlodot developed an alternative strategy. First, *the Commission* should be asked to identify the passages to which it took exception. Second, the Commission's right to review the book at all should be challenged. The censorship of books was the responsibility of the Holy Office, not of the Pontifical Biblical Commission. If van Rossum had concerns about the book, he should take them to the Holy Office, rather than taking the matter into his own hands, for example by himself trying to put pressure on authors.[65] Even as he was drafting his reply to the Biblical Commission, de Dorlodot and Ladeuze began trying to make a preliminary assessment of attitudes in Rome.[66]

By May 15, De Dorlodot had integrated his various drafts into a single reply. At Ladeuze's request, he dropped his insistence that the matter be passed on to the Holy Office.[67] This reply Ladeuze sent on to van Rossum.[68] De Dorlodot there emphasized that he had been careful *not* to assert that the Commission shared his views or even that the Commission had declared that Catholics were free to hold them. He went on to defend what he had said in the passage about the probability of views the affirmation of which had been forbidden, the only passage that the Commission had identified as problematic. He asked that the Commission point out to him any other passages that it had found objectionable. He did not challenge the authority of the Commission in these matters, though anyone who has read his private letters to Ladeuze will notice that, when he wrote "if the competent authority should find anything in his book unacceptable . . . ," he had underlined the words "competent authority."

---

64 These passages were *Darwinisme*, 26, 30, and 33 (trans., 18, 21, and 23–24), as de Dorlodot's reply makes clear.

65 This alternative is articulated first in Letter II. He sent a second draft of a reply (acting on the first point only) to Ladeuze the next morning (Letter III) and second letter (Letter IV), reiterating his desire to pursue the second point, later the same day (de Dorlodot to Ladeuze, May 13 (evening) and 14 (two letters), 1923 (De Dorlodot Papers, AKUL)).

66 De Dorlodot, Post-script to Letter I. The fruits of this effort can be seen in various letters among the Dorlodot Papers: De Dorlodot to Ladeuze (May 22, 1923), Fournier to Ladeuze (June 2 and undated), Laminne to Ladeuze (June 22, 1923), and Vermeersch to de Dorlodot (July 11) (De Dorlodot Papers, AKUL).

67 De Dorlodot to Ladeuze, June 18, 1923 (De Dorlodot Papers, AKUL).

68 Ladeuze to van Rossum, June 27, 1923 (doc. 1c, CL 1922–23/904, ADDF). De Dorlodot's final version can also be pieced together from his letters to Ladeuze (undated letter marked "from M. de Dorlodot to be transmitted to Cardinal van Rossum," but drawing on his drafts of May 13 and 14 [De Dorlodot Papers, AKUL]).

Van Rossum next had someone at the Pontifical Biblical Commission examine the book. The result, dated June 8, 1923, was a ten-page report citing, over the course of its first eight pages, about a dozen passages to which the author of the report took exception.[69] That reviewer thought that when de Dorlodot said that Scripture is consistent with absolute evolution, and that some Fathers supported the idea, he had meant to include in that doctrine also the origin of the human body, even though de Dorlodot had left discussion of *that* point for later, to an as yet unwritten book.[70] The report also took exception to the way de Dorlodot treated the decrees of the Commission.

It concluded with a short summary ("What should one think about this theory?") and a recommendation for the disposition of the case ("What should be done?"). "The theory of *absolute* natural evolution, extending 'from inorganic matter right *up to the body of man inclusive*' ([Engl.] p. 63) is *at least rash*," and, "although, to be sure, no *ex cathedra* document has addressed this question, the Church has shown its aversion to the theory in putting on the *Index* several works of Mivart." The author was wrong about Mivart, of course; he should have put "Mivartism," for he cited (*somewhat* more accurately) the cases of Dalmace Leroy, Zahm, and Bonomelli, as well as the decree of the Council of Cologne. Finally, he mentioned "the decree of the Biblical Commission, which enumerated among the points the historicity of which one must absolutely defend … *peculiaris creatio hominis*."[71] In this objection we find precisely a case (the kind of which de Dorlodot had complained) in which the Commission seemed to extend the reach of its earlier official statements. The decree of 1909 had said that the literal historical sense may not be called into doubt in the case of the "distinctive [*peculiaris*] creation of man." According to de Dorlodot:

> Janssens … when already secretary of the Biblical Commission, having been asked semi-officially [*officieusement*] by the University's Professor of Dogmatics, Msgr. De Becker, about the meaning which the Commission attached to the words "peculiaris creatio hominis," replied that the Biblical Commission had chosen these words *in order to leave the question open*, as long as one safeguards the essential truths of the creation of the spiritual soul and those connected to original sin, which are enumerated in Question III of the Decree of 30 June 1909.[72]

In the complaint against de Dorlodot's book, however, "one may not call into doubt" had become "one must absolutely defend" and the "distinctive creation of man" is taken to exclude the possibility of an evolutionary origin of the human body, even though direct divine creation of the human soul alone (wherever the body had come from) would

---

69 Pontifical Biblical Commission Report, June 8, 1923 (doc. 1a, CL 1922–23/904, ADDF). The author is unidentified.

70 De Dorlodot seems to have discussed this point in the last two of his wartime lectures, and one can presume that the Belgian Janssens had heard from friends at Louvain what the content of those lectures had been. (His brother Frans was a prominent cytologist at the university, though he seems not to have been in Leuven during the war years.) Still, the object under review was the book, not the author.

71 Pontifical Biblical Commission Report, 9.

72 Letter I, page 4 of the draft reply (emphasis de Dorlodot's).

surely also constitute a *distinctive* creation of man.[73] It is, after all, a specific origin that no dog, ape, or dolphin can claim. The report added that de Dorlodot's theory was already common in Catholic periodical literature and that the book had gotten favorable reviews in the Catholic press, which was true.

What should be done? The report offered two alternatives.[74] The first was an official retraction, along the lines of the formula that had been given to Leroy: "I learned today that my thesis, examined here in Rome by the competent authority, has been judged untenable, above all with respect to the human body, incompatible as it is both with scriptural texts and with the principles of sound philosophy." The second alternative was to put the book on the *Index*. The book could not just be corrected; special intervention by God being admitted in the case of the first human body, the author's entire thesis would collapse. In any case, the book should be withdrawn from sale.

Van Rossum wrote back to Ladeuze on June 10, apparently including a copy of this report, and threatened to refer the matter to the Holy Office.[75]

De Dorlodot articulated his thoughts on van Rossum's letter in three letters of his own, written to Ladeuze over the course of four days.[76] He would not sign the statement proposed by van Rossum. Van Rossum could send his concerns to the Holy Office, as he threatened to do; that is where de Dorlodot thought the matter should be handled anyway. With respect to the substance of the matter, de Dorlodot wrote:

> I know, from a trustworthy source that the question of whether evolution extended to the human body should be considered contrary to Catholic orthodoxy was twice subjected to thorough examination and twice the supreme authority decided *to leave the question open*. I knew that already, Monsignor, before you told me. But the trustworthy information which you gathered on this subject, from the best authorized sources, during the trip you made to Rome after your promotion to the Rectorate of our university, and which you communicated in detail to me. . . . You were told, among other things, that professors at the Catholic universities could use this liberty without any fear of being troubled by the Holy See, which wanted to leave the question open and which would not revisit its decision.[77]

Finally, he expressed his concern that repudiating the ideas defended in the book would have the effect of alienating Catholic scientists from the Church.

---

73 No one involved in the controversy thought that the human body had been directly *created* (i.e., brought into being out of nothing). Scripture says that "the LORD God formed man of dust from the ground" (Genesis 2:7).

74 Pontifical Biblical Commission Report, 10.

75 Van Rossum to Ladeuze, June 10, 1923 (De Dorlodot Papers, AKUL; reprinted in part in Lambert, "Acteur majeur," 518–19).

76 De Dorlodot to Ladeuze, June 16, 18, and 19, 1923 (De Dorlodot Papers, AKUL).

77 De Dorlodot to Ladeuze, June 18, 1923 (emphasis de Dorlodot's) (De Dorlodot Papers, AKUL). For a direct account of Ladeuze's visit to Rome, discussed above, see "Visite du recteur au Rom en 1911" (De Dorlodot Papers, AKUL).

On June 27, Ladeuze wrote back to van Rossum,[78] informing him that de Dorlodot could not, in good conscience, make the declaration that he had been asked to make. The thesis attributed to him by van Rossum—that one could defend the natural origin of the first human body—was not one that he had included in the book and therefore was not one that he could retract. In this, of course, he was technically correct. If he had not (as I argued above) always written as carefully as he could have done, the officials at the Commission had not read as carefully as they should have done either. Nevertheless, the idea that St. Augustine had held to the natural formation of the first human body (which de Dorlodot certainly had asserted[79]) would surely have seemed to van Rossum to be, at least, offensive to pious ears. Perhaps van Rossum would have been content with de Dorlodot's assurance that he had not *intended*, in the book, to assert the proposition in question. That was, however, a compromise that de Dorlodot did not offer.

At the same time as they were preparing a response to van Rossum, Ladeuze and de Dorlodot began making inquiries and otherwise contacting people to forecast the course of events, if not to influence them.

Shortly after May 28, Ladeuze heard back ("very confidentially") from Placide de Meester, a Benedictine from the Abbey of Maredsous. De Meester had talked with Francis Aidan Cardinal Gasquet as well as with van Rossum.[80] In general, the members of the Commission (or at least the cardinals[81]) would examine the book. Although the prohibition of books was not part of their mandate, they certainly could put questions to the Commission's consultors and, on that basis, propose authoritative guidance on the interpretation of Scripture.

Gasquet was an English Benedictine, Vatican librarian and archivist, and, since 1914, a member of the Biblical Commission. He was already familiar with the case, having heard about it both from Janssens and from Bertram Windle. The cardinal had found de Dorlodot's views on the origin of man "very sound and very sensible" [*juste et sensé*]. He went on to say, however, that de Dorlodot "should have said what he said without trying to interpret (indeed, without even mentioning) the decision of the Biblical Commission." (Windle also had found de Dorlodot's interpretation of the decrees "very strange.") Gasquet thought, however, that a condemnation of the book would be inopportune.

Van Rossum told de Meester that de Dorlodot had misinterpreted the decree of the Commission. He repeated what he had already told Ladeuze: De Dorlodot should make a written retraction. The Commission would examine the case fairly and with good will. De Meester thought that a compromise was possible as long as de Dorlodot did not write anything more about the scope of the decree.

---

78 Ladeuze to van Rossum, June 27, 1923 (doc. 1c, CL 1922–23/904, ADDF).

79 De Dorlodot, *Darwinisme*, 80 (trans., 63).

80 "Du P. Placide" (De Dorlodot Papers, AKUL).

81 That would mean van Rossum, Rafael Merry del Val, Aidan Gasquet, and the two newly-appointed members, Franz Ehrle and Louis Billot.

By June, Artur Vermeersch, a Jesuit moral theologian then teaching at the Gregorianum, had managed to secure an audience with the pope, apparently with the assistance of Franz Cardinal Ehrle.[82] His purpose was to apprise the pope of the gravity of the case, but not to try to get a response.[83] Vermeersch reported back to de Dorlodot immediately after the audience, on July 11.[84] Vermeersch had, as instructed, reviewed the events surrounding de Dorlodot's book. The pope, unsurprisingly, focused on the question of the origin of man. "That would interest me; I myself wrote about that in my time," he said,[85] and went on to mention favorably both neo-scholastic philosopher Tilmann Pesch and paleontologist Joachim Barrande.[86] Different systems have been tried, he concluded, none satisfactory. Returning to de Dorlodot's book, he said, "Tell Cardinal Ehrle that I will watch this case," which (as we shall see) he appears to have done. Vermeersch offered to send a copy of the book. Pius replied that he would enjoy reading if it were not for the fact that he had a church to govern. Despite the fact that both of the authors Pius had cited were anti-evolutionists, de Dorlodot was encouraged by this interview and on July 16 said as much in a letter to Ladeuze.[87]

De Dorlodot also asked his bishop, Thomas-Louis Heylen (bishop of Namur) to look into the matter on his upcoming visit to Rome (in January 1924). That visit was primarily concerned with a Eucharistic Congress Heylen was organizing, but the bishop raised the matter of de Dorlodot's book during his audience with the pope on January 12.[88] The pope told Heylen that de Dorlodot should not publish his second book until he had heard back about the first. He also said that the Holy See would have the question examined in depth ("au fond").[89]

✳ ✳ ✳ ✳ ✳

In the end (on November 6, 1923), van Rossum did write to the Censor of Books at the Holy Office, sending, in support of his complaint about *Darwinisme*, the final letter

---

82 Ehrle, a Jesuit, was a leading medievalist but is best known for his work as a Vatican archivist and librarian. Pope Pius (then Achille Ratti) had held a position subordinate to Ehrle for several years at the Vatican Library (1911–14). Ehrle had just been appointed to the Pontifical Biblical Commission.

83 Vermeersch to De Becker (draft), June 24, 1923 (De Dorlodot Papers, AKUL).

84 Vermeersch to de Dorlodot, July 11, 1923 (De Dorlodot Papers, AKUL).

85 The reference is surely to the scholium that he had prepared for Sala's *Institutiones*, discussed above.

86 Vermeersch did not name the two-volume German work of Pesch, but presumably it was *Die großen Welträthsel*. There Pesch had written that "Genesis ascribes to man an origin quite different from that of animals, not only with respect to his soul, but also to his body" (2:168).

Barrande's finds in Bohemia were published in his *Système silurien du centre de la Bohême*. Barrande, a Cuvierian fixist and catastrophist until the end of his days, claimed to have found evidence of a disappearance and reappearance of species, a phenomenon that Darwin had suggested would not happen (*Origin of Species*, 313).

87 De Dorlodot to Ladeuze, July 16, 1923 (De Dorlodot Papers, AKUL).

88 Journal de Mgr Thomas-Louis Heylen, année 1924 (A. 36, Archives de l'Évêché de Namur). While in Rome, he also saw van Rossum, Janssens, and Vermeersch, but if he discussed the case with them, he does not say so. See also the letter from Ladeuze to Mercier, April 14, 1925 (De Dorlodot Papers, AKUL).

89 Ladeuze to Mercier, April 14, 1925 (De Dorlodot Papers, AKUL) (on the basis of what de Dorlodot had written to Ladeuze).

from Ladeuze, de Dorlodot's May defense of his book, and the ten-page report prepared by the Biblical Commission.[90]

Two qualificators at the Holy Office were asked to write *vota*; a third opinion was solicited from outside the Congregation. The first of the qualificators was Hildebrand Höpfl, OSB, a Scripture scholar ("of unconcealed conservatism," said the historian of his university). Höpfl taught at the Pontificio Ateneo Sant'Anselmo in Rome; he had been a consultor at the Pontifical Biblical Commission since 1905.[91] His *Buch der Bücher* (1905) had been characterized by the book review editor at *Catholic World* as "the best manual of introduction to the study of Holy Writ that we at present possess."[92] The textbook on Scripture that he had published the year before this assignment was characterized by scripturalist Bruce Vawter as typical for the period.[93] The second qualificator, Jean-Baptiste Frey, CSSp, was a specialist in Jewish epigraphy and literature. He had been a consultor at the Pontifical Biblical Commission since 1910 and was appointed secretary to the Commission on Janssen's death in 1925.[94] The outsider was Agostino Gemelli.

The *vota* came in rather slowly. Höpfl's was submitted in January 1924; Frey's in April of that year; Gemelli's, dated December 2, 1924, was printed only in January 1925. Each of the three *vota* expressed concerns about the book.

Höpfl thought that de Dorlodot took the principles articulated by St. Augustine and Pope Leo XIII—Leo had said, "The principles here laid down will apply to cognate sciences, and especially to History"—too far: "Above all, one has to distinguish the question of the *internal constitution of visible things* (or of their *nature*) and the question *of their origin*; the former can be left to free human investigation, but the latter is at least in some respect connected *with the dogma of creation* and thus can pertain to faith and salvation."[95] Indeed Pope Benedict XV had said, Höpfl pointed out, that Leo "does not lay this [principle] down universally."[96] Höpfl summarized the point he was making as follows: "It is one thing to illustrate the life of some great man by means of an allegorical poem . . . ; it is another *to propound under the appearance and form of history an allegory or some other form far removed from the proper literal or historical meaning of the words.* Here it is the second that is being suggested."[97] Höpfl also took exception to de Dorlodot's treatment of the decrees of the Biblical Commission and to his extension of his Christian naturalism from the ordinary operations of nature to the *formation* of the natural world. Finally, he expressed his doubts about whether the evolution of all species from

90 Attachments, van Rossum to Index (docs 1, 1a, and 1c, CL 1922–23/904, ADDF).

91 Pius Engelbert, *Benediktinerkolleg St. Anselm*, 144–48, at 148 (trans., 137–41, at 140).

92 *Catholic World*, Review of Höpfl, 123.

93 Höpfl, *Compendium*, 73–75.

94 Janko Oberški, "In memoriam," 393.

95 Höpfl, *Votum*, 2–3 (doc. [green] 1, CL 1922–23/904, ADDF). The passages at issue are St. Augustine, *De Genesi ad litteram*, 2.9.20; Leo XIII, *Providentissimus Deus*, 287–89 (trans., ¶20) (the source of the quotation); and de Dorlodot, *Darwinisme*, 20–21 (trans., 13).

96 Benedict XV, *Spiritus Paraclitus*, 395–96 (trans., ¶23).

97 Höpfl, *Votum*, 4. Emphasis Höpfl's.

a common ancestor was consistent with Catholic philosophy. He did not deny the more modest idea of the evolution of one "systematic species" from another. Here he surely has in mind something like common ancestry for all species of squirrels, though the example is mine. His concern is with the evolutionary origin of "natural species." He takes explicit exception only to common ancestry for plants and animals, but his concerns sound as though they are probably more extensive than that.

In *his votum*, Frey objected to de Dorlodot's approach to Biblical interpretation, which he thought was not in conformity either with *Providentissimus Deus* or with the decrees of the Pontifical Biblical Commission.

On the question of evolution itself, he acknowledged that many Catholics do accept the evolutionary origin of some currently existing species from species now extinct. Such arguments had been adequately answered by others, he thought,[98] but he conceded that that is of no concern to theologians. What he thought was theologically problematic (being contrary to Scripture and to Catholic tradition), however, was the idea that God had acted directly only in the creation of inorganic matter and that all living things had gradually evolved without any further divine intervention. Against this idea, he cited various authorities: Gerard Van Noort had denied that a Catholic could assert either the natural origin of living things, or the natural evolution of animals from plants; Janssens had written of the evolutionary origin of plants and animals (man alone, body as well as soul being excepted) that "a Catholic author can maintain this, even though ... it is anti-philosophical and anti-scientific, and does not agree very well with the obvious sense of Scripture."[99] Frey thought that de Dorlodot overstated the scientific status of Darwinism and that it had not yet won general scientific acceptance in 1924.[100]

De Dorlodot's argument from the "teaching of the Fathers" was in fact, Frey objected, only "the teaching of three Fathers," Origen, Gregory, and Augustine, one of whom is not a Father and none of whom offered an *evolutionary* account of the origin of life or of species.[101]

Frey summarized his long *votum* with the assessment that it was rash to say that the first human body was the product of evolution. "No one can have any doubt that the Holy See opposes this doctrine," he said,[102] citing not only various theologians, but the Pontifical Biblical Commission and the cases of Leroy, Bonomelli, and Zahm as reported in *La Civiltà cattolica*. In addition, the idea that absolute natural evolution is compatible with Scripture gives up a doctrine generally held among Catholic exegetes; to say that many of the Fathers favored it is false (and injurious to them).

---

98 Frey, *Votum*, 18–19, ¶41 (doc. [green]) 2, CL 1922–23/904, ADDF), relying on Ioannes Lottini, *Introductio*, 72–104.

99 Frey, *Votum*, 19–22 (¶¶42–44), with quotation from p. 21, ¶44, citing Gerardus Van Noort, *Tractatus*, 26–30; Laurent Janssens, *Summa theologiae*, 707–8.

100 Frey, *Votum*, 23–24, ¶¶47–50.

101 Frey, *Votum*, 27–33, ¶¶57–66.

102 Frey, *Votum*, 36, ¶69.

Gemelli, like Höpfl, allowed some rôle for evolutionary processes; almost no naturalist thinks that every species was separately created, he said. He, however, preferred what he called a polyphylogenetic account to Darwin's and (as one might expect from a scientist) was a little more specific on the question of how deep common ancestry goes. He doubted, for example, that common ancestry extends to reptiles and birds, and cited the work of Louis Vialleton.[103] Gemelli emphasized that SS. Gregory and Augustine, "the battlehorses of evolutionists like Zahm, Fogazzaro, etc.,"[104] were the only two Fathers who took the view that the evolutionists found so congenial to their thesis.

The recommendations of the three reviewers diverged. Frey thought it best to put de Dorlodot's book on the *Index*:

> Would it be sufficient to condemn [*reprobare*] a few propositions containing the substance of de Dorlodot's work as *not safe*? It would perhaps be difficult to state those propositions in a way that would not seem to interfere with the liberty due to Catholics in the natural sciences or that would not affirm more than the defense of Catholic truth would require. If, for example, one excludes the theory of absolute natural evolution, one would seem to be opposing a merely scientific theory. And if one excludes some proposition about the immediate formation of the human body by God, de Dorlodot would say that he had not addressed that topic. Therefore it would seem best to censure [*notare*] de Dorlodot's work directly lest it continue insinuating false doctrines and opinions into the minds of the faithful.[105]

Höpfl and Gemelli thought the book was dangerous and should be withdrawn from circulation.[106] Gemelli also thought the book was, in itself, dangerous enough to forbid, but thought that a condemnation would nevertheless be inopportune for two reasons—one general and one personal. His general concern was that the Church had not addressed the question in the sixty-five years since the publication of the *Origin* and to do so now would just put another argument in the hands of the Church's critics. Absolute and atheistic evolutionism had already been implicitly condemned and in a way that left scientists free to pursue properly scientific research. The personal reason was respect for de Dorlodot. A public condemnation of the book would be too harsh given all the good work that de Dorlodot had done; he should be instructed just to withdraw the book from sale.[107]

※　※　※　※　※

---

103 Vialleton, anatomist at Montpellier, was a saltationist and a finalist, not, as Harry Paul has pointed out, "in the anti-evolutionary camp [, but rather] a convinced *évolutionniste* who opposed the idea of continuous and mechanistic *transformisme*" (*Edge of Contingency*, 99). Lucien Cuénot called Vialleton's *Origine des êtres vivants*, "the last *serious* book to speak of the transformist illusion" (*Évolution biologique*, vi). For more on Vialleton, see Tort, "Vialleton."

104 Gemelli, *Votum*, 6 (no doc. no., CL 1922–23/904, ADDF).

105 Frey, *Votum*, 38.

106 Höpfl, *Votum*, 20; Gemelli, 8.

107 Gemelli, *Votum*, 6–10.

The preparatory congregation was held on January 12, 1925,[108] shortly after the Congregation received Gemelli's *votum*. It apparently reviewed the actions of the Index on previous evolution cases, for documents from four of those—Caverni, Odón de Buen, Leroy, and Zahm—are included in the Congregation's dossier on this case.

Wilhelm Arendt, SJ, since 1909 official theologian of the Sacred Penitentiary as well as being a consultor for the Holy Office, focused the issue on the question of whether it was safe to teach either of the following two theses:

1. The origin of life is found exclusively in natural evolution from created but non-living things, without any intervention of God.

2. The body of the first human being was made not by the immediate intervention of God but by natural evolution from a lower living being.

He answered both questions in the negative and suggested that both propositions be publicly condemned [*reprobata*] in the *Acta Apostolicae Sedis*. He also wanted the archbishop of Mechlin (Mercier) to inform de Dorlodot privately, in the name of the Holy Office, that the Holy See disapproved of the book. The decree of disapproval would not, however, be made public, in the expectation that de Dorlodot would bring his teaching into conformity with the decrees of the Pontifical Biblical Commission. Mercier and the archbishop of Westminster (Francis Cardinal Bourne) were to notify the rectors of Louvain and of the Catholic College at Cambridge, as well as the editors of *The Tablet*,[109] that the Holy See did not approve of Catholic participation in the Darwin centenary. A public condemnation, however, would only bring more harm than good.

Giuseppe Latini, whose office was that of promoter of justice, thought the work was at least close to heresy. Although it was dangerous, it should not be directly and formally condemned, "all the more since in the hundred years or more that evolutionism—Darwinism (i.e., natural selection) preceded by Lamarckism—had been around, the Holy See had never thought it was necessary to issue a direct and formal condemnation." De Dorlodot should be invited to withdraw his book from sale and Ladeuze should be severely admonished for having sent a delegation from Louvain to the Cambridge centenary.[110]

These recommendations were not, however, endorsed by the other consultors present. The rest wanted to postpone the decision. Mercier should tell de Dorlodot not to publish his second volume without consulting the Holy Office and, in the meantime, should invite him to send it the text. In addition, there should be an internal study of the two theses mentioned by Arendt.

✳ ✳ ✳ ✳ ✳

---

108 Seventeen consultors attended the congregation (Acta Congregationum generalium, CL 1924–25, ADDF). The details of the meeting are recorded in "Del Volume di Henry de Dorlodot 'Le Darwinisme,' etc." (CL 1923/904, ADDF).

109 That magazine had printed de Dorlodot's remarks in 1909, a fact that was mentioned in *Darwinisme*, 7 (trans., 2). It had published a moderately favorable, but still reserved, review of the book on October 14, 1922, but it is presumably the former that had come to Gemelli's notice.

110 "Del Volume di Henry de Dorlodot."

A general congregation took the matter up on February 4 and approved a three-point resolution:[111] First, the book should be withdrawn from circulation and removed from the Lovanium collection of which it formed a part.[112] Second, de Dorlodot's second volume should not be published without consulting the Holy Office. Finally, the cardinals deplored the involvement of the University of Louvain at the Cambridge Darwin commemoration. The decree was to be sent to the president of the University with copies to Mercier and to the prefect of the Congregation of Seminaries and Universities, Gaetano Cardinal Bisleti. When the recommendation was presented to the pope on the following day, however, Pius directed the Holy Office first to get the opinion of Mercier.[113] And so, on March 14, 1925, Cardinal Merry del Val, secretary of the Holy Office, wrote to Cardinal Mercier, reporting the concerns and recommendations of the Holy Office and asking for his thoughts on the matter.[114]

Mercier turned to Ladeuze and (through him) to de Dorlodot for help in preparing a reply.[115] In a series of letters to Ladeuze, de Dorlodot took the occasion to reiterate and elaborate his views on the compatibility of Genesis and transformism.[116] To these, Ladeuze added some generally supportive remarks of his own and forwarded them to Mercier.[117]

Mercier decided to make a special trip to Rome to discuss the matter with the pope and with Merry del Val.[118] Merry del Val assured Mercier that the Holy Office would not address the question of evolutionism considered exclusively from the scientific point of view and that the Biblical Commission would refrain from making a judgment on plant or animal evolution.[119]

In a letter written on his return home, Mercier told the Holy Office that de Dorlodot had agreed not to publish the second volume of his book. Withdrawing the book already published, however, would be impractical (since he did not own the unsold copies) and

---

111 A general congregation had met on January 28, but had deferred the matter to a later meeting.

112 This was a series of books published in 1921–26 which the university had aimed at a general educated audience.

113 "Del volume di Enrico Dorlodot."

114 Merry del Val to Mercier, March 14, 1925 (De Dorlodot Papers, AKUL).

115 The communication itself is not in the de Dorlodot Papers in AKUL. De Bont, in his history of the affair (pp. 474 (Engl.) and 290 (Dutch)), says Mercier "leaked [the] letter." Did the Cardinal in fact violate the instructions of the Holy Office, as de Bont's "leaked" and "lekte" suggest? Merry del Val's letter had said, "antequam haec executioni mandari jubeantur, visum est Emi[nentibu]s Patribus eadem cum Eminentia Tua secreto communicare, . . ." but that could mean that Merry del Val is writing "privately" (*secreto*), "before the proposed course of action is put in writing" (*antequam haec executione mandari jubeantur*). It was clear to the principals that the issue was not to be discussed widely, not even with Heylen or with Bourne, who had granted the permission to publish the English translation, since de Dorlodot suggested that Mercier should *get permission* from the Holy Office to discuss the matter with them (letters of de Dorlodot to Ladeuze, April 2, and Ladeuze to Mercier, April 14, 1925 [De Dorlodot Papers, AKUL]). It is simply not clear that the preliminary decision of the Holy Office was to be kept secret from de Dorlodot. It is clear that Mercier was in any case eventually authorized to discuss the matter with de Dorlodot (Mercier to Merry del Val, June 29, 1925 [CL 1922–23/904, ADDF]).

116 De Dorlodot to Ladeuze, April 2, then May 12 and 17, 1925 (De Dorlodot Papers, AKUL).

117 Ladeuze to Mercier, April 14 and May 15, 1925 (De Dorlodot Papers, AKUL).

118 Mercier to Ladeuze, May 18, 1925; Ladeuze was invited to come as well, but he declined (Ladeuze to Mercier, May 20, 1925) (De Dorlodot Papers, AKUL).

119 Mercier to Merry del Val, June 29, 1925, ¶4.

ineffective (since so many copies had already been sold). On the more general question, Mercier put into writing the wish (*voeu*) that he had expressed orally, both to Merry del Val and to Pope Pius:

> Transformism, in its general sense, is accepted by the majority of scientists, both Catholic and non-Catholic, either as an established theory or as an hypothesis. If theology and Biblical exegesis should judge it to be worthy of condemnation, were it only because of the ease with which it could be applied to the formation of our first parents, then ecclesiastical Authority should condemn it, but overtly, without circumlocution.
>
> If the ecclesiastical Authority should judge that there is no reason to condemn it clearly, then for mercy's sake, it should not give the appearance of disguised condemnations by indirect, occasional interventions, by pin-pricks.
>
> In view of the extreme gravity of the matters at issue, would it not be wise to set up a commission of competent men—scientists, philosophers, theologians, and exegetes—with the special task of studying the question of the origin of living things and of the differentiation of organisms, in the relation which these two questions could have with revealed doctrine?[120]

The university archives do not show what exactly Mercier said to Ladeuze after his visit to Rome.

Mercier's was not, however, the only intervention on behalf of de Dorlodot, for meanwhile, somehow, a rumor had begun to spread that the Vatican was about to issue some kind of general condemnation of the theory of evolution. Perhaps the rumor originated in Rome; perhaps it originated with something that Breuil had heard when he had visited Mechlin and Louvain early that year. In any event, priest-paleontologist Hugo Obermaier invited Breuil, Bégouën, and Teilhard to come to Altamira, where he was in the middle of archeological excavations at the famous cave. Teilhard, busy getting ready for his return to China, declined, but the other two went and, over the course of four days, "in a spirit of scientific objectivity and religious faith," discussed the various aspects of transformism.[121] At the end of this "Council of Altamira," they decided to send a report of their thoughts to the pope. The report, a six-page handwritten document (with a two-page cover letter from Henri Bégouën) was personally transmitted by Archbishop Bonaventura Cerretti (apostolic nuncio to France) to Pope Pius.

"The word evolution," they wrote,

> has to be taken in its broadest sense without entering into the discussion of the theories of various schools—Darwinism, Lamarckism, transformism, etc. Let us make our thought precise. Evolution is not a theory or an hypothesis. Its principle is the scientific method itself because it consists in thinking of things in their normal order of succession, recognizing that they are—at least partially—the results of

---

120 Mercier to Merry del Val, June 29, 1925, ¶7.

121 For a brief account, see Henri Bégouën, *Quelques souvenirs*, 37–39. For two historians' accounts, see Arnaud Hurel, *Breuil*, 280–86, and Jacques Arnould, *Breuil*, 188–96.

the events and the beings that preceded them; events and beings that are—at least partially—the source [*principe*] of what follows. That has nothing to do with the ontological cause or with the principle of creation by God. The theory of evolution only gets as far as the external aspect of that which the permanent creative act of God realizes successively in time and in space. It is, therefore, in no way materialist. If it is considered to be so . . . , that is because it has been deformed and disfigured in the course of emotional discussions, seldom having anything to do with science.[122]

The issue arose again in Louvain in early October, when Matthias Winzen, spiritual rector of a school in Nideggen (Germany) asked for permission to translate *Darwinisme* into German in order to counter the dominance of monistic philosophy in that country.[123] De Dorlodot immediately wrote to Ladeuze to ask his advice. How could he make a polite refusal without betraying the secret of possible adverse action by the Holy Office? De Dorlodot suggested that he might cede his authorial rights to Joseph Cardinal Schulte, archbishop of Cologne and so Winzen's ordinary.[124] Ladeuze passed the matter on to Mercier, who emphasized the risks of the plan. Schulte might write to Merry del Val, who could in turn think that Louvain was trying to force his hand. In general, further publication might give rise to a new round of polemics that it would be best to avoid. "The silence of the last months," Mercier concluded, "has been a good sign. We should hope that it lasts."[125] And so, in mid-November, de Dorlodot wrote back to Winzen. It was a difficult letter for him to write. Mercier had suggested that he write a brief letter, ending with the idea that the academic authorities (and de Dorlodot himself) wanted just then to avoid further polemics "at all costs." De Dorlodot wrote back (to Ladeuze) that "it is not exactly true that, for my part, I want to avoid those difficulties at any cost. I would prefer to go to the stake than to betray the truth or the interests of the Church. I will not follow the shameful example of Galileo."[126] In his letter to Winzen, he said that there were a couple of errors that he wanted to correct, one of which would require some revision of the book.[127] These were not, one might add, the same as the "great errors" that he mentioned to O'Brien in his letter of the following year. Since the book had been published under the auspices of his university, he would have to get their advice before authorizing the translation. In the end, he wrote just what Mercier had suggested that he

122 Bégouën, "Note on the disastrous consequences which a condemnation of the theory of evolution could have for ecclesiastical authorities," August 1925, 3 (fol., 34–40, CL 1922–23/904, ADDF).

123 Winzen to de Dorlodot, October 3, 1925 (De Dorlodot Papers, AKUL).

124 De Dorlodot to Ladeuze, October 7, 1925 (De Dorlodot Papers, AKUL).

125 Mercier to Ladeuze, November 11, 1925 (see also de Dorlodot to Ladeuze, November 15, 1925 [De Dorlodot Papers, AKUL]).

126 De Dorlodot to Ladeuze, November 15, 1925 (De Dorlodot Papers, AKUL).

127 The first error, a minor one, concerned the order of publication of the works of Albert the Great (Appendix IV). It had already been corrected in the English translation. The second, "more serious" error was saying that "the Sacerdotal Cosmogony does not trouble itself with the question of whether God made use of the activity of secondary causes." Subsequent study, he said, led him to conclude that "for terrestrial plants and animals, at least if one understands it in the obvious sense, it affirms that the earth had *actively produced* them" (emphasis de Dorlodot's) (de Dorlodot to Winzen [copy], November 14, 1925 [De Dorlodot Papers, AKUL]).

write: for "extrinsic" reasons, they had advised him to avoid giving cause for any further polemics. He made no mention of either the Biblical Commission or of the Holy Office.[128]

The next move in the fate of the book itself, if there had been one, would have had to come from Rome, but none came. Mercier died shortly thereafter, on January 23, 1926.

Another invitation to speak came early in 1927, when the Association des professeurs catholiques de l'Université de Lille decided to devote its annual Journées universitaires catholiques to the question of "the origins of man from the point of view of science and of dogma," and French geologist Pierre Pruvost, organizer of the event, invited de Dorlodot to come to Lille for the occasion.[129] The archives at Louvain do not include a draft of his reply, but we can learn something from Pruvost's second letter.[130] De Dorlodot had apparently written that he was obliged to remain silent. He had also sent Pruvost a manuscript that it seemed inopportune to publish. Was this a draft of the second volume of *Darwinisme*? Pruvost's letter is too vague to confirm this conjecture.

The compromise articulated in his letter to Merry del Val seems to constitute the final resolution of the case. The book itself remained available. Nevertheless, de Dorlodot decided (or perhaps just agreed) not to revisit the issue, as the story of his final years, retold above, shows.

The thesis of the immediate divine formation of the first human body still had, in the mid-1920s, committed adherents, as one can see from the deliberations at the Index, but it had not prevailed.

3. THE JESUIT CURIA: TEILHARD DE CHARDIN (1924–37)[131]

Teilhard's troubles with ecclesiastical authorities began early and continued throughout his life. It is, however, important to note that they did not extend to everything he wrote. No complaints were ever raised against his purely scientific work. Indeed he was sent by his superiors to China, not to be a missionary, but precisely to carry out scientific research. His first round of troubles arose in consequence of some writings that were indisputably theological—on the doctrine of original sin. What makes the Teilhard case complicated is the existence of mixed questions, questions to which both science and theology are relevant, as well as differences of opinion not only over the existence of mixed questions (something that Stephen Jay Gould, for example, denied by asserting "non-overlapping magisteria"[132]), but over exactly which questions were mixed, and how.

128 De Dorlodot to Winzen.

129 Pruvost to de Dorlodot, January 5, 1927 (AUCL).

130 Pruvost to de Dorlodot, March 25, 1927 (AUCL).

131 Much of the material in the following section appeared previously in my "Teilhard and the Holy Office." That article was a reply to David Grumett and Paul Bentley, "Teilhard and the Six Propositions." Grumett replied to my article in "Teilhard: A Response."

132 Gould, "Magisteria." See also his *Rocks of Ages*.

Some of the complaints that precipitated Teilhard's troubles came directly from Jesuits and were addressed to the Jesuit Curia in Rome. Others came from Gemelli, who sent his complaints directly to the Holy Office or to the pope, but those cases were forwarded to the Jesuit Curia for investigation and disposition.

* * * * *

The first official objection to Teilhard's ideas came in reaction to the notes on original sin that Teilhard had sent to Louis Riedinger in 1922. By 1924, someone—it is not clear who—had sent a copy of the Note to the Jesuit Curia in Rome. Teilhard, some of whose work had already been the subject of other Jesuits' complaints to the superior general, was suspected of being the author, but this was at first uncertain.[133] Gabriel Huarte (professor of dogmatic theology, and dean, at the Gregorian University) was asked to review the Note and said that, in his judgment, its main idea—that the original sin (*peccatum original originans*) was not an act that had been committed by an individual human being—was heretical.[134]

Boynes was to meet with Teilhard when the latter returned from China in September. If Teilhard was the author of the Note, he was to be given an opportunity to explain himself. Beauregard was also to get "a written promise that Teilhard would not say or write, either publicly or for purely private use, anything contrary to dogma, or to its traditional explication, on the topic of original sin."[135]

After the meeting, both Teilhard and Beauregard submitted replies to Rome. Teilhard replied on November 21.[136] The Note, he said, had not been intended to provide any "firm solutions," but merely to present "provisional orientations that would permit a temporary reconciliation of the data of dogma with that of scientific knowledge [*expérience*]."[137] He promised that, in the future, he would speak only "with great caution" and, "as much as possible, only with professionals." He would also "as faithfully as possible, conform his explications *de fortuna* to the commonly accepted representations of original sin." Beauregard felt reassured after meeting with Teilhard and wrote the superior general to that effect on November 25.[138] He emphasized Teilhard's loyalty to the Church and wrote that, in his opinion, no formal censure would be necessary.

---

133 Suspected: Teilhard began to hear about the problem in May 1924, when he was still in China, doing field work with Licent (Teilhard to Breuil, May 26, 1924, quoted in *Lettres intimes*, 113–14n5; also Teilhard's letter of May 20, 1924, *Letters to Léontine Zanta*, 67).

    Uncertain: On September 2, 1924, Norbert de Boynes (the French assistant to Ledóchowski) wrote to Jean-Baptiste Costa de Beauregard (the Jesuit provincial of Lyons) that "everything points to Teilhard as the author" and asked Beauregard to confirm whether that was so (doc. 254, fol. 132–33, Provincia Lugdunensis, X (1921–28), ARSI). A letter written by Henry Pinard de la Boullaye (formerly professor of the history of religion at the Enghien scholasticate) suggests that that inquiry was not a mere formality (letter to an unidentified priest, October 8, 1924 (no. 5, Censurae 27–I, ARSI).

134 Huarte to Henricus Carvajal (Secretary of the Society of Jesus), June 9, 1924 (no. 3, Censurae 27–I, ARSI).

135 Boynes to Beauregard (no. 4, Censurae 27–I, ARSI).

136 Teilhard, Statement to Beauregard (no. 7, Censurae 27–I, ARSI).

137 Teilhard had said as much in a letter to his friend Auguste Valensin on November 13, 1924 (cited by Bruno de Solages, *Teilhard de Chardin*, 42).

138 Beauregard to Ledóchowski, November 25, 1924 (no. 7, Censurae 27–I, ARSI).

Ledóchowski was not satisfied and said as much in his reply to Beauregard on December 18.[139] The ideas in question were objectively heretical. If Teilhard actually held them to be true (as opposed to merely proposing them "hypothetically"), he would have to be expelled from the Society and delated to the Holy Office. They were objectionable even as mere hypotheses, since it makes no sense to advance hypotheses that are contrary to faith. Ledóchowski attached a critique [*censure*[140]] of the Note, almost surely the one Huarte had prepared in June.[141] Teilhard should send back to Rome any reservations or objections that he had and these would be submitted to theologians for review. He should, however, "clearly and explicitly reject (even as hypotheses) everything which the critique indicated to be contrary to the faith." The general would decide later what other measures might be necessary.

Teilhard submitted his reply on January 13, 1925.[142] He would not be able to subscribe to the critique in its entirety. He expressed a number of concerns—for example, that the dogmatic texts, the truth of whose content he did not deny, left some outstanding problems, which needed to be addressed. In the end, he hoped that, rather than writing a full account of his views, he could meet in person, if not with the general himself, then at least with some theologian in whom they both had confidence. That, he hoped, would remedy any misunderstandings or concerns.

As he had said he would do, Ledóchowski asked two theologians for their assessment of Teilhard's reply. The theologians, Augustin Bea and Henry Pinard de la Boullaye, both returned negative evaluations. Bea thought that the root of Teilhard's Note lay not so much in geology as in a modernist theology that verges on pantheism.[143] Whatever might be its roots, Teilhard's account of original sin was undoubtedly heretical.[144] In addition, Bea had concerns about two other points. One was the idea that the human race gradually evolved from animals. The idea of the direct creation of a human soul without which a human being would not be human (whatever external form it might have) was theologically certain, if not *proxima fidei*.[145] That would make the origin of the human race not *gradual*. In addition, Bea thought that the descent of all human beings from Adam and Eve (i.e., from a single original couple) was *de fide*, even if it had never been explicitly defined. Teilhard's version of evolutionism (Mivart's, according to which God made the first man by giving some evolved animal a human soul) was, though being

---

139 Ledóchowski to Beauregard, December 18, 1924 (no. 8, Censurae 27–I, ARSI).

140 The letter was written in French, in which the word *censure* does not invariably have the note of disapproval that its English counterpart has. The Latin *censura* has its semantic center even closer to mere assessment.

141 The archival copy of Huarte's letter is labelled in pencil, "Censura scripti P. Teilhard de Peccato originale." Although it is not put next to Ledóchowski's letter in ARSI's relevant file, I was not able to find any other document that matches this description in the archive.

142 Teilhard to Ledóchowski, January 13, 1925 (no. 9, Censurae 27–I, ARSI).

143 Bea, "Animadversiones in opus auctoris cuiusdam quod inscribatur 'Notes sur quelques représentations historiques possibles du Péché originel,'" 1 (no. 10, Censurae 27–I).

144 Bea, "Animadversiones," 6.

145 Bea, "Animadversiones," 4.

a matter distinct from his views on original sin, still at least improbable, if not rash.[146] Pinard's evaluation[147] was not substantially different from Bea's.

Ledóchowski seems next to have gone back to Huarte on the matter, since the latter, in a letter to Ledóchowski on April 2, had proposed a list of six propositions to which Teilhard should be expected to subscribe "without any tergiversations."[148] The first three propositions, on original sin, were drawn directly from the canons of the Council of Trent;[149] the last two, on faith and reason, were from Vatican I.[150] The last of the six—Proposition 4 on the list—required him to acknowledge that "the entire human race has its origin in one protoparent, Adam."[151] This, the document acknowledged, was "nowhere explicitly defined, but was clearly contained in the first three propositions;" it is explicitly introduced with the word "ergo." If he would not accept the six theses, said Huarte, he should be delated to the Holy Office.[152]

On April 13, 1925, Ledóchowski expressed his concerns in a letter to Beauregard.[153] Teilhard "seems to want to accommodate faith to science [*scientia*] and not the other way around." "If we allow the case to continue on as it has, then Teilhard will get more and more entangled in his errors until it ends with a condemnation."

Huarte's six propositions were communicated to Teilhard.[154] Five of them Teilhard said that he could accept. About monogenesis, however, Teilhard hesitated:

> Everything that I know about science, and all the knowledge [*expérience*] of the last three centuries, make me think that this last proposition contains one part of "appearance" (which will little by little be recognized) which will be modified (as was geocentrism, the universality of the Deluge, the 4000 years, etc.) as we uncover the true dogmatic substance included in the traditional "representation."[155]

In the end, however, on July 1, he signed.[156] Ledóchowski was not, however, convinced that the problem would not recur. He later told Alfred Baudrillart (rector of the Institut

146 Bea, "Animadversiones," 5.

147 Pinard, "Judicium R[everend]is H. Pinard" (no. 11, Censurae 27–I, ARSI).

148 Huarte to Ledóchowski, April 2, 1925 (no. 13 [2nd item], Censurae 27–I, ARSI). For the exact formulation, see Grumett and Bentley, "Teilhard and the Six Propositions," 313–14.

149 Trent, Session 5 (June 17, 1546), "Decretum super peccato originale," 1–3 (Alberigo, *Concilium decreta*, 641–42; or Schroeder, *Canons and Decrees*, 21–24).

150 Vatican I, Session 3 (April 24, 1870), "Constitution dogmatica de fide catolica," chap. 3–4 (Alberigo, *Concilium decreta*, 783–87).

151 Huarte to Ledóchowski, April 2, 1925 (no. 17, Censurae 27–I, ARSI). For the exact formulation, see Grumett and Bentley, "Teilhard and the Six Propositions," 313–14.

152 Grumett and Bentley, "Teilhard and the Six Propositions," 310, put "denounced *by* the Holy Office," incorrectly, where the original says "*au* Saint-Office," i.e., "*to* the Holy Office" (emphases mine).

153 Ledóchowski to Beauregard, April 13, 1925 (fol. 157, Provincia Lugdenensis X (1921–28), ARSI).

154 When and how they were communicated is not clear. Ledóchowski's letter of April 13 does not mention them, although that should be about when the propositions were sent.

155 Teilhard to Valensin, June 12, 1925 (*Lettres intimes*, 123).

156 The text accompanying the signature is reprinted by Grumett and Bentley, in "Teilhard and the Six Propositions,"

catholique de Paris) that Teilhard "would never want to remain silent about the burning questions which preoccupied him."[157] He ended Teilhard's teaching assignment at the Institut catholique and ordered him to return to China to resume his scientific fieldwork.[158]

After the events of 1924–25, Teilhard largely refrained from further public speculation about the question through the rest of the 1930s.[159] He returned to the subject, and to something like his original views, only in an unpublished article, circulated "*à la critique des théologiens*" in 1947.[160]

＊　＊　＊　＊　＊

He had more trouble remaining within the bounds expected of him on another aspect of the question of the origin of the human race. Although Teilhard had told Ledóchowski in 1925, at the end of the original-sin affair, that he accepted the doctrine that "the whole human race takes its origin from one protoparent" "in the full sense which the Holy Church gives [it]," those propositions had not addressed a second thesis concerning the origin of the race, the controversy over whether evolutionary processes had played any rôle in the formation of the body of Adam or whether that body was formed directly by God from non-living matter. To put the question in the vague (and therefore exacerbating) way in which it was sometimes put—did man originate from animals?

Between 1929 and 1937, Teilhard's writings, and some public lectures, led to a series of complaints, first from within the Society directed to the Jesuit Curia, and then from other Catholics, usually directed to the Holy Office, but also occasionally directly to Pope Pius XI.

The first of these later controversies arose in 1930, on the publication of his "Que faut-il penser du Transformisme?" in which Teilhard had emphasized the explanatory power of evolution. Towards the end of 1929, Antonio Tissoni (superior of the Jesuits' Pengpu [Pinyin: Bèngbù] Mission) sent to Leandro Gaia (who taught science at the Jesuit colleges in Genoa and Chieri, and was a member of the same Jesuit province as was Tissoni) a copy of Teilhard's article, together with a request for Gaia's opinion of it. Gaia thought that Teilhard's ideas were at least rash. Two months later, he received another letter about Teilhard, this time from one N. Dubois, an acquaintance and, according to Gaia, a fervent Catholic. Gaia wrote to his rector (on February 4), passing on Dubois's letter with the idea that it should be forwarded to Rome.[161]

Ledóchowski solicited two opinions on the article, one from Paul Bornet (superior of the Mission at Sienhsien [Pinyin: Xiànxiàn]) and the other from Peter Hoenen (editor

<hr>

313–14. On this, see also René d'Ouince, *Prophète en procès*, 1:117.

157 Baudrillart, *Carnets*, 498.

158 Some authors, e.g., d'Ouince, in *Prophète en procès*, 1:106–7, and, more recently Grumett and Bentley, in "Teilhard and the Six Propositions," have claimed that the Holy Office played a rôle in this case. I showed that this is not the case in my "Teilhard and the Holy Office" (though Grumett remained unconvinced).

159 For an exception, see a brief mention in "Que faut-il penser du transformisme?," 96 (trans., 156–57).

160 Teilhard, "Réflexions sur le péché originel" (1947).

161 Gaia to his rector, February 4, 1924 (no. 3, Censurae 27–II, ARSI) and Dubois to Gaia, January 26, 1924 (no. 2).

of the *Gregorianum*).[162] Bornet thought that Teilhard's article presented a treatment of his topic that was, especially in the *Dossiers de la Commission synodale*, "inadequate and unsafe [*dangereux*]." Teilhard had said nothing about what the Church had to say about the distinctive creation of the human race (and about the origin of Eve) and made a strange distinction between the results of exegesis and the "Pauline conception of original sin." Hoenen thought that Teilhard's conclusions ran farther than the arguments for them would bear, but he "did not see in them anything with which to find positive fault" and continued:

> Where he takes up the evolutionary origin of the human *body*, he poses the problem from a purely philosophical point of view in considering this *process* [*devenir*] as something that is philosophically possible, which seems to me to be completely irreproachable; then he very nicely disentangles the difficulties that need to be resolved, as much from the scientific point of view as from the theological one; he wants the question to be studied from both sides and he energetically affirms that, for the believer, "Faith guarantees that there will be no contradiction between his Credo and his human knowledge."

Hoenen concluded that he did not know whether the Biblical Commission would approve of what Teilhard had to say about the origin of the human body, but Teilhard had, he noted, already published his ideas in the Catholic press.

Perhaps because the first two reviewers differed in their evaluation of the article, Ledóchowski requested a third evaluation from Biblicist Alberto Vaccari.[163] His evaluation was, like Bornet's, negative. Where Teilhard had written

> For reasons that are not ultimately [*en définitive*] either philosophical or exegetical, but are essentially theological (the Pauline conception of the Fall and Redemption) the Church holds to the historical reality of Adam and Eve.

Vaccari thought that Teilhard should put

> The Church firmly holds the historical truth of Adam and Eve for reasons that are both exegetical and strictly dogmatic (and not merely theological).

Ledóchowski decided that Teilhard's article was unacceptable and, on August 2, Boynes asked Bornet to inform Teilhard that "he should absolutely make a retraction because of the harm that his article could do to his readers."[164]

---

162 Bornet's review, June 3, 1930 (no. 4, Censurae 27–II, ARSI); Hoenen's, July 6, 1930 (no. 5).

163 Vaccari, "Judicium censoris de articulo Patris Teilhard de Chardin" (no. 7, Censura, 27–II, ARSI). Someone wrote "Nov. 1930" at the top of the document. This is hard to reconcile with Bornet's statement (mentioned above) that a decision about the case was ready in early September, but in June 1931, a letter of Ledóchowski (no. 4, Censurae 27–III, ARSI) also indicates that his instructions to Teilhard were made in November 1930. Perhaps a document that was ready immediately before Teilhard left China to return home (in September) only reached him in November.

164 De Boynes to Bornet, August 2, 1930 (fol. 250, *Missiones Galliae* VIII, ARSI) and Bornet to Beauregard (passing on the responsibility of informing Teilhard, which Bornet was unable to do before Teilhard left China), September 12, 1930 (no. 6, Censurae 27–II, ARSI).

* * * * *

Meanwhile, before Teilhard had been informed of Ledóchowski's decision, he had sent off several other articles for publication. Two of these ("Une Importante Découverte en paléontologie humaine: Le Sinanthropus pekinensis" and "Le Sinanthropus de Péking: État actuel de nos connaissances sur le fossile et son gisement") were versions of the same basic article on *Sinanthropus,* one for a general and the other for a professional readership. The third ("Le Phénomène humain"[165]) discussed human exceptionalism in light of evolution. Those became the subject of another complaint. This time, the Holy Office was involved.

The files of that Congregation contain two complaints about Teilhard's work from Gemelli.

The first was a letter dated April 29, 1931, addressed directly to Pope Pius and was brought, by instruction of the pope, to the Holy Office.[166] Although the focus of that letter had been Édouard Le Roy, it included a complaint about the work of Teilhard as well: "On the basis of his studies of human fossils which were found in China last year he has written in some journals published in China relatively advanced affirmations from which one infers that he believes in the simian derivation of man."[167]

The second was a twenty-page "Voto sulle pubblicazioni dal P. Teilhard de Chardin SJ sull'origine dell'uomo," which Gemelli had sent, apparently on his own initiative, the following month.[168] He summarized his own views on the issues by saying:

> The paleontological and biological sciences in general, at the current state of acquired knowledge, certainly admit evolutionism in general—namely the plasticity of living species and the non-identity of systematic and natural species; but they have not brought us any decisive proof, nor have they spoken the definitive word on the monogenesis of living things or on the derivation of the human species from a zoologically similar species.[169]

"The derivation of man from brute animals," he said, was at the time he wrote, "a scientific hypothesis which has the same value as the contrary hypothesis." That equiprobability had, Gemelli wrote, this consequence: "If the view of the scientist is speculative [*posizione aspettativa*], then the view adopted by Teilhard shows, at least, bad judgment [*è imprudente*]. His authority as an anthropologist will make people think that the admission or rejection of the animal origin of man is a matter of indifference to Catholic philosophy and theology."[170]

---

165 This article is different from the book Teilhard later published with the same title.

166 Gemelli to Pius XI, April 29, 1931 (doc. 3, CL 1930/461, ADDF).

167 Gemelli to Pius XI (fol. 20, doc. 3, CL 1930/461, ADDF).

168 Gemelli, *Votum* (fol. 14–34, doc. 6 CL 1931/1528, ADDF). This *votum* made reference to the three articles mentioned above, as well as a few others on the same topic.

169 Gemelli, *Votum,* 18.

170 Gemelli, *Votum,* 18–19.

What should the Holy Office do? He recommended: "a reminder [*richiamo*] to Fr. Teilhard that, while he continues with his (surely important) anthropological studies, he should be more circumspect and above all more respectful of philosophy and of Catholic tradition in expressing his conclusions."[171]

On June 9, Donato Raffaele Sbaretti (secretary of the Holy Office) advised Ledóchowski that a complaint had been received, adding that "Before making a decision in the matter, the Congregation is turning to you to get more ample and precise information on the person and on the activity of the priest in question. We would, in particular, like to have a complete list of the priest's publications and to know about the reception and criticism which they have received from scholars, especially Catholic ones."[172]

A complaint from Gemelli also came to Ledóchowski from the pope himself, by way of the secretary of state. This time, the focus was directly on the article in *L'Anthropologie*.[173] On June 10, 1931, Ledóchowski wrote to Christophe de Bonneville, who had by then taken charge of the Lyons province and was, therefore, Teilhard's superior: "The Holy Father himself recently sent me a complaint he received concerning an article Teilhard published in *L'Anthropologie* at the beginning of this year."[174] Bonneville was to arrange a review of Teilhard's article, which Ledóchowski could pass on to the Holy Father. When Sbaretti's letter arrived, on the 13th, Ledóchowski wrote to Bonneville again, adding the items Sbaretti had requested to the list of agenda.[175] The work went slowly. Teilhard was inaccessible due to his participation in the Haardt Scientific Expedition ("La Croisière Jaune," May 1931 to February 1932), which was by then deep in Central Asia.

Bonneville disagreed with Ledóchowski over what to make of the article in *L'Anthropologie*, which was the focus of the inquiry: "It was simply a descriptive account of the discoveries made at Choukoutien by the Black Scientific Mission .... The Father abstained from philosophical considerations and conclusions."[176] Ledóchowski replied: "I am amazed that you wrote that the article in question contained nothing but a description of what was found at Choukoutien. Indeed, it is immediately apparent to the attentive reader that the author presupposes hypotheses on the antiquity and origin of man that are considered rather unsafe [*periculosus*], if not worse, in Catholic schools."[177]

---

171 Gemelli, *Votum*, 20.

172 Sbaretti to Ledóchowski, June 9, 1931 (no. 3, Censurae 27–III, ARSI; the letter is also in Minutarii 1931/I, 760, ADDF).

173 Gemelli to Pius XI (no. 1, Censurae 27–III, ARSI [the complaint itself] and no. 4 [how it got to Ledóchowski]). ARSI's copy of the complaint is unsigned. It was clearly clipped from the original to remove the signature and (probably) the letterhead identifying Gemelli's Sacred Heart University, stationery that he ordinarily used. The handwriting is identical to that in Gemelli's letter to the pope. The letter begins "Some time ago, I allowed myself to mention to Your Holiness some writings of Fr. Teilhard de Chardin, who maintains the simian origin of man," and Gemelli had done that. (On both points, see doc. 3, CL 1930/461, ADDF.)

174 Ledóchowski to Bonneville, June 10, 1931 (no. 2, Censurae 27–III, ARSI).

175 Ledóchowski to Bonneville, June 13, 1931 (no. 5, Censurae 27–III, ARSI).

176 Bonneville to Ledóchowski, July 9, 1931 (no. 6, Censurae 27–III, ARSI).

177 Ledóchowski to Bonneville, July 24 (also no. 6, Censurae 27–III, ARSI).

On August 10, 1931, Bonneville and Ledóchowski had completed their work and Ledóchowski wrote back to Sbarretti.[178] This included the list of Teilhard's publications and Ledóchowski's answers to the questions that had been put to him. What did Catholic scientists think of his work? Ledóchowski reported: "As far as I know, simply from having heard it said, Catholics are divided on the questions treated by the Father, some of them highly praising his scientific work and others having reservations about some of the hypotheses he has articulated." What about his person and his activities?

> Teilhard is neither a philosopher nor a theologian by profession, but a geologist and a paleontologist, two fields in which he has acquired true competence in the scientific world. To that is due his nomination to the chair of geology at the Institut catholique de Paris in 1921, a chair which he held for five years to general satisfaction; Msgr Baudrillart was able to attest to the fact that his public instruction was unobjectionable [*irreprensibile*] and that, despite the fact that he was a Jesuit (a fact that he never hid), he enjoyed a good reputation in scientific circles.

Ledóchowski went on to summarize the story of the Note on original sin and of the article published in the *Dossiers*. Since even Teilhard's profound attachment to the doctrines of the Church and his loyalty had not been sufficient to keep him from going doctrinally astray, Ledóchowski would now require a review of his articles by two reliable priests, and a review much stricter than that ordinarily applied by journals.

Meanwhile, Nicola Canali, then assessor of the Holy Office, apparently suggested to Gemelli that perhaps Gemelli was being too severe in his judgment of Teilhard; Gemelli acknowledged the suggestion in a letter of February 10, 1932, but held his ground. Teilhard's writings, he asserted again, were "unjustified and unsafe [*pericoloso*]." Gemelli's letter makes clear the exact nature of the concerns of Teilhard's critics:

> First, Fr. Teilhard has not limited himself to a strictly scientific treatment of the question. Nor has he limited himself to expounding his bold hypotheses, contrary to the traditional teaching of the Church on the origin of man, in technical publications for anthropologists and paleontologists. If he had limited himself to technical articles, the formulation of such hypotheses could have been considered to be part of the work of a scholar. But Fr. Teilhard has also written popular articles. . . . With respect to an hypothesis which could be accepted by some scholars but rejected by others, or one which has some facts in its favor but has not been proven, or one which is usable by a scientist as a working hypothesis today (but might tomorrow fall as a result of the work of science itself, as happens to many hypotheses), the duty of a Catholic scholar is without a doubt to discuss such an hypothesis. A Catholic scholar can take part in this examination without danger to his Faith because his honesty, his good judgment, and his circumspection will defend him. But the Catholic scholar also has the obligation of circumspection, i.e., not to discuss it in articles for the general public. Such popularization is unwise and dangerous: those who are not

178 Ledóchowski to Sbarretti, August 10, 1931 (no. 12, Censurae 27–III, ARSI; also at fol. 75–78, Epistolae ad Romanam Curiam VII [1930–34], ARSI). A preliminary reply had been made on June 26 (no. 4, Censurae 27–III, ARSI).

specialists in the subject matter, who do not have sufficient scientific preparation and who lack the mental habits of a scholar trained to evaluate hypotheses (e.g., as temporary research tools) could easily mistake a new hypothesis, presented in an attractive way, for a scientifically established truth. If then, in our case, it is a matter of an hypothesis contrary to the traditional teaching of the Church, then there is indubitably a danger to the religious life of many readers and an occasion of disturbance for many consciences.

Second, I think that Teilhard's publications are dangerous [*periculoso*] because of the authority he enjoys in the Catholic world, given his position as a scholar, a religious, and a Jesuit. [179]

Despite Gemelli's re-articulation of his concerns, the Holy Office does not appear to have taken any further action. Perhaps it considered Ledóchowski's planned remedy to be correct, and sufficient.

* * * * *

That was not, however, the last that the Holy Office was to hear from Gemelli about Teilhard. On July 22, 1933, he wrote again, this time with a complaint about Teilhard's review of Othenio Abel's *Die Stellung des Menschen im Rahmen der Wirbelthiere*.[180] The review was, for the most part, favorable, reporting the Austrian paleobiologist's summary of the state of scientific research on the origins of man, but it began with Teilhard's comment that "No paleontologist now doubts that Man is attached historically, 'evolutionarily,' to the Primates. The matter has been settled."

The Holy Office passed the matter on to Ledóchowski with the request that he have the article examined by two theologians.[181] Ledóchowski chose for the task Charles Boyer and Arnaldo Parenti, the former of whom taught philosophy and theology, and the latter Sacred Scripture, at the Gregorian University.

Boyer had just published his *Deo creante and elevante*.[182] About the evolution of plant and animal species, Boyer had been skeptical ("but willing . . . to accept anything that is established," added one reviewer). The idea that the human body was the product of evolution, however, he had adjudged to be rash, a verdict for which he was criticized by another reviewer.[183] Boyer noted in his report[184] that Teilhard had defended a theistic form of evolution with explicit acknowledgment of the creation of the human soul, but with an evolutionary origin for the human body. That last, Boyer said (as he had said

---

179 Gemelli to Nicola Canali (assessor at the Holy Office), February 10, 1932 (fol. 38–42, doc. 8, CL 1931/1528, ADDF).

180 Gemelli to Canali, July 22, 1933 (fol. 51–52, doc. 12, CL 1931/1528, ADDF).

181 Ledóchowski to Bonneville, March 8, 1934 (no. 6, Censurae 27–IV, ARSI; or fol. 354–55, Epp. regg., Prov[incia] Lugdun[ensis] XI, ARSI).

182 He had been distributing versions of this text to his students since 1929; the book was published by the Gregorian University Press in 1933.

183 The first reviewer quoted is from Bernard Leeming; the second from Jules Gross.

184 Boyer, "Iudicium de recensione Patris Teilhard de Chardin in librum qui titulus Abel, *Die Stellung des Menschen im Rahmen der Wirbelthiere*," February 21, 1934 (fol. 59, doc. 15, CL 1931/1528, ADDF).

286

in this textbook), must be adjudged rash on the basis of three facts. The first was that ecclesiastical authorities had prohibited several recent books that defended that view. Boyer must have been referring to Dalmace Leroy's *L'Évolution restreinte aux espèces organiques* (1891) and John Zahm's *Evolution and Dogma* (1896), though he did not name either book. The second was that the view seemed to be inconsistent with the unity of the human race, the formation of the first woman from the first man, and original justice. These are among the theses that the Pontifical Biblical Commission had said should not be called into doubt in 1909.[185] The third was that the arguments Teilhard adduced were not sufficient to produce certainty. There was still too much controversy among experts on Piltdown Man, on Peking Man, and in general on the transition from animal to human being.

Parenti thought that what Teilhard had said did not seem consistent with Genesis 2:7, was opposed to the *responsa* of the Pontifical Biblical Commission of 1909, and was not in harmony with common understanding of the Fathers and theologians. In making this judgment, Parenti thought, he was following the line taken by the Holy Office.[186]

On March 8, 1934, Ledóchowski, after repeating the severe admonitions that had already been made, required that Teilhard "not publish anything even remotely related to the subject without its first being submitted to two censors of sound doctrine."[187] That apparently satisfied the Holy Office.

The last of the complaints about Teilhard's ideas on the origin of the human race came in 1937, in the wake of a short visit to the United States. He had been invited to Philadelphia to attend the International Symposium on Early Man, organized by the Academy of Natural Sciences of Philadelphia and by the Carnegie Institute. Held on March 17–20, 1937, its significance is indicated by the fact that most of the world's leading paleoanthropologists (Eugène Dubois, G. H. R. von Koenigswald, Robert Broom, and V. Gordon Childe, among others) were in attendance. His visit to Philadelphia included one other event. Villanova College, run by the Augustinian Friars, had, in 1928, established a Mendel Medal. Named in honor of the order's most famous member, it was to be awarded annually to a scientist who had "advanced the cause of science ... [and] demonstrated that between true science and true religion there is no intrinsic conflict." Early recipients had included Georges Lemaître; more recently they have included Francis Collins, George Coyne, and Kenneth Miller. In 1937, the Medal was given to Teilhard. After the symposium and the Villanova ceremony, he had gone to Boston, where Harvard anthropologist Ernest A. Hooton had invited him to speak (on March 31) to a group of about two hundred students and faculty.

What did he say at these talks? The proceedings of the symposium include Teilhard's paper on "Late Cenozoic Correlations Between North China, Malaysia and Central Europe" and a paper by his Chinese colleague, Pei Wen Chung, on "The Palaeolithic

---

185 Pontifical Biblical Commission, "De charactere historico," 568.

186 Parenti, "Animadversiones in notam 'L'Anthropologie,'" February 24, 1934 (no. 5, Censurae 27–IV, ARSI).

187 Norbert de Boynes (*Assistens Galliae*) (?) to Bonneville, March 8, 1934 (no. 6, Censurae 27–IV, ARSI).

Industries in China," which Teilhard presented in Pei's absence.[188] Beyond, possibly, the assumption of the antiquity of the Paleolithic toolmakers, neither paper presents anything of theological interest. However, at some point during the conference, he said something more. An article by *New York Times* science reporter William L. Laurence[189] says both that Teilhard discussed *Sinanthropus* "before the international symposium" and that, in addition, he agreed to "an interview following the paper." In the remarks "before the conference," Teilhard distinguished *Sinanthropus* from his Neanderthal and modern successors. Still, *Sinanthropus* is "definitely below the Neanderthal, [but] too far above the apes to be regarded as the link between ape and man." A "still earlier type" will someday be found. In the interview, Teilhard also addressed the question of science and religion and said, "I find absolutely no barriers between my beliefs as a scientist and my beliefs as a priest." He also said: "As a scientist, I must admit the evidence that man was born from the animal kingdom. But he was not an animal," and "I might compare [the emergence of thought in the material world] to the crisis that takes place in the tea kettle when water is heated." A reporter from the Associated Press added that, in reply to the question, "How do you, a Jesuit, reconcile evolution with the religious belief of the special creation of man?", Teilhard had answered, "As a scientist, I must put aside personal feelings and accept the facts. From the facts I must believe in evolution."

At Villanova, he gave an acceptance speech at the faculty dinner that accompanied the presentation of the award. The *New York Times* reported him as describing "man as 'nothing but evolution becoming conscious of itself'" and adding that "we are on the eve of a spiritualistic evolution." Cuénot added that "he spoke briefly of Mendel, emphasizing how important it is to relate biological research and experimentation with a paleontological approach to the problem of human evolution."[190] He made the same remarks at his Harvard talk, but a reporter put one point in slightly different terms: "The process of evolution is not ended. I believe that man will probably reach a higher stage of intelligence."[191]

Teilhard was quite explicit not only about his compatibilism, but about his exceptionalism (however much the boiling-water analogy obscured that point). Nevertheless, reporters, and especially headline-writers, are not always good at fine distinctions. A story by Howard W. Blakeslee, science editor for the Associated Press, appeared on page one of the *Washington Post* under the headline, "Man Descended From Apes, Jesuit Says Evidence Proves."[192] Blakeslee's story only made it to page three of the Toronto *Globe and*

---

188 Minutes of the symposium were published as Edgar B. Howard, "Minutes."

189 Laurence, "China Cave." Laurence was a well-informed reporter, who later won two Pulitzer Prizes.

190 Cuénot, *Teilhard*, 200n5.

191 This report is from the *Boston Globe*. The *Boston American* reported Teilhard's remark that "Man, 'a thinking animal,' has a long way to go yet before utilizing his mental process to its extreme." Both stories bore the dateline of April 1, 1937. Similar remarks were reported from Philadelphia in Laurence, "China Cave."

192 *Washington Post*, March 20, 1937.

Mail, but with an even more provocative headline, "Jesuit Agrees with Darwin."[193] Both newspapers did acknowledge Teilhard's compatibilism in secondary headlines.

Such press coverage could hardly fail to evoke a reaction. On April 1, William McGarry, SJ, the prefect of studies at Weston College, sent to Ledóchowski clippings from the Associated Press and from several Boston newspapers.[194] The newspaper interviews, and the resultant headlines, are just an example of the lack of pedagogical prudence that d'Ouince described some years later:

> Teilhard [would] talk to a young scholar practically incapable of understanding him in the way in which he talked to a member of the Pontifical Academy of Sciences. . . . He would give a response which, to be understood correctly, required a long familiarity with his thought. Like the rest of us, he was perfectly capable, in the course of a conversation or of a letter written in haste, of using a formula that was objectionable, was literally indefensible, and mispresented his thought.[195]

On April 16, Ledóchowski sent a telegram to New York: "TELL DE CHARDIN CEASE CONFERENCES; LEAVE STATES."[196]

193 Also published on March 20, 1937.

194 The *Post*, the *Herald*, and the *Globe*, all April 1, 1937.

195 D'Ouince, *Prophète en Procès*, 1:104–5.

196 Ledóchowski to Teilhard, April 16, 1937 (no. 4, Censurae 27–V, ARSI).

CHAPTER 13

NON-OFFICIAL FORA
(1909–1931)

1. PERIODICAL LITERATURE

The Catholic periodical press continued to be receptive to articulations of Catholic evolutionism as the new century progressed. The *Revue des questions scientifiques* published an article entitled "Un Demi-siècle de darwinisme" by Robert de Sinéty, SJ, biologist and a student of Alfred Giard (one of the leading French Darwinists of the nineteenth century), in 1910, and later various articles on science and on science and religion by Teilhard de Chardin (mentioned above).

In 1911, Désiré-Joseph Cardinal Mercier's *Revue néo-scolastique de philosophie* published an exchange between Paul le Guichaoua (professor of philosophy at the Grand Séminaire de Poitiers) and Amédée Bouyssonie on the philosophical conditions of evolution.[1]

Le Guichaoua's thesis was that "evolutionism can be interpreted in accordance with the principles of traditional philosophy. One can allow scientists to use this conception if they deem it appropriate; one can follow their efforts with interest and safety."[2] One central challenge that the traditional philosophy posed to evolutionism was, of course, the alleged impossibility of a lower species producing a higher one. Le Guichaoua

---

1 Le Guichaoua, "Conditions philosophiques"; Bouyssonie, "À Propos des conditions philosophiques"; and le Guichaoua, "Réponse à M. Bouyssonie ."

2 Le Guichaoua, "Conditions philosophiques," 211.

argued that God could use a determinate material being to produce a material being of a superior species. Scholastic philosophers had admitted the spontaneous generation of lower plants and animals from non-living matter. They were mistaken about the case, but the point is their acceptance of a metaphysical principle important to the later debate about evolution. "God can make a living being act, not just by assimilating nutrients, but by ascending to a higher species, by generating not offspring like itself, but offspring of a higher species."[3] He went on to say that "this purely philosophical consideration seems not to force us to back off even from the formation of the human body from a lower animal. God could have made it that an ape, rather than generating a simian body, generated a human body. It would not have first to produce a baby ape which would then be killed by the substitution of a human form for its soul. God could have used the reproductive activity of the parents to produce a human body into which He infused a human soul."[4] In a footnote, he emphasized that he was speaking here only of what was metaphysically possible; the text of Genesis, he emphasized, said that God did not in fact form the first human body in this way. In general, the perfection of species does not require immediate divine intervention: "the instrumental power can be imparted one time for all and then deployed bit by bit, according to necessity or opportunity."[5]

Bouyssonie agreed with le Guichaoua's general thesis about the compatibility of evolutionism and traditional philosophy, but not with the details of the arguments that le Guichaoua had offered. In particular, while le Guichaoua had used a species concept that distinguished, for example, donkeys and horses, Bouyssonie suggested that the relevant concept was *metaphysical* species, of which there might be as few as four (mineral, plant, animal, and man). Life, consciousness, and liberty marked distinctions that were metaphysically important in a way that the difference between gracefulness and awkwardness did not.

> If one accepts my hypothesis of four metaphysical species, the problem of the transition from an inferior to a superior species exists only in three cases—the ascension of matter to life, of vegetative to conscious life, and from animal to intellectual [*spirituelle*] life. M. le Guichaoua admits that this transition is theoretically possible in the first two cases if the lower nature is used by God as an instrumental cause.[6]

One or a few original plants and animals, structurally simple but highly malleable, would be enough.[7] Evolution would, therefore, be the product of changes that were prodigiously diversifying, but without affecting the essence of the beings affected.[8] Nevertheless,

3 Le Guichaoua, "Conditions philosophiques," 209.

4 Le Guichaoua, "Conditions philosophiques," 210.

5 Le Guichaoua, "Conditions philosophiques," 211.

6 Bouyssonie, "Conditions philosophiques," 573.

7 Bouyssonie, "Conditions philosophiques," 568.

8 Bouyssonie, "Conditions philosophiques," 577.

a minimum of heterogeneity at the origin of the world would be necessary; Bouyssonie had his doubts about the details of le Guichaoua's theory of causality.

In the United States, the *Catholic Fortnightly Review* published Erich Wasmann's reply to an attack on him (by Simon Fitzsimons) that had appeared in the pages of the *American Catholic Quarterly Review*.

In 1929, Bernard Conway published a completely rewritten second edition of *The Question Box*, in which he wrote

> As the Church has made no pronouncement upon evolution, Catholics are perfectly free to accept evolution, either as a scientific hypothesis or as a philosophical speculation. . . . "It is good [however] to remember that evolution is not a proved fact. . . . it has given us many a new fact, but it suggests more problems than it solves. . . . [Still,] evolution is in no sense at variance with the theistic or Christian theory of life. . . . [Finally, man's] body *may* have been evolved from an existing animal organism, but the so-called proofs from zoology and paleontology are absolutely inconclusive.[9]

In 1921, the *American Ecclesiastical Review* published an article on "Facts and Theories of Modern Biology as Viewed by a Catholic Priest," by Ulrich Hauber, priest-biologist (and later president) of St. Ambrose College in Davenport (Iowa). He presented a brief, but fairly standard, articulation of Catholic evolutionism:

> The evolutionist believes that . . . the whole class of animals we call birds [for example] descended or developed from a simple ancestor in *natural* fashion.

> Once accepted as a tentative working basis, everything seems to fall in line with the theory.

> Those who are fearful lest such a doctrine is incompatible with Scripture and Revelation will do well to read carefully the first chapter of Genesis and to consult the reflections of St. Augustine and St. Gregory of Nyssa.[10]

He was not willing, in the absence of more fossil evidence than the "half dozen bones" that had been found in Java and at Heidelberg, to extend the theory to anthropogenesis, but he reminded his readers that "the Church has not condemned the proposition that . . . in fashioning man's body to become a fit habitation for the soul, God made use of natural laws," acknowledging, however, that "the best one can say is that it is barely tolerated."[11] He added that "We do not like the idea of brute ancestors. Of course not. Did you ever see a two-month old human embryo? Did it appeal to your sense of propriety that you were once such a creature?"[12]

His most interesting remark is perhaps the final one:

9 Conway, *Question Box*, 2nd ed., 8–10.

10 Hauber, "Facts and Theories," 136, 137, and 139.

11 Hauber, "Facts and Theories," 142–43. *Sententia tolerata* was a fairly standard theological note for theses for which not much of a case could be made, but that were nevertheless allowed.

12 Hauber, "Facts and Theories," 142.

The ground must be prepared before such novel ideas can be sowed broadcast. Before that ground is prepared, we shall need a twentieth-century Saint Thomas; one who can so combine sacred and profane learning that both will draw benefit therefrom; one, perhaps, who can make Darwin and Huxley become to modern Catholic thought what Aristotle and Avicenna were to Scholastics.[13]

* * * * *

The events of 1925 provided, for American Catholics in particular, an occasion to address the question with a particular focus. William Jennings Bryan had for some time been campaigning for legislation prohibiting state educational institutions from teaching the evolutionary origin of man. On March 21 of that year, Tennessee Governor Austin Peay signed into the law the Butler Act, which did more or less what Bryan, and other anti-evolutionist Protestants, had been asking to have done.[14] Within a month, prompted by a general appeal from the American Civil Liberties Union, high-school teacher John T. Scopes and some of the citizens of the city of Dayton had arranged a test case, in which Scopes would be charged with violating the law and the state's courts would be asked (by the defense) to rule the Butler Act unconstitutional. The drama of a trial, artificial though it may have been,[15] provided the occasion for much commentary in the press, foreign[16] as well as domestic.

American Catholics generally kept their distance from both sides of the ensuing controversy.[17] The editors of *Commonweal*, a lay Catholic review then in its second year of publication, wrote:

> *The Commonweal* considers that the Dayton case is hardly likely to advance genuine knowledge of this highly complex and technical matter, but is very likely to confuse the real issues involved through the stirring up of a raucous and heated debate between such emotional extremists as Mr. W. J. Bryan and Mr. Clarence Darrow, to the accompaniment of the jazz-band to be installed in Dayton's baseball field among the batteries of radio machines and newspaper cameras.[18]

13 Hauber, "Facts and Theories," 143.

14 The Act made it illegal "to teach any theory that denies the Story of the Divine Creation of man as taught in the Bible, and to teach instead that man has descended from a lower order of animals." Later anti-evolutionist legislation in Mississippi and in Arkansas did the same, but avoided any direct reference to the Bible.

15 Scopes was not sure that he had actually taught the prohibited idea in his classes, but Dayton (including Scopes) was eager to have the honor of hosting the test of the law, and the ACLU was interested in a verdict on the Butler Act, so the case went ahead without worrying much about that detail. For a fuller account of the case, see my *War that Never Was*, chapter 5, or Edward Larson's *Summer for the Gods*, for which he won a Pulitzer Prize.

16 See, for example, Thomas F. Glick's "Juicio de Dayton ante la opinión pública española," the epilogue to his *Darwin in España*, 69–79.

17 For a contemporary confirmation of this, see *America*, "Middle Road to Dayton." For a historian's account, see John L. Morrison, "American Catholics and the Crusade Against Evolution."

18 *Commonweal*, "Concerning Evolution," 121. *Commonweal* covered the law and the trial fairly closely, beginning at least as early as April 22, 1925, with many articles in the June and July issues.

The Jesuit *America* summed the trial itself up this way: "It was no more than an episode in the struggle between a party that wishes to establish Protestant Fundamentalism as a State religion and another impersonated by Clarence Darrow that aims at no less than an overturn of all Christianity. For that reason moderates of all kinds were well justified in saying: 'You're both wrong. A plague on both your houses!'"[19] Catholic neutrality was noted by outside observers. H. L. Mencken, no greater friend of Catholicism than of religion generally, observed:

> the current discussion of the Tennessee buffoonery, in the Catholic and other authoritarian press, is immensely more free and intelligent than it is in the evangelical Protestant press. In such journals as the [*Commonweal*], the new Catholic weekly, both sides were set forth, and the varying contentions are subjected to frank and untrammeled criticism. Canon de Dorlodot whoops for Evolution; Dr. O'Toole denounces it as nonsense.... The [*Commonweal*] itself takes no sides, but argues that Evolution ought to be taught in the schools—not as an incontrovertible fact but as a hypothesis accepted by the overwhelming majority of enlightened men. The objections to it, theological and evidential, should be noted, but not represented as unanswerable.[20]

Catholics were not, of course, completely silent on the larger issue. Hauber took the opportunity to restate what he had said earlier, this time in a pamphlet entitled *A Catholic Opinion on the Evolution Controversy*. Here his phrasing was perhaps slightly more accommodating of evolutionary anthropogenesis—"The body, indeed, may have evolved; that is a scientific problem waiting for data towards its solution"[21]—but at the same time acknowledged the concerns that had led Tennessee to pass the Butler Act:

> No wonder the whole theory has a bad reputation; we are asked by such false philosophers to give up all our most sacred convictions, belief in God, a future life, and personal responsibility. And what are we offered in their place? Blind forces and brute ancestry. That is what the anti-evolutionists justly fear and rightly condemn. If this is the kind of evolutionary teaching that Tennessee has banned, Catholics have no choice of sides in the controversy. It is a doctrine hostile to all religion and surely public schools may not teach it.[22]

19 *America*, "Post-Mortems on Dayton," 376.

20 Mencken, "The Tennessee Circus," 17. Mencken wrote "*Conservator*," but there was no such Catholic periodical in 1925. University of St. Thomas librarian Anne Kenne suggested to me that Mencken might have meant to write "*Commonweal*," since that magazine was founded in 1924. I think that she is correct. Mencken had probably just read *Commonweal*'s editorial "Concerning Evolution," cited above, which mentions both authors. Bertram A. C. Windle's survey "Books on Evolution," published a few months later, shows the same even-handedness.

21 Hauber, *A Catholic Opinion*, rev. ed., 20; see also 28.

22 Hauber, *A Catholic Opinion*, rev. ed., 24–25.

2. ENCYCLOPEDIAS

The 1920s saw a major revision of one Catholic encyclopedia and the appearance of the first volumes of a second.

The first of these was the completely revised fourth edition of the *Dictionnaire apologétique de la foi catholique.*[23] The publication history of this edition is particularly complex. In 1907, Adhémar d'Alès, SJ, theology professor at the Institut catholique de Paris, decided that it was time to redo the old *Dictionnaire apologétique*, by then nearly twenty years old, and undertook the task of a complete revision. The first fascicle of the work appeared in 1909, followed by 24 more fascicles, the last of which appeared in 1928.[24]

Transformism was, d'Alés said in his epilogue, a "delicate question."[25] Indeed in a letter to the editor published in the supplementary volume of the *Dictionnaire*, Pietro Cardinal Gasparri, then Vatican secretary of state, mentioned among the "modern errors" that it was the purpose of the work to combat precisely "modernism, evolutionism, pantheism, and idealism."[26] The task of treating the delicate question was given to de Sinéty; the article appeared in 1928.

The perhaps even more delicate article on Man, already published in 1912, was divided among several authors. D'Alès himself wrote two pages on man according to Genesis; Jean and Amédée Bouyssonie, along with Breuil, wrote fifteen pages on prehistoric man according to the paleontological evidence. Jean Guibert wrote five pages on the unity of the human race. Finally, Teilhard wrote seven pages on man in the teachings of the Church and in spiritualist philosophy. In a book review of these articles for the American *Catholic University Bulletin*, Charles F. Aiken wrote that "the story of primitive man is told with a freedom of treatment not generally found in Catholic works dealing with this difficult subject."[27]

The approach of the *Dictionnaire* was emphatically compatibilist about the evolutionary origins of plants and animals. De Sinéty wrote: "Transformism, to tell the truth, is of interest in apologetics only to the extent that it concerns the human species. . . . [Otherwise] it is entirely with the province of biology and of the philosophy of nature."[28] De Sinéty, following the lead of Teilhard, subjected the direct creation of new species to a

---

23 The work's subtitle describes it as *"contenant les preuves de la vérité de la religion et les réponses aux objections tirées des sciences humaines."*

24 The work is most commonly available in a four-volume edition, with individual volumes dated between 1922 and 1926. A fifth volume, including an epilogue, index, and some other material, was published in 1931.

The *imprimatur*, which is printed only in Volume V: Table Analytique, is dated 1909. The copyright date for the first three volumes is given as 1911; for the fourth, 1922. The last volume must have been printed later than that, however, for the bibliography of at least one article near the end of the volume includes an item published in 1928.

25 D'Alés, Épilogue, *Dictionnaire*, 5:xii.

26 Gasparri to d'Alés, September 10, 1929 (*Dictionnaire*, 5:i). Gasparri's reference to evolutionism, I think it is fair to say on the interpretive principle *noscitur a sociis*, is to Haeckel's Monism and other atheistic philosophies of nature, and not to the purely scientific theory of the evolutionary origin of species.

27 Aiken, Review, 334.

28 De Sinéty, "Transformisme," 4:1793–94.

severe critique. He does not, of course, deny that God could create new species directly, but rather argues that He *did* not:

> Suppose, for example, that one would like to offer an account of the manner in which oak trees first appeared on earth. Does one say that one fine day God produced a fully-grown plant with its roots fixed in soil into which they did not themselves grow, with its trunk showing concentric rings of woody formations which apparently correspond to its age, with its vessels full of sap the elements of which were not drawn from the soil, with its leaves and its buds at different stages of development? All of that seems extremely implausible. . . . Is there any less difficulty with the direct creation of an acorn? Absolutely not.[29]

The alternative, of course, is evolutionary origins for plants and animals.

Man, however, is different from other animals: "Man is the only animal which has abstract and general ideas, who knows formally the relation of cause and effect, who is capable of making a judgment or an inference, of free choice, of having a conceptual language, morality, and religion."[30] He declined to make a *theological* evaluation of the thesis of the evolutionary origin of the human body,[31] but did say that "man is not the product of evolution." For this he gave the standard Catholic argument: "the set of human mental capacities . . . is the operation of an immaterial principle, of an intellectual [*spirituel*] and individual soul. The origin of that soul requires the creative intervention of God."[32] De Sinéty also, following González's suggestion rather than Mivart's account, gave God some rôle even in the formation of the human body:

> God intervened at the origin of the human race not only in order to create an intellectual [*spirituelle*] soul, but to compose the human type in its total human reality, the infusion of the intellectual [*spirituelle*] soul having been transformative, in the full sense of the word, of a pre-existing organism which would never, of itself and left to the laws of nature, have reached the bodily type characteristic of the human race.[33]

> God intervened in a special manner to make the body of the first man and the first woman. It is not necessary for us to specify the exact "how" of that intervention.[34]

God did not need to form the human body directly from the slime of the earth, however. A supernatural modification of an animal body would do:

> If someone finds it more satisfying to the scientific mind to think that the Creator, in order to make the body of the first man, used matter that was already organized [i.e., that was already a biological organism], that he more or less profoundly transformed

29 De Sinéty, "Transformisme," 4:1805–6.

30 De Sinéty, "Transformisme," 4:1837.

31 De Sinéty, "Transformisme," 4:1844.

32 De Sinéty, "Transformisme," 4:1837.

33 De Sinéty, "Transformisme," 4:1840.

34 De Sinéty, "Transformisme," 4:1846.

that organism by the infusion of an intellectual [*spirituelle*] soul, we do not see what theological objection could be raised against this. The Church has never pronounced, either directly or indirectly, on the state of the matter which, according to the text of Genesis itself, was used to make the human body.[35]

He points out, correctly, that "No apodictic scientific argument can be opposed to the traditional thesis … according to which the Creator intervened in a special way to establish the bodily constitution of the first human couple."[36] About this view, he wrote that "infallible authority has not … rejected the hypothesis of a circumscribed [*restreint*] anthropological transformism."[37]

✳ ✳ ✳ ✳ ✳

The second Catholic encyclopedia to appear during those two decades was the monumental *Enciclopedia universal ilustrada europeo-americana*, popularly known just as the *Enciclopedia Espasa* and identified by historian Robert Collison as "one of the outstanding encyclopedias of the [twentieth] century."[38] Appearing in seventy volumes beginning in 1908 and ending only in 1930, the encyclopedia is, like *Herders*, a general encyclopedia with a decidedly Catholic orientation. The size of the encyclopedia allowed thorough treatment of its subjects. Its article "Transformismo," thirty-eight pages in length and unsigned, was published in 1928. The *Espasa* was, of all the twentieth-century Catholic encyclopedias, the most negative in its assessment of evolution. It nevertheless begins on what might be called a semi-compatibilist note: "Transformism is, above all, a scientifico-philosophical question, and as such can be discussed without grounding oneself in any way in revelation and dogma. … The question of transformism does nevertheless have a theological aspect, since some transformationist theses are intimately related to truths clearly revealed in Sacred Scripture."[39] About the origin of man, the *Espasa* wrote that "It is not about the possibility that the body of the first fathers of the human race could have arisen by evolution from lower organic beings, but rather has to do with a historic fact, namely how in reality the formation of the body of the first rational beings took place."[40] With respect to the suggestion first advanced by Cardinal González thirty years before, it said first that "a special intervention of God, which transcends the forces and the laws of nature, is in no way different from that which the anti-transformists admit in the production of the first man,"[41] and then added that the idea had theological

35 De Sinéty, "Transformisme," 4:1847.

36 De Sinéty, "Transformisme," 4:1847.

37 De Sinéty, "Transformisme," 4:1844.

38 Collison, *Encyclopaedias*, 201.

39 *Espasa*, "Transformismo," 981.

40 *Espasa*, "Transformismo," 984.

41 *Espasa*, "Transformismo," 959.

problems: "It is a *sententia communis et certa* that God did not make the body of man by taking the body of a brute animal and preternaturally transforming it into a human body."[42]

3. TEXTBOOKS

Let us begin in Venezuela, with Bl. José Gregorio Hernández's short book *Elementos de filosofía* (1912). Hernández (1864–1919), perhaps best known as "physician of the poor," was also a university professor. He was born in the town of Isnotú in the Venezuelan Andes on October 26, 1864. Inspired by his shopkeeper-father's interest in herbal medicine, he got a formal education in medicine, first at the Central University of Venezuela, and then at the Pasteur Institute in Paris. It was, of course, his generosity in his medical work, and his personal piety, that led to his beatification, but his intellectual work is also of interest.

In his chapter on "Rational Cosmology," Hernández contrasted a fixist account of the origin of the world (in which "everything that now exists was created from nothing in the very state of development which it has today, with fixed species, separate and independent from one another"[43]) with a comprehensive "doctrine of descent," "much more admissible from the scientific point of view . . . and perfectly harmonizable with revelation."[44] The powers of nature, he thought, were sufficient to organize matter into organic bodies that could be animated by God; in any case the idea that they did was not contrary to a doctrine of creation.[45] The multiplicity of plant and animal species in the world can be traced back to just a few initial species, which then evolved under the influence of a variety of factors, including natural selection.[46] He adopts the Mivartist line on the origin of man:

> [It] includes two successive operations: the first, in reference to the body, which is produced by the proper arrangement of the terrestrial minerals which, constituting the anatomical elements and natural tissues, receive the organization sufficient and indispensable for the second operation, the creation of the spiritual, rational, and immortal soul which will animate it.[47]

Although he does not explicitly say that natural forces themselves did the arranging, neither did he say that it was beyond their power. His general emphasis on compatibility suggests that he had no reservations in this respect.

※ ※ ※ ※ ※

42 *Espasa,* "Transformismo," 984.

43 Hernández, *Elementos,* 173.

44 Hernández, *Elementos,* 173–74. See also 176: "As we see, then, the doctrine of descent is in perfect agreement with the philosophical and religious truth of Creation."

45 Hernández, *Elementos,* 176–77.

46 Hernández, *Elementos,* 175.

47 Hernández, *Elementos,* 176.

Sympathy towards Catholic evolutionism can also be found in Cracow (then in Austrian Poland), where, in 1916, Polish Jesuit Stanisław Bartynowski expanded his *Apologetyka podręczna* to include a chapter on "the theory of evolution and the origin of man," divided into three parts.[48]

With respect to the evolutionary origin of plants and animals, Bartynowski said that the Hexaemeron teaches that God created the world, but says nothing about how many species of plants and animals God created or whether those first species were the same as those that exist today. Those are questions for biologists and paleontologists, and their answer favors evolution. Bartynowski defended (1) the polyphyletic theory of Wasmann and others over what he thought to be the less well-grounded monophyletic alternative promoted by Haeckel and (2) the predominance of internal causes of that evolution, giving Darwin's natural selection a much more limited rôle. In both respects, of course, his views are those of his fellow-Jesuit Wasmann, whom, of course, he cited.

He concluded by contrasting the more generic concept of evolution (transformation of species) with Darwinism (selectionism). The popularity of *Darwinism*, he said, was the result of the use to which it could be put by materialists to characterize a world ruled by chance, and more generally to ground an attack on Christianity.[49] The unjustifiable identification of materialism and evolution had given rise to a certain reservations, and even mistrust, about the latter among Catholic authors: "Today, however, in view of the more precise definition of these concepts by science, no Catholic authors speaks out against what is scientifically affirmed in the theory of evolution."[50]

Bartynowski began his discussion of human origins by reviewing the psychological and morphological differences between man and animal, as well as the still-modest fossil evidence. By way of summary, he wrote:

> Since there is not sufficient evidence of the origin of the human body from an animal, but, on the contrary, weighty scientific reasons, both morphological and paleontological, tell against such an origin, it is understandable why theologians, relying on the constant Tradition of the Church, maintain that the body of the first man was created from inorganic matter. However, the highest authority of the teaching Church has not yet settled this question in the form of an *explicit dogma*.[51]

The book went through six more editions, the last appearing in 1948, the year after the author's death.

✳ ✳ ✳ ✳ ✳

---

48 The first edition (1911) appears to have been a translation of Jakob Linden, *Kleine Apologetik*, a work the popularity of which had already given rise to translations into French and Italian. Bartynowski's second ("greatly enlarged") edition is twice the length of the first; its preface suggests that the discussion of evolution is new to this edition.

49 Bartynowski, *Apologetyka podręczna*, 2nd ed., 138–40.

50 Bartynowski, *Apologetyka podręczna*, 2nd ed., 140.

51 Bartynowski, *Apologetyka podręczna*, 2nd ed., 136. See also 141.

At about the same time in Ireland, Michael Sheehan (teacher at St. Patrick's Seminar in Maynooth and later coadjutor archbishop of Sydney), addressed the topic of evolution in the second part of his widely-used *Apologetics and Catholic Doctrine*, first published in 1922:

> The Church … leaves us free to hold either the theory of Permanentism or the theory of Theistic Evolution…. [T]he extreme form which derives all plants and lower animals from one and the same common origin … is so far entirely unsupported by scientific evidence … but if … the theory … should become an established truth, it would but serve to give us a more exalted idea of the power and wisdom of the Creator who so framed His laws as to draw inert or primitive organic matter slowly upwards to higher and higher forms of life.[52]

On the theory of Natural Selection, he added that "if the process described by Darwin really took place, it was due to the operation of natural laws imposed by the Creator on living things."[53] In other words, natural selection is compatible with Catholic doctrine. On the origin of man, he was more cautious: "The doctrine that the body of the first man was evolved from the lower animals has not been officially condemned by the Church, but it is opposed to the all but unanimous teaching of Fathers and theologians."[54] We might call this a presumptive incompatibilism with respect to evolutionary anthropogenesis. Nevertheless, he went on to say that "in thus following the immemorial practice of the Church, never to reject the old in favour of the new and unproved, their [sc., Catholic teachers'] action [sc., acceptance of the traditional and obvious interpretation of the second chapter of Genesis] must commend itself as reasonable and prudent even to those who are not of the faith."[55] On the previous page, he had made the *presumptive* character of this judgment explicit: "If the proof were forthcoming to-morrow that the body of the first man was evolved from the lower animals, it would not be found to contradict any solemn, ordinary, or official teaching of the Church."[56] There is, however, more to human origins than the appearance of the first human body. Sheehan made explicit his (and the predominant) view that "the Church teaches that God directly created the soul of Adam; that he directly creates every human soul; and that the human soul is spiritual."[57] So there we have, in one of the leading textbooks for schools and converts from the 1920s, compatibilism about the evolutionary origin of plants and animals (even by natural selection), only a presumptive incompatibilism about the evolutionary origin of the human body, and a categorical theological rejection only about the evolutionary origin of the human soul, a proposition that is in any case out of the reach of scientific inquiry.

52 Sheehan, *Apologetics: Part II*, 43–44.

53 Sheehan, *Apologetics: Part II*, 49. Recall that natural selection had not yet attained general scientific acceptance in 1922.

54 Sheehan, *Apologetics: Part II*, 51.

55 Sheehan, *Apologetics: Part II*, 55.

56 Sheehan, *Apologetics: Part II*, 54.

57 Sheehan, *Apologetics: Part II*, 51.

* * * * *

In 1926, Bedřich Augustin published in Prague, with ecclesiastical approval, a school textbook in theology under the title *Základní náboženská nauka (Apologetika)*, part 5 of which treated the topic of creation. With respect to man, after identifying some central points from Scripture—origin in God, body-soul composition—Augustin added that Scripture does not add anything else about *how* man originated, leaving that to science.[58] After reviewing the problematic speculations of Haeckel and the scientific controversy over what to make of Java Man, Augustin acknowledged that the prevailing scientific view was that, although man was not descended from an anthropoid ape, man and those apes did have a common ancestor, giving the arguments for and against the latter view. He concluded by saying that "If the theory of evolution applied to man does not deny God the Creator or the essential difference between human and animal souls, then it is not in contradiction with the theological truth contained in Holy Scripture. Holy Scripture does not address the bodily evolution of man, but also does not exclude it. It teaches only, in popular terms, that man is the work of God, and that he differs in his soul from the rest of creation."[59]

58 Augustin, *Náboženská nauka*, 53.

59 Augustin, *Náboženská nauka*, 59–60.

PART V

EVOLUTION ACCOMMODATED:

MIVARTIAN ANTHROPOGENESIS, BUT NOT TEILHARDIAN THEOLOGY OF NATURE (1931–1955)

CHAPTER 14

SCIENTISTS & THEOLOGIANS
(1931–1950)

1. ERNEST CHARLES MESSENGER (1888–1951)

Ernest Messenger was born on July 5, 1888, at Ilford (England). He converted to Catholicism in 1908 and six years later was ordained to the priesthood. In 1919, he entered the Université catholique de Louvain, where he studied for two years under Henry de Dorlodot. Upon completion of his doctoral studies there, he returned to England and taught philosophy for seventeen years at St. Edmund's College in Ware. He also served (from 1935) on the Westminster Diocesan Board of Censors. He died in 1951.[1]

Although much of his scholarly work was devoted to general apologetics and to controversies associated with the history of the Catholic Church in England, he made three contributions to the Catholic discussion of evolution. The first was the translation of de Dorlodot's *Darwinisme* into English. The second was a work of his own—*Evolution and Theology: The Problem of Man's Origin* (1931). The third was an anthology on the same topic—*Theology and Evolution: A Sequel to "Evolution and Theology"* (1952).

In *Evolution and Theology*, Messenger, who had, as mentioned above, received a copy of de Dorlodot's unfinished manuscript, built on and extended de Dorlodot's

---

1 *The Tablet*, Messenger Obituary.

ideas.[2] The book was divided into four parts, of unequal length. It begins with a brief articulation of some general principles regarding the Church, revelation, and Genesis. The next two parts, which constitute the bulk of the book, address the questions at the heart of Catholic evolutionism—the origin of species (including the origin of the first species, i.e., the origin of life) and the origin of man. A final brief part addresses the origin of Eve. The second and third (and to some extent the fourth) parts address their subjects on the basis of Scripture and of theology (Patristic, Scholastic, and modern). Unlike Mivart and Wasmann, Messenger devoted little attention to scientific aspects of his questions.

On the question of the origin of life, Messenger argued, as had de Dorlodot, that Scripture itself attributes this to secondary causes, i.e., "to powers implanted in inorganic matter by the Creator." This view, he said, was unanimous among Patristic theologians and was only set aside in the thirteenth century, under the influence of scientific ideas associated with Aristotelian Scholasticism. Messenger thought that the Scholastics were mistaken on that point, and that the nineteenth-century scientific evidence against spontaneous generation (the experimental work of Louis Pasteur) showed only that no such process was operative in the world as presently constituted. It did not show that such generation could *never* have taken place. The theological evidence, he argued, still pointed rather to a natural origin of life: "If science could prove the reality of spontaneous generation, a Catholic should welcome this, for it would enable him to give complete assent to the teaching of the Fathers on this point."[3]

He applied the same general theological considerations to the question of the evolutionary origin of particular species. In addition, on the basis of scientific evidence that provides "a fairly high degree of certitude concerning the *fact* of, at any rate, *some* evolution," he concluded that "evolution is the only reasonable way of harmonizing our modern knowledge of the succession of geological epochs … with the Scriptural statement that the earth produced all the present-day species."[4] So, "there is no reason whatever to prevent a Catholic from adopting [evolution as a hypothesis applied to the origin of plants and animals] if he wishes to do so."[5]

Both Scriptural and philosophical considerations, in his judgment, require that he give the origin of the human body separate treatment. He rejected the idea, defended by some theologians, that Adam's body was formed *directly* from the slime of the earth: "We

2 Messenger did not mention having incorporated much of de Dorlodot's manuscript into his own book, but confirmed that he had done so in print in a bibliographic notice in 1950: "A projected second volume, dealing with man, was never published, and only in fact partly written. All the available material was used in *Evolution and Theology* by E. C. Messenger" (Messenger, Bibliography, 166).

Groessens-VanDyck and Lambert found further evidence of Messenger's use of de Dorlodot's manuscript in some unpublished notes of Canadian botanist Brother Marie-Victorin, FSC, who visited Louvain in November 1929. In his travel journal (now in the possession of the Archives des Frères des Écoles Chrétiennes à Laval, but cited here from Groessens-VanDyck and Lambert, "Le Darwinisme d'un chanoine," 67) the friar wrote that "the second volume of de Dorlodot—not yet published—will be very freely translated into English by Messenger."

For more on this, see Groessens-VanDyck and Lambert, "Le Darwinisme," 82–84.

3 Messenger, *Evolution and Theology*, 84.

4 Messenger, *Evolution and Theology*, 274.

5 Messenger, *Evolution and Theology*, 84.

can at least infer that Catholic theology is by no means opposed, either to the possibility of Adam's body being formed as a result of a process requiring time, or, secondly, to the partial collaboration of active secondary causes in that process."[6] The secondary causes imagined by Scholastic theologians were, to be sure, the angels, but the exact nature of the secondary causes Messenger regarded as a "comparatively minor point." While he thus gave evolutionary processes a rôle in the origin of man, he nevertheless identified transitions that, in his judgment, were (in two cases) and probably were (in a third) beyond the reach of natural processes. The first was the creation and infusion of a rational soul. This was not a "*special* Divine intervention," he said; it belonged to "the ordinary sphere of Divine Providence." The second was the raising of man to a supernatural state, which, he said, "affected both the body and the soul." The third, about which he was less certain, was "Divine intervention in the *un-supernaturalized* body of Adam": "These," he said, "are all questions which *Science* cannot answer. *Scripture* does not answer them completely and satisfactorily. *Tradition* is somewhat divided, and *Church* authority seems only on the whole to have laid it down that the formation of the first man was '*peculiaris.*'"[7] For the necessity of some direct Divine action even in the formation of the first human body he gave two arguments. The first was this: "the *human soul* can only exist in the *human* body, and such a body is specifically distinct from any other animal body. Accordingly, ... the formation of the human body may well have required a 'special Divine intervention,' at least to give it the last disposition necessary for the infusion of the human soul." The second, "the fact that one and only human being was produced implies that such production was beyond the powers of created nature."[8]

✳ ✳ ✳ ✳ ✳

The final part of Messenger's book addresses the question of the origin of Eve. The Pontifical Biblical Commission's statement on this point seems more explicitly non-evolutionist than does its statement about Adam. It required that "the formation of the first woman from the first man" be taken in the literal historical sense; the statement on Adam, by contrast only requires that sense for the "distinctive [*peculiaris*] creation of man."[9] Messenger followed de Dorlodot's unpublished manuscript[10] in saying that the kind of divine involvement required in the formation of Eve's body did not count against a significant rôle for evolutionary processes in the formation of Adam's. Messenger devoted about twenty pages of his book to a defense of that view.

---

6 Messenger, *Evolution and Theology*, 224.

7 Messenger, *Evolution and Theology*, 276 (italics Messenger's).

8 Messenger, *Evolution and Theology*, 276 (for both passages).

9 Pontifical Biblical Commission, "De charactere historico," III.

10 Drawing, for this section of his book, heavily on de Dorlodot, *Darwinisme: 2. L'Origine de l'homme*, 159–78. Mivart and Zahm seem to have been silent on the question of Eve, but Presbyterian theologian James Woodrow had taken this position many years before. See his "Speech before the Synod of South Carolina," 46–47.

The idea that Eve was formed with material "taken from the side of Adam," to quote the appendix to Pius X's catechism,[11] Messenger thought, was "so clearly taught in both Scripture and Tradition, that it may well be *de fide*."[12] "At the very least," he said later, "it cannot prudently be called into question."[13] Its importance, he went on to say, is in its mystical interpretation: "This story signifies that the Church can only take its origin from Christ; that the Church is so closely united to Christ that it forms with him one single body."[14] And so, Messenger tried to develop what he called a "possible explanation of the formation of Eve" on the basis of the asexual reproduction that is seen in some animals. "Every cell in an ordinary organism contains, at least radically, the virtuality of the species and the race."[15] Although his account tries to include a quasi-natural process, it is still in part supernatural. Does that make Messenger's a non-evolutionary account of the origin of the human race? It surely makes it less evolutionary than a thoroughgoing naturalist would want. But it does leave Adam's body at least partly a product of evolutionary processes (and Eve's, as somehow a product of his), which is much more evolutionary than Messenger's anti-evolutionist critics were willing to allow.

$$* \quad * \quad * \quad * \quad *$$

Messenger's conclusions about the origin of the human body, then, were broadly compatibilist, without being fully evolutionist. They are, in a certain sense, negative: "From the *scientific* point of view, there is so far no *conclusive* evidence that man has evolved. . . . But as an inference, it is very attractive" and "from the *theological* point of view, . . . *Scripture neither teaches nor disproves the doctrine of the evolution of the human body*."[16] They are also cautious. Messenger organized his summary of the book around the interrogatory triad—*potuit, decuit, fecit?* Could God have used evolutionary processes in the formation of the first human body? He could have done so. Would it have been fitting for Him to have done so? It would have been fitting. Did He in fact do so? Messenger's final verdict on the question of the evolutionary origin of the human body, indeed the very last words of the book, after his answering the first two questions in the affirmative, is: "We think it on the whole preferable for a Catholic to suspend his judgment on the matter at the present moment, or at least not to give any unqualified assent to the evolutionary hypothesis. And so, we end on a note of interrogation: 'Fecit?'"[17]

The book, as one might expect, evoked a lively, but mixed, reaction in the Catholic press, some of which Messenger republished, with replies, in *Theology and Evolution* twenty years later. As we shall see in the next chapter, some of Messenger's critics delated *Evolution and Theology* to the Index.

---

11 Pius X, *Catechismo della dottrina cristiana*, 112.

12 Messenger, *Evolution and Theology*, 252.

13 Messenger, *Evolution and Theology*, 273.

14 Messenger, *Evolution and Theology*, 257.

15 Messenger, *Evolution and Theology*, 269–74; the passage quoted is on 269.

16 Messenger, *Evolution and Theology*, 275 (italics Messenger's).

17 Messenger, *Evolution and Theology*, 280.

In addition to continuing the discussion of evolutionism *per se*, Messenger's 1952 book included a part entitled "The Soul of the Unborn Babe." This topic might at first seem out of place in a book about evolution, but Messenger emphasized a connection between the two topics: "if a human being at the present time goes through first a vegetative and then a sensitive or animal stage, it is difficult not to think it likely that the human race as a whole may have had a similar history."[18] In a footnote, he added that "it is scarcely a coincidence that the keenest defenders of the *Immediate Animation theory*, which denies the evolution of forms in the human embryo, are generally also strenuous opponents of the idea of human evolution at the beginning of things." Messenger might better have expressed his meaning with the word "succession," rather than "evolution," of forms. In any case, the connection had been emphasized by de Dorlodot as well: "The gap between plant and animal which, it is said, cannot be crossed is one that nature crosses every day in the course of the generation of animals."[19] De Dorlodot had added that continued defense of immediate animation in the twentieth century was "one of the greatest disgraces of human thought."[20] Indeed three of the seven chapters of this part of Messenger's book were from de Dorlodot's *Nachlaß*, which de Dorlodot had left with Messenger to use as Messenger judged suitable;[21] most of the rest was written by Messenger. De Dorlodot's preferred delayed-hominization embryology continued to lose ground, however, and this theme has not figured particularly prominently in subsequent defenses of Catholic evolutionism.

2. JULES PAQUIER (1864–1932)

Jules Paquier (1864–1932), curate of Saint Pierre de Chaillot in Paris, had been interested in evolution from his years as chaplain at the Lycée Saint-Louis and at the Sorbonne; that is, from about 1901. In the years that followed, he had written on a number of topics in Church history, but only in the last years of his life, in 1929–1931, did he put together a formal exposition of his thoughts on evolution and religion. That he did, first in a series of lectures at his parish church, and then as a book, *La Création et l'évolution: La Révélation et la science.*[22]

Central to Paquier's analysis is a distinction between two different theories of "evolution." The scientific theory of evolution, which had won general acceptance, is theologically neutral, but must be distinguished from a philosophical theory of evolution, focused on religion, morality, and progress. That latter theory is materialist, subjectivist,

18 Messenger, *Theology and Evolution*, 195.

19 De Dorlodot, *Darwinisme*, 131 (trans., 107).

20 De Dorlodot, *Darwinisme*, 131n1 (trans., 107n1)

21 Messenger, *Theology and Evolution*, 219–20.

22 A first fascicle had been published in 1931. The biographical information is at Paquier, *Création*, 8–10.

and individualist, with roots not in science, but in the subjectivism of Immanuel Kant and the pantheism of Johann Gottlieb Fichte and Georg Wilhelm Friedrich Hegel.[23]

His book is divided into three parts. The first addresses "the origin of the universe, of life, and of man." The second, on "the evolution of man," addresses the antiquity and the unity of the human race. The third addresses "philosophical evolutionism"—religion, morality, and progress. That first part includes four chapters on origins (to chapters on the three things named above is added an additional chapter on the origin of species) and a final chapter on God and the theory of evolution.

About the origin of the universe, Paquier wrote that "it is no longer permissible to place in doubt the slow and progressive formation of the universe by the natural action of physical forces."[24] About the origin of life, that "if life has come from matter, that is just one miracle less. But I have plenty of other proofs of divine action in the world; that question is, for me, of no particular importance."[25] And about the evolutionary origin of species, that "the Bible says nothing in favor of the direct and immediate creation of each species."[26] He modified a judgment made by French zoologist (and evolutionist) Yves Delage in 1895 to the effect that "one is, or is not, an evolutionist, not for reasons drawn from the natural sciences, but on the basis of one's philosophical opinions": "Fifty years ago," Paquier wrote, "it was no doubt thus. It is often still so on two capital points—the origin of life and the origin of man. . . . But with respect to species inferior to man, the opposition affirmed by Delage no longer exists."[27]

That brought him, of course, to the question of the origin of man. The human capacity for abstract thought, he said, makes man different in kind from all other animals. The soul that makes such thought possible is not a possible subject of scientific inquiry. Its existence is known from philosophy and from revelation,[28] but it cannot be a product of evolutionary processes.[29] The acceptance of the thesis that it is directly created by God is required, but it is all that is required, by the Pontifical Biblical Commission in its *responsa* of 1909.[30]

With respect to the origin of the first human body, he had already said that "whether the human body came from inanimate soil or from soil already organized [i.e., from a living being], there is nothing there inconsistent with the presence in that body of a principle of thought, capable of general ideas and religious sentiment."[31] He acknowledged both the increasing paleontological evidence in favor of the evolutionary

---

23 Paquier, *Création*, 360–61.

24 Paquier, *Création*, 41.

25 Paquier, *Création*, 49.

26 Paquier, *Création*, 73.

27 Paquier, *Création*, 74; the passage from Delage is in his *La Structure du protoplasme*, 184. See also Paquier, *Création*, 65.

28 Paquier, *Création*, 88–89.

29 Paquier, *Création*, 103.

30 Paquier, *Création*, 105; see also 121–23.

31 Paquier, *Création*, 75.

origins of man and the problems that still had to be faced.[32] The emphasis on secondary causality in St. Thomas's philosophy of nature was, he thought, friendly to the theory of evolution, as was St. Thomas's more particular views about spontaneous generation and embryological development, since both were cases of the emergence of a greater being from a lesser one. "That which St. Thomas says of the individual," he wrote, "Transformism says of the species."[33]

How could the first *human* body have been formed? He reviewed three possibilities. The first, that God "fashioned it like a clay statue and then infused into it a soul," he dismissed: "No one holds this view any longer, if ever anyone did. 'He Who Is' is not a great giant with hands and a mouth."[34] He was, of course, incorrect in suggesting that all Catholics gave some rôle to evolution in the origin of the human body. The other two possibilities were both evolutionist. The first of those held that "the human body came from a pre-existing organism, the elevation being produced by way of a slow and practically unobservable evolution." He acknowledged, but was not convinced by, the concern that such an account would undermine the distinction between man and animal. Nevertheless, he rejected the gradualist view as overly bold (*hardi*). Scientifically (*de point de vue physique*), paleontologists had not turned up a progressive series of fossils. Theologically, the account would create problems both for the origin of the first woman and for the unity of the human race. It had not, however, he pointed out, been condemned by the Church.[35] His own view was that the first human body was the product of a rapid transformation of the kind at the heart of Hugo de Vries's more general mutation theory.[36] He added that the forces of nature that effected those mutations would themselves be under divine direction.

He added a brief note on the origin of the first woman in which he attempted to reconcile his presumption of natural causality with the Biblical Commission's judgment that the production of the first woman's body from that of the first man is a historical fact: "It would have been by an analogical replication (*un dédoublement d'un genre analogue*), a rapid replication, that the body of the first woman would have come from (*sorti de*) the first man."[37] The passage is, to be sure, somewhat unclear. *Dédoublement* can also mean division, without losing the force of the coming-from, and so J. Gross described Paquier's idea as "*dédoublement embryonnaire*" in a review; Messenger translated Gross's phrase as "embryonic division,"[38] which would seem to make Adam and Eve twins. This is not, as an *interpretive* point, impossible; the chromosomal basis for sex-differentiation was

---

32 Paquier, *Création*, 110.

33 Paquier, *Création*, 118.

34 Paquier, *Création*, 127.

35 Paquier, *Création*, 127–28.

36 He cited de Vries's "Transformisme et mutation."

37 Paquier, *Création*, 132.

38 J. Gross, "Problème des origines," 64, and the translation in *Theology and Evolution*, 144.

not universally accepted when Paquier wrote,[39] but the idea that Adam and Eve were, in this sense, twins seems implausible enough to make one wonder whether that could have been what Paquier meant. What else he might have had in mind is, however, not clear; he did not elaborate.

Finally, before turning to the second theme of his book, Paquier devoted a chapter to arguing that transformism laid at least as good a foundation for arguments for the existence of God as had pre-transformist theories.[40] Arguments for a first cause of being and of motion were still good, he said, as were arguments for the general order of the universe and the finality (particularly the "internal finality, the convergence of the parts and functions of a being on the life of that being"[41]) that is still to be found in nature.

This book, like Messenger's, was delated to the Holy Office. The response of the congregation will be discussed in chapter 15.

3. FELIX RÜSCHKAMP, SJ (1885–1957)[42]

Felix Rüschkamp was born on October 8, 1885, in Lüdingshausen (Prussian Rhineland). He entered the Jesuit novitiate at the relatively late age of 22 and was ordained in 1920. By the time he entered the Society of Jesus, he had already developed a strong interest in biology; his early years as a Jesuit brought him first into contact with Wasmann (at Valkenburg in 1912) and then with the Dutch coleopterist Edouard Everts during a period of study at Maastricht (in 1920–1922). His earliest scientific work was thus, unsurprisingly, primarily in entomology. In 1927, when the Jesuits reopened Sankt-Georgen, their *Hochschule* for philosophy and theology in Frankfurt-am-Main, Rüschkamp was assigned to teach organic cosmology.

* * * * *

In addition to his preparation for the priesthood and to his teaching, Rüschkamp found time both for popular-science writing (among other places, in the pages of the old *Stimmen aus Maria-Laach*, since its return to Germany in 1914 renamed *Stimmen der Zeit*, and in *Aus Natur und Museum: Bericht über die Senckenbergische Naturforschende Gesellschaft*) and for scientific research.[43]

He published his first paper, on ants, in 1912 and then several more on that subject over the next few years. Beginning in about 1920, his interest shifted toward the beetles

---

39 See Stephen G. Brush, "Discovery of Sex Determination," 163: "This conclusion [sc., chromosomal determination] was not accepted by all biologists in subsequent decades; during the 1920s and 1930s there was strong support for a quantitative 'balance' theory of sex determination, with no sharp turning point in development."

40 Paquier, "Dieu et la théorie de l'évolution," in *Création*, 135–72.

41 Paquier, *Création*, 155.

42 For general biographic information, see his obituary, Wilhelm Bönner, "Rüschkamp."

43 For a review of his scientific work, see the summary prepared by Adolf Haas for Bönner's "Rüschkamp," 239–45.

that soon became his specialty. His doctoral dissertation on the wings of beetles, for example, made an important contribution to that field.

Although his skills as an observer yielded a fruitful research harvest, he was also, from the first, interested in theoretical questions. He also wrote occasionally on the philosophy of nature, defending a teleological approach to biology against the mechanistic alternative.[44] His interests came, however, more and more to focus on the question of evolution.

Indeed his very first article, although focused on the description of a particular ant colony containing a queen of one species and workers of another, concluded with the remark that "these bionomic questions are of recognized importance for the problem of the evolution of instinct, and their solution on the basis of rich factual material promises to shed valuable light on comparative animal psychology and the theory of evolution."[45] He later wrote, of his acceptance of that idea: "relearning is always difficult and requires mental struggle. I also was not spared this when in 1910 I recognized the untenability of fixism on the basis of my own observations and clear experimental results."[46] In the end he published, by one count, some ninety-one articles on evolutionary topics over the course of his career. The greater share focused on comparative morphology and related topics, with a lesser number devoted to questions of biogeography.

His general views on evolution can be found in the popular-science articles he wrote, particularly for *Stimmen der Zeit*. In "Zur biologischen Entwicklungslehre" he wrote: "Of how many or of how few original species shall each of these two kingdoms, after all, be built? This is a pure question of fact. To solve it is the task of historical research,"[47] and "The smaller was the number of original created species, the higher must have been their potentiality, and the higher shines the wisdom and the power of the Creator. To the speculative need of the philosopher, it is enough to realize that an extensive evolution is possible on the basis of a structure of potency-act; the empiricists prove that it has taken place."[48]

Neither his extensive scientific work nor his occasional contributions to the philosophy of nature, nor even his general work applying the theory of evolution to the plant and animal kingdom, provoked any adverse reaction from ecclesiastical authority. The same cannot, however, be said about his interest in the origin of the human race, which began to develop as he took up his teaching position at Sankt-Georgen. About the rôle of evolution in anthropogenesis, he later wrote: "Over the course of almost thirty years, I recognized the application of the theory of descent to man as possible, probable,

44 Rüschkamp, "Zweckursachen und Wirkursachen."

45 Rüschkamp, "Rufa-fusca-Adoptionskolonie," 215–16.

46 Rüschkamp to Ledóchowski, March 31, 1939, 3–4 (doc. 7, "De doctrina anthropologica a P. F. R. Rüschkamp propugnata 1938–1947," Germania Inferiora 2009 (hereafter, "Rüschkamp Dossiers"), ARSI).

47 Rüschkamp, "Biologische Entwicklungslehre," 230–31.

48 Rüschkamp, "Biologische Entwicklungslehre," 232.

and then certain. In the thunderous battle of opinions, alarm and doubt gave way like mist before the sun."[49]

His next article, on the origin of mammalian flight, relying on the just-published ideas of Hans Böker,[50] gave to the organism a more active rôle in evolution than did the Darwinian-Mendelian emphasis on mutations. Regardless of the cause, however, Rüschkamp concluded, "a wide-ranging evolution is a proven fact." Yet more revealing of his larger worldview is his remark that "the mysterious activity of the living organism [sc., the ability to adapt to its environment] is, ostrich-like, ignored and denied out of existence. Why? Because behind it is revealed an inconceivably great intelligence as its originator?"[51]

✳ ✳ ✳ ✳ ✳

What exactly did Rüschkamp say about *human* evolution? In a lecture that he delivered to some teachers in Düren in 1928, he argued that, although the descent of man from animals had not yet been scientifically proven, it was compatible with revelation: "Which distance is greater, that between God and man or that between us and the animal? The former distance is infinite; the latter, only finite. Now, if God's Son did not consider it to be beneath His dignity to become man in the womb of a virgin, would it be beneath our dignity if God allowed the first human body to be prepared by the animal kingdom?"[52]

In addition to his promotion of the thesis about the animal origin of the human body, an idea that had been both defended and attacked by Catholics already for half a century, Rüschkamp also put some effort into introducing the Catholic educated public to new scientific developments relevant to the origin of the race. In 1932, he wrote an article on the newly-discovered Peking Man for *Stimmen der Zeit*. Peking Man, he said, was already a true man. Morphological similarity to the bones that Dubois had found at Trinil made Java Man a true man as well. These were, of course, different enough even from Neanderthalers to make them a "pre-Neanderthal race ... from which the Neanderthalers can and must be derived,"[53] an evolutionary series. "There is no doubt that *Sinanthropus* and with him *Pithecanthropus* [sc. Java Man] takes the morphological evolutionary series of the human form from Primigenius (Neanderthalers) in a straight line down [i.e., back] into the past."[54] He did not explicitly address the question of whether man had an animal ancestry, but did say that "a number a features can be brought in proof of the truth that man is subject to the law of evolution just as are all of the living beings around him."[55] He concluded with the remark that, although popular reconstructions

49 Rüschkamp, "Mensch als Glied der Schöpfung," 385.

50 On Böker, see Alejandro Fábregas-Tejedal, "Hans Böker's 'Species Transformation.'"

51 Rüschkamp, "Wirbeltiere erobern die Luft," 329–30.

52 Rüschkamp to Johannes Lauer (provincial for Lower Germany), January 13, 1929, 4 (fol. 011–14, doc. 2696, Abt. 252 C 2283, APECESJ).

53 Rüschkamp, "Sinanthropus," 55.

54 Rüschkamp, "Sinanthropus," 56.

55 Rüschkamp, "Sinanthropus," 56.

depicted Peking Man as of limited intelligence, "the man that mastered the Ice Age, and held his own against much stronger animals, was no idiot."[56]

That article precipitated a complaint to the Index in 1933, to be discussed in chapter 15. In conformity with instructions from the Index, Ledóchowski prohibited Rüschkamp from addressing the origin of the human body from an animal species either in teaching or in writing.[57] The restriction did not, however, forbid him from writing on general evolutionary topics or on human prehistory and over the next few years he published, in *Stimmen der Zeit* and elsewhere, articles on both topics, apparently without provoking further controversy.

Indeed the popular-science articles mentioned above were published after the restrictions put in place after the appearance of the Peking-Man article as were several articles on paleoanthropology.

His views on general evolution were mentioned above. His thoughts on evolution and paleoanthropology can be drawn from four articles published between 1935 and 1938,[58] articles in which he addressed fossil man, the age of the race, and monogenism. The topic, he emphasized, was definitely a mixed one: "among all the branches of knowledge that undertake a reconstruction of universal history, two reach directly back to the … phylogenetic root of the human race—theology and biology (*Erbbiologie*). They offer us the *terminus a quo*."[59]

The gap between the earliest forms of fossil man and animal fossils was large enough to allow him to address the question of human evolution without addressing the question of animal ancestry. Piltdown Man he dismissed, correctly, as a composite of a human skull and a simian jaw.[60] About the other results of paleoanthropological research he wrote:

> Modern man [*Jetztzeitmenschheit*] came from an earlier, Neanderthal phase [*Altzeitmenschheit*] and that from an even earlier, pre-Neanderthal [*Frühzeitmenschheit*] of which we have only the few remains from Heidelberg, Peking, and Java. *In the forms from Java we have before us the absolutely earliest [ursprünglichste] human forms yet known.* If our unsuccessful search for even older forms has not deceived us, we have, in Java Man, anatomically as well as temporally, as good as found the ancestral form of the race. The day on which God called the first man into being must have belonged to a subtropical *Altdiluvium* [i.e., lower Pleistocene].[61]

---

56 Rüschkamp, "Sinanthropus," 57.

57 Ledóchowski to Wilhelm Klein (Rüschkamp's provincial), June 18, 1934 (fol. 135–36, Lettere Generali—Germania Inferiora (RLG-GI), XIII), ARSI).

58 Rüschkamp, "Geschichte der Menschheit," "Früh-Anthropologisches," "Erscheinungsbild Adams und Evas," and "Wie alt ist das Menschengeschlecht?"

59 Rüschkamp, "Geschichte," 188.

60 Rüschkamp, "Nicht Morgenrötenmensch." The idea that it was not just an interpretive error but a *forgery* still lay in the future.

61 Rüschkamp, "Geschichte," 198 (emphasis Rüschkamp's).

Humanity, he said, is determined by the capacity for reason (*Vernunftbegabung*), not by bodily form.[62] So, Peking Man, tool- and firemaker, despite the morphological difference between him and modern man, was a member of the human race, which therefore, has been around for perhaps 250,000 years.[63]

That meant, of course, that our first parents would have looked different from any modern race—they were "phenotypically pre-Neanderthalers"[64]—but that did not matter. "What raised them above the most similar animal forms in nature was their rational soul, and what lifted them beyond their natural state was the supernatural grace of being children of God."[65] To this he added two points: "[There is no point in wanting] to search for the original human form among the human races of today" and "accidental racial differentiation . . . directly affects only the material, animal part of man."[66]

Finally, he addressed the theologically sensitive question of monogenism.

He had first written about that issue fourteen years earlier, in 1921, while he was still studying at Maastricht, in a short article published in the Dutch Jesuit *Studiën* as a review of a special issue of the German weekly *Die Naturwissenschaften* commemorating the fiftieth anniversary of the publication of Darwin's *Descent of Man*. He began by calling the idea that the entire human race is descended from a single ancestral couple a theological opinion (*gevoelen*), but one that had not been solemnly proclaimed. He next said that all fossil men (including Neanderthalers and Heidelberg Man[67]) were absolutely human and then quoted Theodor Mollison, one of the four contributors to the issue that he was reviewing to the effect that there could be no doubt about "the monophyletic (i.e., single [*einheitlicher*] origin [of the human species], i.e., an origin only one time [*einmal*] *from one branch* of primates *in one place*."[68] Rüschkamp took this to mean that "mankind forms a single family *and comes from a single forefather*,"[69] though this does not seem to be Mollison's conclusion.[70] He concluded by noting the disagreements among the four contributors, adding that "every layman sees how wise and dignified is the cautious posture of the Church."[71]

In the 1935 article, he wrote:

62 Rüschkamp, "Wie alt ist das Menschengeschlecht?," 164–65.

63 Rüschkamp, "Wie alt ist das Menschengeschlecht?," 167.

64 Rüschkamp, "Erscheinungsbild Adams und Evas," 54.

65 Rüschkamp, "Erscheinungsbild Adams und Evas," 55.

66 Rüschkamp, "Geschichte," 189.

67 He does not explicitly mention Java Man or Piltdown Man. One of the articles in the issue (Theodor Mollison, "Abstammung des Menschen") had emphasized the difference between Java Man and apes and had expressed strong doubts that the Piltdown skull and jaw belonged to the same being. Australopithecines and Peking Man had not yet been discovered when Rüschkamp wrote this article.

68 Mollison, "Abstammung des Menschen," 140 (emphasis Rüschkamp's, on his p. 155).

69 Rüschkamp, "Stamt de Menschheid van één of van meer ouderparen af?," 155 (emphasis mine).

70 I think that Rüschkamp misread Mollison's "once" (*einmal*) as meaning in one individual case, when Mollison only meant at one particular point in phylogenetic history.

71 Rüschkamp, "Stamt de Menschheid . . . ?," 155.

> Theology, in the light of revealed truth, shows and teaches us monogenism, the descent of all men from a single first pair [*Einpaarigkeit des Ursprungs*]. Biology, with the light of reason, comes to an analogous finding.... *Man's specific unity of origin* [*Einartigkeit des Ursprungs*] *is today a matter of biological fact*, independent of whether its root lies four or forty millennia, or however far, in the past. The only biologically undecided point is whether the human race began with one or many conspecific parental couples. Theoretically, both were possible. Here theology supplements our biological knowledge. All mankind comes from a single parental couple.[72]

In 1937, he made the same point in a brief article in which he said: "Science has no definite answer to give to the question of how many conspecific ancestral pairs there were at the beginning of human history. One such pair is the minimal biological requirement. That there was *only one original pair*, Adam and Eve, is a fact drawn from the sources of revelation, a fact that is sacred to Catholics as a dogma of their faith. On this, dogma gives us knowledge that science cannot give."[73] To this, however, he added in a footnote: "Catholics know very well that infallibility belongs only to actually defined doctrines or dogmas, not to every belief or received opinion in the Church, not even to those which are thought to be supportable by reference to Holy Scripture.... It is simply a misleading when, in the fight against the Church, the refutation of a received opinion is presented as a refutation of dogma."

By 1939, he apparently felt, "despite the clear instructions that he had been given," Ledóchowski said,[74] that he could take up some more delicate questions. Early in the year, he submitted to *Stimmen der Zeit* an article on what theology has to say about certain problems in modern anthropology, an article that, according to Paul Schütt, rector at Sankt-Georgen, "showed that Rüschkamp had problems about the creation of the soul and the unity of the human race (with respect to the origin of the body)."[75] The article did not pass censorship and Rüschkamp withdrew it, but, Schütt added, "he seems not to have changed his opinion. Nor do I know with certainty whether he is fully silent about his opinions, even in private conversations with outsiders [*externi*]."[76]

Evidence that Rüschkamp had not changed his opinion, at least on monogenesis, came early in 1941, when he raised with Ledóchowski the question whether it is a revealed truth that Adam is the physical ancestor of all living men, writing up his own thoughts on the state of that question and suggesting that the question be put to the theologians

---

72 Rüschkamp, "Geschichte," 188–89. In the passage quoted, Rüschkamp sometimes used the term *Erbbiologie*, and sometimes merely, *Biologie*, a variation that I have not maintained in the translation.

73 Rüschkamp, "Adam und Eva," 54.

74 Ledóchowski to Wulf, March 18, 1939 (doc. 3, Rüschkamp Dossiers).

75 Schütt to Ledóchowski, March 16, 1939 (doc. 5, Rüschkamp Dossiers).

76 Schütt to Ledóchowski, March 16, 1939 (doc. 5, Rüschkamp Dossiers).

at the Gregorianum.[77] Ledóchowski had replied that there was no need to put such a question to theologians since it is doctrine, even if it has not been formally defined.[78]

Despite the problems with that article, the journal did publish in its March 1939 issue Rüschkamp's article on "man as part of creation." Rüschkamp began the article by acknowledging that the question was a mixed one. The article was, Rüschkamp said, a scientific complement to Périer's theological *Transformisme* (discussed below), even though the article was already in press when Périer's book appeared.[79] Rüschkamp acknowledged that mixed character again mid-article, where he said that an idea that was biologically possible, and was in fact defended by some, was ruled out by the sources of revelation.[80]

His particular point was to present the *corporeal* aspect of human being as a product of the natural processes of biological evolution—"Science is as good as unanimously convinced of the fact of evolution."[81] The evidence for this was sixfold, including the following: First is the fact that the human body, like all other living bodies, was fully subordinated to the laws of biology. Second is the similarity between man and animals, with respect to which he cited a metaphysical principle that "even the most limited kind of agreement suffices for application of the principle of unity of origin."[82] Third, "the systematic rank-order [of primates] corresponds to the order of the historical appearance of the type-representatives." None of this constitutes a challenge to the doctrine of creation—"without the acceptance of an omniscient and omnipotent Creator, the mystery of life and of its 'hierarchical' development cannot be solved."[83]

Bringing this directly to bear on the question of the origin of the first human body, he wrote:[84]

> Man is not only conceptually [*begrifflich*], but also organically and genetically, a part of creation. The difference between man and beast lies not in the animal aspects [of human being], but only in the intellectual [*geistig*]. Our understanding requires, for the formation of abstract concepts, sense-perception and sensory centers [in the brain], but nothing different from what animals (as beings with sense powers only) [*reine Sinneswesen*] already have. Consequently, any creative intervention or patching up of the human body or brain would be superfluous.

77 Rüschkamp to Ledóchowski, Feb 12, 1941 (doc. 29, 30, & 30A, Rüschkamp Dossiers).

78 Ledóchowski to Rüschkamp, Feb 21, 1941 (doc. 31, Rüschkamp Dossiers).

79 Rüschkamp, "Der Mensch als Glied der Schöpfung," 367.

80 Rüschkamp, "Mensch," 376n4.

81 Rüschkamp, "Mensch," 371.

82 Rüschkamp, "Mensch," 378. He cited Cajetan ("Cajetan zu Thom., De pot. 3, a. 6 c") as the source of the principle he quoted, but Cajetan seems never to have written such a commentary. The reference to St. Thomas's own *De Potentia Dei* is apt. In Q. 3, a. 6 (on whether there is but one principle of creation), Thomas had written: "Whenever different things have one thing in common, they must be referred to one cause with respect to that common thing, since either one is the cause of the other, or they both proceed from a common cause."

83 Rüschkamp, "Mensch," 371.

84 Rüschkamp, "Mensch," 384–85.

This article, unlike most of his articles from the preceding few years, provoked an immediate reaction, both from his provincial authorities and at the Jesuit curia in Rome, and had severe consequences—immediate suspension from teaching and restrictions on further publication. For the details, see chapter 15.

After the war, Rüschkamp was allowed to resume teaching, writing, and speaking. His views on evolutionary anthropogenesis seem not to have changed, for in a public lecture that he gave at Landau he said:

> At a certain moment in evolution, when the animal body was so far developed that it could become a worthy instrument to be the carrier of a rational [or spiritual] soul [*Geistseele*], that animal body was, by a creative act of God, infused with a rational soul and in that way the animal was transformed into a man. The moment of transition cannot, of course, be scientifically determined. But it is essentially on account of his rational soul that man differs from an animal and whether old (primeval) fossil finds are early human or prehuman (so, animal) finds cannot be immediately decided, but must rather be judged by whether the find also includes cultural remains (tools, weapons, the use of fire). For such remains cannot be explained without the presence of a rational soul. That does not exclude the Lord God from the evolutionary history of animals and man.[85]

At about the same time, he published an article entitled "Zur Art- und Rassengeschichte des Menschen" in *Stimmen der Zeit*, focused on the relationship between the various stages of human phylogeny along the lines he had defended already in 1935. In addition to the fact that he cited the article that had brought him so much trouble in 1939,[86] two things are worth noting. The first is his strict monogenism. Whatever reservations he might have had in 1941, in this article he wrote: "We Catholics are in possession of a truth of faith which assures us with absolute certainty that *all living men go back to a primordial human couple*."[87] He repeated his earlier thoughts about what Adam and Eve had (or rather, had not) looked like: "There is a delightful naïveté and historical impossibility in the fact that every race, insisting on its present ideal of beauty when illustrating the Biblical creation story, depicts our first ancestors according to this ideal."[88] However understandable such a depiction might be, it completely neglected the fact that those first human beings would have looked rather more like the human beings whose fossil remains had been found in the Neander Valley, in the Peking caves, and along the riverbeds of Java, fossil men of whom Adam and Eve were also the ancestors.

There is no mention of the article in the files of the Jesuit curia in Rome, but the lecture did come to their attention and resulted in a renewed prohibition on his addressing the question. Again, details are presented in chapter 15.

---

85 Weigel, "Artgeschichte und Ursprung des Menschen," so these are Rüschkamp's words as reported by Weigel.

86 Rüschkamp, "Art- und Rassengeschichte," 292n3

87 Rüschkamp, "Art- und Rassengeschichte," 295 (emphasis Rüschkamp's).

88 Rüschkamp, "Art- und Rassengeschichte," 298.

Despite the concerns of his superiors, however, Rüschkamp continued to write on evolutionary questions, without having changed his opinion. In 1944, Munich ethnologist Ferdinand Birkner had argued that Neanderthalers stood on a side line of human phylogenetic history.[89] A couple of years after the Landau incident, when Birkner's view was defended by another author, Rüschkamp re-stated his view that Neanderthalers were not only rational men, but our direct ancestors. Perhaps the question of the Neanderthalers itself was not covered by the prohibition, but the article did not entirely avoid the question of animal ancestry. Its final paragraph said:

> Thus is man a part of creation. The fact that animal and human bodies are made from matter that is essentially the same, united by bonds of blood, does not diminish the essential difference between animal and human soul. It is blood of the same nature that pulses in and makes all hearts beat—the heart of the creature below us, the heart of the man next to us, the heart of the God-Man above us—for us and for all His creatures. Many have opened their eyes and hearts to this truth; when will the rest be convinced?[90]

Mid-article, however, he went a bit further, referring to "the position taken by all researchers (including Catholics) for whom the applicability of the theory of evolution to the human body is an hypothesis or, more usually, an established fact."[91]

⁂ ⁂ ⁂ ⁂ ⁂

In 1949, he published with the approval of Jesuit authorities as well as that of the archiepiscopal ordinariate of Freiburg, an expanded (eighty-page) version of his 1947 article, as a book entitled *Zur Artgeschichte des Menschen*. Rüschkamp began by arguing that, despite the contrary claims of scientists such as George Montandon and Franz Weidenreich, the human race originated at a single place and at a single time.[92] Although its origin in a single couple is theologically certain, it is impossible for science to verify (or to contradict) that claim.[93] He then went on to address the question of the age of the human race (which he put at 250–600 thousand years), the location of its origin, the specific designation of various phylogenetic stages, and racial differentiation. He supplemented his argument for the animal origin of the human body with an acknowledgment of the philosophical case for "the underivability of the spiritual-intellectual [*Geistiges*] from the biological and sensitive [*Sinnliches*]" and the place for "God's instantaneous creative act" in the origin of the human race.[94]

---

89 Birkner, "Zum Erscheinungsbild von Adam und Eva."

90 Rüschkamp, "Artgeschichtlicher Wandel," 402.

91 Rüschkamp, "Artgeschichtlicher Wandel," 396.

92 Rüschkamp, *Artgeschichte*, 12. For this he sometimes uses the term "monogenetic," which he identified with "monophylesis" (13).

93 Rüschkamp, *Artgeschichte*, 13.

94 Rüschkamp, *Artgeschichte*, 79.

In 1950, he published an article on the origin of life in which he argued that, although "Everything that occurs in the natural world must be explained, as far as possible, by natural forces,"[95] the qualification "as far as possible" matters. "That primitive organisms are self-produced . . . is in all probability biologically impossible, and . . . is very certainly impossible philosophically."[96] The question of the origin of life is "cosmogonic, philosophical, and religious."[97]

Rüschkamp died in 1957.

4. PIERRE-MARIE PÉRIER (1865–1938)

Yet another Catholic defense of evolutionary anthropogenesis appeared in 1938, when Pierre-Marie Périer published his *Le Transformisme: L'Origine de l'homme et le dogme catholique: Étude apologétique*.[98] Périer was a theologian and a canon of the diocese of Coutances (Normandy). He served at various times director of its grand seminary and as its vicar-general.

Périer's interest in the connection between science and apologetics dates back at least to 1919–22, when he began a series of articles for the *Revue pratique d'apologétique*.[99] This he followed in 1933–37 with another series of articles in the same journal, this time on evolution and on the origin of man. He reworked the latter articles for *Transformisme*, which appeared shortly after his death.

Many Catholics, he thought, continued to feel misgivings about evolution. For this there was a fourfold cause—poor understanding of the evidence in favor of the theory, the use to which the theory was put by some of its proponents in anti-Christian polemics, adhesion to servilely literal (and assumedly traditional) exegetical principles, and finally an insufficient grounding in metaphysics.[100] There was a need for a book addressed to a general audience in order to undo the resultant religious anxiety.

His book is, as its subtitle emphasizes, an "apologetic study." A *scientific* critique he thought would be "inopportune and dangerous;"[101] safeguarding Catholic doctrine in any case required something different. The problem was not purely scientific ideas, controversial as they might be, but the presentation of philosophical ideas—about God,

---

95 Rüschkamp, "D'où vient la Vie?," 195 (trans., 88).

96 Rüschkamp, "D'où vient la Vie?," 179 (trans.,77).

97 Rüschkamp, "D'où vient la Vie?," 198 (trans., 90).

98 The book appeared in three separate editions over the course of the year. Périer had forty years earlier published another book on science and religion, *Une Religion astronomique*.

99 For a list, see L'abbé Tissier, *Tables générales*, 14 and 22.

100 Périer, *Transformisme*, 91–99. The physical copy from which I am quoting says "third edition," but I have found no reason to believe, and good reason to doubt, that there was anything earlier, other than the articles in the *Revue pratique d'apologétique*.

101 Périer, *Transformisme*, 10.

creation, the human soul, the nature of human intellectual powers, and the origin of life—as though they were scientific conclusions.[102]

The first part of the book, on the general question of evolution, is devoted to "specifying what parts of the transformist theories are compatible with Catholic dogma, and what parts must be absolutely rejected."[103] The problem was, in part, that "a fear of diminishing the rôle of the first cause provided a motive for suspicion with regard to transformism." That fear was, however, ill-grounded: "Christian philosophers of the Middle Ages, . . . gave a very large place to the action of secondary causes."[104] His conclusion is this double affirmation: "There is nothing in the *purely scientific doctrines* of the evolutionists which could upset our faith; there are, among the *philosophical considerations* to which some transformists so boldly and recklessly devote themselves, *a number of errors* which we have the duty energetically to combat."[105] If, he concluded, the theory is correct, then "transformism is, in fact, nothing but the phenomenal form under which the action of the first cause is manifest."[106]

The origin of man, he went on to argue in the second part of the book, is not entirely due to evolution. In the case of animals, one might understand the Biblical description—"Let the earth bring forth the living creature in its kind" (Genesis 1:24)—as meaning that "God put into the earth and waters the virtualities, powers, or germs of life, which, at the moment fixed by His eternal decrees and when everything was properly prepared for their conditions of existence, underwent their normal course of development."[107] That mode of origin would not be sufficient for the production of the first human being. Intellectual powers being more than just the powers of material body, the production of man required the creation of a human soul *ex nihilo*. That soul could then be infused into a material body, one that might well be the product of secondary causes such as evolutionary processes, but, until the soul was so infused into it, it would not really be a *human* body. The question of whether the slime of the earth into which God breathed the first human soul was first organized by biological evolution (i.e., was a living body) or not was not, theologically, particularly important. There was in any case a metaphysical discontinuity between animal and man, one sufficient to necessitate special divine intervention in the formation of the first human being, and that was all that theology required.[108]

Human transcendence of the biological (indeed of the whole natural) world does not, of course, mean that there is no connection between man and nature, that secondary causes played no rôle in the origin of man:

---

102 Périer, *Transformisme*, 12–13.

103 Périer, *Transformisme*, 197.

104 Périer, *Transformisme*, 98.

105 Périer, *Transformisme*, 197 (emphasis his).

106 Périer, *Transformisme*, 198.

107 Périer, *Transformisme*, 233.

108 Périer, *Transformisme*, 234–36.

> I daresay that we render unto God an homage just as complete, and more intelligent, in supposing that He did not disdain to associate already existing secondary causes with the production of the human body and we do so in trying to penetrate the secret of the part those secondary causes played in that production. We thus maintain the true notion of creation, distinguishing it more clearly from miracle, with which it is so easily confused.[109]

That does, of course, leave the question of the details. What can that connection add to our understanding of the origin of man? That question, Périer thought, was insoluble, but not so much so that discussion would be fruitless. So, "How is the human organism associated with the series of animal organisms?"[110]

> One should begin by remembering that *hominization* ... could not be effected except by the substitution of a human soul, created *ex nihilo*, for the animal form and that God did not lack the means either to bring about such changes in substantial forms—changes, incidentally, which St. Thomas thought occurred in the ordinary course of embryological development—or to produce the indispensable anatomical mutations in the animal organism.[111]

He summarized the issue by contrasting two opposed opinions about the formation of the body:

> One, in which one must acknowledge the merit of being traditional, excludes from that formation any action of secondary causes and sees it, consequently, as absolutely miraculous.
>
> The other, suggested by the progress of the empirical sciences and which every day gains new adherents, grants, to the contrary, a rôle to natural forces, sustained and directed by divine power, in the indirect preparation of the human organism, an organism that becomes human only with its substantial union with a human soul.[112]

How can one choose between the two? "No archeological discovery, no paleontological find, would strictly require proponents of the first to change their opinion and give up their belief," and "No decision of the Church condemns those to adopt the second, as long as the necessary governance [*droits nécessaires*] of God is fully respected."[113]

Périer concluded the book with a chapter on prehistory—the paleontological record (what he called the prehistoric races), three problems (and their solution), and three hypotheses then current in Catholic literature. The first of the "problems" was the antiquity of man. Périer acknowledged the range of proposed scientific answers to the

---

109 Périer, *Transformisme*, 255.

110 Périer, *Transformisme*, 257.

111 Périer, *Transformisme*, 259. The relevant passage of St. Thomas is *Summa theologiae*, 1a, 118.2.

112 Périer, *Transformisme*, 264–65.

113 Périer, *Transformisme*, 265.

question, but denied that it was of any theological importance. The other two problems, concerning the specific and the original unity of the human race, by contrast, were theologically important. Were the human fossils that had been discovered (ranging from Java and Peking Man through the Heidelbergers and Neanderthalers to Cro-Magnon Man) all members of the same species? Did they have a common ancestor? These were, of course, distinct questions. Differential transformations over many generations could divide the descendants even of a single original couple into different species.

The question of specific unity was complicated by scientific disagreements about exactly how to distinguish "species" from mere "races." Darwinists were largely nominalists, not realists, on that point. In the end, however, scientific controversies over, for example, whether the Neanderthalers constituted a biological species distinct from *Sapientes* or not, was not, he said, *theologically* important. The theologically relevant concept was the metaphysical species, characterized not by details of skull or jaw, but by intellect and free will, powers found in all primitive peoples. Even the splitting of a once single species into two separate biological species (a possibility that was, of course, at the heart of the theory of evolution) would not create two separate *metaphysical* species.

The third problem is that of *original* unity, common descent from a single couple. Périer is careful not to rule out the possibility of pre-Adamites,[114] but argues from the doctrine of original sin to the thesis that everyone who lived after Adam was descended from him. He recognized the extent to which paleontologists still favored a polyphyletic (and *a fortiori* a polygenetic[115]) account of human origins, but thought that the anatomical arguments in favor of monophyletism overrode paleontological objections. In any case, science had not, and no doubt would never, be able to prove that the human race (present and fossil) was not descended from a single human couple.[116]

Finally came a discussion of three hypotheses about prehistoric races then in the air as attempts to clarify the relation between those races and Adam.

The first was that some of those races (Neanderthalers, for example) are not primitive, but degenerate. "This is not," Périer emphasized, "a *scientific* hypothesis": "It is justified by apologists' desire to retain the widely-accepted theological doctrine [*sententia communis*] that the first man should have had a certain physical perfection."[117] The idea that the fall of Adam had such deleterious physical effects on some of his descendants, Périer said, should not raise any scientific *problems*, even if it could also not be provided with any scientific *support*.

The second hypothesis was that some prehistoric races, though *morphologically* similar to us, are not really human. This hypothesis, he argued, should be rejected. Périer

---

114 Périer, *Transformisme*, 291: descent from that couple is common to "all those who lived on our earth since the elevation of man to a supernatural state, since Adam and Eve . . . ."

115 Périer uses both "-phyletism" and "-genism," sometimes interchangeably. Although he is clear that theology is inconsistent with any kind of polygenism, he sometimes says of arguments that are clearly only antipolyphyletist that they are arguments for monogenism (e.g., 300–302).

116 Périer, *Transformisme*, 301.

117 Périer, *Transformisme*, 310. The theological note of *sententia communis* seems to be asserted on 311.

did not want to underestimate the reach of purely animal powers, but, given what even Peking Man (much less the Neanderthalers) seemed to be able to do, he was not willing to make the distinction between *Homo faber* and *Homo sapiens* proposed, for example, by the priest-paleoanthropologists Amédée and Jean Bouyssonie.[118]

The third hypothesis was that some prehistoric races were really human but lived before God bestowed preternatural gifts on Adam and Eve (so, a version of Pre-Adamitism). This, he thought, was not clearly theologically safe and had best be left alone absent authoritative theological clearance.[119]

5. ALBERT DE LAPPARENT (1905–1975)

Albert-Félix de Lapparent (1905–1975), a grandson of Catholic geologist Albert-Auguste de Lapparent, was a Sulpician priest. Shortly after his ordination in 1929, he was encouraged by his superiors to take up the study of geology himself in order to assume the position that his grandfather had once occupied at the Institut catholique de Paris. He was a specialist in vertebrate paleontology, with a particular emphasis on dinosaurs.[120] Having among his duties that of director of catechetics at the Séminaire Saint-Sulpice, in 1944 he published a booklet entitled *Nos Origines: Les Données de la Bible et de la science*.[121] The work covered five topics: the Hexaemeron, anthropogenesis, the antiquity of man, polygenism, and the Flood.

His determinedly anti-concordist approach, in which even the attempt to correlate the six days of creation week with particular geological epochs is rejected, left him free to state the theological doctrines of Genesis—monotheism, the transcendence and omnipotence of God, etc.—without needing to do more than mention the idea that the chapter is in any sense anti-evolutionist.

The book suggests a Mivartist approach to anthropogenesis, noting the analogy between this and the origin of each human individual. Genesis 2 uses vivid anthropomorphic images to present its central doctrines—the nature of man, human exceptionalism, the special (not immediate) creation of *man* (not of the human body), and the relation between man and woman.

His discussion of polygenesis begins, as did that of so many other Catholic authors, by juxtaposing monogenism with *polyphyletic* polygenism.[122] He acknowledged that a scientific proof of monogenism would be more difficult than would a proof of the broader, monophyletic, thesis.

---

118 Bouyssonie, "Polygénisme," at 2533.

119 Périer, *Transformisme*, 320–21.

120 See Pierre Bordet, "Albert F. de Lapparent"; Xabier Pereda-Suberbiola, "Dinosaurs from Spain"; and Christian Montenat, *Une Famille de géologues*.

121 See also his "Moïse et les géologues modernes."

122 Like Périer, de Lapparent does not always distinguish "-phyletism" from "-genism." See, for example, de Lapparent, *Nos Origines*, 33.

Science, he thought, despite Boule's idea that Neanderthalers constituted a species distinct from *Sapientes* and Teilhard's insistence that the human species could not emerge from a single couple, was not then in a position to settle the matter. Although he acknowledged that the magisterium had not made a definitive statement on the question, he emphasized that theologians were nearly unanimous in rejecting polygenism for reasons connected with the doctrine of original sin. The idea that prehistoric men (*les humanités successives*) were rough drafts of an eventual, definitive, humanity he thought both forced a philosophically inadmissible distinction between *Homo faber* and *Homo sapiens* and risked excluding some true humans (for example, Australian aborigines if, as some then were suggesting, they were the descendants of Neanderthalers) from the universal offer of salvation. It was not entirely clear, he concluded, how the question was to be resolved. It was enough, at the time, to distinguish what theology required and what remained within the realm of science.

6. PIERRE TEILHARD DE CHARDIN (CONT'D.)

The ideas for which Teilhard is best known, his theology of nature, needs to be distinguished both from his purely scientific work (i.e., from the contributions he made to geology and paleontology) and, though the distinction is less sharp, from much of his earlier work on the compatibility of scientific evolutionism and Catholic doctrine.

That theology of nature can be characterized as a kind of cosmic evolutionism, a spiritualist alternative to Haeckel's Monism, something more in the tradition of Henri Bergson and Édouard Le Roy than in that of Licent, Breuil or his other scientific colleagues. This was work that Teilhard himself described (in a letter) as "a kind of new Mystics based on 'the Love of Evolution.'" In the same letter, he described himself as a "would-be 'prophet.'"[123] Robert T. Francoeur, in a preface to his collection of some of Teilhard's writings, wrote: "In attempting to take evolution seriously as a cosmic reality, Teilhard realized that it is more than a simple scientific theory or fact; it is indeed a dimension of thought coloring everything we think and understand. This realization led him to essay a re-expression of the essentials of our Christian revelation in terms of an evolutionary world-vision."[124]

At other times, however, Teilhard emphasized the scientific character of this work, writing in *Le Phénomène humain*: "In order to be understood properly, this book must be read not as a work of metaphysics, and even less as some kind of theological essay, but solely and exclusively as a scientific treatise. The very title indicates as much—nothing but the Phenomenon, but still the whole Phenomenon."[125] He must have been using the term "scientific" in a Pickwickian sense, for the ideas he there developed were not something

---

123 Teilhard to an unnamed friend, October 10, 1945 (*Letters to Two Friends*, 162–63).

124 Francoeur, "Preface," second (unnumbered) page, Teilhard, *Appearance of Man* (1956).

125 Teilhard, *Le Phénomène humain* (1955), 21 (cf. Wall trans., 29).

he deduced from scientific discoveries, or even something required in order to reconcile theology and the paleoetiological sciences. Indeed in a reviewer's report prepared for the Jesuit curia, fellow-Jesuit Édouard Dhanis wrote that "the author claims only to be doing science, not philosophy. I think that hardly any scholar would agree with him on that. In my opinion, he definitely enters the domain of philosophy, not only because of the problems which he treats, but also because of the principles to which he frequently has recourse. His statements on the purely scientific method he followed will be hotly disputed."[126]

The distinction Church officials made between his scientific work (including some, but not all, of the compatibilist commentary that he sometimes added to his popular-scientific articles) and the philosophico-theological work for which he is now best remembered, was maintained until the end of Teilhard's life. It was explicitly applied in 1947, as Teilhard acknowledged in a letter to a friend: "My 'General' Father [then Jean-Baptiste Janssens] has decided that I should . . . refrain from any publication for the time being in the line of philosophy and theology. On scientific matters, no restriction."[127]

"But where does the limit lie for those people?" Teilhard went on to ask. Abbé Paul Grenet echoed Teilhard's uncertainty, commenting that "the frontiers between theology and science were not always as well defined as those in high places wished them to be."[128] In the article that Grenet, and Claude Cuénot, cited as an example of a hard case, "Le Rebondissement humain de l'évolution et ses conséquences,"[129] we find (as a summary) the remark that:

> If social totalization and scientific technology are regarded as they should be, as constituting a direct prolongation, in a human context, of the grand process of the vitalization of Matter, it follows that, from the coming of Man, biological evolution not only rebounds (on a new scale and with new resources) but that it rebounds reflectively upon itself. The Darwinian era of survival by Natural Selection (the vital thrust) is thus succeeded by a Lamarckian era of Super-Life brought about by calculated invention (the vital impulse).[130]

The line is perhaps not as hard to draw as Teilhard and his friends seemed to think.

Perhaps Teilhard persuaded himself that the ideas at issue were scientific in order to see them as being in conformity with his superiors' instructions (given in 1938)[131] that he restrict himself to scientific topics. Whatever the reason for his saying (or thinking) that they were science, they were in fact rather an attempt to synthesize an idiosyncratic

---

126 Dhanis, "Censure du *Phénomène humain*," October 11, 1948, 8 (doc. 6a, Censurae 27–X, ARSI).

127 Teilhard to an unnamed friend, September 24, 1947 (*Letters to Two Friends*, 177); see also his letter of February 8, 1949 (196–97).

128 Grenet, *Teilhard*, 39.

129 The comment from Cuénot is in his *Teilhard*, 325 (trans., 268).

130 Teilhard, "Rebondissement" (1948), 184–85 (trans., 221).

131 Ledóchowski to Charles Chamussy (rector of the College of St. Joseph in Lyons), October 15, 1938 (doc. 6, Censurae 27–VI, ARSI).

Christian mysticism and eschatology with an evolutionary history of the world based (in some way) on the paleoetiological sciences. They were, that is to say, a supplement to Teilhard's more strictly scientific work rather than a presupposition or a logically derivable consequence. Some parts of his *Weltanschauung* were more theological than others. His work sometimes sounds like a philosophy of nature with little, if any, connection to theology. Teilhard, and his editors, however, insisted that there was a connection. Pierre Charles, SJ, added to Teilhard's "Une Interprétation biologique plausible de l'histoire humaine: La Formation de la noosphère," when it was published in *Revue des questions scientifique*, a note to the effect that:

> To avoid any misunderstanding, it is perhaps good to notify the reader that the general synthesis outlined on these pages does not claim either to replace or to exclude a theological account of human destiny.... Quite the contrary.... It is obvious to those willing to place themselves in the perspective indicated by the author that the biological converges with the theological and that the Incarnation of the Word appears, not as a scientific postulate—which would be absurd—but as finding its place, a mysterious alpha and omega, in the entire plan of the Universe.[132]

The editors of a posthumous collection of his works added to his "Les Singularités de l'espèce humaine" a note that "the author reserved the religious elucidations of his thesis for his less exclusively scientific works."[133]

* * * * *

Teilhard's interest in an evolution-centered theology of nature seems to have begun no later than his Hastings years when, in addition to continuing his geological excursions in the time he could spare from his theological studies, he found time to read Bergson's *L'Évolution créatrice*. The book had been published in 1907, but was not put on the *Index* until 1914. Teilhard later wrote: "I remember well having avidly read Bergson's *Creative Evolution*.... I can now see quite clearly that the effect the book had on me was only to kindle,... for a brief moment, a fire that was already consuming my heart and mind."[134] Teilhard began to develop his own ideas shortly thereafter. They found their earliest expression in "La Vie cosmique" (1916), which he wrote while still serving as a stretcher bearer on the Western Front during World War I. It developed after the war when, in about 1921, Breuil introduced him to Le Roy. Teilhard and Le Roy saw one another frequently through the 1920s. Unlike in the case of Teilhard and Bergson, in this case the influence was mutual.[135] Le Roy later wrote of Teilhard, "I have talked over the views expressed here with Father Teilhard so often and at such length that we ourselves can no longer

---

132 Teilhard, "Formation" (1947), 7n (trans., 161).

133 Teilhard, "Singularités" (1955), in *Apparition* (1956), 369 (trans., 270). The editors of *Annales de paléontologie* did not include any such note when the article was first published.

134 Teilhard, *Cœur*, 33 (trans., 25). This autobiography was written in 1950. For an account of the influence of Bergson on Teilhard, see Charles E. Raven, *Teilhard* or Madeleine Barthélemy-Madaule, *Bergson et Teilhard*.

135 See Cuénot, *Teilhard*, 81–82 (trans., 58–59).

pick out our individual contributions."[136] Teilhard continued work on these ideas when he returned to China.

Some of the ideas appeared in an article entitled "Le Phénomène humain" (1930) in *Revue des questions scientifiques*. About 1937, he began to expand them into a book that was to have the same title, a first draft of which was finished in 1940. He completed a second version of a theology (or perhaps in this case of just a philosophy) of nature, somewhat developed and (in his judgment) more strictly scientific, in *La Place de l'homme dans la nature: Le Groupe zoologique humain*, in 1949. His Jesuit superiors did not allow him to publish either of these works in his lifetime. He did publish a further revised (and more purely scientific) version of his ideas in "Les Singularités de l'espèce humaine" in the *Annales de paléontologie* shortly before he died. The earlier books appeared only after his death—*Le Phénomène humain* in 1955 and *La Place de l'Homme dans la Nature* in 1956. Four themes can be distinguished.

The first theme is historical—Teilhard's integrated version of the paleoetiological sciences. It is, that is to say, the same kind of project as that undertaken by Ernst Haeckel, but this time in a way that was, in Teilhard's judgment, more congenial to Catholic doctrine. This is evident in the very titles of the first three parts ("books") of *Le Phénomène humain*. The first, "Before Life Came," culminates in a discussion of "the crystallizing world" and "the polymerizing world." The second, "Life," begins with chapters on "the advent of life" and "life expanding" and culminates with a discussion of "the rise of consciousness." The third, "Thought," features a chapter on paleoanthropology.

Teilhard's account of the history of life (and indeed of the world) is not only theological, but teleological—more Lamarckian than Darwinian in its fundamental orientation, though not Lamarckian in its details. Despite modern evolutionism's commitment to anti-progressionism—to the idea that the history of life is (at least in principle) just one darned species after another—it is an empirical fact that more recent geological ages include species that are more complex and more mindful than were any of the species found in the ages that preceded them.

Lamarck had proposed an account of evolution in which progress was an essential part of the theory. Darwin recognized the empirical fact of progress in the closing paragraphs of *On the Origin of Species*: "Whilst this planet has gone cycling on according to the fixed law of gravity, from so simple a beginning endless forms most beautiful and most wonderful have been, and are being, evolved."[137] Nevertheless, such progress as can be discerned in the history of life is, on Darwin's view, a by-product of more fundamental laws and processes—variability, inheritance, the geometrical ratio of population increase, the struggle for existence, and (consequently) natural selection. Darwin's intellectual heirs, emphasizing that variability occurs in all directions and that greater complexity is not adaptive in all environments, have made anti-progressionism something of a shibboleth.

---

136 Le Roy, *Exigence idéaliste*, 82n1. Also: "We have discussed the views presented here so often and so closely, he and I, that we have come to arrange them in the same order, to express them in almost the same words, and that we ourselves now no longer know how to distinguish each of our own contributions," in Le Roy, *Origines humaines*, 8.

137 Darwin, *Origin of Species*, 490.

Teilhard, by contrast, embeds the progress that is a general feature of faunal succession (even if not of the phylogenetic history of each individual species) into a larger "cosmic law of complexity-consciousness" introduced in the postscript of *Le Phénomène humain*:

> the substance of these long pages can be summed up in this simple affirmation: ... the universe presents itself to us, physico-chemically, as being in the process of organic involution upon itself (from the extremely simple to the extremely complex)—and, moreover, this particular involution "of complexity" is empirically connected to a correlative increase of interiorization, that is to say of the psyche or consciousness.... The particular property, possessed by terrestrial substances, of becoming ever more vitalized as they become increasingly complex is only the local manifestation and expression of a trend as universal as (and no doubt even more significant than) those already identified by Science, trends which cause the cosmic layers not only to expand explosively as a wave but also to condense into corpuscles under the action of electromagnetic and gravitational forces, or even to dematerialize, the different trends probably being strictly interconnected, as we shall one day realize.[138]

The second theme in Teilhard's theology of nature is anthropological. Although Teilhard's work is fundamentally and insistently diachronic, one can detach from it an ahistorical account of the nature of human being. *Le Phénomène humain* is perhaps an odd title for a book that is fundamentally a philosophical history of the universe. So perhaps we should use the title to recall that the work also presents a version of human exceptionalism. Already in his correspondence of 1926–27 he wrote: "I have in mind a work on Man—not specifically prehistoric Man, but Man as the greatest telluric and biological event of our planet.... Geology has, that is to say, some human extensions, which we must begin to disentangle" and "More and more, I am coming to think of Man as *the great terrestrial phenomenon*, the one in which the great geological events and the great progress of life reach their culmination."[139] Human thought constitutes "a 'threshold' or a change of state."[140] Just as the emergence of life had added a biosphere to the cosmos, the emergence of self-conscious beings had added a noosphere.

The third theme returns to diachrony but concerns not the past, but the future. Teilhard's vision is not merely an attempt to see the past history of the world in an orderly way. In 1950, he even wrote that "For some time now the principal interest of my life is no longer Fossil Man, but the Man of tomorrow."[141] The final part of *Le Phénomène humain* is called "Survival" and presents the reader with an account of the destiny of the human race and, more broadly, of all of creation:

138 Teilhard, *Phénomène humain* (1955), 334 (Walls trans., 301).

139 Teilhard in letters of January 16, 1927, and of October 15, 1926, quoted in Cuénot, *Teilhard*, 96n1 and 95 (trans., 71 and 70).

140 Teilhard, *Phénomène humain*, 336 (Walls trans., 303).

141 Teilhard to an unnamed friend, August 30, 1950 (*Letters to Two Friends*, 114).

A harmonized community [*collectivité*] of consciousnesses, equivalent to a kind of super-consciousness; the Earth not only covering itself with myriad grains of thought, but enveloping itself with a single thinking envelope, until, on the sidereal scale, functionally it forms only one vast Grain of Thought; the many individual reflections grouping and strengthening one another in the act of a single unanimous Reflection.[142]

The fourth salient feature of his account of nature is its explicit integration with theological doctrines. The first theme gets only as far as the compatibilism that was, as Teilhard recognized, being defended by de Dorlodot and many others. As early as 1925, Teilhard had written that "far from being incompatible with the existence of a First Cause, transformist views, as outlined here, are rather the most noble and the most uplifting way of representing its influx to us[.] For the Christian transformist, God's creative action is no longer conceived as intrusively forcing his works into the midst of pre-existent beings, but of *causing them to be born* in the womb of things, the successive stages of his work."[143] It also, to be sure, included Teilhard's commitment to finalism (i.e., teleology). His friend Bruno de Solages expressed it well in the context of a larger controversy with Réginald Garrigou-Lagrange over the value of Teilhard's work:

Biological evolution was mechanistic and materialistic. The profound Christian significance of the work of this great scientist [sc. Teilhard] . . . is to have, more than anyone else, succeeded in showing that evolution itself was not able to be anything other than "finalist," that it was moving towards mind [*esprit*], that it could only be explained by mind, and that it postulated at the beginning of things, as it postulated at their end—a transcendent God.[144]

* * * * *

Teilhard's philosophical and theological writings received a mixed reception, among both Catholics and non-Catholics. Among those who appreciated his work were his fellow Jesuit Henri du Lubac, SJ.[145] Among non-Catholics were Theodosius Dobzhansky, who appreciated Teilhard's efforts despite disagreements with significant aspects of his thought, characterizing it as "science illuminated by . . . mystical insights."[146] Julian Huxley (grandson of Thomas Huxley), secretary of the Zoological Society of London and the first president of the British Humanist Association, wrote that "the linking of evolutionary biology with Christian theology is his unique contribution to thought, enabling thousands of Christians to accept the greatest scientific discovery since Newton . . . and so pave the way for the eventual reconciliation of science and religion."[147] On the

---

142 Teilhard, *Phénomène humain*, 279 (cf. Walls trans., 251).

143 Teilhard, "Paradoxe transformiste," 80n1 (trans., 102n1).

144 Bruno de Solages, "Honneur de la théologie," 83.

145 See Du Lubac, *Religion of Teilhard* and *Teilhard: The Man and his Meaning*.

146 Dobzhansky, *Biology of Ultimate Concern*, 115.

147 Julian Huxley, "Foreword," to George B. Barbour, *In the Field with Teilhard*, 8.

other side, Peter Medawar, British biologist and Nobel laureate in Physiology or Medicine (1960), called it "nonsense, tricked out with a variety of metaphysical conceits."[148] Among Catholics who did not appreciate Teilhard's work were the traditional Thomist Reginald Garrigou-Lagrange[149] and Dietrich von Hildebrand.[150] Étienne Gilson called Teilhard's work "theology-fiction."[151]

* * * * *

Although Teilhard was never prohibited from publishing his purely scientific work, he was denied permission to publish his philosophical and theological books, for reasons that will be explained in chapter 15.

148 Medawar, Review of *Phenomenon of Man*, 99.

149 Garrigou-Lagrange, "La Nouvelle Théologie."

150 Hildebrand, *Trojan Horse*, 90, 96, 139–40, and 176.

151 Gilson, *Tribulations de Sophie*, 68.

THE OFFICIAL CHURCH
(1931–1950)

Lack of success in suppressing de Dorlodot's book did not put an end to efforts to keep Catholic evolutionists from extending evolutionary biology to the origin of the human body. Over the course of the 1930s, several more books were delated to Rome.

1. POPE PIUS XII (R. 1939–1958)

Pope Pius XII first addressed the questions raised by the paleoetiological sciences early in his pontificate, in an address to the Pontifical Academy of Sciences delivered on November 30, 1941. There he said: "Multiple lines of research on problems concerning the origin of man, both in paleontology and in biology and morphology, have not yet yielded any positively clear and certain results. So nothing remains to do but to leave to the future the resolution of the problem of whether one day science, informed and guided by revelation, will be able to give trustworthy and definitive results on a matter of such great importance."[1]

Some commentators have read much more into the address than can be found there. Maurizio Flick, in a passage that has unfortunately worked its way into the Anglophone secondary literature, said that the pope indicated three "elements [which] must

---

1 Pius XII, Allocutio III, 506.

be retained as certainly attested by the sacred author, without any possibility of an allegorical interpretation."[2] On this, Flick is incorrect. The address does clearly teach the first of Flick's three elements—"the essential superiority of man in relation to other animals," but neither there nor anywhere else does it make any reference whatsoever to allegorical interpretation.

Two passages address the question of human origins.

In the first, Pius said: "And as the heavens and the earth were made, and the earth was formless and void, and the Spirit of God moved upon the waters; so was man formed out of the mud of the earth, and God breathed into his face the spirit of life, and man became a living person. Here is the macrocosm, which is the universe of worlds, before the microcosm, which is man."[3] The choice of words follows closely (but not perfectly) Antonio Martini's translation of the Vulgate, too closely, I think, to conclude that Pius intended to insist on a non-allegorical interpretation. All the more is that true because Pius's point was not to address the question of evolution, but to articulate the theme of macrocosm and microcosm.

The second passage relevant to the elements on Flick's list comes in a passage immediately after a reference to the Garden of Eden and the naming of the animals. There Pius went on to say that "Even in the midst of that multitude of beings subject to him, he felt sadly alone and sought in vain for a face that resembled him and had a ray of that divine image, with which the eye of every son of Adam shines. Only from man could there come another man who would call him father and progenitor; and the helper given by God to the first man comes also from him."[4] I think that Pius here probably did intend that Flick's second element, "the derivation of the body of the first woman from the first man," should be taken literally (as the *responsum* of the Biblical Commission in 1909 had said should be done), but Pius does not *explicitly* rule out an allegorical interpretation.

What cannot be defended, however, is Flick's comment on the third element, the one perhaps the most important to the topic of this book: "the impossibility that the father and progenitor of a man can be other than a man, i.e., the impossibility that the first man could have been the son of an animal, generated by the latter in the proper sense of the term." Augustin Bea, in an article quoted by Flick, had said the same thing a few years before. The passage from the allocution is not, however, about the origin of *the first* man, but how God will respond to the problem of Adam's loneliness; its reference is quite explicitly about the origin of *other* men, and indeed "another man *who would call him father and progenitor*." Obviously the first man could not himself have come from other men and the only men who could call the first man father would be those who came from him. It is worth noting that Bea's emphasis on Adam's not having an animal as "father and ancestor [*Ahn*]" does not keep him from adding that "whether the animal

2 Flick, "Origine del corpo del primo uomo," 402. The Anglophone literature in question is Messenger, "Evolution and Theology Today," 187–88, and Don O'Leary, *Roman Catholicism and Modern Science*, 142.

3 Pius XII, Allocutio III, 506.

4 Pius XII, Allocutio III, 506.

world made some contribution to the formation of one part of the human being, of the body, is left open,"[5] as one among the yet unsolved subjects of the sciences mentioned by Pope Pius above.

Pope Pius addressed these questions again in 1943, the fiftieth anniversary of the publication of Pope Leo's seminal *Providentissimus Deus*, in another seminal encyclical, entitled *Divino afflante Spiritu*. There he reaffirmed the principles articulated in the earlier encyclical, but also emphasized the value to Catholic exegesis of new work in archeology and in literary studies. His emphasis was not on questions raised by the natural sciences. Still, one should note this remark (made with explicit reference to history, but applicable to scientific questions as well): "For a number of things . . . have been explained either not at all or not satisfactorily by the commentators of past ages, since they generally lacked the knowledge necessary to make them clear. How difficult, and almost unintelligible, it was, even for the Fathers, to handle certain questions is shown, for example, by the repeated efforts of many of them to interpret the first chapters of Genesis."[6]

In about 1947, Emmanuel Cardinal Suhard, then archbishop of Paris, sent to Pope Pius two questions about the interpretation of Scripture, one explicitly about the historicity of the first eleven chapters of Genesis. These Pope Pius passed on to the Biblical Commission and, on January 16, 1948, the Commission published, with the pope's approval, their reply: "The question of the literary forms of the first eleven chapters of Genesis is very obscure and complex. . . . The first duty in scholarly exegesis . . . is to assemble, without prejudgments, all the material of the paleontological and historical, and of the epigraphical and literary, sciences. It is only in that way that one can hope to see more clearly the true nature of certain narratives in the first chapters of Genesis."[7] The texts in question contain "a popular description" of the origin of the human race. It would not be quite correct to call the narratives *un*historical, but it would not be correct either to see them as "historical" if that meant classifying them in either the classical or the modern sense of that term.

For more on Pius XII, see chapter 16.

2. THE HOLY OFFICE

a. The Bergounioux Case (1932)

On November 27, 1931, Fréderic-Marie Bergounioux (b. 1900), a Franciscan priest recently ordained and newly appointed to teach paleontology at the Institut catholique de Toulouse, gave at that Institute an introductory lecture to a public course in geology, a lecture in which he had offered a stylistically rather poetic account of the progressive history of life on earth (and the associated fact of evolution), culminating in "the crown

---

5 Bea, "Neuere Probleme," 77.

6 Pius XII, *Divino afflante Spiritu*, 313 (trans., ¶31).

7 Jacques M. Vosté (secretary of the Pontifical Biblical Commission), "Epistula," 47.

of creation," man. Publication of the lecture in the Institute's *Bulletin* led to another letter from Gemelli to the Holy Father.

Gemelli complained to the pope that Bergounioux's account of the finalism found in nature—"a progressive march of living things towards an ever more complex organizations of the nervous system, i.e., an orientation of all creation towards man"[8]—implies (even though it does not explicitly say) that human beings had animal ancestors. That thesis, representing the ideas of Édouard Le Roy and Teilhard, seemed to Gemelli to be a grave danger for the integrity of Catholic doctrine.[9]

Responsibility for reviewing the book was given to Giovanni Pepe, who submitted his *votum* in November 1932,[10] emphasizing that Bergounioux had not committed himself with regard to the animal ancestry of man. It would be better to wait and to judge his ideas on what he might actually write in the future, rather than to make suppositions about his ideas on these questions.

At the preparatory congregation (on March 6, 1933), the consultors voted unanimously not to act on the case (*reponatur*).[11] At the general congregation (March 15), the cardinals concurred, but also asked that that the nuncio "paternally admonish professor Bergounioux to be careful in the treatment of such dangerous matters," a recommendation that was approved by the pope the following day.[12]

b. The Rüschkamp Case (1934)

Rüschkamp came to the attention of the Holy Office in 1933, when Agostino Gemelli, in one of his complaints about the ideas of Teilhard de Chardin, mentioned that Felix Rüschkamp had also supported an evolutionary account of human origins in his article on Peking Man in *Stimmen der Zeit*.[13] The Holy Office prepared a *pro-memoria* in which, although it recognized that Rüschkamp had not defended the animal origins of the human body, it said that it was clear from what Rüschkamp had said that he was sympathetic to the idea. The Society of Jesus was to prohibit him from addressing the matter either in teaching or in writing.[14] It then added:

> At a time when this question troubles so many people, there are many who want the
> Holy Office to issue directive norms about how to proceed in recent discussions on
> the origin of the human body from an animal species. This seems very opportune,

8 Bergounioux, "Rythme dans la création," 223.

9 Gemelli to Pius XI, January 22, 1932 (doc. 1, CL 1932/148, ADDF).

10 Mons. Giovanni Pepe, "Intorno alla prolusione del Prof. F. Bergounioux all'Università Cattolica di Tolosa, su 'Le rythme dans la Création'" (doc. 4, CL 1932/148, ADDF).

11 Present were Giuseppe Pizzardo, Giuseppe Palica, Marco Sales, Luigi Santoro, Guglielmo Arendt, Lorenzo di San Basilio, Ernesto Ruffini, Pietro Vidal, Alfredo Ottaviani, Luigi Hudal, Alfonso Gasperini, and Giuseppe Latini (Minutes [fol. 21, doc. 5, CL 1932/148, ADDF]).

12 Minutes.

13 Gemelli to Nicola Canali (assessor at the Holy Office), July 22, 1933 (doc. 12, CL 1931/1528, ADDF).

14 Holy Office, *Pro memoria*, August 3, 1934 (fol. 62, doc. 17, CL 1931/1528, ADDF).

since there are those who draw from the silence of the Holy Office the conclusion that there is no objection, at least in light of recent events, to saying that, science having discovered it to be so, the evolution of the human body from an animal one can be openly defended by Catholic authors in books and periodicals.

However opportune the issuance of such norms may have seemed to the author of the *pro-memoria*, no such norms were in fact ever produced by the Holy Office.

The *pro-memoria* containing the personal prohibition was sent to Ledóchowski. Rüschkamp's name did not come to the attention of the Holy Office again; later adverse reaction to his lectures and articles was handled by the curia of the Society of Jesus, as will be discussed below.

c. The Messenger & Paquier Cases (1933–1938)

In January 1933, two more complaints against Catholic-evolutionist books arrived at the Holy Office.

The first of the two letters concerned Messenger's *Evolution and Theology*. On January 19, 1933, Gaetano Cardinal Bisleti, president of the Pontifical Biblical Commission and prefect of the Congregation for Seminaries and Educational Institutions, delated Messenger's *Evolution and Theology* to the Holy Office, commenting that "the author . . . deviates substantially from the Catholic tradition in the matter of the creation of the human body, giving a large rôle to the theory of evolution" and that "the book is clearly dangerous, above all for young clerics." He added that Alexis Cardinal Lépicier "had recently requested this Holy Dicastery [the Sacred Congregation of Seminaries and Universities] for permission to forbid it in the English and Bede Colleges, of which he is the Protector."[15]

The second complaint concerned Paquier's *La Création et l'évolution*. The complaint in this case came from a Countess de Fondeville by way of the abbot of the Three Fountains in Rome. It was in the hands of the Holy Office by January 9, 1933.[16]

✳ ✳ ✳ ✳ ✳

The task of reviewing Paquier's book was first assigned to Ernesto Ruffini (on February 4, 1933), but, despite several requests, he never submitted a *votum*.[17] On February 3, 1934, Gemelli wrote a two-page letter (whether on request or at his own initiative is not clear) expressing his concerns about the book:

> In this book, the author maintains the same ideas on the origin of man as does Fr. Teilhard de Chardin (which I have already mentioned to the Holy Office), namely that "while the soul of man was created by God, the body could have had its origin

---

15 Bisletti to Sbarretti, January 19, 1933 (fol. 1, doc. 1, CL 1933/246, ADDF).

16 Note, registered January 9, 1933 (fol. 1, doc. 1, CL 1933/51, ADDF). The letter of complaint itself is not in the archives of the Holy Office. The note says only that the book was delated on account of its evolutionism.

17 Minutes of the preparatory congregation of February 4, 1933 (fol. 2, doc. 3, CL 1933/51, ADDF).

337

in an evolutionary process." As with Fr. Teilhard, what is asserted is not explicitly evolutionary, although no doubt would arise in a competent reader.

It seems to me that the case of this author is even more serious than that of Fr. Teilhard de Chardin because this is a work of popularization . . . . All the more is it dangerous because the teaching on the problem of the origin of man defended here is said to be in harmony with the decisions of the Biblical Commission.[18]

At the next meeting of a preparatory congregation (February 17, 1934), however, the consultors decided to seek the opinion of a specialist. The case was folded into the Messenger case.[19]

＊ ＊ ＊ ＊ ＊

The task of reviewing Messenger's book had meanwhile been assigned already (on January 28, 1933) to Irish Dominican Michael Browne.[20] Browne had been teaching philosophy at the Pontifical University of Saint Thomas Aquinas since 1919, but, unfortunately for the prompt resolution of the case, had just been appointed *rector magnificus* of his university. As a result, the case remained on hold nearly two years, awaiting Browne's *votum* (which arrived only at the beginning of 1935). Apologizing for the delay, Browne noted not only his other duties, but also the "intrinsic difficulty of the examination of the book."[21]

Browne began his *votum* with a brief review of Messenger's main conclusions, and then offered some general remarks about the book. He acknowledged that there was much there that would be of value to theologians interested in the question, but thought that the author was in some places too bold (*audax*) and that other passages were badly worded (*male sonans*, one of the standard ecclesiastical censures). For example, in emphasizing the importance of caution, Messenger wrote: "Should the Church decide that Adam's body was formed immediately and exclusively by God from inanimate matter, a Catholic author who had hitherto held the contrary would at once wholeheartedly admit that his own interpretation of Scripture had been incorrect and that those Fathers whose ideas he adopted and developed *were not safe guides* in the matter"[22] (emphasis Browne's, not Messenger's). But Browne began the concluding section of his *votum* cautiously in the face of what he emphasized was a difficult question. He acknowledged the orthodoxy of a mitigated evolutionism on a number of points. The issue turned on two others: One was "the absolute immediacy or unicity of Divine efficient causality for the formation of body of the first man, since they insert another cause, instrumentally co-acting with God and below God." The other was "the absolute immediacy of the 'slime of the earth'

---

18 Gemelli to Canali, February 3, 1934 (folio 3–4 (at 3), doc. 4, CL 1933/246, ADDF).

19 Minutes of preparatory congregation of February 17, 1934 (fol. 5, doc. 5, CL 1933/51, ADDF).

20 Minutes of preparatory congregation of February 3, 1933 (fol. 3, doc. 3, CL 1933/51, ADDF).

21 Browne to Index, June 12, 1935, and *Votum*, (fol. 4, doc. 4, CL 1933/246, ADDF).

22 Browne, *Votum*, 4; Messenger, *Evolution and Theology*, 280.

(*limus terrae*) as the kind of material cause."[23] He cited as relevant to the question the decree of Cologne, the handling of the Leroy, Zahm, and Bonomelli cases, and the 1909 *responsum* of the Biblical Commission. Next, he included a list of fifteen Catholic philosophers and theologians who had addressed the issue, ranging from a few who thought that immediacy *was* a matter of faith, through rather more who qualified it only as the prevailing view (*sententia communis*), to a few compatibilists who emphasized that the Church had not addressed the issue.

He acknowledged that there was a general tendency to favor immediate formation, but emphasized, with respect to the statement of the Biblical Commission, that the origin of the first human being would be distinctive even if a body adapted to the reception of a human soul were produced by natural processes. In the end, he said that he would not advise the Congregation to put the book on the *Index*.

A preparatory congregation met on May 25, 1936, and agreed on a recommendation for disposition of the case. Several of the consultors emphasized the connection between this case and that of de Dorlodot. In the end, eight consultors[24] wanted the author's bishop to enjoin him not to reprint the book without a review of the matter by ecclesiastical authorities; two[25] wanted the bishop to have the author withdraw the book from sale. Giuseppe Latini, Promoter of Justice at the Holy Office, who voted on the prevailing side, submitted his own thoughts on the matter in writing.[26] He thought that question needed to be subjected to careful study in light of the most recent historical, physical, physiological, astronomical, and especially geological discoveries. All the consultors agreed that an internal study of evolutionism in general would be in order.

The general congregation met on June 10, 1936. Two of the cardinals present[27] recommended "silence, or ignoring the book [*dissimulandum*] for now;" the others[28] agreed with the secretary that "the bishop should enjoin the author to withdraw the book from sale and, as is his obligation, not to publish any books without a special authorization and an *imprimatur* from his bishop."[29]

At the papal audience the next day, Pope Pius XI accepted the recommendation of the two and requested that the Holy Office get from Wilhelm Schmidt "an authoritative account of the scientific data of anthropological paleontology."[30] Schmidt was asked to

---

23 Browne, *Votum*, 7–8.

24 Alfredo Ottaviani, Giuseppe Palica, Celso Costatini, Giovanni Lottini, Luigi Santoro, Pedro Vidal, Timoteo Schaefer, and Ernesto Ruffini (fol. 8, doc. 6, CL 1933/246, ADDF).

25 Lorenzo di S. Basilio and Alfonso Gasperini (fol. 8, doc. 6, CL 1933/246, ADDF).

26 Latini, "Impressions of the Promoter of Justice," May 22, 1936 (fol. 9, doc. 6A, CL 1933/246, ADDF).

27 Francesco Marchetti Selvaggiani (later secretary of the Holy Office) and Pietro Fumasoni Biondi (prefect of the Congregation for Propagation of the Faith) (fol. 10v, doc. 6, CL 1933/246, ADDF).

28 Cardinals Donato Sbarretti, Gaetano Bisleti, Lorenzo Lauri, Raffaello Carlo Rossi, Nicola Canali, as well as Alfredo Ottaviani (assessor), Giovanni Lottini (commissioner), and Giuseppe Latini (promoter of justice) (fol. 10, doc. 6, CL 1933/246, ADDF, and (for the identification of those present) Acta C[ongregationis] G[eneralis] 1936 (unpaginated but in imperfectly chronological order), ADDF).

29 Minutes of the general congregation of June 10, 1936 (fol. 10v, doc. 6, CL 1933/246, ADDF).

30 Minutes of the general congregation of June 10 and (for the identification of those present) (Acta CG 1936).

prepare a study of the question (or to suggest to the Holy Office someone else who could do so), but he expressed reservations about the project, which the notes in the archives of the Holy Office summarize as follows:

> It would, for now, be inopportune for the Holy Office to issue a document on a question on which the scientific data remain very uncertain and are subject to constant revision.
>
> The same question has, in addition to its scientific aspect, this dogmatic one: how could the evolutionistic hypothesis of the origin of the human body from an inferior animal species be reconciled with revealed doctrine? This second, dogmatic, aspect, should be taken up by a theologian.[31]

Schmidt nevertheless agreed to write a report, with the assistance of his colleagues, but then dragged his feet. The preparatory congregation that met on April 17, 1937, wanted an answer from Schmidt as to what he had done to prepare the requested study.[32] He had to be asked again the next April, and promised that it would be ready soon.[33]

By summer, Schmidt had given to the Holy Office a sixty-seven page report entitled "Älteste Menschheit," written, the notes at the Holy Office comment, some ten years earlier.[34] The document's focus was the more general question of primitive man and most of it had little direct relevance to the question put to him by the Holy Office. The relevant comments came in the final pages,[35] where, in the document's original form, he had expressed his doubt that science had yet provided much evidence in favor of the animal origins of the human body. Nevertheless, he did not rule out the possibility that the situation would change:

> Our best attitude with regard to the question of the descent of man, so far as his bodily form is concerned, must be a patiently expectant one, with an evenly balanced mind, waiting till further discoveries and researches give us such a decisive result as has already been attained with regard to the question of the descent of the soul of man from some earlier existing forms of life. This latter question has already been settled in the negative with complete certainty.[36]

Minutes of the general congregation of June 10, 1936.

31 "Colloquio del sostituto alla censura dei libri con il P. Schmidt," June 13, 1936 (fol. 11, doc. 6bis, CL 1933/246, ADDF).

32 Note, April 17, 1937 (fol. 12, doc. 7, CL 1933/246, ADDF) and letter from the Holy Office to Schmidt, April 22, 1937 (fol. 13, doc. 8).

33 Notes, June 3, 1937, and April 26, 1938 (fol. 15, doc. 9, CL 1933/246, ADDF).

34 Schmidt, "Älteste Menschheit" (fol. 18–89, doc. 10, CL 1933/246, ADDF). Schmidt had published an English version of this essay as "Primitive Man," the first chapter in volume 1 of Edward Eyre, *European Civilization*, 1–82. Joseph Henninger, who found a version of the paper in a microfilmed collection of Schmidt's papers, has suggested that the paper was written in 1931 and revised in 1937 (Schmidt, *Wege der Kulturen*, xv–xvi). He published the version from the microfilm in *Wege*, 45–88. The English translation, in Henninger's opinion, is not always reliable. The three versions vary in ways that do not affect the passages relevant to our topic.

35 Schmidt, "Älteste Menschheit," typescript, 61–67 (published versions: German, 85–88; English, 76–82).

36 Schmidt, "Älteste Menschheit," typescript, 66 (published versions: German, 88; English, 81).

Once the significance of Peking Man became known, however, Schmidt added an additional thought:

> The principle of patient waiting and diligent research has already been confirmed in the case of the most recent prehistorical find, *Sinanthropus pekinensis*. This anthropological find, currently the earliest, . . . shows strong development of the so-called lower bodily traits—receding forehead, eyebrow ridges, etc. However, his true human nature is assured by the rich array of bone, horn, and stone tools, through his knowledge of fire, and through undeniable signs of the burial of the dead.[37]

The records of the Holy Office summarize the report as follows: "Fr. Schmidt concluded, that, according to the current state of science in the matter of the origin of man from a lower species of animal: the evolutionary hypothesis must be ruled out for the origin of the human soul, but it cannot be absolutely ruled out in the case of the human body. On that point, science is uncertain and subject to continuous revision. It would, therefore, be best to continue waiting."[38]

The report was taken up at the next preparatory congregation, on June 18, 1938, and, as Schmidt had recommended, a second opinion was solicited from Breuil, who was to be asked where the question of human evolution stood in general and in particular what he thought of Schmidt's *votum*. On June 22, 1938, the general congregation recommended that the matter be set aside (*reponatur*). At the audience on the following day, Pope Pius asked to see Schmidt's report before making his decision.[39]

Messenger's book was not, in the end, placed on the *Index*.

d. The de Lapparent Case (1944–1946)

Shortly after de Lapparent's *Nos Origines* was published, a parishioner from Nanterre, one Jean-Baptiste Wilfrid, wrote two intemperate letters denouncing the book to Emmanuel Cardinal Suhard, then archbishop of Paris. Philosophical and scientific questions concerning the origin of the world and particularly of man were being much discussed by French theologians and scientists, and this was not the only work on the topic that had come to the attention of the chancery.

The year before, a Franciscan press had published Georges Salet and Louis Lafont's *L'Évolution régressive*, a rather strange book proposing, for both scientific and theological reasons, to replace the conventional theory of evolution with the idea that all living things had been created immortal, a feature they had lost as a consequence of the original sin. The *imprimatur* had come from Auguste Gaudel, long professor of theology at the Université de Strasbourg and author of the article on original sin in the *Dictionnaire de*

---

37 Written by hand at the end of the typescript, 67; added as a footnote to the paragraph just quoted in Henninger, 88; not included in the published English version.

38 Memorandum "Circo uno studio sull'evoluzionismo," undated, but (on internal evidence) the week following Schmidt's submission of his report, so in mid-1938 (fol. 99, Varie [without document number], CL 1933/246, ADDF).

39 Minutes of the congregations, June 1939 (fol. 91, doc. 11, CL 1933/246, ADDF).

théologie catholique, but since 1941 bishop of Fréjus and Toulon. Gaudel had expressed his doubts about the thesis in a letter to the authors, but, since the book was not inconsistent with Catholic doctrine, he thought the authors should be free to express their views. He pointed out that most spiritualist (i.e., non-materialist) paleontologists found the idea of an evolution guided by Providence quite plausible, but he hoped that Salet and Lafont's book would succeed in drawing greater attention to some of the as-yet unresolved problems facing moderate evolutionism.[40] The appearance of the book led to spirited complaints to Suhard (from de Lapparent, Bégouën, and five other scientists, both clerical and lay), in whose archdiocese the book had been published.

Suhard asked Guy de Broglie, SJ, professor of dogmatic theology at the Institut catholique de Paris, to write a report on the matter for the archdiocesan Conseil de Vigilance, which took the matter up at its meetings of July 19 and 26, 1944.[41] All the complainants agreed that the book's fundamental thesis contradicted everything that paleontology tells us about faunal succession. All but one said that even the critique of evolution was full of errors. Theologically, the complainants added, the book showed the authors' lack of theological formation. It interpreted magisterial documents in the strictest way (integralism) and saw the Bible as an infallible mine of scientific information (concordism). Finally, publication of the book was inopportune. Many readers would get the idea that the Church was recommending the book to readers, a problem for which the Church should prepare.

De Broglie emphasized that a scientific evaluation of the book was beyond the competence of the council. Since the magisterium had never addressed the question of the initial immortality of plants and animals, the central thesis of the book could hardly be said to merit a theological censure. Nevertheless, the book's theology, its tendencies more than any explicit statements, left something to be desired. Though this should not be exaggerated, publication of the book had been inopportune for two reasons. First, it would encourage in pious but uninformed Catholics an excessive suspicion of science and then a renewed integralism and concordism. Second, unbelievers would use the book to discredit Catholic theology and science.

What should the council do about the book? De Broglie thought that any official explicit objection to the book would also be inopportune. It would injure the bishop who had permitted its publication. Worse, an official censure would be interpreted by some Catholic evolutionists as supporting *their* sometimes excessive claims to scientific and philosophical liberty. If a response is needed it all, it would be best just to publish a general statement (with only an opaque reference to the book in question), that "the diocesan authorities wish to remind everyone that an ecclesiastical *imprimatur* . . . is nothing more than a permission to publish. Such a permission certifies that the work which has

40 Gaudel to Salet and Lafont, published in their *Évolution régressive,* 299–301.

41 De Broglie, Rapport on *L'Évolution régressive* to the Conseil de Vigilance, undated, but before July 19, 1944 (fol. 3–11, doc. 3, CL 62/1945, ADDF). De Broglie is "E. de Broglie" in the documents of the Conseil.

received it contains nothing heterodox, but does not in any way guarantee the scientific, exegetical, philosophical, or even theological soundness of the views there proposed."[42]

The same meeting also took up the complaint against de Lapparent's *Nos Origines*. In this case, too, Suhard asked de Broglie for his opinion of the booklet. De Broglie wrote that, despite the merits of the work, it had a serious and overarching flaw. The principle that guided the work was that the impossibility of conflict between theology and science was a consequence of a heterogeneity of domains (as between ethics and algebra). If only each stuck to its own domain, de Lapparent had said, there would be no problem. De Broglie replied that, although the Church agreed with the impossibility thesis, which had been asserted at Vatican I, the justification was not heterogeneity of domains, but simply the harmony of truth. God would not reveal anything that contradicted the *truths* discovered by science, though He might well reveal things within the domains explored by secular inquiry (scientific, philosophical, or historical). Indeed He had done so when knowledge of those truths was important to salvation. This became particularly important in the question of the origin of the human race, with respect to which de Lapparent had said that "how man appeared is a matter of anthropology, and is of no religious importance." De Broglie thought that de Lapparent's principles kept him from being firm and precise in his rejection of polygenism.[43]

What should the Church do about the pamphlet? De Broglie said that a public condemnation of the pamphlet would not only be hard on the author and the Institut catholique, where he taught, but would only irritate Catholics who had some sympathy with what de Lapparent had said. Better would be an exposition of the principles relevant to such discussions.[44]

In July, Suhard convened two meetings of the archdiocesan Vigilance Committee. In full agreement with de Broglie, the committee prepared a draft of such a note, irenic in tone and without reference to any particular author or publication. It began with the articulation of principles (and the importance of avoiding both excessive literalism and excessive liberalism). It then proceeded to identify what it saw as the principal historical facts affirmed in the first chapters of Genesis. It began with the list of facts proposed by the Pontifical Biblical Commission in 1909, but thought that it was important to go beyond that *responsum*, both offering reasons why those facts had the importance ascribed to them and acknowledging that the facts varied both with respect to their importance and their certainty. About evolution and anthropogenesis, it affirmed the doctrines of supernatural gifts (and more generally, divine preparation of "conditions of life far superior to anything required by human nature") and original sin. Monogenism seems, therefore, to be closely linked to dogma. Finally, the origin of Adam has some kind of priority, both historical and causal, to that of Eve. In conclusion, "as long as these

<hr>

42 De Broglie, Rapport, 7.

43 De Broglie, Report to Suhard, mid-1944, included in "Circa l'opuscolo 'Nos Origines' del Rev. Prof. Albert F. de Lapparent," 2–9 (fol. 21, doc. 6, CL 61/1945, ADDF).

44 De Broglie, Report to Suhard, 9–10.

principles and points are respected [*restent saufs*], Catholics have the right to propose any hypotheses and theories that seem to them to be scientifically well-founded, with regard to the manner in which certain laws of evolution have been able (under the sovereign action of the Creator and His providence) to cooperate in the development of the present world and of the first human beings."[45]

The concerns of the committee were passed on to de Lapparent, who expressed his willingness to rewrite the booklet in light of the objections that had been raised against it.[46]

Suhard also forwarded the draft, by way of the nuncio, to the Holy Office.[47] The Holy Office focused not the Committee's proposed general guidance, but on de Lapparent's booklet, and asked Agustin Bea to prepare a *votum*.

Bea agreed with de Broglie that de Lapparent's heterogeneity-of-domains principle would not work as an explanation of the impossibility of contradiction between theology and science. He added that de Lapparent seemed to limit inerrancy to things that God intended to teach us, i.e., to religious truths, but not to historical facts connected with those truths. The latter were, according to de Lapparent, only the "necessary vehicle" of the great revealed teachings.[48]

With regard to the particular topics addressed by de Lapparent, Bea saw problems in his treatment of anthropogenesis. The presentation seemed too close to assuming the truth of evolutionism despite the reservations about evolutionary anthropogenesis expressed by Pope Pius XII in his address of 1941.[49] It was not ready enough to acknowledge that the relevant chapters of Genesis, whatever else they taught, also taught some historical facts.[50] De Lapparent was also too ready to apply his account of the separation of the fields to the question of polygenesis, and did not seem ready to accept monogenesis as *de fide divina et catholica*.[51]

Bea concluded his *votum* by suggesting that a work on these topics would be useful to catechists, but it should not be, as *Nos Origines* was, a booklet of a mere forty pages and should not be written by de Lapparent. The content of the book was sufficiently objectionable to warrant a formal condemnation by the Holy Office, but the facts that the booklet was no longer available and that a public prohibition would be a severe blow to the Institut catholique de Paris suggested that such a disposition of the case would be neither necessary nor advisable. De Lapparent should not be permitted to undertake

---

45 Conseil de Vigilance, "Projet d'une note officielle, rappelant les principes dont doivent s'inspirer les catholiques dans les questions philosophiques ou scientifiques qui concernent les origines du monde et de l'homme," July 19 and 26, 1944, 10 (fol. 23–32, doc. 7, CL 61/1945, ADDF).

46 Conseil de Vigilance, "Remarques sur l'opuscule intitulé 'Nos Origines,'" August 6, 1944 (fol. 5, doc. 3, CL 61/1945, ADDF) and letter of de Broglie to Suhard, reprinted as Sommario no. 2 in "Circa l'opuscolo 'Nos Origines,'" 11.

47 Suhard to Angelo Giuseppe Roncalli (nuncio), 10–11 (reprinted as Sommario no. 1 in Holy Office, "Circa l'opuscolo 'Nos Origines'").

48 Bea, *Votum*, March 27, 1945, 4–5 (fol. 47, doc. 8, CL 61/1945, ADDF); De Lapparent, *Nos Origines*, 20.

49 Bea, *Votum*, 7–8.

50 Bea, *Votum*, 9.

51 Bea, *Votum*, 6.

to rewrite the booklet. If the Archdiocese of Paris were to issue instructions on how the question of anthropogenesis should be treated in catechesis and from the pulpit, and Bea was not certain that such a note should be issued at all, it should be in very general terms, since "a number of the questions have not been well-enough thought through to allow a positive and determinate statement from ecclesiastical authorities."[52]

The reports were reviewed by the consultors at the Holy Office in a preparatory congregation held on April 30, 1945. Thirteen of the sixteen in attendance thought that it would not be opportune to put the booklet on the *Index*, but that the author should make a correction of the errors in question, either by a new edition or by an entirely new book. Three thought that the author should be advised of the errors in the booklet and asked to write another booklet correcting them. The cardinals, at the general congregation held on May 9, wanted Suhard to tell de Lapparent that, if the book was not put on the *Index* it was only out of concern for the reputation of the Institut. He was to be prohibited from writing a new edition, or indeed anything else on this topic. The curia should publish some appropriate remarks on the booklet in the *Semaine religieuse* and should encourage publication of a better book on the subject. The pope approved this resolution of the case on May 10.[53]

The actions of the Holy Office occasioned two reactions from France. The first came in October 1945, from Marcel Bith, SJ, the Society's Paris provincial.[54] Bith was particularly concerned about the rise of Communism in France and a certain "divorce" of the clergy from the currents of French political and intellectual life. French Communists were using science to attack the Church. The Church needed to launch a counter-attack, but "too often our scientists are unwilling to act, because they have the impression that, not only are they not encouraged to do so, but often they are threatened with being delated to the authorities as soon as they venture to propose a philosophical interpretation of their research."[55] The second, in December 1945, was a letter from the French ambassador to the Holy See, philosopher Jacques Maritain, to Giovanni Battista Montini (then *sostituto* at the Secretariat of State).[56] Both Bith and Maritain emphasized that de Lapparent's good will, his readiness to rewrite the booklet in response to the criticisms that had been raised, made the actions of the Holy Office particularly inappropriate.

In February 1946, the Holy Office gave the matter renewed consideration, at the preparatory congregation held on the 4th and at the general congregation on the 13th.[57] It decided to allow de Lapparent to continue his work on this topic, but with an

---

52 Bea, *Votum*, 12–14.

53 Holy Office, Memorandum summarizing disposition of the case (fol. 49, doc. 10, CL 61/1945, ADDF).

54 Bith, Rapporto "L'Église face à l'atheisme contemporain" (included in Holy Office Protocol doc. 5/46, "I: Correnti ateistiche in Francia [and] II: Dopo la condanna dell'opuscolo 'Nos Origines' del Rev. de Lapparent," January 1946, 2–11 (fol. 61, CL 61/1945, ADDF)).

55 Bith, "Église," 8–9.

56 Maritain to Montini, December 20, 1945 (fol. 52–56, doc. 13, CL 61/1945, ADDF; reprinted in Holy Office, "Correnti ateistiche," 11–14).

57 Minutes of particular congregation: "Correnti ateistiche in Francia: Circa la condanna dell opuscolo 'Nos origines' del

admonition to do so in cooperation with experts in theology and in Biblical studies. They added an internal note about the importance of "proceeding with caution in such cases in order not to give the impression that ecclesiastical authorities are repressing or suffocating any scientific movement, etc."[58] The lifting of the restrictions on de Lapparent was communicated (orally) to Suhard, but apparently de Lapparent did not hear about this, for in a letter of May 5, 1953, Eugène Cardinal Tisserant, papally appointed protector of the Sulpicians, wrote to Ottaviani at the Holy Office asking that the restrictions be lifted.[59] After a review of the case by Bea,[60] Ottaviani wrote back that the restrictions had been lifted in 1946.[61]

e. Another Teilhard Case (1945–47)

Questions about Teilhard's work arose at the Holy Office again right after the war. On August 21, 1945, Garrigou-Lagrange wrote to the Holy Office to express his concern about Teilhard: "He writes a lot about the evolutionary theory of the origin of man. He *categorically denies the existence of a first human couple and presents original sin as a symbol.*"[62] The next year, on June 8, 1946, Roger Beaussart, auxiliary bishop of Paris, wrote to the Holy Office to express his concern about "doctrinal and practical deviations which he had observed in the contemporary clergy."[63] He forwarded several documents illustrating his concerns. Among those was Teilhard's "Vie et planètes." Materials of concern were also forwarded by Angelo Roncalli (later Pope John XXIII), then Papal nuncio in Paris.[64]

Pietro Parente was assigned to write the *votum*, in which he included both a general report reviewing the earlier complaints about Teilhard's work and an examination of two published works, "Le Cône du temps"[65] and "La Formation de la noosphère." His concerns about the article that had been the subject of the first complaint, "Vie et planètes," were the same, he said, as those he had about "La Formation de la noosphère" and had in any case been covered in a separate document distributed in typescript with the formal

---

sac. de Lapparent," February 4, 1946 (fol. 69, doc. 16, CL 61/1945, ADDF); minutes of general congregation: "Gallia—circa opusculum 'Nos Origines' autore Sac. Alberto Lapparent," February 13, 1946 (fol. 71 [misnumbered, should be fol. 78], doc. 17).

58 At the preparatory congregation, consultor Pietro Parente had been particularly insistent about the importance of this mitigation (fol. 70, doc. 16, CL 61/1945, ADDF).

59 Tisserant to Ottaviani, May 5, 1953 (fol. 73, doc. 18, CL 61/1945, ADDF).

60 Bea, "Circa l'opuscolo 'Nos Origines' di A. F. de Lapparent," June 12, 1953 (fol. 80–82, doc. 19, CL 61/1945, ADDF).

61 Ottaviani to Tisserant, June 23, 1953 (fol. 83, doc. 20, CL 61/1945, ADDF).

62 Letter from Garrigou-Lagrange to the Holy Office, August 21, 1945, 1 (doc. 7, SO 293/1946, ADDF). Garrigou-Lagrange wrote again in December 1946 (doc. 27).

63 Letter from Beaussart to the Holy Office, June 8, 1946, 1 (doc. 1, SO 293/1946, ADDF).

64 Including Teilhard, "Quelques Réflexions" (1936), a typescript, and "Un Grand Événement" (1945), apparently written while Teilhard was still in Peking (Cuénot, *Teilhard,* xv and xx [trans., 433 and 440]) (fol. 252–75 and 281, doc. 48 and 50, CL 1528/1931, ADDF).

65 The article had originally appeared as a typescript in Peking, dated February 15, 1942, as "L'Esprit nouveau" (Cuénot, *Teilhard,* xviii (trans., 438)).

votum.[66] That his concern was with Teilhard's philosophical and theological ideas, rather than with the more strictly scientific aspects of evolution, can be seen from the *votum.* About "Le Cône du temps" he wrote:

> It is exultation of the theory of evolution made not by way of scientific evidence and findings, but by way of insights partly philosophical, partly religious and partly poetic. Evolutionism is a theory which does not have universal acceptance in the scientific world; nevertheless, Teilhard, in the garb of a scientist, does have the right to defend it scientifically. As a Christian and as a religious man, however, he should keep an eye on our truths, those of faith and those which form the heritage of our philosophy (so intimately linked with theology). So, for example, one cannot say that Time has no limit, before or after.... Nor is it orthodox to say that the evolution of the world and of man has no limit. He, however, has no hesitation about so indulging in the scientifico-poetic side of things that he puts those truths in danger. Moreover, Teilhard brings matter and spirit so close, indeed fusing them together, that he seems to want to defend an evolutionary transition from one to the other on the strength of the increasing organic complexity of beings.... Many phrases used carelessly here and there demand an explanation in order to remain harmless and not to offend Christian doctrine.

And:

> His is an evanescent image of Jesus Christ, who has become in a certain sense a cosmic reality which does not respond to that of the Gospel and of Christianity.[67]

Then, about "La Formation de la noosphère":

> There would be no objection to such conceptions if the author merely noted human progress by virtue of the *collectivization* of thought and the free will of individuals.

> But the Reverend Father seems to give his noosphere an organic structure which absorbs and transcends human individuals, as if it were a superhuman Reality, which brings to mind the transcendental Ego of the Idealists, in which case the thought, the freedom and the personality of the individual are compromised if not eliminated.

> Finally, it is strange that he indulges, in the name of science, in so many fantasies about the indefinite future of a planetized Humanity while he says little or nothing about religion and never shows any concern for Christian truths about the destiny of Humanity, something which for him, both as a priest and as a scientist, should be the norm, the limit and the touchstone in his evolutionary excursions.[68]

In conclusion, he wrote:

---

66 Parente, typescript comments on "Vie et planètes" (doc. 40, CL 1528/1931, ADDF).

67 Parente, *Votum*, June 10, 1947, 4–5 (fol. 223, doc. 41, CL 1528/1931, ADDF.

68 Parente, *Votum*, 7.

One has the impression of being in the presence of someone uninfluenced by traditional judgments (*spregiudicato*) and a lover of extravagance. His writings are not scientific work, but paradoxical essays which, if they do not lack a foundation in truth, are clouded by attitudes, conceptions, and expressions which are not always reconcilable with the simple and straightforward truths of Christian doctrine. Even if they are not erroneous, some of Teilhard's statements lend themselves to multiple meanings and to false interpretations. It is open to doubt whether science can draw any real benefit from such lucubrations, which, when they are not overly subjective, are at least not objectively well-documented. Nor can one think of them bringing any benefit to religion.[69]

Parente thought that there was a good reason for the Holy Office to intervene, with a *monitum* and a prohibition on Teilhard publishing or speaking without prior review by competent and secure censors. If the unpublished materials were in fact his, he should be expected to write some kind of retraction or clarification. This should, however, all be done "delicately, so as not to harm the honor and respect he has earned among the educated laity."[70]

The matter was taken up by the consultors at the preparatory congregation that met on June 30, 1947. Their recommendation was that Teilhard be forbidden by the superior-general from publishing anything in theology without its having been subjected to strict review. He was, they emphasized, educated in paleontology but not well-formed in theology and should, as far as possible, stick to his own field of competence. The cardinals at the general congregation (July 9) agreed, and that restriction was approved by the pope.[71] The Holy Office informed Janssens of the restriction a few days later.[72]

f. An Appraisal of Ruffini's Anti-Evolutionism

A folder of miscellaneous documents on evolutionism in the archives of the Holy Office[73] contains an orphaned document of particular interest, a *votum* dated November 1949 written by Bea as an evaluation of something by Ruffini entitled "Responsabilità dei paleoantropologi cattolici." Bea says that he was asked to write the *votum*, though it is not clear from the document by whom, or why.[74]

Ruffini had been engaged in an exchange of views with Gregorian paleoanthropologist Vittorio Marcozzi. It began with publication of Marcozzi's *Evoluzione o*

---

69 Parente, *Votum*, 8–9.

70 Parente, *Votum*, 8.

71 Minutes (fol. 230–41, doc. 42, CL 1528/1931, ADDF).

72 Holy Office to Janssens, July 15, 1947 (fol. 242, doc. 43, CL 1528/1931, ADDF).

73 "Evolutionismus in genere (materiale)" (CL1953/224).

74 At the top of the first page of this *votum* is written "His Eminence Cardinal Ernesto Ruffini, 'Responsibilità dei paleoantropologi cattolici.'" Some seven months after the date of the *votum*, on June 3, 1950, *L'Osservatore Romano* published an article by Ruffini with that title. Perhaps the newspaper sent the article to the Holy Office for review before it was willing to publish it. The published version does not include the words quoted by Bea in his *votum*.

creazione?,[75] which led Ruffini to publish an old manuscript of his as *La teoria della evoluzione secondo la scienza e la fede*, to which Marcozzi replied in an article in the *Gregorianum*, all in 1948. On June 3, 1950, *L'Osservatore Romano* published an article by Ruffini entitled "Responsabilità dei paleoantropologi cattolici," but without one phrase to which Bea took exception. Although the article does not name Marcozzi explicitly, historian Agnès Desmazieres, quite reasonably, places the article in the context of that dispute. Most plausible is that the newspaper asked the Holy Office to review the draft before it was willing to publish it.

As a *votum*, of course, it cannot be said to present the official position of the Holy Office. It is not clear what that office did with the *votum* once it had been submitted. Nevertheless, since Bea was a priest on whom both the Jesuit curia and the Holy Office relied in thinking through the question of evolution, his views are worth noting.

Bea began by acknowledging that

> It would certainly be appropriate to provide a warning to theologians and exegetes not to abandon too readily the traditional positions on the formation of the human body, but to take into consideration not only scientific, but also the theological and philosophical arguments against the theory of evolutionism.[76]

Ruffini, however, had gone beyond that:

> Theologians and exegetes will be surprised to see a thesis which the Holy See has tolerated without censure (i.e., a mitigated theistico-finalistic evolutionism) judged [*qualificata*] . . . to be "rash, heretical, or near to heresy" (p. 6), when even the Holy Father, in an address to the Academy which was also cited by His Eminence [sc. Ruffini], did not want to censure it. [In the address, Pope Pius had said] "let us leave to the future the answer to the question, whether one day science, illuminated and guided by revelation, will be able to give a definitive answer in a matter of such importance." In that way, Pius had characterized the attitude Catholics, whether theologian, exegete, or scientist, should take on the question, namely that each can propose and discuss answers on either side of the question, but with the calm and moderation that the gravity and importance of the question demands, while at the same time being willing to submit to the judgment of the Church if it ever should make one. I fear that it would not make a good impression, if, in this matter, an eminent cardinal were to demand, on behalf of tradition, more than the Supreme Pontiff demands in a statement certainly well thought out and proposed on so solemn an occasion.[77]

"The applicability of the general laws of evolution to man" was widely accepted by scientists. "The force of the paleoanthropological argument lies precisely in the undeniable fact that there have been found remains," "many new and important discoveries," which

---

75 Described as the "third edition," this is a reorganized edition of his earlier *Origini dell'uomo*, augmented with new paleoanthropological data.

76 Bea, *Votum*, 1 (fol. 3–6, CL1953/224).

77 Bea, *Votum*, 1–2.

Ruffini had ignored. "That does not decide the question of fact, since the formation of the human body was a free act of God, who could have produced the body of Adam immediately from inanimate earth.... One can cite that against the scientific argument, but one should not minimize the significance of the scientific argument."[78]

He concluded with the judgment that "In the current situation, both those who take the evolutionary origin of the human body as proven and those who exclude it *a priori* are equally to be criticized for insufficient argumentation. In this matter, it would be highly desirable for theologians and exegetes quietly to await the results of rigorously conducted scientific research done by scholars who combine undoubted technical competence with a proven Catholic conscience."[79]

3. THE PONTIFICAL BIBLICAL COMMISSION

In a letter to Emmanuel Célestin Cardinal Suhard, archbishop of Paris,[80] the Pontifical Biblical Commission addressed a question on the historical character of the first eleven chapters of Genesis, one that had been entrusted to it by the pope. The Commission began by emphasizing the hermeneutical liberty promised in *Divino afflante Spiritu*, in light of which its *responsa* of 1909 should in no way be seen as constituting a hindrance to further truly scientific examination of the problems raised by those chapters:

> The question of the literary forms of the first eleven chapters of Genesis is ... obscure and complex. These literary forms do not correspond to any of our classical categories and cannot be judged in the light of either Greco-Latin or modern literary types. One cannot, therefore, either deny or affirm their historicity as a whole without unjustifiably applying to them norms of a literary type to which they do not belong. If it is agreed not to see in these chapters history in the classical and modern sense, one must also admit that current scientific data do not allow a *positive* solution of all the problems which they present. The first duty of scientific exegesis in this matter is the careful study of all the literary, scientific, historical, cultural, and religious problems connected with these chapters; next, it is necessary to make a close examination of the literary methods of the ancient oriental peoples, their psychology, their manner of expressing themselves, and even their notion of historical truth; it is, in short, necessary to assemble without preformed judgments all the material of the paleontological, historical, epigraphical, and literary sciences. It is only in this way that there is hope of attaining a clearer view of the true nature of certain narratives found in the first chapters of Genesis. To declare *a priori* that these narratives do not contain history in the modern sense of the word might easily be understood to mean that they do not contain history in any sense, whereas they relate the fundamental truths underlying the divine scheme of salvation, as well as a popular description of the origins of the human race and of the chosen people

---

78 Bea, *Votum*, 2–3.

79 Bea, *Votum*, 4.

80 Vosté to Suhard, January 16, 1948. The letter was explicitly approved by the pope.

in simple and figurative language, adapted to the understanding of mankind at a lower stage of development. In the meantime it is necessary to practice the patience which is part of the wisdom of life. This also is taught by the Holy Father in the Encyclical already quoted: "No one should be surprised that all the difficulties have not yet been clarified or solved."[81]

4. THE JESUIT CURIA

a. Teilhard's Theology of Nature

Teilhard was, as I have already said, never restricted from publishing his purely scientific work. He was, by contrast, never permitted to publish his theology of nature, a prohibition that also covered articles of a mixed character (including articles on monogenesis). What might be distinguished as a third round of challenges to Teilhard's work[82] began as he finished *Le Phénomène humain*, which he wrote in 1937–1940[83] and sent from Peking to the Jesuit curia in Rome for permission to publish on March 9, 1941.[84]

Two reviewers were appointed.

The first was Charles Boyer, dean of the theology faculty at the Gregorianum, whose general lack of sympathy for evolutionary ideas was clear from his published work. Boyer characterized Teilhard's manuscript as a mix of science, philosophy, theology, and poetry that did not allow rigorous arguments or firm conclusions. He objected that, although the author wrote as though the book was for scientists, it would in fact be read by non-scientists, in whom it would create false ideas and incurable confusions. In addition, he thought that Teilhard gave insufficient attention to divine action (e.g., in the origin of life, in the various stages of evolution, and in the creation of the soul) and to what faith teaches about our protoparents.[85]

The second reviewer was René Arnou, dean of the philosophy faculty at the same university. Arnou had concerns about Teilhard's eschatology (his "Omega Point") and the way in which he distinguished the natural from the supernatural, but two other comments are of more relevance to the subject of this book. Although Arnou acknowledged that "evolution limited to the origin of the human body can be proposed, as long as it is supported by good arguments," he thought that such an evolution should be finalistic, which (in his view) Teilhard's was not. The second comment relevant to our interest

---

81 Vosté, 47–48 (with the quoted sentence from *Divino afflante Spiritu*, 319 (trans. ¶44)).

82 The first two being the challenge to his views on original sin and on monogenesis, both discussed in chapter 12.

83 The cover of the typescript submitted for review after the war says that the work was written from June 1938 to June 1940 (fasc. 5, OPP.NN. [Opera Nostrorum] 1432, ARSI). That this typescript is the postwar typescript is clear from the page numbers cited in the earlier and later reviews. Teilhard's letters to Max Bégouën, September 26, 1937, and May 23, 1938, indicate an earlier starting date (*Letters from a Traveller*, 232 and 241).

84 Teilhard to Morits Schurmans (Vicar General), March 9, 1941 (doc. 16, Censurae 27–VI, ARSI). Canon Law (§1385) required that he get permission from his superiors prior to publication. Teilhard mentioned this in two letters—one to an unidentified friend, August 4, 1941 (*Letters to Two Friends*, 99), and the other to Henri Breuil, July 12, 1941 (*Letters from a Traveler*, 283–84).

85 Boyer, Censura, October 26, 1942 (doc. 20, Censurae 27–VI, ARSI).

concerns Teilhard's apparent polygenism. Teilhard had said explicitly that "as far as science is concerned, the 'first man' can only be a *crowd*."[86]

Both reviewers having judged that the book affirmed propositions that could not be reconciled with Catholic doctrine, the Jesuit curia asked Georges Marin, visitator to the Jesuit establishment in Peking, to inform Teilhard that the book had not been approved for publication. Teilhard was to be sent a summary of the *censurae*, "as far as circumstances permitted."[87] The curia's reply was not, however, Teilhard thought, so negative as to remove all hope of eventually getting the work published.[88] That his hope was not without foundation is suggested by a remark of Albert Dauchy (secretary to the *assistens* for France) to Auguste Décisier (Teilhard's provincial at Lyons), that Teilhard had already been told "that the work could not be published *as it is*."[89]

On his return to France after the war, in May 1946, Teilhard was encouraged to find that "the demand for [his] 'gospel' is just as big as before" and optimistic that the Jesuit curia, under the new superior general, Jean-Baptiste Janssens, would be more sympathetic to his ideas than the previous one had been.[90] Three weeks after his return to France, he wrote to a friend that "a first step [in his resumption of activities] should be to get the ecclesiastical permission for publishing my book on the 'Human Phenomenon' and a few selected papers."[91] By March 1947 he had "retouched" his old manuscript in hopes of getting permission to publish it.[92] The campaign for approval was launched with a letter of support sent to the Jesuit curia by Jules Cardinal Saliège (archbishop of Toulouse) and a nine-page brief on "La Signification philosophique et la portée apologétique de l'œuvre du P. Teilhard de Chardin," written by Bruno de Solages (rector at the Institut catholique de Toulouse). De Solages wrote:

> It is difficult to deny the immense apologetic range [*portée*] of these views, which transform from within
> • a materialist evolution into a spiritualist one,
> • a deterministic [*nécessaire*] evolution into one directed by God,
> • an immanent evolution into one postulating something transcendent,
> • an anti-Christian evolution into one which so harmoniously makes way for Christianity.[93]

---

86 Arnou, Censura, March 23, 1944 (doc. 25, Censurae 27–VI, ARSI), with the quoted passage (emphasis Teilhard's) from Teilhard, *Phénomène humain* (1955), 206 (Walls trans., 186).

87 Norbert de Boynes (*Assistens* for France) to Marin, April 12, 1944 (doc. 26, Censurae 27–VI, ARSI). The *censurae* were sent on July 5, 1946 (doc. 4, Censurae 27–VIII, ARSI).

88 Teilhard to an unidentified friend, October 10, 1945 (*Letters to Two Friends*, 163).

89 Dauchy to Décisier, July 5, 1946 (emphasis added) (doc. 4, Censurae 27–VIII, ARSI).

90 Teilhard to an unidentified friend, November 1, 1946 (*Letters to Two Friends*, 168–69).

91 Teilhard to an unidentified friend, May 26, 1946 (*Letters to Two Friends*, 165). See also an undated letter, probably from July 1946 (p. 166).

92 Teilhard to an unidentified friend, March 19, 1947 (*Letters to Two Friends*, 170).

93 De Solages, "La signification philosophique et la portée apologétique de l'œuvre du P. Teilhard de Chardin," 8–9 (doc. 3, Censurae 27–IX, ARSI).

Meanwhile, the Jesuits' formal approval process began at Lyons, where Émile Delaye (one of the Society's French censors) and Henri Rondet (the prefect of studies) were appointed to review the manuscript. Delaye wrote a brief (three-page) appraisal with a positive verdict: *imprimi potest*.[94] Rondet, who, despite being (according to Décisier) opposed to some of Teilhard's ideas, also wrote a favorable report, though suggesting that the work be published with accompanying essays to protect against tendentious interpretations.[95]

Meanwhile, Bernard de Gorostarzu (*assistens* for France) solicited further evaluations of the manuscript in Rome.

Rudolf Walter de Moos, SJ, whose assignments included serving as a qualificator at the Holy Office, found the work interesting, well-written, and important, but thought that publication would have two results: It would lead many people to say that at last the Church accepts evolution, but it would lead others to refer it to the Holy Office, where a condemnation could not be excluded. "It would lead directly to another Galileo case," he said. In conclusion: "I would not venture to say yes to an *Imprimatur* unless the Jesuit consultors at the Holy Office (Creusen, Hürth, and Tromp), who know the present situation there better, do not share my hesitations. In that case, I would be very happy to see this fine book published."[96]

De Gorostarzu went to seek the opinion of Hürth, who told him he thought that the book included statements contrary to dogma and *he* would not say *imprimi potest*. Nevertheless, Hürth said that, given the concerns he already had about the matter (*non liberum ab omni preoccupatione mentis*), he thought it was perhaps best that he not serve as censor.[97]

Janssens was not as sympathetic as Teilhard had hoped he might be. The superior general wrote to de Gorostarzu in June that the French provincials should take into account the fact that Teilhard had committed grave wrongs and did not have a good reputation either among the Catholic public or at the Holy Office. He (Janssens) could not risk, either for himself or for Teilhard, the prospect of a condemnation.[98] Nevertheless, he arranged for a third review, as required by usual Jesuit practice.[99]

Heinrich Lennerz's *censura* was short (five pages) and included two parts—one on the idea that all things have at least a certain level of consciousness, the other on the origin of man. On the latter point, he said:

> It clearly holds that the human body originated from the body of a brute animal. But did this happen in just one case such that the whole human race traces its origin

---

94 Delaye, Censura, May 13, 1947 (doc. 4, Censurae 27–IX, ARSI).

95 Rondet, Censura, May 20, 1947 (doc. 5, Censurae 27–IX, ARSI). Décisier's comment was in his cover letter to Janssens, June 4, 1947 (doc. 6, Censurae 27–IX, ARSI).

96 De Moos, Note, July 11, 1947 (doc. 9, Censurae 27–IX, ARSI). The document (typed) has "R. G. de Mos." "R. G." would be "Rodolfo Gualtiero," but, there being no Jesuit named "de Mos," this must be a typographical error.

97 Hürth to de Gorostarzu, July 13, 1947 (doc. 11, Censurae 27–IX, ARSI).

98 Janssens to de Gorostarzu, June 16, 1947 (doc. 8, Censurae 27–IX, ARSI).

99 Janssens to de Gorostarzu, July 15, 1947 (doc. 12, Censurae 27–IX, ARSI).

to that one first man, or did it happen more than once? The author tries to restrict the opinions of the anthropologists a bit, but the reasons he gives for doing so do not touch the question of a single father for the whole human race. One passage seems to show quite clearly that the author does not think that all men originated from a single father and mother. Nor does he in any way indicate that men who may have lived before Adam and have an origin independent of him, all died, along with all of their descendants, so that everyone who lived with Adam, or after him, were children of Adam. He proposes his doctrine in a completely universal way; he admits that not everyone who lived with or after Adam were his children. And I think that readers will also understand the author's meaning in that way.

Lennerz thought that the book's ideas should not be taught and so was not willing to grant a *nihil obstat*.[100]

On July 15, 1947, Janssens was told by the Holy Office that Teilhard was to be forbidden to write or speak on topics outside his professional competence. He could write on science, but not on philosophy or theology.[101] Janssens prohibited publication of *Le Phénomène humain* and strengthened somewhat the prohibitions on Teilhard that had been imposed in 1938. He wrote to Marcel Bith (provincial in Paris): "*For the future, Fr. Teilhard is forbidden to publish anything on philosophy or theology*; review of his writings on those subjects should be refused without examination and *a priori*. What applies to his publications, applies equally to lectures and teaching." He added: "*He is limited to publications that are purely scientific*. These should be submitted to a competent and rigorous review."[102] Teilhard wrote to a friend:

> Apparently, I have offended more people than I realized by my old papers. On the whole, the fundamentalist offensive of last year has been repelled, but someone has to pay something for it. And, in order to protect me from something dreadful (probably to be inscribed on the *Index*?), my "General" Father has decided that I should keep quiet (that is to refrain from any publication) in the line of philosophy and theology for the time being. On scientific matters, no restriction.[103]

✳ ✳ ✳ ✳ ✳

There matters rested for about a year. Then they seem to have changed. The first sign of this came in an exchange of letters between Teilhard and Janssens. The Collège de France had been expressing interest in Teilhard's taking the chair in prehistory. In addition, Teilhard had returned from the United States with the idea of delivering six lectures at American universities in the spring of the following year.[104] In June 1948, probably on

---

100 Lennerz, Censura, July 7, 1947 (doc. 13a, Censurae 27–IX, ARSI).

101 Holy Office to Janssens, July 15, 1947 (fol. 242, doc. 43, CL 1931/1538, ADDF).

102 Janssens to Bith, August 22, 1947 (emphasis Janssen's) (doc. 15c, Censurae 27–IX, ARSI).

103 Teilhard to an unidentified friend, September 24, 1947 (*Letters to Two Friends*, 177).

104 Teilhard to an unidentified friend, July 8, 1948 (*Letters to Two Friends*, 105–6).

354

the 23rd,[105] Teilhard wrote to Janssens to ask whether he would be permitted to accept the position, and to give the American lectures.

In his reply, Janssens suggested that Teilhard come to Rome for one or two months in October or November to discuss both those possibilities and the publication of *Le Phénomène humain*.[106] All that might be possible, but conversations in Rome would be required first. Teilhard wrote to one friend that "these are obviously peace offers," but added, "I have no doubt about the sincerity of their sentiments, but I am somewhat dubious about the possibility of a real agreement."[107] To another, he wrote "this invitation to go to Rome is perhaps the chance of my life, and the turning point for a broader and more direct type of activity."[108]

Why things changed in the middle of 1948 is unclear. Teilhard, in the passage quoted above, as well as in other letters, thought that Janssens was very (in fact, overly) sensitive to the political winds blowing through Rome.[109] Passages in some of Janssens's official correspondence also suggest this. It is worth noting that in early June 1948 de Solages submitted a confidential memorandum to Pope Pius urging that Teilhard be allowed to publish *Le Phénomène humain*.[110] Though I have found no direct evidence of this, it is surely possible that the pope asked Janssens to give the matter a second look.

In any case, Teilhard did go to Rome in October. Meanwhile his book was sent, it is not clear by whom, but probably by de Solages or by de Gorostarzu, to Édouard Dhanis and to Pierre Charles (professors at Louvain) for review.

Dhanis wrote that there were many good things to say about the book, but that it could not be approved until some corrections and some important clarifications had been made.[111] His concerns ranged from the transcendence of God to the end of the world. Two are of particular relevance to our topic. The first was that Teilhard's account of matter and spirit seemed to put the doctrine that the human soul was created *ex nihilo* into doubt.[112] The second concerned evolution. While Dhanis "could not reproach [Teilhard] for proposing that the extension of evolution to all forms of life, including the human form, as a fact supported [*garanti*] by very serious arguments," he objected to Teilhard's claim that it was obvious, which he thought was more than most scientists would be willing to say. In addition, "Perhaps it would be appropriate to note that the scientific doctrine of evolution does not contradict the scientific or theological idea of a special intervention of God in the production of the body of man, especially since this

---

105 "Tomorrow, I will write to Rome . . . ." (Teilhard to an unidentified friend, June 22, 1948, [*Letters to Two Friends*, 181]).

106 Janssens to Teilhard, July 7, 1948 (doc. 2, Censurae 27–X, ARSI).

107 Teilhard to an unidentified friend, August 13, 1948 (*Letters to Two Friends*, 106).

108 Teilhard to an unidentified friend, July 11, 1948 (*Letters to Two Friends*, 182–83).

109 E.g., in a letter to an unidentified friend, Teilhard wrote: "The General is pretty narrow and strict for political reasons" (*Letters to Two Friends*, 197).

110 De Solages, "Le P. Teilhard de Chardin et l'orientation des esprits dans la France contemporaine," 1, about June 8, 1948 (Studia 1060, ARSI).

111 Dhanis, "Censure du *Phénomène humain*," October 11, 1948, 1 (doc. 6a, Censurae 27–X, ARSI).

112 Dhanis, "Censure," 2.

intervention may not be detectable at the level of phenomena. Some statements from ecclesiastical authorities have asked for the admission of such an intervention."[113] Finally, having let his polygenist sentiments show, should Teilhard not at least acknowledge that this was grounded in an exclusively scientific point of view, and that other disciplines (theology in particular) could shed light on the matter? He ended his report with the hope that author would be able to make the needed changes.

Charles's report was shorter, but more favorable. Like Dhanis, he expressed concern about what Teilhard had said in favor of polygenism, suggesting instead that the book say only that, "from the paleontological point of view, . . . the hypothesis is plausible." He concluded by saying that "With those modifications, all of which, it seems to me, would be acceptable to the author, I believe that the work of Teilhard is of a kind to do immense good and to rehabilitate the Christian faith itself in lay scientific circles. I judge it to be my duty to take the responsibility of saying *imprimi potest*."[114]

Both sets of comments were sent to Teilhard, who made some changes in light of the comments that he received.[115]

A revised version of the manuscript was sent to Lennerz sometime in November. On December 2, Lennerz returned his *censura*. It had been difficult for him to come to a definitive conclusion about whether the work should be published. With respect to monogenism, he emphasized one point on which he remained uncertain. Was Teilhard proposing that monogenism be understood as asserting that the first man, from whom everyone else is descended, is already himself *Homo sapiens*, or as asserting that that first man is some kind of older, antecedent form, from whom not only *H. sapiens*, but also other beings that do not lead to *H. sapiens* are descended? If he means the former, then there is no problem. The second, however, does not seem to be in agreement with the monogenism taught by the Church. According to the figure,[116] *H. sapiens* does not seem to descend from *one* ancestral *H. sapiens*. Nevertheless, it being possible to give the passage in question an orthodox interpretation, Lennerz said that he did not have the right to stand by the negative judgment that he had returned the year before.[117]

In February, although Teilhard was still forbidden to publish anything not of a strictly scientific character[118]—something which, he said, would be "psychologically impossible"—he thought that the manuscript still had "a shadow of a chance" of being published and that he would hear within a month, but the month went by without his getting a response.[119]

---

113 Dhanis, "Censure," 6–7.

114 Charles, Censure de *Phénomène humain* (October 20, 1948) (doc. 8a, Censurae 27–X, ARSI).

115 Teilhard, "À propos de la révision no. 1 du PH [Dhanis]" and "Response to censura no. 2 [Charles]," October 28, 1948 (docs. 7 and 9, Censurae 27–X, ARSI)).

116 The diagram is the one found in Teilhard, *Phénomène humain* (1955), 212 (Walls trans., 192).

117 Lennerz, *Censura*, December 2, 1948 (doc. 16a, Censurae 27–X, ARSI)).

118 Janssens to Teilhard, January 31, 1949 (doc. 3, Censurae 27–XI, ARSI).

119 Teilhard to an unidentified friend, February 8, 1949, *Letters to Two Friends*, 196. See also the entire letter and those of February 14 and 22, 1949 (*Letters to Two Friends*, 196–200).

Guy de Broglie (dogmatic theologian at the Gregorianum) returned a second report on May 29, 1949. The first two parts of the manuscript,[120] those concerning the world's, and humanity's, *past*, he said, were acceptable:

> Provided that one keeps to the phenomenal point of view which he said that he is taking (and not a metaphysical one), it seems that no theological objection concerning the substance of things can be made to this fine work. One cannot complain about the fact that he admits an evolutionary origin of humanity, a thesis which (as long as one leaves aside, as the author does, the question of *monogenism*) is in no way opposed to the Christian faith.... Nor can one complain about its pan-psychism. In any case the question of the distinction between living and non-living things has nothing to do with dogma.[121]

The only problem to be found there is "an excessive tendency to apply to the material world and its evolution certain terms which linguistic usage quite legitimately reserves for the world of spiritual beings." In sum, "these corrections are only about details.... The publication of such a work *seems to me highly desirable.*"[122]

The last part of the manuscript, by contrast, was not acceptable. "In spite of its undeniable merits, this third part, in which the author speaks much less as a *man of science* endeavoring to discover the past history of the sensible world than as a *philosopher* trying to understand the mentality of his time and to foresee the destiny of the human race, calls for many reservations, and would require deeper corrections."[123] In particular, "evolution is not just presented as *one of the fundamental laws* of the universe, but as *the supreme norm of the universe and of thought.* ... It tends, whether he intends this or not, to discredit and undermine a number of traditional philosophical and theological truths, which will be criticized for having been conceived in an atmosphere of non-evolutionary thought."[124] Since "the *nihil obstat* of the Society is generally considered by the faithful as a guarantee of complete doctrinal safety," the third part (unlike the first two) should not be published without eliminating both its immoderate enthusiasm for Evolution conceived as the supreme key to being and thought and its systematically optimistic prognostications about the terrestrial future promised to humanity.[125]

Teilhard put his assessment of the problem over publication of *Le Phénomène humain,* and more generally over whether he should be allowed a greater latitude in writing, in a letter as follows: "The fundamental question really at issue is whether or not official authority is willing to accept (and to integrate into the Christian faith) 'faith' in

---

120 The parts (*cahiers*) here referred to are surely the three physical parts of the typescript. The first two parts (OPP. NN. 1432/5–6, ARSI) include Books I, II, and the first part of Book III of the published version; the final part (OPP.NN. 1432/7) begins at the middle of Book III and includes all of Book IV.

121 De Broglie, *Censura,* May 29, 1949, 1 (doc. 5, Censurae 27–XI, ARSI).

122 De Broglie, *Censura,* 3 (emphasis de Broglie's).

123 De Broglie, *Censura,* 4.

124 De Broglie, *Censura,* 8 (emphasis de Broglie's).

125 De Broglie, *Censura,* 11.

a future (i.e., a superevolution) of Humanity on earth."[126] To the extent that Teilhard is correct about *that* being the fundamental question, the difference between him and his opponents is not over the compatibility of Catholic theology with evolutionary biology (even with the origin of the human body), but a question of the orthodoxy of Teilhard's eschatology. In the end, despite everything—his hopes, his revisions of the text, a favorable reception by provincial officials in Lyons, and his friendly reception in Rome—permission to publish *Le Phénomène humain* was never granted.

✳ ✳ ✳ ✳ ✳

On August 4, 1949, when he was still awaiting a final decision on the earlier manuscript, Teilhard submitted for review a new work, *Le Groupe zoologique humain: Structure et directions évolutives*,[127] which he described as "a shorter and better focused version of the long *Phénomène humain*." He estimated his chance of getting permission to publish it as fifty-fifty.[128]

The manuscript, like *Le Phénomène humain*, was reviewed by de Broglie, who had several concerns about the work. It expressed too much confidence in the idea of evolution. The continuity between the material and the spiritual world was "enigmatic," with the transition from animality to man presented as merely the advent of the power of "reflection," of "foresight," and of "invention." The origin of man being said to be "in conformity with the general laws of all 'speciation'" seemed to de Broglie to be a "discreet, but quite clear enunciation" of polygenism.[129] In a letter to his friend Pierre Leroy, Teilhard was a bit contemptuous of de Broglie's concerns—they were "unintelligent, of course, but well-meaning" and only required that he "touch up some details."[130] He made the changes requested and de Broglie then recommended publication, though with a few more corrections.[131] Nevertheless, the final decision was against permission to publish.[132] Teilhard had tried to re-present the ideas developed in his earlier manuscript in more strictly scientific terms, but his idea of where the line lay apparently differed from the curia's. He decided to reproduce the book on his own and to distribute it to his colleagues at the Institut de France, of which he had recently been appointed a member.[133]

He undertook what he called "a second rewrite of *Le Phénomène humain*, but better focused" at the end of the year. He would deliver it as a series of lectures at the

---

126 Teilhard to an unidentified friend, August 13, 1948 (*Letters to Two Friends*, 106).

127 ARSI, OPP.NN. 1432/8.

128 Teilhard to unidentified friends, January 25 and May 29, 1950 (*Letters to Two Friends*, 110–11).

129 De Broglie, *Censura* of *Le Groupe zoologique humain*, February 15, 1950 (doc. 2a, Censurae 27–XII, ARSI).

130 Teilhard to Pierre Leroy, March 31, 1950 (*Letters from My Friend*, 50).

131 De Broglie, Second *Censura* on *Le Groupe zoologique humain*, May 6, 1950 (doc. 3, Censurae 27–XII, ARSI).

132 I was unable to find the documents that usually accompany the implementation of a decision like this at ARSI. Cuénot put the date at June 28 (*Teilhard*, 329 [trans., 271]). This must be at least approximately correct, as Teilhard's letters indicate that no decision had been made before May 29 (*Letters to Two Friends*, 112–13) and he had heard that it was disapproved on July 6 (*Letters from My Friend*, 57–58).

133 Teilhard to Pierre Leroy, July 6 and October 19, 1950 (*Letters from My Friend*, 57–58 and 65–66).

358

Sorbonne and then, "without asking anything of Rome" although he had mentioned it twice to de Gorostarzu, send it to *Annales de paléontologie*. It was, he said "a specifically scientific essay," "different from what was stopped six months [before]." "What appears there cannot be criticized as 'unscientific'!"[134]

Was that work in fact scientific? There are certainly reasonable definitions of science on which it was not. It begins with a summary of paleoanthropology and ends with "a vision of a universe in which each thinking planet would represent, at its end, by the concentration of its noosphere, a point of breakthrough and of escape from the temporo-spatial envelope of things." Teilhard added that "from the moment in which, resolutely trying ultimately to see in the Human, not a superficial modality of the Biosphere, but rather a superior and extreme form, taken evolutionarily by the Fabric of the World, how can one avoid perspectives of this vast scale?"[135] Scientific or not, the *Annales* published them later that year.

He wrote for *Annales de paléontologie* again in the last year of his life, sending them "Les Singularités de l'espèce humaine." This also was not a scientific work in the traditional sense of that term. In the conclusion of the essay, he wrote that "if the entire sphere of things is found to have the essential property of gradually contracting onto its center by an increasingly reflective connection of the elements which compose it, then how can one not see that the Universe, as much as we see it grow around us, both in its power and in its size, does not at all tend, as we might have feared, to crush our individual values, but on the contrary to exalt them by its vastness?" The editors of the posthumous collection of his works added that "the author reserved the religious elucidations of his thesis for his less exclusively scientific works."[136]

✳ ✳ ✳ ✳ ✳

The two books appeared in print only in 1955 (after Teilhard's death), as a result of the efforts of his literary executors. Their popularity among certain Catholics led the Holy Office to issue in 1962 the following *monitum*:

> Several works of Fr. Pierre Teilhard de Chardin, including some edited posthumously, are being published with a good deal of favorable notice. Leaving to the side any judgment about matters that pertain to the positive sciences, it is sufficiently clear that the above-mentioned works abound in such ambiguities, and indeed even in serious errors, as to violate Catholic doctrine. For this reason, the most eminent and most revered Fathers of the Holy Office exhort all ordinaries as well as the superiors of religious institutes, rectors of seminaries and presidents of universities, to protect the minds, particularly of the youth, against the dangers posed by the works of Fr. Teilhard de Chardin and of his followers.[137]

---

134 Teilhard to Pierre Leroy, November 11, 1950 (*Letters from My Friend*, 68).

135 Teilhard, "La Structure phylétique du groupe humain" (1951), 79 (trans., 171).

136 Teilhard, "Les Singularités de l'espèce humaine" (1955), 54 (trans., 270).

137 Congregation of the Holy Office, "Monitum," 526.

An unsigned article published in *L'Osservatore Romano* on the same day emphasized philosophical and theological concerns about Teilhard's handling of the concepts of creation and the supernatural, and his account of the connection between the doctrines of creation, Incarnation, and Redemption, but made no mention of any scientific questions. In a commentary on the *monitum*, Gaston Isaye, SJ, offered this explanation of its meaning: "Teilhard's vocabulary is not precise, but suggestive. This scientist, who is a poet and whose interior life is therefore extremely rich, is attempting to make one 'see' rather than demonstrating. And he emphasizes resemblances without saying a lot about differences."[138]

Teilhard has continued to have Catholic defenders and admirers.[139]

Some years later, on the more appreciative side, on the centennial of Teilhard's birth, the Institut catholique de Paris, where he had once taught, organized a commemoration of his life. Agostino Cardinal Casaroli, Vatican secretary of state, took the occasion to send to the rector of the Institut, on behalf of Pope John Paul II, a message in homage to Teilhard.[140] Casaroli, while praising Teilhard's "powerful poetic insight into the deep value of nature, . . . keen perception of the dynamic of nature, [and] wide view of the becoming of the world," also took care to acknowledge those aspects of Teilhard's work that made it necessary to read the books with caution. Nevertheless, when those positive remarks about Teilhard led to rumors that the *monitum* was no longer in force, the Press Office of the Holy See published a communiqué in *L'Osservatore Romano* reminding readers that the *monitum* of 1962 was still in effect.

✳ ✳ ✳ ✳ ✳

Teilhard's friend and fellow-Jesuit, René d'Ouince saw, in the long-running conflict between Teilhard and ecclesiastical authority, a conflict between two competing understandings of the work of a priest-scientist.

> For the Roman theologians, a priest who had acquired authentic renown as a scientist, was, so to speak, a living *apologia*. His loyalty to the Church—and no one could doubt Teilhard's loyalty—showed clearly enough that there was no incompatibility between science and faith. That silent witness was enough. What good was to be had by risking it by differences in language? If Teilhard should incur public censure from ecclesiastical authority, his life would cease to bear such witness; worse yet, it could become an argument against the cause that he was trying to serve.
>
> In Teilhard's mind, the presence of a religious in the world of research was an incomplete witness. Atheists and believers met there every day, doing valuable scientific work without it being possible to draw from that any argument either in favor of the ideology of the one or of the faith of the other. To bear true witness, a priest devoted to science had to be able to give an account of the unity of his life.[141]

---

138 Isaye, "Avertissement," 867.

139 For example, Henri de Lubac, *Religion of Teilhard de Chardin*.

140 Casaroli's letter to Poupard, *L'Osservatore Romano*.

141 D'Ouince, "L'Obéissance du Père Teilhard de Chardin," 338.

The concept of silent witness is nicely illustrated by an anecdote told by Henri Brémond:

> When Maurice Barrès visited the Museum and was shown our venerable ancestors, he was at first quite moved and then, turning towards Boule, who was doing the interpretation, asked, among other things, what effect such impressive discoveries could have on the religious belief of our country. For his response, the illustrious professor, smiling, only pointed to a young Jesuit—it was Teilhard—moving with a serene familiarity among the bones.[142]

It is also illustrated in the lives of Hugo Obermaier and Breuil. That d'Ouince was right about its application to Teilhard is suggested by a comment Teilhard made in one of his late letters: "It looks as if Rome has almost forgotten me, partly, perhaps, because I've talked up my plan to go and study Australopithecus."[143]

b. Rüschkamp's Evolutionary Anthropogenesis

Neither his Jesuit superiors nor the Holy Office ever expressed any concerns either about Rüschkamp's purely scientific work or about his popular presentation of evolutionary accounts of phyto- and zoogenesis. They did have concerns about his views on anthropogenesis, views that he expressed in his teaching, in public lectures, and in print.

Rüschkamp's readiness to give a place to evolution in anthropogenesis had raised concerns on the part of his Jesuit superiors almost from the start of his teaching at Sankt-Georgen. In mid-June 1928, Ludwig Kösters, then rector, wrote to Superior General Włodzimierz Ledóchowski that "Fr. Rüschkamp is completely unsuitable for philosophy (not biology) and his lectures on the theory of evolution [*Abstammungslehre,* so literally 'theory of descent'] could cause us great embarrassment, even if it has so far been possible to avoid any trouble through supervision and guidance, which he willingly puts up with."[144] Ledóchowski replied that

> [the problem] to which you have referred in regard to certain professors is very grievous, and I earnestly ask that you watch over them, especially Fr. Rüschkamp. Everyone should remember that he teaches in the name of the Society and that therefore, for this reason alone, he ought to present sound Scholastic doctrine. Otherwise the name of the Society is exposed to the greatest danger, all the more since our friends and foes undoubtedly observe us most diligently in this seminary; but there can be nothing of greater harm than an accusation of excessively liberal teaching coming from the Holy See.[145]

---

142 Henri Brémond, "Les 'Batailles d'Idées,'" 31. Brémond (1865–1933), a Jesuit until 1904, had been Teilhard's teacher at secondary school. Barrès (1862–1923) was a nationalist political thinker.

143 Teilhard to an unidentified friend, January 2, 1951 (*Letters to Two Friends,* 115).

144 Kösters to Ledóchowski, June 3, 1928 (Germania Inferiora [hereafter, GermInf] 1023 [Ex officio 1928], ARSI); answered on June 27 (fol. 410–11, Registro Lettere dei Generali—Germania Inferiora [hereafter, RLG-GI] XI, ARSI).

145 Ledóchowski to Kösters, June 27, 1928 (fol. 410–11, RLG-GI XI, ARSI).

An early occasion for addressing Rüschkamp's evolutionism came with Rüschkamp's Düren lecture, after which Johannes Lauer, his provincial, told Rüschkamp that he did not think that the animal ancestry of man was a theologically open question and that any work that clearly contained such a view would immediately be put on the *Index*, especially since Rüschkamp acknowledged that the thesis had not yet been scientifically proven.[146]

* * * * *

Concerns came from another quarter after publication of Rüschkamp's article on Peking Man, which precipitated a complaint to the Index in 1933. The inquiry from that congregation led Ledóchowski to write to Wilhelm Klein (Rüschkamp's provincial) asking what Rüschkamp was saying to students about the difference between man and animal and to arrange for a review of the article on Peking Man.[147]

In response to the inquiry into the content of his teaching, Rüschkamp submitted some lecture notes that he had prepared on the essential difference between man and animal.[148] In those notes, he had said that that essential difference is easy to prove with respect to the soul, but, given that man's exceptional place among living things is not due to bodily features, it seems that no *essential* difference can be proven with respect to the body. Indeed *science*, he went on to say, thinks that the parents of the first human being were animals. While there does not seem to be any philosophical reason to deny this, theology has long been opposed to the idea. Although no one says that the contrary idea (immediate formation of Adam's body by God) is an article of faith, some say that it is a *sententia proxima fidei*, while others do not even give it that qualification.[149] Supporters of the evolutionary origin of the human body say that the relevant scriptural text is anthropomorphic, ascribing directly to God what He did only through secondary causes, while opponents of that view continue to claim that the evolutionist view cannot be safely taught.

Rüschkamp's lecture notes were reviewed by three members of the province in March and early April. Two found the notes unobjectionable, but the third did not. He conceded that the evolutionist view defended by Rüschkamp was gaining ground among Catholics, but thought that, given that a Catholic must accept an original pair and the creation of the human soul, the absence of compelling evidence for the evolutionary view made its defense rash. Rüschkamp replied that "we have the duty to acquaint future priests, who are to work in a world informed by dishonest (Haeckel) as well as by honest science, with what natural science says if we want to prevent obvious harm to the Church and to souls."[150] He was, he added, willing to add the theological judgment that the thesis could not safely be taught. Klein's decision, provisionally supported by

146 Lauer to Rüschkamp, January 19, 1929 (fol. 017r-v, Nr. 2696, Abt. 252 C 2283, APECESJ).

147 Ledóchowski to Klein, June 18, 1934 (fol. 135ff., RLG-GI XIII, ARSI).

148 Rüschkamp, "De essentiali differentia inter animalia et hominem" (Censurae 13, ARSI).

149 Rüschkamp mentioned, as examples of those who evaluated the thesis less definitively, Christianus Pesch, *Compendium*, 2:164 (Rüschkamp cited the 1920 edition); or the Pontifical Biblical Commission.

150 Rüschkamp to Brust, April 15, 1934 (Censurae 13).

Ledóchowski, was that Rüschkamp was not to teach the evolutionary theses contained in the notes, and not to write on the subject. Ledóchowski also wanted the question to be subject to a careful review.[151]

That review was entrusted to Heinrich Lennerz and Josef Donat. Lennerz's evaluation was favorable to Rüschkamp. The question remained open, so students should hear the various sides as long as the relevance of theological considerations was recognized.[152] Donat's *votum* was not favorable. He thought that the question of bodily differences should be handled with more caution. About animal ancestry he wrote that "this view cannot cite any valid evidence and what is presented is almost like a calculation with nothing but unknowns. At the same time, there are very serious theological considerations against it, as a consequence of which it is quite generally rejected by expert theologians. Therefore, it is not appropriate for us to recommend it."[153] Ledóchowski left the earlier, provisional, prohibitions on teaching and writing in place.[154] The restriction appears not to have applied either to discussing the evolutionary origin of plants and animals or to such related questions as the antiquity of the human race, topics on which, as noted earlier, Rüschkamp published a number of articles over the course of the 1930s.

Concerns about what he was teaching in his classrooms, however, continued through the decade. They were raised by Ludwig Kösters on the occasion of an official visit to the college, although they were denied in a response from Klein, who was by then provincial.[155]

✳ ✳ ✳ ✳ ✳

Trouble for Rüschkamp came again only in 1939, with his publication of "Der Mensch als Glied der Schöpfung." Ledóchowski was greatly surprised by the article and wanted to know who had approved it for publication.[156] It had not, he was told, been approved locally; Rüschkamp had sent it directly to *Stimmen der Zeit* and it had been approved there.[157] Theodor Wulf (provincial, as well as a physicist specializing in the study of the atmosphere) wrote to Ledóchowski that he had already expressed his own concerns about the article to Rüschkamp and that the latter had accepted the warning well.[158]

At the same time, Ledóchowski asked Augustin Bea to review the article. In a *votum* submitted on March 12, Bea began by acknowledging that a proper judgment about the

---

151 Ledóchowski to Rüschkamp, May 14, 1934, and to Klein, June 18, 1934 (fol. 135ff., RLG-GI XIII, ARSI).

152 Lennerz, *Votum* and cover letter, May 2, 1934 (Censurae 13).

153 Donat, *Votum*, June 9, 1934, 6 (Censurae 13).

154 Ledóchowski to Klein, June 18, 1934 (Censurae 13; also fol. 135–36, RLG-GI XIII).

155 Concerns: Kösters, February 14, 1937: "The professor of cosmology (Rüschkamp) continues to teach quite eloquently that a brute animal is the origin of the human body" (22 [Francofurt], GermInf 1027–IV [Consultores], ARSI); denied: Klein, June 21, 1937: "The professor of cosmology, Fr. Rüschkamp, was again forbidden to mention [*proferre*] theories about the origin of the human body (*which he thereafter did not do in his lectures*)" (emphasis added) (22 [Francofurt], GermInf 1027–II [Elenchi Visitorum], ARSI).

156 Ledóchowski to Wulf, March 18, 1939 (doc. 3, Rüschkamp Dossiers).

157 Schütt to Ledóchowski, March 16, 1939 (doc. 5, Rüschkamp Dossiers).

158 Wulf to Ledóchowski, March 22, 1939 (doc. 4, Rüschkamp Dossiers).

363

article would be difficult, since it would require good scientific knowledge on the part of the evaluator. One should, however, note that at most Rüschkamp's arguments only show what nature *can* do, but not that what it actually *did*. On the one hand, Bea acknowledged that the case for evolution was not designed to exclude a creator, and was not based on *a priori* postulates, but rather on factual evidence:

> one should not fail to note that the arguments which the theory of evolution offers today are much more cogent than they were in the time of materialistic Darwinism. The course of evolution in the animal world today leads to an organism not far from the form of Neanderthalers and pre-Neanderthalers (*Pithecanthropus* and *Sinanthropus*). If we find human tools (fire, bone tools) for *Paranthropus* ..., then his bodily form will probably not hinder us from recognizing him as true man.[159]

He cited nearly a dozen Catholic authors who accepted the evolutionary origin of the human body.

On the other hand,

> when the sources of revelation, Scripture and Tradition, show the necessity of believing that the human body was formed by the immediate intervention of God directly from inorganic matter, there is nothing compelling left for the scientist to say against it. So, a Catholic cannot take up the question without regard to the verdict of the sources of revelation, and it seems to me to be a defect of the article, that, in a Catholic periodical, it hardly says a word about this.

So, the idea of an evolution willed and directed by God is not scandalous [*unerhört*] or even rash, but the fact that the Holy See has not taken a position "should at least indicate that one should treat the problem as not ready to be decided and that one should not anticipate the result of scientific research."[160] Still, Rüschkamp should at least have acknowledged such scientific counterevidence as the lack of evidence of predecessors to the pre-Neanderthalers and as the sudden appearance of culture some ten thousand years ago.

Finally, Bea emphasized the question of the opportuneness. He was simply not sure how relevant to the needs of German Catholics clarity on this matter really was. If teachers really were drawing anti-religious conclusions from the theory of animal ancestry, it would be better to have an article that was less one-sided. Best, however, would be not to address the issue before the Church itself did so.

By the end of the month, Ledóchowski decided that the Society's commitment to (and reputation for) teaching "safer and more approved doctrine"[161] required that Rüschkamp be removed from his teaching position, effective immediately (i.e., in

---

159 Bea, "Bemerkungen zu dem Artikel 'Der Mensch als Glied der Schöpfung' von P. F. Rüschkamp" ["Annotationes in ... articulum" in the Archive's index], (doc. 2, Rüschkamp Dossiers), 1–2.

160 Bea, "Bemerkungen," 3.

161 The phrase is that of the *Epitome Instituti Societatis Iesu*, n.314§1.

mid-semester).[162] Rüschkamp requested to be transferred, to the Jesuits' Scientific Institute in Tientsin,[163] but Ledóchowski decided that it would not be opportune to send him to China and wanted him instead assigned to "mechanical-scientific" work (e.g., organizing a collection) in Germany, partly to keep him under better supervision and partly for reasons of his health.[164]

✳ ✳ ✳ ✳ ✳

The prohibition on Rüschkamp's writing and teaching, however, did not last long; it was canceled as a result of two events that occurred over the course of the next two years.

The first event was a critique of the idea of the evolutionary origin of the human body written by Rüschkamp's fellow-Jesuit, Gustav Closen and published in the pages of the Pontifical Biblical Institute's journal, *Verbum Domini*. In June 1940, Rüschkamp wrote to Ledóchowski and asked for a review both of Closen's article and of a reply to that article that Rüschkamp had drafted.[165] Ledóchowski again turned to Bea.

Bea thought that neither author was without blame. "Fr. Closen in fact exaggerated a bit in his article; there are now a number of good Catholic scientists who accept transformism in a form attenuated enough that one cannot say that they violate Catholic teaching. That much, at least, should have been admitted. But our youngest generation leans sometimes too categorically to the conservative side." On the other hand, "Father Rüschkamp has too little understanding of anything that lies outside the domain of natural science and it is difficult or impossible to teach it to him."[166] In particular, Bea said, Rüschkamp gave insufficient weight to the theological case against the evolutionary origin of the human body.[167]

Ledóchowski sent Bea's *votum* on to Rüschkamp.[168] Rüschkamp wrote back that the descent from animal bodies was a scientific question on which there was a morally universal consensus in favor of such descent. The alternative, immediate creation, would have unacceptable consequences—the creation of extremely conservative bits of germ-plasm as senseless and misleading pseudo-hereditary traits, all of which would be absurd and incompatible with God's wisdom and truthfulness.[169]

In October, Rüschkamp wrote to Ledóchowski again: "Fr. Closen's article was well-intended but missed its target and has aroused, among exegetes and dogmatic theologians,

---

162 Ledóchowski to Wulf, March 27, 1939 (doc. 6, Rüschkamp Dossiers).

163 Wulf to Ledóchowski, April 6, 1939 (doc. 10, Rüschkamp Dossiers)

164 Maurits Schurmans (vicar) to Wulf, April 18, 1939 (doc. 11, Rüschkamp Dossiers).

165 Rüschkamp to Ledóchowski, June 17, 1940 (doc. 17 [the letter] and 17A [Rüschkamp's reply to Closen], Rüschkamp Dossiers).

166 Bea to Janssens, cover letter for his *votum*, August 3, 1940 (doc. 19, Rüschkamp Dossiers).

167 Bea's *votum*, August 3, 1940 (doc. 19a, Rüschkamp Dossiers).

168 Ledóchowski to Rüschkamp, August 28, 1940 (doc. 20, Rüschkamp Dossiers).

169 Rüschkamp, "Zum Gutachten bei Aufsatz von Closen und Antwort von Rüschkamp" ["Annotationes in iudicium…" in the Archive's index], sent to Ledóchowski, September 14, 1940 (doc. 21a1, Rüschkamp Dossiers).

both astonishment and amazement [*Verwunderung und Kopfschütteln*]."[170] He asked for permission to resume writing on scientific matters, adding that many theologians and philosophers do not see anything dangerous in the idea of the evolution of the human body. Ledóchowski granted the permission, provided that Rüschkamp first sent his manuscripts to his provincial, who was, in turn, to send them on to Bea for approval.[171]

The second event that led to some loosening of the restrictions on Rüschkamp was the address that Pope Pius XII had given to the Pontifical Academy of Sciences in November 1941, which seemed to suggest that science might have a greater rôle to play in the study of human origins than some evolution-suspicious Catholics had been willing to grant to it. Karl Brust (*assistens* for Germany) wrote to Paul Schütt, then rector at Sankt-Georgen, for his opinion.[172] He then wrote to Rüschkamp that the pope's speech to some extent justified Rüschkamp's views on the question.[173] In 1943, the prohibition on teaching was also formally lifted, but, due to the war, during which the Allied bombing of Frankfurt had destroyed the facilities of Sankt-Georgen, he was able to resume teaching only in November 1945.

＊ ＊ ＊ ＊ ＊

Within a year of his return to teaching, however, Rüschkamp ran afoul of the expectations of the Society again. He was beginning to receive invitations to give public lectures on evolutionary questions to Catholic audiences.[174] Albert Weigel, the pastor at Landau, explained why *he* had issued such an invitation: "it should be clearly shown that, as far as the Church is concerned, there is freedom on this question. Fortunately, we are beyond the time when some people lost their faith over this and others were led into a great crisis of conscience because they did not believe that they could reconcile the results of natural science (paleontology) with the Bible."[175]

Rüschkamp had delivered only two such lectures, one at Bamberg and one at Landau, when someone complained to Jesuit authorities.[176] Rüschkamp said two things in his own defense. First, he had steered clear of theological questions in his lectures and had stuck to the clarification of scientific questions.[177] Second, although he had expected

---

170 Rüschkamp to Ledóchowski, October 6, 1940 (doc. 23, Rüschkamp Dossiers).

171 Ledóchowski to Rüschkamp, October 31, 1940 (doc. 24, Rüschkamp Dossiers); Ledóchowski to Wulf, October 31, 1940 (doc. 25, Rüschkamp Dossiers).

172 Brust to Schütt, September 28, 1942 (doc. 33, Rüschkamp Dossiers).

173 Brust to Rüschkamp, October 31, 1942 (doc. 33, Rüschkamp Dossiers).

174 Bamberg: Rüschkamp to Wilhelm Flosdorf (then his provincial), February 16, 1947 (Rüschkamp Dossiers, doc. 36 [Annex III]); other invitations: Rüschkamp to Janssens, October 13, 1947 (doc. 39, Rüschkamp Dossiers).

175 Weigel, "Artgeschichte."

176 Bea to Ledóchowski, December 20, 1946. The complaint originated with Otto Lutz, *regens* of the episcopal seminary in Spires, to a Fr. Holzmeister, his former teacher, December 4, 1946 (doc. 34 [incl. Annex I], Rüschkamp Dossiers).

177 Rüschkamp to Flosdorf, February 16, 1947, and to Janssens, October 13, 1947 (doc. 36 [Annex III] and 39, Rüschkamp Dossiers).

to be addressing a mature audience of priests, the lecture was in fact attended by students from a local school and their relatively unsophisticated [*einfache*] parents.[178]

Jean-Baptiste Janssens, who had become superior general in 1946, in reviewing the statement that Pope Pius XII had made some years earlier, doubted that the pope had intended to allow the kind of open discussion of these questions in which Rüschkamp was engaging, and in the end forbade Rüschkamp from giving any more public lectures on the topic.[179] Although subsequent correspondence between Rüschkamp and the Jesuit curia in Rome suggests that restrictions remained in place,[180] Rüschkamp continued to write on scientific questions, as noted in chapter 14.

* * * * *

The essence of the controversies between Rüschkamp and his superiors can be captured in passages drawn from the correspondence surrounding the events just discussed. Rüschkamp began with an emphasis on a commitment to truth and ended with a strong version of the autonomy of science.

The former is captured in a line from Bernhard Bavink, marked in a copy of an article by Bavink that Rüschkamp sent to Ledóchowski in the wake of the termination of his teaching post at Sankt-Georgen: "The exact professional ethic of researchers and science teachers is, and cannot be other than, the unconditional will to truth."[181] Rüschkamp wrote to Janssens: "My opinion—subject to the Church judging otherwise—is that the descent of the human body from a living being [*materia organica*] is a divinely produced fact. It is a tragedy that many people, lacking the light of revelation, misinterpret this fact and many others, even with that light, do not yet recognize it."[182] Rüschkamp expressed his frustration about a remark that had been made to him by Schütt in 1939: "What matters is not whether what you think is true or not (sic!), but whether it is acceptable to the authorities [*tragbar*]."

178 Rüschkamp to Wulf, February 16, 1947 (doc. 36 [Annexes I and III], Rüschkamp Dossiers).

179 Ledóchowski to Flosdorf, April 4, 1947 (doc. 37, Rüschkamp Dossiers).

180 Rüschkamp to Peter van Gestel (*assistens* for Germany), June 18, 1947 (doc. 41, Rüschkamp Dossiers), and between Ledóchowski and Rüschkamp, October 13 and 23, 1947 (doc. 39–40, Rüschkamp Dossiers).

181 Bavink, "Sinn und Ethos der Wissenschaft," 257 (doc. 8, Rüschkamp Dossiers). Bavink, a Protestant and a science teacher with an international reputation for his work on science and religion, was editor of *Unsere Welt*.

182 Rüschkamp to Janssens, October 13, 1947 (doc. 39, Rüschkamp Dossiers).

The latter point—Rüschkamp's view about the autonomy of science—is revealed in something that he wrote to Ledóchowski in the midst of his controversy with Closen: "The sooner theologians stand together on the ground of the results of scientific research and recognize that natural science is the appointed interpreter of the natural revelation of the Creator, the better."[183]

Of course those who were placing limits on what Rüschkamp was allowed to say—that means, at root, Ledóchowski and Janssens (as superiors-general) and Bea (on whom Ledóchowski relied for evaluation of Rüschkamp's work)—would certainly not have denied that they too were committed to seeking the truth. While it is probable that neither of his superiors agreed with Rüschkamp about what the truth of the matter was in the case of evolution and the human body,[184] the difference will best come into focus if we attend to two particular aspects of the affair.

Ledóchowski, as head of a worldwide organization, emphasized a practical matter: public confidence that the work of the Society would not feature speculative, and possibly unorthodox, new ideas. That certainly does *not* mean that he valued the power or influence of the Society for which he was responsible more than he valued the truth. He did not, after all, require that Rüschkamp teach anything that he, or for that matter Rüschkamp, deemed to be *false*; only that he refrain from teaching something controversial about which ecclesiastical authority still had reservations.

A remark of Bea's, also quoted above, highlights another aspect of the difference. In his cover letter (to Ledóchowski) accompanying his appraisal of the controversy between Rüschkamp and Closen, he wrote: "Father Rüschkamp has too little understanding of anything that lies outside the domain of natural science and it is difficult or impossible to teach it to him."[185] And Janssens, in the wake of the Landau lecture, wrote that "it also has a theological aspect which is perhaps more difficult. So, in any case, great caution is called for."[186]

The correspondence allows us to see something of Rüschkamp as a person and it is perhaps worth concluding with that. Throughout the controversy, from the Düren lecture of 1929 to the Landau lecture of 1946, Rüschkamp reveals two things. First, an expressed willingness to submit to authority, which his authorities recognized as sincere even if not always predominant. Second, if stubbornness is too harsh a word, at least a strong determination to establish the orthodoxy of his position of the animal origin of the human body.

183 Rüschkamp to Ledóchowski, February 12, 1941 (doc. 29, Rüschkamp Dossiers).

184 For Ledóchowski, see his letter to Wulf, February 19, 1941 (doc. 28, Rüschkamp Dossiers); for Bea, see his *Il problema antropologico*, 55.

185 Bea to Ledóchowski, August 3, 1940 (doc. 19, Rüschkamp Dossiers).

186 Janssens to Rüschkamp, October 23, 1947 (doc. 40, Rüschkamp Dossiers).

c. Two Notes on Monogenism

The question of polygenism and original sin came up at the Jesuit curia twice in 1947. Evaluations of the view were solicited from two of the men who were about to be involved in the drafting of *Humani generis.*

The first time was in March, when Janssens, as a result of Dominican criticism of some ideas then being promoted by Jesuit theologians (both in print and in privately circulated typescripts), asked several Jesuit theologians for an evaluation of four published works. Included in one of the books to be reviewed was Henri Rondet's "Les Origines humaines et la théologie," an article in which he had suggested that polygenism might be reconciled with the doctrine of original sin by positing that the original sin (*peccatum originale originans*) might have been a collective one.

Denis Nerney (theologian at Milltown Park, Dublin, but later at the Gregorian University) thought that it could not.[187] Frederick Copleston also doubted that it could and went on to suggest an analogy with the medieval discussion of the eternity of the world. The two ideas might have in common that, although they could not be proven or disproven by reason, they were known by revelation to be false.[188] Édouard Dhanis addressed the question in more detail, writing:

> There is also the note on polygenism (n. 44, p. 250 of the article, a note which was not included in the later study). It seems to me that it is not unlawful to speak as the author has done. The situation is certainly extremely delicate. Perhaps most theologians think that monogenism (a couple from whom everyone alive today is descended) is a truth of the faith, and reasons for that view are very weighty. Are they entirely decisive? It does not seem to me that they are. Certainly monogenism should be held under pain of grave lack of judgment [*imprudence grave*], but I do not see that revelation definitively commits us for the future. Of course, Genesis, St. Paul, and the Council of Trent speak of Adam, and that binds us, but they did not examine the question of monogenism *ex professo.* Is it not possible that they did not intend to affirm this point? ... Are we obliged to say that the matter was certainly and definitively settled, no matter what paleontological discoveries might be made? There are theologians who seem not to take complete account of the great problems which the very disconcerting discoveries of paleontology now pose. Fr. Rondet does not seem to put monogenism in doubt; he only suggests [*donne à entendre*] that, in his view, this does not have the certainly irreformable character of a truth of faith.[189]

The question arose again at the very end of the year, when Alexandre Durand, at the seminary for the Syrian missions in Lyons, wrote to Janssens for advice about how to teach original sin and the origin of man. He sent a seven-page summary of his own thoughts on the question.[190] Polygenism, he had written, should perhaps not be judged

---

187 Nerney to Janssens, November 24, 1947 (doc. 46 bis, De doctrina, anno 1947 [praesertim], ARSI).

188 Copleston to Janssens, June 22, 1947 (doc. 46, De doctrina, anno 1947 [praesertim], ARSI).

189 Dhanis to Janssens, March 26, 1947, 1–2 (doc. 42, De doctrina, anno 1947 [praesertim], ARSI).

190 Durand to Janssens, November 25, 1947, and Durand, "Péché originel et polygénisme" ("P. Alexandre Durand,

a priori inconsistent with the faith. He was not trying to make a case for polygenism, but merely to show that it is not as important as it is sometimes thought to be. Janssens asked Bea to send his thoughts on the matter. Bea thought that Durand's opinions could not safely be taught. If the view were evaluated by the Holy Office it would surely be condemned.[191]

Polygénisme [mars 1948]," Assistentia Galliae 2012, ARSI [hereafter, "Durand File"]).

191 Bea, "Péché original et polygénisme," March 7, 1948. See also Bea's letter to Gorostarzu, March 7, 1948, forwarding the similar opinions from two Jesuit Old Testament scholars, Alberto Vaccari (like Bea, a consultor to the Biblical Commission) and Robert Dyson. (All are in the Durand File).

NON-OFFICIAL FORA
(1931–1950)

It was in about 1930 that overall Catholic appraisal of the idea of an evolutionary origin of the human body began to change. Theologian Maurizio Flick wrote in 1948 that "for more than twenty years there has been an extraordinary increase in the number of theologians, above any suspicion of unorthodoxy, who affirm that reconciliation on this point is possible, even if one restricted within determinate limits," though he acknowledged there were others who still regarded any attempt to effect a reconciliation on this point as offensive to pious ears.[1]

1. PERIODICAL LITERATURE

In the early 1940s, the new American journal *Theological Studies* published two articles touching on human evolution by Thomas J. Motherway, SJ, of Chicago's St. Mary of the Lake Seminary in Mundelein (Illinois). The first, "The Creation of Eve in Catholic Tradition," emphasized the use to which theologians (both Latin and Greek) had made of the creation of Eve (e.g., as a type of the sacramental grace flowing in the form of blood and water from the side of Christ at the Crucifixion) before concluding:

---

1 Flick, "Origine del corpo," 394.

> What is of importance in the question is to exclude an exegesis which would reduce the words describing the creation of the first woman to a merely symbolic expression of the physical and moral relation existing between her and her husband, the first man. Such an exegesis cannot be squared with the consensus of the Fathers of the Church and the great number of Catholic writers who have followed in their footsteps. We must hold as unquestionable that Eve's body was produced by a special operation of God's power from matter taken from the side of Adam.[2]

The second, "Theological Opinion on the Evolution of Man," was a survey of theological opinion published since 1930. He summarized the *status questionis* in two points:

> many very respectable authorities among the theologians consider it allowable to hold that the matter which God used in producing Adam's body may have been living matter, even the body of a brute animal. These authorities in general do not positively maintain that God used the body of an animal, but they do not see that such a stand should be prohibited to scientists.

But still,

> there must have been a special intervention above and beyond the operations of nature to prepare the *materia ex qua* for the infusion of the soul. Even if that matter was an animal body, God's action did not consist merely in the creation and infusion of the soul but also in giving the ultimate preparation necessary to the matter into which the soul was infused. For many theologians, the principal reason why this special action is insisted upon is the decree of the Biblical Commission under date of June 30, 1909.[3]

Later in the decade, Maurizio Flick, SJ, addressed both polygenism and the origin of the body of the first man in the pages of the Jesuit *Gregorianum*. The article on the former topic suggested that the increased acceptance of the rôle of evolutionary processes in anthropogenesis had put some pressure on the doctrine of monogenesis. He argued that the traditional doctrine on this point was the logical consequence of the central dogmatic components of the doctrine of original sin (universal guilt, transmission by natural generation, and singularity of the original sin itself). It was "a truth that, even though not yet solemnly defined, has always belonged, and will always belong, to faith."[4]

The second article was written, not to argue for anthropological evolutionism, but only to show that a restricted version of the theory (basically, that suggested by González, though Flick does not mention him) could not be excluded on the basis of the fonts of revelation. He chastises both those too eager to insist on evolution as the only possible explanation of the origin of the human body and those who reject it as incompatible with Catholic doctrine.[5]

---

2 Motherway, "Creation of Eve," 116.

3 Motherway, "Evolution of Man," 219.

4 Flick, "Poligenismo," 563.

5 Flick, "Origine del corpo," 412, with the key paragraph in italics.

He began by distinguishing three aspects of the question—scientific, philosophical, and theological. He pointed out, as Copleston had done, that in one respect the question resembled the medieval debate over whether the world had a beginning in time, in which St. Thomas taught that, whatever natural philosophy [i.e., science] shows to be possible, only faith can inform us that the created universe had a beginning in time:

> A similar case has now arisen with respect to the origin of the human body. The sciences might give us facts suggesting the hypothesis of a more or less extensive participation of lower living species in the formation of the first human body, and philosophy might not only accept such an hypothesis, but even see in it a certain suitability, while faith nevertheless teaches that things in fact came about otherwise.[6]

Then he proceeded to address the philosophical and theological aspects of the question.

There were three philosophically possible accounts of the origin of that first human body—direct creation, infusion of a human soul into inanimate matter with the features suitable to such an infusion, and infusion into the body of an already existing animal. None seemed to him to be obviously more suitable than any of the others. The elaboration of that third possible account, however, requires some care in its formulation: "If one wants to speak of a true generation of the first human being from a lower living species, the response has to be negative, not because the human soul is created by God alone, something which is true even in the case of human reproduction, but because an individual belonging to a determinate species cannot, as principal cause, transmit a nature superior to its own."[7] He also noted that science can never have the last word: "It might perhaps one day present an ever more perfect series of animal fossils preceding the appearance of man on earth, but it would not be able to determine the nature of the divine action [*decidere di quale natura sia stata l'azione divina*] if God had in fact wanted to make use of lower animals in producing a higher one."[8]

Does theology provide a reason to prefer one of the accounts over the others? The relevant passages of Scripture rule out direct creation (i.e., exnihilation) and require some direct divine action in the formation of the first human body. Whether God formed that body from unorganized (i.e., non-living) matter or from a living being, indeed whether he made use of secondary causes at all, is a theologically open question.[9]

Would any other theological arguments tell against a rôle for evolutionary processes in the formation of the human body? The only official documents relevant to the question were the *responsa* of the Biblical Commission and the address given by Pope Pius XII to the Pontifical Academy of Sciences in 1941.

In the case of the former, although he doubted that creation of the first human soul would be sufficient to make the creation of man "distinctive" in the sense required

---

6 Flick, "Origine del corpo," 395–96. He compares this to what St. Thomas says about the possibility of God creating a world that has existed from all eternity (cf. *Summa theologiae*, I, 46.2).

7 Flick, "Origine del corpo," 400.

8 Flick, "Origine del corpo," 400.

9 Flick, "Origine del corpo," 406–8.

by the Commission, direct divine action in adapting an animal body to the infusion of a human soul would be sufficient to do so. In any case, the *responsa* had to be interpreted in light of the more recent encyclical *Divino afflante Spiritu* (1943), which weakened the case against a rôle for evolution.

Nor could a case be made on the basis of a consensus of the Fathers, whose statements about the formation of the human body from mud was simply a case of their following the obvious sense of Scripture without intending to make adherence to that interpretation a matter of faith. Every religious doctrine that they deduced from it can equally well be deduced from the formation of the first human body by direct divine modification of an animal body.[10]

Finally, analogy of faith could not be deployed to resolve the issue.[11] Three bases for such an argument could be imagined, but none of them would work: Adam's being raised to a supernatural state only required a particular perfecting agent (God); any starting point (mud or animal) would do. The monogenetic unity of the human race required by the doctrine of original sin did not turn on the material basis (slime or animal) of the first human beings. Nor did the derivation of Eve's body from Adam's depend on that material basis.

2. ENCYCLOPEDIAS

Several new encyclopedias were published over the course of these two decades.[12]

In the Netherlands, a 25-volume Dutch *Katholieke Encyclopaedie*, appeared under the editorship of Dr. Jan Sassen, OP, and Bl. Titus Brandsma, OCarm, who died a martyr at Dachau in 1942. The *Encyclopaedie* saw no problem with the theory of evolution as applied to plants and animals, which its author (Theodorus van der Bom, priest of the diocese of Breda) declared to be "in complete agreement with the conclusions of natural theology and with revealed truth."[13] The question of the origin of man it left to its article on man, the theological part of which was assigned to Gerhardus Kreling, OP, theologian at the University of Nijmegen. There, after a several-page review of the fossil record, he said,

> The statement of the Bible Commission [which it quoted] does not establish a
> dogma with infallible authority. A Catholic is not, therefore, obliged by it to deny the
> evolution of man's body by virtue of his faith. But since the Bible Commission has
> official teaching authority, the Catholic is obliged to abide by [*houden*] its statement.
> Although it is not a definitive church statement, its significance for Catholics is this:
> in the present state of science there is no reason and therefore it is not permitted to

---

10 Flick, "Origine del corpo," 408–10.

11 Flick, "Origine del corpo," 410–12.

12 The two not discussed below are *Lexikon für Theologie und Kirche* (1931), a revision of *Kirchliches Handlexikon*, and a fourth edition of *Der Große Herder* (1931–32).

13 Van der Bom, "Afstammingsleer," 558.

question [*in twijfel te trekken*] the literal sense of the Bible concerning the origin of the human body. This leaves science with complete freedom to conduct further research.[14]

Still, "the acceptance of evolution with regard to the human body does not conflict with faith," he concludes, though "to explain the appearance on earth of *homo rationalis* as a whole, i.e., in soul and body, by virtue of evolution is not in accordance with the Catholic faith." He also emphasizes that polygenism also is contrary to faith.

In Italy, the *Enciclopedia cattolica* took an anti-evolutionist position about the human body. Fr. Wilhelm Koppers (1886–1961), priest and cultural anthropologist at the University of Vienna, who wrote the article on the evolution of man, acknowledged that "the ecclesiastical magisterium leaves us free with respect to the question of the origin of the human body,"[15] but on the substance of the question said that "man, even considered just in his body, appears fully . . . characterized by intellect [*spirito*]. . . . It is not possible to get to the formation of man simply by infusing a [human] soul in place of an animal soul in an animal body, even in an animal body of the most developed kind."[16]

On the other side was the most recent volume of the monumental *Dictionnaire de théologie catholique*. Underway since the end of the previous century, and by the mid-twentieth under the editorship of medievalist Father Émile Amann,[17] it reached the letter "T" (for *transformisme*) only in 1946. Despite the fact that he was a historian, not a scientist, he decided to write the article on evolution himself. He wrote that "as for transformism strictly limited to plant and animal species, it does not seem to us that official teaching has ever addressed it. For such a transformism concerns the purely scientific order, which, as such, falls outside the competence of the Church" and that "with certain adjustments, transformism, theistic evolutionism, does not seem at all opposed to the great truths which the *philosophia perennis* claims to make secure."[18]

3. TEXTBOOKS

In 1932, John A. O'Brien, then professor at the Newman Foundation at the University of Illinois, published *Evolution and Religion: A Study of the Bearing of Evolution upon the Philosophy of Religion*, a textbook the general thesis of which was that the Bible should not be used as a textbook of science. Attempts to do so in the past (saliently, in the case of Galileo, to which he devoted many pages) had only harmed religion and, however much the more recent opponents of evolution might be men of good will, the consequences of

---

14 Kreling, "Homo (C)," 474.

15 Koppers, "Evoluzionismo," 913.

16 Koppers, "Evoluzionismo," 913–14.

17 Amann's scholarly work included *Le dogme catholique dans les Pères de l'Église* (1922) and *L'Église au pouvoir des laïques, 888–1057* (1940).

18 Amann, "Transformisme," 1394 and 1377.

their opposition will be equally harmful. O'Brien made reference, of course, to the work of Mivart, Zahm, Wasmann, and de Dorlodot. The book offers some good insights into its subject, but is occasionally inaccurate with respect to some of its historical details.[19] Curiously, he does not distinguish the comprehensive opposition to evolution (which his treatment emphasizes) from the more limited concerns about the idea of an evolutionary origin of the human body that were the focus of concern of those Catholics who had for many years been objecting to the version of Catholic evolutionism proposed by authors from Mivart through Zahm to de Dorlodot.

O'Brien devoted the last half of his book to the philosophy and theology of nature, what he calls "the implications of [scientific] findings upon our concepts of the intelligibility of nature, of the rational organization of the universe and of the Supreme Intelligence behind it."[20] There he defended in particular the idea that the universe was a product of design, an idea that he defended against two challenges. The first was from materialism's mechanistic conception of nature, which "eliminat[es] the concept of plan or purpose from the universe." "Far from [doing that]," he replied, mechanism "renders it more imperative than ever before." "The structure of the machine, the delicate coordination of its parts, the synchronization of their various movements into a unified whole to attain a definite end, give unmistakable evidence both of the perception of the end and of the intelligent arrangement of parts to achieve the purposed objective."[21] The second challenge was that natural selection showed design to be unnecessary, to which he responded by citing (among others) University of California biologist Joseph LeConte, who had written many years before that "the removal of the result from man-like directness of separate action can not destroy the idea of design, but only modify our conception of the Designer. What science, and especially evolution, destroys, therefore, is not the idea of design, but only our low anthropomorphic notions of the mode of working of the Designer."[22] After two more chapters on the teleology of life, O'Brien concluded his book with a chapter on divine administration and natural law. His general theme, here a theology of nature again, is this: "By making nature autonomous, and infusing into the universe a network of laws which operate it with an uninterrupted sway, the Divine Administration has manifested a power far greater than that which would be entailed by direct and immediate intervention."[23]

Another indication of the place of evolution in American Catholic education comes not from a textbook but from the 1933 meeting of the Franciscan Educational Association. There Jerome Kobel, a Capuchin priest and himself a teacher, gave a long report on the evolution of man to his fellow Franciscans, "a survey," as he put it, "of the outstanding trends

---

19 Examples include his misunderstanding the concept of hypothesis in the controversy over heliocentrism (O'Brien, *Evolution and Religion*, 80) and his misstatement of the content of the 1925 Tennessee law challenged in the Scopes Trial (118).

20 O'Brien, *Evolution and Religion*, 123.

21 O'Brien, *Evolution and Religion*, 130.

22 LeConte, *Evolution*, 323; quoted at O'Brien, *Evolution and Religion*, 155.

23 O'Brien, *Evolution and Religion*, 215.

of anthropological evolutionary thought."[24] Kobel's report is not invariably unsympathetic to the idea of human evolution. He provided his fellow friars with a detailed review of the evidence and of the arguments on both sides of the question. In the end, however, he emphasized his concern about a broader "evolutionism," among the consequences of which, he thought, were the nihilism of Yevgeny Bazarov (in Ivan Turgenev's *Fathers and Sons*) and the militarism of Friederich von Bernhardi's *Deutschland und der nächste Krieg*, a militarism partly responsible for Kobel's death eleven years later.[25]

Kobel's brief outline was followed by a three-page comment from Father Hubert Vecchierello (also printed in the *Report*), whose tone was different:

> Today we are on the threshold of a period when ... more than a passing effort will be made to attempt to fit the theory of evolution into our general scheme or view of the universe.... At the present time, no one of any importance in the various branches of science doubts the truth of evolution.[26]

And what does the Church have to say about this? On this, he relied on Sheehan not only on the general compatibility of theistic evolution with Catholic doctrine, but even about the possible evolutionary origin of the human body. About the latter, he said two things. First, "the Church demands that we believed in the creation of Adam, but it has never defined what is meant by the 'slime of the earth' nor are we asked to believe that God actually shaped a figure of clay into which He instilled the breath of life."[27] Second, he repeated the passage quoted from Sheehan in chapter 13, that "if the proof were forthcoming to-morrow that the body of the first man was evolved from the lower animals, it would not be found to contradict any solemn, ordinary, or official teaching of the Church,"[28] but added, that "until it has been established as a fact, the Church will go on teaching the direct creation of Adam's body by God."[29] Vecchierello concluded by quoting, not Bernhardi, but another German—Erich Wasmann.

✳ ✳ ✳ ✳ ✳

Two Czech textbooks published during this period explicitly denied that there were any theological reasons for denying the evolutionary origin of the human body.

In 1938, Dominican theologian Reginald Dacík published a five-part textbook *Věrouka pro laiky*, in the second part of which he took up the question of evolution. The book received an *imprimatur* both from his Dominican provincial and from the

---

24 Kobel, "Brief Outline," 47.

25 Germany, like Japan, Bernhardi had written in that book, can only fulfill its duty to civilization "by the sword" (*Deutschland*, 309 [trans., 258]). When the United States entered the Second World War, Kobel left his classroom for a billet as a Navy chaplain. He was killed in a kamikaze attack while serving aboard the *USS Curtiss* on June 21, 1945. (As it happens, I am writing this paragraph on Memorial Day.)

26 Vecchierello, "Discussion [of Kobel's 'Brief Outline']," 121.

27 Vecchierello, "Discussion," 122.

28 Sheehan, *Apologetics: Part II*, 54.

29 Vecchierello, "Discussion," 123.

diocese of Olomouc. He began by pointing out that, once we accept the idea that the first material being,[30] from which everything else evolves, was created by God, then it does not matter how we present the development of the material world into its present state. As for man, we cannot just imagine God as an artisan making a statue into which He would breathe a soul (he drew on St. Augustine here). The body of the first man was composed of the same matter as was the body of animals and indeed every other material thing; his soul was the immediate product of the creative power of God. That is all that Scripture teaches us.[31] He acknowledges that some theologians[32] have argued that God took the most highly-evolved animal body and prepared it to receive a rational soul. Admitting as it does both the creation of the soul and the final modification of the animal body (presumably by direct divine action, though he does not say that explicitly), such a theory does not contradict the Catholic doctrine of creation. He did doubt that the theory corresponded to the latest science, which, he thought, was more and more abandoning the idea of animal ancestry due to lack of evidence. He also thought that the theory was in some tension with Thomistic philosophy. It would be hard to think of God depriving an animal of its substantial form and transforming its body into one suitable for the reception of a human soul.

In 1946, Bedřich Augustin published a fourth, "newly revised" edition of his widely-used textbook *Základní Náboženská Nauka*. After several pages of review of the fossil record, he wrote that "as long as the theory of evolution, applied to man, does not deny God the Creator or the fundamental difference between human and animal souls, it does not contradict the theological truth contained in Holy Scripture. Holy Scripture does not talk about the evolution of man, but also does not exclude it."[33]

---

30 Dacík used the term *první látka*, which ordinarily means "prime matter," but here he clearly means the first material thing that God created.

31 Dacík, OP, *Věrouka pro laiky*, 28–29.

32 He cited Johannes Peter Junglas, *Lehre der Kirche*, 90.

33 Augustin, *Základní Náboženská Nauka*, 4th ed., 36–37.

CHAPTER 17

HUMANI GENERIS
(1950)[1]

1. THE ENCYCLICAL

Official silence on the question of biological evolution and the origin of man, a silence that the Church had maintained since the ideas were first advanced in the late eighteenth century, ended on August 12, 1950, when Pope Pius XII published his encyclical *Humani generis*. Preparatory work on that letter, a letter on what it called (in its formal title) "some false opinions which threaten to undermine the foundations of Catholic doctrine," began on March 18, 1949, with the pope's appointment of a Commission on Religious Studies in France.[2]

---

1 This chapter is an expanded version of my "*Humani generis* & Evolution."

2 The Commission's working documents are available in the Archive of the Dicastery of the Doctrine of the Faith (D[ubia] V[aria] 1950 n.3-I, 293/1946, ADDF) (hereafter, HG Box-I). Documents of the Secretariate for Briefs to Princes and for Latin Letters, which was responsible for the final preparation of encyclical letters, are available in the Vatican Apostolic Archive (doc. 44, Positiones et minutae 179, Epistolae ad principes, AAV).

The members of the commission were: Augustin Bea, SJ (director of the Pontifical Biblical Institute and confessor to Pius XII); Mariano Cordovani, OP (Pius XII's personal theologian); Joseph Creusen, SJ (a consultor at the Holy Office); Josef Grendel, SVD (former superior general of his order); Franz Hürth, SJ (moral theologian at the Gregorian University); Pietro Parente (professor of dogmatics at the Lateran University and the first to call the tendencies which it was the object of the encyclical to evaluate "la nouvelle théologie" [in "Nuove tendenze teologiche," *L'Osservatore Romano*, February 9–10, 1942, p. 1]), and Sebastian Tromp, SJ (the chief drafter of two previous encyclicals) (Nota d'Ufficio [21 marzo 1949] relativa alla formazione della Commissione per lo studio delle correnti dottrinali in Francia, approvata dal Pontefice "Ex Audientia Sanctissimi" il 18 marzo 1949 [fol. 1, HG Box-I]). In June 1950, the secretary of the Holy Office, Francesco Marchetti-Selvaggiani, invited two Jesuit theologians from the Gregorian to take part in the work of the Commission as

What false opinions did Pope Pius have in mind? Communism, of course, which had just taken over much of Central Europe by force and had a significant following in France and in Italy, was one concern. Another was the existentialism that had become such a prominent aspect of European philosophical thought in the years before the encyclical was published. It had led, according to theologian Gustave Weigel, to a "zeal [that] may make [some theologians] willing to risk the dangers of an existentialist reconstruction [of Catholicism] in order to reach more effectively the human beings engulfed in an existentialist environment."[3]

And evolutionism? In a note prepared as part of another investigation (in 1945), Bea had commented that "in France many Catholics, not excluding the clergy, are favorable to evolutionistic theories."[4] A few years later, Bruno de Solages, in a memorandum that he submitted to the pope, said that "in French public opinion the evolution question [was] fundamental."

> Everyone, from intellectual to schoolteacher and worker, is thinking more and more in an evolutionary way. And every Christian, from the Union catholique des scientifiques français to the Jeunesse ouvrière chrétienne [i.e., from scientists to student-workers] is thinking about the question of the compatibility of Christianity and evolutionism. The evolutionary perspective is something much larger and of a more fundamental nature than the simple problem of the evolution of living species.[5]

This was not an idea completely distinct from the two just mentioned. Dialectical materialism constituted a kind of bridge between evolutionism and Communism. De Solages added, in the memorandum just quoted, that "[French Catholics] are asking to be shown how a spiritualist evolutionism is possible. They are asking all the more because the Marxists are going around proclaiming that the Christian view of the world is out of date and that only the Marxist view is in agreement with modern science."[6] The perceived connection between more general versions of evolutionism and existentialism is perhaps made clear in two passages of a document that Parente submitted to the Commission in the early stages of the drafting process: "The evolutionistic climate, animated by the dynamic concept of a perennial becoming opposed to any idea of an absolute, of substance, and of specific fixed essence, has been propitious to the development of the now fashionable philosophical current of Existentialism."[7] Versions of the evolutionism

---

informal consultants. The first was René Arnou, dean of theology; the second was Édouard Dhanis, newly appointed to the faculty after a number of years teaching at Louvain, probably invited as a result of work which he had done for the Jesuits—a visit to, and report on, the Jesuit scholasticates in France and then preparation of a list of theses to be condemned. (Memorandum [fol. 191, doc. 16, HG Box-I]).

3 Gustave Weigel, "Historical Background," 230.

4 Bea, "Nota sull'opera *L'Évolution régressive*," March 27, 1945 (doc. 4, CL 62/1945, ADDF).

5 De Solages, "Le P. Teilhard de Chardin et l'orientation des esprits dans la France contemporaine," 1, about June 8, 1948 (Studia 1060, ARSI).

6 De Solages, "Teilhard et l'orientation des esprits," 2.

7 Parente, "Saggio per uno schema di *Lettera Apostolica*," 9 (fol. 25, doc. 7, HG Box-I).

then popular in France raised theological concerns in other ways as well. In that same document, Parente also wrote that "others, under the pressure of Evolutionism, approach a dangerous monism, eliminating any substantial distinction between matter and spirit, between the natural and the supernatural orders, between truth and error."[8]

There was perhaps a connection to evolutionary anthropogenesis as well. On July 10, 1944, Emmanuel Célestin Suhard, cardinal-archbishop of Paris, had written in a letter to Rome that "various recent publications in Paris on the origin of man have created a certain amount of turmoil among theologians and scientists."[9] The roots of that turmoil, related to the more purely scientific use of the idea of evolution, could also be blamed in part on excessive enthusiasm for existentialism. Weigel explained why: "Existentialist thinking . . . would be prone to make of narration a secondary concern, not to be scrutinized for detail. . . . The sacred writer [of the first three chapters of Genesis] was only communicating the symbolic or mystical aspects of the origin of man. His narration is not so much concerned with the details of the historical event but rather with the existentialist meaning of creation."[10] But the Biblical narrative concerning the origin of man, Catholic theology insisted, has aspects that are not merely symbolic or mystical.

Addressed though it was to a rather broader array of questions, the encyclical is perhaps *now* best remembered precisely for its remarks on evolution,[11] even though at most five of the encyclical's forty paragraphs address the subject. On that topic, it had three things to say—one on the kind of cosmic evolutionism a Catholic version of which had been promoted by (or at least imputed to) Édouard Le Roy and Pierre Teilhard de Chardin and two on evolution and anthropogenesis.

✳ ✳ ✳ ✳ ✳

The encyclical's first mention of evolution came early in the text, in a passage less concerned with science than with philosophy—"from Hegel to Sartre," Hugo Rahner said.[12] The first draft, which Tromp had ready by October 1949, had made no reference to cosmic evolutionism,[13] but at the Commission meeting at the end of the month Grendel suggested that there probably should be a warning "against the excessive evolutionism which involves not only material matters, but spiritual and religious ones, even Christology."[14] Hürth had by then already proposed to the Commission a list of theses to condemn, including that "one single universal and continuous evolution reigns supreme in every

---

8 Parente, "Saggio," 10.

9 Suhard to Valerio Valeri (apostolic nuncio to France), August 19, 1944 (doc. 1, CL 62/1945, ADDF).

10 Weigel, "Historical Background," 226.

11 That was not the case at the time of its publication. In his "Gleanings from the Commentaries on *Humani Generis*," Weigel wrote that "When the commentators reached the paragraphs on evolution (35–37), the majority had surprisingly little to say" (p. 543).

12 Hugo Rahner, "Hemmschuh des Fortschritts?," 164.

13 Tromp, "Gallia: Instructio" (Progetto [Draft] I), October 1949 (fol. 8, doc. 5, HG Box-I)

14 Commissione speciale per gli studi religiosi in Francia, Verbale dell'adunanza del 31 ottobre 1949 (fol. 25, doc. 6, HG Box-I).

field of life and science, an evolution in which some primordial and fundamental being, going from state to state by its own power over the course of the ages, evolves into some kind of single collective organized being in which all individuation is absorbed."[15] Tromp added that to his second draft's list of theses to be proscribed.[16]

The third draft contained some of the ideas and even the phrases that made it into the final text—the idea that evolution enjoyed only some degree of probability even in the natural sciences, a general concern about the "monistic and pantheistic" versions of evolution, and the idea that it is "something pertaining to the origin of all things." Its tenets, the published version went on to say, were being used to reject "all that is absolute, firm, and immutable."[17]

＊ ＊ ＊ ＊

Pius took up the narrower idea of *biological* evolution as an explanation of the origin of species only late in the encyclical, and only with respect to anthropogenesis. The origin of plant and animal species was not addressed. On human origins, the encyclical made two points.

The encyclical's first point was that "the Teaching Authority of the Church does not forbid that, in conformity with the present state of human sciences and sacred theology, research and discussions, on the part of men experienced in both fields, take place with regard to the doctrine of evolution, in as far as it inquires into the origin of the human body as coming from pre-existent and living matter."[18] The encyclical went on to add two important qualifications. First, though the human body might be the product of evolutionary processes, human souls are immediately created by God. Second, discussion must be conducted judiciously, by experts and with moderation. It would be rash to "act as if the origin of the human body from pre-existing and living matter were already completely certain and proved by the facts which have been discovered up to now . . . and as if there were nothing in the sources of divine revelation which demands the greatest moderation and caution in this question."[19]

Four features of the drafting history are worth explicit notice.

First, the question of the origin of the human body is not mentioned in the first three drafts of the document that was to become the encyclical.[20] The first possible reference to the topic is in a note penciled into the third draft at the meeting of April 30:

15 Hürth, List of 26 theses to be condemned (fol. 21–23 (at 21), doc. 5, HG Box-I; identified by a reference in notes to the Commission minutes of October 31, 1949 (fol. 25, doc. 6)).

16 Thesis 6, in Tromp, "Francia: De Nova Theologia" (Progetto II), January 6, 1950, p. 9 (fol. 32, doc. 7, HG Box-I).

17 Compare Tromp, "Doctrinalia: Novum Schema Instructionis" (Progetto III), March 3, 1950, p. 2 (fol. 64, doc. 10, HG Box-I) with *Humani generis*, 563 (trans. ¶6)

18 Pius XII, *Humani generis*, 575 (trans., ¶36).

19 Pius XII, *Humani generis*, 576 (trans., ¶36).

20 The Commission on France was not immediately committed to writing precisely an encyclical, as opposed to an instruction or a syllabus of proscribed theses, and was directed in either case to an audience more limited than is implicit in the concept of an encyclical.

382

"Fr. Hürth proposed [including] a text on scientific evolutionism."[21] The issue is addressed explicitly first in the fourth draft,[22] in language differing only stylistically from that of the published text.

Second, there is no indication of controversy over this, a thesis that the consultors at the Index had considered rash in the 1890s and that Rüschkamp's Jesuit superiors had told him not to defend even in 1946. Still, the failure of the attempt to suppress Messenger's work in the 1930s does suggest that tolerance of the view was beginning to emerge.

Perhaps the position taken in the encyclical shows the influence of Bea, who had given two lectures on the question of the origin of Adam's body during the Settimane bibliche conferences held at the Biblicum in 1948, subsequently published as *Il problema antropologico*. In the first of those lectures, devoted to the scientific side of the question, he had said the evolutionist account had not yet been incontrovertibly demonstrated. In the second lecture, devoted to exegesis, he had denied that one could draw from the work of the Fathers a decisive argument for the idea that the human body was formed directly from the slime of the earth: "It is not enough simply to adduce a more or less large number of relevant patristic texts. One has to examine and evaluate them in accordance with the criteria of the treatise *De locis theologicis*. . . . Unfortunately, no such critico-theological study has yet been made, and so the patristic argument remains uncertain."[23]

He acknowledged that "a calm examination of the text of Genesis 2:7 . . . seems to show that the words of the Sacred Author do not *per se* exclude that moderate form of transformism which admits a special intervention of God for the formation of the body of Adam from an already living being [*una materia organica*], even though the obvious sense suggests rather that it was formed from the opposite [*una materia inorganica*]."[24] In his concluding remarks, Bea wrote that "the possibility [. . .] authorizes the exegete to re-examine the texts and to see whether they do or do not exclude transformism. If this transformist hypothesis is ever, even in its application to the human body, scientifically proven, then it will certainly become necessary to combine it with Sacred Scripture, since natural knowledge and divine revelation cannot contradict one another."[25] The encyclical agreed that the question was open and that theological considerations were relevant to its resolution. It seems more open to Mivart's version of anthropogenesis than did Bea's lecture, which referred rather to "a special intervention of God for the formation of the body of Adam," along the lines suggested by González and others, as the encyclical did not.

Bea went on, however, to express reservations about whether the evolutionary account of anthropogenesis was correct: "The obvious and most natural sense of the texts of Genesis *makes one think rather of a special production of the human body as*

---

21 Tromp, Progetto III, 13 (fol. 86, doc. 11, HG Box-I).

22 Tromp, "Novum Schema Instructionis (Reformatum)" (Progetto IV), May 1950, p. 12 (fol. 159, doc. 14, HG Box-I).

23 Bea, *Problema antropologico*, 32–33. The work mentioned is Melchior Cano's *De locis theologicis* (1563).

24 Bea, *Problema antropologico*, 45. I think that putting "a living being" for Bea's "una materia organica" is best, given that the controversy is over whether the human body *evolved* from some earlier species, not whether the "slime of the earth" from which God formed it was, say, a pile of rotting leaves or silicate clay.

25 Bea, *Problema antropologico*, 56.

well, without an immediate physiological connection with the animal kingdom. It is very difficult, if not impossible, to give a satisfactory reply to the objections which arise when one tries to get a concrete idea of how the body of Adam could have been produced by way of descent."[26] The encyclical, although cautious, did not express such reservations. Early drafts of the Commission's document had included, at the end of the paragraph that we are discussing, the remark that "it is very clear that the words of Scripture, if read in their obvious sense, are rather unfavorable to evolution," but that remark was dropped from the published text. An annotation in a printed version of Draft V says that Bea (and Hürth), while agreeing with the idea, thought that it would be inopportune to express it.[27]

It is perhaps also worth noting that, on January 2, 1950, as the commission was still in the early stages of drafting a document, Carlo Brivio (a priest of the Pontifical Institute for Foreign Missions, an entomologist and student of theology at the Gregorian University) submitted a dissertation entitled *L'Origine del corpo umano secondo la dottrina dei principali teologi post-Tridentini.* The dissertation itself, as its title suggests, is fundamentally historical, but the author, of course, recognized the relevance of his work to issues under discussion in his own day. Brivio summarized post-Tridentine thought by saying that "it does not seem to be opposed either to the possibility of a successive formation of Adam's body[28] or, what is more important, to the possibility of a partial co-operation by created causes.... There were even theologians positively open both to successive formation and to angelic co-operation."[29] Although the secondary causes under consideration by the theologians who were the subject of Brivio's study were the actions of angels, Brivio thought that it was clear that their arguments could be extended to secondary causes that were not only created, but natural: "Can we and must we, in light of the statements of the assertions common to all the theologians, exclude all forms of evolutionism? We think not.... It is not possible to draw from the doctrines of that period any truly theological argument against the possibility of the cooperation of secondary causes in the formation of man."[30] It is surely possible that the commissioners, several of whom were Jesuits with connections to the Gregorian University, were aware of Brivio's work. I have not, however, been able to find any direct evidence on that point.

The third interesting feature of the drafting history concerns the degree to which, or at least the tone in which, the Church should express its openness to the idea of an evolutionary origin of the human body. Drafts IV and V said, with only slight variation: "Whereas the doctrine of evolution, insofar as it studies the origin of the human body from previously existing organic matter . . . , <u>has until now been left by the ecclesiastical Magisterium, and is now also left</u>, to the investigation of experts in both fields, in

26 Bea, *Problema antropologico,* 55 (emphasis Bea's).

27 "Doctrinalia: Schema instructionis (Denuo reformatum)" (Progetto V), June 1950, p. 14n13 (fol. 192, doc. 16, HG- Box-I).

28 A successive (as opposed to an instantaneous) formation was one in which "the transition from shapeless mud (*terminus a quo*) to a body perfectly organized and suited to the reception of the soul (*terminus ad quem*)" took place gradually, with "intermediate grades of perfection" (Brivio, *L'origine del corpo umano,* 25).

29 Brivio, *Origine del corpo umano,* 31.

30 Brivio, *Origine del corpo umano,* 30.

conformity with the present state of the positive sciences and of sacred theology ....”[31] Antonio Bacci, at the Secretariate for Latin Letters, thought that the draft sounded generally “too scholastic.” After he had finished polishing the draft it read: “For these reasons <u>the Magisterium of the Church permits</u> men experienced in the human sciences and in sacred theology to research and discuss, in conformity with the present state of both fields, the doctrine of evolution, insofar as it inquires into the origin of the human body from pre-existent, living matter.”[32] In the last days before publication of the encyclical, Pope Pius replaced the word “permits” with the “does not forbid” of the published text.[33] Successive drafts thus seem to manifest an increasing aversion to the concession.

The final interesting feature of the drafting history concerns the origin of human souls. Draft V had said that “we are obliged to hold *as a matter of faith* that souls are directly created by God.”[34] Dhanis objected that “typically, approved authors say only that it is a matter of Catholic doctrine. Of course there are those who are more strict when it comes to the soul of the *first* man, but in the text of the draft, the word is plural, ‘souls.’”[35] So he wanted the text to replace “a matter of faith” with the weaker “as a matter of Catholic doctrine.” The published text of the encyclical says that “the Catholic faith obliges us to hold that souls are immediately created by God.”[36] So the plural was deliberate and the stronger ground was retained.

∗　∗　∗　∗　∗

The next paragraph of the encyclical took up the encyclical’s second point about anthropogenesis—“another conjectural opinion,” namely polygenism, about which it said that “the children of the Church by no means enjoy such liberty” as was conceded with respect to the evolutionary origin of the first human body.[37] The word “polygenism” had, to be sure, been used variously over the course of its history. Some authors had used it to mean only that various groups of human beings (e.g., human races) had entirely distinct phylogenetic origins, a concept that, in an effort at disambiguation, Catholic authors were just beginning to call *polyphyletic* polygenism.[38] Others used the term “polygenism” more broadly, to include even multiple original pairs within a single human *group*, i.e., *monophyletic* polygenism. The text of the encyclical on this point is as follows:

---

31 See Progetti IV, 12–13, and V, 13. The version quoted is from “the definitive text, being sent to Bacci for editing” (fol. 454, HG Box-I) (italics mine).

32 “Bozze di stampa rivedute ed approvate [non definitive] dal Pontefice, con alcune correzioni autografe” (fol. 504, HG Box-I) (underlines showing the key change mine).

33 Bacci to Crovini, August 13, 1950 (fol. 289, HG Box-I).

34 Progetto V, 13 (emphasis mine). For more on this question, see chapter 3, where I discuss the treatment of this topic at Vatican I.

35 Dhanis, “Osservazioni del padre Dhanis,” May 25, 1950, 8 (fol. 211, HG Box-I) (emphasis his).

36 Pius XII, *Humani generis*, 575 (trans., ¶36).

37 Pius XII, *Humani generis*, 576 (trans., ¶37).

38 For more on the development of terminology, see below.

The faithful cannot embrace that opinion which maintains that either after Adam there existed on this earth true men who did not take their origin through natural generation from him as from the first parent of all, or that "Adam" signifies [*significare*] a certain number of first parents. Now it is in no way apparent how such an opinion can be reconciled with that which the sources of revealed truth and the documents of the Teaching Authority of the Church propose with regard to original sin, which proceeds from a sin actually committed by an individual Adam and which, through generation, is passed on to all and is in everyone as his own.[39]

Formal discussion of (monophyletic) polygenism was already underway at the Holy Office when work on the encyclical began. Unlike the provisional openness to the evolutionary origin of the human body, the rejection of any form of polygenism (and the corresponding reaffirmation of the Tridentine formulation of the doctrine of original sin) was already included in the first draft of the encyclical.[40]

✳ ✳ ✳ ✳ ✳

That discussion was precipitated by some lectures that had been given by a French Dominican, Louis Dumeste. Dumeste had been teaching Genesis, both to his Dominican brothers at the university-level provincial *studium* at the convent of Saint-Maximin, near Aix, and to a small, select, group of lay auditors at Aix and at Marseilles under the patronage of the archbishop of the latter city. It came to the notice of the Holy Office as the result of a two-part lecture—"Genèse et enseignement religieux" and "Comment présenter aux enfants les premiers chapitres de la Genèse"—presented to priests and lay catechists on June 24, 1948. That lecture covered topics ranging from the authorship of the Pentateuch to the Flood of Noah. Although he did not explicitly raise the question of the evolutionary origin of the human body, that was surely presupposed in what he had to say about polygenism. Its acceptance, Dumeste said, would depend on scientific evidence (beyond what was then available) and its compatibility with the doctrine of original sin (strictly understood). If there had been more than one original couple, the original sin would have had to have been the actual sin of each couple.[41] A handout summarizing the lecture was sent to diocesan clergy and made available at the diocesan center for religious education.

On October 6, 1948, Louis Hemour, a parish priest from Marseilles, complained to the Holy Office about Dumeste's ideas and, on October 14, the Holy Office sent a letter of inquiry to the Dominican master-general, Emmanuel Suárez.[42] Suárez, in turn promptly wrote to Marie-Joseph Nicolas, as the responsible provincial, and received in reply both

---

39 Pius XII, *Humani generis*, 576 (¶37). The standard (NCWC) English translation has "represents" for *significare*, which seems to me to be an error and which I have therefore corrected. Ronald Knox, in his translation (p. 190), put "Adam was the name given to some group."

40 Tromp, Progetto I, 6.

41 Dumeste, "Genèse et enseignement religieux" (doc. 2–3, CL 97/1949, ADDF [hereafter, Dumeste File]).

42 Hemour to the Holy Office, October 6, 1948 (doc. 1, Dumeste File) and Francesco Marchetti-Selvaggiani (secretary to the Holy Office) to Suárez, "Minuta di lettera inviata al maestro generale dei Predicatori," October 14, 1948 (doc. 4).

a summary of what Dumeste had been teaching and an account of the instructions that Nicolas, on his own initiative, had given to Dumeste.[43]

First, Nicolas told Dumeste to use better judgment in discussing these matters, as the idea of a single original human couple seemed to be *proxima fidei*. Second, Dumeste was to submit anything he made available to the public, even hand-outs, to Nicolas for review. Nicolas added that Dumeste's principal goal in detaching monogenism from the sacred text was "to respond to the concerns of those to whom the writings of intemperate evolutionists had done a lot of harm" and that he had felt justified in doing so in light of the remark of Achille Cardinal Liénart that (in Nicolas's words) "in the unlikely event that polygenism were demonstrated, the Church would know how to find a theological interpretation of original sin which would preserve the entirety of the Dogma without contradicting science."

On March 10, 1949, the master-general reported back to the Holy Office.[44] At a meeting on April 2, the consultors decided to take up the case.[45] As Bea later put it in the cover letter to his *votum*, "Dumeste's writing can be considered to be a characteristic expression of an anti-traditional tendency manifest in a number of francophone exegetes."[46] Bea was assigned to write the *votum*, one which, he hoped, would also be of use to the Commission on France, dealing as it did with a question that had not yet received much emphasis in the Commission's discussions.[47]

In his *votum*, Bea said that, even though Dumeste acknowledged the unproven status of polygenism, he took the truth of transformism itself too much for granted and gave too little attention to the necessity or non-necessity of any particular intervention by God in the formation of the human body.[48] The idea of a single original human couple would be hard to reconcile with purely natural processes (it being unlikely that the sudden mutation would occur only twice, once in a man and once in a woman), but, for the Christian transformist for whom God's intervention transforms an animal into a man, there would be no particular problem.[49]

In Bea's judgment, the ideas expressed in Dumeste's lecture notes were rash. Perhaps they could be allowed as part of a contribution to serious academic discussion, but not, as in this case, as ideas proposed for schoolroom teaching.[50] He recommended that the notes should be removed from the education center and that the author should be prohibited from any further writing or speaking on the topic.[51]

---

43 Nicolas to Suárez, November 19, 1948 (Série 1 C 15402, Archive Dominicain de la Province de Toulouse).

44 Suárez to Marchetti-Selvaggiani, "Risposta del generale dei predicatori," March 10, 1949 (doc. 5, Dumeste File).

45 Minutes of the preparatory congregation, April 2, 1949 (doc. 7, Dumeste File).

46 Bea to Ottaviani (assessor at the Holy Office), June 6, 1949 (doc. 8, Dumeste File).

47 Bea to Ottaviani, June 6, 1949 (doc. 8, Dumeste File).

48 Bea, *Votum*, June 5, 1949, 11 (doc. 9, Dumeste File).

49 Bea, *Votum*, 11–12.

50 Bea, *Votum*, 17.

51 Bea, *Votum*, 18.

Suárez, meanwhile, had come to the same conclusion, and on June 30, he wrote to Nicolas that Dumeste was to cease teaching at the end of the year and to avoid further comments on polygenism and original sin.[52] He also wrote to the Holy Office requesting that no public measures be taken against Dumeste personally because (among other reasons), there being other theologians who were saying the same thing, "it would surely be regarded as a strong swipe at the poor little puppy, while the great lion remained unperturbed."[53]

Suárez's actions seem to have satisfied the Holy Office as a resolution of the particular case, but, as Bea had pointed out in the letter quoted above, the problem was not so limited. The consultors, in the preparatory congregation that met on July 4, agreed that the matter needed to be addressed at a higher level, possibly by the Commission on France. As it happened, all seven members of that commission were, as consultors to the Holy Office, present at that meeting. They had in hand a draft of two *dubia* that had been prepared by Bea. The cardinal members of the Holy Office, meeting on July 13, were in general agreement with the consultors on the issue, but were in no hurry about the *dubia*, which they thought could wait for the resolution of more general questions. The pope approved those decisions on the following day.[54]

Six months later, on January 30, 1950, the consultors, unhappy with the time it was taking the Commission on France to address the question of polygenism, passed (13–2) a resolution that a separate decree on polygenism should be published without delay. Again (on February 15) the cardinals decided to wait.[55] On March 24, the pope stated his preference for including the rejection of polygenism in the encyclical; the topic made its first appearance in Draft III, in March 1950.

More important than the disagreement about whether the topic should be addressed in an encyclical or in a separate decree was the question of what should be said. The formulation found in Drafts IV and V (which do not differ from one another on the issue)[56] was turned over to a committee for final drafting before being sent on to the Secretariate of Briefs to Princes and of Latin Letters, which would do the final stylistic editing. The committee did not come to complete agreement, however, and so, on August 3, the Secretariate had in hand two versions of the passage on monogenesis, one recommended by the majority of the committee and another proposed by Dhanis. A review of the successive and alternative formulations can add to our understanding of the issue for two reasons. First, it shows something about what respected theologians thought about the matter in question. Second, not only did the drafting of the encyclical

---

52 Suárez to Nicolas, June 30, 1949 (two letters). See also Nicolas's reply of July 17 (XIII.36104 Dumeste, AGOP).

53 Suárez, "Relazione di padre Suarez per la consulta," July 4, 1949, 3 (fol. 54–55, doc. 11, Dumeste File).

54 "Circa quaedam scripta P. M. L. Dumeste, OP, sub titulo: 'Genèse & enseignement religieux: Comment présenter aux enfants les premiers chapitres de la Genèse'" (fol. 53–62, doc. 11, Dumeste File).

55 Nota della Cancellaria, "Dubbio circa il Poligenismo," April 22, 1955, 3 (fol. 44–51, D[ubia] V[aria] 1950 n.3-IV, 221/1955, ADDF [hereafter, HG Box-IV]).

56 Progetto IV, 13; and Progetto V, 14.

include some consultation with the pope,[57] but in three cases the choice between the formulation proposed by Dhanis and that proposed by the majority was made directly by Pope Pius himself. Three issues (each, as it happens, connected to a choice between those alternative formulations) merit comment.

✶ ✶ ✶ ✶ ✶

The first issue is the exact content of the opinion that Catholics are not at liberty to hold. The *positive* teaching that forms the basis for the prohibition is twofold—that Adam was one person and that he was the ancestor of all of the rest of us.

The assertion that Adam was one single person was aimed at correcting two views that were beginning to gain some currency in the 1940s—that the word "Adam" named not a single individual, but a certain number of first parents, or even that it just meant the human race taken collectively. The various formulations considered by the Commission differ only in how explicitly they make that point—one Adam? one individual Adam? a physical person? The published text says "*uno Adamo,*" "one Adam,"[58] which the pope chose over the majority's "*Adae, hominis individui*" and Dhanis's "*uno homine Adamo,*" but covered the point more explicitly by specifying (at Dhanis's recommendation) a second unembraceable opinion, namely "that Adam represents a certain number of first parents."

The consultors at the Holy Office, considering how to put together a general response to the Dumeste case, and the Commissioners, drafting what should at this point just be called the document on France, had had more trouble deciding exactly how to say that Adam was "the protoparent of all." The problem was specifying the exact extension of the descent from Adam. Whom did it include? Tromp's early drafts just put "the human race," but perhaps that was not as clear as it at first appears to be. Versions of pre-Adamitism (in its usual Catholic sense, i.e., human beings existing *before* Adam, whether his human ancestors or other populations of men entirely separate from us) had received occasional notice in Catholic theological literature. Jules Fabre d'Envieu, priest and theologian at the Université de Paris in the late nineteenth century, for example, had emphasized the possible existence of pre-Adamites unrelated to us as a possible way of explaining certain scientific data without creating theological problems.[59] Domenico Palmieri, SJ, of the Jesuits' Collegium Romanum, agreed that such a view would create no theological problems and refused to assign the idea any note of theological censure.[60] Based as it usually was on a restitutionist hermeneutics that left a gap between the creation of the world and the hexaemeron, it was a view that, by 1950, had few Catholic, and few scientific, defenders.

Nevertheless, the consultors and commissioners, careful about the implications of what they wrote, differed over what account should be taken of pre-Adamitism. In their meeting of January 31, the consultors at the Holy Office appointed Hürth, Parente, Tromp,

---

57 For example, on February 23, March 14, April 24, and May 27. ("Dubbio circa il Poligenismo").

58 "*Uno Adamo*"; the English translation's "individual Adam" is thus slightly at variance with the original.

59 Fabre d'Envieu, *Origines de la terre et de l'homme,* 329–30.

60 Palmieri, *De creatione,* Thesis XXX, 272–78.

389

and Bea to draft "a formula which clarifies the version of polygenism to be condemned, in order not to include pre-Adamites or other forms, perhaps contemporary to Adam, which have now died out."[61] The same concern perhaps underlay the proposal made by Alfredo Ottaviani, assessor at the Holy Office, at a meeting of the consultors at the Holy Office on February 16, to put that Adam was the protoparent of "all men born after [him]."[62] Despite the universal approval of Ottaviani's suggestion reported in the minutes of the meeting, there remained some difference of opinion over exactly how the idea should affect what the final product should say.

Heinrich Lennerz did not want to seem to leave the question open and wrote in March that:

> If the formula which explicitly prescinds from pre-Adamism could be understood to mean that the Holy Office countenances pre-Adamism, then it would seem to me better not to use it; if, however, there is no danger of that, then the wording of the formula, "all men living on earth after him" [rather than merely "the human race"] insofar as it is clearer and more distinct would seem to me to be preferable.[63]

Parente, by contrast, had argued (in a document circulated just before Ottaviani's suggestion) in favor of putting "the entire human race, according to its ordinary meaning" (rather than "all men living after him [Adam] on earth" precisely because it *would* leave the door open to pre- or co-Adamitism in case there later turned out to have existed such beings (it being understood that they would not be covered by the ordinary meaning of the term "human race").[64]

Bea thought that a distinction between two kinds of non-Adamites was theologically important. The existence of *co*-Adamites, "men in such contact with the descendants of Adam that they could interbreed with them," he thought, was theologically inadmissible. Although the text of Genesis was not favorable to the idea of pre-Adamites, the exegetical difficulties, he thought, were not insurmountable.[65] He was concerned that "the actual state of paleoanthropological science does not exclude the possibility that, before Adam, there were other beings of a human nature not related to Adam's stock, who disappeared long ago."[66] He preferred, therefore, wording that would "not prejudge the delicate question, scientifically still under discussion, of the relation of fossil humans to *H. sapiens*." He wanted a formula that would "stay strictly within the field of theology without touching the scientific question, even with respect to the human race."[67]

61 "Dubbio circa il Poligenismo," 3.

62 Minutes of preparatory congregation, February 16, 1950 (fol. 60, doc. 9, HG Box-I).

63 Lennerz, Memorandum, March 31, 1950 (fol. 91–2, HG Box-I).

64 Parente, "Schema di Decreto sul poligenismo," February 13, 1950 (fol. 27, HG Box-IV).

65 Bea, "Pro-memoria sulla questione del Poligenismo," Apr 2, 1950, 2 (fol. 1–6, HG Box-IV).

66 Bea, "Pro-memoria," 3–4.

67 Bea, Memorandum "De poligenismo: forma proposta del Rev.mo P. Bea," April 2, 1950 (fol. 94, HG Box-I).

Over the course of the deliberations, a number of alternative ways of describing the descendants of Adam without raising the question of pre-Adamitism were proposed:[68]

> Tromp: all men existing after Adam here on this earth
> Hürth: the human race with which Sacred Scripture, both Old and New Testament, as well as the doctrine and practice of the Church, is concerned
> Bea: the human race now diffused around the world
> Dhanis: the whole human race

There were others—"all men living (or born) after Adam," "the present human race." Although all formulations agreed in asserting common descent from Adam for everyone now alive, they did not all have the same implications with respect to pre- and co-Adamites. The published version of the text of the encyclical rules out the existence of co-Adamites without ruling out the possible existence of pre-Adamites none of whose descendants lived after Adam.

✳ ✳ ✳ ✳ ✳

The second issue was this: What were the grounds for rejecting polygenism? The problem was not primarily Genesis 1–2, but rather the doctrine of original sin. The textual ground is thus Romans 5:12–19, guided by Tradition in general and by the Council of Trent in particular: "original sin ... proceeds from a sin actually committed by an individual Adam, ... is passed on to all through generation, and is in everyone as his own."[69] Here also there were some differences among the drafters about the proper characterization of the problem with polygenism. The fourth draft, the first that is close enough to the published text to allow such direct comparisons, had proposed saying that it was contrary to "Catholic dogma."[70] In a memorandum submitted to the Commission on May 25, 1950, Dhanis objected that "some of the best-known theologians do not say that monogenism is exactly a dogma, but say rather that it is a *sententia proxima fidei.*" He cited Reginald Garrigou-Lagrange in defense of his point[71] and proposed that the weaker term "doctrine" replace the word "dogma."[72]

What is the significance of this change? Ludwig Ott wrote that "by dogma in the strict sense is understood a truth immediately (formally) revealed by God which has been proposed by the Teaching Authority of the Church to be believed as such."[73] Sixtus

---

68 The formal context was a condemnation of the idea that there was anyone who fit that description without being descended from Adam ("Dubbio circa il Poligenismo," 6–7). See also "Propositiones condemnandae et cum ordinariis communicandae," 5 (fol. 344, doc. 20, HG Box-I).

69 *Humani generis,* 576 (trans., ¶37).

70 Progetto IV, 13.

71 Garrigou-Lagrange had written that "according to Scripture, Tradition, and theology, monogenism appears more and more to be a truth *proxima fidei*" ("Le Monogénisme," 202).

72 Dhanis, "Osservazioni," 9 (fol. 212, HG Box-I).

73 Ott, *Grundriss,* 5 (trans., 5). Or see Cartechini, *De valore notarum theologicarum,* 11. The Code of Canon Law of 1917 (Bk. III., Pt. IV, c. 1323.3), which was in force in 1950 said, "Nothing can be understood to be dogmatically declared or defined, unless it is manifestly presented as such" (*Declarata seu definita dogmatice res nulla intelligitur, nisi id manifeste constiterit*).

391

Cartechini offered a particularly illuminating explication of the concept of *sententiae proximae fidei*. They are propositions which, "although not altogether certain, are nevertheless probable and, as it seems to many, are *de fide*."[74]

So was the problem the reconciliation of polygenism with dogmas made explicit at Trent, or merely reconciliation with the (perhaps only apparent or at least less authoritative) presumptive presuppositions or consequences of those dogmas? The commissioners differed over how specifically the point of contrast should be identified.[75] At the preparatory congregation held at the Holy Office on February 6, thirteen of the consultors wanted to say that "denying that all men living on earth after Adam derive their origin from him" would "contradict (or be contrary to) what the Church has defined and proposes for belief about the origin and transfusion of original sin." Of the four others, two wanted to say only that it "could not be reconciled with the doctrine defined at Trent," while the other two wanted only a bare parenthetic reference to Trent, thinking that further precision would only give rise to further controversy.

No doubt connected to that issue is an omission from the end of the paragraph. The fourth and fifth drafts had put, immediately after the summary of the teaching in question: "Nor is there any reason to fear that this doctrine, proclaimed by the Council of Trent, will be disturbed by new advances in the sciences. For there cannot be any danger of a true conflict between a scientifically certain conclusion and a divine revelation given by Him who is the Lord of all the sciences."[76] Dhanis proposed, in addition to the change of "dogma" to "doctrine," to replace those last few words of that paragraph with the phrase "a proposition so well established in the teaching of the magisterium of the Church."[77] The encyclical omitted the two sentences altogether.

Dhanis further proposed, as the final draft was being prepared for papal approval, that the term "Catholic doctrine," which he had earlier proposed as a replacement for "Catholic dogma," be replaced in turn, by the phrase "that which the sources of revealed truth and the documents of the Teaching Authority of the Church propose." Pius chose this phrase over the majority's (i.e., over Dhanis's earlier) "Catholic doctrine" for the final document. No theological degree of certainty was assigned; the Council of Trent (and the passage from St. Paul) was cited in a footnote.

✳ ✳ ✳ ✳

The third issue is the definitiveness of the encyclical's verdict on polygenism. Commentators on the encyclical have long pointed out that the exact wording of this passage—"it is no way apparent how such an opinion can be reconciled with ..." (*nequaquam appareat quomodo huiusmodi sententia componi queat ...*)[78]—is weaker

---

74 Cartechini, *De valore notarum theologicarum*, 67. Cartechini used monogenesis as an example of a *sententia proxima fidei*. For an explanation of "theological notes," see Appendix II.B.

75 "Dubbio circa il Poligenismo," 4–5.

76 Progetto IV, 13.

77 Dhanis, "Osservazioni," 9 (fol. 212, HG Box-I).

78 Pius XII, *Humani generis*, 576 (trans., ¶37).

than it could have been, though the significance of this has been minimized by those who would give the encyclical a more definitive anti-polygenist reading.[79]

Bea's first draft of a *dubium* on polygenism (from July 1949) had asked only "whether polygenism can safely be taught."[80] A *votum* written by Hürth some months later offers some clarification:

> What was proposed was a decree in which nothing was immediately decided concerning the *truth* of the propositions. The immediate judgment would only be about their *safety*, declaring authoritatively that they included the danger of deviating from *Catholic truth*. That danger is asserted only given *the present state of knowledge* of the case. The formula used, "cannot safely be taught," neither affirms nor denies, but prescinds from the question, whether further scientifico-theological inquiry can be expected to eliminate any serious danger.[81]

On January 30, however, the consultors changed the wording from "cannot be safely taught" to "cannot be held" (*non teneri potest*).[82] When the idea of issuing a *dubium* on the question separate from the encyclical was eventually dropped, the new language became part of later drafts of the encyclical (though "held" was eventually replaced with "embraced" (*amplecti*)).[83]

On the definitiveness of this judgment about inconsistency, however, Dhanis and the majority again offered alternatives. The majority was content with a minor revision of the drafts IV and V—"*quippe quia haec opinio componi nequeat*" became "*cum huiusmodi sententia componi nequeat*," in either case "since that thesis [sc., polygenism] could not be reconciled";[84] Dhanis proposed instead what Mario Crovini (deputy notary at the Holy Office) called "the less rigid"[85] "*cum non appareat quomodo huiusmodi sententia componi queat*," that "it was not apparent how it could be reconciled."[86]

"Only the Holy Father," Crovini said in an internal memorandum, "will be able to decide which text should be preferred." Bacci was to find out what was the mind of Pope Pius.[87] In the end, the pope replaced the wording suggesting the impossibility of reconciliation with what it would be best to call a mere *presumption* of inconsistency, though strengthening slightly the formulation proposed by Dhanis: "it is in no way

---

79 See, for example, Charles Boyer, "Leçons de l'encyclique 'Humani generis,'" 533. Other examples could be cited.

80 Reported in "Dubbio circa il Poligenismo," 2–3.

81 Hürth, *Votum*, January 19, 1950 (fol. 10–11, HG Box-IV).

82 Meeting Minutes, January 30, 1950 (fol. 14v, HG Box-IV).

83 See, for example, Progetto IV, 13; and Progetto V, 14.

84 Progetto IV, 13; Progetto V, 14; and draft forwarded to the Secretariate for Latin Letters (no. 44, Positiones et minutae 179, Epistolae ad principes, AAV). Here I correct an inconsequential error made in my earlier paper, "*Humani generis*," where I labeled as Progetto IV the words of another early draft. This does not affect the point I made there (or here).

85 Crovini, Note to an unidentified monsignor (probably Bacci), August 3, 1950 (no. 44, Positiones et minutae 179, Epistolae ad principes, AAV).

86 Fol. 511, HG Box-IV, and no. 44, Positiones et minutae 179, Epistolae ad principes, AAV.

87 Crovini, Note, and Bacci, August 4, 1950 (no. 44, Positiones et minutae 179, Epistolae ad principes, AAV).

[*nequaquam*] apparent how such an opinion can be reconciled with that which the fonts of revealed truth and the acts of the Magisterium of the Church propose."[88]

* * * * *

The task of writing a general history of Catholic evolutionism after 1950 I will leave to another author. Nevertheless, it does seem appropriate to offer (both at the end of this chapter and in an afterword) a brief account of several matters that have a particularly close association with the encyclical and its themes.

2. THE HOLY OFFICE

Three incidents in the immediate post-encyclical history of the Church shed further light on our topic. Two concerned polygenesis; the third, the origin of the human body. Two are cases of alleged transgression of the norms laid down by the encyclical, the third, a proposal for a clarificatory document from the magisterium.

a. The Muller Case: *The Index of Prohibited Books*

In September 1950, the month after the publication of the encyclical, *Synthèses: Revue européene* published Th. Masson's critique of *Humani generis*, an article in which the author argued that the encyclical would "forever discourage those open and generous minds who still nourished illusions about the rigidity of Catholic views."[89] In a later issue, Canon Camille Muller, a botanist at the Université catholique de Louvain, was given space to come to the encyclical's defense. Muller had addressed the question of science and faith previously, in a 1948 article entitled "La Science et la foi." There he had argued that Catholics' freedom in scientific research extended to the origin of the human race and on that basis had defended the possibility of polygenism.[90] In "L'Encyclique 'Humani Generis' et les problèmes scientifiques," he addressed three points: Catholic freedom with respect to scientific research, the degree of certainty that the evolutionary hypothesis had attained, and whether the human race was descended from a single couple.

On the independence of biological and theological research, Muller wrote that "biological evolution must first be studied scientifically, even by a Catholic scientist, without a preliminary examination of the data which theology might be able to provide."[91]

On the question of certainty, he wrote that there could be no doubt about the fact of evolution, even though the details of the process and about the origin of particular species were less certain. The general certainty extended to the evolution of man—"the rejection

---

88 Pius XII, *Humani generis*, 576 (trans., ¶37).

89 Masson, "Unique salut du monde?," 4.

90 Muller, "Science," 81–89 (trans., 20–29).

91 Muller, "Encyclique," 13.

of the evolution of man constitutes a rejection of biological evolution altogether."[92] The encyclical, he suggested, had undervalued the evolutionary hypothesis.[93]

With respect to monogenesis, Muller had several things to say. First, he thought that the problem was less urgent than was usually supposed and that the Fathers at Trent had been concerned only with existing humanity [*l'humanité actuel*], and not with prehistory.[94] Second, he thought that the encyclical did not rule out a conception of monogenesis slightly different from the usual one, "less strict, but nevertheless efficacious":

> By the successive unions of the descendants of several primitive couples (including the first couple of Genesis), it would only take a very few generations until every human being would be descended from the first human being, the one mentioned in Genesis (without the necessity of marriages between brothers and sisters), and until, perhaps, the entire present [*actuel*] human race (the only one the Fathers of the councils could have had in mind) would be tainted by original sin and saved by Christ.[95]

Muller saw himself as defending the encyclical against Masson's critique, but nevertheless, the article was delated to the Holy Office for possible placement on the *Index.*

The task of writing the *votum* was given to Bea, who submitted it on June 9, 1953. Bea wrote that Muller was "not a theologian, but a scientist, and lacks the breadth of mind and vision necessary to assess either theological or scientific arguments against his theory." Despite his good will and eagerness to defend the encyclical, "his way of speaking is all the more irreverent, not to say arrogant, and the insinuations which he makes are unworthy of a Catholic."[96] Due to its extremely limited circulation, Bea recommended against placing the article on the *Index.* Both author and publisher should be told not to prepare further editions and the author should do something to minimize the damage and scandal involved. Finally, Bea recommended arranging for some Catholic journal or review to publish a scientific critique of the article.

The preparatory congregation met on November 23, 1953, with the commissioner at the Holy Office (Cristoforo Bigazzi), and fifteen consultors present.[97] Support for following Bea's recommendation was unanimous. The cardinals, meeting in a general congregation held on December 2, however, wanted the article put on the *Index,* a recommendation approved by Pope Pius eight days later.[98] This was done on December 14, 1953, with an

---

92 Muller, "Encyclique," 15.

93 Muller, "Encyclique," 29.

94 Muller, "Encyclique," 19.

95 Muller, "Encyclique," 21–22.

96 Bea, *Votum,* June 9, 1953, 6 (fol. 2–6, doc. 2, CL 389/1952, ADDF).

97 Carlo Balić (OFM), Agostino Bea (SJ), Ulrico Beste (OSB), Michele Browne (OP), Emanuele Caronti (OSB), Mario Castellano (OP), Enrico Corrà (OFM Conv), Giuseppe Creusen (SJ), Giuseppe Graneris, Luigi Hudal, Francesco Hürth, Francesco Morano, Pietro Parente, Luigi Traglia, and Sebastian Tromp (SJ) (Minutes of the preparatory and general congregations, November 27 and December 2, 1953 [fol. 8, doc. 3, CL 389/1952, ADDF]).

98 Decretum (doc. 3–4, CL 389/1952, ADDF).

explanation provided in an unsigned article published in *L'Osservatore Romano*.[99] The article was presented not as having come from the Holy Office (although the files in the archives included a draft of the article), but as the opinion of the (unnamed) author.[100] The reason for the action, the anonymous author suggested, was "Muller's having taken insufficient account of certain doctrinal points contained in the encyclical." In particular, "Professor Muller thinks that it was incorrect of the Encyclical to speak of evolutionism as though it was an hypothesis, undemonstrated and still uncertain." The article cited several scientists who had recently emphasized the merely probable character of evolutionary ideas.[101] Muller, the article went on to say, failed to recognize that, "in mixed questions, one must attribute their due weight and necessary preeminence to the data of faith"; he should think more closely about the encyclical's stated reservations concerning the animal origins of the human body. I had expected an explicit reference to Muller's less than fully monogenistic account of the origin of the human race, but there was none. Of course his views on that question presupposed the views to which they had already objected. Muller promptly submitted to the decision.[102]

b. The Marcozzi Case: A Prohibition on Speaking and Writing

On April 1, 1951, an article entitled "Le Origini dell'uomo: Insufficienza scientifica del poligenismo specifico," written by Gregorian University paleontologist Vittorio Marcozzi, SJ, appeared in *L'Osservatore Romano*.[103] Marcozzi's books on human origins had gone through three editions in the 1940s. This article, an abridged version of a public lecture that Marcozzi had recently given at his university, had been supportive of the position taken in the encyclical. He rejected polyphyletic (in his terminology, "specific") polygenism on scientific grounds alone; the polygenism of couples alone, he said, was incapable of scientific proof or refutation.

In the judgment of some, however, it had not been supportive enough. Two days after the article was published, a complaint was in the hands of the Holy Office.[104] In the copy of the article preserved in the archives of the Holy Office, two passages in particular are marked: "What is certain is that even on the hypothesis of spiritualistic evolutionism, the power and wisdom of God can be seen as clearly as in the immediate creation of the human body" and "The scientist, therefore, can raise no difficulties for the teaching

---

99 *Osservatore Romano*, "Un esempio."

100 "Pensiamo che il motivo principale della condanna sia . . . ."

101 Walter Zimmermann, "Methoden der Phylogenetik," 31 ff.; paleontologist G. Heberer, *Allgemeine Abstammungslehre*, 57 ff.; and Basel biologist Adolf Portmann, *Biologische Fragmente* and "Ursprungsproblem der Menschheit," 21–32.

102 Holy Office, "Decretum: Proscriptio libri" and "Submissionis notificatio."

103 Marcozzi, "Origini dell'uomo." This was not the first time that the newspaper had presented Marcozzi's views on evolution. It had published a summary of a public lecture which he had given to the Sezione romana dell'associazione medici catolici the previous year, i.e., before the release of the encyclical. There he had said, in the words of the reporter, that human evolution "does not appear to conflict with the date of Revelation provided that it retains a special intervention of God for the creation of the human soul as well as for the preparation of the body."

104 "Breve relazione d'ufficio," April 3, 1951 (doc. 2, SO 296/1951, ADDF [hereafter "Marcozzi File"]).

of the Church. He can safely continue to ask of nature what the book of Revelation has not handed down to us." The complainant, while conceding that Marcozzi had not said anything inconsistent with Catholic doctrine, nevertheless posed a twofold objection. First, Marcozzi "seems persuaded that this is not a matter *of an hypothesis*, but of a theory approaching certainty." Second, the passage about what scientists were allowed to do (quoted above) omitted the encyclical's qualification about being prepared to submit to the judgment of the Church.

On May 4, 1951, the consultors at the Holy Office judged that Marcozzi's lectures were "not always faithful to the wise norms contained in the encyclical" and recommended that he be prohibited from giving lectures and that his scientific work should be subjected to rigorous review, a decision approved by Pope Pius six days later.[105] There was some interest among the consultors in having *L'Osservatore Romano* publish another article by way of reply. They invited Serafino Dezani, a chemist with a special interest in science-religion issues, to write one, but were unsatisfied with the draft that he sent them. If Marcozzi's article had been too friendly to evolution, Dezani's draft went too far in the other direction. Not only was its science a bit antiquated, but its Biblical literalism, while not unorthodox, seemed itself not sufficiently appreciative of the rôle of metaphor in the relevant Biblical texts. Worse, it seemed almost to accuse Catholic evolutionists of heresy. In neither respect was it quite in line with the thought of Pope Pius.[106] So that part of the response was dropped and the Holy Office contented itself with informing Janssens of the restrictions that were to be placed on Marcozzi.[107]

* * * * *

The question returned to the Holy Office in 1953, when Janssens asked whether Marcozzi might be allowed to accept an invitation to participate in a Biblical conference that fall,[108] but the decision was negative.[109] In September, however, Marcozzi approached Giuseppe Pizzardo (secretary of the Holy Office) with a renewed request. Pizzardo reported that Marcozzi seemed tractable [*docile*], but remained convinced of his earlier views about evolution.[110] At the preparatory congregation held on September 5, 1953, the consultors asked that he clarify his views on evolution. "Then," said Bea, "we will see."[111]

---

105 Minutes of preparatory congregation, May 4, 1951 (fol. 6, doc. 3, Marcozzi File). The decision was communicated to Janssens as Jesuit superior-general on June 19 (Holy Office to Janssens, June 19, 1951) (fol. 10, doc. 7, Marcozzi File). The quotation is from their letter to Janssens.

106 Minutes of the preparatory congregation, May 12, 1951 (fol. 8–9, doc. 5–6, Marcozzi File).

107 The Holy Office notified Janssens at the Jesuit curia on June 19 (fol. 10, doc. 7, Marcozzi File), who replied on June 27 (fol. 11, doc. 8).

108 Janssens to Pizzardo, March 4, 1953 (fol. 14–15, doc. 11, Marcozzi File).

109 Minutes, March 4–14, 1953 (fol. 16, doc. 12, Marcozzi File) and letter to Janssens, March 25 (fol. 17, doc. 13).

110 Pizzardo, *Pro-memoria*, September 4, 1953 (fol. 19, doc. 15, Marcozzi File).

111 Minutes of the preparatory congregation, September 5, 1953 (fol. 20, doc. 16, Marcozzi File).

So, on September 9, Marcozzi sent the Holy Office three papers indicative of his views on evolution.[112] He supported a finalistic and theistic version, one that extended common ancestry, in the case of plants and animals, only as far as systematic species, i.e., one that was not comprehensively monophyletic. Despite the indications in favor of evolutionary anthropogenesis, he acknowledged the remaining difficulties in establishing an absolute Quaternary chronology: "The genetic connection is scientifically uncertain, all the more since the finds are relatively few. For that reason, there is no difficulty, precisely from the scientific point of view, to conclude, with the encyclical *Humani generis*, that the evolution of the human body is an hypothesis not yet *certo omnino demonstrata*."[113] Scientists could, therefore, "continue their research to try to answer the question of whether the human body was formed from inanimate or from living matter."[114]

As it happened, two days after the meeting of the preparatory congregation, Pope Pius gave a talk to the First International Symposium on Medical Genetics, in which he said:

> In recent works on genetics, one reads that nothing explains the affinity among all living things better than does a common genealogical tree. But at the same time one must note that this is only an image, an hypothesis, and not a demonstrated fact.... No one knows any natural process by which a being can produce another being of a different nature. The process by which one species gives rise to another species is absolutely inscrutable, regardless of the number of intermediate stages and no one has yet experimentally succeeded in bringing one species from another. Finally, we absolutely do not know at what point in evolution a hominid all of a sudden crossed the threshold of humanity.[115]

But he also said about the evolutionary origin of the human body: "We have invited further research in the hope of one day achieving definite results because, up until now, nothing definitive has been attained. We have urged that these questions be treated with the caution and maturity of judgment that their great importance demands."[116]

Hürth, who was asked to prepare a *votum* on the Marcozzi case, emphasized these final remarks, saying that the pope "therefore permits and approves research into the problem," albeit with the caution emphasized in the remarks just quoted.[117] Although the consultors at the preparatory congregation held on November 23 were willing, following Hürth's recommendation, to relax the restrictions, the cardinals at the meeting

---

112 Marcozzi, "La mia posizione riguardo all'evoluzionismo," (fol. 50–51, doc. 26, Marcozzi File); "Le origini dell'uomo secondo l'enciclica *Humani generis* e secondo la scienza," a report to the Accademia di S. Tommaso given on February 20, 1952 (fol. 52–67, doc. 27); and "Spiegazione più ampio delle idee espresse nella confernza tenuta all'Accademia di S. Tommaso" (fol. 68–74, doc. 28).

113 Marcozzi, "Mia posizione" (fol. 50–51, Marcozzi File).

114 Marcozzi, "Origini dell'uomo" (fol. 67, Marcozzi File).

115 Pius XII, Allocutio I: "Iis qui interfuerunt," 599–600.

116 Pius, Allocutio I, 604.

117 Hürth, *Votum*, October 30, 1953 (fol. 76–90, doc. 30, Marcozzi File).

on December 2 were concerned about what they thought were doctrinal deficiencies and tendentious deductions in Marcozzi's views as reported by Hürth. They asked that Janssens provide more detail about Marcozzi's teaching at the Gregorian.[118]

Pope Pius initially approved the recommendation of the cardinals at the audience he held on December 10, but that evening suddenly changed his mind. He had just received some documents at which he wanted to take a closer look; the approval of the recommendations of the Holy Office was provisionally revoked.[119] Ten days later, he asked that Ulrico Beste, OSB, consultor at the Holy Office, interview Marcozzi and report back to him.[120] Beste conducted the interview, along with Giovanni Pepe (deputy at the Holy Office's Section on the Censorship of Books).[121] Pius, being satisfied with the results of the interview, granted Marcozzi's request for a prudent liberty to speak and write on topics within his area of expertise, with the provision that Janssens, as superior general, would be particularly vigilant and renew the permission annually, or cancel it, as appropriate.[122]

c. The Kuiper Case (1954)

The Muller and Marcozzi cases show a fairly strict application of *Humani generis*. A complaint from the Netherlands submitted in 1954 show more openness to a Catholic evolutionism. One A. Kuiper, who taught science at the Philosophicum in Dijnselburg, published an article, in the Catholic newspaper *De Volkskrant*, on whether man could be descended from animals.[123] The article argued that research of the last twenty-five years (i.e., since Peking Man) provided evidence of a "non-negligible probability" of such a descent, though the article acknowledged both the relevance of theology to the question and the residual scientific uncertainty. It also defended the human nature of Peking Man on the basis of behavioral evidence, a point, of course, separate from the question of whether Peking Man had animal ancestry. Paolo Giobbe, apostolic internuncio to the Netherlands, delated the article to the Holy Office.[124] The Holy Office did not seem to share Giobbe's concern about the article; the files on the case show no evidence of official action.

118 Minutes of the meetings of the congregations, November 23 as well as December 2 and 10 (fol. 113–19 [esp. fol. 114 and 119], doc. 31, Marcozzi File).

119 Angelo dell'Acqua (deputy secretary of state) to the Holy Office, December 10, 1953 (fol. 144, doc. 39, Marcozzi File); see also Breve relazione "Pro secreta," March 1954 (fol. 155–61 [at 157], doc. 44).

120 "Nota Ex Audientia Sanctissimi," December 20, 1953 (fol. 145, doc. 40, Marcozzi File).

121 "Verbale dell'interrogatorio di padre Vittorino Marcozzi," March 2, 1954 (fol. 151–54, doc. 43, Marcozzi File).

122 Wilhelm Hentrich (consultor at the Holy Office), Relazione "Circa P. Marcozzi," April 4, 1954 (fol. 162–63, doc. 45, Marcozzi File); see also Breve relazione (fol. 157) and Holy Office to Janssens, April 10, 1954 (fol. 167–68, doc. 48).

123 Kuiper, "Stamt de mens van de aap af?," 12. The article was followed with a reply from Leo M. van Nieuwenhoven, SJ, "Enige Notities bij de Vraag" on May 29, and Kuiper's reply to the reply, "Dr Kuipers antwoordt" on June 1 (doc. 6a-6c, RV 1954/48, ADDF).

124 Giobbe to Giuseppe Pizzardo, July 10, 1954 (fol. 2, doc. 1, RV 1954/48, ADDF).

d. A Proposed Clarificatory *Dubium* (The Holy Office, 1955)

The final incident relevant to the history of the encyclical is the Holy Office's decision to revisit the question of polygenism in 1955 in the wake of a recent apostolic visit to Austria. On March 23, the Holy Office proposed to prepare a *monitum* or *dubium* on polygenism, a plan that was approved by Pope Pius on April 15. Augustin Bea was to prepare the *dubium* and a brief *votum* justifying the response to the *dubium*.[125]

Bea's draft asked "whether it can be held that: The encyclical *Humani generis* of August 12, 1950, does not definitively establish that the hypothesis of polygenesis as there described cannot be reconciled with that which the fonts of revealed truth and the acts of the Magisterium of the Church state about original sin."[126] The draft replied that it could not be held that the question was in any respect open. Bea's justification for the action proposed was as follows:

> A provision in this regard seems to be necessary since the assertion of the reformability of the decrees of the Council of Trent is becoming more and more common. As early as September 1950, some Catholic authors said that the words of the encyclical allow the possibility of interpreting it in the sense that the intent of the decrees of the Council is not yet entirely certain. That interpretation is finding more and more adherents. Fr. [Karl] Rahner [then dogmatic theologian at the Universität Innsbruck] is only one of the representatives of that opinion, and not the only one. Since he has discussed this idea theologically in a highly-respected review, there is a danger that this tendency will only become more emphasized from now on.
>
> There is no doubt that the intent of the Holy Father was to assert that polygenism, as described in the encyclical, *cannot be reconciled* with Catholic doctrine on original sin.

He went on to add that such other questions as that of pre-Adamites or co-Adamites were not addressed in the *dubium*, as they had not been in the encyclical. His proposed formulation of the *dubium* "leaves open the question of whether the proposition in question was 'erroneous,' 'offensive to pious ears,' or 'rash.'"

The *dubium* was subjected to a thorough discussion at the Holy Office on May 23, after which the consultors present unanimously instructed Bea, Tromp, and Parente to revise the *dubium*.[127]

On June 1, the group met, with Hürth replacing Tromp, and proposed a new draft: "Whether the passage from *Humani generis* which concerns the hypothesis of Polygenism is to be understood to mean that the Christian faithful are prohibited from adhering to it (as there described) inasmuch as it cannot in any way be reconciled [*nequaquam componatur*] with divine revelation and the documents of the Magisterium of the Church. Reply: AFFIRMATIVE." This, they hoped, would "eliminate the ambiguity inherent in the

---

125 "Dubbio circa il Poligenismo," 1.

126 "Voto del Rev.mo P. Agostino Bea, SJ, Consultore" (fol. 44–45, HG Box-IV).

127 Bea, Hürth, and Parente, "Relazione," June 1, 1955 (fol. 64–65, HG Box-IV).

language of the encyclical (*cum nequaquam appareat, &c.*)" without going any further than the encyclical itself had done.

On June 20, the consultors at the Holy Office approved the new formulation, and requested that the Holy Father approve it *in forma specifica* (i.e., in a way that made the formulation his own). The cardinal-members of the Holy Office met on June 28, but were divided on whether to endorse the proposed *dubium* and *responsum*. Three wanted to do so; the other two would also do so, but wanted the final phrase of the *dubium* (from "inasmuch as . . .") to be dropped. The three thought that, without that final phrase, the *dubium* would only reinforce the doubts raised by the encyclical.[128] In the papal audience held on July 4, Pope Pius, however, rejected the proposed *dubium*, saying:

> There was no need for any clarification of the quoted passage from the encyclical *Humani generis*, the formulation of which was deliberately cautious and it is good for it to remain as it is, without any further clarifications, except—of course—the absolute "irreformability" of the dogma of original sin in the descendants of Adam. The two cardinals (Ciriaci and Ottaviani) rightly observed that "one needs to be very careful in the matter, as the words of the encyclical are."[129]

And there the matter ended.

---

128 Memorandum "De Poligenismo," June 21, 1955 (fol. 68, HG Box-IV). The three were: Giuseppe Pizzardo (the secretary), Clemente Micara, and Adeodato Piazza; the two: Pietro Ciriaci and Alfredo Ottaviani.

129 "Ex Audientia Sanctissimi," July 4, 1955 (fol. 70v–72, HG Box-IV). The passage quoted is from a summary approved by the pope (fol. 72).

PART VI

CONCLUSION & AFTERWORD

CHAPTER 18

CONCLUSION

As I said in the introduction, if it is true, as one historian has claimed, that "many Catholics experienced great difficulties when they struggled to reconcile the narratives of Genesis with progressive developments in the historical, geological, and biological sciences," it is also true that many other Catholics did not. The history that shows this can be summarized in seven points:

1. Catholic evolutionism was not an all-or-nothing proposition. Catholic discussion of the evolutionary origin of biological species included a range of distinct views.

The first dimension of variation was substantive. Two theses constitute the minimal core of Catholic evolutionism—transformism and a human exceptionalism grounded in the direct creation of each (and *a fortiori* of the first) human soul. Without the first thesis, it would not be evolutionist; without the second, it would not be Catholic. Catholic evolutionists differed on the question of whether evolutionary processes played a rôle in the formation of the first human body. The weakest version of Catholic evolutionism limited transformism to phyto- and zoogenesis. Stronger versions of Catholic evolutionism gave evolutionary processes at least *some* rôle in the formation of the first human *body*. Those versions differed with respect to whether those processes were or were not supplemented by direct divine intervention in the final preparation of the first human body for the infusion of a created rational soul. No Catholic evolutionist, of course, thought that evolutionary processes were sufficient to bring into being the first complete human *person*. Catholic evolutionists also differed over such peripheral issues as the depth of common ancestry and the prominence of natural selection in effecting evolutionary change.

Connections—between the core theses of Catholic evolutionism and the details of anthropogenesis as well as between those theses and the peripheral theses—were logically loose enough to permit separate assessment of each thesis. Non-evolutionist Catholics agreed in rejecting the truth of transformism (some for scientific, others for philosophical, reasons), but differed among themselves over whether it, or any kind of evolutionary anthropogenesis, was compatible with Catholic doctrine. That yields (even leaving aside the peripheral theses) five different views—incompatibilism, mere compatibilism, and three kinds of evolutionism (weak, intermediate, and robust—varying in their account of the rôle of evolutionary processes in anthropogenesis).

The second dimension of variation was in the degree of confidence with which any particular thesis was held. One does not have to deny the law of the excluded middle to realize that the true-false dichotomy must give way to a more nuanced distinction among degrees of confidence in the acceptance or rejection of any particular thesis. As I have shown, Catholic evolutionists varied in the degree of certainty that they ascribed to the various evolutionary theses. This, of course, conforms to standard scientific, and theological, practice. For scientists, there are well-established theories and working hypotheses; for theologians, theses that are *de fide definitae* and those that are merely *sententiae communes*.

2. The history of some scientific theories is characterized by the *development* of a seminal idea over the course of the theory's history. That seems not to be true of Catholic evolutionism. The components of the robust version (the fully evolutionary origin of the first human body), now the Catholic consensus, emerged early—in the work of de Filippi (1864) and of Mivart (1871)—although it did not immediately win general acceptance.

The robust version of Catholic evolutionism was, however, eventually able to overcome the objections of its opponents without significant modification. The history of Catholic evolutionism is thus not so much that of the *development* of a seminal idea, as one of *increasing acceptance*, increasing confidence that Catholic objections (both hermeneutical and Thomistic) could be answered. It is perhaps, at least in part, another instance of Planck's Principle at work—"A new scientific truth does not triumph by convincing its opponents and making them see the light, but rather because its opponents eventually die, and a new generation grows up that is familiar with it"[1]—but there is more to say than that.

3. The magisterium never condemned the theory of evolution, though it did prohibit some evolutionist works and suppress some others.

Three kinds of evolutionist work were put on the *Index* by Vatican congregations or disapproved in pre-publication censorship by the Jesuit curia. First, some overtly materialist treatments of the topic were so treated. Second, works by Catholic authors who tried to resolve alleged tension between evolutionary processes and the Biblical text in *ways* that the Church judged to be hermeneutically unacceptable were also put on the

---

1 Planck, *Scientific Autobiography*, 33–34.

Index. Third, works that one might loosely classify as Bergsonian were also prohibited, for defending a comprehensive evolutionism too much at odds with the Catholic account of the relation between God and the world.

No work focused on Catholic evolutionism as defined above that did not also raise more general hermeneutical problems was ever listed in the *Index of Prohibited Books.* Some works of Catholic evolutionism were never delated to the Index. Others, in the 1890s, were judged to be rash in their treatment of anthropogenesis. Although some of the consultors and cardinals at the Index would have put those books on the *Index* itself, Pope Leo XIII only allowed them to go so far as to require the authors to make a public retraction of their views and to withdraw their books from sale. Anti-evolutionists continued their attempts to have works of Catholic evolutionism prohibited in the 1920s and 1930s, i.e., under Pope Pius XI, but with less success. In the early 1930s, the pope instructed officials at the Index to look into the *scientific status questionis* before coming to a decision. He suggested that they ask the opinion of Austrian priest-anthropologist Wilhelm Schmidt, whose earlier writings had expressed some openness to evolutionary ideas. In the end, no action was taken against the books.

4. The theory of the evolutionary origin of plant and animal species was quickly and generally judged to be a theologically open question, even by most of those who believed it to be false for scientific or philosophical reasons; any tensions with Thomistic philosophy of nature were left to the philosophers to work out. The truth of the new scientific ideas was subject to debate in Catholic periodicals, encyclopedias, textbooks, and popularizations.

5. The philosophical integration of transformism and Thomism was a persistent, but secondary, theme in the articulation of a Catholic evolutionism. In a 1949 editorial, *The New Scholasticism* wrote: "Of all scientific theories, perhaps the one that comes nearest to being of philosophical fiber is the belief in evolution," and added that "as a doctrine, popularized by the sciences and yet dealing at least indirectly with origins and purposes, matter and its mobility, evolutionism is in a twilight zone between science and philosophy."[2] For Catholics, especially after 1879, "philosophy" meant "Thomistic philosophy." Catholic evolutionists generally thought that, in the end, the integration of some kind of evolutionism into a Thomistic philosophy of nature could be effected. By 1950, leading Thomistic philosophers—e.g., Jacques Maritain[3] and Charles De Koninck[4]—seemed confident that a Thomistic philosophy of nature could include some kind of a theory of evolution, even if they were sometimes vague about the details of how that could be done. The editors of *The New Scholasticism,* to be sure, complained in their 1949 editorial that "Scholastics have not accorded [evolution] the treatment it merits"[5] and in an article

2 *New Scholasticism,* "The Problem of Evolution," 255.

3 Maritain, "Philosophical Co-Operation," 6–7.

4 De Koninck, *Cosmos.*

5 *New Scholasticism,* "The Problem of Evolution," 255.

that it published the next year, Charles A. Hart wrote that "the factors bringing about the evolution of species are still shrouded in much mystery, however well the fact itself seems established."[6]

Still, Mivart had made clear how human exceptionalism could be integrated with even a fully evolutionary account of the origin of the human body. The less theologically charged species problem—preserving the insights of Thomistic essentialism, while resisting the apparently nominalist implications of Darwinian transformism—may have been more of a challenge, but clarification of the concept of a species was a challenge in scientific biology as well. If natural selection was not a teleological process in the way that digestion and perspiration are, at least it could be subordinated to a larger, external teleology. It (even with its incorporation of *random* variations) could be shown to serve God's purpose in creating the world. It had, after all, (the evolutionists argued) produced human bodies.

6. The magisterium judged the theory of evolution to be incapable of providing a full account of the origin of man, because each human soul, starting with the first, requires direct creation by God. Whatever hesitation there may have been among the bishops at the First Vatican Council about declaring the thesis to be a matter of faith, very few Catholic evolutionists ever challenged the point. That doctrine insured that nearly all versions of Catholic evolutionism were fully exceptionalist.

7. The heart of the Catholic controversy over evolution was over whether the formation of the first human body was the result of evolutionary processes. Even some Catholics who accepted the evolutionary origin of plant and animal species thought, usually for Scriptural reasons, that God had formed Adam's body directly from non-living ("un-organ-ized") matter. Many Catholic evolutionists in the first half of the twentieth century were content to accept a mixed theory in which God acted directly to modify an evolved animal body in order to prepare it for the reception of a rational soul. Their concern was the *inclusion* of evolutionary processes in anthropogenesis, not its *maximization*. Mivartists were eager to emphasize the place of secondary causes (as efficacious, but also precisely as *secondary*) in the economy of nature, and certainly *not* the *exclusion per se* of divine action. Leo XIII's *Providentissimus Deus*, and in particular Pius XII's *Divino afflante Spiritu*, although they did not address evolution directly, surely made it easier for theologians to abandon the Scriptural warrant for the mixed account of anthropogenesis.

---

6 Hart, "Twenty-five Years of Thomism," 24.

CHAPTER 19

AFTERWORD
CATHOLIC EVOLUTIONISM AFTER *HUMANI GENERIS*

Catholic discussion of evolutionism did not end with the publication of *Humani generis*. Although it is not my intention to write a history of the three quarters of a century since publication of the encyclical, a few words about subsequent Catholic thought on the two issues that the encyclical addressed seem nevertheless to be appropriate, not as a conclusion, but as an afterword.

1. THE EVOLUTIONARY ORIGIN OF THE HUMAN BODY

No subsequent document that has the authority of an encyclical has returned to the question of evolution and the origin of man. Reservations about the evolutionary origin of Adam's body gradually faded. One can, to be sure, still find Catholics defending anti-evolutionist views. An English translation of Cardinal Ruffini's book was published in 1957; a new edition of Carlo Boyer's *De Deo creante et elevante* (still anti-evolutionist on this question) was published the same year.[1] Michał Chaberek, OP, published his *Aquinas and Evolution* in 2017. Nevertheless, the view provisionally acknowledged in

---

1 Boyer, *De Deo creante*, 5th ed., 168–92.

the encyclical eventually seems to have won general, if not universal, consensus among Catholics who addressed the issue.

One can take as a sign of this acceptance two statements made by St. John Paul II, and one issued by the International Theological Commission in 2004.

John Paul first addressed the question of evolution in his General Audience of April 16, 1986, where he said that

> from the point of view of [Catholic] doctrine, there is no apparent difficulty in explaining the origin of man, as far as concerns the body, by the hypothesis of evolutionism. However, it must be added that that hypothesis puts forward only a probability, not a scientific certainty. [Catholic] doctrine, on the other hand, invariably affirms that man's spiritual soul is directly created by God. That is, it is possible, according to the hypothesis just mentioned, that the human body, as a result of the order impressed by the Creator in the powers of life, was gradually prepared in the forms of antecedent living beings. The human soul, however, on which man's humanity ultimately depends, being spiritual, cannot have emerged from matter.[2]

He addressed it again on October 22, 1996, when, as part of the celebration of the sixtieth anniversary of the founding of the Pontifical Academy of Sciences, he gave an address (on evolution and on broader questions associated with the relation between science and religion) to a plenary assembly of the Academy. The particular question of evolution was one that it had chosen for some of its own work. St. John Paul began by recalling *Humani generis*. His address developed the work of his predecessor on one important point:

> Taking into account the state of scientific research at the time as well as of the requirements of theology, the Encyclical *Humani Generis* considered the doctrine of "evolutionism" to be a serious hypothesis, worthy of careful investigation and reflection, equal to that due to the opposing hypothesis. . . . [But] today, almost half a century after the publication of the Encyclical, new knowledge has led to the recognition that the theory of evolution is more than an hypothesis. . . . The convergence . . . of the results of lines of work conducted independently of one another constitutes by itself a significant argument in favor of the theory.[3]

There is, he went on to acknowledge, variation in detail between one scientific theory and another. More importantly for his purpose, there are various philosophical "readings" of evolution—materialistic-reductionist, as well as spiritualist. St. John Paul re-emphasized, in his own words, a point central to Pius: "In the case of man, we find ourselves faced with an ontological difference, one might even say with an ontological leap."[4] The intellect and the will make man a kind of being different from any other. The spiritual soul that underlies these powers could only have been created by God.

2 John Paul II, "Created Things Have a Legitimate Autonomy," 216–20.

3 John Paul II, "Ad Pontificiae academiae scientiarum sodales," ¶4.

4 John Paul, Address, ¶6.

* * * * *

A few years later, the International Theological Commission addressed the question in its "Communion and Stewardship: Human Persons Created in the Image of God,"[5] in which it emphasized that "Christians have the responsibility to locate the modern scientific understanding of the universe within the context of the theology of creation."[6] It reiterated St. John Paul II's acceptance of scientific theories of the evolutionary origin of species, including man:

> While there is little consensus among scientists about how the origin of this first microscopic life is to be explained, there is general agreement among them that the first organism dwelt on this planet about 3.5–4 billion years ago. Since it has been demonstrated that all living organisms on earth are genetically related, it is virtually certain that all living organisms have descended from this first organism. Converging evidence from many studies in the physical and biological sciences furnishes mounting support for some theory of evolution to account for the development and diversification of life on earth, while controversy continues over the pace and mechanisms of evolution. While the story of human origins is complex and subject to revision, physical anthropology and molecular biology combine to make a convincing case for the origin of the human species in Africa about 150,000 years ago.[7]

The document also, of course, warned against "theories of evolution . . . of a neo-Darwinian provenance which explicitly deny to divine providence any truly causal rôle in the development of life in the universe" as well as "materialistic theories of human origins."[8] The document later emphasizes that the rôle given to chance by Neo-Darwinism is not *per se* incompatible with the doctrine of divine providence.[9]

2. MONOGENESIS

Pius XII's affirmation that the evolutionary origin of the human body was a theologically open question, even despite its cautious and provisional character, seems, for most Catholics, to have resolved the central question of the compatibility of the theory of evolution and Catholic doctrine, but the encyclical did not resolve every question. There was, after all, still the question of monogenesis. There Pius had reaffirmed, even if not definitively, a theological doctrine inconsistent with a presumptive consequence of the theory of evolution and, as it later turned out, some surprising similarities between

---

5 See especially ¶¶62–70. The authority of the document is suggested by the following statement, appended to the document: "The present text was approved *in forma specifica*, by the written ballots of the International Theological Commission. It was then submitted to Joseph Cardinal Ratzinger, the President of the Commission, who has given his permission for its publication."

6 International Theological Commission, "Communion and Stewardship," ¶62.

7 International Theological Commission, "Communion and Stewardship," ¶63.

8 International Theological Commission, "Communion and Stewardship," ¶64.

9 International Theological Commission, "Communion and Stewardship," ¶69.

chimpanzee and human genomes. Three points about the post-encyclical discussion of the question are worth noting.

i. The Clarification of Terminology

The first point concerns the gradual emergence of a uniform terminology for discussion of the question. Shortly before 1950, Catholic authors had already begun to make a more explicit acknowledgment that, however unified the concept of polygenism was in its rejection of monogenism, it came in two quite different scientific forms. Shortly thereafter, they began to use the "suffixes" -phyletism and -genism to distinguish theories about the number of first human groups from those about the number of first human couples in a way that clarified Catholic discussion of the issue.

The first step was taken in 1948, in two articles in the same issue of the *Gregorianum*. Vittorio Marcozzi wrote in his "Poligenesi ed evoluzione nelle origini dell'uomo" that:

> Today the problem of polygenism can mean either of two things. The first meaning: Must the human races, living and extinct, be considered to be descendants of a single, already human, stock or must they be considered to have originated from diverse stocks? The second meaning: If it is proven that all the races are derived from the same stock, is it necessary to maintain that they were born from a single couple, or must one admit that there were originally many couples?[10]

Heinrich Lennerz made the same point in "Quid theologo dicendum de Polygenismo?"[11] Marcozzi went on to review geographical pluralism in some detail before returning his verdict: "There is not a single positive argument in favor of the simultaneous appearance of Man in multiple places on earth."[12] He then turned briefly to the second question, on which he wrote only a single paragraph, saying:

> Whether many couples appeared in that center of origin, or only one, is not, in our modest judgment, a problem that can be resolved, at least not with certainty, with the resources of natural science alone since, in our opinion, one will never be able to know, from paleontology or biology, if there was only one couple or more than one at the origin of the species. The problem will have to be resolved by way of something other than the natural sciences.[13]

Within a few months of the publication of *Humani generis*, Teilhard wrote (but did not publish) a short paper entitled, "Monogénisme et monophylétisme: Une Distinction essentielle à faire." His introductory remarks—"one must insist once again"—suggest both that the distinction was not new and that not everyone was bothering to make it. Four points (of his) are important here.

10 Marcozzi, "Poligenesi," 343–44.

11 Lennerz, "Quid dicendum?," 420.

12 Marcozzi, "Poligenesi," 361.

13 Marcozzi, "Poligenesi," 361.

First, "polygenism" should be defined by reference to plurality of primitive *couples*; it has nothing to do with the question of how many distinct branches or phyla lay at the base of humanity. Polyphyletism, that is to say, stands in contrast to two forms of monophyletism, one poly*genistic* and the other monogenistic.

Second, since science (paleontology) can only see populations, mono- and polygenism are "purely theological" concepts. The *scientific* conception of the unity of man can be a matter only of *phylogenetic* unity (i.e., monophyletism), independent of questions of population size and morphology.

Third, the scientific indeterminacy with respect to population size leaves the theologian with a certain freedom with respect to whatever seems dogmatically necessary.

Fourth, all that we think we know about "the biological laws of 'speciation'" renders monogenism "scientifically untenable." Teilhard did not publish this note, though he may well have circulated it among his fellow Jesuits.

At that point, the now-standard Catholic terminological formulation of the trichotomy—polyphyletic polygenism, monophyletic polygenism, and monophyletic monogenism—was nearly in place. Marcozzi had distinguished two forms of polygenism; Teilhard, two forms of monophyletism. The combination of these two taxonomic categories appeared, shortly after the publication of *Humani generis*, in an article by another Jesuit, Guy Picard, whose article "La Science expérimentale est-elle favorable au polygénisme?" was published in *Sciences ecclésiastiques*. He wrote that "the name *monogenism* has been given to the doctrine according to which the present (*actuel*) human species has its origin in a single couple; and *polygenism* to the contrary opinion, which affirms many initially independent couples."[14] In a footnote, he added:

> One can add another distinction. In fact, if a polygenistic origin began with several different species, it could be called *polyphyletic*; if came from a single species, it would be *polygenistic* in the strict sense. *Polygenism* is therefore a [logical] genus of which the [logical] species are *polygenism* (an [older] species producing several couples of a new species) and *polyphyletism* (several [older] species producing, by convergence, several couples of a single new species).

By 1960, a number of other authors had begun to make Teilhard's "essential distinction" in a way that made the now-standard trichotomous taxonomy terminologically easy. Teilhard did so in print in his posthumously published *Le Phénomène humain* (1955).[15] Léon Cristiani, priest, historian at the Université de Lyon, and popularizer, writing under the pseudonym Nicolas Corte, made it in his *Les Origines de l'homme* (1957), published as part of the *Encyclopédie du catholique au XXème siècle*.[16] So did Frédéric-Marie Bergounioux in his *La Préhistoire et ses problèmes* (1958).[17]

14 Picard, " Science expérimentale," 65 (incl. n1).

15 Teilhard, *Phénomène humain*, Bk. III, Ch. 1, Sec. 2.

16 Cristiani, *Origines de l'homme*, 74–76 and 116–17 (trans., 83–84 and 133–340).

17 Bergounioux, *Préhistoire et ses problèmes*, 41–42.

The distinction, did not, to be sure, meet with universal approval. Jules Carles complained that distinguishing the "suffixes" -genism and -phyletism is "a subtlety whose only significance is to muddle a problem which is already a bit confused."[18] Other authors simply ignored it. Of those, some simply worked around the trichotomous nomenclature; others continued to use the term "polygenism," in particular, as they always had done (in many cases, alas, imprecisely). Some of the resistance may have been connected to a fact noted by Léon Renwart of Louvain:

> Theologians and scientists often use the words "monogenism" and "polygenism" in very different senses.
>
> For theologians, monogenism is the doctrine that "all men now alive on this earth are descended from a single human couple, Adam and Eve." For the scientist, the same word refers to the conception "according to which all hominids are derived from the same stock [*souche*], i.e., independent of the number of individuals], which had already attained the human level."
>
> Theologians define the term "polygenism" as meaning "that the origin of modern man is to be found in a multiplicity of first ancestors, while scientists use the same term for "the scientific conception in accordance with which human races come from parallel lineages which were detached from a common trunk before they had attained the human level."[19]

In 1960, Edouard L. Boné commented that, useful as adhering to the essential distinction would be, it still had by no means become general in the academic literature.[20] Over the course of the next decade, however, it seems to have done so.[21]

ii. Evolutionary Monogenism after the Encyclical

The second point worth noting is that, in the years following the publication of *Humani generis*, there were several attempts to accommodate the populational account of human origins suggested by the scientific evidence with the strict monogenism of the encyclical. Muller's attempt to do this was mentioned above. There were at least four others.

The first, appearing only a few months after the encyclical itself, was Swiss theologian (and later cardinal) Charles Journet's brief *Petit Catéchisme sur les origines du monde*. Journet sketched two possible ways to imagine the origin of the human race.

> First, from among the transitional beings (whose existence is uncertain), who are similar to man in their morphology and instincts but who, lacking a spiritual and

---

18 Carles, "Polygénisme ou monogénisme," 87.

19 Renwart and Georges Vandebroek, "Humani generis," 348, where the quotations about theological meaning are from Alois Janssens, *God als Schepper*, 3rd ed., 214 and 223; those about the scientific meaning are from Vandebroek, "Origine de l'homme," 106–7.

20 Boné, "Polygénisme et polyphylétisme," 105.

21 See Paul Overhage, in Overhage and Karl Rahner, *Problem der Hominisation*, 3rd ed., 179; Boné, "Evolution, Human: 1. Biological Aspect," 5:680; O. W. Garrigan, "Monogenism" and "Polygenism"; and Ervin Nemesszeghy and John Russell, *Theology of Evolution*, 51–52.

immortal soul, are not philosophically human, God chose two, who became the first human couple. He made them in his image and likeness.

In his image: that is to say that He infused in them a spiritual and immortal soul which, entering into the body, made it a human body.

In his likeness: that is to say that He enfolded them with original grace.[22]

His second, and more complex, possibility was that God infused spiritual and immortal souls into a larger number of these transitional beings (at different times and in different places). These philosophically human beings, made in the image of God, played some rôle in preparing for the arrival of Adam. It was from them that God would choose a single couple whom He formed in his likeness in order to inaugurate the order of grace. Only the descendants of Adam survived the catastrophes of prehistory; the rest became extinct. The idea that human beings are not descended from a single couple, but from multiple different couples, he said, would require separate original sins for each lineage and would require an interpretation of certain passages of Scripture different from those of the Church.[23] He quoted from the encyclical and concluded by saying that science could not resolve the question of monogenesis. That view was neither scientific nor anti-scientific, but trans-scientific.[24]

Camille Muller's idea (discussed in chapter 17) that, within a few generations, everyone within a small population that included Adam and Eve would be descended from them and thus tainted by original sin appeared again in a lecture at the Istituto de Paleontologia Umana dell'Università de Ferrara on July 7, 1962.[25] In that lecture, Italian Jesuit Giovanni Blandino presented two alternative hypotheses (as well as a detailed mathematical proof of just how quickly descent from an Adam and Eve inserted into a larger population would become universal).

According to Blandino's first hypothesis, the human race was the product of a gradual corporeal evolution from an earlier anthropoid population supplemented, at a certain point, by a general infusion of created spiritual souls. These first human beings were probably not able to exercise their intellectual powers to any great extent, but once they could do so, God raised two of them to a supernatural state by giving them sanctifying grace and revealing to them the fundamental truths of religion. He also subjected them to a test, which they failed. They and their descendants bred only among themselves and the co-Adamites gradually became extinct, leaving us with the entire species exclusively descended from Adam and Eve.

Blandino's second hypothesis varies from the first by allowing interbreeding with the larger human population, with any descent from either Adam or Eve being sufficient for the inheritance of original sin and the promise of redemption.

22 Journet, *Petit catéchisme*, 41–42.

23 Journet, *Petit catéchisme*, 45–46.

24 Journet, *Petit catéchisme*, 46–47.

25 Blandino subsequently published the text privately as "Deux hypothèses sur l'origine de l'homme: Observations théologiques et scientifiques."

Blandino thought that both hypotheses were consistent with the three dogmatic theses about original sin as one in origin, transmitted by generation, and present in everyone (anyway, "all men now being born") at birth. He interpreted that "now" "broadly," he said, but that breadth reached only as far back as the calling of Abraham. In a typescript tipped into at least some copies of the pamphlet,[26] Blandino acknowledged that a more comprehensive version of universal guilt (as expressed, for example, in *Humani generis*) was inconsistent with his second hypothesis, but he expressed doubt that that encyclical was part of infallible magisterial doctrine.

Neither Muller nor Blandino succeeded in articulating a scenario in which all human beings (in the sense of beings with rational souls) are descended from the first couple. Both include co-Adamites that the encyclical said did not exist. A new hypothesis, one that did not include the kind of co-Adamites found in those earlier scenarios, was proposed by Josephite priest Andrew Alexander in 1964.[27] On his account, a final crucial genetic mutation renders the body of pre-human beings suitable for the infusion of a rational soul without rendering them incapable of interbreeding with the other members of the pre-human population from which they emerged. If only descendants of Adam and Eve had that mutation, one would have a scenario that respected both the polygenism suggested by ordinary science and the monogenism required by Catholic theology.

Some years later, I proposed a variant of Alexander's hypothesis, arguing that the genetic mutation that Alexander used to distinguish Adam and Eve from the larger population with whom they interbred, was not strictly necessary. The infusion of a rational soul into Adam, Eve, and all (or even most) of their descendants would be sufficient to make all fully human beings descendants of Adam.[28]

iii. Magisterial Silence

The third point worth noting is the relative neglect of the question of monogenesis in official statements on evolution and theology. The two documents mentioned above illustrate this.

St. John Paul II's address to the Pontifical Academy of Sciences reemphasized the central point made by Pius forty-six years before, differing primarily in the greater certainty that he thought was due to the scientific argument in favor of evolution. The address did not, however, address a third point that was important to Pius, namely the monogenetic origins of the human race.

The second is the International Theological Commission's "Communion and Stewardship." With respect to the origin of man, the Commission asserted the "natural unity of the human race,"[29] but in two passages seems open to polygenetic (though not

---

26 For example, those in the Pius XII Memorial Library at Saint Louis University and the Feehan Memorial Library at St. Mary of the Lake Seminary in Mundelein, Illinois.

27 Alexander, "Human Origins and Genetics."

28 Kemp, "Monogenesis." See also my "Body of Adam."

29 International Theological Commission, "Communion and Stewardship," ¶65.

polyphyletic) accounts of the origin of the human race. First, it concluded the long passage quoted above with the phrase "in a humanoid population of common genetic lineage." Second, when it returned to the matter several paragraphs later, it referred to "the emergence of the first members of the human species (*whether as individuals or in populations*)."[30] It did not propose a response to the problem of the original sin which had worried Pope Pius. Although some readers see in this parenthetical remark a new theological openness to monogenetic polygenism, that is perhaps too strong a conclusion. It can, in light of its failure to address the concerns raised by Pius XII, more plausibly be read to assert only that what the Commission was saying in that paragraph—"that that the emergence of the first members of the human species … represents an event that is not susceptible of a purely natural explanation and which can appropriately be attributed to divine intervention"—does not depend precisely on a monogenistic account of human origins.

30 International Theological Commission, "Communion and Stewardship," ¶70 (emphasis mine).

APPENDICES

THE HISTORY OF SCIENCE

Despite the piecemeal precedents to be found in ancient and medieval authors,[1] there was something new in René Descartes's seventeenth-century proposal to understand the natural world by reference to natural processes that would (or could, Descartes was explicitly hypothetical in this) constitute its formational economy. He asked:

> what would happen in a new world, if God were now to create somewhere in imaginary space enough matter to put it together, and if He moved the various parts of this matter about without any order, in such a way as to form of it a chaos as confused as the poets can imagine, and if He afterwards did nothing else but to lend to nature His ordinary support and to leave it to act according to the laws which He had established.

He went on to suggest that

> The greater part of the matter of this chaos would, following these laws, have to organize itself in such a way as to make it resemble our heavens.... Some of its parts must compose an earth, some compose planets and comets, and some others a sun and fixed stars.... There would be nothing in our world which would not, or at least which could not, appear in the same way in the world I was describing.[2]

---

1 E.g., Lucretius, *De rerum natura*, Bks. 5–6; and Aristotle, *Meteorologica*, 1.14.

2 Descartes, *Discours*, V (*Œuvres de Descartes*, 6:42–44; *Works of Descartes*, 107–8).

This laid the foundation for a new kind of science, one to which nineteenth-century historian and philosopher of science, and inveterate neologist, William Whewell gave the name "paleoetiological sciences," the sciences of ancient causes.[3]

This form of natural science was applied first to geology and then to cosmology. The first serious attempt to do historical geology was made by Danish scientist Niels Stensen in his *De solido intra solidum naturaliter contento dissertationis prodromus* (*Forerunner to a Dissertation on a Solid Naturally Contained within a Solid*) (1669), in which he addressed the problems of geological strata and of the fossils they contained.[4] Work along these lines was continued by (Catholic) Italian geologists over the course of the eighteenth century—for example by Antonio Vallisneri in *De' corpi marini, che su' monti si trovano* (1721), by Anton-Lazzaro Moro in *De' Crostacei e degli altri marini corpi che si truovano su' monti* (1740), and by Giuseppe Cirillo Generelli in his summary of Moro, "De' crostacei e dell'altre produzioni marine, che sono ne' monti" (1757).[5] All three were singled out for praise by Charles Lyell in the historical chapters with which he began his *Principles of Geology*.[6] Stensen was ordained a priest, and then a bishop, by the Catholic Church shortly after he had finished the *Prodromus*. He was beatified by Pope St. John Paul II in 1988. Moro was a diocesan priest; Generelli was a Carmelite.

None of that work gave rise to theological objections. Censors who reviewed Descartes's works for the Holy Office in 1663 raised theological and philosophical concerns about other aspects of the work, but not about his prospectus for a paleoetiological science.[7] All the other works passed ecclesiastical censorship.

A. THE ORIGIN OF SPECIES

The eighteenth century saw the appearance of several attempts to explain the origin of species—Benoît de Maillet's *Telliamed: Entretiens d'un philosophe indien avec un missionnaire françois sur la diminution de la mer, la formation de la terre, l'origine de l'homme, &c.* (1748) and Erasmus Darwin's *Zoonomia* (1794).

The empirical foundations for the scientifically most plausible version of evolutionary biology lie, however, rather in some new geological insights made at the very beginning of the nineteenth century, when William Smith (in England) and, independently, Georges Cuvier and Alexandre Broingnart (in France) came to recognize that each geological stratum has its own distinctive faunal content. Combining this with Stensen's

---

3 Whewell, *The Philosophy of the Inductive Sciences*, 1:xxxv–xxxvi. Whewell used a haplological version, *palætiology*, which seems to me to be both less euphonious and less clear than the form I will use.

4 For an account of Stensen's work, see my *War That Never Was*, 50–61; or Steven J. Gould, "Titular Bishop of Titiopolis."

5 The works in question were Vallisneri, *De' corpi marini, che su' monti si trovano* (1721); Moro, *De' crostacei e degli altri marini corpi che si truovano su' monti* (1740); and Generelli, "De' crostacei e dell'altre produzioni marine, che sono ne' monti" (1757).

6 Lyell, *Principles of Geology*, 1:41–48.

7 See Jean-Robert Armogathe and Vincent Carraud, "La première condamnation."

recognition that each stratum represented a distinct epoch in the history of the earth led directly to the conclusion that each epoch was characterized by its own distinct set of plants and animals and raised the question of the origin of species. If the animals that lived in later epochs (i.e., animals whose fossil remains were found in higher strata) did not leave any fossil remains in lower strata, then they might reasonably be presumed not to have existed at those earlier epochs of earth history. So where did they come from?

* * * * *

That question, that "mystery of mysteries" as Sir John Herschel called it in 1836,[8] had received two evolutionary answers in the first half of the nineteenth century. The first, proposed by Jean-Baptiste Lamarck in his *Philosophie zoologique* (1809) and his *Histoire naturelle des animaux sans vertèbres* (1815), began with the spontaneous generation of micro-organisms which, in partial response to an inner drive and in partial response to environmental pressures, produced ever more complex organisms over the course of many generations. The process of spontaneous generation still being operative, the simpler organisms do not simply recede into the past, but are replaced by the descendants of more recently generated lineages. The second, proposed (anonymously) by Scottish publisher Robert Chambers in his *Vestiges of the Natural History of Creation* (1844), had new species emerge as the result of modification during an extended period of gestation at some point in a species' phylogenetic history. Neither of these provided, in the judgment of contemporary scientists, a satisfactory solution to the question, which was still open when Charles Darwin and Alfred Russel Wallace advanced a third evolutionary answer to the question in 1858.[9]

Darwin's answer, published at book length in *On the Origin of Species by Means of Natural Selection, or the Preservation of Favoured Races in the Struggle for Life* (1859), can be summarized, for our purposes, as consisting of three theses, to which a fourth was added in *The Descent of Man* in 1871.

The first of these is the thesis that "existing forms of life are the descendants by true generation of pre-existing forms."[10] In 1845, Darwin had already written that

> The relationship, though distant, between the Macrauchenia and the Guanaco, between the Toxodon and the Capybara,—the closer relationship between the many extinct Edentata and the living sloths, ant-eaters, and armadillos, now so eminently characteristic of South American zoology,—and the still closer relationship between the fossil and living species of Ctenomys and Hydrochærus, are most interesting facts. This relationship is shown wonderfully . . . by the great collection lately brought to Europe from the caves of Brazil by MM. [Peter Wilhelm] Lund and [Peter] Clausen. In this collection there are extinct species of all the thirty-two genera, excepting

---

8 The phrase comes from a letter of Herschel to Charles Lyell, on February 20, 1836. Darwin quoted it on the first page of his *Origin of Species*, attributing it only to "one of our greatest philosophers." The full letter was published in Walter F. Cannon, "Impact of Uniformitarianism."

9 Charles Darwin and Alfred Wallace, "Tendency of Species to Form Varieties."

10 Darwin, *Origin of Species*, 4th ed., xiii.

four, of the terrestrial quadrupeds now inhabiting the provinces in which the caves occur. . . . This wonderful relationship in the same continent between the dead and the living, will, I do not doubt, hereafter throw more light on the appearance of organic beings on our earth . . . than any other class of facts.[11]

In the *Origin*, published fourteen years later, he offered an explanation: "On the theory of descent with modification, the great law of the long enduring, but not immutable, succession of the same types within the same areas, is at once explained; for the inhabitants of each quarter of the world will obviously tend to leave in that quarter, during the next succeeding period of time, closely allied though in some degree modified descendants."[12] So, "descent with modification," transformism, is the first of Darwin's theses.

The second is Common Ancestry: "all living species have been connected with the parent-species of each genus . . . and these parent-species, now generally extinct, have in their turn been similarly connected with more ancient species; and so on backwards, always converging to the common ancestor of each great class."[13] This thesis requires two comments.

First is the question of its *logical* relation to transformism. Common ancestry is not implied by transformism. Lamarck's transformism, for example, at least in the simpler versions of his theory, was linear (rather than branching) in a way that did not include common ancestry for distinct species. But common ancestry does presuppose (and therefore imply) transformism. Its explanatory power (at least at lower taxonomic levels) quickly won acceptance for both theses, despite a few prominent fixist hold-outs (such as Harvard geologist Louis Agassiz and, though less committedly, Würzburg biologist Rudolf Virchow).

Second, one should note Darwin's acknowledgment that the Common Ancestry Thesis could take stronger and weaker forms:

> I believe that animals have descended from at most only four or five progenitors, and plants from an equal or lesser number. Analogy would lead me one step further, namely, to the belief that all animals and plants have descended from some one prototype. But analogy may be a deceitful guide. Nevertheless all living things have much in common . . . . Therefore I should infer from analogy that probably all the organic beings which have ever lived on this earth have descended.[14]

Ernst Haeckel called these two versions of the thesis "monophyletism" and "polyphyletism."[15] While comparative morphology and embryology make it easy to imagine

---

11 Darwin, *Voyage of the Beagle*, 173.

12 Darwin, *Origin of Species*, 340.

13 Darwin, *Origin of Species*, 281–82. Although Darwin there says that this is so, "by the theory of natural selection," suggesting that this theory is a consequence of the theory of natural selection that he had articulated in the early chapters of the book, there is good logical reason to distinguish his causal explanation (natural selection) from the pattern of the history of life (common ancestry), as many of his contemporaries recognized.

14 Darwin, *Origin of Species*, 484.

15 Haeckel, *Schöpfungsgeschichte*, ch. 11.

prototypes for each class of organisms—for mammals, birds, and reptiles, or even, more ambitiously, just for radiates (such as jellyfish and starfish), articulates (such as insects and annelid worms), molluscs, and vertebrates; or for monocotyledonous and dicotyledonous plants—the idea of "*one* primordial form into which life was first breathed" could only be called conjectural.

The evidence for common ancestry within a class was homology, i.e., observed similarity such as that between the skeletal structure of human arms and canine forelimbs.[16] Or, to put the point differently, common ancestry was the *explanation* of homology. Philosophical enthusiasts for Darwinism such as Herbert Spencer and Haeckel tended to emphasize the idea of universal common ancestry, illustrated in Haeckel's famous Monophyletic Family Tree of Organisms.[17] Other evolutionists seem not to have emphasized the question of whether the family tree of organisms was *monophyletic*, but did point to homologies that reached the level of phyla (e.g., Darwin on swim bladders and lungs[18]), kingdoms (e.g., Huxley on the dermal and intestinal layers of hydrozoa and the germinal layers in vertebrate embryos[19]), or even further. Darwin wrote that "all living things have much in common, in their chemical composition, their germinal vesicles, their cellular structure, and their laws of growth and reproduction,"[20] and Huxley that cell theory "involves the admission of a primitive conformity, not only of all the elementary structures in plants and animals respectively, but of those in the one of these great divisions of living things with those in the other."[21] Jesuit metaphysician Thomas Norton Harper also noted

> the striking similarity between the process and organs of fecundation, or reproduction, in plants and in animals. There are in both the germ-cells and sperm-cells, and the fertilization of the former by the latter,—that which may be called in both the nutritive yolk to support the embryo in the beginning of its growth . . . , in both the same gradual development of organism. It is further curious to notice, that a great part of the nutritive matter, reserved in the endosperm and cotyledons (where these latter exist) for the service of the plant-embryo is albuminous, like that reserved for some animal-embryos,—for instance the yolk in the eggs of birds.[22]

Darwin's third thesis proposes a *cause* of the transformation of one species into another—Natural Selection, i.e., the "preservation of favourable variations and the

---

16 Richard Owen (in his *Invertebrate Animals*, 379) had defined "Homologue" to mean "the same organ in different animals under every variety of form and function." Darwin used the word in that sense: "We find in distinct languages striking homologies due to community of descent" (*Descent of Man*, 1:59). Modern biologists use the term differently; for them, homologous parts are those that (*by definition*) derive from a common ancestral part.

17 Haeckel, *Generelle Morphologie*, in the tables on the unnumbered pages at the end of the volume.

18 Darwin, *Origin of Species*, 190–91.

19 Huxley, "Medusæ."

20 Darwin, *Origin of Species*, 484.

21 Huxley, "Evolution. I. Evolution in Biology," 8:750.

22 Harper, *Metaphysics of the School*, 558.

rejection of injurious variations"[23] from one generation to the next until the descendants are so different from their ancestors as to constitute a distinct species. "Natural Selection," Darwin went on to say, "has been the main but not exclusive means of modification,"[24] a judgment that he weakened slightly in later work.[25] Some biologists, "neo-Darwinists"[26] such as A. R. Wallace or August Weismann, for example, made natural selection the only agent of change. Others ("neo-Lamarckians") gave it a distinctly weaker rôle. Alternative mechanisms were proposed including macromutations, the inheritance of acquired characteristics, and orthogenesis (i.e., an innate tendency to evolve in a pre-established direction). Peter Charles Mitchell, then secretary to the Zoological Society of London, wrote, in his 1910 *Encyclopaedia Britannica* article on "Evolution," that "how far 'natural selection' suffices for the production of species remains to be seen."[27] The matter was not resolved until the synthesis of Darwinism and Mendelian genetics in the 1930s.

* * * * *

Despite the philosophically-driven association of a purely natural origin of life with evolutionary accounts of the origin of species (an association prominent in the thought of Herbert Spencer and Haeckel), it is important to note that all three of the Darwinian theses just identified are, both logically and scientifically, distinct from the question of whether natural processes could have given rise to the first living things.

The actualist scientific methodology at the heart of Lyellian (and *a fortiori* of Darwinian) science might naturally connect the question about the origin of life to the question of whether what was variously called heterogeny, spontaneous generation, or abiogenesis can be found in nature today. On that question, science had vacillated over

---

23 Darwin, *Origin of Species*, 81.

24 Darwin, *Origin of Species*, 6.

25 See, for example, the change, in Darwin's *Variation under Domestication*, between the first edition, 2:419, and the second, 2:414, where the crossed out passages are deleted and the bracketed passages added:

> ~~We must not exaggerate the importance of the definite action of changed conditions in modifying all the individuals of the same species in the same manner, or of use and disuse.~~ As [almost] every part of the organisation ~~is~~ [becomes] highly variable, and as variations are ~~so~~ easily selected, both consciously and unconsciously, it is ~~very~~ difficult to distinguish between the effects of the selection of indefinite variations, and the direct action of the conditions of life.

26 The usage is that of George Romanes, who used it to make a three-way contrast between the extreme selectionism of Wallace and August Weismann, "Neo-Darwinism," which held "that natural selection is the only possible cause of adaptive modification;" the Neo-Lamarckianism of certain American biologists, "that much greater importance ought to be assigned to the inherited effects of use and disuse than was assigned to these agencies by Darwin;" and Darwin's own view ("Darwinism"), "standing ... between those extremes," "that natural selection has been the main means of modification [even though] it has not been the only means[,] but has been supplemented or assisted by the co-operation of other causes" (Romanes, *Darwin, and After Darwin*, 2:12, 13, and 7).

This term has been used variously over the history of Darwinism. When Samuel Butler coined the term, he used it to contrast "the original Darwinism of Dr. Erasmus Darwin," in which "the variations whose accumulation results in species [is] due to the wants and endeavours of the living forms in which they appear," to "the neo-Darwinism of to-day," in which those variations are "ascribed to chance, or, in other words, to unknown causes, as by Mr. Charles Darwin's system" (Butler, *Unconscious Memory*, 280–81). In today's usage, the term "Neo-Darwinism" generally refers to the synthetic (Mendelian-Darwinian) theory that emerged in the 1930s.

27 Mitchell, "Evolution," 10:34. For a fuller contemporary account, see Stanford biologist Vernon L. Kellogg, *Darwinism To-day*. For a historical survey, see Peter J. Bowler, *Non-Darwinian Revolution*.

426

the course of the last several centuries. The evidence cited by Aristotelians in favor of spontaneous generation (of, for example, insects from putrefying matter[28]) was refuted by Francesco Redi (in his *Esperienze intorno alla generazione degl'insetti* [1668]). Robert Hooke and Antoni van Leeuwenhoek's discovery of microbes (1665–83) raised the issue again, but the subsequent, late eighteenth-century, controversy—between two Catholic priests, John Needham and Lazzaro Spallanzani—was again settled against spontaneous generation. The idea was proposed for a third time in 1858, by Félix-Archimède Pouchet, director of the Muséum d'histoire naturelle at Rouen,[29] but refuted by the work of another Catholic scientist, Louis Pasteur.

That did not raise direct problems for the Darwinian theses articulated above. Darwin himself carefully distinguished his account of the origin of species from the question of the origin of life. About the latter he maintained a careful agnosticism: "our ignorance is as profound on the origin of life as on the origin of force or matter."[30] Nevertheless, a more comprehensive evolutionism, philosophical rather than scientific, was in the air. The general view was articulated by Spencer: "If we must form any conclusion respecting the general course of things, past, present, and future, . . . the only one for which there is any justification is, that the change from an indeterminate uniformity to a determinate multiformity which we everywhere see going on, has been going on from the first, and will continue to go on."[31]

And so, despite the lack of direct *logical* connection with Darwin's evolutionary account of the origin of species, at least some leading evolutionists placed their bets on an abiogenetic account of the origin of life on earth. August Weismann wrote that "spontaneous generation, in spite of all vain efforts to demonstrate it, remains for me a logical necessity."[32] Thomas H. Huxley, only slightly more cautious, wrote:

> Expectation is permissible where belief is not; and if it were given me to look beyond the abyss of geologically recorded time to the still more remote period when the earth was passing through physical and chemical conditions, which it can no more see again than a man can recall his infancy, I should expect to be a witness of the evolution of living protoplasm from not living matter.[33]

All the details of how this happened (i.e., a *scientific* theory of the origin of life) is a matter of ongoing scientific research.

---

28 Aristotle, *Generation of Animals*, 5.31.

29 Pouchet, *Hétérogénie*.

30 Darwin, "Doctrine of Heterogeny," 554.

31 Spencer, *First Principles*, 1st ed., 218. Spencer later wrote that "Evolution is an integration of matter and concomitant dissipation of motion; during which the matter passes from an indefinite, incoherent homogeneity to a definite, coherent heterogeneity." *First Principles*, 3rd ed., 396.

32 Weismann, "Duration of Life," 34.

33 Huxley, "Presidential Address," lxxxiii–lxxxiv.

B. THE ORIGIN OF MAN

Darwin's fourth thesis was that the first three theses (asserting the evolutionary origin of species) applied not only to plants and animals, but to man as well.

The idea of an evolutionary origin of the human race was not new with Darwin. It had appeared in Lamarck's *Philosophie zoologique* and in Chambers's *Vestiges*. Darwin carefully avoided explicit assertion of the thesis in the *Origin*, but he did make three remarks that strongly suggest it:

> I can, indeed, hardly doubt that all vertebrate animals having true lungs have descended by ordinary generation from an ancient prototype, of which we know nothing, furnished with a floating apparatus or swimbladder.

> I should infer from analogy that probably all the organic beings which have ever lived on this earth have descended from some one primordial form into which life was first breathed.

> In the distant future I see open fields for far more important researches. Psychology will be based on a new foundation, that of the necessary acquirement of each mental power and capacity by gradation. Light will be thrown on the origin of man and his history.[34]

The implication of those remarks was clear from the start, as was evident in the famous exchange of views between Samuel Wilberforce (Anglican bishop of Oxford) and Huxley.[35] Evolutionary anthropogenesis was publicly defended in three works that appeared in the 1860s—Huxley's *Evidence as to Man's Place in Nature* (1863), Carl Vogt's *Vorlesungen über den Menschen, seine Stellung in der Schöpfung und in der Geschichte der Erde* (1863), and Giovanni Canestrini's, *Origine dell'uomo* (1866). Darwin explicitly made the thesis his own in *The Descent of Man* (1871), arguing that it was the logical consequence of similarities between man and animal in mental powers as well as bodily structure.

Comparative anatomy played an important rôle in the defense of Darwin's fourth thesis. Haeckel wrote in 1895:

> We can only partially acknowledge the great weight which laymen or narrow specialists give to the evidence of "fossil men" and "forms transitional between ape and man." Those who have a comprehensive knowledge of comparative anatomy and of ontogeny, as well as of paleontology, and who are able to make an impartial *comparison* of the phenomena, do not need those fossils in order to recognize the "historical descent of man from apes" as an *historical fact*. For us, that idea is already a *fully empirically grounded* hypothesis, regardless of whether later paleontological discoveries include intermediate forms or not.[36]

And in 1920, French paleontologist Marcellin Boule wrote:

---

34 Darwin, *Origin of Species*, 191, 484, and 488.

35 For details, see my *War That Never Was*, 72–82.

36 Haeckel, *Phylogenie der Wirbelthiere*, 3:618 (italics Haeckel's).

The significance and importance of these rudimentary organs have been clearly brought out by Darwin. They furnish the strongest arguments that comparative anatomy, on its own authority, can bring forward in support of the transformist theory in general, and of the animal descent of Man in particular.

Physiology likewise contributes evidence in its favor. There is now a science of comparative bio-chemistry, according to which each group of beings possesses a specific chemical constitution accompanying its specific morphology, and distinguishing it, like the latter, from neighboring groups. The very striking experiments made in the last few years by the method of serum precipitation by numerous physiologists, have enabled an accurate estimation to be made, in a marvelously delicate manner, of the degrees of consanguinity between the different Primates. The relationship of Man especially with the anthropoid apes, and with the Chimpanzee in particular, has been confirmed. With other monkeys of the Old World, such as the Macaque, his relationship is much less close and it is still more distant with the Flat-nosed (Platyrrhine) Monkeys of the New World.[37]

Nevertheless, this fourth thesis had the antiquity of the human race as an "indispensable basis," said Darwin,[38] and raised in many minds the possibility of finding fossil evidence of such evolution.[39] The establishment of such antiquity and the finding of those fossils are each relevant enough to our story to merit review and important enough to require more detail than was necessary on points less controversial in the construction of Catholic evolutionism.

✳　✳　✳　✳

Nineteenth-century paleontology could not generally assign absolute (i.e., numerical) ages to fossils, so the answerable version of the question of the antiquity of man was this: "whether or no we have sufficient evidence in caves, or in the superficial deposits commonly called drift or 'diluvium,' to prove the former co-existence of man with certain extinct mammalia."[40] Cuvier wrote in 1826 that "it is certain that human bones have not yet been found among the fossils," though he was not quite ready to say that no human beings had existed in previous epochs.[41] Lyell wrote in 1830 that "the low antiquity of our species … is not controverted by any geologist."[42]

---

37 Boule, *Hommes fossiles*, 437 (trans., 440).

38 Darwin, *Descent of Man*, 1:3.

39 Darwin did not overemphasize such finds as a test of his idea: "With respect to the absence of fossil remains, serving to connect man with his ape-like progenitors, no one will lay much stress on this fact, who will read Sir C. Lyell's discussion, in which he shews that in all the vertebrate classes the discovery of fossil remains has been an extremely slow and fortuitous process. Nor should it be forgotten that those regions that are the most likely to afford remains connecting man with some extinct ape-like creature, have not as yet been searched by geologists" (Darwin, *Descent of Man*, 1:201).

40 Charles Lyell, *Antiquity of Man*, 1. For an excellent brief general history of the history of ideas on this topic, see James A. Sackett, "Human Antiquity and the Old Stone Age." For a more detailed account, see Donald K. Grayson, *Establishment of Human Antiquity* or A. Bowdoin Van Riper, *Men among the Mammoths*. Also valuable is Nicolaas A. Rupke, *Great Chain of History*, chap. 8.

41 Cuvier, *Discours sur les révolutions de la surface du globe*, 65 and 68.

42 Lyell, *Principles of Geology*, 1:153.

429

Some of the early evidence of the antiquity of the human race was found by John MacEnery (1796–1841), a Catholic priest employed as a private chaplain by a Catholic family at Torre Abbey in Devonshire.[43] He was not, however, the only researcher to have discovered tools that suggested the antiquity of man. François Jouannet, in 1810 and for some years following, was finding stone tools in the rock shelters of the Périgord, enough to make the distinction between what were later called Paleolithic and Neolithic technologies.[44] The turning point came, however, with the finds of Jacques Boucher de Perthes, master of customs at Abbeville (France) and amateur antiquary, who, working not in caves but in the gravel terraces of the Somme, also discovered flint tools together with the fossils of extinct fauna.[45]

The establishment of the antiquity of man, *congenial* as it may have been for the proponents of an evolutionary anthropogenesis, was not direct *evidence* for human evolution. That would require not human artifacts, but human bodies.[46] These also were beginning to emerge from the ground as three researchers on the continent—Paul Tournal and Jules de Christol in southern France, and Philippe-Charles Schmerling in Belgium—found human bones in circumstances similar to those that had yielded the artifacts just mentioned.[47]

Oxford professor William Buckland, one of England's most prominent paleontologists, was interested. He wrote to U.S. government geologist George William Featherstonhaugh that:

> There is one Discovery of infinite Importance to my Views of the diluvial question … Human Bones in two caves near Sommières under circumstances which seem to shew that Men were coeval with the Hyenas and Elephants.… It seems to me a Case not to be explained but by admitting what, if it can be well-established, is the most important Geological Discovery that I can ever hope to witness.[48]

As historian Nicolaas Rupke has pointed out, such a discovery would have been of "bipartisan interest": "To Buckland and his school the occurrence of antediluvial human remains … would provide the missing link between geological and biblical history. To the opponents of the diluvial theory, the early presence of man on earth would provide a

---

43 MacEnery's work and ideas are accessible through his *Nachlaß*, published by William Pengelly as "Literature of Kent's Cavern." A. S. Kennard, "Early Digs in Kent's Hole," provides a guide to their contents. The best account of MacEnery's life is Leo Kevin Clark, OP, *Pioneers of Prehistory*.

44 See André Cheynier, "Précurseur amateur en préhistoire," or Cheynier, *Jouannet*.

45 Boucher de Perthes, *De l'Industrie primitive* (1846); republished the next year as *Antiquités celtiques et antédiluviennes*, with a second volume published in 1857. See also his retrospective *Homme antédiluvien et de ses œuvres*. For a brief biography, see James Sackett, "Boucher de Perthes."

46 For a detailed history, see John Reader, *Missing Links*; or Peter J. Bowler, *Theories of Human Evolution*.

47 Tournal, "Considérations théoriques"; De Christol, *Notice sur les ossemens humains fossiles*; Schmerling, *Recherches sur les ossemens fossiles*. For an overview, see John Lyon, "The Search for Fossil Man."

48 Buckland to Featherstonhaugh, November 4, 1829, Adam Sedgwick: Letters and Papers, Department of Manuscripts and University Archives, MS Add. 7652.II.LL.23, Cambridge University Library (quoted from Rudwick, *Worlds before Adam*, 232). It was Christol's work to which Buckland was referring.

mechanism for piecemeal extinction, removing the need for a cataclysmic inundation."[49] Nevertheless, the scientific community remained skeptical through the 1850s.[50] Why was this so? Charles Lyell wrote retrospectively that "a discovery which seems to contradict the general tenor of previous investigations is naturally received with much hesitation."[51] But there were particular reasons for scientific caution. In his 1860 presidential address to the British Association for the Advancement of Science, Lyell said:

> extreme reluctance was naturally felt on the part of scientific reasoners to admit the validity of such evidence, seeing that so many caves have been inhabited by a succession of tenants, and have been selected by man, as a place not only of domicile, but of sepulture, while some caves have also served as the channels through which the waters of flooded rivers have flowed, so that the remains of living beings which have peopled the district at more than one era may have subsequently been mingled in such caverns and confounded together in one and the same deposit.[52]

About Boucher de Perthes, Huxley later wrote that "eminently generous, truthful, hearty, and enthusiastic, Boucher de Perthes paid for these virtues by a certain facility of belief, which is as terrible a drawback to scientific weight as it is advantageous in the struggle against neglect and adverse criticism when a man happens to have laid hold of a truth."[53] Historian Donald Grayson summarized the problem this way: "It was clear that no change in the belief in human recency was going to come about in Britain as a result of data derived from a cave unless that cave possessed outstandingly well-stratified deposits, and unless the excavation of those deposits was carried out by someone outstandingly well-qualified to make the case."[54]

Just those *desiderata* turned up in 1859, with the discovery of Brixham Cave, not far from Kent's Hole, where a careful excavation of the previously sealed site by Hugh Falconer and William Pengelly, expert investigators both,[55] yielded flint tools in unambiguous association with extinct fauna and led to a general scientific acceptance first of the coexistence of man and the extinct animals, and then of the antiquity of man.[56]

British paleontologist George Busk, in some remarks he attached to his translation of one of the early reports on the first discovery of Neanderthalers, wrote:

> The fact of the geological antiquity of Man, or, to use other words, of his having been cotemporary with extinct animals whose remains are universally regarded by

---

49 Rupke, *Great Chain*, 94.

50 See, for example, Buckland (in 1836), *Geology and Mineralogy*, 103–6 and 597.

51 Lyell, *Antiquity of Man*, 68.

52 Lyell, "Human Art in Post-Pliocene Deposits," 93–95. See also his remarks on the Languedocian caves in *Principles of Geology*, 2:224–27.

53 Huxley, "Anniversary Address," xxxi. See also Jules Desnoyers's case against the Languedocian finds in a paper originally delivered to the Société géologique de France—"Considérations sur les ossemens humains," or "Human Bones and Works."

54 Grayson, *Establishment of Antiquity*, 83.

55 For a history, see Jacob W. Gruber, "Brixham Cave."

56 Joseph Prestwich, "Flint-Implements."

> geologists as "fossil," has apparently been fully established, though rather, perhaps,
> from the discovery of his works than of his actual remains, under certain geological
> conditions. It has become a matter, therefore … of extreme interest to determine
> how far it may be possible, from the scanty remains of his bones as yet discovered, to
> ascertain whether, and in what respects, the priscan race or races may have differed
> from those which at present inhabit the earth.[57]

As it happened, the first such evidence was recognized almost simultaneously with the establishment of human antiquity.

Despite Schmerling's isolated finds of human skeletal material in the Engis caves in Wallonia (1829–30), the story of human fossils begins in 1856, when quarrymen clearing a cave in Germany's Neander Valley found a skull cap and assorted other bones in the mud that it was their task to remove. These they passed on to a local schoolteacher, one Johann Carl Fuhlrott, who in turn passed them on to Hermann Schaaffhausen, professor of anatomy at the University of Bonn. Schaaffhausen prepared and presented reports on the find, which they thought was an early, but still modern, human being. Nevertheless, the remains were heavy-boned enough, and had brow-ridges prominent enough, to distinguish them from modern specimens. While some scientists argued that these distinctive features were pathological and required a medical explanation (such as rickets or arthritis), the scientific consensus was that the differences made them, as Schaaffhausen had ventured to suggest, comparable to those of "the most ancient races of man."[58]

Might the Neanderthalers be a hitherto missing link in human evolution? Thomas Henry Huxley addressed the question in his *Man's Place in Nature* (1863). After examining a plaster cast, and after correspondence with Fuhlrott, he answered the question in the negative: "In no sense … can the Neanderthal bones be regarded as the remains of a human being intermediate between Men and Apes. At most, they demonstrate the existence of a Man whose skull may be said to revert somewhat towards the pithecoid type."[59] The cranial capacity (75 in³, or 1229 cc), he thought, was too large to allow him to draw any other conclusion. William King, professor of geology and mineralogy at Queen's College, Galway, by contrast, thought that the Neanderthalers represented at least a different species within the genus *Homo* and gave it the name *Homo neanderthalensis*.[60]

The pathology theory was done in decisively, if not immediately, by the appearance of more Neanderthalers. Two had come unrecognized in the years before 1856—first at Liège, where one of the skulls found by Schmerling turned out to be a Neanderthaler and then (in order of recognition) again in 1848 at Forbes Quarry on the peninsula of Gibraltar. Within a few decades, relatively complete skeletons had been found—by the priest-paleoanthropologists Amédée and Jean Bouyssonie at Chappelle aux Saints (Aquitaine) (1908). The debate over whether Neanderthalers were members of an ancestral

---

57 Busk, "Crania," 172.

58 Schaaffhausen, "Älteste Rasseschädel," 471 (trans., 167).

59 Huxley, *Man's Place*, 181–82.

60 King, "Reputed Fossil Man." For more on King, see John Murray et al., "Contribution of King."

species, members of a sister species, or members of our own species has still not reached consensus, but it was clear that, whatever their exact place relative to modern man in the history of life, they were too close to modern man to close the gap between man and ape. In their report, Fraipont and Lohest wrote that "The distance which separates the Spy man from modern anthropoids is incontestably enormous; it is a little less large between the Spy man and dryopithecus."[61] And so, through most of the nineteenth century, Haeckel's comment in his *Natürliche Schöpfungsgeschichte* still stood: "We as yet know of no fossil remains of the hypothetical primæval man (*Homo primigenius*) who developed out of anthropoid apes during the tertiary period."[62]

Three candidates for link in the chain of human ancestry emerged in the last decade of the nineteenth and the first half of the twentieth century—two out of the ground and the third, sad to say, out of a forger's workshop.

The first of those candidates appeared in 1890 as a result of the efforts of Eugène Dubois, a Dutch physician who had gone to the Dutch East Indies in 1887 precisely to search for fossil evidence of human evolution.[63] In 1891–1892, at a Solo River site near the village of Trinil on the island of Java, he found first a molar and a skull cap and then (a year later and at a distance of 10–15 meters from the earlier find) a thigh bone. These he first took to be a new species of chimpanzee (*Anthropopithecus erectus*), but then identified as a new genus, intermediate between ape and man, to which he gave a name that had been coined by Haeckel in 1868—*Pithecanthropus*. Controversy over the exact significance of Dubois's Java Man continued for several decades. As late as 1928, Garrit S. Miller, then curator of the Division of Mammals at the U.S. National Museum, wrote:

> Opinions differed to an astonishing degree. Some accepted the belief of Dubois that the remains came from one individual; others regarded the circumstances of the discovery as giving no support to it. About the skullcap some agreed with Dubois that it clearly represented a transition stage between ape and man; others pronounced it human, and still others were as fully convinced that it was simian. In April, 1896, Dubois gave a summary of the opinions of 19 writers (p. 425): 5 regarded the skullcap as simian, 7 as human, and 7 as intermediate.[64]

The second putative link came from Piltdown, in Sussex, and was first presented to the scientific community in 1912. The skull fragments, the partial jawbone, and the teeth that constituted "Piltdown Man" (formally, *Eoanthropus*) showed a mix of human and simian features. "The announcement," Miller wrote, "gave rise to a contest of opinion which is probably unequaled in the history of paleontology."[65] Some scientists doubted that the skull and the jawbone had belonged to the same individual. In fact, those doubters

---

61 Fraipont and Lohest, "Race humaine de Néanderthal," 755.

62 Haeckel, *Schöpfungsgeschichte*, 4th ed., 620 (trans., 2:326).

63 For a biography of Dubois, see Pat Shipman, *Man Who Found the Missing Link*, or L. T. Theunissen, *Eugène Dubois*.

64 Miller, "Missing Links," 425.

65 Miller, "Missing Links," 434.

were correct; Piltdown Man was revealed in 1953 to be a forgery. The perpetrator of the forgery, and his motives, have never been established.[66]

Miller summarized the state of the question in 1928 as follows:

> As the result of 70 years of effort these tireless workers have made exactly two "finds"—no more—which are of such a nature that they can be seriously regarded as furnishing the looked-for direct evidence of man's blood relationship with animals resembling in some general manner the present-day gorilla and chimpanzee.

> We should not hesitate to confess that in place of demonstrable links between man and other mammals we now possess nothing more than some fossils so fragmentary that they are susceptible of being interpreted either as such links or as something else.... The things most needed now are more fossils and many of them.[67]

In the context of the history of paleoanthropological thought, Piltdown Man stood as an anomaly and a distraction for many years. Acceptance of the intermediate character of Dubois's *Pithecanthropus* came shortly after Miller wrote, with the discovery of similar fossils—Peking Man (1929) and then more fossils from Java (1937–1941).

In fact a third candidate, not yet noticed by Miller, had already been discovered in the lime-pits of Taung (South Africa), where, in 1924, Raymond Dart, anatomist at the new University of Witwatersrand, recovered some fossil remains of a young child. The circumstances of its discovery left the fossil with no geological context, but various features of its morphology, ranging from dentition to evidence of upright posture and "improved quality of the brain," led Dart to see in his fossil "an extinct race of apes *intermediate between living anthropoids and man*"[68]—*Australopithecus africanus*. Dart's claim that australopithecines were ancestral to man met scientific resistance for some years. Among other grounds for the resistance was the fact that *Australopithecus*'s small brain and nearly human jaw showed a pattern exactly the opposite of that found in Piltdown Man. Some critics insisted that Dart's find was in fact a chimpanzee. *Australopithecus* gained a somewhat better reception only once further examples were found, by Robert Broom at Starkfontein (1936) and at Kromdraai (1938). Over the course of the next few years, the place in the human lineage that Dart had attributed to australopithecines won general acceptance.

In 1951, Harvard biologist Ernst Mayr, whose *Systematics and the Origin of Species from the Viewpoint of a Zoologist* (1942) had helped lay the foundations of the New Evolutionary Synthesis, offered a reorganization of the human fossils in question into three species—*Homo transvaalensis* (for all of the australopithecines), *H. erectus* (including both Java and Peking Man), and *H. sapiens* (including both Neanderthalers and modern

---

66 For a scholarly account of Piltdown Man, see Frank Spencer, *Piltdown*. For a more popular history, see Evangelist John Walsh, *Unraveling Piltdown*.

67 Miller, "Missing Links," 415–16, 446.

68 Dart, "*Australopithecus africanus*," 198 and 195 (emphasis Dart's). For Dart's autobiographical account of his work, see his *Adventures with the Missing Link*.

man).[69] Much progress has, of course, been made in the past six decades, but by 1951, the compatibility of evolutionary anthropogenesis and Catholic theology had been given official recognition.

C. MONOGENISM & POLYGENISM

One other topic played a rôle in the history of the relation between Catholic theology and the natural sciences: whether the human race originated in a single couple from whom all other human beings are descended. That reading of the Genesis narrative of Adam and Eve was reinforced by theological considerations related to the doctrine of original sin presented by St. Paul in his Epistle to the Romans (5:12)—"by one man sin entered into this world, and by sin death; and so death passed to all men, in whom all have sinned." The existence of such a couple is connected to the doctrine of original sin as articulated by the Council of Trent: "The sin of Adam is in its origin one, and being transfused into all by propagation, not by imitation, is in all men and proper to each."[70] Clarification of two key terms in that sentence connects it to a monogenetic account of the origin of the human race. First, "in its origin one" means that the first, or original, sin (the *peccatum originale originans*) was a single act. Second, "by propagation" means "through biological descent." This would place all ancestors, collateral relatives, and neighbors of the original sinner (and his wife) outside the scope of the *peccatum originale originatum*, the universal human sinfulness that is the effect of that first sin.

Alternatives to this view of the origin of the race have come in two forms of what one might call (using an early term to avoid ambiguities associated with later terms) "pluralism"—in one form of which the human race originated separately in many different places and in another of which it originated in a single place, but from an entire initial population rather than from a single original couple.[71]

The idea that the human race had its origins in a group, or even in many groups, or that the Biblical Adam had ancestors, only occasionally came to the attention of Christian theologians before the modern age, and not from sources that commanded their respect. Julian the Apostate had defended a pluralist account of human origins in his "Letter to a Priest": "The facts show many men came into existence at the same time. . . . If they were all descended from one man and one woman, then our laws would probably not vary as much as they do, nor is it likely that the whole world was filled with the descendants

---

69 Mayr, "Taxonomic Categories in Fossil Hominids," 114: The exposure of the Piltdown hoax was still several years in the future when Mayr wrote, but it was already anomalous enough that Mayr refused to classify it: "It may take a long time before the Piltdown puzzle is completely cleared up. . . . [Its] phylogenetic and chronological relationship [to other hominid finds] . . . remains to be determined."

70 Trent, "Decretum super peccato originali" (Alberigo, *Conciliorum decreta*, 641–43, or Schroeder, *Canons and Decrees*, 21–23).

71 For a more comprehensive historical overview, see Jindřich Matiegka, "Monogenismus a Polygenismus"; Claude Blanckaert, "Monogénisme et Polygénisme"; or David N. Livingstone, *Adam's Ancestors*.

of one person."[72] The most prominent, if not the very first, *modern* exposition of what might be called *geographical* pluralism is the work of Isaac La Peyrère. Peyrère, born in Bordeaux in about 1596, was possibly, but not certainly, descended from a family of converted Spanish Jews; by religious conviction, he was a Calvinist.[73] In 1655, he published two works relevant to our topic, *Præ-adamitæ sive Exercitatio super versibus duodecimio, decimotertio, & decimoquarto, capitis quinti Epistolæ D. Pauli ad romanos* and *Systema theologicum: Ex præadamitarum hypothesi.* His idea was that Adam was the ancestor of the Jews, but not of all human beings, the rest having independent origins in what he called "men before Adam," or "Pre-Adamites." This hypothesis, he thought, solved a number of problems, both scientific and theological.

On the scientific side, there was, first, the problem of the origin of the indigenous "Skraelings" whom the Vikings had encountered when they discovered Greenland. Doubts about their connection with Old World peoples had already occurred to Peyrère in 1644–45, as he was writing his *Relation de Groenland.* This was augmented "from the most ancient accounts of the Chaldeans; from the oldest records of the Egyptians, Ethiopians, and Scythians; from the recently discovered parts of the frame of the world; and from those unknown regions which the Dutch have just reached, the inhabitants of which, it seems likely, are not descended from Adam."

On the theological side, the hypothesis would solve exegetical puzzles—"Where Cain went after he had killed his brother, . . . [and] where, far from his native land, he found a wife and built a city." It would also, he thought, explain how "sin was in the world before it was imputed to men."[74]

That idea, along with his idea that Moses was not the author of the Pentateuch, was regarded, by both Calvinists and Catholics, as heretical. He was arrested by Catholic authorities in Brussels in 1656 and, after many months of interrogation, agreed to become a Catholic. He retracted his pre-Adamitism, not because he had been *shown* that it was false, he said, but on the authority of the pope.[75] The idea, however, continued to be the subject of theological critique, by Catholics and Protestants alike, for many years.

When a more exclusively scientific approach to the question did arise, with the emergence of the sciences of man in the eighteenth century, opinion was at first decidedly on the side of unitary origin, though over the course of the century that followed, the question of polygenism became entangled with another question—what to make of human racial differences, in particular their cause, their permanence, and their significance. Some scientists even raised the question of whether all human beings were members of the same species, as they had always been thought to be, or whether, as some nineteenth-century anthropologists began to suggest, human races in fact constituted distinct species.[76] The

---

72 Julian the Apostate, Fragment of a letter to a priest, 2:306.

73 For a comprehensive account of his life and thought, see Richard H. Popkin, *Isaac La Peyrère.*

74 Peyrère, *Systema theologicum*, I: Prooemium, C4 (trans. F).

75 Peyrère, *Suite des lettres*, 127.

76 One must be careful to distinguish specific diversity from two other raciological theses current in the nineteenth

questions of *original* and *specific* unity are logically distinct from one another (as well as from the question of the fixity or evolutionary transformability of species). Peyrère, for example, despite his endorsement of original diversity, did not believe that there was more than one human species.[77]

Most prominent among the scientific defenders of specific unity of man were Karl von Linné, in his *Systema naturae* (1735), and the Comte de Buffon, in his *Histoire naturelle de l'homme* (1749). Specific unity was defended late in the eighteenth century by Johann Friedrich Blumenbach in *De generis humani varietate nativa* (1775), in the first half of the nineteenth century by James Cowles Prichard in *Researches into the Physical History of Man* (1813), and at mid-century by Jean Louis Armand de Quatrefages, in *L'Unité de l'espèce humaine* (1861).

Specific pluralism, of which one can find traces among the less-scientific thinkers of the eighteenth century (for example in Voltaire's *Traité de metaphysique* [1734] or in Lord Kames's *Sketches of the History of Man* [1774][78]) received more determined support in the first half of the nineteenth century. In France, it was defended by Julien Joseph Virey in *Histoire naturelle du genre humain* (1801), by Jean Baptiste Bory de Saint-Vincent in *L'Homme, Essai zoologique sur le genre humain* (1827), by Louis Antoine Desmoulins in *Histoire naturelle des races humaines* (1827), and, later in the century, by Paul Broca in *Recherches sur l'hybridité animale en général et sur l'hybridité humaine en particulier considérées dans leurs rapports avec la question de la pluralité des espèces humaines* (1860). In the United States, its defenders constituted what came to be called the American school of ethnology—Philadelphia scientist Samuel Morton, Mobile (Alabama) physician Josiah Nott, and Anglo-American showman and amateur Egyptologist George Gliddon, the latter two of whom jointly prepared *Indigenous Races of the Earth* (1857).[79]

It was Gliddon who, in 1857, gave us the terms "polygenism" and "monogenism,"[80] though unfortunately, he never gave the terms exact definitions. Gliddon's "polygenism" included both specific and geographic diversity, the latter of which would require many foundational couples. Subsequent usage of these terms has varied from one author to another. Although some people associated the term "polygenism" with Gliddon's *specific*

---

century. The first is that some races are inferior to others. The second is a justification for race-based slavery. Specific diversity did not imply either of those other theses and specific unity was logically compatible with both. Karl Vogt, for example defended specific diversity but condemned slavery (*Vorlesungen*, 1:110; trans., 92), and many defenders of slavery accepted specific unity.

77 Peyrère did write that "Judae species hominum distincta a specie gentilium [est]" (*Systema Theologicum*, 87; trans., 115), for which his English translator of 1655 put "the Jews [are] a kind of men distinct in species from the Gentiles," but the translator should have put just "distinct from the Gentiles." The term "species" here only means something more like "ethnic groups." (For another seventeenth-century author using the word in the same way, see the English translation of Adam Olearius's *Reyse*, in which John Davies rendered Olearius's distinction of four *Horden* or *Hauffen* of Tatars—Volga, Crimean, etc. [p. 372]—as "four species of Tatars" [p. 126]). There is no reason to think that Peyrère meant biological species; elsewhere (e.g., *Systema theologicum*, 221), he referred to the human species in the singular.

78 Voltaire, *Traité*, ch. 1; Kames, *Sketches*, bk. I, sk. 1.

79 For a history, see William Stanton, *Leopard's Spots*.

80 Chapter 5 of *Indigenous Races* was on "Monogenists and the Polygenists: Being an Exposition of the Doctrines of Schools Professing to Sustain Dogmatically the Unity or the Diversity of the Human Races."

pluralism, others use it to refer merely to geographical, or polycentric, pluralism or even to origin in anything more than a single couple (even in a single location). And so Jean Louis Armand de Quatrefages, for example, called geographical pluralist Louis Agassiz a "*mitigated*" polygenist for his hesitation about *specific* pluralism.[81] The term "monogenism," although generally used to refer to the traditional, single-couple view, was sometimes extended to mere geographic unity, regardless of the number of first human beings. Dictionaries reported (or authorized) this range of usage.[82] In the end, as Léon Renwart, SJ, noted rather later,[83] theologians, who needed a name for the single-couple view, adopted the narrower definition of monogenesis, while scientists, who did not, adopted the broader definition.

Haeckel proposed a second pair of terms in his *Natürliche Schöpfungsgeschichte* (1868). He had already introduced the neologisms, "monophyletic" and "polyphyletic" to denominate alternative views on the question of whether various taxa of protists, plants, and animals had "single centers of creation" or whether they arose independently at a number of different places.[84] For Darwin, *species* were monophyletic, but, as noted above, it was for him an open question whether *all* living things had a common origin in a single first species, i.e., whether life itself was mono- or polyphyletic. When Haeckel came to "the much-discussed question of the unified [*einheitlich*] or plural [*vielheitlich*] origin of the human race," he added Gliddon's terms "monogenism" and "polygenism," which were already in use, parenthetically as alternatives to "monophyletism" and "polyphyletism."[85]

Perhaps the pluralist with the strongest scientific credentials was the Swiss-American geologist Louis Agassiz, whose account of the origin of the human race was embedded in a more comprehensive theory of the origin and distribution of other species. That account, first articulated in a lecture delivered to the Académie de Neuchâtel, was based on the idea that "all living things [*êtres organisés*], plants as well as animals, have their own native country [*patrie*]"[86] within about a dozen different "zoological provinces." Each was specially created for the country that it would inhabit, making the fauna differ from one province to another. Asia, Europe, and North America, for example, each have its own distinct species of bears, wolves, and foxes.

How does this look when applied to man? In Neuchâtel, he had said that man is exceptional with respect to the rule. First, "man alone is spread over the entire surface of

---

81 Quatrefages, *Unité de l'espèce humain*, 386.

82 For "monogenism," some dictionaries offered a broad definition. Émile Littré's *Dictionnaire de la langue française*, Camille Flammarion's *Dictionnaire encyclopédique universelle*, and James Murray's *Oxford English Dictionary* all said that it signified descent from a single couple *or* common ancestry. *Chambers's Twentieth-Century Dictionary of the English Language* narrowed the term in one direction—"the descent of the whole human family from a single pair"; but Claude Augé's *Nouveau Larousse illustré* had "from a single primitive type." Similarly for "polygenism" and related terms. While Murray mentioned both original and specific diversity, Littré and Flammarion mentioned only the former and Augé only the latter.

83 Georges Vandebroek and Renwart, "L'Encyclique 'Humani Generis,'" at 348.

84 Haeckel, *Schöpfungsgeschichte*, 1st ed., 344 (cf. trans., 2:44–45).

85 Haeckel, *Schöpfungsgeschichte*, 1st ed., 511 (cf. trans., 2:303).

86 Agassiz, *Notice* (an extract from the lectures given by Professor Agassiz at the Académie de Neuchâtel), 3.

the earth."[87] Second, "although animals are of distinct species in the different zoological provinces to which they belong (e.g., New World and Old World monkeys, Asian and African carnivora), man, despite the diversity of human races, constitutes one and the same species across the surface of the globe."[88] Nevertheless, he later wrote, "the boundaries, within which the different natural combinations of animals are known to be circumscribed upon the surface of our earth, coincide with the natural range of distinct types of man."[89]

Five years after the Neuchâtel lecture, after he came to America, he published two articles, "The Geographical Distribution of Animals" and "The Diversity of Origin of the Human Races," for a Boston Unitarian readership. There he was emphatic in his insistence that "the Unity of Mankind, and the Diversity of Origin of the Human Races . . . are two distinct questions, having almost no connection with each other."[90] His primary focus was the latter; about the former, his views are less clear and seem to have drifted over time. In Neuchâtel, he had said that all men were members of a single species. In Boston, he just said that there was a unity, "a reflection of that Divine nature which pervades their whole being," one constituted by a "consciousness of . . . higher moral obligations."[91] At remarks made from the floor at a meeting of the American Association for the Advancement of Science, at Charleston, South Carolina, in March 1850, he said (according to the minutes of the meeting) that "he regarded all the races of men as one in the possession in common, of all the attributes of humanity; as one in the possession of moral and intellectual powers, that raise them above the brutes, and by which they are allied to the Deity."[92] He later, however, rejected any definition of species (and criterion of specific identity) dependent on "genetic succession" in favor of Samuel Morton's "primordial organic forms," adding that "the differences existing between the races of men are of the same kind as the differences observed between the different families, genera, and species of monkeys or other animals."[93] In the end, he said, "whether the natural groups which can be recognized in the human family are called races, varieties, or species, is of no great importance."[94]

✳ ✳ ✳ ✳ ✳

87 Agassiz, *Notice*, 3.

88 Agassiz, *Notice*, 31.

89 Agassiz, "Natural Provinces of the Animal World," lviii.

90 Agassiz, "Diversity of Origin," 110. See also page 139.

91 Agassiz, "Diversity of Origin," 111.

92 Agassiz, Remarks, 106–7. The remarks, offered just after the reading of the abstract of a paper on racial differences by Josiah Clark Nott, were made, Agassiz said, in order to "correct some misapprehensions of his [own] views."

Recognition of that unity did not, he later said, obviate the appropriateness, indeed the obligation, of "settl[ing] the relative rank among these races." The different races are "equally endowed with the same superior nature," but they "do not rank upon one level in nature" ("Diversity of Origin," 142, 135, and 144).

93 Agassiz, "Sketch," lxxiv. See also his "Prefatory Remarks" to Nott and Gliddon, *Indigenous Races of the Earth*.

94 Agassiz, "Diversity of Origin," 141. It is worth noting his similarity, on this point, to Darwin, whose views are elaborated below.

Darwin's thoughts on the question follow directly from his more general thesis that each species has a single center of origin.[95] And so he wrote in *The Descent of Man* that "those naturalists . . . who admit the principle of evolution . . . will feel no doubt that all the races of man are descended from a single primitive stock; whether or not they think fit to designate them as distinct species."[96] The distinction between varieties (which would include races) and species was, he thought, often "vague and arbitrary." He had made this point already early in the *Origin*, where he had written that "few well-marked and well-known varieties can be named which have not been ranked as species by at least some competent judges"[97] and he repeated it in the *Descent of Man*.[98] And so, with respect to man, he wrote that "it is almost a matter of indifference whether the so-called races of man . . . are ranked as species or sub-species; but the latter term appears the most appropriate."[99] Huxley agreed, saying that "the Polygenists . . . have as yet completely failed to adduce satisfactory positive proof of the specific diversity of mankind."[100] By way of conclusion, Darwin added that "when the principles of evolution are generally accepted . . . the dispute between the monogenists and the polygenists will die a silent and unobserved death."[101] Huxley seconded him on this point as well, saying that Darwin "reconcil[es] and combin[es] all that good in the Monogenistic and Polygenistic schools."[102]

* * * * *

Not all generally Darwinian evolutionists shared the monophyletism of Huxley and Darwin, however. Two major figures, each sometimes called "the Darwin of Germany," denied both the specific and the original unity of mankind.

Karl Vogt, despite his general enthusiasm for Darwin's ideas, not only had reservations about divergence of human lineages over the course of evolutionary history, but had a greater positive openness to convergence than did Darwin. That allowed him to say:

> Let us think of the three anthropomorphic apes extended to the human type which they have not and probably never will reach. From those parallel lineages of apes would evolve three distinct foundational races [*Urrassen*] of man—two dolichocephalic races, descended from the gorilla and chimpanzee, and one brachycephalic race, descended from the orang.[103]

---

95 Darwin, *Origin of Species*, 351–56.

96 Darwin, *Descent of Man*, 1:229.

97 Darwin, *Origin of Species*, 48 and 47, remarks followed by several pages of examples and comment.

98 "We have a practical illustration of the difficulty in the never-ending doubts whether many closely-allied mammals, birds, insects, and plants, which represent each other in North America and Europe, should be ranked species or geographical races" (Darwin, *Descent of Man*, 1:228–29).

99 Darwin, *Descent of Man*, 1:235.

100 Huxley, "Ethnology," 275.

101 Darwin, *Descent of Man*, 1:235.

102 Huxley, "Ethnology," 275.

103 Vogt, *Vorlesungen*, 2:282 (trans., 465).

and

> If, in different places, anthropomorphic apes could emerge from different phylogenetic trees [*Stammbäume*], we cannot see why these various lineages should not develop into man, and why only one lineage should be so favored. In short, we cannot see why American species of man may not be derived from American apes, Negroes from African apes, and Negritos, perhaps, from Asiatic apes![104]

Nevertheless, "by the unrelenting working of his brain, man . . . begins to recognize as his brothers other lineages, races, and species, with whom he finally commingles and interbreeds. . . . In spite of the tenacity with which the foundational races resist alteration, they are slowly led on the way to coalescence into a unity."[105] That coalescence was, however, only partial: "The differences between well-marked species of apes are in no case greater, and are more often much smaller, than those proven in human races . . . the races of mankind must either be considered as different species, or the species of apes must be designated only as races."[106]

Haeckel offered a different account of the origins of human species. His begins with the divergence of what he called *Pithecanthropus alalus*, the speechless ape-man, from the *Menschenaffen* (the family that includes today's gibbons, gorillas, chimpanzees, and orangutans).[107] *Pithecanthropus alalus* is different from the apes, but is not quite human. Two key ideas guide his further account. The first is that "the origin of articulate language [*gegliederte Wortsprache*] is the essential step [*der eigentliche Hauptakt*] in hominization."[108] It is that which turns *Pithecanthropus alalus* into true man. The second, from August Schleicher, is that "human language probably had a multiple, i.e., polyphyletic, origin."[109] The consequence would be that "human language, as such, probably first evolved after the separation of the genus of alinguistic proto-men or ape-men into several species. In each of these species, and perhaps even in the various subspecies, language evolved independently."[110] So, is the origin of man monophyletic or polyphyletic? "In a broader sense, the monophyletic view is certainly correct, . . . but in a narrower sense, one can agree with the polyphyletic view, since the various original languages probably evolved quite independently from one another."[111] Does man share at least a specific unity? Haeckel's answer here was negative. The consequence of diversity of origin was specific diversity: "One can . . . just as well see the various so-called human 'races' as 'good species.'"[112]

---

104 Vogt, *Vorlesungen*, 2:284 (trans., 466–67).

105 Vogt, *Vorlesungen*, 2:286 (trans., 468).

106 Vogt, *Vorlesungen*, 1:270; see also 1:285 (trans., 213–14 and 222).

107 Haeckel, *Schöpfungsgeschichte*, 1st ed., 492–93 (cf. trans., 2:295).

108 Haeckel, *Schöpfungsgeschichte*, 1st ed., 511 (cf. trans., 2:303).

109 Haeckel, *Schöpfungsgeschichte*, 1st ed., 510 (cf. trans., 2:302). He was relying on Schleicher, *Über die Bedeutung der Sprache*.

110 Haeckel, *Schöpfungsgeschichte*, 1st ed., 510 (cf. trans., 2:302).

111 Haeckel, *Schöpfungsgeschichte*, 1st ed., 511 (cf. trans., 2:303).

112 Haeckel, *Schöpfungsgeschichte*, 1st ed., 512.

Despite the prominence of Haeckel, not only in Germany, but abroad as well, neither the polyphyletic aspect of his account of anthropogenesis nor his views about specific diversity in man lasted long into the new century. Augustus Henry Keane, as it happens a Catholic, wrote in his article on "Ethnology" in James Hastings's *Encyclopedia of Religion & Ethics*:

> Polygenism, which postulates a given number of distinct groups independently originating in so many distinct geographical areas—the actual number of these distinct groups and areas ranging from about four to sixteen or even more—is certainly not yet extinct. But the tendency of modern thought is undoubtedly towards Monogenism, which postulates only one such distinct group and one such distinct area, with four main or relatively fundamental divisions separately evolved in four corresponding geographical areas reached by migration from a single cradle-land.[113]

One can, to be sure, find a few anthropologists who continued to support pluralist accounts of human origins in the early twentieth century—in Germany, Hermann Klaatsch and Theodor Arldt; in Italy, Giuseppe Sergi and Gioacchino Leo Séra; and in the United States, later and in a mitigated form, Carleton Coon. Those authors were a distinct minority.

That raciological pluralism soon came to be supplemented (or perhaps replaced) by paleoanthropological questions of unity and plurality as fossil human beings began to emerge from the ground in the middle of the nineteenth century. Neanderthalers, for example, were noticeably (though not radically) different from modern human beings, and generated debate both over whether they constituted a distinct human species (discussed above) and over exactly how they, apes, and modern races of human being were related to one another on phylogenetic trees. While some scientists put the separation of man from apes first, then the separation of modern man from Neanderthalers, and finally the differentiation of races, others proposed early divisions that placed one combination of apes, fossil men, and modern races on one branch of the phylogenetic tree and another combination on another.

✳ ✳ ✳ ✳ ✳

Polyphyletism (and the associated idea of specific diversity) were subjected to a fairly thorough critique in 1927–29, by Henri-Victor Vallois, professor of anatomy at Toulouse, and, from 1931, editor of *L'Anthropologie*.[114] He argued, on the basis of comparative anatomy, that "it is absolutely impossible to establish between the variations of the diverse races of men and those of various genera of apes that systematic parallelism which is at the very base of polyphyletic theories."[115]

---

113 Keane, "Ethnology," 522.

114 Vallois, "Plusieurs Souches?" and "Preuves anatomiques." For a later account of his views, see his "Monophyletism and Polyphyletism in Man."

115 Vallois, "Preuves anatomiques," 98; repeated in his "Monophyletism and Polyphyletism," 73.

A second, entirely different, challenge to the unitary account of human origins, came from those who conceded specific unity and a geographical original unity, but denied that human origins can be traced back to a single first couple.

Such a single first couple would have been impossible for geographical pluralists to maintain, but Agassiz had taken care to reject the idea of single couples even for animals within a zoological province. As a general matter

> Evidence could be accumulated to show, we will not say the improbability only, but even the impossibility, of supposing that animals and plants were created in single pairs .... [They were created rather] in large numbers, in such proportions as suits their natural mode of living and the preservation of their species.... The idea of a pair of herrings or of a pair of buffaloes is as contrary to the nature and habits of those animals, as it is contrary to the nature of pines and birches to grow singly and to form forests in their isolation. [116]

With respect to this rule, man was no exception.

Darwin's version of the evolutionary origin of species, focused as it was on *populations*, would also incline rather against the idea that the human species began with a single couple. Nevertheless, Huxley conceded that "whether [man] arose singly, or a number of examples appeared contemporaneously, is ... an open question for the believer in the production of species by the gradual modification of pre-existing ones."[117] Haeckel, at least in later editions of the *Schöpfungsgeschichte*, was less tolerant of the idea:

> We do not want to say that "all men are descended from a single pair." That view ... is certainly untenable. The whole celebrated question of whether mankind is descended from a single couple or not is based on a completely wrong way of formulating the question.... No "first human couple" or a "first man" ever existed, just as there was never a first couple or a first individual Englishman or German. [118]

116 Agassiz, "Geographical Distribution," 190, 193, and 188.

117 Huxley, "Ethnology," 275–76.

118 Haeckel, *Schöpfungsgeschichte*, 4th ed., 600–601 (cf. trans., 2:304).

CATHOLIC EPISTEMOLOGY

A second element of the background to the Catholic reception of evolutionary biology is the theory of knowledge that underlies Catholic thought in general, and Catholic theology in particular.

A. FOUNDATIONS

The foundation of Christian theology, like that of Jewish and Muslim theology, is, of course, revelation. Nevertheless, Catholic theology differs not only from its Jewish and Muslim counterparts, but even from non-Catholic (and especially Protestant) forms of Christian theology in the details of where revealed truths are to be found and of how its sources are to be discerned and interpreted.

First, of course, Catholics differ from other Christians over the exact canon of the Bible, though the books the canonicity of which is at issue (e.g., Tobit and Maccabees) do not play much rôle in the controversies that we are about to discuss.

Second, Catholics differ from Protestants in their denial that Scripture alone (*sola Scriptura*) is the locus of revealed truths, and in asserting that some truths (the Assumption, for example), not explicitly contained in any passage of Holy Scripture, are nevertheless revealed—and therefore known—according to a principle articulated in the fifth century by St. Vincent of Lérins, sc., because they have been believed "everywhere, always, by all."[1]

Third, Catholics differ from Protestants in the authority they give to doctrines that have been formally promulgated, for example by pope or council. They also place great importance on the Church Fathers as interpreters of Scripture, the Council of Trent having declared that "No one should … dare to give Holy Scripture a meaning of his own invention, contrary either to the meaning that Holy Mother Church … held and holds or contrary to the unanimous agreement of the Fathers."[2]

Catholicism's distinctive doctrines—on revelation in general, on Scripture in particular, and on the teaching authority of the Church—framed rather differently from Protestantism the task of separating the wheat from the chaff among the new ideas that were emerging in the middle of the nineteenth century, whether in Darwin's *Origin of Species* or in the *Essays and Reviews*[3] (and their German counterparts). These distinctive features facilitated theology's reaction to evolutionary biology in some ways, but complicated it in others.

B. DEGREES OF CERTAINTY

That some scientific ideas are better established—more certain—than others is generally recognized. One can illustrate this fact by citing a passage from Darwin (the italics, of course, being mine):

> *I cannot doubt that* the theory of descent with modification embraces all the members of the same class. *I believe that* animals have descended from at most only four or five progenitors, and plants from an equal or lesser number. *I should infer from analogy that probably* all the organic beings which have ever lived on this earth have descended from some one primordial form, into which life was first breathed.[4]

Catholic doctrines must also be so distinguished. Long-standing Catholic theological practice, in use throughout the period that is our subject, assigned to various doctrines theological qualifications (or notes) indicating their evidence, their degree of certainty, the extent to which Catholics were required to believe them, and their irreformability. The exact range of choices of qualifications and the exact definition of each varied somewhat from one theologian to another. The imprecision in definitions of the various qualifications is surely an attempt to provide a descriptive guide to practice rather than a prescriptive template. As an abridged guide, sufficient for our purposes, we can note

---

1 Vincent of Lérins, *Commonitoria*, 2.

2 Trent, "Decretum secundum: recipitur vulgata editio bibliae præscribiturque modus interpretandi sacram scripturam etc." (Alberigo, *Conciliorum decreta*, 640; or Schroeder, *Canons and Decrees*, 18–20) (trans., 8–10, 94–96, and 103–5).

3 Frederick Temple et al., *Essays and Reviews*.

4 Darwin, *Origin of Species*, 483–84.

the following terms, definitions, and examples, drawn from Ludwig Ott's *Grundriss der katholischen Dogmatik* (1952):[5]

GRADE	DEFINITION	EXAMPLE
Sententia de fide definita	A truth defined in a solemn declaration of the pope or of an ecumenical council	The first man was created by God.
Sententia fidei proxima	A doctrine that is almost universally judged by theologians to be a revealed truth	The supernatural endowment of the first men included freedom from irregular desire.
Sententia theologice certa	A doctrine the truth of which is guaranteed by its intrinsic connection to revealed doctrine (theological conclusions)	The whole human race stems from one single first couple.
Sententia communis	A doctrine that *per se* belongs to the realm of free opinion, but is generally held by theologians	The supernatural endowment of the first men included freedom from suffering.

We should also note one more qualification, included near the lower end of the scale—*sententia certa*, or *communis et certa*, which Sixtus Cartechini defined as "a doctrine that is certain, but less immediately deduced from a revealed truth [than is a *sententia theologice certa*]."[6]

To these grades of certainty correspond a set of theological censures. A proposition contrary to one *de fide definita* would be heretical. Propositions could also be judged near to heresy or error (*hæresi proxima* or *errori proxima*). One denying a *sententia theologice certa* (e.g., a conclusion drawn from one premise *de fide definita* and one known only with natural certainty) would be adjudged merely erroneous. Finally, propositions could be judged rash (or temerarious) if they were contrary to a *sententia communis* and asserted for insufficient reason.[7]

The moral importance of avoiding rashness was nicely summarized by Bl. John Henry Cardinal Newman:

> In certain cases there may be a duty of silence, when there is no obligation of belief. Here no question of faith comes in. We will suppose that a novel opinion about Scripture or its contents is well grounded, and a received opinion open to doubt, in a case in which the Church has hitherto decided nothing, so that a new question needs a new answer: here, to profess the new opinion may be abstractedly permissible, but is not always permissible in practice. The novelty may be so startling as to require a full certainty that it is true; it may be so strange as to raise the question whether it will not unsettle ill-educated minds, that is, though the statement is not an offence against faith, still it may be an offence against charity. It need not be heretical, yet at a particular time or place it may be so contrary to the prevalent opinion in the

---

5 Ott, *Grundriss*, 9–12 (for the definitions), 108–11 and 119–22 (for the examples).

6 Cartechini, *De valore notarum theologicarum*, 99.

7 Joseph Sollier, "Theological Censures."

Catholic body, as in Galileo's case, that zeal for the supremacy of the Divine Word, deference to existing authorities, charity towards the weak and ignorant, and distrust of self, should keep a man from being impetuous or careless in circulating what nevertheless he holds to be true, and what, if indeed asked about, he cannot deny. The household of God has claims upon our tenderness in such matters, which criticism and history have not.[8]

Those tempted to think that the very notion of rash ideas is at least offensive to academic ears will be able to reconcile themselves to the concept, if not fully to the associated precept, by imagining the reaction of a senior referee at a prestigious academic journal to a submission from a young scholar who denies without serious argument an established scholarly consensus.

Due to the inherently traditional character of Catholic theology, inconsistency with a *sententia communis* would constitute a problem, but it would be a problem qualitatively different from inconsistency with a *sententia de fide definita*. The doctrine of the infallibility of the Church extends to the latter, but not to the former.

So, it is too imprecise to ask simply whether some new scientific idea is compatible or incompatible with Catholic theological doctrine. One must distinguish at least two kinds of incompatibility—categorical (i.e., incompatibility with a *sententia de fide definita*) and presumptive (e.g., incompatibility with a *sententia communis*).[9] A verdict of merely presumptive incompatibility would raise the further question of whether the evidence in favor of some new scientific idea was sufficiently strong to override the presumption against it, a matter that might be reassessed in light of a deeper understanding of the dogmas in question, of strengthened evidence for the truth of the scientific thesis, or of both. A verdict of compatibility would of course still leave anyone interested in the idea with the further question of whether the thesis in question was not only compatible with Catholic doctrine, but actually true, but at that point the discussion among Catholics may not look any different from the discussion among anyone else interested in the question.

C. PRINCIPLES OF SCRIPTURAL INTERPRETATION

Two fundamental principles underlie Catholic hermeneutics—inspiration and inerrancy. The second is generally held to be consequent on the first. These principles have always been implicit in the theology of Scripture. They were articulated explicitly as they came under attack in the nineteenth century. And so we find in the First Vatican Council's dogmatic constitution *De Fide Catolica* (1870): "These books of the Old and New Testaments . . . the Church holds to be sacred and canonical . . . because, having been written under the inspiration of the Holy Spirit, they have God for their Author" and

---

8 Newman, "Inspiration of Scripture," 187.

9 How *sententiae fidei proximae* or *certae* should be classified would depend on how exactly one understood closeness and certainty.

"they contain revelation without error."[10] The doctrines were reasserted at the Second Vatican Council in its dogmatic constitution on Divine Revelation *Dei Verbum* (1965): "Holy Mother Church ... holds that the books of both the Old and New Testaments in their entirety, with all their parts, ... were written under the inspiration of the Holy Spirit, [and] have God as their author" and "since everything that the inspired authors or sacred writers assert must be held to have been asserted by the Holy Spirit, it follows that the books of Scripture must be acknowledged as teaching solidly, faithfully, and without error that truth which God ... wanted put into them."[11]

The doctrine of inerrancy established the framework within which interpretive questions had to be addressed. The text itself posed certain interpretive problems, as early Christians recognized. There were, for example, questions of internal consistency. "How," St. Augustine asked, "can it be demonstrated that God, without any change to Himself, produces effects subject to change and measured by time?"[12] But there were also questions of external consistency. Although the central teachings of Scripture may be purely theological matters (such as the universality of God's salvific will or the necessity of baptism for salvation), the text also seems to make statements on matters about which we might also know something on the basis of historical or natural-scientific inquiry (such as the life of Nebuchadnezzar or the origin of biological species).

This problem of external consistency had already arisen in the ancient world. Manichean critiques of the Genesis account of creation, on the basis of Greek philosophical cosmology, led St. Augustine of Hippo to write his *De Genesi ad litteram* (415). The medieval recovery of Aristotelian science had raised the question of whether the world had a beginning in time.[13] The early modern period posed new questions. Seventeenth-century Aristotelians asked how the new heliocentric astronomy promoted in Nicholas Copernicus's *De Revolutionibus orbium coelestium* (1543) could be squared with the geostatic cosmos that they claimed was taught in (or at least presupposed by) certain scattered passages of Scripture. The discoveries that accompanied the Age of Exploration raised questions about the story of the Flood. The development of the paleoetiological sciences raised questions about the age of the earth, the Hexaemeron, and (eventually) the origin of man.

Along with those scientific questions came historical ones, in particular from archeology.[14] As philologists learned to read Akkadian and Sumerian, the great libraries of Mesopotamia were finally able to yield up their secrets. Egyptian and Mesopotamian historical texts, although sometimes in accord with Biblical narratives, raised questions about the doctrine of inerrancy when they were not. Newly-discovered Mesopotamian

---

10 Vatican I, *Dei Filius*, chap. 2 (in Alberigo, *Conciliorum decreta*, 782).

11 Vatican II, *Dei Verbum*, ¶11.

12 Augustine, *De Genesi ad litteram libri duodecim*, 1.1.2.

13 See, for example, the texts of Thomas Aquinas, Siger of Brabant, and Bonaventure collected in Cyril Vollert et al., *On the Eternity of the World*.

14 For an overview, see Jean Levie, *The Bible, Word of God in Words of Men*.

epics, counterparts to the Biblical accounts of creation and of the Flood of Noah, raised further questions, about the proper understanding of the Hexaemeron and of the Genesis proto-history and even about the nature of Biblical inspiration.

These problems did not necessarily force Christians to abandon the doctrines of inspiration and of inerrancy or the Bible itself. St. Augustine had emphasized the range of options: "I most firmly believe that the authors [of the canonical books of Scripture] were completely free from error. And if in these writings I am perplexed by anything which appears to me opposed to truth, I do not hesitate to suppose that either the manuscript is faulty, or the translator has not caught the meaning of what was said, or I myself have failed to understand it."[15] The problems did require Christians to ask what exactly it is that the inspired authors asserted. Of particular relevance to our story, of course, are the Hexaemeron and the story of Adam and Eve.

Already in the fifth century St. Augustine had warned against advancing interpretations of Scripture that are inconsistent with our knowledge of "the earth, the heavens, and the other elements of this world."[16] But that was a negative heuristic. What positive heuristic was appropriate to a Catholic elucidation of the meaning of the Biblical texts in question? A comprehensive history of the Catholic answer to this question would be too ambitious for a book whose main subject is something else. Here, I will concentrate on the foundations laid by St. Augustine.

He was not the first to address either the general question of hermeneutic methodology or the particular question of the interpretation of Genesis, but he is important for three reasons. First, he had a special interest in exactly the passages most relevant to Catholic evolutionism. Second, he has had a singular influence on later interpreters. Third (if this is not just an elaboration of the reasons just given), he was an explicit subject of interest on hermeneutical questions in the controversy over evolution and Catholic doctrine.

* * * * *

St. Augustine took up the interpretation of the creation narratives in Genesis five times over the course of his life.[17] Like Origen, St. Augustine had an appreciation for allegorical interpretation of Scripture. Unlike Origen, however, he granted a certain priority to literal interpretation (in his sense of the term[18]) and this was in particular true of the creation narrative in Genesis, which he called "a faithful history of events that happened"[19] and of which he wrote that "the narrative in these books is not written in

---

15 Augustine to Jerome, dated 405, no. 82, 1.3 (Migne, *Patrologia* 33:275–91, at 277; trans., Philip Schaff, *Fathers*, 1st ser., 1:349–61, at 350).

16 Augustine, *De Genesi ad litteram*, 1.19.39.

17 The first two attempts—*De Genesi contra Manichaeos* (388) and *De Genesi ad litteram imperfectus liber* (391)—he never finished. He returned to the task, however, in Books 11–12 of his *Confessiones* (397–401), in *De Genesi ad litteram libri duodecim* (401–15), and in Book 11 of *De Civitate Dei* (417). See Taylor's introduction to his translation of *De Genesi ad litteram*, 1–9.

18 The "literal sense" is the meaning conveyed by the words; it does not exclude metaphor or other figurative uses.

19 Augustine, *De Genesi ad litteram*, 9.12.22.

449

a literary style proper to allegory, as in the Canticle of Canticles, but from beginning to end in a style proper to history, as in the Books of Kings and other works of that type."[20] And so, St. Augustine thought, there really was, for example, a "real material tree [of life]" and a naming of the animals.[21]

St. Augustine relied on a number of distinct interpretive principles, laid out his literal interpretation of Genesis. He did not gather them into any one place, but cited them as the need for them arose. For our purposes, we can distinguish six.[22]

His first principle might be called Difficulty of Interpretation. Scripture, he had said elsewhere, is "veiled by mysteries," "a thing neither accessible to the proud nor bared to children."[23] He said on more than one occasion that "It is a laborious and difficult task for the powers of our understanding to see clearly the meaning of our sacred writer."[24] The immediate referent here is the matter of the Six Days. This is an explicit rejection of the perspicuity of Scripture (*claritas Scripturae*) that features so prominently in some Protestant approaches to hermeneutics. St. Augustine sometimes offers a literal interpretation that is by no means perspicuous;[25] sometimes he admits that he simply is not certain what the literal sense of a passage might be.[26]

His second principle might be called Presumption of Natural Causality. In his discussion of the firmament in the midst of the waters, he wrote that "No one should argue against [an interpretation] by appealing to the power of God, to whom all is possible. . . . For now it is our business to seek in Holy Scripture how God made the universe, not what He might produce in nature or from nature by His miraculous power."[27] Obviously, St. Augustine does not deny that God performs miracles;[28] he does suggest that the formational economy and fundamental structure of the world make use of the natural powers of created things (in the passage at hand, water).

His third principle might be called Deference to Science, where "science" (my term) in this context just refers to our naturally acquired knowledge of the world.[29] He did this on more than one occasion. At one point he wrote:

---

20 Augustine, *De Genesi ad litteram*, 8.1.2.

21 Augustine, *De Genesi ad litteram*, 8.5.10 and 9.12.20.

22 For an earlier scholar's account, see Ernan McMullin, "How Should Cosmology Relate to Theology?," esp. 18–22, and McMullin's later "Galileo on Science and Scripture."

23 Augustine, *Confessiones*, 3.5.9.

24 Augustine, *De Genesi ad litteram*, 4.1.1. See also 4.14.25.

25 Augustine, *De Genesi ad litteram*, 4.22.39. See also 2.1.4: "Even in a literal interpretation, one cannot take the words, *He established the earth above the water*, to mean that in nature a mass of water was placed underneath a mass of earth to support it."

26 Augustine, *De Genesi ad litteram*, 5.1.1 and 5.5.16.

27 Augustine, *De Genesi ad litteram*, 2.1.2.

28 He addresses this, for example, at *De Genesi ad litteram*, 6.13.23.

29 He makes use of both "the facts of experience" (*De Genesi ad litteram*, 3.8.12) and of theory-laden claims (e.g., about the nature of oil, 2.1.2).

> When they [directly "those who try to defame our Holy Scripture," but more broadly, surely, anyone] are able, from reliable evidence, to prove [*demonstrare*] some fact about the nature of things [so, a fact of physical science], we shall show that it is not contrary to our Scripture. But when they produce from any of their books something contrary to Scripture, and therefore contrary to the Catholic faith, either we shall have some ability to demonstrate that it is absolutely false, or at least we ourselves will hold it so without any shadow of a doubt.[30]

"Showing that it is not contrary to our Scripture" can here only mean finding an interpretation that is consistent with the scientific knowledge in question. Later, in a discussion of the shape of the material heaven, he wrote that "if they are able to establish their doctrine with proofs that ought not to be doubted, we must show that this statement of Scripture . . . is not opposed to the truth of their conclusions."[31]

That formulation is perhaps an invitation to controversy, especially in light of what Ernan McMullin identified as a countervailing principle of the priority of Scripture (i.e., of a presumption of literal interpretation in the absence of demonstration).[32] What does St. Augustine mean by "ought not to be doubted"? It is unlikely that he had in mind a standard as demanding as that found in Aristotle's account of knowledge and demonstration (ἐπιστήμη and ἀπόδειξις), what we might call "mathematical certainty." Anything less, however, will raise not only theoretical, but practical, problems. What is needed here is an epistemology of probable knowledge, a scientific counterpart of what American courts have worked out under the head of "standards of proof"—proven whether beyond a reasonable doubt, with clear and convincing evidence, or by (mere) preponderance of evidence; or just suspected on the basis of probable cause—and this St. Augustine did not develop. Probable reasoning being what it is, this principle lays the foundation for possible institutional conflict. To whose judgment is deference due on the question of how probable some item of putative natural knowledge is—to theologians' or to scientists'?

The fourth principle might be called Theological Relevance. About the shape of the material heaven, St. Augustine wrote that "Such subjects are of no profit for those who seek beatitude. . . . [T]he Spirit of God, who spoke through [the Sacred Writers], did not wish to teach men these facts that would be of no avail for their salvation."[33] What did St. Augustine mean by "did not wish to teach"? Are the things the Spirit of God does not wish to teach things that are omitted altogether (as is suggested a few lines above the passage just quoted)? Or does Scripture sometimes refer to things without wishing to teach about them? Does Scripture, in saying that the LORD had "stretched out the heavens like

---

30 Augustine, *De Genesi ad litteram*, 1.21.41. I have replaced the phrase "theory contrary . . ." of Taylor's published translation with "something contrary;" the Latin just says *quidquid . . . contrarium.*

31 Augustine, *De Genesi ad litteram*, 2.9.21. I have replaced Taylor's "cannot be denied" with "ought not to be doubted." St. Augustine's words are *ut dubitari inde non debeat.*

32 McMullin, "Galileo on Science and Scripture," 295–96.

33 Augustine, *De Genesi ad litteram*, 2.9.20.

a tent,"[34] teach that the heavens were flat? Does it teach that Abraham had two sons? That Tobit had a dog? Of course Abraham's sons and Tobit's dog are safe from the requirement of Deference to Science. Does one have to believe them? Could denying that Tobit had a dog endanger one's salvation? Perhaps, as St. Robert Bellarmine suggested, it would endanger one's salvation to start denying what is found in Scripture,[35] but reliance on that principle alone would beg the question. Acceptance of the Theological Relevance Principle leaves room for much disagreement about how exactly it applies.

The fifth principle might be called Accommodated Language. In an attempt to explain a puzzle about Genesis 2:5–6, St. Augustine wrote that "Perhaps Sacred Scripture in its customary style is speaking with the limitations of human language in addressing men of limited understanding."[36] He denied that St. Paul's comment that "star differs from star in glory"[37] requires one to think (contrary to a view with some currency in his day) that the stars are not all equally bright. "They differ in glory to the eyes of men on earth."[38]

One might here notice a related principle, one not, as far as I can tell, articulated in the commentary on Genesis. In his *Harmony of the Gospels*, St. Augustine rejected *verbal* inspiration:

> To understand [why there are variations between the Septuagint and the Hebrew Old Testament] … is useful to faith, lest we think that the truth is protected by consecrated sounds, as though God committed to our care not only the thing itself but also the words which we use to express it. Rather, the thing expressed is to be preferred to the words in which it is expressed. We would not have to ask about that at all were it possible for us to know without the words, as do God and his angels.[39]

The sixth principle, which St. Augustine stated repeatedly, could be called the Caution Principle. "We should not rush in headlong and so firmly take our stand on one side that, if further progress in the search of truth justly undermines this position, we too fall with it. That would be to battle not for the teaching of Holy Scripture but for our own."[40] This is especially true in the case of scientific knowledge, for here there is real danger of doing harm to the Church:

> Usually, a non-Christian knows something about the earth, the heavens, and the other elements of this world, about the motion and orbit of the stars and even their size and relative positions, about the predictable eclipses of the sun and moon, the cycles

---

34 Psalms 104 (103):2.

35 "If it [sc., the motionlessness of the earth] is not a matter of faith 'as regards the topic,' it is a matter of faith 'as regards the speaker'; and so it would be heretical to say that Abraham did not have two children and Jacob twelve, … because [it] is said by the Holy Spirit through the mouth of the prophets and the apostles" (Bellarmine to Paolo Foscarini, April 12, 1615 [translation in Maurice A. Finocchiaro, *The Galileo Affair*, 68]).

36 Augustine, *De Genesi ad litteram*, 5.6.19.

37 1 Corinthians 15:41.

38 Augustine, *De Genesi ad litteram*, 2.16.33.

39 Augustine, *Harmony of the Gospels*, 2.66.128.

40 Augustine, *De Genesi ad litteram*, 1.18.37 and 2.18.38.

of the years and the seasons, about the kinds of animals, shrubs, stones, and so forth, and this knowledge he holds to as being certain from reason and experience. Now, it is a disgraceful and dangerous thing for an infidel to hear a Christian, presumably giving the meaning of Holy Scripture, talking nonsense on these topics; and we should take all means to prevent such an embarrassing situation, in which people show up vast ignorance in a Christian and laugh it to scorn. The shame is not so much that an ignorant individual is derided, but that people outside the household of the faith think our sacred writers held such opinions, and, to the great loss of those for whose salvation we toil, the writers of our Scripture are criticized and rejected as unlearned men. If they find a Christian mistaken in a field in which they themselves know well and hear him maintaining his foolish opinions about our books, how are they going to believe those books in matters concerning the resurrection of the dead, the hope of eternal life, and the kingdom of heaven, when they think their pages are full of falsehoods on facts which they themselves have learnt from experience and the light of reason? Reckless and incompetent expounders of Holy Scripture bring untold trouble and sorrow on their wiser brethren when they are caught in one of their mischievous false opinions and are taken to task by those who are not bound by the authority of our sacred books.[41]

* * * * *

Not surprisingly, the principles articulated in St. Augustine's *De Genesi ad litteram* had a great influence on later Catholic exegesis. One can find similar ideas in the writings of St. Albert the Great and in St. Thomas Aquinas. First, there is a presumption of natural causality: "It belongs to the dignity of a ruler to have many ministers and a variety of executors of his rule, for, the more subjects he has, on different levels, the higher and greater is his dominion shown to be. But no ruler's dignity is comparable to the dignity of the divine rule. So, it is appropriate that the execution of divine providence be carried out by diverse levels of agents."[42]

Second, there is a respect for the natural sciences: "In matters of faith and morals, Augustine is more to be believed than are the philosophers, if they disagree. But if it is medicine that is under discussion, I would put more trust in Galen or Hippocrates and if it is the natures of things, in Aristotle or in some other expert in the natures of things."[43]

And third, a recognition of accommodated language: "Moses was speaking to ignorant people, and because of their limited knowledge [*imbecilitati condescendens*] he put before them only such things as are apparent to sense.... He avoids setting before ignorant persons something beyond their knowledge."[44] During the Catholic Reformation, the great Jesuit exegete Benito Pereira drew on Augustine's principles in presenting the

---

41 Augustine, *De Genesi ad litteram*, 1.19.39. See also 2.9.20.

42 Thomas, *Summa contra Gentiles*, 3.77.4.

43 Albert, *Commentarii in II sententiarum*, dist. 13, art. 2 (Jammy ed., 15: 137).

44 Thomas, *Summa Theologiae*, 1a, 68.3c.

453

four rules that would guide his work in the *Commentariorum et disputationum in Genesim tomi quattuor* (1591–1599):

First Rule: The narration of Moses is historical and is to be interpreted historically.

Second Rule: One should not resort to miracles or to God's absolute omnipotence without necessity.

Third Rule: Stubborn defense of one's own opinions is to be avoided.

Fourth Rule: What is transmitted by Sacred Scripture cannot be contrary to sound human reasoning and experience.[45]

Discussion of these principles became particularly important in the evaluation of Copernicus's *De revolutionibus orbium cœlestium* (1543). First to offer a compatibilist defense of Copernicanism was Diego de Zúñiga (Didacus a Stunica) in his *In Iob commentaria* (1584), which relied on the Principle of Accommodated Language to handle Scriptural objections to heliostatic (and geokinetic) astronomy. His critics accepted the principle, but rejected the application. Some went further and seemed to reject the importance of Deference to Science: "Philosophy and physics are to be adapted to Sacred Scripture and to the word of God ... Sacred Scripture is not to be twisted to fit the opinions of philosophers or the light and prescriptions of nature."[46]

The next compatibilist contributions to the debate came only in 1615—Paolo Foscarini's "Lettera sopra l'opinione de' pittagorici e del Copernico della mobilità della Terra e stabilità del Sole, e del nuovo pittagorico sistema del mondo" and Galileo Galilei's (privately circulated) "Lettera a Madama Cristina di Lorena Granduchessa di Toscana."[47] When *De Revolutionibus* was placed on the *Index of Prohibited Books*, de Zúñiga's *Commentaria* and Foscarini's "Lettera," were also condemned. Galileo's letter, not being a publication, did not fall within the authority of the Congregation of the Index.[48]

✳ ✳ ✳ ✳ ✳

Nineteenth-century attacks on Scripture and on Catholicism in particular focused, in a way that Enlightenment attacks on religion (those of David Hume, Voltaire, Thomas Paine, and Ethan Allen, for example) had not, precisely on history and science—on the new developments in archeology and in the paleoetiological sciences. One example was William Draper's *History of the Conflict between Religion and Science* (1874), the thesis of which was that "The history of Science is not a mere record of isolated discoveries; it is a narrative of the conflict of two contending powers, the expansive force of the human intellect on one side and the compression arising from traditionary faith and human

---

45 Pereira, *Commentariorum*, Bk. 1, ch.1 (Jammy 1612 ed., 3–4).

46 Cornelius van den Steyn [à Lapide], Canon 2 of the "Canones facem præferentes Pentateucho," *In Genesim* (Vivès 1866 ed., 28).

47 Written in 1615, the letter circulated only privately for many years. It is now widely available, for example in Maurice A. Finocchiaro, *The Galileo Affair*, 87–118.

48 For more details, see Irving A. Kelter, "The Refusal to Accommodate"; MacMullin, "Galileo"; and Richard J. Blackwell, *Galileo, Bellarmine, and the Bible.*

interests on the other."[49] The "religion" of the title, one comes to see, is Catholicism. Another is Ernest Renan, who wrote in his *Souvenirs d'enfance et de jeunesse* (1883):

> A single error proves that a Church is not infallible; one single weak part proves that a book is not revealed. Outside of rigid orthodoxy, there was nothing, so far as I could see, except eighteenth-century French free-thought .... The masters of St. Sulpice were quite right in refusing to make concessions, since to admit a single error would ruin the whole edifice of absolute truth, and reduce it to the level of human authorities in which each person makes his own choice in accordance with his personal taste.[50]

Newman summarized the charge as being that Roman Catholicism demands of its converts "an assent to views and interpretations of Scripture which modern science and historical research have utterly discredited."[51]

This, of course, required a rearticulation of the traditional principles of Catholic hermeneutics in light of these new attacks and in light of the new ideas emerging from scientific work.

---

49 Draper, *The Conflict between Religion and Science*, vi.

50 Renan, *Souvenirs*, 292 (trans., 255).

51 Newman, "Inspiration of Scripture," 185.

LOCI OF
THE DEBATE

It is natural, as one reads the works of leading Catholic evolutionists, to wonder what kind of reception their ideas received.

It is, of course, impossible to determine what ordinary Catholic laymen thought about biological evolution. Perhaps many would have given the answer Bl. Matthew Lambert gave to his Elizabethan tormentors in an earlier century about another matter: "I am unable to debate with you, but I can tell you that I am a Catholic and I believe what our Holy Mother the Catholic Church believes."[1] That answer would, of course, be remarkably similar to the answer that one would get from many ordinary Americans about modern science today: "If science says it, I believe it." Or perhaps Catholics in the pews would not have given Lambert's answer. We have no way of knowing.

We can, however, learn a great deal about the Catholic reception of evolutionary ideas both by reading the Catholic publications that hosted the debate over the issue and by inspecting archival materials. A few words about the Catholic press, and about the workings of the relevant offices of the Church, may help readers new to the subject to understand the relevant chapters of this work.

---

1 John Holing, "Irish Martyrs during the Reign of Elizabeth," 103.

A. THE CATHOLIC PRESS: PERIODICALS, TEXTBOOKS, AND ENCYCLOPEDIAS

First, the topic was discussed in the Catholic periodical press. Authors included Catholic scientists as well as non-scientist priests and, occasionally, bishops. Some of these periodicals (such as *The Rambler* in England and *Commonweal* in the United States) were strictly lay and private undertakings; others, such as the Jesuit-owned *Month* in England and *Stimmen aus Maria-Laach* (from 1914, *Stimmen der Zeit*) in Germany, and the Dominican-owned *Revue thomiste* in France, were the work of particular religious orders. Some, such as *The Dublin Review* in England and the (Jesuit) *Civiltà Cattolica* in Italy, were widely (though not always accurately) regarded as being reliable guides to the thought of the hierarchy on the issues that they addressed.

In light of the prominence of *Civiltà cattolica* in the debate over Catholic evolutionism, it is important to note that that periodical, in particular, does not have quite the authority that has sometimes been attributed to it, even by some generally careful historians.[2] Its limits as an authoritative source of Catholic thinking were made clear in an exchange of letters on the American school question between Archbishop John Ireland (of St. Paul, Minnesota) and Mariano Cardinal Rampolla (secretary of state) in 1892. Ireland's controversial attitude towards public and parochial schools had just been criticized on the pages of the journal. On May 22, 1892, Ireland wrote to Rampolla:

> I read [from my opponents in the American press] clear and positive declarations . . . that the articles of the *Civiltà* have an extraordinary authority from the fact that they are read and approved in the Vatican before being printed. I myself know very well that this is not the case, and that the articles of this review have no other authority than that of the pen which traces them out. But . . . in order to dissever the Holy See from this war of discord, I beg your Eminence to send me a few lines assuring me that the Vatican never has assumed and does not assume any responsibility for the articles of the *Civiltà* on the school question in the United States.[3]

Rampolla replied on May 23, 1892: "Having brought to the knowledge of the Holy Father what your Grace related to me in your letter of yesterday, . . . I find it my duty to inform you that it is in no way correct to say the articles of this periodical are, as it is held by some, submitted before being printed to the revision and the approval of the Holy See."[4]

In the periodicals just mentioned, one can find both book reviews of the works of Darwin and of others and freestanding treatments of the question of biological evolution from a Catholic point of view. Discussions of the question sometimes also appeared in books devoted primarily to other topics.

---

2 E.g., by Artigas, who wrote that "while it was still in proofs, each number of the journal was sent to the Vatican Secretariat of State for its approval" (*Negotiating Darwin*, 27 and, more broadly, 27–30).

3 Ireland to Rampolla, May 22, 1892 (John Ireland Papers, Reel 4, Minnesota Historical Society).

4 Rampolla to Ireland, May 23, 1892 (John Ireland Papers, Reel 4).

* * * * *

The topic also comes up in the textbooks prepared for seminaries and universities, as well as in books for use in apologetics courses offered in various university and other contexts to lay audiences. Although the ideas that constituted evolutionary biology could be raised in commentaries on Genesis, they were often raised in systematic theology under the title *De Deo creante* or the like. Sometimes Darwinism was taken up in the context of the history of philosophy. These textbooks, unlike their twenty-first-century counterparts, were no mere puréed composite of glossy pictures, text boxes, and review questions; they were often works of genuine scholarship in which the author made his own contribution to the resolution of the questions addressed. The significance of these works lies in the expectation of author and publisher that they would be used in seminaries, where their adoption would be a sign of what views received, at least locally, a degree of official toleration, if not necessarily support.

Finally, the topic was discussed in the numerous Catholic encyclopedias published during this period. Although the idea of preparing an encyclopedia of human knowledge dates back to classical antiquity, the eighteenth century had seen a new approach to this work when Ephraim Chambers published his two-volume *Cyclopaedia, or, An universal dictionary of arts and sciences* (1728), a book that won Chambers recognition from one historian as "the father of the modern encyclopedia."[5] His approach differed from most of his predecessors in his reliance on specialists to write the articles that made up the work. Until that date, encyclopedias had generally been entirely the work of one or a few authors.[6] Chambers's approach was first applied to the task of producing a distinctively Catholic encyclopedia only in the following century, by Benjamin Herder, son of the founder of the Herder publishing house. Then, over the course of the nineteenth and early twentieth centuries, major Catholic encyclopedias were published (some in several successive editions) in Germany, Poland, France, the United States, Spain, the Netherlands, and Italy. As products of editorial judgment, as (usually) the bearers of an *imprimatur*, and as a first point of reference for Catholic nonspecialists,[7] these works provide a meaningful indication of mainstream educated Catholic thought about evolution. Some of these articles constituted original contributions to the discussion of their subject.

B. OFFICIAL PRONOUNCEMENTS

There were a variety of what might be called official reactions to the new ideas.

One might, of course, first look to the pope (in his statements and in his actions) and to the ecumenical council held at the Vatican in 1869–1870. That council did not,

---

5 Robert Collison, *Encyclopaedias*, 103.

6 For a late Catholic example, see Gaetano Moroni, *Dizionario di erudizione*.

7 John L. Morrison said of the American *Catholic Encyclopedia* in 1951, "No single publication rivals this work in its effects upon American Catholic thought. Virtually every rectory in the country has a set . . . in its library" (*History*, 312).

however, address the issue. Neither did any pope offer any formal statement until 1950. There were, however, actions on the part of several popes that bear on the issue.

There were also, occasionally, statements made and actions taken by local bishops and councils. Provincial councils had played an important rôle in the history of the early Church. In 1563, the Council of Trent had mandated their convocation every three years "for the regulation of morals, for the correction of excesses, for the composition of controversies, and for other purposes permitted by [earlier] sacred canons,"[8] but practice did not follow the mandate. In Cologne, for example, there were councils in 1536 and 1549, but then not again either in that century or in the two that followed. The nineteenth century, however, saw the emergence of strong interest in the practice, and councils were held in Baltimore (first in 1829 and regularly thereafter), in Paris (in 1849), in Vienna and Esztergom (in 1858), and in Cologne and Prague (1860).[9] Although the proper work of such councils was more disciplinary than doctrinal,[10] that line was somewhat blurred by the task of identifying and correcting errors of the day. The Council of Vienna, for example, devoted some of its efforts to a critique of materialism, pantheism and deism.[11] Only one such council addressed the question of evolution directly.

Third would be the statements and actions of other offices of the Church. There were three such offices in the period of interest to us—the Holy Office,[12] the Sacred Congregation of the Index of Prohibited Books (after 1917 not an independent congregation, but a section of the Holy Office), and the Pontifical Biblical Commission (from its establishment in 1902). The Holy Office (the Vatican Congregation responsible for doctrinal matters) never directly addressed the question of the relationship between the theory of evolution and Catholic doctrine, though it occasionally reviewed evolutionist works in the context of other, larger investigations. For official action at this level we must look rather to the actions of the Index (indirect and *ad hoc* though they were) and to statements issued by the Pontifical Biblical Commission.

* * * * *

What was the nature of these two offices?

First, the Index.[13] Practically from the beginning of its institutional existence, the Church has recognized that books have not only the power to instruct minds and

---

8 Trent, "Decretum de reformatione," Canon 2 (Alberigo, *Conciliorum decreta*, 737; Schroeder, *Canons and Decrees*, 192–93).

9 The acts of all of these councils are collected in *Acta et decreta: Collectio lacensis*, vol. 5.

10 See Dominique Bouix, *Du Concile provincial*, 20–23; or Joseph Fessler, *Provincial-Koncilien und Diözesan-Synoden*, 132–44.

11 *Acta et decreta: Collectio lacensis*, 5:134–39.

12 Formally, the Sacred Roman and Universal Inquisition until 1908, when it was renamed the Sacred Congregation of the Holy Office. In 1965, it was renamed the Congregation for the Doctrine of the Faith and, in 2022, renamed again, as the Dicastery for the Doctrine of the Faith.

13 "The Index" can refer either to the Congregation (whose function it was to identify books that Catholics should be prohibited from possessing or reading) or to the list of those books. I distinguish the two meanings by italicizing references to the list, which was from time to time published as a book.

459

improve character, but also the power to subvert faith and corrupt morals. It has therefore long made a practice of the public and formal evaluation of books. This practice was formalized in several ways, including prohibition of the keeping or reading of books that it judged to be objectionable.[14]

In 1571–1572, in the wake of the Council of Trent, Popes St. Pius V and Gregory XIII established the Congregation of the Index of Prohibited Books. That Congregation existed as an independent department of the Curia from 1572 until 1917, when its separate existence was brought to an end and its work entrusted to the new Section for the Censorship of Books within the Holy Office. In 1966 the *Index of Prohibited Books* was abolished.[15]

It was the task of the Index to determine whether books (or other published writings) that came to its attention were objectionable. Its primary interest, of course, was a book's theological orthodoxy. As one consultor put it in one of his *vota*: "It not my responsibility to address the literary, philological, and scientific merits of the book in question. My charge is restricted to seeing whether the book is pernicious, harmful, and censurable. My entire review must therefore be directed to its dogmatic and doctrinal worth."[16]

Formal ecclesiastical objection to a book might be based on doctrinal error, but it could also be based on rashness alone. Fr. David Fleming, consultor to the Holy Office, made this very point in a letter to John Zahm, discussed in chapter 6: "It is not necessary that there should be anything against faith and morals; it is enough that the thesis may be looked upon as inopportune or premature."[17] John Cavanaugh, CSC, a close friend of Zahm's, reported a second possible ground of objection: "The distinguished Dominican, Father Esser, an official of the Index, once told me, in speaking of Father Zahm, that among the functions of the Congregation is the suppression of books calculated to arouse undue controversy among Catholics."[18]

John Gmeiner's *The Church and Foreignism* (1891) provides an example unconnected to evolutionism. Gmeiner, whose views on evolution I discussed in chapter 2, was born in Bavaria, but raised in the United States. Though ordained in the diocese of Milwaukee, one of the anchors of the German Triangle at the heart of the American Catholic Midwest, he took the assimilationist side in the bitter late-nineteenth-century fight between German- and Irish-American Catholics over the relation between culture and religion. Against those Catholics who were still living by Milwaukee Archbishop John Martin Henni's motto that "Die Sprache rettet den Glauben," Gmeiner had written

---

14 For a history of the Index, see J. M. De Bujanda, *Index Librorum Prohibitorum*, 29–44; or Joseph M. Pernicone, *Ecclesiastical Prohibition of Book*, 26–67. For general information about its operations, see Hubert Wolf, *Index*.

15 On June 14, 1966, the Congregation for the Doctrine of the Faith announced that "the *Index* remains morally binding, in light of the demands of natural law, in so far as it admonishes the conscience of Christians to be on guard for those writings that can endanger faith and morals. But, at the same time, it no longer has the force of ecclesiastical law with the attached censure. In this matter, the Church trusts in the mature conscience of the faithful" (Congregation of the Doctrine of the Faith, "Notificatio").

16 Settimio Maria Vecchiotti, *Votum* on Stefano Zecchini's *Dio*, 2 (fol. 175, Protocolli 1875–1878, CL, ADDF).

17 Fleming to Zahm, October 20, 1898 (CJZA 1/12, UNDA).

18 Cavanaugh, "Father Zahm," 583n2.

that "The Catholic Church is no literary club ... nor any ethnological society ... but a divinely instituted organization to bring men of 'all nations ...' to eternal salvation."[19] As if that were not offensive enough to *fromme Ohren*, he went on to write, "Let our German infidels who ignore the One True God worship their idol 'Deutschtum'; to us as Catholics our German language is not an object of religious veneration."[20] In 1891, Gmeiner, having managed to secure a transfer to more friendly territory on the far side of the St. Croix River (in John Ireland's Archdiocese of St. Paul), continued his assault on German-American Catholicism in the booklet just mentioned, and Milwaukee Archbishop Frederick Katzer complained to Rome.[21] Dom Bernard Smith, an Irish Benedictine with extensive American connections and a consultor to the Index, wrote: "Monsignor Katzer, Archbishop of Milwaukee, ... referred the book to this Sacred Congregation [sc., the Index], not because it contains anything contrary to faith and morals, but for reasons that that he considers grave enough to make it deserving of condemnation."[22] He continued:

> I think that Msg. Katzer has good reason to make his complaint against this as a dangerous and scandalous book, in which not only priests, but also bishops are presented to the people as though they were in league with foreign powers and little less than traitors to the republic.... This book is scandalous, as I have said: now, to eliminate a public scandal, it will require public reparation.[23]

The secretary of the Index summarized the disposition of the case to Mieczysław Cardinal Ledóchowski (whose responsibility it would be to act on the decision) as follows:

> Even though the Congregation could for various reasons have prohibited this work, especially because it inflames an already existing mistrust and injures people worthy of respect (including ecclesiastics); nevertheless it did not think it would be opportune to go as far as a decree of prohibition, and wanted to find some other way of undoing the scandal and of avoiding harm.
>
> Therefore, it is the will of this Holy Congregation that the author's ordinary call the author in and make known to him the judgment of this Holy Congregation, require him to withdraw from sale (insofar as possible) all copies of the work, and order him not to publish any similar works in the future.[24]

The recommendation of the Congregation was accepted by the Holy Father on April 7, 1892.

One can find yet another ground of objection cited in Don Francesco Zanotto's *votum* on Antonio Fogazzaro's last novel, *Leila* (1911). Zanotto acknowledged that "There

---

19 Gmeiner, *Church and Various Nationalities*, 6–7.

20 Gmeiner, *Church and Various Nationalities*, 21.

21 Katzer to the Index, undated (doc. 14, Protocolli 1891–1894, CL, ADDF).

22 Smith, *Votum*, March 12, 1892, 1 (doc. 12, Protocolli 1891–1894, CL, ADDF). The insistence that this is not a matter of doctrine is repeated on p. 6.

23 Smith, *Votum*, 6 and 7.

24 Minuta del Communicato al Prefetto della Propaganda, April 7, 1892 (doc. 15, Protocolli 1891–1894, CL, ADDF).

are no explicitly heretical doctrines in this work,"[25] but he had other concerns: "We can conclude, therefore, without looking further, that in some parts of the novel there prevails a spirit of satire against the clergy and their friends, and which therefore feeds in the mind of the reader a sentiment of aversion which disposes them to the anticlericalism now so much in vogue."[26] *Leila* was placed on the *Index* on May 11, 1911.

In addition to making these judgments (formally, recommendations to the pope, for the final decision was his), the Congregation maintained a list of books condemned by the Church, a list that it published at irregular intervals under the title *Index Librorum Prohibitorum*. That list was never intended to be a comprehensive catalog of objectionable books—John Stuart Mill's *Principles of Political Economy* (for example) was on the *Index*, but Karl Marx's *Das Kapital* was not; most of Voltaire's works were on the *Index*, but none of Thomas Paine's were. The officials responsible for the *Index* were, of course, aware of this. In writing his *votum* on Salvatore di Bartolo's *Criteri teologici*, Giuseppe Maria Granniello, anticipating the objection that other authors' books had said what di Bartolo's said without being placed on the *Index*, replied "Other books were not delated [sc. reported to the Index]; this one was."[27]

There were also general norms intended to guide Catholics in their reading. Canon 1399 of the 1917 code of canon law, based on Leo XIII's apostolic constitution *Officiorum et munerum* (1897) and other earlier documents, listed twelve kinds of books that Catholics were forbidden from reading.[28]

✳ ✳ ✳ ✳ ✳

How exactly did something get put on the *Index*? First, we should note that the Index was focused on published books (or occasionally articles), rather than on authors, though it occasionally put into the *Index* a prohibition on all of an author's works (examples include Giordano Bruno [in 1603], Émile Zola [in 1894–1895], and Jean-Paul Sartre [in 1948]).

Although the pope could put a book on the list on his own initiative (or on the recommendation of the Holy Office or of other curial congregations), and occasionally did so,[29] the usual process of condemnation began when a book was referred (or, in the language of the day, delated) to the Congregation from the outside. (In 1908, Pope St. Pius X authorized the Congregation for the first time to take the initiative in identifying books that should be condemned.[30]) A complaint about a book sometimes came from a

---

25 Zanotto, *Votum*, 23 (doc. 234, Protocolli 1910–1911, CL, ADDF).

26 Zanotto, *Votum*, 22.

27 Granniello, *Votum*, ¶50 (doc. 79, Protocolli 130 [1889–1891], CL, ADDF).

28 For an example of the practical promulgation of this law, see the relevant chapters of Francis S. Betten, *Roman Index*; or Redmond A. Burke, *What is the Index?*

29 For numerical totals, see Bujanda, *Index*, 37.

30 Pius X, *Sapienti Consilio*, 1.7.1. The number of condemnations increased each year, from about five (1902–1908) to about eleven (1909–1914). After 1914, the last year in the pontificate of Pius X, the number fell back to its previous level.

462

bishop, often but not always from the author's ordinary.[31] Complaints might also come from the Pontifical Biblical Commission.[32] Sometimes, a complaint came from the laity.[33]

When a book or article was brought to its attention, the Index evaluated the item in question in accordance with procedures established by Pope Benedict XIV in his apostolic constitution *Sollicita ac provida* (1753), a procedure updated slightly by Leo XIII in *Officiorum ac munerum*. The Congregation, in the late nineteenth and early twentieth centuries, included a cardinal prefect, a secretary responsible for organizing its work, about thirty consultors (and relators), and about the same number of cardinals.[34] The master of the Sacred Palace (an official now called the Theologian of the Papal Household) also took regular part in the work of the Congregation. Not all of the consultors, nor all of the cardinal members, took part in every case.

The secretary of the Congregation must have had some discretion as to whether to act on a complaint at all. Although the constitution establishing the procedures for the Index[35] does not explicitly allow for this, the practice is suggested by the fact that complaints recorded in the Diaries of the Index are relatively few. That the Index must have received complaints not worth its attention is suggested by one letter that *has* been preserved in the archive, a letter from one Ch. Chalmel, apparently a teacher in France but otherwise unknown. In 1894, Chalmel wrote to the Index "submitting two questions [about the suitability of books] of extreme importance for the faith."[36] One question (discussed in chapter 6) was about Dalmace Leroy's *Évolution des espèces organiques*; the other asked whether Hervé Faye, a Catholic astronomer at the Paris Observatory, had been correct in saying that the decree (of 1632) against the movement of the earth had been revoked.[37] The second question was merely crossed out by someone at the Index. Perhaps in other cases, complaints were simply discarded by the secretary or by the prefect, though I have found no *direct* evidence that this was done.

Hubert Wolf did find evidence of discretion at the next stage—a case in which the secretary himself dismissed a case after reading the consultors' *vota*, without sending it on for further review.[38] Such cases seem, however, to have been rare.

31 The books of Odón de Buen, Raffaello Caverni, and Pietro Martinelli were referred to the Index by their ordinaries; that of John Zahm by a bishop in the Curia, though not in connection with that bishop's official duties.

32 As did those about the books of Henry de Dorlodot and of Ernest Messenger.

33 Dalmace Leroy's book was delated by a French schoolteacher.

34 Names of the year's individual members, consultors, and relators were listed each year in *La Gerarchia cattolica* (1872–1911) and its successor, *Annuario Pontificio* (1912 onwards).

35 See Benedict XIV, *Sollicita ac provida* (1753), §8. Wolf, *Index*, seems to come to the same conclusion.

36 Chalmel to the Index, June 20, 1894 (doc. 71, Protocolli 1894–1896, CL, ADDF).

37 The book in question was surely Faye's *Origine du monde*, which makes the statement in question on page 26 using the same word (*rapporté*) used by Chamel in his letter; Chamel called it only "his treatise on astronomy."

38 The book was Adolph Knigge's *Umgang mit Menschen*, the Italian translation of which was delated to the Index in about 1820. For details, see Wolf, *Index*, 69–83.

Books referred to the Index were first assigned to a consultor (or relator), whose responsibility it was to prepare a written *votum* presenting the consultor's summary of the book's contents and his recommendation on the disposition of the case.

Two or three times a year, a group of about a dozen consultors met (as a "preparatory [or particular] congregation") to review those *vota* (a typical congregation reviewed about half a dozen items) and to make their own recommendation for the disposition of the cases. We do not generally have detailed accounts of the discussions that took place. The *vota* do not consist of a list of charges on which the consultors voted item by item. At the end of the discussion, the consultors in attendance took a vote on what should be done about the book; that vote was then passed on to a meeting of (usually about five to ten) cardinal members of the Index (a "general congregation"). These cardinals reviewed the work of the preparatory congregation and made a recommendation to the pope, who had the final responsibility for the disposition of the case.

If the pope approved the condemnation of a book, that fact was published in the *Acta Sanctae Sedis* (renamed *Acta Apostolicae Sedis* in 1909), often with the explicit admonition that "no one, regardless of rank or condition, may republish, retain or read the above-named condemned and prohibited books in any place or in any language, but [those who possess them] must hand them over to the local ordinary or to an inquisitor under penalty as prescribed in the *Index of Prohibited Books*."[39] In the case of Catholic authors, the author was ordinarily notified in advance of publication of the decree and given the opportunity to accept the decision. If the author did so, that fact was noted, usually with the phrase "The author laudably submitted, and reproves [i.e., forsakes] the work"[40] either when the decree itself was first published, or subsequently in a separate note in the *Acta Sanctae* (or later, *Apostolicae*) *Sedis*. The book was later included in the next published edition of a comprehensive *Index of Prohibited Books*.

What effect did placement of a book on the *Index* have? Catholics were bound in conscience not to keep or read books listed in the *Index* without permission. Catholic university students were reminded of the existence of the *Index* and of the importance of adhering to its norms. The library of my own (Catholic archdiocesan) institution,[41] for example, put on top of the date-due slip a note saying

> This book is on the Index and may not be read unless permission has been granted by the Archbishop.

> Direct questions regarding use of the book to the Librarian.

---

39 For an example, see *Act Sanctae Sedis* (1878) 11:206.

40 The Latin read *opus reprobavit*. The word *reprobavit* can, of course, have a stronger sense than "forsakes." Should the translation not rather be "the author *repudiates* the work"? Since condemnation of the book did not constitute a judgment that the book was in error, it being sufficient reason to condemn a book that its publication was judged inopportune, the author's "reprobation" of the work cannot necessarily be construed as more than abandonment or withdrawal of approval from the work.

41 Then called the College of St. Thomas, in St. Paul, Minnesota.

Books not listed explicitly in the *Index*, for example the works of Vladimir Lenin, were sometimes marked "This book is prohibited by Canon 1399." Many libraries put prohibited books in a part of the library to which access was restricted.

✳ ✳ ✳ ✳ ✳

Sometimes, for practical reasons, an objectionable book was not put on the *Index*. The matter might be returned to the author's ordinary for local disposition, as in the case of Pietro Martinelli (discussed in chapter 9). In other cases, a book might be condemned without public notice of any prohibition. That was the fate, for example, of a book written by Irish priest (and Maynooth professor) Walter McDonald. His *Motion: Its Origin and Conservation* was prohibited in 1898–99, with the decree, out of consideration for the good name of the author's institution and the author's presumed good disposition, not to be published. The author was instructed (through the archbishop of Dublin) to withdraw the book from sale, to renounce the ideas that had led to the book's condemnation, and to refrain from teaching them.[42]

Strictly speaking, that second type of resolution was addressed only to the author (and the ordinary or religious superior through whom it was transmitted). Librarians had no formal notice to restrict the circulation of those books; potential readers had no formal notice that these were among the books that they should not read. If the author was required, as some were, to make a public announcement of their withdrawal of a book from the market, the announcement might, but would not necessarily, come to the attention of librarians. Librarians would not, in such cases, have been explicitly required to restrict access to the books, though they might do so anyway.

It is important to keep in mind that the Congregation was in the business of regulating the circulation of books, not of articulating or of promulgating doctrine. The *Index* listed only the titles of prohibited books, not the reasons why they were prohibited.[43] In addition, the participants in the work of the Congregation were bound by an oath of secrecy not to discuss their deliberation.[44]

✳ ✳ ✳ ✳ ✳

In addition to the offices whose responsibility was to watch over the Church as a whole, there were also offices with more local responsibilities. Catholic authors (and in particular the clergy) were required to submit books on religion, theology, or morals to the bishops of their dioceses for approval (a *nihil obstat* and an *imprimatur*) before publication.[45]

Religious orders such as the Jesuits and the Dominicans also made efforts to ensure that their members did not publish works inconsistent with Catholic doctrine.

---

42 Walter McDonald, *Reminiscences*, 130–31.

43 Rarely, but not in the cases most important to our story, a brief explanation of the condemnation was provided in *Acta Apostolicae Sedis*.

44 Benedict XIV, *Sollicita et provida*, §12.

45 For a history of this practice, see Donald H. Wiest, *Precensorship of Books*.

465

Concerns about transgressions were sometimes brought directly to the attention of the order itself, rather than being sent to the Congregation of the Index. In those cases, review and sanctions were often handled internally.

Finally, religious orders had the authority to regulate the research and publication of their members, and occasionally acted on their own initiative. Whether one considers that an action of the "official Church" or not, such permissions and restrictions do shed light on the reception of Catholic evolutionism.[46]

* * * * *

In 1902, Pope Leo XIII established a Pontifical Biblical Commission[47] to guide Catholic interpretation of Sacred Scripture. Like the Congregation of the Index, the work of the Commission was done by appointed consultors (in this case, Biblical scholars) and the cardinals who were its members. Its task included not only the identification of some interpretations as unorthodox, but also the identification of others as merely rash, a defect against which measures would also be taken. Decisions of the Commission usually came in the form of *responsa* to questions that had, or could have been, put to the Commission. Although the *responsa* were published with the approval of the pope, they remained decisions of the Commission itself.

The *responsa* were not infallible, but they were official norms requiring not only obedience, but interior assent. In 1910, Pope St. Pius X wrote in his *motu proprio Praestantia Scripturae*:

> All are bound in conscience to submit to the decisions of the Pontifical Biblical Commission, whether already issued or to be issued in the future, in the same way as they are bound to submit to decrees of the Sacred Congregations which pertain to doctrine and have been approved by the Pontiff; nor can they avoid the charge both of disobedience and rashness or be free from grave sin who impugn these decisions either verbally or in writing.[48]

---

46 For an account of Jesuit practice, see Eugene J. Ahern, "The Society's Rules."

47 Leo XIII, *Vigilantiae studiique*.

48 Pius X, *Praestantia Scripturae*, 724. For background, see John Corbett, "The Biblical Commission."

ARCHIVES

AANY	Archives of the Archdiocese of New York
AAV	Archivio Apostolico Vaticano
ADDF	Archivio del Dicastero per la Dottrina della Fede
AGOP	Archivum Generale Ordinis Praedicatorum
AKUL	Universiteitsarchief, Katholieke Universiteit Leuven
APECESJ	Archiv der Zentraleuropäischen Provinz der Jesuiten
APG	Archiv der Deutschen Provinz der Jesuiten
	Archive Dominicain de la Province de Toulouse
	Archives de l'Évêché de Namur
ARSI	Archivum Romanum Societatis Jesu
ASPF	Archivio Storico de Propaganda Fide
ASSR	Archivio Storico della Sezione dei Rapporti con gli Stati della Segreteria di Stato
AUCL	Archives de l'Université catholique de Louvain
IPA	Indiana Provincial Archives of the Congregation of Holy Cross
UNDA	University of Notre Dame Archives

BIBLIOGRAPHY

Abel, Othenio. *Die Stellung des Menschen im Rahmen der Wirbeltiere.* Jena: Fischer, 1931.

Académie royale de Belgique. "Programme du concours pour l'année 1907." *Bulletins de la classe des lettres et des sciences morales et politiques et de la classe des beaux-arts* 3rd ser., 42, no. 8 (1904): 450–52 and 463–65.

Acta et decreta sacrorum conciliorum recentiorum: Collectio lacensis, vol. 5. Freiburg im Breisgau: Herder, 1879.

Adam, Karl. *Das Wesen des Katholizismus.* Augsburg: Haas & Grabherr, 1924.

Adam, Karl. *Christus unser Bruder.* Regensburg: Habbel, 1929.

Agassiz, Louis. "Essai sur la géographie des animaux." *Revue suisse* 8 (1845): 441–52 and 538–55. Republished as *Notice sur la géographie des animaux.* Neuchatel: Wolfrath, 1845.

Agassiz, Louis. "The Geographical Distribution of Animals." *Christian Examiner and Religious Miscellany* 48, no. 2 (1850): 181–204.

Agassiz, Louis. "The Diversity of Origin of the Human Races." *Christian Examiner and Religious Miscellany* 49, no. 1 (1850): 110–45.

Agassiz, Louis. Remarks. *Proceedings of the American Association for the Advancement of Science* 3rd Meeting (1850): 106–7.

Agassiz, Louis. "Sketch of the Natural Provinces of the Animal World and their Relation to the Different Types of Man." In Nott and Gliddon, *Types of Mankind,* lviii–lxxvi.

Agassiz, Louis. "Prefatory Remarks." In Nott and Gliddon, *Indigenous Races,* xiii–xv.

Ahern, Eugene J., SJ. "The Society's Rules of Censorship." *Woodstock Letters* 92, no. 4 (1963): 383–94.

Aiken, Charles F. Review of *Dictionnaire apologétique de la foi catholique,* Fascicule VIII, edited by A. D'Alès. *Catholic University Bulletin* 19, no. 4 (1913): 332–34.

Alba Sánchez, Ricardo. "La evolución de las especies según Juan González Arintero." Ph.D. diss. Universidad de Navarra, 2005.

Alberigo, Joseph, et al. *Conciliorum œcumenicorum decreta*. Freiburg im Breisgau: Herder, 1962.

Albertus Magnus. *Commentarii in II sententiarum*. Vol. 15 of *Opera omnia*.

Albertus Magnus. *De vegetabilibus libri VII*. Vol. 5 of *Opera omnia*, 508–27.

Albertus Magnus. *Opera omnia*. Edited by Petrus Jammy. Lyons: Prost, 1651.

Albertus Magnus. *Summa theologiae*. Vol. 17–18 of *Opera omnia*.

Alexander, Andrew, CJ. "Human Origins and Genetics." *Clergy Review* 49 (1964): 344–53.

Allievi, Cristoforo. "Un contributo poco noto di Pio XI alla sismologia d'Italia." *Sapere: Quindicinale di divulgazione di scienza, tecnica, e arte applicata* 9, no. 100 (1939): 146–47.

Allen, Grant. *Charles Darwin*. London: Longmans, Green, 1885.

Altholz, Joseph. *The Liberal Catholic Movement in England: The "Rambler" and its Contributors 1848–1864*. London: Burns & Oates, 1960.

Álvarez, García. *Discurso leído en la solemne apertura del curso académico de 1872 a 1873 en el Instituto de segunda enseñanza de la provincia de Granada*. Granada: Ventura, 1872.

Amann, Émile. *Le Dogme catholique dans les Pères de l'Église*. Paris: Beauchesne, 1922.

Amann, Émile. *L'Église au pouvoir des laïques, 888–1057*. Paris: Bloud & Gay, 1940.

Amann, Émile. "Transformisme." In *Dictionnaire de théologie catholique, contenant l'exposé des doctrines de la théologie catholique, leurs preuves et leur histoire*, edited by A. Vacant, E. Mangenot, et al., 15.1:1365–96. Paris: Letouzey et Ané, 1899–1950.

America. "Post-Mortems on Dayton." Editorial. 33, no. 16 (1925): 376.

America. "The Middle Road to Dayton." Editorial. 33, no. 15 (1925): 352.

American Catholic Quarterly Review. Review of *Bible, Science, and Faith*, by John A. Zahm. 19, no. 76 (1894): 892–93.

Appel, Toby A. *The Cuvier-Geoffroy Debate: French Biology in the Decades before Darwin*. Oxford: Oxford University Press, 1987.

Appleby, R. Scott. "Between Americanism and Modernism: John Zahm and Theistic Evolution." *Church History* 56, no. 4 (1987): 474–90.

Aquinas, Thomas. "Responsio de 43 articulis ad magistrum Ioannem de Vercellis." In *Opera Omnia Iussu Leonis XIII P.M. Edita*, 42: 327–35. Rome: Editori di San Tommaso, 1979.

Aquinas, Thomas. *Summa contra gentiles*.

Aquinas, Thomas. *Summa theologiae*. 3rd ed. Madrid: Biblioteca de autores cristianos, 1961. Translated by the Fathers of the English Dominican Province. New York: Benziger, 1947.

Arcelin, Adrien. "L'Homme tertiaire." In Congrès scientifique de 1888, *Compte rendu*, 2:638–67.

Arduin, Alexis. *La Religion en face de la science, II: Géologie et géogénie, Tome second*. Lyon: Vitte et Perrissel, 1883.

Arintero, Juan González de, OP. "El paraíso terrenal." *El movimiento católico* (April 18 to May 6, 1890).

Arintero, Juan González de, OP. *El diluvio universal de la Biblia y de la Tradición, demostrado por la geología y prehistoria*. Vergara: El Santísimo Rosario, 1891.

Arintero, Juan González de, OP. *La evolución y la filosofía cristiana*. Madrid: del Amo, 1898.

Arintero, Juan González de, OP. "La evolución ante la fe y la ciencia." *Soluciones católicas* 1 (1899–1900): 342–48, 383–90, 410–17, 444–50, 465–72, 497–506.

Arintero, Juan González de, OP. *La crisis científico-religiosa. Discurso inaugural leído en la solemne reanudación de los estudios superiores exegéticos-apologéticos de San Gregorio de Valladolid*. Valladolid: Cuesta, 1900.

Arintero, Juan González de, OP. "La creación y la evolución." *Revista iberoamericana de ciencias eclesiásticas* 1 (1901): 18–27, 94–99, 280–82, 404–7, 507–13; and 2 (1901): 20–28, 508–19.

Arintero, Juan González de, OP. *El Hexámeron y la ciencia moderna.* Valladolid: de la Cuesta, 1901.

Arintero, Juan González de, OP. *Evolución mística.* Salamanca: Calatrava, 1908.

Arintero, Juan González de, OP. *Mecanismo divino de los factores de la evolución eclesiástica.* Salamanca: Calatrava, 1911.

Aristotle. *Generation of Animals.* Translated by A. L. Peck. The Loeb Classical Library, 366. Cambridge, MA: Harvard University Press, 1942.

Aristotle. *Meteorologica.* Translated by H. D. P. Lee. Loeb Classical Library, 397. Cambridge, MA: Harvard University Press, 1952.

Arkansas Gazette. "Evolution Law Held Not Violated." July 11, 1929, 11.

Arldt, Theodor. *Die Stammesgeschichte der Primaten und die Entwicklung der Menschenrassen.* Heidelberg: Springer, 1915.

Armogathe, Jean-Robert, and Vincent Carraud. "La Première Condamnation des œuvres de Descartes, d'après des documents inédits aux archives du Saint-Office." *Nouvelles de la république des lettres* 2 (2001): 103–37.

Arnould, Jacques. *L'abbé Breuil: Le Pape de la préhistoire.* Tours: CLD, 2011.

Arriaga, Roderigo de. "De opere sex dierum." In *Disputationes theologicae in primam partem D. Thomae. Tomus secundus, qui continet tractatus tres,* 316–466. Antwerp: Moreti, 1643.

Artigas, Mariano, Thomas F. Glick, and Rafael A. Martínez. *Negotiating Darwin: The Vatican Confronts Evolution, 1877–1902.* Baltimore: Johns Hopkins University Press, 2006.

Atteridge, A. Hilliard. "Periodical Literature: England." In *The Catholic Encyclopedia,* 11:673–75.

Augé, Claude. *Nouveau Larousse illustré.* Paris: Larousse, 1898.

Augé, Claude. *Petit Larousse illustré.* Paris: Larousse, 1918.

Augustin, Bedřich. *Základní náboženská nauka (Apologetika).* Prague: Českoslovanská akciová tiskárna, 1926. 4th ed. Prague: Vyšehrad, 1946.

Augustine. *De Genesi contra Manichaeos libri II.* 388. Republished in Migne, *Patrologia latina,* 34:173–220. Translated as "Two Books on Genesis against the Manichees" by Roland J. Teske, SJ, in *On Genesis,* 45–141. Washington, DC: The Catholic University of America Press, 1991.

Augustine. *De Genesi ad litteram imperfectus liber.* 391. Republished in Migne, *Patrologia latina,* 34:219–246. Translated as "On the Literal Interpretation of Genesis: An Unfinished Book" by Roland J. Teske, SJ, in *On Genesis,* 143–88. Washington, DC: The Catholic University of America Press, 1991.

Augustine. *Confessiones.* 397–401. Translated by R. S. Pine-Coffin as *Confessions.* London: Penguin, 1961.

Augustine. *De consensu evangelistarum libri quatuor.* Translated by S. D. F. Salmond as *The Harmony of the Gospels.* In *Nicene and Post-Nicene Fathers,* edited by Philip Schaff, 1st ser., 6:65–236. Christian Literature Company, 1886.

Augustine. *De Civitate Dei.* 417. Translated by Marcus Dodds et al. as *The City of God.* New York: Modern Library, 1950.

Augustine. *De Genesi ad litteram libri duodecim.* Translated by John Hammond Taylor, SJ, as *On the Literal Meaning of Genesis.* New York: Newman Press, 1982.

Ave Maria. "With Authors and Publishers." 75, no. 11 (1912): 351.

Aveling, Francis. "Man." In *The Catholic Encyclopedia,* 9:580–83.

Baranzke, Heike. "Erich Wasmann (29.5.1859–27.2.1931): Jesuit und Zoologe in Personalunion." *Jahrbuch für Geschichte und Theorie der Biologie* 6 (1999): 77–140.

Barrande, Joachim. *Système silurien du centre de la Bohême.* Prague: Privately published, 1852–94.

Barthélemy-Madaule, Madeleine. *Bergson et Teilhard de Chardin.* Paris: Seuil, 1963.

Bartolo, Salvatore di. *I criteri teologici.* Turin: San Giuseppe, 1888.

Bartynowski, Stanisław, SJ. *Apologetyka podręczna.* Cracow: Nakładem wydawnictw Towarzystwa Jezusowego, 1911. 2nd ed. 1916.

Baudrillart, Alfred. "Apostolat intellectuel de Mgr d'Hulst." *La Quinzaine* 8, no. 171 (1901): 369–92. Published as a booklet. La Chapelle Montligeon: Notre-Dame, 1901.

Baudrillart, Alfred. *Vie de Mgr D'Hulst.* 3rd ed. Paris: Gigord, 1921.

Baudrillart, Alfred. *Les Carnets du Cardinal Baudrillart (13 avril 1925–25 décembre 1928).* Paris: Cerf, 2002.

Baur, Ludwig. "Abstammungslehre." In *Kirchliches Handlexikon,* 1:29–33.

Baur, Ludwig. "Entwicklung." In *Kirchliches Handlexikon,* 1:1307–9.

Bavink, Bernhard. "Die Sinn und Ethos der Wissenschaft." *Unsere Welt: Zeitschrift für Naturwissenschaft und Weltanschauung* 30, no. 9 (1938): 241–65.

Bea, Augustin. "Neuere Probleme und Arbeiten zur biblischen Urgeschichte." *Biblica* 25, no. 1 (1944): 70–87.

Bea, Augustin. *Il problema antropologico in Gen. 1–2: Il trasformismo.* Rome: Pontificium Institutum Biblicum, 1950.

Beaumont, Élie de. "Recherches sur quelques-unes des révolutions de la surface du globe." *Revue française* 15 (1830): 1–58.

Bégouën, Charles-Maximilien. *La Création évolutive.* Toulouse: Privat, 1879.

Bégouën, Henri. "La Préhistoire à la Société archéologique du Midi de la France." *Mémoires de la Société archéologique du Midi de la France* 18 (1932): 96–106.

Bégouën, Henri. *Quelques Souvenirs sur le mouvement des idées transformistes dans les milieux catholiques.* Paris: Bloud & Gay, 1945.

Benedict XIV. *Sollicita ac provida.* 1753. In *Index librorum prohibitorum Sanctissimi Domini Nostri Leonis XIII,* 4th ed., xxix–xxxix. Turin: Marietti, 1892.

Benedict XV. *Ad beatissimi Apostolorum. Acta Apostolicae Sedis* 6, no. 18–19 (1914): 565–81 and (in translation) 647–60.

Benedict XV. *Spiritus Paraclitus. Acta Apostolicae Sedis* 12, no. 10 (1920), 385–422.

Bennett, Alfred W. Review of *On the Genesis of Species,* by St. George Mivart. *Nature* 3 (1871): 270–73.

Beretta, Francesco. "Monseigneur d'Hulst, les Congrès scientifiques internationaux des catholiques et la question biblique." In *Monseigneur d'Hulst, fondateur de l'Institut catholique de Paris,* edited by Claude Bressolette, 75–136. Paris: Beauchesne, 1998.

Beretta, Francesco. "Les Congrès scientifiques internationaux des catholiques (1888–1900) et la production d'orthodoxie dans l'espace intellectuel catholique." In *Le Catholicisme en congrès (XIXe–XXe siècles),* edited by Claude Langlois and Christian Sorrel, 155–203. Paris: Cerf, 2008.

Bergounioux, Fréderic-Marie. "Le Rythme dans la création." *Bulletin de littérature ecclésiastique* 32, no. 9–10 (1931): 211–27.

Bergounioux, Fréderic-Marie. *La Préhistoire et ses problèmes.* Paris: Fayard, 1958.

Bergson, Henri. *Essai sur les données immédiates de la conscience.* Paris: Alcan, 1889. Translated by F. L. Pogson as *Time and Free Will: An Essay on the Immediate Data of Consciousness.* London: Macmillan, 1912.

Bergson, Henri. *Matière et mémoire: Essai sur la relation du corps à l'esprit.* Paris: Alcan, 1896. Translated by Nancy Margaret Paul and W. Scott Palmer [pseud.] as *Matter and Memory.* New York: Allen, 1911.

Bergson, Henri. *L'Évolution créatrice*. Paris: Alcan, 1907. Translated by Arthur Mitchell as *Creative Evolution*. New York: Holt, 1911.

Bergson, Henri. *Correspondances*. Edited by André Robinet. Paris: Presses universitaires de France, 2002.

Bernard, Claude. *La Science expérimentale*. Paris: Ballière, 1878.

Bernhardi, Friedrich von. *Deutschland und der nächste Krieg*. 6th ed. Stuttgart: Cotta, 1913. Translated by Allen H. Powles as *Germany and the Next War*. New York: Longmans, Green, 1914.

Betten, Francis S. *The Roman Index of Forbidden Books Briefly Explained for Booklovers and Students*. St. Louis: Herder, 1920.

Beumer, Johannes. "Pater Wilhelm Wilmers, SJ, und seine Tätigkeit auf dem Kölner Provinzialkonzil von 1860 und auf dem Ersten Vaticanum." *Annuarium historiae conciliorum: Internationale Zeitschrift für Konziliengeschichtsforschung* 3 (1971): 137–55.

Biblische Zeitschrift. Notice of *I primi tre capitoli della Sacra Bibbia annotati secondo il sistema delle apparenze*, by Pietro Martinelli. 5, no. 3 (1907): 322.

Binchy, D. A. *Church and State in Fascist Italy*. Oxford: Oxford University Press, 1941.

Birkner, Ferdinand. "Zum Erscheinungsbild von Adam und Eva." *Haec loquere et exhortare: Monatsschrift für homiletische Wissenschaft und Praxis vereinigt mit dem Klerusblatt* 38, no. 5 (1944): 155–59.

Blackwell, Richard J. *Galileo, Bellarmine, and the Bible*. Notre Dame, IN: University of Notre Dame Press, 1991.

Blakeslee, Howard W. "Man Descended from Apes, Jesuit Says Evidence Proves." *Washington Post*, March 20, 1937, 1 and 4.

Blanc, Elie. "Le Transformisme est-il une question purement scientifique?" *Revue du clergé français* 31 (1902): 50–55.

Blanckaert, Claude. "Monogénisme et Polygénisme." In Tort, *Dictionnaire du darwinisme*, 2:3021–37.

Blandino, Giovanni. "Deux Hypothèses sur l'origine de l'homme: Observations théologiques et scientifiques." Florence: Self-published, 1962. Republished in his *Questioni dibattute di teologia 1* (Rome: Città Nuova, 1977), 205–26.

Blandino, Giovanni. "Il peccato originale." In *Questioni dibattute di teologia 1*, 46–105. Rome: Città Nuova, 1977.

Blum, Christopher. "St. George Mivart: Catholic Natural Philosopher." PhD diss., University of Notre Dame, 1996.

Blumenbach, Johann Friedrich. *De generis humani varietate nativa*. Göttingen: Rosenbusch, 1775. Translated by Thomas Bendyshe as "On the Natural Variety of Mankind." In *The Anthropological Treatises of Blumenbach and Hunter*, edited by Thomas Bendyshe, 65–143. London: Longman, Green, Longman, Roberts, & Green, 1865.

Blumenbach, Johann Friedrich. *Handbuch der Naturgeschichte*. 8th ed. Göttingen: Dieterich, 1807.

Boiteux, Jules. "Sur la Genèse évolutionnaire des types zoologiques." In Congrès scientifique de 1900, *Akten*, 441–42.

Bom, Th. van der. "Afstammingsleer." In *De Katholieke Encyclopaedie*, 1:556–58.

Boné, Édouard L. "Polygénisme et polyphylétisme: Orientation présente de la pensée scientifique en matière d'apparition de l'homme." *Archives de philosophie* 23, no. 1 (1960): 99–141.

Boné, Édouard L. "Evolution, Human: 1. Biological Aspect." In *The New Catholic Encyclopedia*, 5:676–81.

Bönner, Wilhelm, SJ. "P. Felix Rüschkamp." *Mitteilungen aus den deutschen Provinzen der Gesellschaft Jesu* 20, no. 125–27 (1963–65): 235–48.

Bonomelli, Geremia. "Roma e l'Italia e la realtà delle cose: Pensieri di un prelato italiano." *Rassegna nazionale* 46 (1889): 3–87. Republished as a pamphlet. Florence: Rassegna nazionale, 1889.

Bonomelli, Geremia. "A proposito de evoluzionismo: Una dichiarazione de mons. Bonomelli." *La Lega Lombarda: Giornale politico quotidiano.* June 22–23, 1898, 1.

Bonomelli, Geremia. *Seguiamo la ragione. Dio creatore e autore dell'ordine naturale.* Milan: Cogliati, 1898. 2nd ed. 1900. 3rd ed. 1906.

Bordet, Pierre. "Albert F. de Lapparent (1905–1975): Notice biographique." In *Livre à la mémoire d'Albert F. de Lapparent (1905–1975) consacré aux recherches géologiques dans les chaînes alpines de l'Asie du Sud-Ouest, Mémoire hors-série № 8 de la Société géologique de France,* 7–18. Paris: Société géologique de France, 1977.

Börsenblatt für den deutschen Buchhandel und die mit ihm verwandten Geschäftszweige. 27, no. 52–53 and 74 (April 4, May 2, and June 11, 1860).

Bory de Saint-Vincent, Jean Baptiste. *L'Homme, Essai zoologique sur le genre humain.* Paris: Rey et Gravier, 1827.

Boston American. Article on Teilhard de Chardin. April 1, 1937. Clipping available in Censurae 27–V no. 3, ARSI.

Boston Globe. "Thinks Two Links are Still Missing." April 1, 1937, 28.

Boston Herald. Article on Teilhard de Chardin. April 1, 1937. Clipping available in Censurae 27–V no. 3, ARSI.

Boston Post. "One Link to Trace Man to Ape." April 1, 1937.

Boucher de Perthes, Jacques. *Antiquités celtiques et antédiluviennes.* Paris: Treuttel et Würtz, 1847–64.

Boucher de Perthes, Jacques. *De l'Homme antédiluvien et de ses œuvres.* Paris: Jung-Treuttel, 1860.

Bouix, Dominique. *Du Concile provincial: ou, Traité des questions de théologie et de droit canon qui concernent les conciles provinciaux.* Paris: Lecoffre, 1850.

Boulay, Nicolas. "La Théorie de l'évolution en botanique." In Congrès scientifique de 1894, *Compte rendu,* 7:127–38.

Boulay, Nicolas. "Les Sciences naturelles et l'anthropologie au dernier Congrès scientifique international des catholiques." *Revue de Lille* 12 (1895): 610–28.

Boulay, Nicolas. "De l'Antiquité de l'homme." In Congrès scientifique de 1897, *Compte rendu,* 9:52–67; discussion reported at 9:11–13.

Boule, Marcellin. Review of *Les Origines: Questions d'apologétique,* by Jean Guibert. *L'Anthropologie* 7 (1896): 331–33.

Boule, Marcellin. *Les Hommes fossiles: Éléments de paléontologie humaine.* Paris: Masson, 1921. Translated by Jessie Elliot Ritchie and James Ritchie as *Fossil Men: Elements of Human Palæontology.* Edinburgh: Oliver & Boyd, 1923.

Bourdier, Frank. "Gaudry, Albert Jean." In *Complete Dictionary of Scientific Biography,* edited by Charles Coulston Gillispie, et al., 5:295–97. New York: Scribner's Sons, 2008.

Bourgeois, Louis. "Étude sur des silex travaillés trouvés dans les dépôts tertiaires de la commune de Thenay, près Pontlevoy (Loir-et-Cher)." In *Congrès international d'anthropologie et d'archéologie préhistoriques: Compte rendu de la deuxième session, Paris 1867,* 67–75. Paris: Reinwald, 1868.

Bouvier, Pierre. *L'Exégèse de M. Loisy: Les Doctrines, les procédés.* Paris: Retaux, 1903. Translated by Pietro Martinelli as *L'esegesi del sig. Loisy: Le dottrine, i metodi.* Siena: San Bernardino, 1903.

Bouyssonie, Amédée. "À Propos des Conditions Philosophiques de l'évolution." *Revue néo-scolastique de philosophie* 18, no. 72 (1911): 564–77.

Bouyssonie, Jean and Amédée Bouyssonie. "Polygénisme." In *Dictionnaire de théologie catholique,* 12:2520–36.

Bouyssonie, Jean and Amédée Bouyssonie, with Henri Breuil. "L'Homme préhistorique, d'après les documents paléontologiques." In *Dictionnaire apologétique de la foi catholique,* 4th ed., 2:462–92.

Bowler, Peter J. *Theories of Human Evolution: A Century of Debate, 1844–1944.* Baltimore: Johns Hopkins University Press, 1986.

Bowler, Peter J. *The Non-Darwinian Revolution: Reinterpreting a Historical Myth.* Baltimore: Johns Hopkins University Press, 1988.

Boyer, Charles. "Les leçons de l'encyclique 'Humani generis.'" *Gregorianum* 31, no. 4 (1950): 526–39.

Boyer, Charles. *De Deo creante et elevante.* 5th ed. Rome: Editrice Pontificia Università Gregoriana, 1957.

Braga, Council of. "Concilium Bracarense II." In Mansi, *Sacrorum conciliorum collectio,* 9:773–80.

Brandewie, Ernest. *Wilhelm Schmidt and the Origin of the Idea of God.* Lanham, MD: University Press of America, 1983.

Brandewie, Ernest. *When Giants Walked the Earth: The Life and Times of Wilhelm Schmidt, SVD.* Fribourg: Presses Universitaires, 1990.

Brandi, Salvatore, SJ. Review of *Evoluzione e domma,* by John A. Zahm. *Civiltà cattolica* 17th ser., 5, no. 1165 (1899): 34–49.

Brandi, Salvatore, SJ. "Evoluzione e domma. Erronee informazioni di un inglese." *Civiltà cattolica* 18th ser., 6, no. 1243 (1902): 75–77.

Brassac, Augustin. *Manuel biblique, ou Cours d'Écriture Sainte à l'usage des séminaires: Ancien Testament.* 14th ed. Paris: Roger et Chernoviz, 1917–20.

Brémond, Henri. "Les 'Batailles d'idées' de M. le chanoine A. Bouyssonie." In *Le Charmes d'Athènes et autres Essais,* edited by Jean Henri and André Brémond, 27–54. Paris: Bloud & Gay, 1925.

British Medical Journal. "Scientific Conciliation." 1 (1871): 71.

Brivio, Carlo. *L'origine del corpo umano secondo la dottrina dei principali teologi post-tridentini.* Milan: Pontificio istituto missioni estere, 1950.

Broca, Paul. *Recherches sur l'hybridité animale en général et sur l'hybridité humaine en particulier considérées dans leurs rapports avec la question de la pluralité des espèces humaines.* Paris: Claye, 1860. Translated by C. Carter Blake as *On the Phenomena of Hybridity in the Genus Homo.* London: Longman, Green, Longman, & Roberts, 1864.

Bronn, Heinrich, translator. *Über die Entstehung der Arten im Thier- und Pflanzenreich durch natürliche Züchtung.* Stuttgart: Schweizerbart, 1860.

Bronn, Heinrich. "Ch. Darwin, *On the Origin of Species* ..." *Neues Jahrbuch für Mineralogie, Geognosie, Geologie und Petrefaktenkunde* (1860), 112–16. Translated by David Hull in *Darwin and His Critics: The Reception of Darwin's Theory of Evolution by the Scientific Community,* 120–24. Chicago: University of Chicago Press, 1973.

Browne, Janet. *Charles Darwin: 2. The Power of Place.* New York: Knopf, 2002.

Brucker, Joseph, SJ. "Les Jours de la création et le transformisme." *Études religieuses, philosophiques, historiques et littéraires* 46 (1889): 567–92.

Brucker, Joseph, SJ. "L'Origine de l'homme d'après la Bible et le transformisme." *Études religieuses, philosophiques, historiques et littéraires* 47 (1889): 28–50.

Brucker, Joseph, SJ. Review of *L'Évolution des espèces organiques,* by Dalmace Leroy. *Études religieuses, philosophiques, historiques et littéraires* 55 (1891): 488–97.

Brucker, Joseph, SJ. *Questions actuelles d'écriture sainte.* Paris: Retaux, 1895.

Brush, Stephen G. "Nettie M. Stevens and the Discovery of Sex Determination by Chromosomes." *Isis* 69, no. 2 (1978): 163–72.

Buckland, William. *Geology and Mineralogy Considered with Reference to Natural Theology.* London: Pickering, 1836.

Buen y del Cos, Odón de. *Tratado elemental de geología.* Barcelona: La Academia, 1890.

Buen y del Cos, Odón de. *Tratado elemental de zoología.* Barcelona: La Academia, 1890.

Bueno Sánchez, Gustavo. "La obra filosófica de Fray Zeferino González." Ph.D. diss., Universidad de Oviedo, 1989.

Buffon, Georges-Louis Leclerc. *Histoire naturelle de l'homme.* Paris: Imprimerie royale, 1749.

Bujanda, J. M. De. *Index librorum prohibitorum: 1600–1966.* Sherbrooke: Centre d'Études de la Renaissance, Université de Sherbrooke, 2002.

Burke, Redmond A. *What is the Index?* Milwaukee, WI: Bruce, 1952.

Burrell, David B., CSC. *When Faith and Reason Meet: The Legacy of John Zahm.* Notre Dame, IN: Corby, 2009.

Burton, Philip, CM. "St. Augustine and the Missing Link." *Irish Ecclesiastical Record* 4th ser., 5 (1899): 450–57.

Burton, Philip, CM. "Was St. Augustine an Evolutionist?" *Irish Ecclesiastical Record* 4th ser., 5 (1899): 102–10.

Burton, Philip, CM. "Was St. Augustine an Evolutionist?" *Irish Ecclesiastical Record* 4th ser., 5 (1899): 521–30.

Busk, George. "On the Crania of the Most Ancient Races of Man." *Natural History Review* 1, no. 2 (1861): 155–76.

Butler, Cuthbert. *The Vatican Council 1869–1870.* London: Longmans, Green, 1930.

Butler, Samuel. *Unconscious Memory.* London: Bogue, 1880.

Calmet, Antoine Augustin, OSB. *Commentarius literalis in omnes libros veteris et novi testamenti.* Venice: Coleti, 1754. Cf. translation by Charles Taylor as *Calmet's Dictionary of the Holy Bible.* 7th ed. Boston: Crocker and Brewster, 1835.

Camerano, Lorenzo. "La vita scientifica di Michele Lessona." *Memorie della Reale accademia delle scienze di Torino* 2nd ser., 45 (1896): 331–88.

Canadelli, Elena. "La morte di Filippo De Filippi a Hong Kong (1867): Il racconto inedito di un missionario." *Atti della Società italiana di scienze naturali e del Museo civico di storia naturale di Milano* 153, no. 1 (2012): 85–110.

Canestrini, Giovanni. *Origine dell'uomo.* Milan: Brigola, 1866.

Cannon, Walter F. "The Impact of Uniformitarianism: Two Letters from John Herschel to Charles Lyell, 1836–37." *Proceedings of the American Philosophical Society* 105, no. 3 (1961): 301–14.

Cappelletti, Vincenzo, and Federico Di Trocchio. "Caverni, Raffaello." In *Dizionario biografico degli italiani,* edited by Alberto M. Ghisalberti, 23:85–88. Rome: Istituto della Enciclopedia Italiana, 1979.

Carbonnelle, Ignace, SJ. "Bulletin scientifique." *Études religieuses, historiques et littéraires* 4th ser., 4 (1869): 472–82.

Carbonnelle, Ignace, SJ. *Les Confins de la science et de la philosophie.* 3rd ed. Paris: Palmé, 1881.

Carbonero y Sol, León, ed. *Índice de los libros prohibidos por el santo oficio de la inquisición española.* Madrid: Pérez Dubrull, 1873.

Carles, Jules. "Polygénisme ou monogénisme: Le Problème de l'unité de l'espèce humaine." *Archives de philosophie* 17, no. 2 (Sciences et problèmes d'unité) (1948): 84–100.

Carroll, Patrick J., CSC. "Mind in Action: Life of Father John A. Zahm, CSC." Published in many parts in *Ave Maria* 63–64 (1946).

Cartechini, Sixtus, SJ. *De valore notarum theologicarum et de criteriis ad eas dignoscendas.* Rome: Editrice Pontificia Università Gregoriana, 1951.

Casamajor, Louis de. "Que la Notion d'espèce précédemment faussée doit être mieux précisées ou mieux appliquée, si l'on veut l'employer comme base des discussions fixistes ou évolutionnistes." In Congrès scientifique de 1897, *Compte rendu,* 9:68–78.

Casamajor, Louis de. *Hétérogénie, transformisme et Darwinisme: Problème de l'espèce.* Bar-le-Duc: St.-Paul, 1898.

Casaroli, Agostino. Letter to Archbishop Paul Poupard of May 12, 1981. *L'Osservatore Romano.* June 10, 1981, 1. Translation in *Weekly Edition in English.* June 22, 1981, 2.

Castagnetti, Giuseppe, and Michele Camerota. "Raffaello Caverni and his *History of the Experimental Method in Italy*." *Science in Context* 14, no. 1 (2001): 327–39.

Caterini, Pietro, SJ. "Dell'origine dell'uomo secondo la scienza e la rivelazione." *Civiltà cattolica*, 10th ser., 5, to 11th ser., 4 (1878–80), in 37 parts. Republished as *Dell'origine dell'uomo secondo il trasformismo: Esame scientifico filosofico teologico*. Prato: Giaccheti, 1884.

Catholic Encyclopedia, The: An International Work of Reference on the Constitution, Doctrine, Discipline, and History of the Catholic Church, edited by Charles G. Herbermann, et al. New York: Encyclopedia Press [originally, Appleton], 1907–14.

Catholic Fortnightly Review. Review of *The Humanizing of the Brute*, by Hermann Muckermann. 14, no. 3 (1907): 73–74.

Catholic World. Review *Bible, Science, and Faith*, by John A. Zahm. 60, no. 355 (1894): 135–37.

Catholic World. Review of *Evolution and Dogma*, by John A. Zahm. 63, no. 373 (1896): 130–32.

Catholic World. Review of *Das Buch der Bücher*, by Hildebrand Höpfl. 81, no. 481 (1905): 123–24.

Catholic World. Review of *The Berlin Discussion of the Problem of Evolution*, by Erich Wasmann. 90, no. 535 (1909): 116–18.

Catholic World. "With Our Readers [Obituary and bibliography of George Searle]" 107, no. 641 (1918): 713–16.

Cathrein, Victor. "Der Entwicklungsgedanke in der Philosophie des 19. Jahrhunderts." In Congrès scientifique de 1900, *Akten*, 233–34. Published in full in *Theologisch-praktische Quartalschrift* 54, no. 11 (1901): 257–74.

Cavanaugh, John, CSC. "Father Zahm." *The Catholic World* 114, no. 683 (1922): 577–88.

Caverni, Raffaello. *De' nuovi studi della filosofia, discorsi di R. C. ad un giovane studente*. Florence: Carnesecchi, 1877. Originally published as "Sulla filosofia delle scienze naturali: Discorsi ad un giovine studente." *Rivista Universale* 21, no. 148 and 152 (1875): 212–29 and 581–603; 22, no. 156 and 158 (1875): 360–377 and 607–630; 23, no. 161 (1876): 255–275; and 24, no. 165, 168, and 170 (1876): 73–87, 408–38, and 626–52.

Caverni, Raffaello. *Dell'antichità dell'uomo secondo la scienza moderna: Saggio di studi*. Florence: Cellini, 1881. Originally published in *La Rassegna nazionale* 1, no. 4–5 (1879): 580–607 and 657–70, and 2, no. 6 (1880): 809–38.

Chaberek, Michael, OP. *Catholicism and Evolution: A History from Darwin to Pope Francis*. Kettering: Angelico, 2015.

Chambers, Ephraim. *Cyclopaedia: or, An Universal Dictionary of Arts and Sciences*. London: Knapton, 1728.

Chambers, Robert. *Vestiges of the Natural History of Creation*. London: Churchill, 1844.

Cheynier, André. "Un Précurseur amateur en préhistoire: François Jouannet." *Bulletin de la Société préhistorique française* 32, no. 2 (1935): 145–47.

Cheynier, André. *Jouannet, grand-père de la préhistoire*. Brive: Chastrusse, Praudel, 1936.

Chil y Naranjo, Gregorio. *Estudios históricos, climatológicos y patológicos de las Islas Canarias*. Las Palmas de Gran-Canaria: Miranda, 1876.

Ciani, John Louis. "Across a Wide Ocean: Salvatore Maria Brandi, SJ, and the *Civiltà Cattolica*, from Americanism to Modernism, 1891–1914." PhD diss., University of Virginia, 1992.

Cimino, Guido. "De Filippi, Filippo." In *Dizionario biografico degli italiani*, edited by Alberto M. Ghisalberti, 33:745–50. Rome: Istituto della Enciclopedia italiana fondata da Giovanni Treccani, 1987.

Civiltà cattolica, La. "Bibliografia." 17th ser., 4, no. 1161 (1898): 332–50.

Civiltà cattolica, La. "Cronaca contemporanea: IV. Cose varie: 2. Il libro 'Evoluzione e domma' del Prof. Zahm." 17th ser., 7, no. 1177 (1899): 125.

Civiltà Cattolica, La. Announcement of *I primi tre capitoli della Sacra Bibbia annotati secondo il sistema delle apparenze*, by Pietro Martinelli. 57th yr., 3, no. 1348 (1906): 512.

Civiltà cattolica, La. "Cronaca contemporanea." 59th yr., 2, no. 1387 (1908): 106–26.

Clark, Leo Kevin, OP. *Pioneers of Prehistory in England.* London: Sheed and Ward, 1961. Originally published as "A Pioneer of Prehistory." *Blackfriars* 6, no. 67–69 (1925): 603–13, 640–48, and 726–38.

Closen, Gustav, SJ. "De Incarnatione imaginis Dei: Notae quaedam criticae et theologicae de origine corporis humani." *Verbum Domini: Commentarii de re biblica* 20 (1940): 105–15.

Coakley, Patrick F., OSA. "St. Augustine: Was he an Evolutionist?" *Irish Ecclesiastical Record* 4th ser., 5 (1899): 342–58.

Cochin, Denys. *L'Évolution et la vie.* Paris: Masson, 1886.

Collard, A. "S. G. Mgr. Jacques Laminne (1864–1924)." *Ciel et terre: Bulletin de la Société belge d'astronomie* 41 (1925): 107.

Collison, Robert. *Encyclopaedias: Their History Throughout the Ages.* New York: Hafner, 1964.

Cologne, Council of. *Acta et decreta sacrorum conciliorum recentiorum: Collectio lacensis,* 5:231–382. Freiburg im Breisgau: Herder, 1879.

Colunga Cueto, Alberto, OP. "El autor de La Biblia y la ciencia." *Ciencia tomista* 43, no. 128 (1931): 145–68.

Commonweal. "Concerning Evolution." 2, no. 5 (1925): 119–21.

Complete Dictionary of Scientific Biography, edited by Charles Coulston Gillispie et al. Detroit: Scribner's Sons, 2008.

Confessore, Ornella. *L'Americanismo cattolico in Italia.* Rome: Studium, 1984.

Congregation of the Doctrine of the Faith. "Notificatio." *Acta Apostolicae Sedis* 58, no. 6 (1966): 445.

Congregation of the Holy Office. "Decretum: Proscriptio libri." *Acta Apostolicae Sedis* 46, no. 2 (1954): 25.

Congregation of the Holy Office. "Submissionis notificatio." *Acta Apostolicae Sedis* 46, no. 3 (1954): 64.

Congregation of the Holy Office. "Monitum." *Acta Apostolicae Sedis* 54, no. 9 (1962): 526.

Congregation of the Index of Prohibited Books. "Decretum: Feria sexta die vigesima quarta Maji." Rome: Camera Apostolica, 1771. Available at the website of Internet Culturale: Cataloghi e collezioni digitali delle biblioteche Italiane (internetculturale.it).

Congregation of the Index of Prohibited Books. *Ad indicem novissimum librorum prohibitorum appendix tertia in qua recensentur libri proscripti a die 3. Decembris an. MDCCLXX. ad diem 14. Maji an. MDCCLXXIX.* Rome: Camera Apostolica, 1779.

Congregation of the Index of Prohibited Books. *Index librorum prohibitorum Sanctissimi Domini Nostri Pii Sexti.* Rome: Camera Apostolica, 1786.

Congregation of the Index of Prohibited Books. *Index librorum prohibitorum Sanctissimi Domini Nostri Gregorii XVI.* Rome: Camera Apostolica, 1835. Rev. ed. 1841.

Congregation of the Index of Prohibited Books. "Decretum." *Act Sanctae Sedis* 11 (1878): 204–7.

Congrès scientifique international des catholiques de 1888. *Compte rendu du Congrès scientifique international des catholiques tenu à Paris du 8 au 13 avril 1888.* Paris: Annales de philosophie chrétienne, 1888.

Congrès scientifique international des catholiques de 1891. *Compte rendu du Congrès scientifique international des catholiques tenu à Paris du 1er au 6 avril 1891.* Paris: Picard, 1891.

Congrès scientifique international des catholiques de 1894. *Compte rendu du troisième Congrès scientifique international des catholiques tenu à Bruxelles du 3 au 8 septembre 1894.* Brussels: Société belge de librairie, 1895.

Congrès scientifique international des catholiques de 1897. *Compte rendu du quatrième Congrès scientifique international des catholiques tenu à Fribourg (Suisse) du 16 au 20 août 1897.* Fribourg: Saint-Paul, 1898.

Congrès scientifique international des catholiques von 1900. *Akten des fünften internationalen Kongresses katholischer Gelehrten zu München* (= *Compte rendu du Ve Congrès scientifique international des catholiques*). Freiburg im Breisgau: Herder, 1901.

Conversations-Lexikon. "Darwin, Charles." 2:81–82. Freiburg im Breisgau: Herder, 1877.

Conway, Bertrand, CSP. *The Question Box: Replies to Questions Received on Missions to Non-Catholics.* 1st ed. New York: Catholic Book Exchange, 1903. 2nd ed. New York: Paulist, 1929.

Coon, Carleton. *The Origin of Races.* New York: Knopf, 1962.

Copernicus, Nicholas. *De revolutionibus orbium coelestium.* Nuremberg: Petreius, 1543.

Corbett, John. "The Biblical Commission." In *The Catholic Encyclopedia,* 2:557–58.

Cosmacini, Giorgio. *Gemelli.* Milan: Rizzoli, 1985.

Cotter, Anthony C., SJ. "The Antecedents of the Encyclical *Providentissimus Deus.*" *The Catholic Biblical Quarterly* 5, no. 2 (1943): 117–24.

Cristiani, Léon [under pseud. Nicolas Corte]. *Les Origines de l'homme.* Paris: Artème-Fayard, 1957. Translated by Eric Earnshaw Smith as *The Origins of Man.* New York: Hawthorn, 1958.

Cuénot, Claude. *Pierre Teilhard de Chardin: Les Grandes Étapes de son évolution.* Paris: Plon, 1958. Somewhat abridged translation by Vincent Colimore as *Teilhard de Chardin: A Biographical Study.* London: Burns & Oates, 1965.

Cuénot, Lucien. *L'Évolution biologique.* Paris: Masson, 1951.

Cüppers, Sebastian M. M. *Das Kölner Provinzialkonzil von 1860: Kanonistische Struktur und Kirchenbild einer Provinzialsynode im 19. Jahrhundert.* Augsburg: Wissner, 1992.

Current Literature. "Review of the World." 48, no. 5 (1910): 463–472.

Cuvier, Georges. *Discours sur les révolutions de la surface du globe et sur les changements qu'elles ont produits dans le règne animal.* Paris: Dufour & Ocagne, 1825. 6th ed. Paris: Ocagne, 1830. Partially translated by Martin S. J. Rudwick in *Georges Cuvier, Fossil Bones, and Geological Catastrophes: New Translations & Interpretations of the Primary Texts.* Chicago: University of Chicago Press, 1997.

Cuvier, Georges. *Le Règne animal.* 2nd ed. Paris: Déterville, 1829. Translated by Henry McMurtrie as *The Animal Kingdom.* London: Henderson, 1837.

Dacík, Reginald, OP. *Věrouka pro laiky. II: Bůh v svém díle.* Olomouc: Krystal, 1938.

D'Alès, Adhémar. "L'Homme après la Genèse." In *Dictionnaire apologétique de la foi catholique,* 4th ed., 2:458–62.

Dart, Raymond. "*Australopithecus africanus:* The Man-Ape of South Africa." *Nature* 115, no. 2884 (1925): 195–99.

Dart, Raymond. *Adventures with the Missing Link.* New York: Harper & Brothers, 1959.

Darwin, Charles. *Journal of Researches into the Natural History and Geology of the Countries Visited during the Voyage of H. M. S. Beagle Round the World, under the Command of Capt. FitzRoy, RN.* 2nd ed. London: Murray, 1845.

Darwin, Charles. *On the Origin of Species by Means of Natural Selection, or The Preservation of Favoured Races in the Struggle for Life.* London: Murray, 1859. 3rd ed. 1861. 4th ed. 1866. 5th ed. 1869. Citation from the 1st ed. unless otherwise noted.

Darwin, Charles. "The Doctrine of Heterogeny and Modification of Species." *The Athenæum* no. 1852 (1863): 554–55.

Darwin, Charles. *The Descent of Man, and Selection in Relation to Sex.* London: Murray, 1871.

Darwin, Charles. *The Variation of Animals and Plants under Domestication.* London: Murray, 1868. 2nd ed. 1875.

Darwin, Charles. *The Life and Letters of Charles Darwin, Including an Autobiographical Chapter,* edited by Francis Darwin. London: Murray, 1887.

Darwin, Charles. *More Letters of Charles Darwin,* edited by Francis Darwin. London: Murray, 1903.

Darwin, Charles. *The Correspondence of Charles Darwin*. Edited by Frederick Burkhardt and Sydney Smith. Cambridge, MA: Cambridge University Press, 1985–.

Darwin, Charles, and Alfred Russel Wallace. "On the Tendency of Species to Form Varieties; and on the Perpetuation of Varieties and Species by Natural Means of Selection." *Journal of the Proceedings of the Linnean Society of London. Zoology* 3, no. 9 (1858): 45–62.

Darwin, Erasmus. *Zoonomia: or The Laws of Organic Life*. London: Johnson, 1794. Translated into Italian as *Zoonomia ovvero Leggi della vita organica*. Milan: Pirotta e Maspero, 1803–5.

De Bonniot, Joseph. "Essai philosophique sur le transformisme." *Études religieuses, philosophiques, historiques et littéraires* 46 (1889): 337–68.

De Bont, Raf. "Rome and Theistic Evolutionism: The Hidden Strategies behind the 'Dorlodot Affair,' 1920–1926." *Annals of Science* 62, no. 4 (2005): 457–78.

De Bont, Raf. "A Serpent without Teeth: The Conservative Transformism of Jean-Baptiste d'Omalius d'Halloy." *Centaurus* 49 (2007): 114–37.

De Bont, Raf. *Darwins kleinkinderen: De omgang met de evolutieleer in België, 1865–1945*. Nijmegen: Vantilt, 2008.

De Bont, Raf. "'Peut-être pas bien vu à Rome': Jacques Laminne and the Theory of Evolution." In *Religious Modernism in the Low Countries*, edited by Leo Kenis and Ernestine van der Wall, 85–101. Louvain: Peeters, 2013.

De Christol, Jules. *Notice sur les ossemens humains fossiles des cavernes du département du Gard*. Montpellier: Martel, 1829.

De Dorlodot, Henry. *Le Darwinisme au point de vue de l'orthodoxie catholique. 1. L'origine des espèces*. Louvain: Ceuterick, 1918 (though with the false date of "1913" to avoid the shame of submitting it to German censorship). 2nd ed. Brussels: Vromant, 1921. Translated (with some supplementary material) by E. C. Messenger as *Darwinism and Catholic Thought*. London: Burns, Oates & Washbourne, 1922.

De Dorlodot, Henry. *Le Darwinisme au point de vue de l'orthodoxie catholique: 2. L'Origine de l'homme*, edited by Marie Claire Groessens-VanDyck and Dominique Lambert. Wavre: Mardaga, 2009.

De Filippi, Filippo. *La creazione terrestre: Lettere a mia figlia*. Milan: Vallardi, 1854.

De Filippi, Filippo. "Il diluvio noëtico." *Il cimento: Rivista de scienze, lettere ed arti* 3rd ser., 6, no. 2, 5 and 6 (1855): 89–104, 341–53, and 472–81. Republished as a book. Turin: Franco, 1855.

De Filippi, Filippo. "La fisiologia di professore Moleschott." *Rivista italiana di scienze, lettere ed arti* 2, no. 57 (1861): 933–35.

De Filippi, Filippo. "L'uomo e le scimie." *Il politecnico: Repertorio mensile di studj applicati alla prosperità e coltura sociale* 21 (1864): 5–32. Republished as *L'uomo e le scimie: Lezione pubblica detta a Torino la sera dell'11 gennaio 1864*. Milan: Daelli, 1864. 3rd ed. (with appendix). 1865.

De Greef, M. G. "Rapport de M. G. de Greef, deuxième commissaire." *Bulletins de la classe des lettres et des sciences morales et politiques et de la classe des beaux-arts* [of the Académie royale de Belgique] 3rd ser., 42, no. 8 (1907): 220–261.

De Koninck, Charles. *Cosmos*. 1936. In *The Writings of Charles De Koninck*, translated and edited by Ralph McInerny, 1:235–354. Notre Dame, IN: University of Notre Dame Press, 2009.

De Lapparent, Albert. "Moïse et les géologues modernes." *La Revue apologétique* 61 (1935): 426–34.

De Lapparent, Albert. *Nos Origines: Les Données de la Bible et de la science*. Paris: Éditions St. Paul, 1944.

De Letter, P., and W. G. Hill. "Theology, History of." In *The New Catholic Encyclopedia*, 2nd ed., 13:902–18.

De Maillet, Benoît. *Telliamed, ou Entretiens d'un philosophe indien avec un missionnaire françois sur la diminution de la mer, la formation de la terre, l'origine de l'homme, &c*. Edited by J. A. G. Amsterdam: L'Honoré, 1748. Translated as *Telliamed, or, The World Explain'd: Containing Discourses between an Indian Philosopher and a Missionary, on the Diminution of the Sea, the Formation of the Earth, the*

Origin of Men & Animals, &c. London: Osbourne, 1750. Retranslated (as an attempt to reconstruct the original version of Maillet's book) by Albert V. Carozzi as *Telliamed, or Conversations Between an Indian Philosopher and a French Missionary on the Diminution of the Sea.* Urbana: University of Illinois Press, 1968.

De San, P. L. *Institutiones metaphysicae specialis.* Louvain: Fonteyn, 1881.

De Serres, Marcel. *De la cosmogonie de Moïse comparée aux faits géologiques.* Paris: Lagny, 1838.

De Sinéty, Robert, SJ. "L'Haeckélianisme et les idées du père Wasmann sur l'évolution." *Revue des questions scientifiques* 59 (= 3rd ser., 9), no. 1 (1906): 226–42.

De Sinéty, Robert, SJ. "Transformisme." In *Dictionnaire apologétique de la foi catholique*, 4th ed., 4:1793–1848.

De Sinéty, Robert, SJ. "Un Demi-siècle de darwinisme." *Revue des questions scientifiques* 67 (= 3rd ser., 17), no. 1–2 (1910): 5–38 and 480–513.

De Solages, Bruno. "Pour l'Honneur de la théologie." *Bulletin de littérature ecclésiastique* 48, no. 2 (1947): 65–84.

De Solages, Bruno. *Teilhard de Chardin: Témoignage et étude sur le développement de sa pensée.* Toulouse: Privat, 1967.

De Tonquédec, Joseph. *Dieu dans "L'Évolution Créatrice" avec deux lettres de M. Bergson.* Paris: Beauchesne, 1912.

De Valroger, Hyacinth. *La Genèse des espèces: Études philosophiques et religieuses sur l'histoire naturelle et les naturalistes contemporains.* Paris: Didier, 1873.

De Vries, Hugo. "Transformisme et mutation." *Revue du mois* 8, no. 45 (1909): 269–302.

De Vries, Hugo. *Species and Varieties: Their Origin by Mutation.* Chicago: Open Court, 1905.

Delage. Yves. *La Structure du protoplasme et les théories sur l'hérédité et les grands problèmes de la biologie générale.* Paris: Reinwald, 1895.

Delsaulx, Joseph, SJ. "Les Derniers Écrits philosophiques de M. Tyndall." *Revue catholique: Recueil religieux, philosophique, scientifique, historique et littéraire* n.s., 15 (1876): 275–303, 337–67, and 441–80. Republished as a book. Paris: Baltenweck, 1877.

Desmazieres, Agnès. "Agostino Gemelli e gli intellettuali cattolici francesi nel secondo dopoguerra. La 'nouvelle théologie' vista da Milano (1946–1951)." *Annali di storia moderna e contemporanea* 13 (2007): 159–92.

Dennert, Eberhard. *Vom Sterbelager des Darwinismus.* Halle an der Saale: Mühlmann, 1902. Translated by John H. Peschges as *At the Deathbed of Darwinism: A Series of Papers.* Burlington, IA: German Literary Board, 1904.

Descartes, René. *Discours de la Méthode pour bien conduire sa raison, et chercher la vérité dans les sciences.* Leyden: Maire, 1637. Republished in *Œuvres de Descartes*, edited by Charles Adam et Paul Tannery, 1–78. Paris: Cerf, 1902. Translated by Elizabeth S. Haldane and G. R. T. Ross as "Discourse on the Method of Rightly Conducting the Reason" in *The Philosophical Works of Descartes*, 1:79–130. Cambridge: Cambridge University Press, 1978.

Desmoulins, Louis Antoine. *Histoire naturelle des races humaines.* Paris: Méquignon, 1826.

Desnoyers, Jules. "Considérations sur les ossemens humains des cavernes du Midi de la France." *Bulletin de la Société géologique de France* 2 (1831–32): 126–33.

Desnoyers, Jules. "Proofs that the Human Bones and Works of Art found in Caves in the South of France, are More Recent than the Antediluvian Bones in these Caves." *The Edinburgh New Philosophical Journal* 16 (1834): 302–10.

D'Hulst, Maurice. "La Question biblique." *Le Correspondant* 170, no. 2 (1893): 201–51. Republished as a pamphlet. Paris: Poussièlgue, 1893.

Dictionnaire apologétique de la foi catholique, edited by Jean-Baptiste Jaugey. Paris: Delhomme et Briguet, 1889. Translated into Spanish as *Diccionario apologético de la fe católica*, edited by Jean-Baptiste Jaugey and Joaquín Torres Asensio. Madrid: Sociedad Editorial de San Francisco de Sales, 1890. Translated into Polish as *Słownik apologetyczny wiary katolickiej*, edited by Jean Baptiste Jaugey and Władysław Szcześniak. Warsaw: St. Niemiery, 1894.

Dictionnaire apologétique de la foi catholique contenant les preuves de la vérité de la religion et les réponses aux objections tirées des sciences humaines, edited by Adhémar d'Alès, SJ. 4th ed. Paris: Beauchesne, 1911–28.

Dictionnaire de théologie catholique, edited by Alfred Vacant et al. Paris: Latouzey, 1902–50.

Dierckx, François, SJ. "L'Homme-singe et les précurseurs d'Adam en face de la science et de la théologie." *Revue des questions scientifiques* 35–36 (= 2nd ser., 5–6), no. 2–3 (1894), 518–89 and 80–121. Republished as a book. Brussels: Retaux, 1894.

Dobzhansky, Theodosius. *The Biology of Ultimate Concern*. New York: New American Library, 1967.

D'Omalius d'Halloy, Jean-Baptiste Julien. "Essai sur la géologie du nord de la France." *Journal des mines* 24, no. 140 and 142–44 (1808): 123–58, 271–318, 345–92, and 439–66.

D'Omalius d'Halloy, Jean-Baptiste Julien. "Notice sur le gisement du calcaire d'eau douce, dans les départemens du Cher, de l'Allier et de la Nièvre." *Journal des mines* 32, no. 187 (1812), 43–64. Summarized in *Nouveau Bulletin des sciences par la Société philomathique de Paris* 3, no. 59 (1812): 123–28.

D'Omalius d'Halloy, Jean-Baptiste Julien. "Mémoire sur l'étendue géographique du terrain des environs de Paris." *Annales des mines* 1 (1816): 231–66.

D'Omalius d'Halloy, Jean-Baptiste Julien. *Éléments de géologie*. Paris: Levrault, 1831.

D'Omalius d'Halloy, Jean-Baptiste Julien. "Note sur la succession des êtres vivants." *Bulletin de la Société géologique de France* 2nd ser., 3 (1846): 490–97. Also *Bulletin de l'Académie royale des sciences, des lettres, et des beaux-arts de Belgique* 13, pt.1 (1846): 581–91.

D'Omalius d'Halloy, Jean-Baptiste Julien. Untitled public lecture. *Bulletin de l'Académie royale des sciences, des lettres, et des beaux-arts de Belgique* 17, pt. 2 (1850): 498–510.

D'Omalius d'Halloy, Jean-Baptiste Julien. "Discours sur l'espèce." *Bulletin de l'Académie royale des sciences, des lettres, et des beaux-arts de Belgique* 2nd ser., 5 (1858): 555–65.

D'Omalius d'Halloy, Jean-Baptiste Julien. "De l'Accord entre les croyances religieuses et les progrès des sciences naturelles." *Bulletin de l'Académie royale des sciences, des lettres, et des beaux-arts de Belgique* 2nd ser., 22 (1866): 555–63.

D'Omalius d'Halloy, Jean-Baptiste Julien. *Précis élémentaire de géologie*. 8th ed. Brussels: Muquard, 1868.

D'Omalius d'Halloy, Jean-Baptiste Julien. "Sur le Transformisme." *Bulletin de l'Académie royale des sciences, des lettres, et des beaux-arts de Belgique* 2nd ser., 36 (1873): 769–79.

Dopp, Katharine Elizabeth. *Tree Dwellers*. New York: Rand McNally, 1904.

Doran, William R. "De corporis Adami origine: Doctrina Alexandri Halensis, sancti Alberti Magni, sancti Bonaventurae, sancti Thomae." Ph.D. diss., St. Mary of the Lake Seminary, 1936.

Dörpinghaus, Hermann Josef. "Darwins Theorie und der deutsche Vulgärmaterialismus im Urteil deutscher katholischer Zeitschriften zwischen 1854 und 1914." Ph.D. diss., Albert-Ludwigs-Universität zu Freiburg-im-Breisgau, 1969.

D'Ouince, René, SJ. "L'Obéissance du Père Teilhard de Chardin." In *L'Homme devant Dieu: Mélanges offerts au Père Henri de Lubac*, 3:331–46. Paris: Aubier, 1964.

D'Ouince, René, SJ. *Un Prophète en procès: Teilhard de Chardin dans l'Église de son temps*. Paris: Aubier-Montaigne, 1970.

Draper, William. *History of the Conflict between Religion and Science*. New York: Appleton, 1875.

Du Lubac, Henri, SJ. *Teilhard de Chardin: The Man and his Meaning*. Translated by René Hague. New York: Hawthorn, 1965.

Du Lubac, Henri, SJ. *The Religion of Teilhard de Chardin*. Translated by René Hague. New York: Desclée, 1967.

Dublin Review. Review of *On the Genesis of Species*, by St. George Mivart. 68 (= n.s., 16), no. 32 (1871): 482–86.

Dubois, Eugène. *Pithecanthropus erectus: Eine menschenähnliche Übergangsform aus Java (Pithecanthropus erectus)*. Jakarta: Landesdruckerei, 1894. Translated as "On *Pithecanthropus erectus*: A Transitional Form between Man and the Apes." *Scientific Transactions of the Royal Dublin Society* 2nd ser., 6, no. 1 (1896): 1–18.

Ducrost, Antoine. *De l'évolution*. Lyons: Vitte et Perrussel, 1884. Originally published in *La Controverse et le contemporain* n.s., 2 [?] (1884).

Duhem, Hélène. *Un Savant français: Pierre Duhem*. Paris: Plon, 1936.

Duilhé de Saint-Projet, François. *Apologie scientifique de la foi spiritualiste et chrétienne*. Toulouse: Privat, 1885.

Duilhé de Saint-Projet, François. "Le Problème anthropologique et les théories évolutionnistes." In Congrès scientifique de 1888, *Compte rendu*, 2:621–33.

Dupont, E. "Notice sur la vie et les travaux de J. B. J. d'Omalius d'Halloy." *Annuaire de l'Académie royale de Belgique* 42 (1876): 181–296.

Dwight, Thomas. *Thoughts of a Catholic Anatomist*. New York: Longmans, Green, 1911.

Dyroff, Adolf. "Hertling." In *Lexikon für Theologie und Kirche*, edited by Michael Buchberger, 4:1007–9. Freiburg im Breisgau: Herder, 1930–38.

Elder, Benedict. "The Tennessee Case." *Fortnightly Review* 32, no. 13 (1925): 274–75.

Elder, Benedict. "A Law that is not a Law." *Commonweal* 2, no. 10 (1925): 245–47.

Elder, Benedict. "The Tennessee School Regulation." *Fortnightly Review*, 32, no. 17 (1925): 358–63.

Elder, Gregory P. *Chronic Vigour: Darwin, Anglicans, Catholics and the Development of a Doctrine of Providential Evolution*. Lanham, MD: University Press of America, 1996.

Enciclopedia cattolica. Vatican City: Ente per l'Enciclopedia cattolica e per il Libro cattolico, 1948–54.

Enciclopedia universal ilustrada europeo-americana. "Transformismo." 63:947–85. Madrid: Espasa-Calpe, 1928.

Encyklopedja kościelna podług teologicznej encyklopedji Wetzera i Weltego z licznemi jej dopełnieniami, edited by Michał Nowodworski et al. Warsaw: Czerwiński, 1873–1933.

Engelbert, Pius, OSB. *Geschichte des Benediktinerkollegs St. Anselm in Rom: von den Anfängen (1888) bis zur Gegenwart*. Roma: Pontificio Ateneo S. Anselmo, 1988. Translated by Henry O'Shea, OSB, as *Sant'Anselmo in Rome: College and University: From the Beginnings to the Present Day*. Collegeville, MN: Liturgical Press, 2015.

Epitome Instituti Societatis Iesu. 3rd ed. Rome: Curia praepositi generalis, 1943.

Eyre, Edward, ed. *European Civilization: Its Origin and Development*. London: Oxford University Press, 1934.

Fabre d'Envieu, Jules. *Les Origines de la terre et de l'homme*. Paris: Thorin, 1873.

Fàbregas-Tejeda, Alejandro, et al. "Revisiting Hans Böker's 'Species Transformation Through Reconstruction: Reconstruction Through Active Reaction of Organisms' (1935)." *Biological Theory* 16, no. 2 (2021): 63–75.

Farges, Albert. "L'Évolution et les évolutions." *Annales de philosophie chrétienne* n.s., 37, no. 3–4 (1897–98): 307–33 and 401–20.

Farges, Albert. *La Philosophie de M. Bergson*. Paris: Bonne, 1912.

Faye, Hervé. *Sur l'Origine du monde: Théories cosmogoniques des anciens et des modernes*. Paris: Gauthier-Villars, 1884.

Federici, M. Review of *I primi tre capitoli della Sacra Bibbia annotati secondo il sistema delle apparenze*, by Pietro Martinelli. *Rivista storico-critica delle scienze teologiche* 2, no. 11 (1906): 878–79.

Federici, M. Review of *I primi tre capitoli della Sacra Bibbia annotati secondo il sistema delle apparenze*, by Pietro Martinelli. *Rivista bibliografia italiana* 12, no. 16 (1907): 243.

Ferrière, Émile. *Essai sur le libre arbitre*. Paris: Balitout-Questroy, 1865.

Ferrière, Émile. *Darwinisme*. Paris: Germer-Baillière, 1872.

Ferrière, Émile. *L'Âme est la fonction du cerveau*. Paris: Baillière, 1883.

Ferrière, Émile. *La Vie et l'âme*. Paris: Alcan, 1888.

Ferrière, Émile. *Les Erreurs scientifiques de la Bible*. Paris: Alcan, 1891.

Fessler, Joseph. *Über die Provincial-Koncilien und Diözesan-Synoden*. Innsbruck: Rauch, 1849.

Finke, Heinrich. *Internationale Wissenschaftsbeziehungen der Görres-Gesellschaft*. Cologne: Bachem, 1932.

Finocchiaro, Maurice A. *The Galileo Affair: A Documentary History*. Berkeley: University of California Press, 1989.

Fitzsimons, Simon. "Fr. Wasmann on Evolution." *American Catholic Quarterly Review* 35, no. 137 (1910): 12–48. Republished as *Revised Darwinism, or Father Wasmann on Evolution*. New York: Kenedy, 1910.

Flammarion, Camille. *Dictionnaire encyclopédique universelle*. Paris: Flammarion, 1894–98.

Fleming, David, OFM. Review of *Evolution and Dogma*, by John A. Zahm. *Dublin Review* 119 (= 4th ser.), no. 20 (1896): 245–55.

Flick, Maurizio. "Il poligenismo e il dogma del peccato originale." *Gregorianum* 28, no. 4 (1947): 555–63.

Flick, Maurizio. "L'Origine del corpo del primo uomo alla luce della filosofia cristiana e della teologia." *Gregorianum* 29, no. 3/4 (1948): 392–416.

Fogazzaro, Antonio. *Per un recente raffronto delle teorie di s. Agostino e di Darwin circa la creazione*. 3rd ed. Milan: Galli, 1892.

Fogazzaro, Antonio. *L'Origine dell'uomo e il sentimento religioso: Discorso letto in Roma il 2 marzo 1893 alla Società per l'istruzione della donna*. Milan: Galli, 1893.

Fogazzaro, Antonio. *Per la bellezza d'un'idea: Conferenza tenuta il 2 maggio 1892 all'Ateneo veneto*. Milan: Galli, 1893.

Fogazzaro, Antonio. *Ascensioni umane*. Milan: Baldini & Castoldi, 1899.

Fogazzaro, Antonio. *Il santo*. Milan: Baldini & Castoldi, 1905.

Fogazzaro, Antonio. *Leila*. Milan: Baldini & Castoldi, 1910.

Foscarini, Paolo. "Lettera sopra l'opinione de' pittagorici e del Copernico della mobilità della Terra e stabilità del Sole, e del nuovo pittagorico sistema del mondo." Naples: Scoriggio, 1615. Translated in Thomas Salusbury, *Mathematical Collections*. London: Leybourn, 1661.

Fourtau, René. "Note sur les échinides fossiles recueillis par M. Teilhard de Chardin dans l'éocène des environs de Minieh." *Bulletin de l'Institut égyptien* 5th ser., 2, no. 2 (1909): 122–55.

Fox, Robert. *The Savant and the State: Science and Cultural Politics in Nineteenth-Century France*. Baltimore: Johns Hopkins University Press, 2012.

Fraipont, Julien, and Max Lohest. "La Race humaine de Néanderthal ou de Canstadt en Belgique." *Archives de biologie* 7 (1887): 587–757.

Frank, Karl, SJ. *Die Entwicklungstheorie im Lichte der Tatsachen*. Freiburg im Breisgau: Herder, 1911. Translated by Charles T. Druery as *The Theory of Evolution in the Light of Facts*. London: Kegan Paul, 1913.

Frayssinous, Denis de. *Défense du christianisme, ou Conférences sur la religion*. 3rd ed. Paris: Le Clère, 1825. Translated by John Benjamin Jones as *Defence of Christianity*. London: Rivington, 1836.

Frohschammer, Jakob. *Über den Ursprung der menschlichen Seelen: Rechtfertigung des Generationismus*. Munich: Rieger, 1854.

Funghini, Luigi. *L'uomo e il trasformismo*. Florence: Mariani, 1898.

Funghini, Luigi. *Risposta al nuovo evoluzionista mons. Geremia Bonomelli, vescovo di Cremona.* Florence: Mariani, 1898.

Galileo. "Lettera a Madama Cristina di Lorena Granduchessa di Toscana." Translated in *The Galileo Affair: A Documentary History*, edited by Maurice A. Finocchiaro, 87–118. Berkeley: University of California Press, 1989.

Gallagher, Idella Jane, and Thomas M. King, SJ. "Bergson, Henri Louis." In *The New Catholic Encyclopedia Supplement 2010*, edited by Robert L. Fastigi, 1:125–28. Detroit: Gage, 2020.

García Álvarez, Rafael, and Leandro Sequeiros San Román. *Granada y el darwinismo: Discurso de Rafael García Álvarez (1872) y la censura sinodal de 1872, presentación científica, histórica y teológica.* Granada: Universidad de Granada, 2009.

Gardeil, Ambroise, OP. "L'Évolutionnisme et les principes de S. Thomas." *Revue thomiste* (1893–96), 1: 27–45, 316–27, and 725–37; 2: 29–42; 3: 61–84 and 607–33; and 4: 64–86 and 215–47.

Garrigan, O. W. "Monogenism." In *The New Catholic Encyclopedia*, 9:1063–64.

Garrigan, O. W. "Polygenism." In *The New Catholic Encyclopedia*, 11:539–40.

Garrigou-Lagrange, Réginald, OP. *Le Sens commun: La Philosophie de l'être et les formules dogmatiques.* Paris: Beauchesne, 1909.

Garrigou-Lagrange, Reginald, OP. "La Nouvelle Théologie, où va-t-elle?" *Angelicum* 23, no. 3/4 (1946): 126–45.

Garrigou-Lagrange, Réginald, OP. "Le Monogénisme n'est-il nullement révélé, pas même implicitement?" *Doctor Communis* 2 (1948): 191–202.

Gaudry, Albert. "Alcide d'Orbigny: Ses Voyages et ses travaux." *Revue des deux mondes* 2nd per., 19, no. 4 (1859): 816–47.

Gaudry, Albert. *Contemporanéité de l'espèce humaine et de diverses espèces animales aujourd'hui éteintes.* Paris: Cosson, 1859.

Gaudry, Albert. *Considérations générales sur les animaux fossiles de Pikermi.* Paris: Savy, 1866. Later incorporated into his *Animaux fossiles et géologie de l'Attique*, 325–370. Paris: Savy, 1862–67.

Gaudry, Albert. "Animaux fossiles du Mont Léberon (Vaucluse): Étude sur les vertébrés." In *Animaux fossiles du Mont Léberon*, edited by Gaudry et al., 1–112. Paris: Savy, 1873.

Gaudry, Albert. *Les Enchaînements du monde animal dans les temps géologiques: Mammifères tertiaires.* Paris: Savy, 1878.

Gaudry, Albert. *Les Enchaînements du monde animal dans les temps géologiques: Fossiles primaires.* Paris: Savy, 1883.

Gaudry, Albert. *Les Enchaînements du monde animal dans les temps géologiques: Fossiles secondaires.* Paris: Savy, 1890.

Gaudry, Albert. *Le Dryopithèque.* Paris: Librairie Polytechnique Baudry, 1892.

Gaudry, Albert. *Essai de paléontologie philosophique.* Paris: Savy, 1896.

Gazzetta ufficiale. "Ultime notizie." March 26, 1867. No. 85: 3.

Gemelli, Agostino, OFM. "Conflitto di tendenze (A proposito di alcune critiche mosse alle mie idee sulla teoria dell'evoluzione)." *La Scuola cattolica* 4th ser., 10 (1906): 54–69 and 135–49.

Gemelli, Agostino, OFM. "Il problema dell'origine delle specie e la teoria dell'evoluzione." In Wasmann, *La Biologia moderna*, xiii–civ.

Gemelli, Agostino, OFM. "Su di un nuovo indirizzo della teoria dell'evoluzione." *La Scuola cattolica* 4th ser., 9 (1906): 21–38, 148–61, 351–66, 451–64, and 529–45.

Gemelli, Agostino, OFM. "Teorie recenti sull'origine dell'uomo." *Rassegna nazionale* 170, no. 22 (1909): 464–94.

Gemelli, Agostino, OFM. "Il P. Erich Wasmann SJ." *Atti pontificia delle scienze nuovi lincei* 84 (1931): 3–6.

Generelli, Giuseppe Cirillo. "De' crostacei e dell'altre produzioni marine, che sono ne' monti." In *Raccolta Milanese dell'Anno 1757*, 1–23.

Gilson, Étienne. *The Philosopher and Theology.* Translated by Cecile Gilson. New York: Random House, 1962.

Gilson, Étienne. *Les Tribulations de Sophie.* Paris: Vrin, 1967.

Gioberti, Vincenzo. *Introduzione allo studio della filosofia.* Brussels: Hayez, 1840.

Giovannozzi, Giovanni. "Un tedesco di Montelupo." *La Rassegna nazionale* 171, no. 2 (1910): 257–74.

Giraudet, Alexandre-Aimé. *Nouveau Traité de géologie.* Tours: Mame, 1843.

Glick, Thomas F. *Darwin in España*, Barcelona: Península, 1982.

Glick, Thomas F. "Spain." In *The Comparative Reception of Darwinism*, edited by Thomas F. Glick, 307–45. Chicago: University of Chicago Press, 1988.

Glick, Thomas F. "Teilhard de Chardin, Pierre." In *Complete Dictionary of Scientific Biography*, edited by Charles Coulston Gillispie et al., 13:274–77. New York: Scribner's Sons, 2008.

Gmeiner, John. *Modern Scientific Views.* Milwaukee: Yewdale, 1884.

Gmeiner, John. *The Church and the Various Nationalities in the United States: Are German Catholics Unfairly Treated?* Milwaukee: Zahn, 1887.

Gmeiner, John. "Doctrina H. Spencer de evolutione rerum: Luce sanae philosophiae spectata." In Congrès scientifique de 1888, *Compte rendu*, 1:179–183. Translated in the *Northwestern Chronicle* 22, no. 26 (May 25, 1888): 1 and 8.

Gmeiner, John. "The Liberty of Catholics in Scientific Matters." *Catholic World* 48, no. 284 (1888): 145–50.

Gmeiner, John. *Cosmology.* Milwaukee: Hoffmann, 1893.

Godinot, Marc. "De la Géologie à l'évolution dans les travaux scientifiques de Teilhard." In *Pierre Teilhard de Chardin face à ses contradicteurs*, edited by Jean Duchesne, 61–82. Paris: Parole et Science, 2016.

Gomez-Heras, J. M. G. *Temas dogmáticos del Concilio vaticano I: Aportación de la Comisión teológica preparatoria a su obra doctrinal.* Vitoria: Eset, 1971.

González y Díaz Tuñón, Zeferino, OP. "La electricidad atmosférica y sus principales manifestaciones." In his *Estudios religiosos filosóficos científicos y sociales*, 2:341–415. Madrid: Lopez, 1873.

González y Díaz Tuñón, Zeferino, OP. "Los temblores de tierra." In his *Estudios religiosos filosóficos científicos y sociales*, 2:125–206. Madrid: Lopez, 1873.

González y Díaz Tuñón, Zeferino, OP. *Estudios sobre la filosofía de Santo Tomás.* Manila: Cortada, 1864.

González y Díaz Tuñón, Zeferino, OP. *Philosophia elementaria.* Madrid: Lopez, 1868, 1877, 1881, 1882, 1885, 1889, and 1894.

González y Díaz Tuñón, Zeferino, OP. *Filosofía elemental.* Madrid: Lopez, 1873, 1876, 1881, 1884, 1886, and 1894.

González y Díaz Tuñón, Zeferino, OP. *Historia de la filosofía.* Madrid: Araque, 1879; 2nd ed. Madrid: Jubera, 1886.

González y Díaz Tuñón, Zeferino, OP. *La Biblia y la ciencia.* Seville: Dubrull, 1891. 2nd ed. Seville: Izquierdo, 1892.

Gottesleben, Nikolaus, and Johann Baptist Schiltknecht. *Die Biblische Geschichte auf der Oberstufe der katholischen Volksschule.* 4th ed. Paderborn: Schöningh, 1905.

Goudge, T. A. "Bergson, Henri." In *Encyclopedia of Philosophy*, edited by Paul Edwards, 1:287–95. New York: McGraw-Hill, 1968.

Gould, Stephen Jay. "Piltdown Revisited." *Natural History* 88, no. 3 (1979): 86–99. Republished in his *The Panda's Thumb*, 108–24. New York: Norton, 1980.

Gould, Stephen Jay. "The Piltdown Conspiracy." *Natural History* 89, no. 8 (1980): 8–28. Republished in his *Hen's Teeth*, 201–226.

Gould, Stephen Jay. "The Titular Bishop of Titiopolis." *Natural History* 90, no. 5 (1981), 20–24. Republished in his *Hen's Teeth*, 69–78.

Gould, Stephen Jay. *Hen's Teeth and Horse's Toes.* New York: Norton, 1983.

Gould, Stephen Jay. "A Reply to Critics." In his *Hen's Teeth*, 227–40.

Gould, Stephen Jay. "Nonoverlapping Magisteria." *Natural History* 106, no. 2 (1997): 16–22. Republished in his *Leonardo's Mountain of Clams and the Diet of Worms*, 269–83. New York: Harmony, 1998.

Gould, Stephen Jay. *Rocks of Ages: Science & Religion in the Fullness of Life.* New York: Ballantine, 1999.

Granderath, Theodor, SJ, and Gerhard Schneermann, eds. *Acta et decreta sacrorum conciliorum recentiorum: Collectio lacensis.* Freiburg im Breisgau: Herder, 1879.

Granderath, Theodor, SJ. *Geschichte des vatikanischen Konzils.* Freiburg im Breisgau: Herder, 1903.

Grayson, Donald K. *The Establishment of Human Antiquity.* New York: Academic Press, 1983.

Grenet, Paul. *Teilhard de Chardin: The Man and his Theories.* Translated by R. A. Rudorff. London: Catholic Book Club, 1965.

Groessens-VanDyck, Marie Claire, and Dominique Lambert. "Le Darwinisme d'un chanoine." In de Dorlodot, *Darwinisme: 2. L'Origine de l'homme*, 11–90.

Groessens-VanDyck, Marie Claire. "Une Théorie iconoclaste fait son entrée à Louvain: De Dorlodot et le Darwinisme." In *Sedes scientiae: L'Émergence de la recherche à l'Université: Contributions au séminaire d'histoire des sciences 2000–2001*, edited by Patricia Radelet-de-Grave et al., 217–46, with references at 319–64. Louvain-la-Neuve: Centre de recherche en histoire des sciences, 2003.

Grogin, Robert C. *The Bergsonian Controversy in France, 1900–1914.* Calgary: University of Calgary Press: 1988.

Gross, Jules. "Le Problème des origines dans la théologie récente." *Revue des sciences religieuses* 13, no. 1 (1933): 38–65.

Gross, Jules. Review of *Tractatus de Deo creante and elevante*, by Charles Boyer. *Revue des sciences religieuses* 15, no. 3 (1935): 453–54.

Große Herder, Der. 4th ed. Freiburg im Breisgau: Herder, 1931–39.

Gruber, Jacob W. "Brixham Cave and the Antiquity of Man." In *Context and Meaning in Cultural Anthropology*, edited by Melville E. Spiro, 373–402. New York: Free Press, 1965.

Gruber, Jacob W. *A Conscience in Conflict: The Life of St. George Jackson Mivart.* New York: Columbia University Press, 1960.

Grumett, David. "Teilhard, the Six Propositions, and Human Origins: A Response." *Zygon: Journal of Religion and Science* 54, no. 4 (2019): 954–64.

Grumett, David, and Paul Bentley. "Teilhard de Chardin, Original Sin, and the Six Propositions." *Zygon: Journal of Religion and Science* 53, no. 2 (2018): 303–30.

Guequier, J. "Omalius d'Halloy." *Biographie nationale de Belgique*, published by the Académie royale des sciences, des lettres et des beaux-arts de Belgique, 16:157–166. Brussels: Bruylant, 1866–1944.

Guettler, Carl. *Naturforschung und Bibel in ihrer Stellung zur Schöpfung: Eine empirische Kritik der mosaischen Urgeschichte.* Freiburg im Breisgau: Herder, 1877.

Guibert, Jean, PSS. *Les Origines: Questions d'apologétique.* Paris: Letouzey, 1896. 2nd ed. 1898. 2nd ed. translated by G. S. Whitmarsh as *In the Beginning.* London: Kegan Paul, 1900.

Guibert, Jean, PSS. "Unité de l'espèce humaine." In *Dictionnaire apologétique de la foi catholique*, 4th ed., 2:492–501.

Guibert, Jean, PSS, and L. Chinchole. *Les Origines: Questions d'apologétique.* Paris: Letouzey, 1923. 8th ed. 1928. Translated into Spanish by Modesto H. Villaescusa, *Los orígenes: Cuestiones de apologética.*

Barcelona: Editorial Litúrgica Española, 1925. Translated into English by Victor A. Bast as *Whence and How the Universe?* Baltimore: St. Mary's Seminary Press, 1928.

Guillemet, Léon. "Pour la Théorie des ancêtres communs." In Congrès scientifique de 1894, *Compte rendu,* 8:19–30.

Gutierrez, Antonio, OP. "El Padre Arintero, escritor." *Ciencia tomista* 105, no. 4 (1978): 581–624.

Gwynn, Denis. "Sir Bertram Windle, 1858–1929: A Centenary Tribute." [*Irish*] *University Review* 2, no. 3/4 (1960): 48–58.

Haas, Reimund. "'… und an die geistlichen Personen und gläubigen Laien unserer Provinz!' 150 Jahre Kölner Provinzialkonzil von 1860." *Pastoralblatt für die Diözesen Aachen, Berlin, Essen, Hildesheim, Köln und Osnabrück* 63 (2011): 121–25.

Haeckel, Ernst. *Generelle Morphologie der Organismen: Allgemeine Grundzüge der Mechanischen Wissenschaft von den Entwickelten Formen der Organismen, begründet durch die Descendenz-Theorie. II: Allgemeine Entwicklungsgeschichte der Organismen.* Berlin: Reimer, 1866.

Haeckel, Ernst. *Natürliche Schöpfungsgeschichte.* Berlin: Reimer, 1868. 4th ed. 1873. Fourth ed. translated by E. Ray Lankester as *The History of Creation.* New York: Appleton, 1880.

Haeckel, Ernst. *Systematische Phylogenie der Wirbelthiere (Vertebrata).* Berlin: Reimer, 1894–95.

Hall, Robert A., Jr. *Antonio Fogazzaro.* Boston: Twayne, 1978.

Hamard, Pierre-Julien. "Antiquité de l'homme." In *Dictionnaire apologétique* (1889), 190–234.

Hamard, Pierre-Julien. "Darwinisme." In *Dictionnaire apologétique* (1889), 722–32.

Hamard, Pierre-Julien. "Homme: II. Origine de l'homme." In *Dictionnaire apologétique* (1889), 1397–412.

Hamard, Pierre-Julien. "Transformisme." In *Dictionnaire apologétique* (1889), 3087–104.

Hamard, Pierre-Julien. *L'Âge de la pierre et l'homme primitif.* Paris: Haton, 1883.

Hammerstein, Ludwig von. *Gottesbeweise und moderner Atheismus.* 6th ed. Trier: Paulinusdruckerei, 1903.

Hardon, John, SJ. *Catholic Lifetime Reading Plan.* New York: Doubleday, 1989.

Harper, Thomas, SJ. *Metaphysics of the School.* London: Macmillan, 1879–84.

Hart, Charles A. "Twenty-five Years of Thomism." *The New Scholasticism* 25, no. 1 (1951): 3–45.

Hartmann, Édouard von. *Wahrheit und Irrthum im Darwinismus: Eine Kritische Darstellung der organischen Entwickelungstheorie.* Berlin: Duncker, 1875.

Harty, John M. "Probabilism." In *The Catholic Encyclopedia,* 12:441–46.

Hauber, Ulrich. "Facts and Theories of Modern Biology as Viewed by a Catholic Priest." *American Ecclesiastical Review* 65, no. 2 (1921): 134–143.

Hauber, Ulrich. *A Catholic Opinion on the Evolution Controversy.* Rev. ed. Davenport, IA: St. Ambrose College, 1925.

Haught, John. "Evolution, In Nature and Catholic Thought." In *Rome has Spoken … : A Guide to Forgotten Papal Statements and How They Have Changed Through the Centuries,* edited by Maureen Fiedler and Linda Rabben, 180–84. New York: Crossroad, 1998.

Haught, John. "Darwin and Catholicism." In *Darwin and Evolutionary Thought,* edited by Michael Ruse, 485–92. Cambridge: Cambridge University Press, 2013.

Heberer, G. *Allgemeine Abstammungslehre.* Göttingen: Musterschmidt, 1949.

Hedley, John Cuthbert, OSB. "Evolution and Faith." *The Dublin Review* 69 (= n.s., 17), no. 33 (1871): 1–40.

Hedley, John Cuthbert, OSB. "Physical Science and Faith." *Dublin Review* 123 (= 4th ser.), no. 28 (1898): 241–61.

Hedley, John Cuthbert, OSB. "Physical Science and Faith. To the Editor of *The Tablet.*" *The Tablet* 93, no. 3062 (1899): 59.

Henninger, Joseph. "P. Wilhelm Schmidt SVD: 1868–1954, Eine biographische Skizze." *Anthropos* 51, no. 1/2 (1956): 19–60.

Herders Konversations-Lexikon, 3rd ed. "Abstammungslehre." 1:46–50.

Herders Konversations-Lexikon, 3rd ed. "Darwin." 2:1074.

Herders Konversations-Lexikon, 3rd ed. Freiburg im Breisgau: Herder, 1902–3.

Hernández, José Gregorio. *Elementos de filosofía*. Caracas: El Cojo, 1912.

Hertling, Georg von. "Entwicklungslehre." *Wetzer und Welte's Kirchenlexikon* (1886), 4:642–61.

Hertling, Georg von. *Die Hypothese Darwins mit Berücksichtigung neuerer Darstellungen geprüft*. Würzburg: Woerl, 1876.

Hervé, J. M. *Manuale theologiae dogmaticae*. 12th ed. Paris: Berche et Pagis, 1935.

Heuser, Herman J. Review of *Evolution and Dogma*, by John A. Zahm. *American Ecclesiastical Review* 14, no. 6 (1896): 568–70.

Hewit, Augustine. "Scriptural Questions." 1st series. *Catholic World* 40 (1884): 145–56, 316–26, 444–54, 635–50. 2nd series. *Catholic World* 44 (1886–87): 351–64, 445–59, 654–67, 741–55.

Hewit, Augustine. Review of *Special Dogmatic Theology*, by Adolphe Tanquerey. *Catholic World* 60, no. 359 (1895): 611–20.

Hildebrand, Dietrich von. *Trojan Horse in the City of God*. Chicago: Franciscan Herald Press, 1967.

Hofmann, James R. "Catholicism and Evolution: Polygenism and Original Sin." *Scientia et Fides*, 8, no. 2 (2020): 95–138, and 9, no. 1 (2021): 63–129.

Hofmann, James R. "Erich Wasmann, SJ: Natural Species and Catholic Polyphyletic Evolution during the Modernist Crisis." *Journal of Jesuit Studies* 7, no. 2 (2020): 244–62.

Hogan, Peter E. "Americanism and the Catholic University of America." *The Catholic Historical Review* 33, no. 2 (1947): 158–90.

Holing, John, SJ. "Irish Martyrs during the Reign of Elizabeth." From the Archives of the Irish College of Salamanca, before 1599. Published in *Spicilegium Ossoriense: Being a Collection of Original Letters and Papers Illustrative of the History of the Irish Church, from the Reformation to the Year 1800*, 1st ser., edited by Patrick Francis Moran, 82–109. Dublin: Kelly, 1874.

Holzammer, Johann Baptist. *Handbuch zur Biblischen Geschichte*. Freiburg im Breisgau: Herder, 1873.

Höpfl, Hildebrand, OSB. *Introductionis in sacros utriusque testamenti libros compendium*. Rome: Pontificia in Instituto Pii IX, 1922.

Howard, Edgar B. "Minutes of the International Symposium on Early Man Held at the Academy of Natural Sciences of Philadelphia. March 17th–20th, 1937. In Celebration of Its One Hundred and Twenty-Fifth Anniversary." *Proceedings of the Academy of Natural Sciences of Philadelphia* 89 (1937): 439–49.

Huarte, Gabriel, SJ. *De Deo creante et elevante*. 2nd ed. Rome: Editrice Pontificia Università Gregoriana, 1935.

Huerga, Alvaro. "La evolución: Clave y riesgo de la aventura intelectual arinteriana." *Studium* 7 (1967): 127–53.

Hummelauer, Franz von. *Der biblische Schöpfungsbericht: Ein exegetischer Versuch*. Freiburg im Breisgau: Herder, 1877.

Hummelauer, Franz von. *Commentarius in Genesim*. Paris: Lethielleux, 1895.

Hurel, Arnaud. *L'Abbé Breuil: Un Préhistorien dans le siècle*. Paris: Centre national de la recherche scientifique, 2014.

Hurter, Hugo. *Theologiae dogmaticae compendium*. 2nd ed. Innsbruck: Wagner, 1878.

Huxley, Julian. "Foreword." In George B. Barbour, *In the Field with Teilhard de Chardin*, 7–9. New York: Herder & Herder, 1965.

Huxley, Thomas Henry. "On the Anatomy and Affinities of the Family of the Medusæ." *Philosophical Transactions of the Royal Society of London* 139 (1849): 413–34.

Huxley, Thomas Henry. *Evidence as to Man's Place in Nature.* London: Williams & Norgate, 1863.

Huxley, Thomas Henry. "On the Methods and Results of Ethnology." *Fortnightly Review* 1 (1865): 257–77.

Huxley, Thomas Henry. "Anniversary Address of the President." *The Quarterly Journal of the Geological Society of London* 25, no. 1 (1869): xxviii–liii.

Huxley, Thomas Henry. "Scientific Education: Notes of an After-dinner Speech [1869]." In his *Collected Essays, III: Science and Education,* 111–33. New York: Appleton, 1897.

Huxley, Thomas Henry. "Address of Thomas Henry Huxley, President." In *Report of the 40th Meeting of the British Association for the Advancement of Science,* lxxiii–lxxxix. London: Murray, 1871. Republished and retitled "Biogenesis and Abiogenesis" in his *Critiques and Addresses,* 218–50. London: Macmillan, 1873.

Huxley, Thomas Henry. "Mr. Darwin's Critics." *The Contemporary Review* 18 (1871): 443–76.

Huxley, Thomas Henry. "Evolution. I. Evolution in Biology." In *Encyclopædia Britannica,* 9th ed., 8:744–51. Edinburgh: Black, 1875–89.

International Theological Commission. "Communion and Stewardship." In *International Theological Commission: Texts and Documents (1986–2007),* edited by Michael Sharkey and Thomas Weinandy, 319–351. San Francisco: Ignatius, 2009.

Isaye, Gaston, SJ. "Avertissement du 30 juin 1962 concernant les œuvres de Teilhard de Chardin." *Nouvelle revue théologique* 84, no. 8 (1962): 866–69.

James, Constantin. *Du Darwinisme, ou l'Homme-singe.* Paris: Plon, 1877. Republished as *Moïse et Darwin: L'Homme de la Genèse comparé à l'homme-singe, ou L'Enseignement religieux opposé à l'enseignement athée.* Paris: Desclée, De Brouwer, 1892.

Janssens, Alois. *God als Schepper.* 3rd ed. Antwerp: Standaard-boekhandel, 1937.

Janssens, Laurent. *Summa theologiae: t.7: De Hominis natura.* Freiburg im Breisgau: Herder, 1918.

Joannis, J. de. "Description de trois nouvelles espèces du genre *Eublemma* Hb. [Lép., Noctuidae]." *Bulletin de la Société entomologique de France* 14, no. 9 (1909): 167–71.

John Paul II. "Created Things Have a Legitimate Autonomy." General Audience, April 16, 1986. In *God, Father and Creator: A Catechesis on the Creed,* 216–220. Boston: Pauline Books & Media, 1996.

John Paul II. "Ad Pontificiae academiae scientiarum sodales." *Acta Apostolicae Sedis* (1997), 89:186–90. Translated as "Message to Pontifical Academy of Sciences on Evolution." In *Origins: CNS [Catholic News Service] Documentary Service* 26, no. 25 (1996): 414–16.

Johnson, H. J. T. "Leo XIII, Newman, and the Inerrancy of Scripture." *The Downside Review* 69, no. 218 (1951): 411–27.

Jones, Spencer. *England and the Holy See.* London: Longmans, Green, 1902.

Journet, Charles. *Petit catéchisme sur les origines du monde.* St. Maurice: St-Augustin, 1950.

Jousset, Pierre. *Évolution et transformisme: Des Origines de l'état sauvage, étude d'anthropologie.* Paris: Baillière, 1889.

Jousset, Pierre. *L'Homme-singe (Pithecanthropus erectus) et la doctrine évolutionniste.* Paris: Baillière, 1901.

Jugie, Martin. Review of *Nouvelle Théologie dogmatique,* by Jules Souben. *Échos d'Orient* 7, no. 48 (1904): 316–17.

Julian the Apostate. Fragment of a letter to a priest. In *Works* 2:297–339. Cambridge, MA: Harvard University Press, 2014.

Junglas, Johannes Peter. *Die Lehre der Kirche.* Bonn: Buchgemeinde, 1936.

Kames, Henry Home, Lord. *Sketches of the History of Man.* Dublin: Williams, 1774–75.

Katholieke Encyclopaedie, edited by Jan Sassen, OP, and Titus Brandsma, OCarm. Amsterdam: Joost van den Vondel, 1933–39.

Keane, Augustus Henry. "Ethnology." In *Encyclopedia of Religion & Ethics*, edited by James Hastings et al., 5:522–32. Edinburgh: T&T Clark, 1913–27.

Kellogg, Vernon L. *Darwinism To-day*. New York: Holt, 1908.

Kelter, Irving A. "The Refusal to Accommodate: Jesuit Exegetes and the Copernican System." *The Sixteenth Century Journal* 26, no. 2 (1995): 273–83.

Kemp, Kenneth W. "Science, Theology, and Monogenesis." *American Catholic Philosophical Quarterly* 85, no. 2 (2011): 217–36.

Kemp, Kenneth W. "With Friends Like Those, Who Needs Enemies: How Aggressive Atheism Impedes the Acceptance of Evolutionary Biology." *Roczniki filozoficzne* 60, no. 4 (2012): 29–39.

Kemp, Kenneth W. "Teilhard de Chardin, the 'Six Propositions,' and the Holy Office." *Zygon* 54, no. 4 (2019): 932–53.

Kemp, Kenneth W. "God, Evolution, and the Body of Adam." *Scientia et Fides* 8, no. 2 (2020): 139–72.

Kemp, Kenneth W. *The War That Never Was: Evolution and Christian Theology*. Eugene, OR: Cascade, 2020.

Kemp, Kenneth W. "*Humani generis* & Evolution: A Report from the Archives." *Scientia et Fides* 11, no. 1 (2023): 7–29.

Kennard, A. S. "The Early Digs in Kent's Hole, Torquay, and Mrs. Cazalet." *Proceedings of the Geologists' Association* 56 (1945): 156–213.

Keogh, James (?). "The Immutability of the Species." *Catholic World* 10, no. 56, 57, and 59 (1869–70): 252–67, 332–46, and 656–73.

King, Thomas M., SJ. "Appendix: Teilhard and Piltdown." in *Teilhard and the Unity of Knowledge*, edited by King and James F. Salmon, SJ, 159–69. New York: Paulist Press, 1983.

King, William. "The Reputed Fossil Man of the Neanderthal." *Quarterly Journal of Science* 1 (1864): 88–97.

Kirchliches Handlexikon: Ein Nachschlagebuch über das Gesamtgebiet der Theologie und ihrer Hilfswissenschaften, edited by Michael Buchberger. Freiburg im Breisgau: Herder, 1907.

Kirwan, Charles de [under pseud. Jean d'Estienne]. "Transformisme et la discussion libre." *Revue des questions scientifiques* 25, no. 1–2 (1889): 76–142 and 373–420.

Kirwan, Charles de. "De l'Évolution progressive de la connaissance depuis les organismes primaires jusqu'à l'homme." In Congrès scientifique de 1897, *Compte rendu*, 9:79–99, with discussion at 7–11.

Kirwan, Charles de. Review of *Hétérogénie, transformisme et Darwinisme: Problème de l'espèce*, by Louis de Casamajor. *Revue des questions scientifiques* 44 (= 2nd ser., 14), no. 3 (1898): 296–99.

Kirwan, Charles de. "Où en est l'Évolutionnisme?" *Revue thomiste* 9 (1901): 379–406 and 540–568.

Klaatsch, Hermann. "Entstehung und Entwicklung des Menschengeschlechtes." In *Weltall und Menschheit: Geschichte der Erforschung der Natur und der Verwertung der Naturkräfte im Dienste der Völker*, edited by Hans Kraemer, 2:1–338. Berlin: Bong, 1902–4.

Kleutgen, Joseph. *Philosophie der Vorzeit*. Münster: Theissing, 1860–63.

Knabenbauer, Joseph. "Glaube und Descendenztheorie." *Stimmen aus Maria-Laach* 13, no. 1 and 2 (1877): 69–86 and 121–38.

Knigge, Adolph. *Über den Umgang mit Menschen*. Hannover: Schmidt, 1788. Translated into Italian by R. A. as *Della condotta da tenersi nella società*. Milan: Stella, 1816.

Knox, Ronald, translator. "The Encyclical 'Humani Generis.'" *The Tablet* 196, no. 5754 (September 2, 1950): 187–90.

Kobel, Jerome. "The Evolution of Man—A Brief Outline of the Opinions for and against the Theory of Anthropological Transformism." *Report of the Fifteenth Annual Meeting* [of the Franciscan Educational Conference], *Marathon, Wisconsin, June 30th, July 1st, July 2nd, 1933*, 47–122.

Koppers, Wilhelm. "Evoluzionismo." In *Enciclopedia cattolica*, 5:897–914. Vatican City: Ente per l'Enciclopedia cattolica e per il Libro cattolico, 1949–54.

Kreling, Gerardus, OP. "Homo (C)." In *De Katholieke Encyclopaedie*, 13:473–74.

Kuhn, Johannes von. "Adam." In Wetzer, *Kirchenlexikon*, 1:92–94.

Kuiper, A. "Stamt de mens van de aap af?" *De Volkskrant*, May 15, 1954, 12.

Kuiper, A. "Stamt de mens van de aap af? Dr Kuipers antwoordt dr Van Nieuwenhoven." *De Volkskrant*, June 1, 1954, 9.

La Peyrère, Isaac. *Relation du Groenland*. Paris: Courbe, 1647.

La Peyrère, Isaac. *Præ-adamitæ sive Exercitatio super versibus duodecimio, decimotertio, & decimoquarto, capitis quinti Epistolæ D. Pauli ad romanos*. 1655. Translated as *Men before Adam: A Discourse upon the Twelfth, Thirteenth, and Fourteenth Verses of the Fifth Chapter of the Epistle of the Apostle Paul to the Romans, By which are Prov'd, that the First Men were Created before Adam*. 1655.

La Peyrère, Isaac. *Systema theologicum: Ex præadamitarum hypothesi*. 1655. Translated as *A Theological Systeme: Upon that Presupposition, That Men were before Adam*. 1655.

La Peyrère, Isaac. *Suite des lettres à Monsieur le Comte de la Suze pour l'obliger par raison à se faire catholique*. Paris: Piget, 1662.

Lacroix, Robert. *L'Origine de l'âme humaine*. Québec: Action catholique, 1945.

Lactantius. *Divinae institutiones*. Translated by Mary Francis McDonald as *The Divine Institutes*. Washington, DC: The Catholic University of America Press, 2017.

Lagrange, Marie-Joseph, OP. "Avant-propos." *Revue Biblique* 1 (1892): 1–16.

Lagrange, Marie-Joseph, OP. *M. Loisy et le modernisme. À Propos des "Mémoires."* Juvisy: Cerf, 1932.

Lamarck, Jean-Baptiste. *Philosophie zoologique*. Paris: Dentu, 1809. Translated by Hugh Elliot as *Zoological Philosophy*. Chicago: University of Chicago Press, 1984.

Lamarck, Jean-Baptiste. *Histoire naturelle des animaux sans vertèbres*. Paris: Verdière, 1815–22.

Lambert, Dominique. "Un Acteur majeur de la réception du darwinisme à Louvain: Henry de Dorlodot." *Revue théologique de Louvain* 40, no. 4 (2009): 500–530.

Laminne, Jacques-Joseph. "Cosmologie matérialiste." *La Revue apologétique* 5, no. 1 (1903): 1–19.

Laminne, Jacques-Joseph. "Que nous enseigne le Ier Chapitre de la Genèse?" *La Revue apologétique* 5, no. 6 (1903): 321–42.

Laminne, Jacques-Joseph. "Psychologie matérialiste." *La Revue apologétique* 5, no. 11–12 (1904): 651–69 and 740–58.

Laminne, Jacques-Joseph. *L'Homme d'après Haeckel*. Paris: Bloud, 1905.

Laminne, Jacques-Joseph. "Morale matérialiste." *La Revue apologétique* 6, no. 11 (1905): 659–76.

Laminne, Jacques-Joseph. *L'Univers d'après Haeckel*. Paris: Bloud, 1905.

Laminne, Jacques-Joseph. *La Philosophie de l'inconnaissable [et] La Théorie de l'évolution: Étude critique sur les "Premiers Principes" de Herbert Spencer*. Brussels: Dewit, 1907.

Laminne, Jacques-Joseph. "L'Idée d'évolution chez Saint Augustin." *Revue des sciences philosophiques et théologiques* 2, no. 3 (1908): 506–21.

Laminne, Jacques-Joseph. *La Situation actuelle du catholicisme en face de la science*. Brussels: L'Action Catholique, 1908.

Laminne, Jacques-Joseph. Review of *L'Évolution créatrice*, by Henri Bergson. *La Revue Apologétique* 10, no. 3–4 (1908): 253–61.

Landucci, Giovanni. "De Filippi, Filippo." In Tort, *Dictionnaire du darwinisme*, 1:1134–39.

Laplace, Pierre-Simon. *Système du monde*. Paris: Cercle-Social, 1796.

Laplanche, François. "Hamard, Pierre-Julien." In his *Les Sciences religieuses: Le XIXe siècle 1800–1914. Dictionnaire du monde dans la France contemporaine*, 316. Paris: Beauchesne, 1996.

Larrañaga, Victoriano. "El Cardenal Zeferino González y Su Santidad León XIII." *Estudios bíblicos* 7, no. 1 (1948): 77–114.

Larson, Edward. *Summer for the Gods: The Scopes Trial and America's Continuing Debate over Science and Religion*. New York: Basic Books, 1997.

Lartet, Édouard. "Note sur un grand Singe fossile qui se rattache au groupe des Singes supérieurs." *Comptes rendus hebdomadaires des séances de l'Académie des sciences* 43 (1856): 219–23.

Lateran Council V. *Apostolici regiminis*. December 19, 1513. Reprinted in Alberigo, *Conciliorum decreta*, 581–82.

Laurence, William L. "China Cave a Lead to 'Missing Link.'" *New York Times*, March 20, 1937, 9.

Laurent, Goulven. *Paléontologie et évolution en France de 1800 à 1860: Histoire des idées de Cuvier et Lamarck à Darwin*. Paris: Comité des travaux historiques et scientifiques, 1987.

Laurent, Goulven. "Les Catholiques face à la géologie et à la paléontologie de 1800 à 1880." In *Christianisme et science: Études*, prepared by the Association française d'histoire religieuse contemporaine, 77–100. Paris: Vrin, 1989.

Laurent, Goulven. "Albert Gaudry et la paléontologie évolutive." In *Le Muséum au premier siècle de son histoire*, edited by Claude Blanckaert et al., 295–311. Paris: Muséum national d'histoire naturelle, 1997.

Laurent, Goulven. "Gaudry, Albert." In Tort, *Dictionnaire du darwinisme*, 2:1802–5.

Le Guichaoua, Paul. "Les Conditions philosophiques de l'évolution." *Revue néo-scolastique de philosophie* 18, no. 70 (1911): 197–211.

Le Guichaoua, Paul. "Réponse à M. Bouyssonie." *Revue néo-scolastique de philosophie* 18, no. 72 (1911): 578–88.

Le Roy, Édouard. "Sur Quelques Objections adressées à la nouvelle philosophie." *Revue de métaphysique et de morale* 9, no. 3 and 4 (1901): 292–327 and 407–32.

Le Roy, Édouard. *L'Exigence idéaliste et le fait de l'évolution*. Paris: Boivin, 1927.

Le Roy, Édouard. *La Pensée intuitive*. Paris: Boivin, 1929–30.

Le Roy, Édouard. *Le Problème de Dieu*. Paris: L'Artisan du livre, 1930.

Le Roy, Édouard. *Les Origines humaines et l'évolution de l'intelligence*. Paris: Boivin, 1928.

LeConte, Joseph. *Evolution and its Relation to Religious Thought*. New York: Appleton, 1888.

Leeming, Bernard, SJ. Review of *Tractatus de Deo creante and elevante*, by Charles Boyer. *Gregorianum* 15, no. 2 (1934): 291–94.

Lennerz, Heinrich. "Quid theologo dicendum de polygenismo?" *Gregorianum* 29, no. 3/4 (1948): 417–34.

Lenormant, François. *Les Origines de l'histoire d'après la Bible et les traditions des peuples orientaux*. 2nd ed. Paris: Maisonneuve, 1880–84. Translated by Mary Lockwood as *The Beginnings of History according to the Bible and the Traditions of Oriental Peoples: From the Creation of Man to the Deluge*. New York: Scribner's Sons, 1881.

Leo XIII. *Aeterni patris*. Acta Sanctae Sedis 12 (1879): 97–115.

Leo XIII. *Providentissimus Deus*. Acta Sanctae Sedis 26 (1893–94): 269–92.

Leo XIII. *Officiorum ac munerum*. Acta Sanctae Sedis 30 (1897–98): 39–53.

Leo XIII. *Testem benevolentiae*. Acta Sanctae Sedis 31 (1898–99): 470–79.

Leo XIII. *Vigilantiae studiique. Acta Sanctae Sedis* 35 (1902–3): 234–38. Translated as "On the Institution of a Commission for Biblical Studies" in *The Scripture Documents: An Anthology of Official Catholic Teachings*, edited by Dean Philip Bechard, 62–66. Collegeville, MN: Liturgical Press, 2002.

Leroy, Dalmace, OP. *L'Évolution des espèces organiques.* Paris: Perrin, 1887.

Leroy, Dalmace, OP. "Discussion sur le mode de la création du premier homme (Correspondance)." *La Science catholique* 6, no. 3 (1892): 241–47.

Leroy, Dalmace, OP. *L'Évolution restreinte aux espèces organiques.* Paris: Delhomme & Briguet, 1891.

Leroy, Dalmace, OP. "Correspondance au R. P. Directeur de la *Revue thomiste.*" *Revue thomiste* 1, no. 4 (1893): 532–35.

Leroy, Dalmace, OP. "Une lettre de soumission." *Le Monde* 39, no. 62 (March 4, 1895): 2–3. Also in Brandi, "Evoluzione e domma," 49.

Leroy, Dalmace, OP. *Lettre à M. l'abbé A. Farges.* Privately published, 1898.

Leroy, Dalmace, OP. Review of *Les Origines*, by Jean Guibert. *Revue thomiste* 7, no. 6 (1899): 735–41.

Leroy, Dalmace, OP. "L'Homme-singe et la doctrine évolutionniste: Réponse à Dr P. Jousset." *Annales de philosophie chrétienne* 142 (1901): 516–35.

Leroy, Dalmace, OP. "L'Évolutionnisme: Fondé sur une ignorance." *Annales de philosophie chrétienne* 144 (1902): 166–98.

Lessona, Michele. "Filippo De Filippi." *Nuova antologia di lettere, arti e scienze* 6, no. 12 (1867): 631–60. Republished in his *Naturalisti italiani*, 161–206. Rome: Sommaruga, 1884.

Levasseur, Stéphane. Review of *L'Évolution et le dogme*, by John A. Zahm. *Annales de philosophie chrétienne* 137, no. 6 (1899): 729–30.

Levie, Jean. *The Bible, Word of God in Words of Men.* New York: Kenedy, 1962.

Lewis, Charlton T., and Charles Short. *A Latin Dictionary.* Oxford: Oxford University Press, 1879.

Lexikon für Theologie und Kirche, edited by Michael Buchberger. Freiberg im Breisgau: Herder, 1931.

Liénart, Achille. "Le Chrétien devant les progrès de la science." *Études* 255, no. 11 (1947): 289–300. Translated as "Science and the Bible." *Commonweal* 50 (1949): 241–43 and 265–67.

Linden, Jakob, SJ [under pseud. Jakob Schmitz]. *Kleine Apologetik.* Regensburg: Pustet, 1895.

Linnaeus, Carolus. *Systema naturae.* Leyden: Haak, 1735. 10th ed. Stockholm: Salvius, 1758.

Littré, Émile. *Dictionnaire de la langue française.* Paris: Hachette, 1874.

Livingstone, David N. *Darwin's Forgotten Defenders: The Encounter Between Evangelical Theology and Evolutionary Thought.* Grand Rapids, MI: Eerdmans, 1987.

Livingstone, David N. *Adam's Ancestors: Race, Religion, and the Politics of Human Origins.* Baltimore: Johns Hopkins University Press, 2008.

Lodiel, Desideratus. "Quelques Appréciations récentes des arguments transformistes." *Études religieuses, philosophiques, historiques et littéraires* 57 (1892): 573–96.

Loriol, P. de. "Note sur quelques stellérides du Santonien d'Abou-Roach." *Bulletin de l'Institut égyptien* 5th ser., 2, no. 2 (1909): 169–84.

Lucretius. *De rerum natura.* Translated by W. H. D. Rouse as *On the Nature of Things.* Revised by Martin F. Smith. Cambridge, MA: Harvard University Press, 1924.

Lustig, A. J. "Ants and the Nature of Nature in August Forel, Erich Wasmann, and William Morton Wheeler." In *The Moral Authority of Nature*, edited by Lorraine Daston and Fernando Vidal, 282–307. Chicago: University of Chicago Press, 2004.

Lyell, Charles. "On the Occurrence of Works of Human Art in Post-Pliocene Deposits." *Report of the 29th Meeting of the British Association for the Advancement of Science: Notices and Abstracts of Miscellaneous Communications to the Section*. London: Murray, 1860.

Lyell, Charles. *Principles of Geology*. London: Murray, 1830. 7th ed. 1847. 9th ed. 1853. 10th ed. 1867–68. Citations to the *Principles*, unless otherwise noted, are to the 1st edition.

Lyell, Charles. *The Geological Evidence of the Antiquity of Man*. London: Murray, 1863.

Lyon, John. "Immediate Reactions to Darwin: The English Catholic Press' First Reviews of the 'Origin of the Species.'" *Church History* 41, no. 1 (1972): 78–93.

Lyon, John. "The Search for Fossil Man: Cinq Personnages à la Recherche du Temps Perdu." *Isis* 61, no. 1 (1970): 68–84.

M., H. (probably Hermann Muckermann, SJ). Review of *Die moderne Biologie und die Entwicklungstheorie*, by Erich Wasmann. *The Fortnightly Review* 11, no. 45 (1904): 705–9.

M., H. (probably Hermann Muckermann, SJ). "Natural Selection or Organic Evolution?" *Catholic Fortnightly Review* 12, no. 2 (1905): 17–21.

Macchi, Mauro. "Non è Possibile." *Il libero pensiero: Giornale dei razionalisti* 2, no. 14 (1867): 221–22.

MacCurdy, George Grant, ed. *Early Man as Depicted by Leading Authorities at the International Symposium, The Academy of Natural Sciences, Philadelphia, March 1937*. Philadelphia: Lippincott, 1937.

Maher, Michael. *Psychology*. 1st ed. London: Longmans, Green, 1890. 4th ed. 1900.

Maisonneuve, Paul. "Création et évolution." In Congrès scientifique de 1891, *Compte rendu*, 8:36–61.

Malbranche, Alexandre François. "Le Transformisme, ses origines, ses principes, ses impossibilités." In *Précis analytique des travaux de l'Académie des sciences, belles-lettres et arts de Rouen pendant l'année 1872–73*, 91–162. Rouen: Boissel, 1873. Republished as a book. Rouen: Boissel, 1874.

Malone, Richard. "Historical Review of the Rosmini Case." *L'Osservatore Romano: Weekly Edition in English*. July 25, 2001, 9–10.

Mano, Camille. "Métaphysique et transformisme." *Revue du clergé français* 31 (1902): 207–10.

Mansi, Joannes Dominicus, et al., *Sacrorum conciliorum nova et amplissima collectio*. Paris: Welter, 1901–27.

Mansini, Guy, OSB. *"What is a Dogma?": The Meaning and Truth of Dogma in Edouard Le Roy and his Scholastic Opponents*. Rome: Editrice Pontificia Università Gregoriana, 1985.

Marcora, Carlo, ed. *Corrispondenza Fogazzaro–Bonomelli*. Milan: Vita e Pensiero, 1968.

Marcozzi, Vittorio, SJ. *Le origini dell'uomo*. Rome: A.V.E., 1942. 2nd ed., 1944.

Marcozzi, Vittorio, SJ. *Evoluzione o creazione?: Le origini dell'uomo* 3rd ed. Milan: Ambrosiana, 1948.

Marcozzi, Vittorio, SJ. "Le origini dell'uomo: Insufficienza scientifica del poligenismo specifico." *L'Osservatore Romano*. April 1, 1951, 3–4.

Marcozzi, Vittorio, SJ. "Poligenesi ed evoluzione nelle origini dell'uomo." *Gregorianum* 29, no. 3/4 (1948): 343–91.

Maritain, Jacques. "L'Évolutionnisme de M. Bergson." *Revue de philosophie* 19 (1911): 467–540.

Maritain, Jacques. "Philosophical Co-Operation and Intellectual Justice." *The Modern Schoolman* 22, no. 1 (1944): 1–15.

Maritain, Jacques. *Bergsonian Philosophy and Thomism*. Translated by Mabelle L. and J. Gordon Andison. New York: Philosophical Library, 1955.

Marselli, Niccola. *L'origini dell'umanità*. Turin: Loescher, 1879.

Marselli, Niccola. *Le grandi razze dell'umanità*. Turin: Loescher, 1880.

Martel, Louis-Charles [under pseud. E. Lefranc]. *Les Conflits de la science et de la Bible*. Paris: Nourry, 1906.

Martens, P. "In Memoriam: Victor Grégoire." *Bulletin de la Société Royale de Botanique de Belgique / Bulletin van de Koninklijke Belgische Botanische Vereniging* 72, no. 1 (1939): 8–14.

Martinelli, Pietro, trans. *L'esegesi del sig. Loisy: Le dottrine, i metodi.* Siena: San Bernardino, 1903. A translation of Bouvier, *L'Exégèse de M. Loisy.*

Martinelli, Pietro. *I primi tre capitoli della Sacra Bibbia annotati secondo il sistema delle apparenze.* San Quirico d'Orcia: Turbanti, 1906.

Martínez Vigil, Ramón. *La creación, la redención y la Iglesia ante la ciencia.* Madrid: Del Amo, 1892.

Marx, Karl. *Das Kapital.* Hamburg: Meissner, 1867.

Masson, Th. "L'Église est-elle l'unique salut du monde?" *Synthèses: Revue européene* (1950).

Matiegka, Jindřich. "Monogenismus a Polygenismus, Monofyletismus a Polyfyletismus, Monogonismus a Polygonismus." *Anthropologie: Časopis Věnovaný Fyzické Antropologii* 1, no. 4 (1923): 298–322.

Mattiussi, Guido, SJ. "L'evoluzione è possibile?" *La Scuola cattolica* 16 (1898): 445–54; 17 (1899): 116–31, 305–16, 504–15; and 18 (1899): 98–111. Republished as a book. Monza: Artigianelli, 1899.

Mattiussi, Guido, SJ. "Le speranze svanite del Darwinismo." *La Scuola cattolica* 4th ser., 16 (1909): 46–65, 153–71, 441–60, 578–89, and 714–27.

Maupied, François-Louis-Michel. *Dieu, l'homme, et le monde connus par les trois premiers chapitres de la Genèse.* Paris: Méquignon junior, 1851.

Mayr, Ernst. *Systematics and the Origin of Species from the Viewpoint of a Zoologist.* New York: Columbia University Press, 1942.

Mayr, Ernst. "Taxonomic Categories in Fossil Hominids." *Cold Spring Harbor Symposia on Quantitative Biology* 15 (1950): 109–18.

Mazzella, Camillo. *De Deo creante.* Ed. altera. Rome: Polyglotta, 1880.

McAvoy, Thomas T. *The Americanist Heresy in Roman Catholicism, 1895–1900.* Notre Dame, IN: University of Notre Dame Press, 1963.

McCarthy, Joseph M. *Pierre Teilhard de Chardin: A Comprehensive Bibliography.* New York: Garland, 1981.

McCorkell, E. J., CSB. "Bertram Coghill Alan Windle, FRS, FSA, KSG, MD, LLD, PhD, ScD." *Canadian Catholic Historical Association Report* 25 (1958): 53–58.

McDonald, Walter. *Reminiscences of a Maynooth Professor.* Edited by Denis Gwynn. London: Cape, 1925.

McDonald, Walter. *Motion: Its Origin and Conservation.* Dublin: Browne and Nolan, 1898.

McDonald, Walter. "The Nature of Species." In Congrès scientifique de 1900, *Akten,* 214–15. [NB: The spelling of the author's name (as "MacDonald") in the *Akten* is incorrect.]

McElrath, Damian. *Richard Simpson, 1820–1876: A Study in XIXth Century English Liberal Catholicism.* Louvain: Publications universitaires de Louvain, 1972.

McMullin, Ernan. "How Should Cosmology Relate to Theology?" In *The Sciences and Theology in the Twentieth Century,* edited by Arthur Peacocke, 17–57. Notre Dame, IN: University of Notre Dame Press, 1981.

McMullin, Ernan, ed. *Evolution and Creation.* Notre Dame, IN: University of Notre Dame Press, 1985.

McMullin, Ernan. "Galileo on Science and Scripture." In *The Cambridge Companion to Galileo,* edited by Peter Machamer, 271–347. Cambridge, MA: Cambridge University Press, 1998.

Medawar, Peter. Review of *The Phenomenon of Man,* by Pierre Teilhard de Chardin. *Mind,* n.s., 70, no. 277 (1961): 99–106.

Mejzlík, Jan. "Jak pohlížíme na nauku o evoluci v biologii?" *Museum: Časopis bohoslovců českoslovanských* 40 (1906): 12–16, 57–62, 113–19, and 173–80.

Mencken, H. L. "The Tennessee Circus." *Baltimore Evening Sun,* June 15, 1925, 2nd sec., 17.

Mendive, José. *La Religión católica vindicada de las imposturas racionalistas.* Madrid: Gutenberg, 1883.

Mercalli, Giuseppe. *Vulcani e fenomeni vulcanici in Italia.* Milan: Vallardi, 1883.

Mercier, Désiré-Joseph. "Rapport de Mgr Mercier, troisième commissaire." *Bulletins de la classe des lettres et des sciences morales et politiques et de la classe des beaux-arts* [of the Académie royale de Belgique] 3rd ser., 42, no. 8 (1907): 261–67.

Messenger, Ernest Charles. Bibliography to "The Origin of Man in the Book of Genesis." In *God, Man, and the Universe: A Christian Answer to Modern Materialism,* edited by Jacques de Bivort de La Saudée, 147–67. New York: Kenedy, 1953.

Messenger, Ernest Charles. *Evolution and Theology: The Problem of Man's Origin.* London: Burns Oates and Washbourne, 1931.

Messenger, Ernest Charles. *Theology and Evolution: A Sequel to Evolution and Theology.* Westminster: Newman, 1949.

Meunier, Fernand. "Les Insectes paléozoïques & mésozoïques." Congrès scientifique de 1897, *Compte rendu,* 7:88–90.

Michelis, Friedrich. "Darwins Theorie der Entstehung der Arten im Thier- und Pflanzenreiche durch natürliche Züchtung theologisch und naturwissenschaftlich geprüft." *Natur und Offenbarung* 7 (1861): 261–71, 313–25, and 374–86.

Migne, Jacques-Paul. *Patrologia Latina.* Paris: Migne, 1844–1902.

Mill, John Stuart. *Principles of Political Economy.* London: Parker, 1848.

Miller, Garrit S. "The Controversy over Human 'Missing Links.'" In *Annual Report of the Board of Regents of the Smithsonian Institution for 1928,* 413–65. Washington, DC: US Government Printing Office, 1929.

Miller, Kenneth R. *Finding Darwin's God: A Scientist's Search for Common Ground between God and Evolution.* New York: Perennial, 2007.

Mitchell, Peter Charles. "Evolution." In *Encyclopædia Britannica.* 11th ed. 10:22–37. Cambridge, MA: Cambridge University Press, 1910.

Mivart, St. George Jackson. "Difficulties of the Theory of Natural Selection." *The Month* 11 (1869): 35–53, 134–53, and 274–89.

Mivart, St. George Jackson. Review of *The Descent of Man,* by Charles Darwin. *The Quarterly Review* 131 (1871): 47–90.

Mivart, St. George Jackson. *On the Genesis of Species.* London: Macmillan, 1871. 2nd ed. 1871. New York: Appleton, 1871. Citations here are from the American edition, the text (but not the pagination) of which corresponds to the first, pre-*Descent,* English edition.

Mivart, St. George Jackson. "Evolution and its Consequences: A Reply to Professor Huxley." *The Contemporary Review* 19 (1872): 168–97.

Mivart, St. George Jackson. *Man and Apes.* London: Hardwicke, 1873.

Mivart, St. George Jackson. *Contemporary Evolution.* London: King, 1876.

Mivart, St. George Jackson. *Lessons from Nature as Manifested in Mind and Matter.* London: Murray, 1876.

Mivart, St. George Jackson. "Modern Catholics and Scientific Freedom." *The Nineteenth Century* 18, no. 101 (1885): 30–47.

Mivart, St. George Jackson. *Introduction générale à l'étude de la nature: Cours professé à l'Université de Louvain.* Louvain: Peeters, 1891.

Mivart, St. George Jackson. "Happiness in Hell." *The Nineteenth Century* 32, no. 190 (1892): 899–919.

Mivart, St. George Jackson. "The Happiness in Hell: A Rejoinder." *The Nineteenth Century* 33, no. 192 (1893): 320–38.

Mivart, St. George Jackson. "Last Words on the Happiness in Hell." *The Nineteenth Century* 33, no. 194 (1893): 637–51.

Mivart, St. George Jackson. "The Index and my Articles on Hell." *The Nineteenth Century* 34, no. 202 (1893): 979–90.

Mivart, St. George Jackson. "Some Reminiscences of Thomas Henry Huxley." *The Nineteenth Century* 42, no. 250 (1897): 985–98.

Mivart, St. George Jackson. "The Continuity of Catholicism." *The Nineteenth Century* 47, no. 275 (1900): 51–72.

Mivart, St. George Jackson. "Some Recent Catholic Apologists." *Fortnightly Review* 67, no. 397 (1900): 24–44.

Mivart, St. George Jackson. *Under the Ban.* New York: Tucker, 1900.

Moleschott, Jacopo. "Cenno biografico sul socio prof. Filippo De Filippi." *Atti della Reale accademia delle scienze di Torino* 2 (1867): 431–53.

Molisso, G. "La figura di Giuseppe Mercalli come docente del Regio liceo Vittorio Emanuele." *Miscellanea INGV* [Istituto Nazionale di Geofisica e Vulcanologia] 24 (2014): 133–36.

Mollison, Theodor. "Die Abstammung des Menschen." *Die Naturwissenschaften: Wochenschrift für die Fortschritte der Naturwissenschaft, der Medizin und der Technik* 9, no. 8 (1921): 128–40.

Molloy, Gerald. "Geology and Revelation." *Irish Ecclesiastical Record* 3 (1866–67): 124–34, 241–61, 358–74, and 448–67; 4 (1867–68): 49–66, 169–87, 326–41, and 373–85; 5 (1866–67): 49–73 and 193–223. Revised and republished as *Geology and Revelation.* London: Longmans, Green, 1870.

Monchamp, Georges. "Rapport de Mgr Monchamp, premier commissaire." *Bulletins de la classe des lettres et des sciences morales et politiques et de la classe des beaux-arts* [of the Académie royale de Belgique] 3rd ser., 42, no. 8 (1904): 195–219.

Monsabré, Jacques-Marie-Louis. *Exposition du dogme catholique: Œuvre de Dieu, Carême 1875.* 9th ed. Paris: Année Dominicaine, 1890.

Montenat, Christian. *Une Famille de géologues: Les Lapparent: Un Siècle d'histoire et d'aventures de la géologie.* Paris: Vuibert, 2008.

Month, The. Review of *On the Genesis of Species,* by St. George Mivart. 14, no. 17–18 (1871): 526–29.

Month, The. Review of *Psychology,* by Michael Maher. 71, no. 319 (1891): 135–37.

Month, The. Review of *Nouvelle théologie dogmatique,* by Jules Souben. 106, no. 495 (1905): 326–28.

Monzón y Martín, Bienvenido. "El Darwinismo—Censura sinodal y condenación del discurso herético leído en el Instituto de Granada en la inauguración de curso 1872 a 1873." *La Cruz, Revista religiosa de España y demás países católicos* 1 (1873): 296–315.

Moore, James R. *The Post-Darwinian Controversies: A Study of the Protestant Struggle to Come to Terms with Darwin in Great Britain and America, 1870–1900.* Cambridge, MA: Cambridge University Press, 1979.

Moran, John, SJ. *Alpha et Omega: Theses quaedam selectae de Deo uno et trino.* Worcester: Harrigan, 1935.

Moro, Anton Lazzaro. *De' crostacei e degli altri marini corpi che si truovano su' monti.* Venice: Monti, 1740.

Moroni, Gaetano. *Dizionario di erudizione storico-ecclesiastica da san Pietro sino ai nostri giorni.* Venice: Emiliana, 1840–79.

Moroni, Gaetano. *Indice generale alfabetico delle materie del Dizionario di erudizione storico-ecclesiastica.* Venice: Emiliana, 1878.

Morris, John. Review of *On the Origin of Species,* by Charles Darwin. *The Dublin Review* 48, no. 95 (1860): 50–81.

Morrison, John L. "A History of American Catholic Opinion on the Theory of Evolution, 1859–1950." PhD diss., University of Missouri, 1951.

Morrison, John L. "American Catholics and the Crusade Against Evolution." *Records of the American Catholic Historical Society of Philadelphia* 64, no. 2 (1953): 59–71.

Morrison, John L. "William Seton: A Catholic Darwinist." *The Review of Politics* 21, no. 3 (1959): 566–84.

Mortillet, Gabriel. *Le Préhistorique: Antiquité de l'homme*. Paris: Reinwald, 1883.

Motherway, Thomas J. "The Creation of Eve in Catholic Tradition." *Theological Studies* 1, no. 2 (1940): 97–116.

Motherway, Thomas J. "Theological Opinion on the Evolution of Man." *Theological Studies* 5, no. 2 (1944): 198–221.

Mourret, Fernand. *Le Concile du Vatican, d'après des documents inédits*. Paris: Bloud et Gay, 1919.

Muckermann, Hermann, SJ. *Attitude of Catholics towards Darwinism and Evolution*. St. Louis: Herder, 1906.

Muckermann, Hermann, SJ. *The Humanizing of the Brute: or, The Essential Difference between the Human and Animal Soul proved from their Specific Activities*. St. Louis: Herder, 1906.

Muckermann, Hermann, SJ. "Evolution, History and Scientific Foundation of." In *The Catholic Encyclopedia*, 5:655–70.

Muller, Camille. "L'Encyclique 'Humani Generis' et les problèmes scientifiques." *Synthèses* 5, no. 57 (1951). Republished, with some slight changes, as a booklet. Louvain: Nauwelaerts, 1951.

Muller, Camille. "La Science et la foi." In *Problèmes d'adaptation dans la chrétienté actuelle*, edited by Robert Waelkens, 73–103. Louvain: Nauwelaerts, 1949. Translated by Hilary Crusz as *Science and Faith, Co-existence or Synthesis?* Louvain: Nauwelaerts, 1962.

Müller, Johannes. *Handbuch der Physiologie des Menschen für Vorlesungen*. Coblenz: Hölscher, 1838–40.

Murphy, Jeremiah. "Darwinism." *Irish Ecclesiastical Record* 3rd ser., 5, no. 9 (1884): 584–94.

Murphy, Jeremiah. "Evolution and Faith." *Irish Ecclesiastical Record* 3rd ser., 5, no. 12 (1884): 756–67.

Murphy, Jeremiah. "Faith and Evolution." *Irish Ecclesiastical Record* 3rd ser., 6, no. 8 (1885): 481–96.

Murphy, Jeremiah. "Faith and Evolution—A Reply." *Irish Ecclesiastical Record* 3rd ser., 6, no. 11 (1885): 723–36.

Murray, James. *Oxford English Dictionary*. Oxford: Clarendon, 1908.

Murray, John, et al. "The Contribution of William King to the Early Development of Palaeoanthropology." *Irish Journal of Earth Sciences* 33 (2015): 1–16.

Nadaillac, Jean-François-Albert du Pouget, Marquis de. Review of *Evolution and Dogma*, by John A. Zahm. *Revue des questions scientifiques* 40 (= 2nd ser. 10), no. 3 (1896): 229–46.

Nadaillac, Jean-François-Albert du Pouget, Marquis de. "Les Progrès de l'anthropologie." In Congrès scientifique de 1891, *Compte rendu*, 8:5–35. Republished as a pamphlet. Paris: De Soye, 1891.

Nadaillac, Jean-François-Albert du Pouget, Marquis de. "Unité de l'espèce humaine prouvée par la similarité des conceptions et des créations de l'homme." In Congrès scientifique de 1897, *Compte rendu*, 9:100–121, with discussion reported on 17–19.

Naturwissenschaften: Wochenschrift für die Fortschritte der Naturwissenschaft, der Medizin und der Technik. Special issue on Darwinism. 9, no. 8 (1921): 121–52.

Necchi, Ludovico. Review of *La biologia moderna e la teoria dell'evoluzione*, by Erich Wasmann. *La Scuola cattolica* 4th ser., 9 (1906): 573–81.

Needham, John. "Lettre de M. de Needham à M. de Buffon." In his *Nouvelles Recherches physiques et métaphysiques sur la nature et la religion*, 1–26. London: Lacombe, 1769.

Nemesszeghy, Ervin, SJ, and John Russell, SJ. *Theology of Evolution*. Notre Dame, IN: Fides Publishers, 1971.

Neveu, Bruno. "Bergson et l'Index." *Revue de métaphysique et de morale* 40, no. 4 (2003): 543–51.

New Catholic Encyclopedia, 2nd ed. Washington, DC: The Catholic University of America Press, 2003.

New Catholic Encyclopedia Supplement 2010, edited by Robert L. Fastigi. Detroit: Gale, 2010.

New Scholasticism. "The Problem of Evolution: An Editorial." 23, no. 3 (1949): 255–56.

New York Times. "De Chardin is Honored." March 23, 1937, 9.

New York Tribune. "Father Zahm Submits to Rome." July 2, 1899, 3.

Newman, John Henry. "On the Inspiration of Scripture." *The Nineteenth Century* 15, no. 84 (1884): 185–99.

Newman, John Henry. *The Philosophical Notebook of John Henry Newman,* edited by Edward Sillem. Louvain: Nauwelaerts, 1969–70.

Newman, John Henry. *The Letters and Diaries of John Henry Newman,* edited by C. S. Dessain and T. Gornall. Oxford: Clarendon, 1973.

Nieuwenhoven, Leo M. van, SJ. "Enige Notities bij de Vraag: Stamt de mens van de aap af?" *De Volkskrant,* May 29, 1954, 11.

Noël, Léon. "Review of *Nouvelle théologie dogmatique,* by Jules Souben." *Revue philosophique de Louvain* 13, no. 50 (1906): 224–25.

Notre Dame Scholastic. Untitled news item. 28, no. 23 (1895): 366.

Nott, Josiah, and George Gliddon. *Types of Mankind.* Philadelphia: Lippincott and Grambo, 1854.

Nott, Josiah, and George Gliddon. *Indigenous Races of the Earth.* Philadelphia: Lippincott, 1857.

Nowodworski, Michał. "Człowiek." In *Encyklopedja kościelna* 3:669–72. Warsaw: Czerwiński, 1874.

Núñez, Diego. *El darwinismo en España.* Madrid: Castalia, 1969.

Obermaier, Hugo. *Der Mensch aller Zeiten. Band I: Der Mensch der Vorzeit.* Berlin: Allgemeine Verlags-Gesellschaft, 1912.

Oberški, Janko. "† P. Jean B. Frey, CSSp." *Ephemerides theologicae Zagrabienses* [*Bogoslovska smotra*] 27, no. 5 (1939): 393.

O'Brien, John A. *Evolution and Religion: A Study of the Bearing of Evolution upon the Philosophy of Religion.* New York: Century, 1932.

Olearius, Adam. *Außfürliche Beschreibung der kundbaren Reyse nach Muscow und Persien.* Schleswig: Holwein, 1663. Translated by John Davies as *The Voyages and Travells of the Ambassadors sent by Frederick Duke of Holstein, to the Great Duke of Muscovy, and the King of Persia.* 2nd ed. London: Starkey and Basset, 1669.

O'Leary, Don. *Roman Catholicism and Modern Science: A History.* New York: Continuum, 2006.

Orban, Alexis-Jules. "Transformism: Lamarck—Darwin." *American Catholic Quarterly Review* 16, no. 62 (1891): 280–97.

Orbán, Ladislao. *Theologia güntheriana et Concilium vaticanum: Inquisitio historico-dogmatica de re güntheriana iuxta vota inedita consultoris J. Schwetz actaque Concilii vaticani exarata.* Rome: Editrice Pontificia Università Gregoriana, 1949.

Orientalistische Literaturzeitung. Notice of *I primi tre capitoli della Sacra Bibbia annotati secondo il sistema delle apparenze,* by Pietro Martinelli. 10, no. 10 (1907): 559.

O'Riordan, Michael. *Draper's "Conflict between Religion and Science."* London: Catholic Truth Society, 1898.

O'Riordan, Michael. "Science and the Scientists." *Freeman's Journal & Catholic Register,* July 30, 1898, 4.

O'Riordan, Michael. "Science, Scientists, and Dr. Seton." *Freeman's Journal & Catholic Register,* September 3, 1898, 4.

O'Riordan, Michael. "Science and Scientists." *Freeman's Journal & Catholic Register,* October 29, 1898, 4.

O'Riordan, Michael. "Darwinism." *Freeman's Journal & Catholic Register,* December 3, 1898, 5.

Osservatore Romano. "Le Origini dell'uomo e le recenti scoperte paleoantropologiche." February 8, 1950, 2.

Osservatore Romano. "Un esempio." January 6, 1954, 1.

Osservatore Romano. "Pierre Teilhard de Chardin e il suo pensiero sul piano filosofico e religioso." June 30, 1962, 1–2.

O'Toole, George Barry. *The Case against Evolution*. New York: Macmillan, 1925.

Ott, Ludwig. *Grundriß der katholischen Dogmatik*. Freiburg im Breisgau: Herder, 1952. Translated (but without Ott's helpful bibliographic notes) by James Bastible and Patrick Lynch as *Fundamentals of Catholic Dogma*. 4th ed. Rockford, IL: TAN, 1974.

Overhage, Paul, with Karl Rahner. *Das Problem der Hominisation*. 3rd ed. Freiburg im Breisgau: Herder, 1965.

Owen, Richard. *Lectures on Invertebrate Animals*. London: Longman, 1843.

Pagnini, Sara. *Profilo di Raffaello Caverni (1837–1900)*. Florence: Pagnini e Martinelli, 2001.

Palmieri, Dominico. *Tractatus de Deo creante et elevante*. Rome: Polyglotta, 1878.

Paquier, Jules. *La Création et l'évolution: La Révélation et la science*. Paris: Gabalda, 1932.

Paredes, Lucas. *El drama político de honduras*. México: Editorial Latinoamericana, 1958.

Parente, Pietro. "Nuove tendenze teologiche." *L'Osservatore Romano*, February 9–10, 1942, 1.

Paul, Harry W. *The Edge of Contingency: French Catholic Reaction to Scientific Change from Darwin to Duhem*. Gainesville: University Presses of Florida, 1979.

Pègues, Thomas-M. "L'Évolution créatrice." *Revue thomiste* 16 (1908): 137–63.

Pelayo López, Francisco. *Ciencia y creencia en España durante el siglo XIX: La paleontología en el debate sobre el darwinismo*. Madrid: Consejo Superior de Investigaciones Científicas, 1999.

Pengelly, William. "The Literature of Kent's Cavern. Part II." *Transactions of the Devonshire Association for the Advancement of Science, Literature and Art* 3 (1869): 191–482.

Pereda-Suberbiola, Xabier, and José Ignacio Ruiz-Omeñaca. "Discovery and Study of Dinosaurs from Spain: The Contribution of Albert F. de Lapparent." *Comptes Rendus Palevol* 11, no. 4 (2012): 315–22.

Pereira, Benito. *Commentariorum et disputationum in Genesim tomi quattuor*. Mainz: Hieratus, 1612.

Périer, Pierre-Marie. *Une Religion astronomique: Doctrines philosophiques et théologiques de M. l'astronome C. Flammarion*. Coutances: Daireaux et Salette, 1895.

Périer, Pierre-Marie. *Le Transformisme: L'Origine de l'homme et le dogme catholique: Étude apologétique*. Paris: Beauchesne, 1938.

Pernicone, Joseph M. *The Ecclesiastical Prohibition of Books*. Washington, DC: The Catholic University of America Press, 1932.

Perrone, Giovanni. *Praelectiones theologicae*. Turin: Marietti, 1839.

Pesch, Christianus. *Compendium dogmaticae theologicae*. Freiburg im Breisgau: Herder, 1913.

Pesch, Tilmann. *Die großen Welträthsel: Philosophie der Natur. Bd. 2, Naturphilosophische Weltauffassung*. Freiburg im Breisgau: Herder, 1884. 3rd ed. 1907.

Pesch, Tilmann. *Institutiones philosophiae naturalis*. Freiburg im Breisgau: Herder, 1880. 2nd ed. 1897.

Petròcchi, Policarpo. *Nòvo dizionàrio universale della lingua italiana*. Milan: Trèves, 1912.

Pfülf, Otto, SJ. *Cardinal von Geissel: Aus seinem handschriftlichen Nachlaß geschildert*. Freiburg im Breisgau: Herder, 1896.

Pianciani, Giovanni Battista. "Della Origine delle specie organizzate." *Civiltà cattolica* 4, no. 7 (1860): 164–79.

Pianciani, Giovanni Battista. *Cosmogonia naturale comparata col Genesi*. Rome: Civiltà cattolica, 1862.

Picard, Guy, SJ. "La Science expérimentale est-elle favorable au polygénisme?" *Sciences ecclésiastiques* 4 (1951): 65–89.

Pictet de la Rive, Jules. Review of *On the Origin of Species*, by Charles Darwin. *Bibliothèque universelle: Revue suisse et étrangère: Archives des sciences physiques et naturelles* n.s., 7 (1860): 233–55.

Pius IX. *Quanta cura*. Acta Sanctae Sedis 3 (1867): 160–76.

Pius X. *Lamentabili sane exitu*. Acta Sanctae Sedis 40 (1907): 470–78. Translated in *All Things in Christ: Encyclicals and Selected Documents of Saint Pius X*, edited by Vincent A. Yzermans. Westminster: Newman, 1954.

Pius X. *Pascendi domenici gregis*. Acta Sanctae Sedis 40 (1907): 593–650. Translated in *All Things in Christ: Encyclicals and Selected Documents of Saint Pius X*, edited by Vincent A. Yzermans. Westminster: Newman, 1954.

Pius X. *Praestantia Scripturae (motu proprio)*. Acta Sanctae Sedis 40 (1907): 723–26.

Pius X. *Sapienti Consilio*. Acta Sanctae Sedis 41 (1908): 425–40.

Pius X. *Sacrorum antistitum (motu proprio)*. Acta Apostolicae Sedis 2, no. 17 (1910): 655–80.

Pius X. *Catechismo della dottrina cristiana*. Rome: Poliglotta Vaticana, 1912.

Pius X. *Codex Iuris Canonici Pii X Pontificis Maximi*. Rome: Polyglottis Vaticanis, 1918. Translated by Edward N. Peters as *The 1917 or Pio-Benedictine Code of Canon Law*. San Francisco: Ignatius, 2001.

Pius XI. *Casti conubii*. Acta Apostolicae Sedis 22, no. 13 (1930), 539–92.

Pius XII. Allucutiones: III. *Acta Apostolicae Sedis* 33, no. 13 (1941): 504–12. Sometimes called "God the Only Commander and Legislator of the Universe," an unpolished translation is available in *Papal Addresses to the Pontifical Academy of Sciences 1917–2002 and to the Pontifical Academy of Social Sciences 1994–2002*, edited by Marcella Sánchez Sorondo, 91–99. Vatican City: Pontifical Academy of Sciences, 2003.

Pius XII. *Divino afflante Spiritu*. Acta Apostolicae Sedis 35, no. 10 (1943): 297–326.

Pius XII. *Humani generis*. Acta Apostolicae Sedis, 42, no. 11 (1950): 561–78.

Pius XII. Allocutiones: I. Iis qui interfuerunt 'Primo symposio internationali geneticae medicae.' *Acta Apostolicae Sedis* 45, no. 12 (1953): 596–607.

Piveteau, Jean. *Le Père Teilhard de Chardin, savant.* Paris: Fayard, 1964.

Planck, Max. *Scientific Autobiography, and Other Papers.* New York: Philosophical Library, 1950.

Plate, Ludwig. *Ultramontane Weltanschauung und moderne Lebenskunde.* Jena: Fischer, 1907.

Poels, Vefie, and Hans de Valk. "A Stranger in the Sacred College of Cardinals: Contextual and Heuristic Problems in Investigating Cardinal van Rossum." *Mélanges de l'École française de Rome—Italie et Méditerranée modernes et contemporaines* 128, no. 1 (2016).

Pohle, Joseph. "Darwinism and Theism." *American Ecclesiastical Review* 7, no. 3 (1892): 161–76.

Pohle, Joseph. *Lehrbuch der Dogmatik.* Paderborn: Schöningh, 1902. Abridgment of the 5th German edition translated by Arthur Preuss as *God: The Author of Nature and the Supernatural.* 2nd ed. St. Louis: Herder, 1916.

Pontifical Biblical Commission. "De Mosaica authentia Pentateuchi." *Acta Sanctae Sedis* 39 (1906): 377–78.

Pontifical Biblical Commission. "De charactere historico trium priorum capitum Geneseos." *Acta Apostolicae Sedis* 1, no. 13 (1909): 567–69.

Pontifical Biblical Commission. *The Interpretation of the Bible in the Church.* Boston: Pauline Books and Media, 1993.

Popkin, Richard H. *Isaac La Peyrère (1596–1676): His Life, Work, and Influence.* Leiden: Brill, 1987.

Portalié, Eugène. "Le R. P. Frins et la *Revue Thomiste*." *Études religieuses, philosophiques, historiques et littéraires* 59 (1893): 37–64.

Portmann, Adolf. "Die werdende Menschheit: Das Ursprungsproblem der Menschheit." In *Historia Mundi: I. Frühe Menschheit*, edited by Fritz Kern, 21–32. Bern: Francke, 1932.

Portmann, Adolf. *Biologische Fragmente zu einer Lehre von Menschen*. Basel: Schwabe, 1944.

Pospíšil, Ctirad V. "The Reaction of Czech Thinkers and Especially of Catholic Theologians to the Evolution Theory of Human Origin in Global Context (1840–1950)." *Anthropos* 111, no. 2 (2016): 607–18.

Pospíšil, Ctirad V. *Průkopníci a jejich odpůrci: Světová katolická teologie 1871–1910 a evoluční vznik-stvoření člověka*. Prague: Karolinum, 2018.

Pottmeyer, Hermann Josef. *Der Glaube vor dem Anspruch der Wissenschaft: Die Konstitution über den katholischen Glauben* Dei Filius *des 1. Vatikanischen Konzils und der unveröffentlichten theologischen Voten der vorbereitenden Kommission*. Freiburg im Breisgau: Herder, 1968.

Pouchet, Félix Archimède. *Hétérogénie, ou Traité de la génération spontanée basé sur de nouvelles expériences*. Paris: Baillière, 1859.

Press Office of the Holy See. Communiqué on Teilhard de Chardin. *L'Osservatore Romano: Weekly Edition in English*, July 20, 1981, 2.

Prestwich, Joseph. "On the Occurrence of Flint-Implements, Associated with the Remains of Animals of Extinct Species in Beds of a Late Geological Period, in France at Amiens and Abbeville, and in England at Hoxne." *Philosophical Transactions of the Royal Society of London* 150 (1860): 277–317.

Preuss, Arthur. "Dr. Zahm and his Book." *The Fortnightly Review* 6, no. 18 (1899): 140.

Prichard, James Cowles. *Researches into the Physical History of Man*. London: Arch, 1813.

Prohászka, Ottokár. *Isten és a világ: Különös tekintettel a természettudományokra*. Esztergom: Buzárovits, 1890.

Prohászka, Ottokár. "Mire kell ma a theológiában súlyt fektetni?" *Magyar Sion* (1899). Citations here from *Összegyüjtött munkái* [Collected Works], edited by Antal Schütz, 15:179–235. Budapest: Szent István, 1928.

Prohászka, Ottokár. *Modern katholicizmus*. Budapest: Szent-István-Társulat, 1907.

Prohászka, Ottokár. *Az intellektualizmus túlhajtásai*. Budapest: Kiadja a Magyar Tudományos Akadémia, 1910.

Prohászka, Ottokár. "Több békességet!" *Egyházi közlöny* [Church Bulletin], December 23, 1910.

Prohászka, Ottokár. *Föld és ég: Kutatások a geologia és theologia érintkező pontjai kórúl*. 3rd ed. Esztergom: Buzárovits, 1906. 4th ed. 1912. 5th ed. Budapest: Szent István, 1927. Citations here from 5th edition, passages in which are substantially equivalent to those in the 3rd edition.

Prohászka, Ottokár. *Naplójegyzetek* [Diary Notes], edited by Barlay Szabolcs et al. Székesfehérvár: Ottokár Püspök Alapítvány, 1997.

Publishers Weekly. Review of *The Jesuit and the Skull: Teilhard de Chardin, Evolution, and the Search for Peking Man*, by Amir D. Aczel. 254, no. 28 (2007): 153.

Pujuila, J. Review of *Die moderne Biologie und die Entwicklungstheorie*, by Erich Wasmann. *Razón y Fe* 11 and 12 (1905): 496–508 and 59–69.

Quatrefages, Jean Louis Armand de. *L'Unité de l'espèce humaine*. Paris: Hachette, 1861.

Rahner, Hugo. "Hemmschuh des Fortschritts? Zur Enzyklika *Humani generis*." *Stimmen der Zeit* 147, no. 3 (1950–51): 161–71.

Ratti, Achille. "Terremoti storici italiani." In *Vulcani e fenomeni vulcanici in Italia 3: Vulcani e fenomeni vulcanici*, by Giuseppe Mercalli, 216–80. Milan: Vallardi, 1883.

Ratti, Achille. "De hominis origine quoad corpus." In *Institutiones positivo-scholasticae theologiae dogmaticae*, by Friderico Sala. 5th ed. Milan: S. Josephus, 1899–1900.

Raven, Charles E. *Teilhard de Chardin: Scientist and Seer*. New York: Harper & Row, 1962.

Reader, John. *Missing Links: The Hunt for Earliest Man*. 2nd ed. New York: Penguin, 1988.

Reany, William. *The Creation of the Human Soul*. New York: Benziger, 1932.

Redi, Francesco. *Esperienze intorno alla generazione degl'insetti*. Florence: Stella, 1668.

Renan, Ernest. *Souvenirs d'enfance et de jeunesse*. Paris: Lévy, 1883. Translated by C. B. Pitman as *Recollections of My Youth*. London: Chapman and Hall, 1883.

Renwart, Léon, and Georges Vandebroek. "L'Encyclique 'Humani generis' et les sciences naturelles." *Nouvelle revue théologique* 73, no. 4 (1951): 337–51.

Reusch, Franz Heinrich. *Bibel und Natur*. Freiburg im Breisgau: Herder, 1862. Translated from 4th ed. by Kathleen Lyttelton as *Nature and the Bible*. Edinburgh: Clark, 1886.

Revilla, Manuel de la. "Revista crítica." *Revista contemporánea* 10, no. 1 (1877): 117–22.

Revue biblique internationale. Review of *I primi tre capitoli della Sacra Bibbia annotati secondo il sistema delle apparenze*, by Pietro Martinelli. N.s. 4, 3 (1907): 454–55.

Revue des questions scientifiques. Prefatory note to Zahm, "Évolution et téléologie." 43 (= 2nd ser., 13), no. 2 (1898): 403–4.

Richards, Robert J. *The Tragic Sense of Life: Ernst Haeckel and the Struggle over Evolutionary Thought*. Chicago: University of Chicago Press, 2008.

Rigg, James McMullen. "Mivart, St. George." In *Dictionary of National Biography, Supplement*, edited by Sidney Lee, 3:179–81. London: Macmillan, 1901.

Rivista contemporanea. "Miscellanea di scienze, lettere ed arti: Inghilterra." 20 (1860): 140–41.

Rivista di studi religiosi. Review of *I primi tre capitoli della Sacra Bibbia annotati secondo il sistema delle apparenze*, by Pietro Martinelli. 6 (1906): 638–39.

Rivista internazionale di scienze sociali e discipline ausiliarie. Review of *I primi tre capitoli della Sacra Bibbia annotati secondo il sistema delle apparenze*, by Pietro Martinelli. 41, no. 164 (1906): 624.

Rohling, August. "Die Inspiration der Bibel in Dingen der natürlichen Erkenntnis." *Natur und Offenbarung* 18 (1872): 97–108.

Rolfes, Eugen. "Die Stelle Gen. II, 7 und die Deszendenztheorie." *Jahrbuch für Philosophie und spekulative Theologie* 18 (1904): 458–63.

Romanes, George. *Darwin, and After Darwin*. London: Longmans, Green, 1895.

Rondet, Henri. "Les Origines humaines et la théologie." *Cité nouvelle: Revue catholique d'étude et d'action* 55 (1943): 961–87. Republished as "Croyons-nous encore au Péché originel?" in his *Problèmes pour la réflexion chrétienne: Le Péché originel. L'Enfer et autres études*, 9–40. Paris: Spes, 1946.

Ronero Gómez, Ena Yolanda, et al. Reforma liberal: relaciones iglesia-estado 1887–1901. Bachelor's thesis, Universidad Nacional Autónoma de Honduras, 1982.

Root, John D. "The Final Apostasy of St. George Jackson Mivart." *The Catholic Historical Review* 71, no. 1 (1985): 1–25.

Rosmini-Serbati, Antonio. *Nuovo saggio sull'origini delle idee*. Rome: Salviucci, 1830. Translated by Robert A. Murphy et al. as *A New Essay Concerning the Origin of Ideas*. Durham: Rosmini House, 2001.

Rosmini-Serbati, Antonio. *Psicologia*. Naples: Romano, 1858. Translated by Denis Cleary and Terence Watson as *Psychology, Vol. 1: Essence of the Human Soul*. Durham: Rosmini House, 1999.

Roure, Lucien. Review of *Le Darwinisme au point de vue de l'orthodoxie catholique*, by Henry de Dorlodot. Études 169 (1921): 365–66.

Royer, Clémence, translator. *De l'Origine des espèces ou des lois du progrès chez les êtres organisés*. Paris: Guillaumin, 1862.

Rudwick, Martin J. S. *Worlds Before Adam: The Reconstruction of Geohistory in the Age of Reform*. Chicago: University of Chicago Press, 2008.

Ruffini, Ernesto. *La teoria dell'evoluzione secondo la scienza e la fede*. Rome: Orbis Catholicus, 1948. Translated by Francis O'Hanlon as *The Theory of Evolution Judged by Reason and Faith*. New York: Wagner, 1959.

Ruffini, Ernesto. "Responsibilità dei paleoantropologi cattolici." *L'Osservatore Romano*. June 3, 1950, 1–2.

Rupke, Nicolaas A. *The Great Chain of History: William Buckland and the English School of Geology (1814–1849)*. Oxford: Oxford University Press, 1983.

Rüschkamp, Felix, SJ. "Eine neue natürliche rufa-fusca-Adoptionskolonie." *Biologisches Centralblatt* 32 (1912): 213–16.

Rüschkamp, Felix, SJ. "Mededeelingen: Stamt de Menschheid van één of van meer ouderparen af?" *Studiën: Tijdschrift voor godsdienst, wetenschap, letteren* 96, no. 2 (1921): 152–55.

Rüschkamp, Felix, SJ. *Der Flugapparat der Käfer*. Stuttgart: Schweizerbart, 1927.

Rüschkamp, Felix, SJ. "*Sinanthropus Pekinensis* Black." *Stimmen der Zeit* 123, no. 1 (1932): 50–57.

Rüschkamp, Felix, SJ. "Nicht Morgenrötenmensch, sondern Nordaffe." *Stimmen der Zeit* 124, no. 4 (1933): 277–78.

Rüschkamp, Felix, SJ. "Von Zweckursachen und Wirkursachen der Lebensvorgänge." *Stimmen der Zeit* 126, no. 5 (1934): 350–52.

Rüschkamp, Felix, SJ. "Geschichte der Menschheit." *Stimmen der Zeit* 129, no. 3 (1935): 187–99.

Rüschkamp, Felix, SJ. "Früh-Anthropologisches aus Italien, Ostafrika, China und Java." *Scholastik: Vierteljahresschrift für Theologie und Philosophie* 11, no. 2 (1936): 250–62.

Rüschkamp, Felix, SJ. " Zur biologischen Entwicklungslehre." *Stimmen der Zeit* 130, no. 4 (1936): 225–33.

Rüschkamp, Felix, SJ. "Wirbeltiere erobern die Luft." *Stimmen der Zeit* 130, no. 5 (1936): 318–30.

Rüschkamp, Felix, SJ. "Wie alt ist das Menschengeschlecht?" *Stimmen der Zeit* 133, no. 3 (1937): 156–71.

Rüschkamp, Felix, SJ. "Zum Erscheinungsbild Adams und Evas." *Stimmen der Zeit* 132, no. 7 (1937): 52–55.

Rüschkamp, Felix, SJ. "Der Mensch als Glied der Schöpfung." *Stimmen der Zeit* 135, no. 6 (1939): 367–85.

Rüschkamp, Felix, SJ. "Zur Art- und Rassengeschichte des Menschen." *Stimmen der Zeit* 139, no. 4 (1946–47): 290–309.

Rüschkamp, Felix, SJ. "Zum artgeschichtlichen Wandel der Menschengestalt." *Philosophisches Jahrbuch* 58 (1948): 395–404.

Rüschkamp, Felix, SJ. *Zur Artgeschichte des Menschen*. Baden-Baden: Knapp, 1949.

Rüschkamp, Felix, SJ. "D'Où vient la vie?" In *Essai sur Dieu, l'homme et l'univers*, edited by Jacques de Bivort de la Saudée, 175–202. Paris: Casterman, 1950. Translated as "The Origin of Life." In *God, Man, and the Universe*, 75–90. London: Burn & Oates, 1954.

S., F. Ch. "Geologie." In *Allgemeine Realencyclopädie oder Conversationslexicon für das katholische Deutschland*, edited by Wilhelm Binder, 4:699–708. Regensburg: Manz, 1846–50.

Sackett, James A. "Human Antiquity and the Old Stone Age: The Nineteenth Century Background to Paleoanthropology." *Evolutionary Anthropology* 9, no. 1 (2000): 37–49.

Sackett, James A. "Boucher de Perthes and the Discovery of Human Antiquity." *Bulletin of the History of Archaeology* 24, no. 2 (2014): 1–11.

Salet, Georges, and Louis Lafont. *L'Évolution régressive*. Paris: Éditions franciscaines, 1943.

Salis Seewis, Francesco, SJ. Review of *Darwinisme, ou l'Homme Singe*, by Constantin James. *Civiltà cattolica* 10th ser., 2, no. 646 (1877): 449–58.

Salis Seewis, Francesco, SJ. Review of *De' nuovi studi della filosofia*, by Raffaello Caverni. *Civiltà cattolica* 10th ser., 4, no. 659 (1877): 570–80 and 5, no. 661 (1878): 65–76.

Salis Seewis, Francesco, SJ. Review of *Evoluzione e dogma*, by John A. Zahm. *Civiltà cattolica* 16th ser., 10, no. 1118 (1897): 201–4.

Salis Seewis, Francesco, SJ. Review of *L'origine dell'uomo e il sentimento religioso*, by Antonio Fogazzaro. *Civiltà cattolica* 15th ser., 8, no. 1040 (1893): 199–211 and no. 1041: 324–39.

Sambucy-Luzençon, Count de. "Séance du 26 Février 1878." In *Bulletin de la Société archéologique du Midi de la France: Séances du 19 juin 1877 au 19 mars 1878 inclus* (1878), 18–19. Toulouse: Privat, 1878.

Scannell, T. B. "Gift, Supernatural." In *The Catholic Encyclopedia*, 6:553–54.

Schaaffhausen, Hermann. "Zur Kenntniss der ältesten Rasseschädel." *Archiv für Anatomie, Physiologie und wissenschaftliche Medicin* [= *Müllers Archiv*] (1858): 453–78. Translated by George Busk as "On the Crania of the Most Ancient Races of Man." *Natural History Review* no. 2 (1861): 155–75.

Schatz, Klaus, SJ. "'Modernismo' tra i Gesuiti: I casi Hummelauer e Wasmann." In *Il Modernismo in Italia e in Germania nel contesto europeo*, edited by Michele Nicoletti and Otto Weiss, 341–59. Bologna: Mulino, 2010.

Schatz, Klaus, SJ. "Pater Erich Wasmann S.J. und die Humanevolution." *Theologie und Philosophie* 85, no. 1 (2010): 81–86.

Scheeben, Mathias. *Handbuch der katholischen Dogmatik*. Freiburg im Breisgau: Herder, 1873–1903. Condensed and translated (from the 3rd ed.) by Joseph Wilhelm and Thomas B. Scannell as *A Manual of Catholic Theology based on Scheeben's "Dogmatik."* London: Kegan Paul, 1906.

Schleicher, August. *Über die Bedeutung der Sprache für die Naturgeschichte des Menschen*. Weimar: Böhlau, 1865.

Schmerling, Philippe-Charles. *Recherches sur les ossemens fossiles découverts dans les cavernes de la province de Liège*. Liège: Collardin, 1833–34.

Schmidt, Wilhelm, SVD. "Primitive Man." In *European Civilization: Its Origin and Development*, edited by Edward Eyre, 1:1–82. Oxford: Oxford University Press, 1935.

Schmidt, Wilhelm, SVD. "Die Uroffenbarung als Anfang der Offenbarungen Gottes." In *Religion Christentum Kirche: Eine Apologetik für wissenschaftlich Gebildete*, edited by Gerhard Esser and Joseph Mausbach, 1:477–632. Kempten: Kösel, 1911. Translated (from the 5th ed.) with supplementation by Joseph J. Baierl as *Primitive Revelation*. St. Louis: Herder, 1939.

Schmidt, Wilhelm, SVD. *Wege der Kulturen: Gesammelte Aufsätze*. St. Augustin bei Bonn: Anthropos-Institut, 1964.

Schroeder, H. J., OP. *The Canons and Decrees of the Council of Trent*. Rockford, IL: TAN, 1978.

Schryrgens, Joseph. "Monseigneur Jacques Laminne." *Revue générale* 58 (1925): 617–28.

Schuster, Ignaz. *Handbuch zur Biblischen Geschichte*. Freiburg im Breisgau: Herder, 1861.

Schütz, Antal. "A kiadó jegyzetei" [Publisher's note]. In Prohászka, *Föld és ég*, 5th ed., 2:257.

Schwetz, Johann. *Theologia dogmatica catholica*. Vienna: Mechitharistica, 1858.

Scuola cattolica, La. Review of *I primi tre capitoli della Sacra Bibbia annotati secondo il sistema delle apparenze*, by Pietro Martinelli. 4th ser., 10 (1906): 533–35.

Searle, George M. "Scientific Dogmatism." *The Catholic World* 33, no. 194 (1881): 274–81.

Searle, George M. "The Supposed Issue between Religion and Science." *The Catholic World* 38, no. 227 (1884): 578–88.

Searle, George M. "Evolution and Darwinism." *The Catholic World* 56, no. 332 (1892): 223–31.

Selbst, Joseph. *Dr. I. Schuster und Dr. J. B. Holzammer[s] Handbuch zur Biblischen Geschichte*. Freiburg im Breisgau: Herder, 1906.

Senff, M. "Jesuitenpater Wasmann. *Pro* oder *contra*?" *Harzer Kurier*, April 27–28, 1907.

Séra, Gioacchino Leo. "L'attuale controversia su poligenismo e monogenismo in Italia." *Archivio per l'antropologia e la etnologia* 40 (1910): 97–108.

Sergi, Giuseppe. "L'apologia del mio poligenismo." *Atti della Società Romana di Antropologia* 15 (1909–10): 187–95.

Serres, Marcel de. *De la Cosmogonie de Moïse comparée aux faits géologiques.* Paris: Lagny, 1838. 2nd ed. 1841.

Seton, William. "Geographical Distribution in Natural History." *The Catholic World* 50, no. 295 (1889): 20–30.

Seton, William. "Disguises of Nature." *The Catholic World* 50, no. 300 (1890): 767–74.

Seton, William. "The Study of Geology and the Summer School." *The Catholic World* 56, no. 336 (1893): 761–69.

Seton, William. "Ancient Mammals and their Descendants." *The Catholic World* 60, no. 357 (1894): 401–8.

Seton, William. "How to Solve One of the Highest Problems of Science." *The Catholic World* 58, no. 348 (1894): 787–93.

Seton, William. "The Museum of the Rocks." *The Catholic World* 61, no. 363 (1895): 395–404.

Seton, William. *A Glimpse of Organic Life, Past and Present.* New York: O'Shea, 1897.

Seton, William. "The Hypothesis of Evolution." *The Catholic World* 66, no. 392 (1897): 198–204.

Seton, William. "Science and the Scientists." *Freeman's Journal & Catholic Register*, August 6, 1898, 4.

Seton, William. "Science and Scientists." *Freeman's Journal & Catholic Register*, September 17, 1898, 4.

Seton, William. "Science and Scientists." *Freeman's Journal & Catholic Register*, November 12, 1898, 5.

Seton, William. "The Century's Progress in Science." *The Catholic World* 69, no. 410 (1899): 146–67.

Seton, William. "Divine Action in Natural Selection." *The Catholic World* 70, no. 419 (1900): 625–31.

Seton, William. "A Plan in the History of Nature." *The Catholic World* 71, no. 423 (1900): 376–80.

Seton, William. "The Sea and its Inhabitants." *The Catholic World* 79, no. 470 (1904): 192–208.

Seton, William. "Darwinism on its Deathbed." *The Catholic World* 80, no. 477 (1904): 348–57.

Seward, Albert Charles. "A Contribution to our Knowledge of Wealden Floras." *The Quarterly Journal of the Geological Society of London* 69 (1913): 85–116.

Shahan, Thomas J. "The Scientific Congress at Brussels." *The Catholic University Bulletin* 1 (1895): 73–85.

Shea, John Gilmary. "Catholic Congresses." In *Souvenir Volume of the Centennial Celebration 1789–1889 and Catholic Congress*, edited by William H. Hughes, 25–27. Detroit: Hughes, 1889.

Sheehan, Michael. *Apologetics and Catholic Doctrine: Part II, Catholic Doctrine.* Dublin: Gill, 1927.

Shipman, Pat. *The Man Who Found the Missing Link: Eugène Dubois and His Lifelong Quest to Prove Darwin Right.* New York: Simon & Schuster, 2001.

Shubin, Neil. *Your Inner Fish.* London: Penguin, 2009.

Siciliani, Pietro. *Sul rinnovamento della filosofia positiva in Italia.* Florence: Barbèra, 1871.

Siciliani, Pietro. *La critica nella filosofia zoologica del XIX secolo.* Naples: Morano, 1876.

Siciliani, Pietro. *Socialismo, Darwinismo e sociologia moderna.* 2nd ed. Bologna: Zanichelli, 1879.

Siciliani, Pietro. *Prolégomènes à la psychogénie moderne.* Paris: Ballière, 1880.

Siciliani, Pietro. *Teorie sociali e socialismo.* Florence: Gazzetta d'Italia, 1880.

Siciliani, Pietro. *La scienza nell'educazione secondo i principii della sociologia moderna.* 2nd ed. Bologna: Zanichelli, 1881.

Siciliani, Pietro. *Sull'insegnamento religioso ai bambini, secondo i dettami della filosofia scientifica.* Bologna: Zanichelli, 1881.

Siciliani, Pietro. *Della psicogenia moderna in servigio degli studi biologici, storici e sociali.* 3rd ed. Bologna: Zanichelli, 1882.

Sickenberger, J. "Joseph Pohle † zum Gedächtnis." *Schlesisches Pastoralblatt* 43, no. 3/4 (1922): 20–22.

Simpson, Richard. "Religion and Modern Philosophy." *The Rambler* 6, pt. 33–36 (1850): 185–204, 279–98, 373–90, and 480–90.

Simpson, Richard. Review of *On the Origin of Species*, by Charles Darwin. *The Rambler* n.s., 2, pt. 6 (1860): 361–76.

Slattery, John P. *Faith and Science at Notre Dame: John Zahm, Evolution, and the Catholic Church.* Notre Dame, IN: University of Notre Dame Press, 2019.

Société archéologique du Midi de la France. "Séance du 26 Février 1878." In *Bulletin de la Société archéologique du Midi de la France: Séances du 19 juin 1877 au 19 mars 1878 inclus,* 18–19. Toulouse: Privat, 1878.

Sollier, Joseph. "Theological Censures." In *The Catholic Encyclopedia*, 3:532–33.

Souben, Jules. *La Création selon la foi et la science.* 2nd ed. Paris: Beauchesne, 1903.

Spahn, Martin, and Thomas F. Meehan. "Congresses, Catholic." In *The Catholic Encyclopedia*, 4:242–51.

Spencer, Frank. *Piltdown: A Scientific Forgery.* Oxford: Oxford University Press, 1990.

Spencer, Herbert. *First Principles.* London: Williams and Norgate, 1862. 3rd ed. 1875.

Spencer, Herbert. *The Principles of Biology.* London: Williams and Norgate, 1864.

Spruit, Leen. *The Origin of the Soul from Antiquity to the Early Modern Era.* Lugano: Agorà, 2014.

Stanton, William. *The Leopard's Spots: Scientific Attitudes Towards Race in America, 1815–1859.* Chicago: University of Chicago Press, 1960.

Stensen, Niels. *De solido intra solidum naturaliter contento dissertationis prodromus.* Florence: Stella, 1669.

Steyn, Cornelius van den [à Lapide]. *In Genesim Prœmium et Commentarium.* Republished in *Commentaria in Scrituram Sacram,* edited by Augustinus Crampon. Paris: Vivès, 1866. Also in J.-P. Migne, *Scripturæ Sacræ cursus completus.* Paris: Migne, 1859.

Sticco, Maria. *Father Gemelli: Notes for the Biography of a Great Man.* Translated by Beatrice Wilczynski. Chicago: Franciscan Herald Press, 1980.

Stöhr, Johannes. "Exempel Köln: 150-jähriges Jubiläum des Provinzialkonzils: Wegweisungen zur Gotteskenntnis." *Forum Katholische Theologie: Vierteljahresschrift für das Gesamtgebiet der katholischen Theologie* 27, no. 2 (2011): 81–102.

Stölzle, Remigius. "Kölliker gegen Darwin." In Congrès scientifique de 1900, *Akten,* 191–92. Published in full as *A. von Köllikers Stellung zur Descendenzlehre.* Münster: Aschendorff, 1900.

Stoppani, Antonio. *Note ad un corso annuale di geologia.* Milan: Bernardoni, 1867.

Stoppani, Antonio. *Geologia d'Italia.* Milan: Vallardi, 1874–81.

Stoppani, Antonio. *Il Dogma e le scienze positive, ossia La missione apologetica del clero nel moderno conflitto tra la ragione e la fede.* Milan: Dumolard, 1884.

Suárez, Francisco, SJ. *De opere sex dierum.* Lyons: Gabriel, 1635.

Surbled, Georges. "Chronique scientifique." *Revue du clergé français* 32 (1902): 69–88.

Synave, P., OP. "Bulletin de théologie biblique: I. — Ancien Testament." *Revue des sciences philosophiques et théologiques* 11 (1922): 122–55.

Szabó, Ferenc, SJ. *The Life and Work of Ottokár Prohászka (1858–1927).* Translated by Attila Miklósházy. Budapest: Szent István, 2007.

Tablet, The. Review of *On the Genesis of Species*, by St. George Mivart. 37, no. 1611 (1871): 232–33.

Tablet, The. "Catholic University College, Kensington," 47, no. 1870 (1876): 182–83.

Tablet, The. "The Dublin Review." 92, no. 3051 (1898): 690.

Tablet, The. "The Darwin Celebration at Cambridge: Address from Louvain." 114, no. 3608 (1909): 15.

Tablet, The. Review of *Darwinism and Catholic Thought,* by Henry de Dorlodot. 140, no. 4301 (1922): 495.

Tablet, The. Obituary of E. C. Messenger. 199, no. 5824 (1952): 15.

Tanquerey, Adolphe, PSS. *Synopsis theologiae dogmaticae.* Tournai: Desclée, 1894.

Tassy, Pascal. "Albert Gaudry et l'émergence de la paléontologie darwinienne au XIXe siècle." *Annales de paléontologie* 92, no. 1 (2006): 41–70.

Tassy, Pascal. "Trees before and after Darwin." *Journal of Zoological Systematics and Evolutionary Research* 49, no. 2 (2011): 89–101.

Taylor, Monica, SND. *Sir Bertram Windle: A Memoir.* London: Longmans, Green, 1932.

Teilhard de Chardin, Pierre, SJ. "L'Éocène des Environs de Minieh." *Bulletin de l'Institut égyptien* 5th ser., 2, no. 2 (1909): 116–21.

Teilhard de Chardin, Pierre, SJ. "Homme: IV. L'Homme devant les enseignements de l'Église et devant la philosophie spiritualiste." In *Dictionnaire apologétique de la foi catholique,* 2:501–14.

Teilhard de Chardin, Pierre, SJ. "La Préhistoire et ses progrès." *Études* 134 (1913): 40–53. Translated as "The Progress of Prehistory." *Appearance,* 11–24.

Teilhard de Chardin, Pierre, SJ. "Les Carnassiers des phosphorites du Quercy." *Annales de paléontologie* 9, no. 3–4 (1914–15): 103–92.

Teilhard de Chardin, Pierre, SJ. "Sur Quelques Primates des phosphorites du Quercy." *Annales de paléontologie* 10, no. 1–2 (1916–21): 1–20.

Teilhard de Chardin, Pierre, SJ. "Les Mammifères de l'Éocène inférieur français et leurs gisements." *Annales de paléontologie* 10 and 11: 1–2 and 3–4 (1916–21): 169–76 and 1–108 (plus plates I–VIII).

Teilhard de Chardin, Pierre, SJ. "La Vie cosmique." Unpublished, 1916. Published posthumously in *Écrits du temps de la guerre,* 17–82. Translated by René Hague as "Cosmic Life," in *Writings in Time of War,* 13–71. New York: Harper & Row, 1968.

Teilhard de Chardin, Pierre, SJ. "Chute, rédemption et géocentrie." Unpublished, 1920. Published posthumously in *Comment je crois,* 47–57. Translated as "Fall, Redemption, and Geocentrism" in *Christianity and Evolution,* 36–44.

Teilhard de Chardin, Pierre, SJ. "Le Cas de l'homme de Piltdown." *Revue des questions scientifiques* 77 (= 3rd ser., 27), no. 1 (1920): 149–55.

Teilhard de Chardin, Pierre, SJ. Review of *Les Hommes fossiles,* by Marcelin Boule. *Études* 166 (1921): 570–77. Translated as "Fossil Man" in *Appearance,* 25–32.

Teilhard de Chardin, Pierre, SJ. "Comment se pose aujourd'hui la question du transformisme." *Études* 167 (1921): 524–44. Translated as "How the Transformist Question Presents itself Today" in *Vision,* 7–25.

Teilhard de Chardin, Pierre, SJ. "La Face de la Terre." *Études* 169 (1921): 585–602. Translated as "The Face of the Earth" in *Vision,* 26–48.

Teilhard de Chardin, Pierre, SJ. "Note sur quelques représentations historiques possibles du Péché originel." Unpublished, 1922. Published posthumously in *Comment je crois,* 59–70. Translated as "Note on Some Possible Historical Representations of Original Sin" in *Christianity and Evolution,* 45–55.

Teilhard de Chardin, Pierre, SJ. "La Paléontologie et l'apparition de l'homme." *Revue de philosophie* 30 (1923): 144–73. Translated as "Paleontology and the Appearance of Man" in *Appearance,* 33–57.

Teilhard de Chardin, Pierre, SJ. "Le Paradoxe transformiste: À propos de la dernière critique du transformisme par M. Vialleton." *Revue des questions scientifiques* 87 (= 4th ser., 7), no. 1 (1925): 53–80. Translated as "The Transformist Paradox" in *Vision,* 80–102.

Teilhard de Chardin, Pierre, SJ. "Les Mammifères de l'Éocène inférieur de la Belgique." *Mémoires du Musée royale d'histoire naturelle de Belgique* 36 (1927): 1–33.

Teilhard de Chardin, Pierre, SJ. "Que faut-il penser du Transformisme?" *Dossiers de la Commission synodale* 2, no. 6–7 (1929): 462–69. Republished in *Revue des questions scientifiques* 97 (= 4th ser., 17), no. 1 (1930): 89–99. Translated as "What Should we Think of Transformism?" in *Vision*, 151–60.

Teilhard de Chardin, Pierre, SJ. "Un Importante Découverte en paléontologie humaine: Le Sinanthropus pekinensis." *Revue des questions scientifiques* 98 (= 4th ser., 18), no. 1 (1930): 5–16. Translated as "Sinanthropus Pekinensis" in *Appearance*, 58–67.

Teilhard de Chardin, Pierre, SJ. "Le Phénomène humain." *Revue des questions scientifiques* 98 (= 4th ser., 18), no. 3 (1930): 390–406. Translated as "The Phenomenon of Man" in *Vision*, 161–74.

Teilhard de Chardin, Pierre, SJ. "Le 'Sinanthropus' de Péking: État actuel de nos connaissances sur le fossile et son gisement." *L'Anthropologie* 41, no. 1–2 (1931): 1–11.

Teilhard de Chardin, Pierre, SJ. Review of *Die Stellung des Menschen im Rahmen der Wirbeltiere*, by Othenio Abel. *L'Anthropologie* 43, no. 1–2 (1933): 103–6.

Teilhard de Chardin, Pierre, SJ. "Les Fouilles préhistorique de Péking." *Revue des questions scientifiques* 105 (= 4th ser., 25), no. 2 (1934): 181–93. Translated as "The Prehistoric Excavations of Peking" in *Appearance*, 68–78.

Teilhard de Chardin, Pierre, SJ. "Quelques Réflexions sur la conversion du monde." Typescript, 1936. Later published in *Science et Christ*, 155–66. Paris: Seuil, 1965. Translated by René Hague as "Some Reflections on the Conversion of the World" in *Science and Christ*, 118–27. New York: Harper & Row, 1968.

Teilhard de Chardin, Pierre, SJ. "La Découverte du Sinanthrope." *Études* 232 (1937): 5–13. Translated as "The Discovery of Sinanthropus" in *Appearance*, 84–92.

Teilhard de Chardin, Pierre, SJ. *Fossil Men: Recent Discoveries and Present Problems*. Beijing: Vetch, 1943. Republished as "The Question of Fossil Man" in *Appearance*, 93–125.

Teilhard de Chardin, Pierre, SJ. "Un Grand Événement qui se dessine: La Planétisation humaine." *Cahiers du monde nouveau* 2, no. 7 (1945): 1–13.

Teilhard de Chardin, Pierre, SJ. "Le Cône du temps." *Psyché: Revue internationale de psychanalyse et des sciences de l'homme* 1, no. 1–2 (1946): 23–27 and 171–79. The article had originally appeared as a typescript in Peking, dated February 15, 1942, as "L'Esprit nouveau" (Cuénot, *Teilhard*, 438).

Teilhard de Chardin, Pierre, SJ. "Vie et planètes: Que se passe-t-il en ce Moment sur la terre?" *Études* 249 (1946): 145–69. Translated as "Life and the Planets" in *Future*, 101–28.

Teilhard de Chardin, Pierre, SJ. "La Formation de la noosphère: Une Interprétation biologique plausible de l'histoire humaine." *Revue des questions scientifiques* 118, no. 1 (1947): 7–37. Translated as "The Formation of the Noosphere" in *Future*, 161–91.

Teilhard de Chardin, Pierre, SJ. "Réflexions sur le péché originel." Unpublished, 1947. Published in *Comment je crois*, 217–30. Translated as "Reflections on Original Sin" in *Christianity and Evolution*, 187–98.

Teilhard de Chardin, Pierre, SJ. "Le Rebondissement humain de l'évolution et ses conséquences." *Revue des questions scientifiques* 119, no. 2 (1948): 166–85. Translated as "The Human Rebound of Evolution" in *Future*, 201–21.

Teilhard de Chardin, Pierre, SJ. *Titres et Travaux de Pierre Teilhard de Chardin*. N.p., 1948. Edited translation as "The Scientific Career of Pierre Teilhard de Chardin" in *Heart of the Matter*, 152–54.

Teilhard de Chardin, Pierre, SJ. "Monogénisme et monophylétisme: Une Distinction essentielle à faire." Unpublished, 1950. Published in *Comment je crois*, 245–49. Translated as "Monogenism and Monophyletism: An Essential Distinction" in *Christianity and Evolution*, 209–11.

Teilhard de Chardin, Pierre, SJ. "La Structure phylétique du groupe humain." *Annales de paléontologie* 37 (1951): 49–79. Translated as "The Phyletic Structure of the Human Group" in *Appearance*, 132–71.

Teilhard de Chardin, Pierre, SJ. *Œuvres complètes*, 13 vols. Paris: Seuil. 1955–76. The volumes cited here are *L'Apparition de l'homme* (1956), *La Vision du passé* (1957), *L'Avenir de l'homme* (1959), *Comment je crois* (1969), *Écrits du temps de guerre* (1976), *Le Cœur de la matière* (Seuil, 1976).

Teilhard de Chardin, Pierre, SJ. *Le Phénomène humain*. Paris: Seuil, 1955. Translated by Bernard Wall, *The Phenomenon of Man*. New York: Harper, 1959. Retranslated by Sarah Appleton-Weber as *The Human Phenomenon*. Brighton: Sussex Academic Press, 1999.

Teilhard de Chardin, Pierre, SJ. "Les Singularités de l'espèce humaine." *Annales de paléontologie* 41 (1955): 1–54. Translated as "The Singularities of the Human Species" in *Appearance*, 208–70.

Teilhard de Chardin, Pierre, SJ. *Les Singularités de l'espèce humaine*. Paris: Masson, 1955.

Teilhard de Chardin, Pierre, SJ. "The Antiquity and World Expansion of Human Culture." In *Man's Role in Changing the Face of the Earth*, edited by W. L. Thomas, 103–12. Chicago: University of Chicago Press, 1956.

Teilhard de Chardin, Pierre, SJ. *The Future of Man*, translated by Norman Denny. London: Collins, 1964.

Teilhard de Chardin, Pierre, SJ. *The Appearance of Man*, translated by J. M. Cohen. New York: Harper & Row, 1965.

Teilhard de Chardin, Pierre, SJ. *The Vision of the Past*, translated by J. M. Cohen. New York: Harper & Row, 1966.

Teilhard de Chardin, Pierre, SJ. *La Place de l'Homme dans la Nature: Le Groupe zoologique humain*. Paris: Union Générale, 1956. Translated by René Hague as *Man's Place in Nature: The Human Zoological Group*. New York: Harper & Row, 1966.

Teilhard de Chardin, Pierre, SJ. *Letters from a Traveller*, translated by René Hague et al. New York: Harper, 1962.

Teilhard de Chardin, Pierre, SJ. *Letters from Paris*, edited by Henri de Lubac. Translated by Michael Mazzarese. New York: Herder & Herder, 1967.

Teilhard de Chardin, Pierre, SJ. *Letters to Two Friends*, translated by Helen Weaver. New York: New American Library, 1968.

Teilhard de Chardin, Pierre, SJ. *Letters to Léontine Zanta*, translated by Bernard Wall. New York: Harper & Row, 1969.

Teilhard de Chardin, Pierre, SJ. *Christianity and Evolution*, translated by René Hague. New York: Harcourt Brace Jovanovich, 1971.

Teilhard de Chardin, Pierre, SJ. *L'Œuvre scientifique*, 10 vols., edited by Nicole and Karl Schmitz-Moormann. Olten: Walter, 1971.

Teilhard de Chardin, Pierre, SJ. *Lettres intimes à Auguste Valensin, Bruno de Solages, Henri de Lubac (1919–1955)*. Paris: Aubier Montaigne, 1972.

Teilhard de Chardin, Pierre, SJ. *The Heart of the Matter*, translated by René Hague. New York: Harcourt Brace Jovanovich, 1978.

Teilhard de Chardin, Pierre, SJ. *Letters from My Friend Teilhard de Chardin 1948–1955*, compiled by Pierre Leroy, SJ. Translated by Mary Lukas. New York: Paulist Press, 1980.

Teilhard de Chardin, Pierre, SJ, and Émile Licent, SJ. "On the Discovery of a Palaeolithic Industry in Northern China." *Bulletin of the Geological Society of China* 3, no.1 (1924): 45–50.

Teilhard de Chardin, Pierre, SJ, and W. C. Pei. "The Lithic Industry of the *Sinanthropus* Deposits in Choukoutien." *Bulletin of the Geological Society of China* 11, no. 4 (1932): 315–58.

Temple, Frederick, et al. *Essays and Reviews*. London: Longman, 1861.

Theologus. "Le idee di un Vescovo sull'Evoluzione." *Rassegna nazionale* 104, no. 2 (1898): 418–20.

Theunissen, L. T. *Eugène Dubois and the Ape-Man from Java: The History of the First "Missing Link" and Its Discoverer*, translated by Enid Perlin-West. Dordrecht: Springer, 1988.

Tijd, De. "Werken en geschriften van Z. H. Paus Pius XI." February 17, 1922, 6.

Tissier, L'Abbé. *Tables générales de la Revue pratique de l' apologétique 1905–1921*. Paris: Beauchesne, 1925.

Tonquédec, Joseph de. *La Notion de vérité dans la "philosophie nouvelle."* Paris: Beauchesne, 1908.

Tonquédec, Joseph de. *Dieu dans "L'Évolution créatrice" avec deux lettres de M. Bergson.* Paris: Beauchesne, 1912.

Toronto *Globe and Mail.* "Jesuit Agrees with Darwin." March 20, 1937.

Tort, Patrick. "James, Constantin." In Tort, *Dictionnaire du darwinisme,* 2:2377–78.

Tort, Patrick. "Vialleton, Louis." In Tort, *Dictionnaire du darwinisme,* 3:4460–62.

Tort, Patrick, ed. *Dictionnaire du Darwinisme et de l'évolution.* Paris: Presses Universitaires de France, 1996.

Tournal, Paul. "Considérations théoriques sur les cavernes à ossemens de Bize, près de Narbonne (Aude) et sur les ossemens humains confondus avec des restes d'animaux appartenant à des espèces perdues." *Annales des sciences naturelles* 18 (1829): 242–58.

Trent, Council of. Canons and Decrees. 1545–63. Republished by Alberigo, *Conciliorum decreta,* 633–775. Translated by H. J. Schroeder, OP, as *The Canons and Decrees of the Council of Trent.* Rockford, IL: TAN, 1978.

Urquinaona y Bidot, José María. *Carta Pastoral.* Las Palmas: Doreste y Navarro, 1876.

Vallisneri, Antonio. *De' corpi marini, che su' monti si trovano.* Venice: Lovisa, 1721.

Vallois, Henri-Victor. "Y-a-t-il Plusieurs Souches humaines?" *Revue générale des sciences pures et appliquées* 38, no. 7 (1927): 201–9.

Vallois, Henri-Victor. "Les Preuves anatomiques de l'origine monophylétique de l'homme." *L'Anthropologie* 39, no. 1–3 (1929): 77–101.

Vallois, Henri-Victor. "Monophyletism and Polyphyletism in Man." *South African Journal of Science* 49 (1952): 69–79.

Van Noort, Gerardus. *Tractatus de Deo Creatore.* 2nd ed. Amsterdam: Langenhuysen, 1912. 3rd ed. Hilversum: Brand, 1920.

Van Riper, A. Bowdoin. *Men among the Mammoths: Victorian Science and the Discovery of Human Prehistory.* Chicago: University of Chicago Press, 1993.

Vandebroek, Georges. "L'Origine de l'homme et les récentes découvertes des sciences naturelles." In de la Saudée, *Essai sur Dieu,* 47–115.

Vandebroek, Georges, and Léon Renwart. "L'Encyclique 'Humani Generis' et les sciences naturelles." *Nouvelle revue théologique* 73, no. 4 (1951): 337–51.

Vatican Council I. *Dei Filius.* April 24, 1870. *Acta Sanctae Sedis* 5 (1869–70): 481–93.

Vatican Council I. *Pastor aeternus.* July 18, 1870. *Acta Sanctae Sedis* 6 (1870–71), 40–47.

Vatican Council II. *Dei Verbum.* November 18, 1965.

Vaughan, Herbert. "Dr. Mivart's Heresy." *The Tablet* 95; no. 3113 (January 6, 1900): 5–7.

Vaughan, John S. "Faith and Evolution: A Further Consideration of the Question." *Irish Ecclesiastical Record* 3rd ser., 6, no. 7 (1885): 413–24.

Vaughan, John S. "Faith and Evolution—A Reply." *Irish Ecclesiastical Record* 3rd ser., 6, no. 10 (1885): 651–64.

Vaughan, John S. "What Nature Says of its Creator." *The Catholic World* 55, no. 325 (1892): 1–13.

Vawter, Bruce. *Biblical Inspiration.* Philadelphia: Westminster, 1972.

Vélez, Manuel Francisco. "El Darwinismo i la Creacion." *El Ateneo: Revista mensual de la Sociedad Científico-Literaria* 1, no. 4 (1881): 72–81. Republished in *Revista conservadora de el pensamiento centroamericano* 26, no. 130 (1971): 72–81.

Vélez, Manuel Francisco. *Lecciones de lógica.* N.p., 1882.

Vélez, Manuel Francisco. *Lecciones de ideología.* N.p., 1884.

Vélez, Manuel Francisco. *Antropogenia, o sea Origen del hombre según la revelación y la ciencia.* San Salvador: Sagrini, 1884–85.

Vialleton. Louis. *Membres et ceintures des vertèbres tétrapodes: Critique morphologique du transformisme.* Paris: Doin, 1924.

Vialleton, Louis. *L'Origine des êtres vivants, L'Illusion transformiste.* Paris: Plon, 1929.

Vienne, Council of. *Fidei catholicae fundamento.* 1312. Republished in Alberigo, *Conciliorum decreta,* 336–37.

Vincent of Lérins, *Commonitoria.* Translated by C. A. Heurtley as *A Commonitory.* In *Nicene and Post-Nicene Fathers,* edited by Philip Schaff, 2nd ser., 11:127–59. New York: Christian Literature Company, 1894.

Virey, Julien Joseph. *Histoire naturelle du genre humain.* Paris: Dufart, 1801.

Vogt, Karl, trans. *Natürliche Geschichte der Schöpfung des Weltalls, der Erde und der auf ihr befindlichen Organismen, begründet auf die durch die Wissenschaft errungenen Tatsachen.* 2nd ed. Brunswick: Wieweg, 1858.

Vogt, Karl. *Vorlesungen über den Menschen, seine Stellung in der Schöpfung und in der Geschichte der Erde.* Giessen: Ricker, 1863. Translated by James Hunt as *Lectures on Man: His Place in Creation and in the History of the Earth.* London: Longman, 1864.

Vollert, Cyril, et al., trans. *On the Eternity of the World.* 2nd ed. Milwaukee, WI: Marquette University Press, 1965.

Voltaire. *Traité de metaphysique.* Unpublished, 1734.

Vosté, Jacques M. "Epistula ad Card. Suhard, De tempore documentorum Pentateuchi et de genere litterario undecim priorum capitum Geneseos." *Acta Apostilicae Sedis* 40, no. 1 (1948): 45–48.

Waagen, Lukas. "Palæontology." In *The Catholic Encyclopedia,* 11:410–14.

Wallace, Alfred Russel. *Contributions to the Theory of Natural Selection.* London: Macmillan, 1870.

Wallace, Alfred Russel. *Letters and Reminiscences,* edited by James Merchant. New York: Cassell, 1916.

Walsh, Evangelist John. *Unraveling Piltdown: The Science Fraud of the Century and Its Solution.* New York: Random House, 1996.

Walsh, James J. "The Present Position of Darwinism." *Catholic World* 80, no. 478 (1905): 499–511.

Walworth, Clarence A. *Gentle Skeptic: or Essays and Conversations of a Country Justice on the Authenticity and Truthfulness of the Old Testament Records.* New York: Appleton, 1863.

Ward, James. *Naturalism and Agnosticism.* Cambridge, MA: Cambridge University Press, 1899.

Ward, Wilfred. *The Life of John Henry Cardinal Newman.* London: Longmans, Green, 1912.

Washington Post. "Science and Theology: Rev. Dr. Pohle's Lecture on Darwinism and Theism." March 4, 1892, 6.

Wasmann, Erich, SJ. "Vorbemerkungen des Verfassers zur italienischen Übersetzung." In Baranzke, "Erich Wasmann," 127–31.

Wasmann, Erich, SJ. *Die Trichterwickler: Eine naturwissenschaftliche Studie über den Thierinstinkt.* Münster: Aschendorff, 1884.

Wasmann, Erich, SJ. *Instinkt und Intelligenz im Thierreich.* Freiburg im Breisgau: Herder, 1897. 2nd ed. 1899. Translated as *Instinct and Intelligence in the Animal Kingdom: A Critical Contribution to Modern Animal Psychology.* St. Louis: Herder, 1903.

Wasmann, Erich, SJ. *Vergleichende Studien über das Seelenleben der Ameisen und der höheren Thiere.* Freiburg im Breisgau: Herder, 1897. 2nd ed. 1900. Translated as *Comparative Studies in the Psychology of Ants and of Higher Animals.* St. Louis: Herder, 1905.

Wasmann, Erich, SJ. "Giebt es tatsächlich Arten, die heute noch in der Stammesentwicklung begriffen sind?" *Biologisches Centralblatt* 21, no. 22 (1901): 689–711.

Wasmann, Erich, SJ. "Zur Anwendung der Deszendenztheorie auf den Menschen." *Stimmen aus Maria-Laach* 65 (1903): 387–409.

Wasmann, Erich, SJ. *Die moderne Biologie und die Entwicklungstheorie.* 2nd ed. 1904. 3rd ed. 1906. 2nd ed. translated into Italian by Agostino Gemelli as *La biologia moderna e la teoria dell'evoluzione.* Florence:

Libreria editrice fiorentina, 1906. 3rd ed. translated into English by A. M. Buchanan as *Modern Biology and the Theory of Evolution*. London: Paul, Trench, Trübner, 1910. 3rd ed. partially translated into Polish by Robert Wierzejski as *Biologia nowoczesna a teoria rozwoju. Część I*. Warsaw: Gebethner, 1913.

Wasmann, Erich, SJ. "Bemerkungen zu dem Dekret der päpstlichen Bibelkommission vom 30. Juni 1909 über den historischen Charakter der drei ersten Kapitel der Genesis." In Baranzke, "Erich Wasmann," 123–26.

Wasmann, Erich, SJ. "Vorbemerkungen des Verfassers zur italienischen Übersetzung" Undated manuscript published in Baranzke, "Erich Wasmann," 127–31.

Wasmann, Erich, SJ. *Der Kampf um das Entwicklungsproblem in Berlin*. Freiburg im Breisgau: Herder, 1907. Translated as *The Berlin Discussion of the Problem of Evolution*. London: Paul, Trench, Trübner, 1909.

Wasmann, Erich, SJ. "Catholics and Evolution." In *The Catholic Encyclopedia*, 5:654–55.

Wasmann, Erich, SJ. *Entwicklungstheorie und Monismus: Die Innsbrucker Vorträge von Erich Wasmann am 14., 16., u. 18. Okt. 1909*. Innsbruck: Tyrolia, 1909. Translated as an appendix to *Modern Biology*, 484–522.

Wasmann, Erich, SJ. "The Rev. Simon FitzSimons' Ideas on Evolution." *The Catholic Fortnightly Review* 18–19 (1911–12): 625–28, 658–60, 697–700, 722–27 and 8–10, 41–45, 70–74, 102–5, 133–36, 178–81, 197–98, 240–45, 265–66. Republished as a book. St. Louis: Herder, 1912.

Wasmann, Erich, SJ. *Das Gesellschaftsleben der Ameisen: Das Zusammenleben von Ameisen verschiedener Arten und von Ameisen und Termiten: gesammelte Beiträge zur sozialen Symbiose bei den Ameisen*. 2nd ed. Münster: Aschendorff, 1915.

Wasmann, Erich, SJ. *Der christliche Monismus: Zeitgemäße Betrachtungen über christliche Glaubenswahrheiten*. Freiburg im Breisgau: Herder, 1920. Translated as *Christian Monism: Meditation on Christian Truths in the Language of Modern Thought*. London: Burns Oates Washbourne, 1923. 3rd ed. republished as *Eins in Gott: Gedanken eines christlichen Naturforschers*. Freiburg im Breisgau: Herder, 1928.

Wasmann, Erich, SJ. *Die Gastpflege der Ameisen, ihre biologischen und philosophischen Probleme*. Berlin: Borntraeger, 1920.

Wasmann, Erich, SJ. *Menschen- und Tierseele*. Cologne: Bachem, 1921.

Wasmann, Erich, SJ. *Die Ameisenmimikry: Ein exakter Beitrag zum Mimikryproblem und zur Theorie der Anpassung*. Berlin: Borntraeger, 1925.

Wasmann, Erich, SJ. *Die Ameisen, die Termiten und ihre Gäste: Vergleichende Bilder aus dem Seelenleben von Mensch und Tier*. Regensburg: Manz, 1934.

Weber, Ralph E. *Notre Dame's John Zahm: American Catholic Apologist and Educator*. Notre Dame, IN: University of Notre Dame Press, 1961.

Weigel, Albert. "Zur Artgeschichte und zum Ursprung des Menschen." *Katholischer Kirchenbote* (Landau), November 3, 1946. Available as no. 34, Annex II, Rüschkamp Dossiers, ARSI.

Weigel, Gustave, SJ. "Gleanings from the Commentaries on *Humani Generis*." *Theological Studies* 12, no. 4 (1951): 520–49.

Weigel, Gustave, SJ. "Historical Background of the Encyclical *Humani Generis*." *Theological Studies* 12, no. 2 (1951): 208–30.

Weinzierl, Hans. *Zur Entwicklungsgeschichte der neueren katholischen Philosophie mit besonderer Berücksichtigung der Philosophie G. V. Hertlings*. Reimlingen: St. Joseph, 1928.

Weismann, August. "The Duration of Life," translated by Arthur E. Shipley. In Weismann's *Essays upon Heredity and Kindred Biological Problems*, 2nd ed., edited by Edwin R. Poulton, et al., 1–66. Oxford: Clarendon Press, 1891.

Wenninger, Frances J. Review of *Darwinism and Catholic Thought*, by Henry de Dorlodot. *American Midland Naturalist* 8, no. 8/9 (1923): 211–14.

Wernz, Franz Xaver, SJ. *Ius decretalium ad usum praelectionum in scholis textus canonici sive iuris decretalium*. 3rd ed. Prati: Giachetti, 1915.

Wetzel, Franz Xaver. *Dr. Otto Zardetti, Erzbischof von Mocissus. Erinnerungsblätter.* Einsiedeln: Benziger, 1902.

Wetzer, Joseph, and Benedict Welte, eds. *Kirchenlexikon oder Encyklopädie der katholischen Theologie und ihrer Hilfswissenschaften.* Freiburg im Breisgau: Herder, 1847–56.

Wetzer, Joseph, and Benedict Welte, eds. *Wetzer und Welte's Kirchenlexikon, oder Encyklopädie der katholischen Theologie und ihrer Hülfswissenschaften.* 2nd ed. Freiburg im Breisgau: Herder, 1886.

Whewell, William. *The Philosophy of the Inductive Sciences.* London: Parker, 1840.

White, Andrew Dixon. *History of the Warfare of Science with Theology in Christendom.* New York: Appleton, 1896.

Wiest, Donald H. *The Precensorship of Books (Canons 1384–1386, 1392–1394, 2318,§2): A History and a Commentary.* Washington, DC: The Catholic University of America Press, 1953.

Wilmers, Wilhelm. *Handbuch der Religion für Studirende an höheren Lehranstalten.* 2nd ed. Regensburg: Pustet, 1875.

Wilson, E. O. *Insect Societies.* Cambridge, MA: Harvard University Press, 1971.

Winchell, Alexander. *Adamites and Preadamites.* Syracuse: Roberts, 1878.

Windle, Bertram. *Facts & Theories: Being a Consideration of Some Biological Conceptions of To-Day.* London: Catholic Truth Society, 1912.

Windle, Bertram. *A Century of Scientific Thought & Other Essays.* New York: Benziger, 1915.

Windle, Bertram. *The Church and Science.* London: Catholic Truth Society, 1917. 3rd ed. 1924.

Windle, Bertram. "Books on Evolution." *Commonweal* 2, no. 20 (1925): 484–85.

Windle, Bertram. *Evolution and Catholicity.* New York: Paulist Press, 1925.

Windle, Bertram. "A Roman Catholic View of Evolution." *Current History* 23, no. 3 (1925): 335–39.

Windle, Bertram. *The Evolutionary Problem as it is Today.* New York: Wagner, 1927.

Wiseman, Nicholas. *Twelve Lectures on the Connexion between Science and Revealed Religion.* London: Booker, 1836.

Wolf, Hubert. *Index: Der Vatikan und die verbotenen Bücher.* Munich: Beck, 2006.

Woodrow, James. "Professor Woodrow's Speech before the Synod of South Carolina." *The Southern Presbyterian Review* 36, no. 1 (1885): 1–65.

Yzermans, Vincent A. *Frontier Bishop of St. Cloud.* Waite Park, MN: Park, 1988.

Zahm, John Augustine, CSC. *The Catholic Church and Modern Science.* Notre Dame, IN: University of Notre Dame Press, 1883. Republished as "Science and the Church" in *Catholic Science and Catholic Scientists,* 9–54. Philadelphia: Kilner, 1894.

Zahm, John Augustine, CSC. *Sound and Music.* Chicago: McClurg, 1892.

Zahm, John Augustine, CSC. *Bible, Science, and Faith.* Baltimore: Murphy, 1894. Translated into French by J. Flageolet as *Bible, science et foi.* Paris: Lethielleux, 1894. Translated into Italian by Luigi Cappelli as *Bibbia, scienza e fede.* Siena: Biblioteca del Clero, 1895.

Zahm, John Augustine, CSC. *Catholic Science and Catholic Scientists.* Philadelphia: Kilner, 1894.

Zahm, John Augustine, CSC. *Evolution and Dogma.* Chicago: McBride, 1896. Translated into Italian by Alfonso Maria Galea as *Evoluzione e dogma.* Siena: Biblioteca del clero, 1896. Translated into French by J. Flageolet as *L'Évolution et le dogme.* Paris: Lethielleux, 1897. Translated into Spanish by Miguel Asúa as *La evolución y el dogma.* Madrid: Sociedad Editorial Española, 1905.

Zahm, John Augustine, CSC. "Évolution and Téléologie." In Congrès scientifique de 1897, *Compte rendu,* 9:166–76, with discussion at 9:8–11. Republished in *Revue des questions scientifiques* 43 (= 2nd ser., 13) (1898), 403–19. Also as "Evolution and Teleology," in *Appleton's Popular Scientific Monthly* 52 (1898), 815–24.

Zahm, John Augustine, CSC. *Along the Andes and Down the Amazon*. New York: Appleton, 1911.

Zahm, John Augustine, CSC [under pseud. J. Mozans]. *Women in Science: With an Introductory Chapter on Woman's Long Struggle for Things of the Mind*. New York: Appleton, 1913.

Zahm, John Augustine, CSC. *Through South America's Southland: With an Account of the Roosevelt Scientific Expedition to South America*. New York: Appleton, 1916.

Zahm, John Augustine, CSC. *Great Inspirers*. New York: Appleton, 1917.

Zahm, John Augustine, CSC. *From Berlin to Bagdad and Babylon*. New York: Appleton, 1922.

Zaremba, Aleksander. "Pentateuch: §7 Zarzuty podniesione w imię nauki przeciwko wiarogodności Pismu." In *Encyklopedja kościelna*, 19: 77–85.

Zecchini, Stefano. *Dio, l'universo, et la fratellanza di tutti gli esseri della creazione*. Turin: Privately published, 1875.

Zigliara, Tommaso. *Della luce intellettuale e dell'ontologismo*. Rome: Chiapperini, 1874.

Zigliara, Tommaso, OP. *Summa philosophica in usum scholarum: II. Cosmologia, psychologia et theologia naturalis*, 12th ed. Paris: Briguet, 1900.

Zimmermann, Walter. "Die Methoden der Phylogenetik." In *Die Evolution der Organismen: Ergebnisse und Probleme der Abstammungslehre*, edited by Gerhard Heberer, 20–56. Jena: Fischer, 1943.

Zúñiga, Diego de. *In Iob commentaria*. Toledo: Rodriquez, 1584.

Życiński, Józef. *God and Evolution: Fundamental Questions of Christian Evolutionism*. Translated by Kenneth W. Kemp and Zuzanna Maślanka. Washington, DC: The Catholic University of America Press, 2006.

INDEX

Flower, William Henry, xi

Fogazzaro, Antonio, **97–99**; novels placed on *Index*, 98–99, 461–62; recommended Zahm to Bonomelli, 93, 127; views on evolution, 97–99, 272

Fonck, Leopold, 182

Fondeville, Countess de, 337

Fontan, Albert, 16

Fontana, Ernesto, 109, 111

Foscarini, Paolo, 454

fossils. *See* paleoanthropological record

Français, Gilbert, 91, 121, 122, 123–24, 125n139

France: anti-evolutionist stance of nineteenth-century French Catholic periodicals, 70–71; evolution question entangled in Catholic-republican political conflicts, 56–57; Leo XIII's condemnation of French Americanism, 122; postwar Communism and existentialism condemned in *Humani generis*, 345, 380. *See also* Bégouën, Charles-Maximilien; Bégouën, Henri; Bergounioux; Cochin; de Lapparent, Albert-Félix; Gaudry; Guibert; Leroy; Le Roy; Martel; Paquier; Périer; Teilhard

Franzelin, Johann Baptist, 52n29, 53

Frayssinous, Denis de, 4

Freddi, Ruggero, 206

Freppel, Charles, 140

Frey, Jean-Baptiste, 270, 271

Frick, Karl, 206, 207, 208, 209

Frohschammer, Jakob, 55n37

Frühwirth, Andreas, 112, 113, 114, 115

Fuhlrott, Johann Carl, 432

Funghini, Luigi, 94

Gaia, Leandro, 281

Galea, Alfonso Maria, 95, 123, 124, 125, 126, 131

Galileo, 106, 127, 276, 353, 375, 447, 454

García Álvarez, Rafael, 56

Gardeil, Ambroise, 151–52

Garrigou-Lagrange, Réginald, 331, 332, 346, 391

Gasparri, Pietro, 295

Gasquet, Francis Aidan, 268

Gaudel, Auguste, 341–42

Gaudry, Albert, **11–18**; biographical information, 12; did not attend International Scientific Congresses, 145; on evolution in general, 12–16, 188; on human origins, 16–18, 142–43; Seton studied under, 99; significance, 11–12

Geissel, Johannes von, 47

Gemelli, Agostino, **173–76**; biographical information, 173–74, 191; complaints about individual authors, 256–57, 278, 283–86, 336, 337–38; on evolutionary biology, 174–76, 213–14; personal acquaintance with Pius XI, 256n15; rejected evolutionary origin of human body, 175–76, 257; translated Wasmann's *Moderne Biologie*, 170, 174, 257; *vota* in Holy Office cases, 257–58, 259, 264n63, 270, 272–73, 283–84, 337–38

Generelli, Giuseppe Cirillo, 422

geocentrism and heliocentrism, 199, 280, 376n19, 448, 452n35, 454

Geoffroy Saint-Hilaire, Étienne, 11, 19, 134, 188, 231

Geoffroy Saint-Hilaire, Isidore, 11

Germany: anti-clericalism in, xv–xvi; monism in, 171–72, 208, 276. *See also* Rüschkamp; Wasmann

Gheyn, Joseph van den, 136, 144

Giard, Alfred, 290

Gilson, Étienne, 250, 332

Giobbe, Paolo, 399

Gioberti, Vincenzo, 31

Giovannozzi, Giovanni, 141–42

Gismondi, Enrico, 198–99

Glick, Thomas F., 59, 60, 81

Gliddon, George, 43, 437–38

Gmeiner, John, **35–36**; biographical information, 460–62; and German-Irish rivalry in United States, 460–61; on intellectual freedom from ecclesiastical authority, xvi; taught at St. Francis Seminary along with Zardetti, 118; views on evolution, 35–36, 107, 110, 135

Golgi, Camillo, 174

González y Díaz Tuñón, Zeferino, **81–86**; assessment of Darwinism, 82–84; biographical information, 81–82; "mixed" account of evolutionary origin of the human body, 84, 170, 188, 236, 296, 297, 372, 383;

Szabó, Szádok, 194–95

Tacci Porcelli, Giovanni, 184

Tanquerey, Adolphe, 155–56

Teilhard de Chardin, Pierre, **239–49**; biographical information, 239–40; connections with Le Roy, 252, 258, 259, 328–29; contributions to *Dictionnaire apologétique de la foi catholique*, 244, 295; on evolutionary anthropogenesis, 244–49, 259, 279–80, 281–89, 330, 336, 337–38, 351, 353, 355–56, 357; Holy Office's investigations of, 278, 281, 283–86, 346–48, 354, 359–60; invited to Altamira by Breuil, 275; Jesuit Curia's oversight of and restrictions on, 277–89, 327, 329, 332, 348, 351–61; on monogenesis, 244, 245, 247, 248–49, 279–81, 326, 346, 351–52, 353–54, 356, 357, 358, 412–13; on original sin, 238, 244, 248–49, 277–81, 282, 285, 346; on origin of "noosphere," 252n125; on Piltdown Man, 241–42, 243n87; purely scientific work, 239–43, 277, 284–85, 326–28, 332; on science and religion, xiii, 243–46, 288; theology of nature (cosmic evolutionism), xx, 249, 326–32, 346–48, 351–61, 381; and Warfare Myth, xiii

teleology: individual authors on, 143, 151, 154, 180, 188, 190, 255, 313, 329, 331, 376; orthogenesis, 157, 251, 426; and philosophical integration of Thomism and transformism, xv, 408

Temple, Frederick, xi

textbooks: overview, 458; 1859–1885, 73–77; 1885–1900, 155–59; 1898–1909, 220–23; 1909–1931, 298–301; 1931–1950, 375–78

theological censures: overview, 446–47; heretical, 110, 163, 170n40, 349, 446; merely erroneous, 110, 400, 446; near to heresy or error, 68, 110, 349, 446; rash, 68, 73, 90, 94, 110, 111, 130, 163, 170n40, 208n55, 239, 266, 271, 281, 286–87, 349, 364, 382, 387, 446–47

theological notes: overview, 445–47; assigned to immediate creation of the human body, 74, 156, 208, 220, 292, 297–98, 362; assigned to monogenesis, 280, 344, 387, 391–92, 400; as matter of variation in Catholic evolutionism, 406; *sententia certa*, or *communis et certa*, 220, 297–98, 446; *sententia communis*, 156, 208, 324, 446, 447; *sententia de fide definita*, 74, 75, 280, 308, 344, 362, 446, 447; *sententia proxima fidei*, 362, 387, 391–92, 446; *sententia theologice certa*, 446; *sententia tolerata*, 292n11

Thill, Ernst, 207, 208, 209

Thomas Aquinas: Buonpensiere thought Leroy's ideas were far removed from, 114; caution with regards to defining dogmas, 104; on creation, 26, 107, 228; on embryology, 311, 323; and González's "mixed" evolutionary anthropogenesis, 84; Hauber on need for a "twentieth-century Saint Thomas," 293; on interpretation of Scripture, 83, 148; on principle of unity of origin, 318n82; on secondary causality, 311; on spontaneous generation, 311; on whether the world had a beginning in time, 373, 448n13; in Zahm's theology of nature, 91–92, 143, 151, 158. *See also* Thomism

Thomism: alternative approaches of Blondel, Valensin, and Przywara, 257n18; compatibility with Darwinism, xv, xvii, 76, 151–52, 407–8; embryology, 35, 76, 169, 234, 311, 323; emphasis on secondary causality in creation, 40, 41, 48n13, 49, 107, 120n106, 237, 307, 311, 384; Hauber on need for a "twentieth-century Saint Thomas," 293; human nature as body and rational soul, xv, 50, 82; principle of successive and graded evolution of forms, 219; principles of scriptural interpretation, 83, 453; "probable," definition of, 93n56; rejected idea of *rationes seminales*, 237–38; renewal promoted by Leo XIII in *Aeterni patris*, xiv–xv, xv, 50, 82, 166, 176; species problem and Thomistic essentialism, xv, 113, 157–58, 186, 188–89, 216–17, 378, 408; species problem of a lower species producing a higher one, 291, 311, 373; spontaneous generation, 291, 306, 311, 427; whether the world had a beginning in time, 369, 373, 448, 488n13. *See also* human exceptionalism; teleology

Tisserant, Eugène, 346

Tissoni, Antonio, 281

tools: as evidence of antiquity of the human race, 16, 17, 288, 430, 431; as evidence of human intelligence, 243, 252, 316, 319, 325, 341, 364, 399